Belhar Confession

The Embracing Confession of Faith for Church and Society

Editors
Mary-Anne Plaatjies-Van Huffel
Leepo Modise

Belhar Confession: The Embracing Confession of Faith for Church and Society

Published by AFRICAN SUN MeDIA under the SUN PReSS imprint.

All rights reserved.

Copyright © 2017 AFRICAN SUN MeDIA and the editors

This publication was subjected to an independent double-blind peer evaluation by the Publisher.

The editors and the publisher have made every effort to obtain permission for and acknowledge the use of copyrighted material. Please refer enquiries to the publisher.

No part of this book may be reproduced or transmitted in any form or by any electronic, photographic or mechanical means, including photocopying and recording on record, tape or laser disk, on microfilm, via the Internet, by e-mail, or by any other information storage and retrieval system, without prior written permission by the publisher.

Views expressed in this publication do not necessarily reflect those of the publisher.

First edition 2017

ISBN 978-1-928357-58-2
ISBN 978-1-928357-59-9 (e-book)
DOI: 10.18820/9781928357599

Set in Fira Sans Light 10/13

SUN PRESS is an imprint of AFRICAN SUN MeDIA. Scholarly, professional and reference works are published under this imprint in print and electronic format. This publication may be ordered directly from www.sun-e-shop.co.za

Produced by AFRICAN SUN MeDIA.

www.africansunmedia.co.za
africansunmedia.snapplify.com (e-books)
www.sun-e-shop.co.za

DECLARATION

For tomorrow's children

CONTENTS

Acknowledgements vii

Meaning of the logo of the Uniting Reformed Church in Southern Africa ix

Introduction xi

SECTION 1
CHRONOLOGICAL OUTLINE OF THE STORY OF BELHAR

Acceptance, adoption, advocacy, reception and protestation:
A chronology of the Belhar Confession 1
Mary-Anne Plaatjies-Van Huffel

The mission of the Dutch Reformed Church as mission for colonisation and
division of the Reformed Church in South Africa (1652–1982) 97
Sipho Mahokoto

Unity and diversity: An overview of the URCSA decisions on church
unity since 1994 119
Willem Saayman

SECTION 2
THEOLOGICAL AND ETHICAL THEMES REGARDING THE BELHAR CONFESSION

The unification process in the Dutch Reformed Church family and the
Uniting Reformed Church in southern Africa: The confessional basis
and Confession of Belhar 135
Leepo Modise

Conversion towards radical inclusivity 153
Ernst Conradie

Yearning for a just and inclusive society 161
David Peter Carelse

Belhar as a therapeutic resource to the Dutch Reformed Church family 185
Eugene Baron

The Belhar Confession of faith: A spirituality sense-making confession 199
Leepo Modise

The Belhar Confession: Addressing racism in church and society 215
  Dawid Kuyler

The Belhar Confession and the establishment of a theology of development 231
  Jacques Walter Beukes

Belhar Confession, children and the Eucharist: Towards restoration of broken relationships 251
  Tipi Jacob Nthakhe

Standing where God stands (outside the gate, with Christ): The Belhar Confession as a call for public pastoral care 273
  Llewellyn L.M. MacMaster

The Belhar Confession and compassionate justice 295
  Henry Gerhardus Platt

The Belhar Confession and internal unity: '[A]nd together fight against everything that may threaten or hinder this unity.' (Belhar Confession) 305
  Daniël Kuys

From a racially-segregated congregation towards a multi-ethnic, multicultural congregation 319
  Dawid Johannes Van Huffel

Living Belhar: Enhancing the reception of Belhar in congregations 331
  J.N.J. (Klippies) Kritzinger

Unwrapping the gift of the Belhar Confession 347
  Motlalentwa Godfrey Betha

The history of Belhar 355
  Johannes Cornelius Adonis

Can justice be embodied in sexist language? A challenge to the Confession of Belhar 363
  Christina Landman

Barmen to Belhar: A contemporary confessing journey 375
  Hayman Russel Botman

The relevance of pedagogical narrative maps: The Confession of Belhar as a practical theological narrative searching for a pedagogic-therapeutic methodology 387
  Gordon Dames

Barmen and Belhar in conversation: A South African perspective 407
  Dirkie Smit

To stand where God stands: Reflections on the Confession of Belhar after 25 years 421
  Allan Boesak

ADDENDA

Addendum 1: WARC Resolution on racism and South Africa 442

Addendum 2: WARC Seoul statement on the DRC and the status confessionis 446

Addendum 3: The Declaration of faith of the Presbyterian Church of Southern Africa 452

Addendum 4: Covenanting for the reunification of the DRC family – Esselenpark Declaration 454

Addendum 5: Declaration of Laudium 457

Addendum 6: The testimony of Vereeniging March 1989 459

Addendum 7: A pastoral letter to the moderamen and our brothers and sisters of the Dutch Reformed Church (NGK) from the 23rd WARC General Council, meeting in Debrecen, Hungary, August 1997 463

Addendum 8: Joint Resolution of the World Alliance of Reformed Churches and the Dutch Reformed Church 465

Addendum 9: Resolutions of the moderamen (expanded) of the DRC on church reunification 11–12 June 2008 Carmelite Retreat Centre 466

Addendum 10: A Statement by the Delegation from the World Alliance of Reformed Churches 2009 471

Addendum 11: Memorandum of agreement between the DRC and URCSA 474

Addendum 12: The roadmap to church reunification: DRC and URCSA 480

Addendum 13: Response of the URCSA with regard to the acceptance/(non)acceptance of the Belhar Confession in the DRC 2015 483

Addendum 14: Press statement of the URCSA on xenophobia 487

Addendum 15: Confession of Belhar 489

Addendum 16: Responsive Litany of the Belhar Confession 495

Websites with material on the Belhar Confession 497
Index 499

ACKNOWLEDGEMENTS

1. General Synod for entrusting the editors, Prof. Mary-Anne Plaatjies-Van Huffel and Leepo Modise with the noble task. It had been an honour to serve the Synod in this regard.
2. Prof. Mary-Anne Plaatjies-van Huffel for compiling the archival documents on the Belhar Confession and editing the manuscript.
3. Prof. Leepo Modise for keeping everyone accountable to honour due dates.
4. Authors for submitting superb chapters on the Confession.
5. The *Ned Geref Teologiese Tydskrif* and *Studia Historiae Eccelsiasticae* for permission granted to republish the articles of Proff. Adonis, Botman, Landman, Dames, Smit and Boesak.
6. The URCSA for permission granted to republish reports, articles, statements and speeches in Acts and Agenda of Synods as well as articles published in the URCSA News.
7. To the churches across the globe for developing excellent resources on the Belhar Confession which are available on various websites.
8. To tomorrow's children for reading and reflecting upon the book and embodying the Belhar Confession.

Meaning of the Logo of the Uniting Reformed Church in Southern Africa

1. The two symbols from the former Dutch Reformed Mission Church (DRMC) and the Dutch Reformed Church in Africa (DRCA) are jointly used in the logo of the Uniting Reformed Church in Southern Africa (URCSA) to showcase our common background and identity:
    a. The anchor was part of the logo of the Dutch Reformed Church in Africa. The anchor is an early Christian symbol. One of the oldest of the symbols of the cross is the anchor. The achor symbolizes atonement through Christ alone (Latin: solus Christus). 'For there is one God and one mediator also between God and men, the man Christ Jesus, who gave Himself as a ransom for all, the testimony given at the proper time'. (1 Timothy 2:5-6).
    b. The lighthouse was part of the logo of the Dutch Reformed Mission Church. We as Christians are called to be the light of the world so that others can see, by the grace of God, the way to eternal life through Jesus Christ. The lighthouse symbolizes justification is by faith alone (Latin: sola fide), not faith plus anything else. 'Therefore, since we have been justified by faith, we have peace with God through our Lord Jesus Christ.' (Romans 5:1). The sinner's entire salvation is by free and sovereign grace only (Latin: sola gratia). 'For it is by grace you have been saved, through faith – and this is not from yourselves, it is the gift of God (Ephesians 2:8).
2. The Bible showcases the centrality of the Word of God. The Uniting Reformed Church in Southern Africa as a reformed church places the Word of God and the preaching of the word in the centre. The Bible symbolizes that Scripture alone is the standard for our beliefs (Latin: sola Scripture). 'All scripture is given by inspiration of God, and is profitable for doctrine, for reproof, for correction, for instruction in righteousness: That the man of God may be perfect, thoroughly furnished unto all good works.' (2 Timothy 3:16-17). The Bible alone is therefore the ultimate authority.
3. The blanket with Africa design is indicative of multi-ethnic-multicultural character of the Uniting Reformed Church in Southern Africa which consists of the language and cultural groups in South Africa, Namibia and Lesotho. 'So in Christ Jesus you are all children of God through faith, for all of you who were baptized into Christ have clothed yourselves with Christ. There is neither Jew nor Gentile, neither slave nor free, nor is there male and female, for you are all one in Christ Jesus.' (Gal. 3:26-28).

4. The name of the Uniting Reformed Church in Southern Africa (which is in the continuous tense) and its logo (which is an incomplete circle) reflects the emphasis on unity and URCSA's hope for an even greater church unification within the reformed family in Southern Africa. 'I pray that they will all be one, just as you and I are one – as you are in me, Father, and I am in you. And may they be in us so that the world will believe you sent me.' (John 17:14). Every activity is therefore to be sanctified unto the glory of God alone. (Latin: Soli Deo Gloria).

INTRODUCTION

The Uniting Reformed Church in Southern Africa (URCSA) is pleased to present this book on the Belhar Confession. On 26 September 2016, the URCSA commemorated the 30th celebration of the Belhar Confession (1986–2016). The moderamen of the General Synod of the URCSA commissioned Mary-Anne Plaatjies-Van Huffel and Leepo Modise to spearhead the book project. This comprehensive anthology expounds on the history of the Belhar Confession and presents the results of a study process, already started in 2008.

The confession gives a strong biblical and Christological foundation to engage on numerous matters. The Belhar Confession is not confined to the issue of racism – rather the language of the Confession implies its application to unity, reconciliation and social justice. While celebrating the gift of the Belhar Confession, we also take note of the reception abroad and the protestation against the confession by the Dutch Reformed Church (DRC), Dutch Reformed Church in Africa (DRCA) and the Reformed Church in Africa (RCA). Churches across the globe took heed of the call of the URCSA in 1997 to include the confession in their confessional basis, while the DRC, DRCA and the RCA, after numerous bilateral and multilateral talks could not come to an agreement on this inclusion.

This book is a call to future generations to take heed of our history and to engage in an informative manner on unity, reconciliation and justice. The Belhar Confession is a declaration of faith that emerged in South Africa when certain practices of the church were so clearly contrary to biblical teaching that the integrity of the proclamation of the gospel was at stake. The Belhar Confession, like other classical confessions, such as the Belgic Confession, the Heidelberg Catechism and the Canon of Dort, originated in a specific historical context. These three confessions were written within a sixty-year period from 1561 to 1619 and were adopted within the then context of conditions in northern Europe. The Belhar Confession is the first and only confessional contribution received from the Reformed community in the Southern Hemisphere.

Structure, method and aim of the book

After an introductory overview, the anthology is divided into two major parts: original scholarly contributions and scholarly work of the URCSA members already published in accredited journals. The authors, two women and twenty-one male ministers of the Word or theologians of the URCSA, come from diverse cultural and language backgrounds. The methodology is multifaceted and interdisciplinary. It is multifaceted in the sense that the contributors are from different backgrounds and their contributions are of different categories and employ different approaches. This publication uses the Belhar Confession as a hermeneutical tool to comment on various aspects of justice in South Africa.

The book does not attempt to give a comprehensive thesis on every sub-theme relating to the Belhar Confession. Rather the reception of the Belhar Confession is narrated in such a manner as to showcase the historical background, drafting, acceptance and adoption of the confession as well as the advocacy, reception and protestation of the confession in South Africa and abroad. The authors considered the theological contributions from the World Council of Churches (WCC) and the World Alliance of Reformed Churches (WARC) on racism, which bear direct reference to the drafting of the Belhar Confession. In addition, the authors take into account the presuppositions of the DRC family of churches (DRC family) regarding the confession. To understand the URCSA stance on the inclusion of the Belhar Confession in the confessional basis of the envisaged unified church, it is important to take cognisance of the troublesome history of the confession. The Belhar Confession has as background the racial, racist, segregationist and apartheid history and theology in South Africa. It is, therefore, important to put the drafting and ultimate acceptance of the confession in a broader historical context.

The first section of the book gives a chronological outline of the story of the Belhar Confession with voices from different backgrounds telling the story from their vantage points. The interpretation of Belhar Confession is like a pattern in a kaleidoscope. When the instrument is turned a bit to get the historical perspective, a different pattern emerges, although the basic elements are the same. Section 1 considers the development of racially-segregated churches in the Reformed tradition in South Africa and Namibia, the theological justification of apartheid, the drafting of the confession and the acceptance, adoption, advocacy, reception and protestation regarding the confession in South Africa, Namibia and in the global North. The lead essay in this section is by Mary-Anne Plaatjies-Van Huffel, moderator of General Synod of the URCSA. Plaatjies-Van Huffel, Sipho Mahokoto as well as Willem Saaylman set Belhar in its historical context. The contributions of the authors depend on whether the author participated in the discourse personally (e.g. Smit, Boesak, Adonis and Botman) or reconstructs the history from the outside (Plaatjies-Van Huffel, Mahokoto, Saayman and Modise, among others).

In Section 2, Leepo Modise, Ernst Conradie, David Carelse, Eugene Baron, Jacques Beukes, Tipi Jacob Nthakhe, Dawid Kuyler, Llewellyn Macmaster, Hendrikus Gerhardus Platt, Daniël Kuys, Dawid Johannes Van Huffel and Klippies Kritzinger reflect on theological and ethical themes regarding the Belhar Confession. These themes include church reunification, inclusivity, economic injustice, therapeutic resource, a theology of development, inclusion of children at the Eucharist, public pastoral

Introduction

care, addressing racism, compassionate justice, multiculturalism and the reception of the confession in local congregations. The premise of the authors is that good and just societies do not just need constitutions and laws, but also a worshipping church, calling people to, among the many things, justice, solidarity and care of the marginalised and suffering.

The book includes chapters taken from articles previously published in accredited journals by URCSA, and the editors recognise the vast array of published work of URCSA members on the Belhar Confession. These chapters are: 'The History of Belhar' by Hannes Adonis, 'Can Justice be Embodied in Sexist Language? A Challenge to the Confession of Belhar' by Christina Landman, 'Barmen to Belhar: A Contemporary Confessing Journey' by Hayman Russel Botman, 'The Relevance of Pedagogical Narrative Maps: The Confession of Belhar as a Practical Theological Narrative Searching for a Pedagogic-therapeutic Methodology' by Gordon Dames. 'Barmen and Belhar in Conversation: A South African Perspective' by Dirkie Smit, and 'To stand Where God Stands: Reflections on the Confession of Belhar after 25 Years' by Allan Boesak. In June 2014, Professor Botman indicated his willingness to partake in this project. He tragically passed on during July 2014. Prof. Adonis also passed on during 2016. The mentioned articles are republished in this book with the permission granted by the _Nederduitse Gereformeerde Teologiese Tydskrif_ (_Dutch Reformed Theological Journal_) and _Studia Historiae Eccelsiasticae_.

The book includes 16 church documents issued by the WARC, DRC, RCA or the URCSA, which will help readers to come to terms with the complex history of the Belhar Confession. The book also offers a list of websites to acquaint readers, both local and global, with the material available on the Belhar Confession

With this publication, the URCSA pays homage to the drafters, communal authors, and advocates of the Confession of Belhar, namely Allan Aubrey Boesak, Isak Mentor, Gustav Bam, Jaap Durand and Dirkie Smit. We hope that the confession continues to invigorate the discourse as well as research regarding confessions at large?

We call upon to future generations to take heed of our history and to engage in an informative manner on unity, reconciliation and justice. We hereby affirm emphatically: Unity is a gift and an obligation for the church; God entrusted reconciliation to the church; justice and peace are revealed in the nature of God. We hereby offer the Belhar Confession as a gift to tomorrow's children. As Rubem Alves (1972) rightly imparts 'We must dream a new dream for tomorrow because we are tomorrow's children.'

MARY-ANNE PLAATJIES-VAN HUFFEL
AND LEEPO MODISE
NOVEMBER 2017

SECTION ONE

Chronological outline of the story of Belhar

ACCEPTANCE, ADOPTION, ADVOCACY, RECEPTION AND PROTESTATION

A chronology of the Belhar Confession

Mary-Anne Plaatjies-Van Huffel[1]

Historical background of the Belhar Confession

On 6 April 1652, Johan van Riebeeck representing the Vereenigde Oost-Indische Compagnie in Holland (Dutch East India Company) arrived in the Cape of Good Hope. His goal was to establish a refreshment station for ships in trade between Europe and Asia. The arrival of Van Riebeeck heralded the introduction of Christianity to the indigenous people of the Cape of Good Hope and the Reformed faith was established in South Africa (Van der Watt 1977:4). Until the end of the eighteenth century, indigenous people and slaves were fully fledged members of the Dutch Reformed Church in South Africa (DRC) and participated fully in the sacraments (Plaatjies-Van Huffel 2011, 2013a, 2013b, 2014). During 1828, several problems arose in Stellenbosch, Calvinia, Caledon, Riversdale and the Swartland relating to the admission of black Christians to the Lord's Table (Loff 1981:18-19). For example, during that year, Bentura Johannes (a black man), after being baptised, became a member of the DRC of Somerset West. His presence challenged the DRC members of the congregation regarding the inclusion of the black people at the Eucharist Table. There was a known practice in the DRC, namely, that 'such persons' will only share the Lord's Supper after the 'born Christians' had been invited, 'as it is done in Stellenbosch and Caledon' (Loff 1981:18-19).

During 1829, the Cape Town presbytery of the DRC dealt with an enquiry from the church council of the Swartland congregation regarding the administering of the Holy Communion to people of mixed descent. At the DRC Synod of that year, the Swartland church council submitted a motion relating to the issue. The question to be considered was, whether 'persons of 'colour', who were confirmed and baptised, should be allowed, together with 'born again Christians' (white people), to take the Lord's Supper or whether these people should take the Holy Communion

---

[1] Prof. Mary-Anne Plaatjies-Van Huffel teaches Church Polity and Ecclesiology at Stellenbosch University. She was the moderator of the URCSA General Synod (2012–2016) and was elected as the Africa President of the World Council of Churches (WCC) in 2013 at the WCC General Assembly in Busan, Korea.

separately: 'Of personen Van de kleur, die door het doen Van de belydenis en de toediening Van den H. Doop tot leden Van de Kerke zijn aangenomen – gelijk met geborene Kristenen het Avondmaal zal bediend worden.'[2] (*Acta NGK* 1829:79, VI(6). The commissioners of politics, D.F. Berrangé and Sir J.A. Truter, also took part in the discussion and ironically stated that the discussion of the question was indeed unworthy of Christianity (Kriel 1963:55). The 1829 DRC Synod unanimously rejected the separation at the Eucharist on the basis of colour. The resolution reads as follows:

> Te verklaren, dat men dit voorstel tot geen onderwerp Van deliberatie of beslissing by de Synode behoorde te maken; maar hetzelve als een onwrikbaren stelregel op het onfeilbaar Woord Van God gegrond, behoort te merken; dat bij gevolg, alle Christen gemeenten, en elk Christen in het bijzonder, verpligt is overeenkomstig te denken en te handelen.
> (*Acta NGK* 1829:71-72)[3]

With this resolution, the synod confirmed that all members, regardless of race, should have access to the sacraments. Although the 1829 Synod formally rejected discrimination on the basis of skin colour there was a growing practice to minister to people of colour at separate worship services and to administer the sacraments (separately from white congregants) to them. For example, the DRC Ceres generated funds to construct a building where the 'heathen' could receive catechism and where the sacraments could be administered to them. According to Chris Loff in Swellendam a separate building for 'heathen' had already been completed during 1838 (Loff 1981:22).

The synods of the DRC 1834, 1837 and 1857, nevertheless raised the issue of separate administration of the sacraments to the 'heathen'. In the *Ontwerp van bepalingen Der Hervormde Zending Genootschappen in de Ned. Herv. Gemeenten in Zuid-Afrika Van 1834*, provisions had been made for the establishment of separate congregations for natives, however, allowance was made for members of mixed descent to join existing DRC congregations (Kriel 1963:49). These provisions regarding mission can be seen as the DRC's first mission policy. The *Ontwerp van bepalingen* provided for racially segregated congregations as well as the integration of races in one church. The first mission policy of the DRC had already been accepted in 1835 and was reviewed in 1837 (Adonis 1982:78). In the policy provision was being made for

---

2   Translation: Whether people of colour, who by being confirmed and having been baptised may be accepted as members of the church – together with born Christians will receive Holy Communion.
3   Translation: To declare that one should not make this recommendation a topic of consideration or decision at the synod; but take into account this topic as an unyielding principle in the infallible Word of God; that consequently, all Christian congregations, and each Christian particularly, are obliged to reason and act accordingly.

establishment of free, but separated seats in the church for so-called heathen. According to Coertzen (2010:51) there is a duality in the mission strategy of the DRC. On the one hand, new converts from the so-called heathendom could become fully-fledged members of the existing congregations of the DRC, while on the other hand provisions had been made for the separate ministry to the 'coloured' church members (Kriel 1963:54).

In 1855, forty-five white members of the DRC applied to the church council of Stockenström DRC to be allowed to celebrate the Holy Communion separately. The church council justifiably rejected the request and referred it to the presbytery of Albany. The latter unanimously recommended to the church council of Stockenström that due to the biases and weaknesses of some of the congregants, the Holy Communion should be administered separately to 'coloureds' and whites (Kriel 1963:58). Nicolaas Hofmeyer, a minister of the DRC and professor at the Theological Seminary of the DRC at Stellenbosch, saw the middle-way approach as the most feasible: 'De middenweg tusschen beide is de verkieslijke' (Coertzen 2010:52). According to Hofmeyer, there should not be separation between so 'coloureds' and whites. With regard to the efficiency of the ministry, members from the 'heathendom' should be minister separately from whites, but they should remain members of the same congregation (Coertzen 2010:52). The issue of having separate Holy Communion services for different racial groups was discussed thoroughly at the DRC Synod in 1857. Rev. R. Shand of the DRC Tulbagh tabled the following with regard to the decision of the presbytery of Albany:

> Of het de goedkeuring der Synode wegdraagt, dat in de Gemeenten der Nederduitsche-Gereformeerde Kerk, waar men het begeert, de gekleurden in een afzonderlijk gebouw, echter onder bestier en opzigt Van den Kerkraad, alle voorregten der Christelijke Godsdiens afzonderlijk genieten zullen. (*Acta NGK* 1857:58, 60, 89, XII(5))[4]

His submission was keenly debated at the synod. The question that had to be considered was whether people of mixed descent who had been baptised and confirmed as fully-fledged congregants should be allowed to partake in the Lord's Supper together with white congregants, or whether the Holy Communion should be administered to them separately. On scriptural grounds, the synod could not approve the request. The DRC Synod of 1857, however, approved, due to the

---

4 Translation: Whether the synod approves that in the congregations of the Dutch Reformed Church, where the desire exists, coloureds can enjoy all privileges of the Christian religion separately in a separate building, but under administration and supervision of the church council.

'weakness of some', to allow the creation of separate buildings for believers from the so-called heathendom. The decision of the synod reads as follows:

> The synod considers it desirable and according to the Holy Scripture that our heathen members (non-whites) be accepted and initiated into our congregations wherever it is possible; but where this measure, as a result of the weakness of some, would stand in the way of promoting the work of Christ among the heathen people, then congregations set up among the heathen, or still to be set up, should enjoy their Christian privileges in a separate building or institution. (*Acta NGK* 1857:58, 60, 89, XII (5))[5]

This decision opened the door for the establishment of separate churches based on colour and led ultimately to the constitution of separate churches in the Reformed Family, namely, the establishment of the Dutch Reformed Mission Church of South Africa (DRMC) in 1881, the Dutch Reformed Church in Africa for Africans (from 1910) and the Reformed Church in Africa for Indians (1968). The 1857 decision officially introduced church apartheid into the DRC. One should, however, take note that many churches for people of mixed descent ('*oefeninghuise*' or '*gentisate*') already existed by 1857. In Wagenmakersvallei and Tulbagh and many other places, the sacraments had been administered separately to people of mixed descent long before the decision of 1857. At the 1857 DRC Synod, praxis merely became church policy. The 1857 decision led to the division of Christians on the basis of colour at the Table of the Lord as a matter of practice and policy and paved the way for the establishment of the first racially segregated Reformed church in South Africa, and ultimately societal apartheid (Plaatjies-Van Huffel 2014). The decision paved the way for the separation of Reformed churches in South Africa along colour and racial lines and the later theological justification of racism. The inability of the DRC Synod to take a qualified stand on the issue smoothened the way for church and societal apartheid.

In 1880, the DRC identified in 1880 twenty mission stations ("*gestichte*") who could become part of the DRMC and invited the missionaries from the selected mission stations to partake in a conference where, amongst other issues, the draft constitution for the envisaged separate church was to be discussed. No people of colour attended the conference. On 12 November 1880, the DRC Synod approved the Constitution for the Nederduitsche Gereformeerde Zendingkerk Van Zuid-Afrika

---

5   Original wording: 'De Synode beschouwt het wenschlijk en schrifmatig dat onze ledematen uit de Heidenen, in onze bestaande gemeenten opgenomen en ingelijfd worden, overall waar zulks geschieden kan; maar waar deze maatregel, ten gevolge van de zwakheid van sommigen de bevordering van de zaak van Christus onder de Heidenen, in de weg zoude staan, de gemeenten uit de Heidenen opgerigt, of nog op te rigten, hare Christelijke voorregten in een afzonderlijk gebouw of gesticht genieten zal.'

(Dutch Reformed Mission Church or DRMC). Soon after the synod, invitations were issued to all mission stations of the DRC to attend the first Synod of the Mission Church. On 5 October 1881, the Constituting Synod of the DRMC met in Wellington. The attendance at the synod was poor with only five congregations represented, namely Wellington, Wynberg, George, Zuurbraak and Beaufort West. Reverend Paul Teske of Beaufort West strongly objected to the constituting of a racially-segregated church controlled by the DRC. Notwithstanding Teske's objections, the synod approved the constituting of the Reformed DRMC of South Africa, primarily for people of mixed descent. Initially, African people could also become members of the DRMC (Plaatjies-Van Huffel 2009:250-265).

From the above, it seems clear that church apartheid developed long before the National Party (NP) took power in 1948 and adopted the policy of apartheid (separateness). In the editorial of *Die Kerkbode*, the official newspaper of the DRC, on 22 September 1948, shortly after the National Party came to power, it became clear that the DRC supported apartheid as state policy and justified it on a scriptural basis. The editorial referred to apartheid as church policy (*'apartheid is 'n kerklike beleid'*) (Van der Watt 1977:84).

The policy of apartheid brought widespread opprobrium. After its election victory, the National Party institutionalised and consolidated existing discriminatory and segregative policies and bills. Numerous apartheid laws were passed from 1948 onwards, which confined the people of South Africa's life in minute detail. These laws were attempts to keep South African citizens apart on racial and ethnic lines. For example, the apartheid laws laid down legal provisions on the specific areas where different population groups could own property, reside, work and even enjoy leisure. The Prohibition of Mixed Marriages Act (No. 55 of 1949) prohibited marriages between white people and people of other races; while the Immorality Amendment Act (No. 21 of 1950) prohibited adultery, attempted adultery or related 'immoral' acts, such as sexual intercourse between white and black people. The primary aim of the Group Areas Act (No. 41 of 1950) was to make residential separation compulsory. The Population Registration Act (No. 30 of 1950) provided that all South Africans be racially classified in one of three categories: white, black or coloured. According to this act, Indians fell in the coloured category. In disputed cases, a Race Classification Board took the final decision on what a person's race was. The Natives (Abolition of Passes and Co-ordination of Documents) Act (No. 67 of 1952), commonly known as the 'Pass Law Act', forced black people to carry passbooks with their fingerprints, photo and information, in order to access non-black areas. It was a criminal offence to be unable to produce a pass when required to do so by the police. No black person could leave a rural area for an urban one without a permit from the local authorities. On arrival in an urban area, a permit to seek work had to be obtained within 72 hours. Families were torn apart due to the racial classification laws. The University Education Act (No. 45 of 1959) provided for the establishment of separate tertiary institutions for blacks, Indians, coloureds and whites, of which the University of the Western Cape (UWC) was one. Black people were not allowed to attend 'white universities' without special permission from the government and vice versa.

Although the members of the congregations of the DRMC and the DRCA suffered directly from the results of apartheid (e.g., forced removals, pass laws, migrant labour, group areas, racially segregated education systems, prohibition of mixed marriages, and 'Bantustans') the decisions of the DRMC and DRCA synods from 1950 to 1974 reflect a perplexing apathy towards the socio-political situation in South Africa (Plaatjies-Van Huffel 2014).

The DRC played a pivotal role in the theological justification of what later became known as 'separate development'. At a conference organised by the Federal Mission Council of the DRC family, which took place from 4 to 6 April 1950 in Bloemfontein, the *'naturellevraagstuk'* (native question) was discussed. The 'native question' tried to spell out exactly how different nations could live equally but separately in one geographical area (Van Schalwyk 1950:12-22). The solution arrived at during that mission conference later became known as the policy of separate development. There was also an inexplicable absence of critique from both the DRMC and the DRCA on the 'native question' (Plaatjies-Van Huffel 2014).

In 1970, the DRC General Synod appointed a permanent commission for the study of race and ecumenical issues (*Agenda Algemene Sinode NGK* 1970:785; Van der Merwe 2010:154). The report from this commission, approved by the General Synod in 1974, was published in 1975 under the title: *Ras Volk en Nasie en Volkereverhoudinge in die Lig van die Skrif* (RVN) (*NGK Algemene Sinode* 1975:1-16). The RVN supported the policy of separate development, of which the outline can be traced back to the 1950 Bloemfontein conference. The RVN in its reflection on racial and human relations emphasis that the church of Jesus Christ must accept the Word of God as the starting point and norm. The presumption is that although the Bible is not a scientific textbook, it provides fundamental principles that have normative meaning for all areas of life, including racial and ethnic relationships (*NGK Algemene Sinode* 1975:1-16). The commission's report (RVN) was translated into English under the title *Human Relations and the South African Scene in the Light of the Scripture* (DRC 1976), as well as into other languages (Dutch, French and German) in order to disseminate the DRC's policy on race and ethnicity both nationally as well as abroad.

Throughout the years the white Afrikaans Reformed churches of South Africa worked out in considerable detail the theological and moral justification for the system of apartheid (Plaatjies-Van Huffel 2014:310). The DRC theologically justified the system of apartheid, which deprived black people of their right to vote, the right to freedom of speech and assembly, and basic labour rights, for example, the fundamental right to live where they please, work, and receive education and social security without discrimination on the grounds of race or gender (*General Synodal Commission of the Dutch Reformed Church* n.d:6-11)[6]

This policy was based on the DRC theological anthropology. According to Christina Landman, the theological anthropology of the DRC is dualistic by nature and can assume one of three forms:

1. In the basic form, a dualistic anthropology accentuates the difference between groups of people; between white and black, between men and women. The distinction is usually made on biological level.

2. In a more developed form, dualistic anthropology acknowledges that people are equal but different. In a dualistic anthropology, it is argued that white and black are equal in value before God, but belong separately because of cultural differences. This anthropology presupposes that men and women are equal but different, precisely to complement/supplement each other. Man and woman are therefore equal, but by divine decree men must lead and women must follow.

3. In the most sophisticated form, a dualistic anthropology acknowledges the liberation of people but still presupposes that groups of people must be polarised to enable emancipation. A dualistic anthropology, therefore, works with the presupposition that people should necessarily be polarised to achieve the expected outcomes (Landman 1991:33).

The RVN was the DRC's first official answer to the call of Cottesloe. The Cottesloe Consultation, initiated by the World Council of Churches (WCC), was held from 7 to 14 December 1960, shortly after the Sharpeville massacre, at the Cottesloe hostel of the University of the Witwatersrand. Representatives of the eight member-churches of the WCC in South Africa attended. At the end of the conference, the so-called 'Cottesloe Declaration' was released. Van der Merwe is correct when he maintains that the content of the document was nothing else than a confirmation of the church's support for the policy of the National Party government, giving separate development a biblical foundation (Van der Merwe 2010:157). Marriages between racial groups were seen as undesirable and forbidden and common worship was only permissible in special situations.

---

6   See also Apartheid laws in the Bibliography.

The DRC sent a delegation spearheaded by F.E. O' Brein Geldenhuys to their partners overseas to enlighten them about the RVN. The Gereformeerde Kerken in Nederland (GKN) and the Swiss Federation of Reformed Churches ('*Reformierter Bund*') condemned the RVN (Geldenhuys 1982:61). The RVN was strongly critiqued for, among other things, the interpretation of Scripture, the biblical foundation and the sanctioning of the political policy of separate development as well as the dualism between theology and practice in the document. In a report published after the discussions, the *Reformierter Bund* declared that they regarded the RVN as a theological confirmation of the political system in South Africa, in which the separation of races meant in practice the dominion of the one and the discrimination, denial of rights and exploitation of the other (*Handelinge Algemene Sinode NGK* 1982:157; Van der Merwe 2013:6). On 22 September 1979, the *Reformierter Bund* released the following press release:

> Against the background of the terrible consequences of the Homeland policy, against the background of the news we get about torture and banning, against a background of a church divided according to race, we have asked their advocating for the disadvantages of the oppressed and their involvement in the struggle for church unity. Our dialogue partner could not give a satisfactory answer, because they had to hold on in general to the present official line of the NGK as outlined in the 1974 Synod report. (Van der Merwe 1990:157)

The churches in Germany as well as the GKN not only severely criticised the RVN, but by 1982 had severed all relations with the DRC (Van der Merwe 2013:56).

Early resistance to apartheid within the DRMC

Not everybody in the DRMC passively accepted the theological justification of apartheid. An early protestation against the apartheid policy and the theological justification of apartheid came from Rev. Isaac David Morkel (1910–1983). Morkel studied at the Stofberg Theological School (for Africans) in the Orange Free State and completed his studies in 1943. On 2 January 1945, he became part-time minister of the Word in charge of the Rondebosch Congregation of the DRMC in Crawford. On 22 December 1945, he was ordained as the full-time minister of the congregation. During the 1940s, only six people of mixed descent had been legitimised by the DRMC, namely, A.D. Andries, P. Solomon, A. Ontong, J. Prinz, W.A. September (who, like Morkel, studied at The Stoffberg Theological School) and Morkel himself. Rev. Morkel, therefore, struggled to let his voice be heard in a church where the missionaries had been members of the DRC and had been trained and commissioned by the DRC to work in the Mission churches. On 7 October 1946, Morkel was elected as chairman of the Presbytery of Wynberg of the DRMC. He was outspoken against discrimination, particularly as it applied to mixed-race communities at the Cape. Subsequently, he became known as an opponent of apartheid and thus an embarrassment to his church (Carstens 1959:48).

On 3 September 1948, Morkel convened a meeting in Crawford to consider means to oppose apartheid. Approximately 116 members from twenty-eight DRMC congregations unanimously supported a motion tabled by him to oppose apartheid on scriptural grounds. They protested the proposed race classification legislation and appealed to the National Party government not to implement these laws. The result of this event resounded within the Presbytery of Wynberg. On 7 October 1948 and under the leadership of Morkel the Presbytery of Wynberg declared that it could not find any grounds for the policy of apartheid in the Bible (Loff 1998:234). The Presbytery rejected the unbiblical implementation of forced apartheid, which gave rise to discrimination against 'coloureds', and in so doing destroys Christlikeness among 'coloureds' (Submission of the URCSA to the Truth and Reconciliation Commission 1997:15). On the contrary, they found that apartheid was evil, sinful, and harmful and out of harmony with human laws. A system that must be rejected in all its forms. Furthermore, under Morkel's leadership, the Presbytery approved an overture to the next synod of the DRMC regarding the biblical justification of apartheid. The premise of the Wynberg Presbytery was that the DRMC should express itself regarding apartheid and the theological justification thereof (*Acta NGSK* 1950:160; Fortein 2016:55). The next year, in a lengthy statement, the Presbytery denounced apartheid as unbiblical (*Notule, Ring Van Wynberg* 1949:1-2).

Furthermore, on the inauguration of the Voortrekker Monument on 16 December 1949, Morkel called or a day of prayer in supplication that the Lord delivers the land from the affliction of apartheid. The official structures of the DRMC did not welcome Morkel's objections against the theological justification of apartheid. Morkel wrote several letters to the editor of the *Cape Times* newspaper, focusing on racial discrimination. Rev. Morkel announced that he could no longer preach love and practise apartheid. He decided to leave the DRMC to establish a separate church. For Morkel, the abolition of the race classification laws was an existential issue. His family has been separated by the apartheid laws. Of his ten brothers and sisters, five were classified white and the rest coloured South ('Africa minister wants race laws changed', published in *The New Courier*, 21 January 1967, p. 3).

It was clear to Morkel that the leadership of the DRMC and congregations were not ready to support the request of the presbytery of Wynberg to denounce of the theological justification of apartheid (Fortein 2016:57; Loff 1998:248; *Notule, Ring Van Wellington* 1948:174). This left Morkel with no choice other than to leave the DRMC. On 30 September 1950, days before the meeting of the DRCM Synod, Morkel announced that he and 26 church council members of the Rondebosch congregation would leave the DRCM to form their own Calvyn Protestante Kerk (Calvin Protestant Church) (Loff 1998:248). Morkel gave his farewell sermon on 8 October 1950 in Athlone from the back of a lorry since the DRMC had forbidden him to use the Rondebosch church building. On 15 October 1950, the Calvin Protestant Church was established in the Glenmoore town hall in Athlone, Cape Town. The Calvin Protestant Church did not differ in its doctrine, rites or confessional basis from the DRCM or the DRC, but strongly denounced the theological justification of apartheid. In due time congregations were constituted in Worcester, Malmesbury, Paarl, Retreat, Newtown, Kommagas, Ravensmead and Macassar.

The Calvin Protestant Church was welcomed enthusiastically by the inhabitants of Komaggas, one of the 'coloured reserves' in Little Namaqualand in the North-West Cape. On 8 December 1956, Rev. Morkel visited Komaggas and held a service in the open. Nearly a third of the population of the reserve attended this service, while only twenty-six people were at the service in the DRMC (Carstens 1959:49). During the first fourteen months after Rev. Morkel was invited to Komaggas, 256 children were baptised and 90 young people confirmed. By 1960, there were about 600 confirmed members and many baptised members who had not yet been confirmed. On 5 May 1957, a petition containing more than 700 signatures was presented to Dr I.D. du Plessis, Commissioner for Coloured Affairs, asking for permission to acquire land on which to erect a church (Carstens 1959:51). The request was refused.

The Calvin Protestant Church met with opposition from the government regarding access to Komaggas. On 25 October 1957, the Minister of the Interior promulgated Regulation 88. According to Carstens, Sub-regulation (i) of Regulation 88 stipulates that any person, without the approval of the commissioner or the magistrate of the area concerned,

> (a) Holds, presides at or addresses any meeting, gathering or assembly at which more than five persons in the area under the control of the Board of Management are present at any one time; or (b) Permits any such meeting, gathering or assembly to be held in his house or on other premises or land under his control, shall be guilty of an offence.
> (Carstens 1959:51)

It was, however, possible for more than five persons to gather, without permission, for events such as funerals, weddings, political meetings presided over by members of parliament and religious services held by the established church or churches in the area (Carstens 1959:51). According to Regulation 88, the Commissioner for Coloured Affairs had first to consult with the established church in the area concerned before granting or refusing the Calvinist Protestant Church permission to continue its work. The regulation was nothing more than a virtual ban on all religious services or meetings held by any denomination other than the DRC. According to Carstens, it could be assumed that also the DRMC did not grant permission to the Calvinist Protestant Church to do missionary work in the area (Carstens 1959:53). When the churches in the area sought approval to do missionary work in the area, only the DRMC was allowed. The others, including the Calvinist Protestant, Anglican and Roman Catholic churches had to obtain permission for every service they held.

In January 1957, shortly after Rev. Morkel had been first invited to the reserves, a party of DRC officials visited the various DRMC congregations, expressly to warn them against what they termed the 'Morkel danger' (Carstens 1959:53) They tried to show that Morkel was an unreliable and irresponsible character and that his church was a new sect completely alien to the DRC. On 7 March 1958, the first prosecution against the Calvin Protestant Church took place. Three members of that church were found guilty of holding a prayer meeting of more than five persons in the Komaggas Reserve. Meetings of more than five persons needed special approval of the Commissioner. The regulation allowed for events such as funerals, weddings and religious services, but only if held by an established church. The three men were fined and suspended for three years. In this way, the government played a role in silencing the voices that objected against apartheid in the church (Carstens 1959; Morkel & Thebus 2011:1-4). Morkel, in vain, called upon the apartheid government to appeal the race laws. He, among others, called for the end of the 'torture and inhumanity created by devilish race classification laws' ('South Africa Minister wants race laws changed', *The Pittsburgh Courier*, 21 January 1967, p. 3). The DRMC was unresponsive to Morkel's objections against apartheid. The present-day Calvinist Protestant Church consists of 35 congregations spread over the Western Cape, Southern Cape, Eastern Cape, Northern Cape (Namaqualand) and Namibia.

The ecumenical movement paved the way (1964–1982)

The international ecumenical movement played a critical role in the anti-apartheid struggle and the ultimate decision of the DRMC during their synod in September 1982 to draft a confession. Race relations had been long on the agenda of the Reformed Ecumenical Council (REC), founded in 1946. Already in 1948, the General Assembly of the United Nations condemned apartheid. From 1958 on, the REC declared there was no scriptural evidence for or against mixed-race marriages. As mentioned, in December 1960, shortly after the Sharpeville massacre, the consultation at Cottesloe took place. At that stage, the DRMC was not a member of the WCC and was, therefore, not obliged to prepare a response to the questions which the WCC had put to the member churches. Even after Cottesloe, both the DRMC and the DRCA did not directly reject the basic philosophy of segregation. Rather a deafening silence on the issue prevailed in the Acts of the Synods of the RCA and the DRMC until 1974.

In 1968, the REC declared that that church and state may not prohibit mixed-race marriages and furthermore stated that the unity of the body of Christ should come to expression in common worship, including Holy Communion, among Christians regardless of race. The REC also held a series of consultations with South Africans in 1971, 1978, 1981, 1982 and 1989, when the REC interim committees met with churches in South Africa to discuss race relations. In 1980, the Council called on its members to work to remove the structures of racial injustice and use their influence with the South African government to effect such changes. The Council did not declare that the South African churches were, in fact, guilty of heresy, but asked the South African member churches to answer whether this applied to them (Luke & Van Houten 1997:4).

In 1964, the General Assembly of the WCC, meeting in Frankfurt, declared that racism is nothing less than a betrayal of the gospel and that the unity in Christ of members, not only of different confessions and denominations but of different nations and races, points to the fullness of the unity of all in God's coming kingdom. The WCC stated clearly that the exclusion of any person on grounds of race, colour or nationality, from any congregation and part of the life of the church, contradicts the very nature of the church. The WCC Programme to Combat Racism was launched in 1969 in response to a 1968 mandate from the council's Fourth Assembly in Uppsala, Sweden. The programme played a highly visible and controversial role in international debate about white-minority rule in South Africa. In 1970, the General Assembly of the WCC held in Nairobi confirmed that the church must recognise racism for the idolatry it is and that the church that by doctrine and/or practice affirms segregation of peoples (e.g. racial segregation) as a law for its life cannot be regarded as an authentic member of the body of Christ. The DRC, as well as the Nederduitse Hervormde Kerk, did not heed to the WCC declarations.

During the 1980s, the DRMC became a member of the REC, the WCC programme, the World Alliance of Reformed Churches (WARC) as well as the South African Council of Churches (SACC) (*Agenda en Handelinge NGSK* 1982:21). TheWCC's Programme to Combat Racism was tabled at the DRMC Synod in 1982 and had a bearing on decisions made regarding racism and apartheid at the synod (*Agenda en Handelinge NGSK* 1982:210-250). According to Russel Botman, the systematic theology class at the University of the Western Cape during 1978 struggled to make theological sense of the resistance to apartheid. Their professor of systematic theology, Jaap Durand, challenged the class to find the theological essence of the judgement on apartheid. The class arrived at the following conclusion: 'Apartheid has as its point of departure the irreconcilability of people of different race groups. It was thus against the heart of the gospel of Jesus Christ, which takes its point of departure in the doctrine of reconciliation' (Botman 1997:1). In October 1978, the DRMC Synod considered the theological conclusion that apartheid was 'anti-evangelical' against the heart of the gospel of Jesus Christ. The synod clearly stated that apartheid, being a system of oppression and injustice, is sinful and incompatible with the Bible (meaning it is against the gospel) because it is based on a fundamental irreconcilability of human beings, thus rendering ineffective the reconciling and uniting power of Lord Jesus Christ (*Agenda en Handelinge NGSK* 1978:200). The racism of apartheid was, therefore, a structural and institutional sin.

The DRMC sent a full delegation, spearheaded by Allan Boesak, to the WARC General Council, which met in August 1982 in Ottawa, Canada. Allan Boesak presented the position of the synod on matters pertaining to racism to the General Council (Botman 1997:1). In his paper 'He made us all, but...', prepared for the assembly, Allan Boesak pointed out that the WARC had a responsibility towards its member churches in South Africa who suffered under the apartheid theology and policy (Boesak 1984:11). Furthermore, Boesak introduced a motion at the assembly requesting that the WARC declare apartheid a heresy. Subsequently, the WARC General Council declared that the situation in South Africa constituted a *status confessionis*. The latter is a Latin term meaning that which is foundational for belief and behaviour and must be affirmed by professing members of the church. The declaration of *status confessionis* becomes necessary when the integrity of the proclamation of the gospel is at stake. The white Afrikaans Reformed churches of South Africa through the years have worked out in considerable detail both the policy itself and the theological and moral justification for the system. Apartheid ('separate development') is therefore a pseudo-religious ideology as well as a political policy (Addendum 1, WARC Resolution on Racism and South Africa). It depends to a large extent on this moral and theological justification. The division of Reformed churches in South Africa on the basis of race and colour was defended by the DRC as a faithful interpretation of the will of God and of the Reformed understanding of the church in the world. This leads to the division of Christians at the Table of the Lord as a matter of practice and policy.

The DRC theologically and morally justified the system of apartheid. Apartheid was institutionalised in the laws, policies and structures in South Africa. This situation brought challenges to the WARC and the WCC. The WARC General Council in Ottawa declared that the apartheid situation in South Africa and the position of both white South African WARC member churches regarding it constitutes a *status confessionis*. The WARC General Council declared as follows:

> The promises of God for his world and for his church are in direct contradiction to apartheid ideals and practices ... We feel duly bound by the gospel to raise our voice and stand by the oppressed ... The Nederduitse Gereformeerde Kerk and the Nederduitse Hervormde Kerk, in not only accepting, but

actively justifying the apartheid system by misusing the gospel and the Reformed confession, contradict in doctrine and in action the promise which they profess to believe. Therefore, the general council declares that this situation constitutes a *status confessionis* for our churches, which means that we regard this as an issue on which it is not possible to differ without seriously jeopardizing the integrity of our common confession as Reformed churches. We declare with black Reformed Christians of South Africa that Apartheid (separate development) is a sin and that the moral and theological justification of it is a travesty of the gospel, and in its persistent disobedience to the word of God, a theological heresy. (WARC 1983:177ff., 1990:173-175, 279-281)

The WARC consequently suspended the membership of the DRC as well as that of the Nederduitsche Hervormde Kerk (NHK) in South Africa (i.e. sending delegates to general council and holding membership in departmental committees and commissions). The WARC General Council reiterated its firm conviction that apartheid ('separate development') is sinful and incompatible with the gospel on the grounds that: (a) it is based on a fundamental irreconcilability of human beings, thus rendering ineffective the reconciling and uniting power of our Lord Jesus Christ; (b) in its application through racist structures it has led to exclusive privileges for the white section of the population at the expense of the blacks; and (c) it has created a situation of injustice and oppression, large-scale deportation causing havoc to family life, and suffering to millions. The WARC stated in the Resolution on Racism and South Africa (Addendum 1). That these two churches would be warmly restored to the full privileges of membership when the following changes have taken place:

1. Black Christians are no longer excluded from church services, especially from Holy Communion.

2. Concrete support in word and deed is given to those who suffer under the system of apartheid ('separate development').

3. Unequivocal synod resolutions are made which reject apartheid and commit the church to dismantling this system in both church and politics (WARC 1983:176-180).

The decisions of REC, WARC and WCC on racism and apartheid paved the way for the declaration of a *status confessionis* by the DRMC during September 1982. The heart of the gospel was at stake. The WARC General Council in Ottawa, 1982 subsequently declared that apartheid represents *a status confessionis*, that it is essentially sinful and its theological justification a heresy. According to Smit, one of the co-drafters of the Belhar Confession, the expression '*status confessionis*' means that

> a Christian, a group of Christians, a church, or a group of churches are of the opinion that a situation has developed, a moment of truth has dawned, in

which nothing less than the gospel itself, their most fundamental confession concerning the Christian gospel, is at stake, so that they feel compelled to witness and act over against this threat. (Cloete & Smit 1984:16)

Apartheid constituted a *status confessionis* in which the truth of the Gospel and the Reformed faith was at stake. This implies that it was impossible to disagree on the issue of apartheid without the integrity of the common confession as Reformed church being seriously endangered. The declaration of the WARC on apartheid was reaffirmed by the WARC General Council held in Seoul in 1989 (see Addendum 2). The WARC indicated the following guidelines for the declaration of a *status confessionis*:

1. Jesus Christ sets us free to confess our faith, to confess our sins and hear God's word of forgiveness, to witness to him and to live in love towards God and our neighbour. This is the primary meaning of Christian confession.

2. Any declaration of a *status confessionis* stems from the conviction that the integrity of the gospel is in danger. It is a call from error into truth. It demands of the church a clear, unequivocal decision for the truth of the gospel, and identifies the opposed opinion, teaching or practice as heretical.

3. The declaration of a *status confessionis* refers to the practice of the church as well as to its teaching. The church's practice in the relevant case must conform to the confession of the gospel demanded by the declaration of *status confessionis*.

4. The declaration of a *status confessionis* addresses a particular situation. It brings to light an error which threatens a specific church. Nevertheless, the danger inherent in that error also calls in question the integrity of proclamation of all churches. The declaration of a *status confessionis* within one particular situation is, at the same time, addressed to all churches, calling them to concur in the act of confessing.

5. When church bodies declare a *status confessionis*, they declare first of all that they themselves are in a situation in which a clear decision for the truth of the gospel must be made. The declaration of *status confessionis* therefore has the character of self-obligation.

6. A declaration of a *status confessionis* must, therefore, be treated as a matter of high seriousness. The fragmented history of Reformed churches is a sober warning against declaring a *status confessionis* on issues that are less than central to the gospel.

7. It is not appropriate to declare a *status confessionis* in order to emphasise commitments which are primarily based on current ethical, social or political concerns ... It is quite unjustifiable to declare a *status confessionis* in order to exert moral pressure upon Christian sisters and brothers who take the call to Christian discipleship as seriously as we do, but give different answers to

such ethical, social or political challenges. Christian confession is always and inevitably particular and historical. It reverberates beyond the particular historical context when it authentically echoes the claim and promises of God, our Creator, redeemer and sanctifier. In this sense, every act of punctual confession and witness has universal import and contributes to the life of the church as a community of witnesses (WARC 1990:279-281).

According to Karel Blei, a 'neutral' position regarding apartheid is not different from, a pro-apartheid position. She maintains that a *status confessionis* is not just a matter of free discussion or of personal moral conviction, but indeed a matter of faith (Blei 1994:1-3). Heresy is not just mistake or error. It is indeed betrayal of the gospel doctrine in contradiction with it. It is false doctrine, which can only be rejected by the church, and for which, by definition, there is no place within the church. In the Christian tradition, confession always goes together with rejection. It is in this rejection that the confession of Jesus Christ, in that given situation, gets its special, concrete focus. The Ottawa resolution put the theological justification of apartheid on the same level as such heretical doctrines as second-century Gnosticism or Marcionism or fourth-century Docetism. Ottawa considered the ideology of apartheid, especially because it was presented as a Christian, biblical position and a threat to the very heart of the gospel. The Ottawa resolution was not just a denunciation of a certain form of apartheid, of a special way of practising apartheid, of a certain outcome of apartheid. No, it is apartheid itself – apartheid as such, that has been denounced unconditionally. According to the Ottawa declaration, these churches, because of their outspoken pro-apartheid position, had become heretical churches, witnessing not to the gospel, but in opposition to it. That Ottawa did not shrink from suspending these two churches indicates how seriously its denunciation of the 'Christian' apartheid ideology and its statement on *status confessionis* were meant.

The drafting of the Confession

The socio-political realities in apartheid South Africa had a bearing on the decisions of the DRMC Synod of 1982, which convened in Belhar. The name 'Belhar' in the confession refers to a township in Cape Town, constituted by the apartheid government for the so-called coloured people in which to live. The apartheid government had set up semi-urban townships for black, Indian and 'coloured' population groups, of which Belhar is merely one. The adoption of the Belhar Confession, therefore, did not take place in a political vacuum. It was adopted in a so-called coloured township, in a racially segregated Reformed church, especially constituted by the DRC in 1881 for people of mixed descent.

The 'Broederkring van NG Kerke' (later called the 'Confessing Circle') was established in 1974 in Bloemfontein by about 60 clergy, evangelists, church council members and lay members of the DRMCA and the DRCA. At the DRMC Synod of 1982, the members of the Confessing Circle played a pivotal role in the deliberations. The Confessing Circle had set itself the goal of guiding and pressuring the church in the struggle against apartheid and attaining church unity, especially affecting debates on a synodical level with regard to social justice issues. Because of its opposition to apartheid, the members of the DRMC and the DRCA became victims of security legislation and the Confessing Circle was viewed as the authentic voice of the oppressed within the two churches. The Confessing Circle period represents the struggle within the church. The Circle swayed the theological thinking of the DRMC and the DRCA and ultimately influenced the drafting and acceptance of the Belhar Confession (Submission of the URCSA to the Truth and Reconciliation Commission 1997:1-5).

The mid-1970s, with the Soweto uprisings as a turning point, overturned just about everything within the DRMC and the DRCA. During the 1970s, the communities served by the DRMC and the DRCA became increasingly involved in protesting against and opposing apartheid legislation in all spheres of life. Youth and student revolts resulted in expulsions and detentions, and ultimately some members of the DRMC and the DRCA even went into exile (Submission of the URCSA to the Truth and Reconciliation Commission 1997:5). These churches did not remain untouched by the realities of the day, and from 1974 onwards, both the DRMC and the DRCA expressed their disapproval of the system of apartheid. During the 1980s, the DRMC and the DRCA strongly opposed the way in which the South African government used banning, detention without trial and solitary confinement to silence those who criticised the unjust system of apartheid. For example, Dr A.A. Boesak, the Reverend R.J. Stevens, A. Beukes, H.R. Botman, J.D. Buys, J. de Waal, E. Leeuw, B. Leuvenink, J. Thyse, A.J. Visagie, P. Moatse, K. E. Leputu, L. Mabusela, L.M. Matsaung, E.M. Tema, elder N.J. Matlakane, and others were convicted and imprisoned (*Agenda en Handelinge NGSK* 1982:25).

During the 1978 and 1982 synods of the DRMC, numerous social justice issues were tabled and extensively deliberated upon. For example, the 1978 DRMC Synod took cognisance of the RVN and stated that apartheid rested to a significant extent on the theological and moral justification of the system. The synod declared that apartheid and the moral and theological justification of it ridiculed the gospel and was a theological heresy (*Agenda en Handelinge NGSK* 1978:2, 21).

A report on black power and black theology was tabled at the DRMC synods of 1978 and 1982 (*Agenda en Handelinge NGSK* 1978:269-298, 1982:377-380.). At the DRMC Synod in September 1982, the role of the church and society in apartheid

South Africa again came under scrutiny and reports on apartheid and racism were tabled (*Agenda en Handelinge NGSK* 1982:32-34, 443-469). Consequently, the DRMC called for the repeal of the Group Areas Act, which made the residential separation compulsory. At the same synod, the Immorality Amendment Act and the Prohibition of Mixed Marriages Amendment Act, which invalidated any marriage entered into outside of South Africa between a male citizen and a woman of another racial group, were critiqued for the first time in the history of the DRMC. The synod urged the government to recall all laws against racially mixed marriages (*Agenda en Handelinge NGSK* 1982:15). The synod also affirmed that the migrant labour system was one of the factors that disrupted the stability of marriage and family life among black people (*Agenda en Handelinge NGSK* 1982:438). The synod of 1982 noted the infringement of human dignity which the congregants had to endure due to the apartheid laws, namely, separate entrances in business places, poor public services, racially divided beaches, poor sport facilities,[7] unequal education,[8] unequal salaries, inadequate housing, job reservation (to protect particular racial and ethnic groups), and so forth. (*Agenda en Handelinge NGSK* 1982, 378-379, 431-443). The synod also noted the strong resentment among blacks against the racially segregated education system. The synod, therefore, affirmed that equal educational facilities and opportunities should be provided for all (*Agenda en Handelinge NGSK* 1982:439). These deliberations, affirmations and decisions set the scene for the decision regarding the *status confessionis* and the acceptance of the draft of the Belhar Confession at the same synod.

The DRMC Synod of 1982 took place shortly after the WARC General Council of 1982. The synod deliberated at length on the WARC's declaration of a *status confessionis* regarding apartheid. There were emotional protestations from clergy and church council members regarding the hardships people had to endure due to the policy and practice of apartheid. The synod declared a *status confessionis* regarding apartheid and reasserted that it was a heresy and a misrepresentation of the gospel. The DRMC affirmed that apartheid contradicted the very nature of the church and saw apartheid as a structural and an institutional synod The DRMC followed the WARC in rejecting the defence of apartheid on moral and theological grounds. It was a '*kairos* moment' for the DRMC.

---

7   The Reservation of Separate Amenities Act (No. 49 of 1953) forced segregation in all public amenities, public buildings, and public transport with the aim of eliminating contact between whites and other races. 'Europeans Only' and 'Non-Europeans Only' signs were put up. The act stated that facilities provided for different races need not be equal.

8   The Bantu Education Act (No. 47 of 1953) and the Extension of University Education Act (No. 45 of 1959) made provision for the establishment of separate tertiary institutions for blacks, Indians, coloureds and whites. Blacks were not allowed to attend 'white' universities unless with special permission by the government. The separation of these institutions was not only along racial lines but also along ethnic lines.

Prof. Gustav Bam, lecturer in Pastoral Theology at the Faculty of Theology at the UWC, showed the synod that the acceptance of the *status confessionis* necessarily should lead to the formulation of a confession (*Agenda en Handelinge NGKA* 1983:22). Bam said, quoting Karl Barth, that confession has certain claims that must be met. First, a confession must always bear the character of an action without an ulterior goal – it will take place only to God's honour. One does not confess with an aim in view nor to effect and to carry out this or that with a confession; the confessor aims not at results and expects none. Second, a merely human statement is wholly inadequate as a protest of faith. Third, a confession is distinguished from lyrical effusion in that it occurs as a definite opposition and therefore as an act of defiance and conflict. Finally, Bam conveyed that confession is a free action. It is a response to a summons and rests on free choice. It proceeds from the Holy Spirit who breathes where He wills (Barth 1969/1951:82, 80). According to Bam, if a church has stumbled upon a heresy it has no option but to confess its faith in the face of such a false doctrine.

Consequently, the DRMC Synod of 1982 following in the footsteps of the WARC declared a *status confessionis*. With this position, it was said that the DRC, in its commitment to apartheid, could not have served the God of the Bible nor the reconciliation that the Bible speaks of. The justification of apartheid was not only a disservice to the kingdom of God; it constituted a heresy, an evil act, which is irreconcilable with the kingdom of God. The DRMC realised that in a situation like this you must confess anew to the truths of the Bible in the light of the pseudo-gospel. The DRMC decided to draw up a confession in order to do that.

The synod appointed a committee consisting of Rev. Isak Mentor, Moderator of the DRMC, Dr Allan Boesak, Vice-Moderator of the DRMC, and three lecturers from the UWC (at the time a racially segregated tertiary institution), namely, Dr Dirkie Smit, Prof. Jaap Durand and Prof. Gustav Bam, to draw up a draft confession of faith, known today as the 'Belhar Confession'. The drafters of the Belhar Confession were all held in high regard in the DRMC. According to an article by Murray la Vita, '*Die belydenis Van dominee Dirkie*' published in *Die Burger*, 26 May 2011, the commission entrusted the young Dirkie Smit to draft a document because most of the others were engaged in commission work during the synod. He played a pivotal role in the drafting of the Belhar Confession. Within days, the committee presented the synod the draft. The Belhar Confession was born in a moment of truth. The draft confession dealt with three issues: (1) unity of the church, (2) reconciliation in Christ, and (3) the justice of God. The synod adopted the draft as well as an official accompanying letter to explain the decision to draft the confession. The letter explains among others the attitudes and expectations behind this deed. The beginning of the accompanying letter states:

> We are aware that such an act of confession is not lightly undertaken, but only if it is considered that the heart of the gospel is so threatened as to be at stake. In our judgement, the present church and political situation in our country and particularly within the Dutch Reformed Church Family calls for such a decision. (Belhar Confession 1986:1)

The synod accepted the draft confession of Belhar. The word 'accepted' used for the reception of the report of the commission does not imply adoption. A long process of discernment by the local congregations, which took four years, followed. The Belhar Confession was a response of the church in faith at a time of tremendous challenge and adversity.

The publishing of Murray la Vita's article in *Die Burger* made it public knowledge that Dirkie Smit played a pivotal role in the drafting of the Belhar Confession. Kritzinger, however, highlights the role that the theological declaration of the Confessing Circle in August 1979 was one of the significant documents used by the authors while formulating the Belhar Confession (Kritzinger 2010:209-231). According to Kritzinger, it did not matter who wrote the confession. I concur with Kritzinger in that confessions are formally approved in the Reformed tradition by a specific church, based on a well-established procedure involving local (church council), regional (presbytery) and national (synod) bodies. The stance of the URCSA is that once a confession has been formally approved by a Reformed church, that church 'speaks' or 'confesses' that particular confession, not the individual authors who formulated it or the committee that proposed it to the church. One should always remember that any text, once written, has little to do with the author. Communal authorship and ownership, therefore, applies to the Belhar Confession. The delegates at the DRMC and DRCA synods were painfully aware of the hardships of apartheid and can rightfully be seen as co-authors of the Belhar Confession. The confession put into words their observation about the situation in South Africa.

The Belhar Confession is indeed the culmination of a variety of factors, processes and efforts in the DRMC, DRCA, Confessing Circle and Alliance of Black Reformed Christians in Southern Africa (ABRESCA). The movement and philosophy of the Confessing Circle found extension in the formation of the ABRECSA in 1981. ABRECSA was a broad Reformed forum constituted by members of the black DRC, Presbyterians and the Congregational Church. ABRECSA reflected on Reformed faith and its implications for opposing apartheid within and outside the church. The members of ABRESCA also influenced the decisions of the DRMC and the DRCA on social justice issues during the 1980s. According to Kritzinger (2010), the first and clearest influence of the Confessing Circle's declaration in relation to the Belhar Confession is the one found in Article 4 of the confession: 'As God's property the church must be busy standing where God stands, viz. against injustice and with those who are denied justice' (Confessing Circle's Declaration of 1979), versus 'We believe: that the church, belonging to God, should stand where God stands, namely against injustice and with the wronged' (Belhar Confession, Art. 4). Chris Loff, as coordinator of the drafting team of the Confessing Circle, presented the draft Declaration of the Circle to the plenary of the Confessing Circle conference held in 1979 in Hammanskraal, for approval. Allan Boesak, one of the co-drafters of the Belhar Confession, was the chairperson of the Confessing Circle at the time. The formulation by Chris Loff was approved at the Confessing Circle's meeting. Kritzinger maintains that although the influence of the Confessing Circle's Declaration on the Belhar Confession is in most cases not verbatim, there are indeed discernible influences to be seen in the Belhar Confession.

With only a few small formal changes to the original formulation, the Belhar Confession and the accompanying letter were officially adopted by the DRMC Synod of 1982. The draft of the Belhar Confession was distributed in a booklet to all the congregations of the DRMC, in order for the church councils of the DRMC to comment. It was a confession in concept form, which was to be finalised at the next synod in 1986. The members of the DRMC were aware that they contributed in one way or another also to the situation, and together they accepted responsibility for that which they confessed. The DRMC rejected the claims of an unjust or oppressive government and denounced Christians who claimed theological justification of the system of apartheid. The DRMC committed themselves to a common witness to injustice and equality in society and to unity at the Table of the Lord. It was a moment of *kairos* for the church to obedience.

The Belhar Confession was adopted during a particularly trying time in South Africa's history. Section 17 (the ninety-day detention law) of the General Law Amendment Act (No. 37 of 1963) authorised any commissioned officer to detain – without a warrant – any person suspected of a political crime and to hold them for 90 days without access to a lawyer. The Act also allowed for further declaration of unlawful organisations. The state president could declare any organisation or group of persons that had come into existence since 7 April 1960 to be unlawful. The Internal Security Act (No. 32 of 1979) empowered the government to declare an organisation unlawful and to control the distribution of publications. Meetings of more than twenty persons were declared unlawful unless authorised by the magistrate. Even some of the presbyteries of the DRMC and DRCA could not meet, due to the unrest in South Africa (Submission of the URCSA to the Truth and Reconciliation Commission 1997:2). The apartheid government had the right to declare areas of 'unrest' and to allow extraordinary measures to suppress protests in these areas. On 12 June 1986, three months before the DRMC Synod where the Belhar Confession would be approved, the government extended the existing state of emergency to cover the whole country. Under these circumstances, the DRMC Synod was constituted.

The delegates at the 1986 Synod knew that under a state of emergency the minister of law and order, the commissioner of the South African Police or a magistrate or a commissioned officer could detain without trial any person for reasons of public safety. For example, DRCA ministers of the Word Peter Moatse and K.E. Leputu were detained the same evening after a debate on apartheid in the Regional Synod of Northern Transvaal in 1986. Notwithstanding this, the delegates at the DRMC Synod of 1986 approved the Belhar Confession. The acceptance of the Belhar Confession as an authority of faith in September of that year can, therefore, be seen as an act of defiance. The state of emergency continued until 1990 when it was finally lifted by then state president F.W. de Klerk.

The adoption of the Belhar Confession during the state of emergency can be seen as a church defying state theology at its best, like the Israelites, who refused to 'sing the Lord's song in a foreign land.' In Psalm 137, the Israelites were sitting on the banks of the rivers of Babylon. They had been in exile. The Babylonians requested the Israelites to sing. Instead of obeying their slave masters the Israelites left their harps hanging on trees. This was indeed an act of defiance. They refused to obey the empire. The delegates at the DRMC Synod did more or less the same. They accepted the Belhar Confession knowing that hardships will follow them immediately after the synod. They refused to listen to their masters' voice and meekly accept the *status quo*. The Belhar Confession is a reformed response to the theological justification of apartheid, namely that the gospel and the integrity of the church had been at stake.

Belhar is a profound confession of faith in the face of the 'heresy' of apartheid (see Cloete & Smit 1984). It includes five articles, with the first and last being short statements of faith in the triune God and a commitment to the confession itself. The other three articles each focus on a key issue at the heart of the heresy of apartheid: unity, reconciliation and justice. Article 2 on unity affirms the oneness in Christ that is at the heart of the church and rejects the way that apartheid has entrenched division in the church. Article 3 affirms that the church is entrusted with the gospel of reconciliation and includes the claim that the credibility of this message is seriously affected and its beneficial work obstructed when it is proclaimed in a land which professes to be Christian, but in which the enforced separation of people on a racial basis promotes and perpetuates alienation, hatred and enmity.

Boesak rightly said that the Confession of Belhar became the bedrock of theological reference and reflection as well as a salient point of theological identity within the URCSA Africa (Boesak 2008:143-172).

On the 26 September 1986, after four years of discernment of the local congregation on the inclusion of the Belhar Confession in the standard of faith, the DRMC formally adopted the Belhar Confession as the fourth confession of the church. Prof. Gustav Bam recited the proposals of the ad hoc commission on the Belhar Confession at the synod. He said retention of the confession would not hinder or accelerate the unification process between the DRC and the DRMC.

> A confession lives in the heart of a church. We cannot for the sake of unity hold it back. If we do, these words are like fire that burn in our hearts. What is at stake is the reality of different religious understanding between us and the DRC. These differences will not disappear if we redeem the confession. (*Die Burger*, 29 September 1986)

On Friday 26 September 1986, 399 of the 470 delegates of the DRMC rose to express their endorsement of the Belhar Confession and thereby adopted the confession (*Agenda en Handelinge NGSK* 1986:718-747). Altogether 71 delegates voted against the adoption of the Belhar Confession, including Rev. Isak Mentor, ironically one of the co-drafters of the confession. Mentor's proposal at the synod that the Belhar Confession should not be accepted, but should rather be referred, for the greatest possible unity, to all other Dutch Reformed churches to reach consensus with the other Reformed churches, was rejected by an overwhelming majority. The acceptance of the Belhar Confession held profound judicial implications for all clergy of the DRMC. Eventually, it was expected of all ministers to sign the Belhar Confession. The synod, however, decided to accompany, with pastoral sensitivity, those who were not ready to accept the confession. The writing, as well as the ultimate adoption of the Belhar Confession, was a risky business. For example, many clergy feared that their financial subsidies by the DRC could be revoked or declined (Plaatjies-Van Huffel 2014:315-316). The acceptance of the Belhar Confession also held repercussions for relations with the DRC. The implications of the acceptance of the Belhar Confession were discussed at the Synod. Many pastors wanted to know what the implications were for ministers of the DRC who worked as missionaries in the DRMC, especially regarding their licence, which had been issued by the DRC. Fears were expressed over the DRC's financial aid to congregations, especially in the countryside. The possibility that the DRC could withdraw its financial support to the DRMC was mentioned (*Agenda en Handelinge NGSK* 1986:718-747).

The Belhar Confession was a response of the church in faith at a time of tremendous challenge and adversity. The DRMC found that the only proper response to the challenge for people of faith was a renewed confession in Jesus Christ our Lord, a renewed understanding of the promises of God's Word, and a new commitment to our covenant with God. The DRMC, therefore, requested the REC Assembly of 1988 in Harare to include the Belhar Confession in the list of Reformed confessions in Article II of the Constitution of the Reformed Ecumenical Council to which all member churches must subscribe (Botha 1991:1). The REC Assembly asked the member churches to consider accepting the Belhar Confession and to report their decisions to the 1992 Assembly. The REC member churches were requested to reflect upon the history of the Belhar Confession; the purpose of the Belhar Confession; the question whether the Belhar Confession can stand alongside the classical confessions; the question whether the Belhar Confession is specifically South African in orientation, and whether that would be a hindrance; and the question whether the Belhar Confession should be approved. The REC constituted a theological forum to promote discussion of the Belhar Confession so that an enlightened decision could be made at the REC Assembly in Athens (Schrotenboer 1991:1). There had been diverse opinions in the member churches of the REC over this issue.

Reception of the Belhar Confession

The Belhar Confession is a living document and is a guiding light in the discourse on race, ethnicity, apartheid and the unification of racially-segregated churches in both the global South and the global North. During the past three decades, the DRMC and later the URCSA engaged, on the basis of the Belhar Confession, on numerous issues, inter alia, church reunification between the DRC family, racism, domestic violence, gender, genetic modification of food, xenophobia and globalisation (Addendum 14). The Belhar Confession identifies unity, reconciliation and justice as problems in apartheid South Africa and attempts to provide a solution for the problems, mainly by trying to persuade the reader in affirmation and rejections. The Belhar Confession endeavours to convince, persuade and to motivate the reader to reject apartheid and to affirm fundamental biblical truths. The Belhar Confession, however, does not simply present information and arguments with regard to apartheid, discrimination, racism, etc. It rather employs rhetorical devices: affirmation and rejections. The Belhar Confession confesses its belief in justice as opposed to the practice of apartheid. The Belhar Confession is a call to action in order to change ideas, beliefs and behaviours on unity, justice and reconciliation.

The confession addresses three key biblical issues of concern to all churches, namely, the unity of the church and among all people, reconciliation within church and society, and God's justice. The relevance of the Belhar Confession is, therefore, not confined to southern Africa, and the use or application of this confession in the life of the church is far wider than its original context. The URCSA gave the Belhar Confession as a gift to the worldwide Reformed community. In 1997, the URCSA General Synod requested Reformed churches around the world to consider adopting the Belhar Confession so as to make it a part of the global Reformed confessional basis (*Acts of CRC Synod* 2007:592; *Agenda for CRC Synod* 1999:197-200, 2003:235, 246). During the past thirty years, churches on the continent as well as abroad embarked upon the process of reception and ultimately adoption of the Belhar Confession. The confession helps churches to approach issues of justice in their own context, and as such, has engendered vigorous debate about the nature of confessions in Reformed churches and the nature of the ministry of the church in the world and in the public sphere.

Various churches, based on their own historical moments, decided to adopt the Belhar Confession as part of their confessional basis. The Belhar Confession has been approved by the Calvin Protestant Church (1988), the Evangelical Reformed Church in Africa in Namibia (ERCA) (1997), United Protestant Church in Belgium (UPCB) (1998), the Seattle First Christian Reformed Church (2007), Iglesia Rerformada Dominicana, the Dominican Reformed Church (2009), the Reformed Church in America (RCA) (2010), the Uniting Presbyterian Church in Southern Africa (UPCSA) (2011), the Lesotho Evangelical Church (2016) and the Presbyterian Church in the USA (PCUSA) (2016). The Christian Reformed Church in North America accepted it as an Ecumenical Faith Declaration in 2012.

Other Reformed churches, such as the Dutch Reformed Church in Africa, the Reformed Church in Africa and the Dutch Reformed Church, unsuccessfully tried to include the Belhar Confession in their confessional basis. Although the Belhar Confession was also being studied during the '*Samen op Weg*' process[9] for possible acceptance in the envisaged unified church in the Netherlands, it was not included with the formation of the Protestant Church in the Netherlands (PCN) in the confessional basis of the PCN (Agenda General Synod URCSA 2005:47). However, the PCN, based on the principles of the Belhar Confession, through '*Kerk in Aktie*'[10] is funding several projects in the URCSA, including theological training as well as several diaconal projects in the Western Cape, Eastern Cape and the Northern Cape and at the Beyers Naude Centre for Public Theology at Stellenbosch University.

---

9 The 'Jointly on the way' process is the name of the attempts at closer co-operation of the Dutch Reformed Church, the Reformed churches in the Netherlands and the Evangelical Lutheran Church in the Netherlands since 1961.

10 'Church in Action' is the programme for missionary and diaconal work of the Protestant Church in the Netherlands and of ten smaller churches and ecumenical organisations.

Calvin Protestant Church

Shortly after the DRMC accepted the Belhar Confession as a fully-fledged confession, the Calvin Protestant Church embarked on a church judicial process to include the confession in their confessional basis. This process resulted in the adoption of the confession in 1988. The Calvin Protestant Church became the first denomination on the African continent to accept the Belhar Confession as part of their confessional basis and the Calvin Protestant Church became part of the unification process between the DRCA and the DRMC (*Agenda and Handelinge NGSK* 1986, 1990, 1994). However, the Calvin Protestant Church indicated that the DRC should be part of the united church. When the DRCA and the DRMC decided to continue church reunification in 1994 without the DRC, the Calvin Protestant Church left the church reunification process. Bilateral talks between the URCSA and the Calvin Protestant Church started on 6 February 2006 (Minutes of bilateral discussion with the Calvin Protestant Church held in Belhar 2006:1). The meeting appointed a small task team to oversee the unification process between the churches. The meeting also encouraged congregations and presbyteries the two churches to seek opportunities to work together, especially on a grassroots level. This included pulpit exchanges, congregations visiting each other, joint services, co-operation on various levels and other joint ventures.

Evangelical Reformed Church in Africa

The Evangelical Reformed Church in Africa (ERCA) was established on 3 July 1975 due to the missionary action of the DRC in Namibia (then known as South West Africa) (Lombard & Tjingaete 1995:23-24.). The DRC used the Theological School at Orumana in Kaokoland as a centre of the mission activities (Lombard & Tjingaete 1995:21). The DRC had constituted autonomous congregations in Orumana, Takuasa in Kavango and in Onuno in Ovambo. Like all the other racial segregated churches constituted by the DRC, the ERCA formed with a white moderamen. According to Reverend Boas Tjingaete, the last moderator of the ERCA, the ERCA was nothing more than apartheid's guinea pig (Lombard & Tjingaete 1995:22). Tjingaete, furthermore, stressed that the ERCA served as a basis (reservoir) for new members who fought as soldiers of the defence force of the South West Africa Army, homeland officials, Angolan refugees and other political aliens (Lombard & Tjingaete 1995:24). This relationship did not work out as the DRC had initially anticipated, for soon the ERCA became critical of its white 'mother' and critically accessed its role within the Namibian society. The DRC tried in vain to suppress the critical voices in the ERCA through financial means. The DRC subsidised the ministers of ERCA and in so doing kept them dependent on foreign funding, however, when it was revealed that liberation theology was accepted by ministers of the ERCA, the mission secretary of the DRC was mandated by the DRC to stop payments of subsidies (*Beraad Van*

NGK in SWA 1986:88). Financial manipulation seemed to be a strong motivation for reaching the aspired aims of the DRC concerning the ERCA.

Critical voices emerged in the ERCA against the political misuse of the church, the non-compliance of Reformed church polity principles and the paternalism of the DRC (for example, the upgrading of evangelists as ministers of the Word without following the correct church-order procedures). The ERCA were also critical of the DRC's financial control over salaries, for example, all power to cease the payment of subsidies to ERCA resided with the Synodical Mission Commission of the DRC. Other areas of criticism concerned theological training (for example, the closing of the Theological School at Orumana and the opening of the Windhoek Theological Seminary, without any input of the ERCA), and the emotional manipulation of members and ministers of ERCA to abide by decisions of the DRC in Namibia. The ERCA were also critical of the DRC paternalism and the divide-and-rule strategy. An example of the latter was the division of the ERCA into four regional synods: Ovambo, Kavango, Central and East, without any input of the ERCA. This was done to enable the DRC to manipulate the four small ethnic-based synods more effectively (Lombard & Tjingaete 1995:23-29).

The DRC in Namibia downgraded the Belhar Confession as liberation theology (Lombard & Tjingaete 1995:27, 29, 34-35). The critical thinkers in the ERCA strongly objected against any form of church apartheid and urged in vain that church reunification and the Belhar Confession should be put on the agenda of the bi-annual consultations between the ERCA, the DRC and the URCSA. The last such consultation between the Dutch Reformed churches in Namibia took place on 10 August 1994 (*Beraad Van NGK in SWA* 1986:88). The August 1994 consultation symbolised a critical turning point in the history of ERCA. The ERCA realised that all the proposals of consultation regarding how to enhance unity on the local congregational level in the DRC family merely affirmed the status quo of division along racial lines (among other things, pulpit exchange) (Lombard & Tjingaete 1995:38).

The General Synod of the ERCA held from 18 to 20 August 1996 decided to unify with the URCSA and with a two-thirds majority approved in principle that the Belhar Confession should be included in their confessional basis. According to the URCSA's Rules for Incorporation of Churches, any church that desires to join the URCSA should accept the Belhar Confession before joining (Lombard & Tjingaete 1995:32; URCSA Church Order Regional Synod Cape 2004:182). The ERCA, therefore, referred the decision to their various regional synods for ratification (*Agenda en Handelinge VGKSA* 1997:57; Lombard & Tjingaete 1995:32;). All four regional synods of the ERCA, namely, Ovambo, Kavango, Central and East, approved the inclusion of the Belhar Confession in the confessional basis of ERCA.

In 1997, the General Synod of the ERCA approved the inclusion of the Belhar Confession in their confessional basis. The decision if ERCA was an act of defiance. At the 1997 General Synod, the application of ERCA to unite with the URCSA was approved with a two-thirds majority as they complied with all requirements of the URCSA's Rules for Incorporation of Churches (*Agenda en Handelinge VGKSA*1997:57, 426). Permission was also given at the same General Synod for the eleven URCSA congregations in Namibia to constitute with the congregations of the ERCA as a separate Regional Synod of URCSA. The ERCA ceased to exist on 16 April 1997 and amalgamated with the URCSA Presbytery of Namibia to constitute the Regional Synod of Namibia.

United Protestant Church in Belgium

The United Protestant Church in Belgium (UPCB) adopted the Belhar Confession in 1998 as well as the *Konkordie Van Leuenberg*[11] with a majority vote to be taken up in the rules and regulations ('*Gewoonteregels*') of the UPCB and used it as a basis for further reflection and sharing between the URCSA and the UPCB (Motivatie tot voorstel wijziging Constitutie Art. 1.2, 2015:1). Since 1998, a partnership agreement has existed between the URCSA and the UPCB, based on the Belhar Confession, which had been taken up in the 'Gewoonteregels' of the UPCB.

In order to reinforce the partnership of the URCSA and the UPCB and to come to a deeper knowledge of each other and a better co-operation, these churches exchange members of their ecclesiastic personnel. This is a great opportunity to develop relationships with brothers and sisters in another part the world and strengthen relationships between the churches. It also offers the opportunity to be involved in the mutual mission of the two churches. The UPCB also contributes financially to several projects in the URCSA, notably home-based healthcare, the publication of a newsletter and the Council for World Mission (CWM) Congress (*Agenda General Synod URCSA* 2005:49). The youth of the two churches attend CAP (comrades, artisans and partners) camps twice a year. The camp is a three-way partnership of the *Eglise presbytérienne au Rwanda* (EPR), the URCSA and the UPCB. The aim of the CAP camp is to help break down barriers between people, churches and cultures.

On Saturday 4 November 2015, the Synod of the UPCB unanimously approved the inclusion of the Belhar Confession in Article 1.2 their constitution. The motivation for the new article was as follows: 'The church recognises the significance of the

---

11 Officially called the 'Concordia of Reformed churches in Europe' is a statement on 16 March 1973 in the Leuenberg Conference Centre. This statement formed the basis for the Church Community of Leuenberg. Since 2003, called the Community of Protestant Churches in Europe.

Barmen Theological Declaration,[12] the *Konkordie of Leuenberg* and the Belhar Confession as confession of the church at present' (Motivatie tot voorstel wijziging Constitutie Art. 1.2, 2015:1).

Reformed churches in Germany

The Evangelisch-reformierte Kirsches (Evangelical Reformed Church), Lippische Landeskirche (Church of Lippe) of Germany, the Reformierter Bund in Deutschland (Reformed Federation in Germany) and the URCSA share a common theological history and legacy in the Barmen Declaration and the Confession of Belhar, to covenant against the theological immorality of the situations from which they emerged (Boesak 2010:1).

Already in 1998, the Church of Lippe and the URCSA approved a partnership agreement based on the Belhar Confession. This includes among others an agreement between the Church of Lippe in Germany and the URCSA with regard to vicariate, partnerships between local congregations and support for various diaconal projects, inter alia, the Light of the Children Foundation, a faith-based organisation – locally owned and organically growing, with the aim of helping orphans and vulnerable children to reach their full potential (Report of the Executive of URCSA to the General Synodical Commission 2015:24).

In 2006, the Evangelical Reformed Church in Germany and the URCSA embarked on a joint project regarding globalisation and justice for humanity and the earth. The aim was to interrogate the issues emanating from the Accra Confession adopted by the World Alliance of Reformed Churches' General Council in Accra, Ghana, 2004; share experiences from within the two churches different historical, social, economic, political and theological contexts; and seek common understanding of the complexities of the challenges confronting the church. The URCSA and the Evangelical Reformed Church in Germany hoped to build, with this project among others, consensus based on their shared faith, presenting shared convictions and common testimony to the ecumenical church and the world (Boesak 2010:1). Dr Allan Boesak was appointed to coordinate the Globalisation Project (*Agenda GSC URCSA* 2009:65-66).

In 2015, the Evangelical Reformed Church in Germany, Church of Lippe in Germany, and the Reformed Federation in Germany embarked on a project to make the Belhar Confession better known to their denominations. For this purpose, a working group

---

12 The 'Barmen Declaration' of 1934 or 'The Theological Declaration of Barmen' (*Die Barmer Theologische Erklärung*) was a document adopted by Christians in Nazi Germany who opposed the *Deutsche Christen* (German Christian) movement.

collected all kinds of material relating to the confession for the use in congregations on different levels and in different settings. For example, the group collected material for catechism classes, worship and liturgy, for synods, church gatherings and group discussions. The material was aimed at helping to address various issues of justice, reconciliation and unity. The outcome was the publishing of a brochure, *'Für das Recht straiten: 30 Jahre Bekenntnis von Belhar (1986-2016)'* (Arguing for the Law: 30 years of the Confession of Belhar) during 2016. The richly illustrated brochure includes contributions regarding the practice in church, community and school, as well as theological texts and information on the historical background of the confession. Themes in this booklet include among others *'Das bekenntnis von Belhar'* (the meaning of Belhar), *'Stimmen aus den Kirchen'* (Voices from the churches), *'Belhar in der Gemeindepraxis'* (Belhar in community practice), *'Belhar im Gottesdienst'* (Belhar in worship,), *'Belhar in der Theologie'* (Belhar in theology) and *'Belhar in der Geschichte'* (Belhar in history).This brochure also includes the URCSA's press statement on xenophobia: *'Wie wir auf Fremde in unserer Mitte reagieren, das berührt das Herz der kirchlichen Lehre'* (How we react to strangers in our midst, touches the heart of ecclesiastical doctrine) (see Addendum 14). On 11 September 2016, the Evangelical Reformed Church held a 'Day of Belhar' in all their congregations focusing on Belhar in worship services and other activities. The Reformed Federation in Germany and the Church of Lippe of Germany are considering adopting the Belhar Confession (Van der Borght 2012:77).

Reformed Church in America

The Reformed Church in America (RCA) had been considering the Belhar Confession since 1985, three years after it was written in South Africa. This in response to divisions in the church during apartheid. The Commission on Christian Unity of the RCA studied the Belhar Confession during 1998–1999 and supported ongoing reflection of the confession. In 2001, the Commission on Race and Ethnicity recommended to General Synod to endorse and use the theological foundation of the Belhar Confession to inform the RCA's commitment to being a church freed from racism. The commission also recommended that the church invites members of congregations and classes to carefully study the Belhar Confession and the implications of its endorsement for life and ministry in the RCA, using materials made available by the Commission on Christian Unity.

Throughout the past decade, the commission has made the Belhar Confession and the church-wide study its highest priority and focussed on the creation of study and worship materials that would allow the RCA, its congregations and members, to engage the Belhar Confession deeply and in multiple ways (*Acts and Proceedings RCA* 2010:206). At the 2009 General Synod, essays on the Belhar Confession were tabled including 'Observations on the Belhar Confession and Scripture', 'Observe All

Things: The Belhar and the Call to Discipleship'; 'The Belhar and Race: The Dream Fulfilled'; 'The Belhar and Reconciliation: The confession's Application to the Church's Work in Sudan'; 'The Belhar and Women: Overcoming Sexism to Embrace Unity'; and 'Belhar Confession: Where Are We Now? Why Confess?' (*Acts and Proceedings RCA* 2009:100-101, 240-257, 263-276, 315-319, 327).

In 2000, the General Synod of the RCA instructed the Commission on Christian Unity to commend the Belhar Confession to the church over the next decade for reflection, study, and response as a means of deepening the RCA's commitment to dealing with racism and strengthening its ecumenical commitment to the URCSA and other Reformed bodies.

In 2007, the General Synod of the RCA voted to provisionally adopt the Belhar Confession for two years of testing in worship, teaching, discernment and confession. This meant that it should be considered for final adoption by the RCA Synod in 2009. Since then, the confession has been referred to RCA congregations and classes for study (*Acts General Synod RCA, Report of Global Mission* 2007:166).

During 2009, the General Synod of the RCA voted to recommend adoption of the Belhar Confession as a standard of unity. This recommendation placed this change in the *Book of Church Order* before the classes for approval. The polity of the RCA required that for the final adoption to take effect synod decision must be ratified by a two-thirds (or more) majority vote of the 46 classes of the RCA. This was to be followed by a declarative vote from the 2010 General Synod in order for the change in the *Book of Church Order* to be ratified. Thirty-two classes voted in favour of the recommendation (over two-thirds), with fourteen classes not in favour (*Acts and Proceedings RCA* 2010:309). During June 2010, the General Synod of the RCA officially declared the Belhar Confession the fourth standard of the RCA. The reasons for the support of the inclusion of the Belhar Confession in the RCA confessional basis include the following:

- The Belhar Confession expands and balances the RCA confessions to encompass the whole of Scripture. It speaks to unity and justice in ways that the other confessions do not.
- The Belhar Confession challenges the church to the hard work of unity and it gives a vision for unity and reconciliation in the global church and society.
- The Belhar Confession will help the RCA to add unity, justice and reconciliation to the denominational DNA of the RCA.
- The Belhar Confession heightens awareness of injustices and brings focus to specific areas of injustice, such as poverty and racism.

- The Belhar Confession strengthens the vision of the RCA (*Acts and Proceedings* RCA2010:206).

The RCA decision to include the Belhar Confession in their confessional basis proves their commitment to be faithful to the Triune God and to live out that faithfulness through addressing lingering issues of racism and the injustice of exclusion.

Christian Reformed Church of North America

The Christian Reformed Church in North America (CRC) includes just over one thousand congregations across the United States and Canada. About 75 percent of the churches are in the United States with 25 percent in Canada. Already in 1984, the CRC considered the request of the DRMC to the member churches of REC regarding the adoption of the Belhar Confession (*Acts of Synod CRC* 1984:172:220). In view of the ecumenical relationship of the CRC with the Reformed churches of South Africa in the REC, it was seen as incumbent on the CRC, out of integrity towards these relationships, to judge the decision of the DRMC concerning apartheid (that it is a sin) and the 'moral and theological justification of it' (that it is a theological heresy) (*Acts of Synod CRC* 1984:602-3). During 1985, further informal discussions were held with the DRC regarding their reactions to the Belhar Confession (*Acts of Synod CRC* 1985:211). In 1989, in response to the request to the REC, the CRC Synod instructed the Interchurch Relations Committee (IRC) to study the Belhar Confession and present recommendations to the 1990 Synod (*Acts of Synod CRC* 1989:497).

In 1990, the CRC took official action on the request of the REC interim committee. The CRC Synod of 1990 declared that the Belhar Confession was in harmony with the Reformed faith as a body of truth as articulated in the historic Reformed confessions, and that it was in basic agreement with the REC and CRC decisions on race made over the last decades. The CRC had, therefore, had no objection to its inclusion in the list of Reformed confessions in Article II of the REC Constitution. (*Acts of Synod CRC* 1990:625). At a later meeting of the REC, the recommendation to add the Belhar Confession to Article II of the REC Constitution was vigorously debated, however, not adopted.

In December 2002, the CRC and RCA delegations met and discussed a unified approach to dealing with the Belhar Confession, as asked for by the URCSA. (*Agenda for Synod URSCA* 2005:240). The RCA produced their study materials in a form that allowed for its use as a discussion guide in the CRC context (*Agenda for Synod CRC* 2005:241). The CRC offered the study guide, *Unity, Reconciliation, and Justice: A Study Guide for the Belhar Confession*, to every congregation in the CRC. In 2007, the CRC Synod mandated the IRC to study and assess the Belhar Confession and to present recommendations concerning it to the 2009 Synod (*Acts of Synod CRC* 2007:592). The IRC initiated a series of focus group discussions about the Belhar Confession.

The Classis Pacific Northwest requested the CRC Synod of 2009 to endorse the recommendation of the IRC to accept the Belhar Confession as a doctrinal standard of the CRC on par with the historic three forms of unity. The Classis urged the synod to recommend to the 2012 Synod that Belhar be adopted as a fourth confession of the CRC. The following arguments were tabled as grounds for the acceptance of the confession:

- There is little mention in the classical confessions of the central biblical principle of God's justice and care for the poor and suffering. The Belhar fills this gap in the standard confessions.
- The unity of the church, reconciliation of people in Christ, and God's justice and care of the suffering and poor are fundamental biblical principles that lie at the core of the Reformed faith.
- The issues addressed by the Belhar Confession, Christian unity, reconciliation, injustice and racism are as relevant for the Reformed Church in North America and the world today as they were for the Reformed churches in South Africa under apartheid. Church splits continue, proliferating new denominations, often pitting brother against brother. The evils of racism following centuries of slavery, discrimination and abuse of minorities linger in most facets of North American society. Growing poverty and injustice are major worldwide issues affecting billions of people in nations around the globe (*Overture to the Synod of the CRC* March 2009:1-2).

The CRC Synod of 2009 proposed that the 2012 Synod adopt the Belhar Confession as part of the standards of unity (what the church believes) of the church as a fourth confession, and authorise the revision of the Church Order Supplement and the Public Declaration of Agreement to reflect that adoption (IRC 2009:13). The General Synod of the CRC finally voted for the amendment of the confessional basis of the CRC in June 2012. The churches used the time between the synods of 2009 and 2012 to 'adequately study and reflect on the proposal. This decision invigorated a discussion on confessional theology and the Belhar Confession. For example, John W. Cooper, professor of Philosophical Theology at the Calvin Theological Seminary stated seven reasons why the CRC should not make the confession one of the denomination's doctrinal standards, namely:

- Insufficient content – the Belhar Confession is much too brief and narrow to be a confession.

- Social gospel/liberation theology – it seems that the Belhar Confession equates the gospel with social well-being and to conflate human reconciliation with reconciliation to God.
- Theological ambiguity – the wording of the Belhar Confession is not sufficient to rule out progressive theologies or to make its intended meaning clear.
- Confessional integrity – adopting the Belhar as a confession will undermine the confessional integrity of the CRC.
- Redundancy – the Belhar adds little to what the CRC already affirms. The contemporary testimony of the CRC addresses ethnic diversity, unity in Christ, and social justice.
- Setting of precedents – if it is necessary for the church to make biblical mandates into confessions in order to take them seriously, then churches should also add confessions about worship, evangelism, lifestyle, and more.
- Potential divisiveness – the Belhar is supposed to promote unity but has the potential to divide the church among those who subscribe to it and those who cannot conscientiously do so (Cooper 2010:11-12, 2011a, 2011b:1-34).

After spending more than three hours debating the Belhar Confession, the CRC Synod of 2012 finally adopted it as an 'Ecumenical Faith Declaration' rather than a confession. The Belhar Confession has engendered vigorous debate about the nature of confessions in the CRC. The CRC affirmed that the three central themes of the Belhar Confession, namely unity, justice and reconciliation, have deep biblical resonance for Reformed Christians. They also offer the church a historic opportunity to stand in solidarity with the voices of the global South. Yet the 2012 Synod, due to a lack of clarity over the definition and nature of a confession, decided to adopt the Belhar Confession and place it in a new category called 'Ecumenical Faith Declarations'. This category for the adoption of the Belhar Confession would set it apart from the 'standards of unity'. The full text of the decision reads as follows:

i. That synod expresses its gratitude to the Uniting Reformed Church in Southern Africa for the gift of the Belhar Confession to the CRCNA and the worldwide Reformed community as an excellent call to unity, justice, and reconciliation.

ii. That synod authorise a formal category called Ecumenical Faith Declarations

iii. This category identifies declarations and statements of faith that speak to global realities and uniquely enable the CRCNA to formally state its commitment to and live out key biblical principles.

iv. Documents in this category, while important and contributing to the CRCNA's worldwide witness and ministry, are not considered part of the confessional basis of the CRCNA, and, therefore, will not be listed in the Form of Subscription (CRC Synod 2012 Advisory Committee 7 2012:1-2).

That CRC adopted the Belhar Confession, the accompanying letter from the Uniting Reformed Church of Southern Africa, and the joint statement of the RCA and CRC as an Ecumenical Faith Declaration and recommended it to the churches for study and for incorporation of its themes into their discipline and liturgical ministries.

The grounds for the decisions were as follows:
- The central themes of unity, justice, and reconciliation in the Belhar Confession reflect biblical teaching and are consistent with the historic Reformed confessions.
- The Belhar Confession addresses important issues that are also pertinent to the CRCNA's own history and context in North America.
- The three-year discussion of the Belhar Confession revealed a lack of consensus in support of adopting the Belhar Confession as a fourth confession on par with the historic confessions adopted by the CRCNA.
- The three-year discussion of the Belhar Confession revealed substantial support for the Belhar Confession to have an official status. (*Acts of CRC Synod* 2012, 766-767, Art. 56 D. 3-5)

Such a category could function like Presbyterian confessions, but they would not have the same weight as the CRC's three main confessions. A delegation of approximately 50 representatives from various denominations associated with the World Communion of Reformed Churches (WCRC) met in Grand Rapids, Michigan from 2 to 4 February 2014 in an Ecumenical Faith Declaration Consultation This consultation arose in the aftermath of the CRC's decision to adopt the Belhar Confession and designate it as a document in a new category entitled 'Ecumenical Faith Declaration'. The Ecumenical and Interfaith Relations Committee of the CRC in conjunction with the WCRC extended invitations to consider in an open and transparent environment whether this new category could serve a broader purpose among Reformed churches. It became clear at the consultation that creeds and confessions function in a variety of ways in the life of Reformed churches across the globe. The Ecumenical Faith Declaration category did not convey a clearly understood meaning to those gathered. Some even wondered whether this category could implicitly discriminate among varied expressions of faith in ways that might contribute to an unhealthy hierarchical classification of the church's varied forms of witness. Most the participants in the consultation did not embrace the concept of the new category (Consultation Issues, Report on Ecumenical Faith Declaration 2014:1-4). The WCRC representatives did not endorse the Ecumenical

Faith Declaration, but they also said they appreciated the opportunity to review and discuss creeds, confessions, declarations and statements of faith are having and can have in the life of the contemporary church.

The CRC Synod of 2016 approved a proposal that the Belhar Confession be recognised as a contemporary testimony of the Christian Reformed Church. This would give it the same status as one of the CRC's own contemporary testimonies namely 'Our World Belongs to God'. Changing the status of the Belhar would make a difference in the Covenant of Office-bearers that all office-bearers in the CRC must sign. This covenant now required office-bearers to affirm the contemporary testimony, Our World Belongs to God, as a current Reformed expression of the Christian faith that forms and guides the CRC. If the CRC gave the Belhar the same status as the contemporary testimony, Our World Belongs to God, then each year the office-bearers of the CRC would be confronted with the contents of the Belhar.[13] The proposal to re-categorise the Belhar Confession was referred to the 2017 Synod, which will make the final decision in the matter.

First Christian Reformed Church of Seattle

The First Christian Reformed Church in Seattle was founded in 1857 and forms part of the CRC in North America. The church was introduced to the Belhar Confession in 2005 during a visit to South Africa. Already in 1984, the CRC had concluded that the Belhar was in accord with the decisions of several synods (1984:602-3). In 2006, the First CRC Seattle prepared an overture to their synod in order start to outline a strategy and a process for congregations, classes and synods to study and consider the adoption of the Belhar Confession as a fourth standard of unity.

The premise of the First CRC Seattle echoed that put forward by the The Classis Pacific Northwest, namely, that issues of Christian unity, reconciliation, injustice and racism, highlighted by the Belhar Confession were as relevant for the Reformed churches in North America and the world today as they were for the Reformed churches in South Africa under apartheid. In 2007, the Christian Reformed Church Synod encouraged the ongoing work of the IRC to inform and engage the churches concerning the Belhar Confession and the issues raised by it through a greater dissemination of the Belhar Confession to the congregations. The synod also proposed that the IRC initiate regional-level dialogues to discuss the confession. In mid-2007, the church council of the First CRC Seattle decided there were no denominational prohibitions against an individual congregation adopting a confession that the synod had declared to be biblical and consistent with the existing confessions. The church

---

13 'Synod proposes re-categorising the Belhar Confession as a contemporary testimony'. In *The Banner*, 16 June 2016.

order of the CRC does not forbid congregations from receiving a confession as binding on their members as long as it is in accordance with Scripture and the Standards of Faith. Therefore, on 21 October 2007, by a 94 percent majority, the First Christian Reformed Church Seattle voted to adopt the Belhar Confession as its own and added it as a fourth 'Standard of Unity'.[14]

Iglesia Rerformada Dominicana in the Dominican Republic

The story of the Iglesia Rerformada Dominicana (IRD) (Dominican Reformed Church) is the amazing story of advocacy of the Belhar Confession. The RCA Global Mission supported the adoption of the Belhar Confession as a provisional confession of the church and became one of the advocates of the Belhar Confession. The Global Mission has been engaged in cross-cultural mission for more than 150 years and has a record of excellence that is well known both within our church and the ecumenical mission world (*Acts General Synod RCA Report of Global Mission* 2008:179). The Iglesia Rerformada Dominicana is one of the global churches born out of the Global Mission endeavours. The RCA began its work in the Dominican Republic several years ago through a co-operative partnership of the General Synod Council's Hispanic Ministries Council, former Global Mission director Bruce Menning, Andres Serrano and the Radio Impacto broadcast ministry, begun through the church he serves (Iglesia Reformada La Senda in Corona, California) and the regional synods of Mid-Atlantic and New York (where the largest concentrations of Dominicans outside of the Dominican Republic reside). During 2004, Rev. Andres Serrano of the IRD from Corona, spoke about reformed theology, history and confessions, including the Belhar Confession over Radio *Impacto*. Christians from across the Dominican Republic were inspired by his teachings. Rev. Victor Castro, the current president of the IRD, began discussions with Rev. Serrano of the RCA, Rev. Brigido Cabrera, the RCA's Hispanic Council and Rev. Bruce Menning of partnering with the RCA. They laid a solid foundation of teaching, inspiration, and relational networks among pastors and leaders of independent churches in the Dominican Republic who intended to become the Iglesia Rerformada Dominicana. The mission was to organise to unite independent churches across all 31 provinces (*Acts General Synod Council Reports RCA* June 2007:172). The Council for Hispanic Ministries fully supported the Reformed Church in America's vision of forming a church in the Dominican Republic.

Rev. Andres Serrano trained a group of 250 pastors and workers in the Dominican Republic on Reformed standards, the Belhar Confession and Reformed church polity. On 9 February 2008, the vision and mission of the Iglesia Rerformada Dominicana was presented to over one hundred pastors (*Acts General Synod Council Reports*

---

14 'Adopting the Belhar'. In *The Banner*, 18 January 2011, p. 1.

RCA 2008:187). The RCA Council for Hispanic Ministries approved that the Heidelberg Catechism, Articles of the Belgic Confession, Canons of Dort as well as the Belhar Confession should form part of the confessional basis of the envisaged Reformed church. Preparation to make it official began in January 2009 with a visit by an RCA delegation headed by General Secretary Wesley Granberg-Michaelson and the RCA leadership team. On 23 May 2009, the formation of the IRD General Synod and the first ordinations of pastors and elders took place. On that date, 21 pastors were ordained, 14 church planters commissioned, and 24 children, ages 5 to 14, were baptised. Andres Serrano, Brigido Cabrera, and Kenneth Bradsell (General Synod Assistant Secretary and Director of Operations of the RCA), representing the RCA, were made temporary members of the IRD, and participated in the ordinations of the new ministers and church planters. The IRD then approved the inclusion of the Belhar Confession in their confessional basis.

Uniting Presbyterian Church in Southern Africa

The Uniting Presbyterian Church in Southern Africa (UPCSA) was formed through the union of the Presbyterian Church of Southern Africa (PCSA) and the Reformed Presbyterian Church in South Africa (RPC). Both former denominations owe their origin to the church of Scotland. The PCSA came into being in 1897 at its first general assembly held in Durban through the amalgamation of a number of different congregations established by Scottish settlers in Cape Town, the Eastern Cape and Natal. The general assembly brought together the presbyteries of Cape Town, Natal and the Transvaal, the white congregations of the Synod of Kaffraria (Free Church of Scotland), the white congregations of the Presbytery of Adelaide (United Presbyterian Church of Scotland) and the two independent congregations at Port Elizabeth and Kimberley. The Free Church Synod of Kaffraria and United Presbyteries, which was preponderantly black in membership, declined to enter into union and chose to stay out of the newly formed PCSA. The PCSA thus became a preponderantly white settler church. A separate denomination called the Bantu Presbyterian Church (BPC) was formed for black members. In 1982, the BPC was renamed the Reformed Presbyterian Church in Southern Africa. Union between the PCSA and the RPC was finally achieved in 1999 with the formation of the Uniting Presbyterian Church in Southern Africa (Vellem 2013:146–162).

At the UPCSA General Assembly of 2010, Dr Jerry Pillay, General Secretary of the UPCSA moved that as many Reformed churches across the world have adopted, or are in the process of adopting, the Belhar Confession of Faith, the General Assembly instruct the Ad Hoc Committee on Confessions to help the UPCSA to understand, reflect on and study the Belhar Confession with a view to possibly including the Belhar Confession among the Statements of Faith of the UPCSA (*Papers, Proceedings and Decisions of the 9th General Assembly* 2010:415, no. 14). During 2011, the committee responded to this proposal in its report with a comprehensive study of Belhar (*Papers, Proceedings and Decisions for the 9th General Assembly* 2010:355). Jerry Pillay motived his proposal on the Belhar Confession at the UPCSA Assembly in 2010 as follows:

i. Reformed Churches in Belgium, Norway, Germany and the USA have adopted the Belhar Confession or are in the process of doing so. They often raise the question why Reformed churches in South Africa are not doing the same;

ii. The confession is considered to have significance for the church and Christians all over the world, because of its attempt to address human dignity and rights and people's responsibilities to one another and to all creation.

iii. The Dutch Reformed Church cannot seem to get the 2/3 majority it needs to accept it as a confession. Perhaps its acceptance by other Reformed churches in South Africa can challenge and enlighten its approach to, and thinking about, this (Supplementary Papers, Proceedings and Decisions for the Executive Commission of the UPCSA 2011:50).

The motion was agreed by consensus (*Papers, Proceedings and Decisions for the 9th General Assembly of the UPCSA* 2010:383).

The ad hoc Committee on Confessions of the UPCSA tabled a fully-fledged report on the Belhar Confession at the Executive Commission 2011 (*Supplementary Papers, Proceedings and Decisions for the Executive Commission of the UPCSA* 2011:49-53). The committee found everything in the Belhar Confession acceptable and praiseworthy. The committee also welcomed the high regard that churches and Christians in other parts of the world showed the Belhar Confession. The committee also appreciated that some of these churches were adopting, or considering adopting and the confession and also recognising the historic significance of the Belhar Confession in South Africa in its role of addressing human dignity and people's rights and responsibilities to one another and to all creation (Supplementary Papers, Proceedings and Decisions for the Executive Commission 2011:50). The premise of the committee was that the UPCSA-owned confessions (the Declaration of Faith and the Confession of the UPCSA) take the same stand as the Belhar Confession does regarding the gospel truths of unity, reconciliation and justice. For example, the Declaration of Faith of the UPCSA, like the Belhar Confession, was specifically formulated, adopted and eventually enacted against the ideology and justification of apartheid (Addendum 3). The Confession of Faith of the UPCSA likewise contains many statements that take a stand for the gospel truths of unity, reconciliation and justice against racism, discrimination and oppression, *inter alia*,

- that Jesus 'proclaimed God's coming victorious rule especially to the poor';
- that Christ 'identified with the poor and oppressed';

- that 'God wants to save sinners – and stands on the side of the poor, the oppressed and the exploited against all social, economic and political structures that oppress them';
- that 'God calls us to a life in which everyone's poverty is our own and our wealth is everyone's. We are to live simply and be faithful stewards of our abilities, time and money and other material resources, using them to be a community of mutual sharing, to support the church in its mission, and to do all we can for the poor as well as our own families';
- that the church 'is Catholic in that it is sent to reach out with the gospel to all the world, to embrace people of every race, culture and class, and be a church also for the poor and those on the margins of society';
- the 'unity and fellowship of the body of Christ is manifested above all at the Holy Table: no believer may be barred from it or separated at it on grounds of race, nationality, culture or class'; and
- that 'peace within a nation is endangered where there is injustice or extreme inequality and little is done to alleviate the suffering of the poor' *(Papers, Proceedings and Decisions for the 9th General Assembly UPCSA* 2010:78; *Supplementary Papers, Proceedings and Decisions for the Executive Commission UPCSA* 2011:51).

According to the committee, the Belhar Confession did not say anything that was not already in the confessions of the UPCSA. The church had already formulated their own declaration against apartheid and their own subordinate standards already said the same as the Belhar Confession. (*Supplementary Papers, Proceedings and Decisions for the Executive Commission UPCSA* 2011:52).

Despite this, the Ad-Hoc Committee on Confessions premise was that the URCSA should give their full and unqualified approval to the Belhar Confession. According to the committee it was imperative that DRC adopt the Belhar Confession for the following reasons:

- Because the DRC lacks any subordinate standard that addresses the critical issues that Belhar does.

- Because whatever admission or confession of guilt the DRC may have made for the decision of 1857 and its support for the ideology and practice of apartheid, the sincerity of its repentance will remain in doubt so long as it refuses to adopt the Belhar Confession as a necessary corrective and so show that it recognises how far it strayed from the gospel.

- Because its declared openness to unite with the URCSA will remain so many empty words until it removes the fundamental obstacle to such union that its refusal to accept the Belhar Confession as a subordinate standard of the United Church constitutes (*Supplementary Papers, Proceedings and Decisions for the Executive Commission of the UPCSA* 2011:53).

The Committee recorded that the UPCSA can and should:

1. Declare its solidarity with the URCSA in the pain and suffering that called forth the Belhar Confession.
2. Declare our esteem for the Belhar Confession and our gratitude for the important historic role it played in the witness of the church in southern Africa.
3. Approve all its contents and embrace all its values and sentiments; and commend it to its ministers and members for study and as a resource document.
4. The Committee would also all favour adopting the confession if that ever becomes a condition for union with the URCSA or to form a wider united Reformed church in southern Africa.
5. A study of the confession and of all the possible motives for our adopting it as one of our own subordinate standards has in the end, however, led the Committee to think that for the time being we should hesitate to do that (*Supplementary Papers, Proceedings and Decisions for the Executive Commission UPCSA* 2011:54).

The UPCSA expressed its solidarity with the URCSA in all the pain and suffering that its members had endured under the system of oppression that made the Belhar Confession necessary. The UPCSA also expressed its gratitude to God for the Belhar Confession and the historic role it has played in the history and witness of the church in southern Africa. The UPCSA, furthermore, approved all the contents of the Belhar Confession and embraced all its sentiments and values and commended the Belhar Confession to all the ministers, sessions and presbyteries of the UPCSA in South Africa, Zambia and Zimbabwe for study and discussion and as a resource for preaching and teaching (*Supplementary Papers, Proceedings and Decisions UPCSA* 2011:40-41).

The General Assembly UPCSA 2013 instructed the Ad Hoc Committee on Confessions to help the UPCSA to understand, reflect on and study the Belhar Confession with a view to possibly including the Belhar Confession among the statements of faith of the UPCSA. The UPCSA mandated the General Secretary, Dr Jerry Pillay, as convener of the Ecumenical Relations Committee, to approach the DRC and the URCSA through their respective general secretaries, Dr Kobus Gerber and Dr Dawid Kuyler, to ask the two churches to consider whether they deemed it appropriate to invite the UPCSA to be represented, even if only by way of observer status, on the combined commission discussing union between them. This representation on the commission would enable the UPCSA to offer any relevant insights they may have from their own experience of unification in their process of moving towards unity. It would also open the way for discussions about unity between the churches; any such unity being subject to all the parties endorsing the Belhar Confession but leaving open the question of whether unity between the DRC, the URCSA and the UPCSA should, 'to begin with, take a simple, federal or confederal form' (*Decisions of General Assemblyof the* UPCSA 2013:2).

Presbyterian Church in the USA

The Presbyterian Church in the USA, or PCUSA was established by the 1983 merger of the Presbyterian Church in the United States (whose churches were located in the southern and border states) with the United Presbyterian Church in the United States of America (whose congregations could be found in every state). The PCUSA is the largest Presbyterian denomination in the United States. The process of preparing the PCUSA for the possibility of adopting the Belhar Confession began with a task force reporting to the General Assembly of the PCUSA in 2004.

Because of the enduring problem of racism in the USA, the 216th General Assembly 2004 asked PCUSA members to consider how the Belhar Confession can address the problem of racism in the USA and in their denomination (PCUSA 2010:6). They built their premise on Durand's notion that racism is not a sin exclusive to Afrikaners, or to white people for that matter. 'It lurks in the hearts of all of us. We have to do battle constantly against it in the power of the Spirit.' (Durand 1994:1).

The General Assembly approved the Belhar Confession to the church as a 'resource for reflection, study and response, as a means of deepening the commitment of the PCUSA to dealing with racism and a means of strengthening its unity' (PCUSA 2010:1). The General Assembly also urged each presbytery and all congregations to undertake a study of the Belhar Confession before the 218th General Assembly (2008) and directed the Office of the General Assembly and the General Assembly Council, Office of Theology and Worship, to receive response, prepare a summary and report results with possible recommendations for further engagement with the Belhar Confession. The Advocacy Committee on Racial Ethnic Concerns (ACREC) and the Advocacy Committee on Women's Concerns both recommended the approval of the Confession of Belhar. In 2008, the General Assembly called for the institution of a special committee on the Confession of Belhar to study whether the Belhar Confession should be adopted into the *Book of Confessions* (PCUSA 2008:62-70).

In 2008, the 218th General Assembly of the PCUSA took the first step in adopting the Belhar Confession. Approval by two consecutive General Assemblies and ratification by two-thirds of the 173 presbyteries between those assemblies was required. The special committee unanimously recommended that the 219th General Assembly

(2010) approve the inclusion of the Confession of Belhar in the *Book of Confessions*, and that the amendment be sent to the presbyteries for their affirmative or negative votes by June 2011. The 219th General Assembly (2010) approved these amendments to the motion and agreed also to send the Belhar Confession to the presbyteries for their votes. The 219th General Assembly in 2010 approved inclusion of Belhar by a vote 525 to 150 with three abstentions. However, the presbyteries could not reach a two-thirds affirmative vote on the adoption of the Belhar Confession by July 2011, falling eight votes short (108 to 63) of the required majority.

The 220th PCUSA General Assembly 2012 approved to test the PCUSA a second time on the inclusion of the Belhar Confession in their confessional basis. Moderator Neal Presa appointed Teaching Elder Clifton Kirkpatrick (Mid-Kentucky Presbytery) and Ruling Elder Matilde Moros (Hudson River Presbytery) to serve as co-moderators of the special committee. The sub-themes of Justice, Unity, and Reconciliation framed their approach to the Confession of Belhar and the development of interpretative materials. The special committee created material to study Belhar both in print and online. In 2014, the special committee unanimously recommended that the 221st General Assembly approve the inclusion of the Confession of Belhar in the *Book of Confessions*, and that this amendment be sent to the presbyteries for their affirmative or negative votes by June 2015. The 221st General Assembly called upon all congregations, councils, seminaries, and denominational conferences to engage in serious and prayerful study of the Confession of Belhar and its accompanying letter as well the accompanying letter to the Confession of Belhar from the General Assembly and to make use of the variety of resources produced by the special committee (PCUSA 2014).

By an overwhelming vote, the 221st General Assembly sent a proposed amendment to the *Book of Confessions of the* PCUSA that would add the Belhar Confession to their confessional basis. Before it could be added to the denomination's confessions, the Belhar would have to be ratified by 115, or two-thirds, of the denomination's 171 presbyteries – each by a two-thirds vote. The committee felt that the accompanying letter to the Confession of Belhar from the 221st General Assembly (2014) of the PCUSA, which highlighted racism in the USA, might give presbyteries reason to not be in favour of the confession. They, therefore, recommended that the Belhar Confession and the accompany letter of the confession should rather be added to the confessional basis of the PCUSA. The 221st General Assembly of the PCUSA approved recommendations from the special committee with 551 to 87, or an 86 percent affirmative vote (PCUSA 2014).

By the end of April 114 of the presbyteries had voted in favour of the amendment of the *Book of Confessions* of the PCUSA, surpassing the two-third majority it required. In doing so, the crucial hurdle with 75% of the presbyteries voting to approve the addition was cleared. Rev. Gradye Parsons, the Stated Clerk of the PCUSA stated that the PCUSA acknowledged the confession to be relevant for such a time as this in the life of the PCUSA and that the PCUSA diligently desired to live into it as part of the body of Christ:

> We recognise our need to confess the ways this denomination has contributed to racism historically and even still today, and mourn all the ways we have fallen short. We believe this Confession, appropriated for this time and place, can bring about reconciliation and justice, and allow us to more fully follow Jesus in ministry and mission. (Parsons 2015:1)

On 22 June 2016, the 222nd PCUSA General Assembly finally approved, by an overwhelming (540 to 33) vote to include the Belhar Confession in their confessional basis. The Belhar Confession joined the 11 Eurocentric creeds and confessions in the *Book of Confessions* of the PCUSA). It was the first addition to the *Book of Confessions* in nearly 30 years. The adoption of the Belhar Confession by the PCUSA clearly demonstrates their commitment to embody the principles of the confession. The Belhar Confession is indeed a guiding light in the discourse on racism and a vast array of social justice issues, among other things, restorative justice, hate speech, incitement, statelessness, atrocity crimes, human rights violations, state capture, land grabbing, gender justice, the neoliberal economic globalisation and eco-justice.

Protestations against the reception of the Belhar Confession

The Dutch Reformed Church in Africa, Reformed Church in Africa and the Dutch Reformed Church tried in vain to include the Belhar Confession in their confessional basis. Numerous reasons had been offered since 1986 why the confession should not be added to the confessional basis of the envisaged unified church. The reservations of affording the Belhar Confession full confessional status in the envisaged unified church included the arguments that the Belhar was not biblical; the Belhar was not Christological; the three Forms of Unity were enough as it was; they were not involved in the drafting of the confession; and that the Belhar Confession was a champion of social gospel/liberation theology. The DRC attempted to admit it to the confessional basis of the DRC following the 2013 General Assembly but it fell short of the two-thirds majority for ratification in the ten regional synods. More than three decades after the drafting, acceptance and inclusion of the Belhar Confession in the confessional basis of the DRMC there is still little consensus about its confessional status within the DRC family.

Dutch Reformed Church in Africa

Missionary work under the jurisdiction of the Mission Commission of the DRC among Africans in the Cape Colony only started in 1859. Racial segregated churched for African people had been established in the different provinces, *inter alia*, the NG Sendingkerk in die Oranje-Vrystaat (1910), the NG Sendingkerk Van Transvaal (1931), the NG Bantoekerk in Kaapland (1951) and the NG Sendingkerk Van Natal (1952). These four churches unified in order to constitute the Dutch Reformed Church in Africa in 1963. The General Synod of the DRCA of 1974 expressed the desire to unite with the RCA, the DRMC and the DRC and instructed the General Synodical Committee to contact them (*Agenda en Handelinge NGKA* 1974:253).

The first unity conference of the DRC family took place on 10 to 12 February 1976 at Turfloop. Approximately 200 ministers, evangelists of the DRCA and DRMC and a few reverends of the DRC attend the conference. The following resolutions were made at the conference:

- Church unity is a biblical demand as well as a gift from God.
- Unity in the DRC family should be more visible (*Agenda en Handelinge NGSK* 1978:53-54).

The DRCA General Synod of 1978 and the DRMC Synod of 1978 strongly objected to an overarching synod. The DRC General Synod, 1978 also found it unacceptable that an overarching synod structure could be able to make bounding decisions (*Agenda en Handelinge* NGSK 1978:51-59).

At the sixth General Synod of the DRCA in Barkly West in 1983 a study document of the DRMC on the 'Church and Apartheid' was tabled in which the DRMC petitioned the DRCA to assist the DRMC in the declaration of the *status confessionis* and to subscribe to the draft the Belhar Confession (*Agenda en Handelinge* NGKA 1983:19-28).

In 1983, a year after the acceptance of the draft Belhar Confession, the DRCA declared migrant labour to be in conflict with the norms of Scripture and formulated a principled decision against it (*Acta NGKA* 1983:116-121, 360-361). Apartheid legislation restricted African people to acquire property in white South Africa. In the case of the DRCA, the ownership and actual possession of ecclesiastical property was determined by the following colonial and apartheid laws: Natives Land Act (No. 27 of 1913), Natives (Urban Areas) Act (1923), Group Areas Act (No. 41 of 1950), Prevention of Illegal Squatting Act (No. 52 of 1951), Bantu Authorities Act (No. 68 of 1951), Native Laws Amendment Act (1952), Promotion of Bantu Self-government Act (No. 46 of 19590, Natives Resettlement Act (No. 19 of 1954), Group Areas Development Act (No. 69 of 1955), Urban Bantu Councils Act (No. 79 of 1961), Preservation of Coloured

Areas Act (No. 31 of 1961), Bantu Homelands Citizens Act (1970),[15] amongst others. These laws made it illegal for blacks to purchase or lease land from whites except in the so-called reserves and restricted black occupancy to less than eight percent of South Africa's land. The Natives Resettlement Act granted powers to the government to remove Africans from any area reserved for whites or 'coloureds.' In so doing Africans became migrants in their own land. This laid the foundations for residential segregation in urban areas and the establishment of black homelands. In these homelands, the DRCA could acquire land for church purposes. The only ownership or occupational rights a black African possessed were restricted to the Bantustans or the black townships. The laws restricted the DRCA from purchasing land for church purposes. The actual control of the ecclesiastical property of the DRCA belonged essentially to the DRC, the local government in the Bantustans or the so-called urban Bantu councils. Ecclesiastical property of the DRCA was held under a lease for ninety-nine years and was renewable forever. Land was also conveyed to the trustees of the Missionary Commission of the DRC and their successors with the proviso that the land was to be used for church purposes by the DRCA.

Notwithstanding the above, the DRCA Synod of 1983 was not willing to adopt the Belhar Confession. The DRCA rather referred the draft confession with the existing decisions of the DRCA about church unity to a commission for further study (*Agenda en Handelinge NGKA* 1983:379). This decision was reaffirmed at the DRCA General Synod of 1987. The synod regretted that the decision of the DRCA on church reunification unity did not produce concrete results and tasked the moderamen to proceed with great urgency to bring the decisions to implementation 'because any sign that the DRC in Africa would be an "apartheid" church, is dangerous to the lives of our youth, physically and mentally' (*Agenda en Handelinge NGKA* 1987:379, 388). The 1987 DRCA Synod referred the Belhar Confession and it to the Commission for Scripture and Confession. This was to test the desirability of the acceptance of the confession and to determine to what extent its acceptance by the DRCA may promote or delay the unification of the DRC family (*Agenda en Handelinge NGKA* 1987:413-414). The new commission was tasked to table their findings during the recess to the Federal Council of the Reformed churches in South Africa, and to serve the next DRCA Synod of the DRCA with proposals regarding the inclusion of the confession in their confessional basis.

---

15   The Bantu Homelands Citizenship Act required all Africans to become citizens of a self-governing territorial authority. And in so doing they were not deemed only longer as South Africa citizens. Africans was only able to occupy the houses bequeathed to them in the urban areas, by special permission of the Minister.

In October 1989, the task teams of the DRMC and the DRCA commenced with a series of meetings regarding the reunification of the two churches (*Agenda en Handelinge NGKA 1990:221, 233; Skema Van Werksaamhede VGKSA Algemene Sinode 1994:8*).

On 1 October 1990, an extraordinary session of the General Synod of the DRCA convened in Cape Town, with representatives from the six regional synods, namely, those of the Orange Free State, Phororo, Southern Transvaal, Northern Transvaal, Cape Province and Natal. The synod, without any dissenting votes approved the inclusion of that the Belhar Confession in the confessional basis of the DRCA. Any objections from members, presbyteries or regional synods against the amendment could through gravamina (of complaint) and/or memoranda be brought to the next meeting of the General Synod for consideration (*Agenda en Handelinge NGKA 1991:392*).

The phrase 'and after each regional synod separately with a two-third majority decided in favour thereof: and after all the churches of the Reformed Church [were] consulted' was deleted at the General Synod of the DRCA in Article 36.2. The new Article 36.2, par. 2.2.4 read as follows: 'The General Synod may amend or supplement the church order with a two-third majority' (*Agenda en Handelinge NGKA 1991:51,*). Article 1 was also amended at the 1991 Synod to include the Confession of Belhar as part of the confessional of the DRCA. The wording of the amended article reads as follows:

> The Dutch Reformed Church in Africa is built on the foundation of Jesus Christ, based on the Bible, the holy and infallible Word of God. The doctrine of the church in accordance with God's Word is expressed as The Forms of Unity as set by the Synod of Dordrecht in 1618–1919, the Heidelberg Catechism, the Canons of Dort and the ecumenical confessions, the Apostles' Creed the Confession of Nicaea and the Confession of Athanasius and the Belhar Confession. (*Agenda en Handelinge NGKA 1991:389*)

In 1998, these decisions were ruled *ultra vires* by the Supreme Court. The Dutch Reformed Church was regarded as a voluntary or mutual association (collegium) whose members are contractually bound by the church order (*Nederduitse Gereformeerde Kerk in Afrika* (Phororo) vs *Verenigende Gereformeerde Kerk in Suider-Afrika*, case number 536/96:13). According to Appeal Judge Harmse, the confession of faith of the DRCA could only be amended in compliance with the three formal requirements in Article 36.1 of the church order of the DRCA, namely (i) consultation of all churches of the DRC family; (ii) a two-thirds majority vote in favour of the change by each Regional Synod separately and only then; and (iii) a two-thirds majority vote of the General Synod (Supra case number 536/96). According Judge Vivier, the General Synod is a temporary and not a permanent governing body (*Supra* case number 536/96:24). The authority of the General Synod ends with dispersal of the meeting. The General Synod of the DRCA was, therefore, not empowered to make decisions that are in conflict with their church order (*Supra* case number 536/96:325). When the DRCA decided to unite, the synodical decision does not *ipso facto* affect the decision by a Church Council. The General Synod does not represent in all respects the will of the 'church' (Supra case number 536/96:3). The General Synod has therefore, according to Harmse, limited powers. The General Synod, according to Judge Vivier (Supra case number 536/96:23) was not entitled to a provision to change the church order to reach a goal beyond its powers. Judge Vivier's assumption was that with the insertion of section 61 in the church order of the DRCA the General Synod acted outside its jurisdiction (*Supra* case number 536/96:28):

> The entire decision of the General Synod of the NGKA at its meeting of July 1991 with the uniting NGSK (decision 1.1.33) as well as the decisions related thereto (decisions 1.1.34 to 1.1.38) was therefore *ultra vires* and void. In addition, the amendment of section 36, as I have found, also invalid. (*Supra* case number 536/96:43)

Judge Vivier highlighted in his ruling that one of the key features of the Reformed system is that every local church and the visible manifestation of the church organisation, and thus in itself fully, 'church' (*Supra* case number 536/96:17). The Supreme Court of Appeal reversed the ruling of the Supreme Court and rendered a verdict on 27 November 1998 in favour of the Oranje Free State Synod and Phororo Synod of the DRCA (*Skema Van Werksaamhede en Handelinge VGKSA* 1997:134). Since 1998, the DRCA and the URCSA had been engaged in numerous court cases about property. This placed a huge strain on the bilateral and multilateral talks.

During the past decade, the DRCA has emphatically claimed that they never made a formal evaluation of the Belhar Confession or decided to accept the confession to be part of the united church. (*Agenda en Handelinge NGKA* 2007:45, 184-185, 223). History, as indicated above, shows a different picture. The 1991 DRCA Synod indeed unanimously adopted the Belhar Confession (*Agenda en Handelinge NGKA* 1991:392).

During the past two decades, the verdict of the Supreme Court of Appeal in 1998 has caused a lot of hostility, stress, mistrust, unease between members of the DRCA and the URCSA on the bi- and multilateral talks regarding church reunification and the place of the Belhar Confession in the envisaged unified church. The DRCA has repeated claimed, especially after 1998, that they cannot accept Belhar Confession as part of the confessional basis of the united church. They, however, affirmed that they accept the Belhar Confession as part of URCSA's confessional basis but are against it as a pre-requisite for church unification. The DRCA strongly objected to the procedure followed at the General Synod of the DRCA 1991 with regard to the changing of the confessional basis of the DRCA in order to include the Belhar Confession.

On 27 February 2009, in a letter to the DRC, URCSA and the WCRC, the DRCA indicated that it, with great concern, took note of the bilateral talks between the DRC and the URCSA. The DRC objected to, among other things, the unification talks at Esselenpark on 22 June 2006 where the DRC and URCSA had made a solemn agreement (called a 'covenant'), which touched on the confessional basis and model for the envisaged unified church (Addendum 4, Covenanting for the Reunification of the Family of DRC – Esselenpark Declaration). The DRCA stated that it was adamant that any consultations on unification, model and confessional basis should involve all four churches, namely the DRC, DRCA, RCA and URCSA. The DRCA premise was that Belhar was not their confession. They did, however, respect Belhar as a confession of the URCSA and recognised the importance of reconciliation between the URCSA and the URCSA on the way to reunification. The premise of the DRCA was that there is still a lot of healing to be done between the DRCA and the URCSA. The Belhar Confession should, however, not be seen a stumbling block for the reunification of the church. The DRCA wanted to retain their regional synods and presbyteries in the envisaged unified church (Minutes of the meeting of the four moderamen of the DRC family 6–7 August 2014:1-4). The DRCA, furthermore, tabled that they respected any agreements between the DRC and the URCSA concerning the Belhar Confession, however, the Belhar Confession was not a confession of the DRCA. The DRC and URCSA needed to indicate how the DRCA would be accommodated in one church without accepting the Belhar Confession. The DRCA felt that they were not part of the drafting of Belhar Confession and that it was, therefore, not fair to expect them to accept it (Minutes of the meeting of the four moderamen of the DRC family 6–7 August 2014:1-4).

Reformed Church in Africa

Mission work among the Indians was carried out from 1946 in Natal (Pietermaritzburg, Durban, Harding, Colenso, Greytown and Glencoe); in the Southern Transvaal from 1955 (Krugersdorp, Lenasia, Johannesburg, Germiston, Benoni, Springs and Society); in the Cape Province from 1960 (Cape Town, Kimberley, Uitenhage and Port Elizabeth); and in Northern Transvaal from 1964 (Pretoria) (*Agenda en Handelinge NGK* 1966:195). The first Indian congregation was constituted in 1957. Already at the first General Synod of the DRC in 1962, the mission among the Indians throughout the Republic had been accepted as part of the mission strategy of the DRC (*Agenda en Handelinge NGK Algemene Sinode* 1962:137-138, 193). Following the decision, a sub-committee for Indian Mission was appointed and assigned to prepare a draft constitution or church order for Indian Mission for the next synod. At the General

Synod of the Dutch Reformed Church in 1966 it was decided to proceed with church planting among the Indian churches of Transvaal, the Cape and Natal and unite them into one denomination (*Acta NGK Algemene Sinode* 1966:215, 521). The DRC General Synod of 1966 approved the draft church order for the Indian Reformed Church as the official document for the Convention of the new church (*Acta NGK Algemene Sinode* 1966:215, 466, 521, 562;193).

On 28 August 1968, the first Synod of the Reformed Church in Africa consisting of the four congregations, namely Pietermaritzburg/Durban West, Transvaal, Durban and Cape constituted. Already in 1970, the RCA had indicated their desire to unite the DRC family (*Agenda en Handelinge NGSK* 1978:51). At the RCA Synod of 1976, mandate was given to their Synodical Commission to initiate unity talks with other churches in the DRC family. On 21 April 1978, under the leadership of the RCA a consultation for church unity in Durban took placed (*Agenda en Handelinge NGSK* 1978:24). The RCA and the DRMC were represented at the consultations by their executive committees, while the DRC was represented as observers. The DRCA did not attend the consultations and their absence of the DRCA was viewed with grave concern. At a consultation between the DRMC and the RCA held between 30 and 31 May 1978 in Cape Town a Memorandum of Agreement between the URCSA and the DRC was drafted (*Agenda en Handelinge NGSK* 1978:57-59, 1986:62). The DRC was absent from a consultation between the DRCA, DRMC and the RCA held in Pretoria on 10 March 1980.

On 26 October of that year, the DRC Synod decided to enter into a fully-pledged union with the DRMC leaving the door open to other members of the DRC family. Based on the Memorandum of Agreement reached in 1978, and in order to unify appropriately, the DRMC and the RCA attended to the church judicial requirements and related issues, such as, property, finances, administration, theological training, ecumenical relations, church polity, church order and confessional basis. The bilateral consultation between the RCA and the DRMC ceased during 1984 due to the change of RCA leadership (*Agenda en Handelinge NGSK* 1986:63-65). Following the WARC decision in 1982 in Ottawa to denouncing apartheid as a heresy, the RCA rejectedthe theological justification of apartheid as unscriptural and any attempt to support it as being unchristian. The synod refrained from labelling it as heresy (*Agenda en Handelinge NGSK* 1986:31).

The sixth Synod of the RCA in October 1990 declared that it could identify with the content of Belhar, but could not accept it as a confession on the same level as the other three Reformed faith confessions as the social issues referred to by the Belhar Confession were continuously subjected to change. According to the RCA, the Belhar Confession is more than doctrinal in nature (*Agenda RCA* 1990:31). Because the Belhar Confession was proposed as confession for the planned new church, the RCA withdraw from the unification process between the DRCA and the DRMC (*Agenda RCA* 1990:40, 41). The synod committed itself, however, to strive for a united, non-racial Reformed Church in Southern and Central Africa (*Acts RCA* 1990:34).

The same synod adopted the Declaration of Laudium (Addendum 5). The Declaration marks the resolve of the RCA to maintain its evangelical character. The denomination worked in predominantly non-Christian settings to, among other things, reach people of Asian descent, especially people from Hindu and Muslim backgrounds. Most of the congregations were predominately Indian and this affected the questions of denominational identity. In this context, Belhar helped to address the sufferings of the past.

A joint discussion group comprising of the URCSA, DRC and RCA was established in 1994. The objective of the discussion group was to facilitate the process of church unity based on a joint church order. The discussion group was mandated to negotiate the confessional basis, a model for a united church and a new name for the united church. No agreement could be reached on the issue of the Confession of Belhar and the URCSA rejected the concept of maintaining separate presbyteries based on ministerial needs as a form of new apartheid.

The RCA Synod of 1998 reaffirmed its belief that church unity is of paramount importance and urgency and requested that the Declaration of Laudium be an integral part of the life and ministry in envisaged united church (*Acts RCA* 1998:73). Furthermore, they supported the reunification of the DRC family and recommended that the Confession of Belhar should form part of the confessional of the envisaged unified church.

> [We] recommend the acceptance in principle or as a Belhar Confession in the new Uniting Church, with the practical implementation to be deliberated in the process of unification. [We] request our Synods to invite representatives of the URCSA to attend the Synod meeting of the Reformed Church in Africa and the DRC in order to help us to understand and accept Belhar, as well as to listen to and understand our deliberations on Belhar. (*Acts RCA* 1998:59)

The RCA changed their viewpoint at the consecutive synods. The RCA did not have a problem with the content of the Belhar Confession. Their problem was that they would never be able to embrace it as a confession of the envisaged unified church as it was accepted in a time when there were very hostile relationships between the two churches, when they lost congregations to the URCSA, when people walked out of their synod, when their theological students and ministers of the Word were ordained by the URCSA without securing permission of the RCA beforehand, and so forth. The RCA's assumption was that the unity of a church rested in a common confessional basis. They saw the Confession of Belhar as a point of difference between the RCA and the URCSA. The RCA believed that the place of the Confession of Belhar in the confessional basis of the envisaged unified church should be clarified before church reunification between the two churches could become a reality. (Achterbergh Declaration I 2006:1).

The RCAs main critique was that there had been no prior consultation with them regarding the drafting of Belhar, which occurred during the DRMC Synod of 1982. At that time, the DRMC and the RCA had already embarked on the road to church reunification. They, therefore, rejected the notion of the acceptance of the Belhar Confession as a precondition for church reunification. The RCA, however, embraced the consensus reached at Achterbergh II regarding the confessional basis of the envisaged unified church. The five points of consensus were as follows:

- Belhar should not be a precondition for church unity.
- That discussions between all four churches continue with the purpose of agreeing to the biblical content of Belhar and writing a joint commentary on it. That would make it possible to preach, teach and use the biblical content of Belhar in a new denomination.
- The doctrinal basis of a new denomination must accommodate all four churches, synods and congregations without forcing anybody to accept or to abandon Belhar (Achterbergh Declaration II 2007:1).

The RCA respected the value that Belhar as a confession has for URCSA, but emphasised that in the envisaged unified church it would not expect members and ministers who were not ready or willing to accept it as a confession. The RCA affirmed that the Belhar Confession was not in conflict with Bible and they saw it as a declaration and not as a confession. They expressed a wish that the DRC family should jointly publish a commentary on the confession (Achterbergh Declaration II 2007:1).

The RCA endured much humiliation, suffering and splits during the church reunification process. As a denomination, they supported the suspension of the DRC by the WARC. However, the RCA never fully recovered from the consequences of this decision and is still dealing with some of the pain, suffering and trauma that came from that experience, including a loss of financial support from the DRC. Due to the strong evangelical focus of the church, the synodical decision of the RCA on the Belhar Confession was generally supported, however, some church members queried Article 4 of the confession, which states that God is especially on the side of the poor and oppressed.

Dutch Reformed Church 1982–2015

The DRC consists of ten regional synods, namely, Western and Southern Cape, Eastern, Eastern Cape, Namibia, Highveld, Kwazulu-Natal, Northern, West Transvaal, Northern Cape and Free State. The discourse on the acceptance of the Belhar Confession in the confessional basis of the envisaged unified church led to robust discussions in the synods during the past three decades. In 1982, the DRMC forwarded the concept Belhar Confession to the DRC for their consideration. According to Piet Meiring, when the DRC Synod convened in Pretoria in October 1982, most delegates clearly did not know what to do with the *status confessionis* and the concept Belhar Confession. Eventually a resolution was passed stating the 'sadness and distress' the synod felt at the 'unfair accusations of theological heresy and idolatry levelled at the DRC,' without analysing the theological merits of the accusations contained in the Belhar Confession. The synod, however, declared itself willing to conduct future discussions with the DRMC on these and related issues (Meiring 1991:18).

In October 1986, the DRC formally approved a new policy statement regarding the socio-political issues in South Africa, entitled 'Kerk en Samelewing, 'n Getuienis van die Nederduitse Gereformeerde Kerk' (Church and Society, a Testimony of the Dutch Reformed Church). In Church and Society, the DRC rejected racism as a serious sin which no person or church may justify or practice (*NGK Algemene Sinode* 1986:22). With regards to the church and human relationships, in particular race and people, the DRC admitted that racial and colour differences play no role in the Bible's judgement of people. The Bible treats concepts like 'people' and 'nation' and the variety of people as part of the existing reality (*NGK Algemene Sinode* 1986:20). The DRC admitted that the Bible does not condemn mixed marriages. (*NGK Algemene Sinode* 1986:35) and DRC General Synod of 1986 withdrew its objections to these marriages. The synod also renounced racism but was still not ready to accept the Belhar Confession. The 1986 Synod took note of the contents of the Belhar Confession and expressed its concern regarding Article 4 of the confession in which God is declared to be the God of the destitute, the poor and the wronged.

The WARC Executive Committee held in Belfast in October 1988 maintained that although the DRC's *Church and Society* on the surface might reveal a significant repentance from and revision of its earlier position, the document, at its best, may indicate that the church was ready to consider so-called reforms of the apartheid system. This, however, did not alter the present situation. The church had recently refused to declare apartheid a sin and its theological justification a heresy. The WARC took note that the Vereeniging Declaration (Addendum 6) issued by the representatives of the various member churches of the DRC family after a consultation held in Vereeniging in March 1989 under the auspices of REC unequivocally rejected apartheid in all its forms as sin. The Declaration had also committed the DRC family of churches to the dismantling of apartheid in both church and state by accepting unification of the various churches into one non-racial Reformed church in southern and central Africa, and by calling on the state to repeal all racist laws and repressive security legislation. All the representatives present, with exception of the white DRC, adopted this declaration (WARC 1990:279-281). The WARC concluded by its own admission that the white DRC has not moved further forward than the position adopted at its synod on the basis of its church and society document. Furthermore, the 1998 WARC Executive Committee clearly stated that this position failed to meet the conditions laid down at Ottawa in 1982, particularly those in clause (b) and (c), and recommended that suspension be maintained. The committee confirmed that the General Council meeting in Seoul had reviewed the situation and affirmed that the decision on *status confessionis* taken in 1982 was and still is appropriate. WARC General Council in Ottawa in 1982 declared that the DRC would be restored to the full privileges of membership of WARC if 'black Christians are no longer excluded from church services, especially from Holy Communion'. In 1989, the DRC assured the WARC that the DRC was an open church that it gave support in word and deed to those who suffer under the system of apartheid (WARC 1990:279-281). Furthermore, the DRC acknowledged that apartheid, as it was theologically justified and supported by the DRC, had largely contributed to a situation of an unequal and unjust distribution of economic resources, which had led to serious discrepancies between white and black in income, standard of living, and education and training. The DRC also acknowledged that there was a notable willingness within the family of Reformed churches to work together in addressing problems of the enormous poverty and unemployment in South Africa.

Regarding the request of the WARC General Council in 1982 that the DRC should issue unequivocal synodical resolutions to reject apartheid and commit to dismantling the system in both church and politics, the DRC General Synod in Bloemfontein, 1990 declared that racism is a grievous sin, that apartheid is an oppressive system and must be rejected as sinful, and that all forms of discrimination and suppression of peoples were to be condemned. The DRC also indicated that whether the situation of apartheid constituted a *status confessionis* in the sense that 'in this issue the confession of Jesus Christ is at stake', it must be acknowledged that there exists a difference of opinion between the interpretation of the DRC (and the Reformed Ecumenical Council) and WARC regarding this matter (WARC 1990:279-281). The DRC also indicated that their commitment to the unity of the DRC family. The DRC Synod of 1990 declared that the Belhar Confession not juxtapose with the three 'Formulas of Unity' (*Agenda Algemene Sinode NGK* 1990:29, 707). The DRC affirmed that some members of the DRC saw the background context of the Belhar Confession as a stumbling block. At the 1990 Synod, the revised edition of *Church and Society* was adopted, with its call for confessing the DRC's role in establishing and practising apartheid. The synod decided to work towards the ideal of structural unity with the DRCA, DRMC and the RCA.

On the matters of the *status confessionis* and the Belhar Confession, the DRC Synod recognised the right of the DRMC to adopt the Belhar Confession, and concurred that the issues involved were extremely important to the DRMC (Meiring 1991:18-23). On the one hand, the synod regarded the Belhar Confession not to be in conflict with the contents of the Belgic Confession, the Heidelberg Catechism or the Canons of Dort. On the other hand, the synod ascertained that *Church and Society* contained the DRC answer to the paragraphs containing 'rejections' in the Belhar Confession. Furthermore, the synod pointed out that after the DRC's adoption of the revised *Church and Society*, some of the accusations levelled against the DRC in the Belhar Confession were no longer applicable (*Agenda en Acta van die Algemene Sinode van die NGK te Bloemfontein* 1990; *Agenda van die Algemene Sinode NGK* 1986).

The 1990 Synod believed that some phrases in the Belhar Confession, such as parts of Article 4, could have been formulated differently. The synod preferred the wording of *Church and Society* concerning the affirmation of the Lord being the God of the poor and the wronged. The synod also emphasised that in future deliberations between the two churches, both documents, the Belhar Confession and *Church and Society*, should be used as a basis for discussion. The 1990 Synod decided as follows:

> [S]ynod took note of the official adoption of the Belhar Confession by the DRMC, and recognised the right of the DRMC to do that. Synod agrees that the issues involved are of extreme importance to the DRMC. The synod considered the Belhar Confession not to be in conflict with the contents of the Belgic Confession, the Heidelberg Catechism or the Canons of Dort. Synod emphasizes the fact that in future deliberations between the two churches both documents, the Belhar Confession as well as the document *Church and Society* should be used as basis for discussions. The DRC declares that Belhar is not in conflict with the other confessions of the family of Reformed churches. (*Acta Algemene Sinode NGK* 1990)

In March 1993, the WARC held a consultation in Johannesburg to review church relations in South Africa and to obtain first-hand information about the process of unification that had started in the family of Dutch Reformed churches (between the DRCA and the DRMC). The WARC was represented by Rev. Hugh Davidson, Prof. Pieter Holtrop, Dr Ed Mulder, Dr Jane Dempsey Douglass, Dr Karel Blei and Prof. Pieter Holtrop. Three South Africans presented papers at the consultation, namely Prof. Jaap Durand, Dr Beyers Naudé and Rev. Russel Botman. Before the meeting, they sent, as requested, a written reply to the questions formulated by the Ottawa

General Council. On the third day of the meeting, they read out a statement, which tried to respond to the questions raised during the discussions. These were open questions that needed to be answered in the ensuing unification process: Does the DRC reject apartheid unequivocally? Is theological justification of apartheid a theological error or is it heresy? Is the DRC ready to work for structural changes in the society of South Africa? Is the DRC prepared to confess publicly its guilt and to ask the victims of apartheid for forgiveness? The most important part of this statement was the willingness to participate in the unification process that had started between the DRCA and the DRMC.

The WARC profoundly regretted that in the past some Reformed churches in South Africa had defended racism and developed a theology of apartheid and that these churches had become accomplices in the system that inflicted immense suffering on millions of people. This situation called for a declaration of guilt, acts of repentance and asking for forgiveness. The WARC appealed to all Reformed Christians to reject apartheid unequivocally as a sin and its theological justification as heresy. According to Prof. Jane Dempsey Douglass, President of the WARC, and Prof. Milan Opocensky, General Secretary of the WARC, it was a matter of life and death. They said:

> If you defend the system of apartheid your salvation is in jeopardy. The Christian approval of racist policies created a situation in which the proclamation of the gospel and its integrity were at stake. This is why the WARC general council in Ottawa declared *status confessionis*. It must be clear that the first and ultimate loyalty of a Christian community goes to Jesus Christ and to the gospel, and not to a cultural or national identity, to the relics of apartheid and its ideology. (Douglass & Opocensky 1994:1)

In 1994, the DRC reported to WARC that they complied with all three requirements of WARC. In that same year, the General Synod of the DRC affirmed a church judicial process regarding the *envisaged unified church* (Agenda NGK Algemene Sinode 1994:144; Besluiteregister NGK Algemene Sinode 1994:16-17).

The 23rd WARC General Council meeting in Debrecen, Hungary in August 1997 wrote a pastoral letter to the DRC (Addendum 7). The WARC communicated that of the three requirements laid down by the 21st General Council at Ottawa, 1982 for the lifting of the DRC's membership suspension, the DRC had only complied with the first two, namely, the opening of worship to Christians of all races and giving aid to victims of apartheid. It had been difficult to find unequivocal synod and moderamen resolutions of the DRC rejecting apartheid and committing the church to dismantling this system in both church and state. The WARC premise was that even *The Story of the Dutch Reformed Church's Journey with Apartheid 1960–1994*, which had been produced by order of the General Synodical Commission of the DRC's submission to the Truth and Reconciliation Commission, suggested that the errors and sinful actions of apartheid resided more in the implementation of apartheid than in its fundamental nature:

> Clearly, however, the suffering, hardship and poverty endured by people in South Africa over the past few decades or more cannot be ascribed to apartheid alone. A variety of social and economic realities contributed to their plight. During this time South Africa, in fact, enjoyed relative prosperity in which everyone could share to a greater or lesser degree. The fact that at the end of the apartheid years South Africa was, economically speaking, a ray of hope in Africa – in spite of sanctions and boycotts – cannot be left unsaid in an evaluation of the period that lies behind us. (*The Story of the Dutch Reformed Church's Journey with Apartheid 1997:72-76*)

According to the WARC, an official resolution from the DRC stating unequivocal rejection of apartheid was still outstanding. The WARC, therefore, proposed that the DRC should approve the joint resolution drafted by the executive committee of WARC as follows:

> Of the three requirements laid down by the 21st General Council in Ottawa in 1982 for lifting of your membership suspension, we can recognise your compliance with the first two: you have opened your worship to Christians of all races and given aid to victims of apartheid. It has been more difficult to find unequivocal synod and moderamen resolutions rejecting *apartheid* and committing the church to dismantling this system in both church and state. Even recent statements, including *Journey with Apartheid* of May 1997, suggest that the errors and sinful actions of apartheid reside more in the implementation of apartheid than in its fundamental nature. Because the very nature of forced separation of people of differing races denies fundamental biblical teaching that all humanity is equally created in the image of God, teaching so central to the Christian faith that it cannot be denied by Christians without denying their Christian commitment, we still seek an official resolution from the DRC stating unequivocal rejection of apartheid. The proposed joint resolution, if approved by the DRC, would meet that last requirement. (Opocenský, Debrecen 1997:186-188)

The WARC Executive Committee believed that passage of the joint resolution of the General Council of WARC in Debrecen and then by the General Synod of the DRC in 1998 would satisfy the remaining requirement laid down by the WARC General Council in Ottawa, 1982 for the lifting of the suspension of the DRC's membership in WARC in 1998, The executive committee, therefore, moved the adoption of the resolution by the General Council of WARC and called upon the DRC Synod to also adopt it. The DRC General Synod of 1998 approved the joint resolution of the WARC and in doing so the General Synod rejected apartheid:

> As part of this action, the Dutch Reformed Church through its General Synod meeting in 1998, within the framework of the decision of WARC, assures the churches of the Alliance that it rejects apartheid as wrong and sinful not simply in its effects and operations but also in its fundamental nature. (Addendum 8)

The approval of the joint resolution at the DRC General Synod of 1998 restored the right to full participation by the DRC in the WARC. The synod, furthermore, stated that the substantive content of Belhar Confession ('our commitment to the biblical witness about the Triune God, the unity of the church, on justice and reconciliation') was widely accepted in the DRC (*Acta Algemene Sinode NGK* 1998:422-425). The synod, therefore, adopted the essential content of the Confession of Belhar The DRC premise was that this did not imply that all churches, pastors, elders and members of the envisaged unified church would be obliged to endorse the Belhar Confession as a confession. The 1998 General Synod declared that the Belhar Confession was not in conflict with the other confessions of the family of Reformed churches. The 1998 General Synod also noted that all the regional synods of the DRC rejected the adoption of the Confession of Belhar as part of the doctrinal standards of a reunited church (*Agenda Algemene Sinode NGK* 1998:422-425; *Besluiteregister Algemene Sinode NGK* 1998:16).

The DRC General Synod of 2004 proposed that the Confession of Belhar be included in the doctrinal standards of the united church in view of having adopted the essence of this confession already in 1998. It stated that this did not mean that every congregant, church council or the ministers would have to subscribe to this confession. The synod ruled that each congregation could make its own decision regarding the confession. Furthermore, it ascribed resistance to this confession to historical, emotional and symbolic factors (*Besluiteregister Algemene Sinode NGK* 2004:1-4). The synod approved a consultative process and referred the decision on the Belhar Confession to the synods, church councils and congregations for comment and further recommendations. The 2004 Synod affirmed that there were many ministers and church members who were ready for unity and would endorse the Confession of Belhar, but there were many ministers and church members who for various reasons did not want to underwrite the Confession of Belhar as a confession. The DRC stance was that the church had a responsibility to all these groups and would instigate a process of church reunification that will embrace the *'ruim huis'* ('spacious house') notion that provides space for all[16] (*Besluiteregister Algemene Sinode NGK* 2004:1).

From 2001 to 2007, conventicles betweenthe regional synods of the DRC and the URCSA in the Cape and Southern /Northern Transvaal created a positive momentum to the church reunification and the inclusion of the Belhar Confession in the confessional basis of the envisaged unified church. In 2003, the Western, Southern and Eastern Cape regional synods of the DRC proposed that the confessional basis of the reunited church be dealt with within the framework of concentric circles with the Confession of Belhar being located as a confession in the fourth circle. It, furthermore, proposed that in line with earlier decisions of the DRC, the Confession of Belhar should have an optional status in the envisaged unified church (*Minutes URCSA GSC* 2004:1). The URCSA strongly objected to the proposal.

The Cape Convention of the DRC in June 2004 rejected the decisions of these synods and replaced these with a resolution stating that the Confession of Belhar be included in the doctrinal standards equal to the formulae of unity, that all ministers sign it and that provision should be made to pastorally accompany those who were not ready or able to sign it (*Minutes URCSA GSC* 2004:1).

In 2004, a second Cape Convention for Unity met in Brackenfell and reaffirmed that the inclusion of Belhar in an envisioned united church was not negotiable. The Convention requested that the resolution be addressed to the General Synod of the DRC and the URCSA for approval and implementation. In July of that year, the moderamen of the URCSA considered the resolution. The moderamen believed that the decision represented a significant step forward in the process of church unity and stated its support for the broad principles of the resolution while raising its concern for the lack of clarity regarding the process of the accompaniment of ministers who are not able or willing to sign the Confession (*Minutes URCSA GSC* 2004:1).

The DRC General Synod of 2004 proposed that Belhar should be accepted as a fourth confession in a united Reformed church. The synod worked with the assumption that the content of the Belhar was widely accepted. Over time, numerous joint ventures based on the principles of the Belhar Confession developed in the regional synods

---

16 Original wording: 'Wat ons eie kerk betref, het ons 'n verantwoordelikheid teenoor baie predikante en lidmate wat gereed is vir 'n hegte eenheid en graag Belhar sou wou onderskryf, maar ook baie predikante en lidmate wat om verskillende redes nie kans sien om Belhar as belydenisskrif te onderskryf nie. Ons glo dat ons 'n verantwoordelikheid teenoor al hierdie groepe het en sou onsself wou gee vir 'n proses waarin ons so gou as moontlik een word in 'n "ruim huis" wat plek maak vir almal van ons – met die baie waaroor ons saamstem, maar ook dit waaroor ons verskil.'

and commissions, for example, diaconal services, the Curatorium of the DRC and the URCSA. A few DRC and the URCSA presbyteries amalgamated. These included the Stellenbosch United Presbytery and the Wesland United Presbytery *(Minutes of General Synodical Commission* Meeting 2004:48).

On 10 May 2011, the Regional Synod of the Western and Southern Cape discussed the following motion put forward by the moderamen:

> The synod is convinced that the biblical call for justice for all people, reconciliation between people, and the unity of the church are at the heart of the gospel. The Belhar Confession gives expression to the call of the gospel in a different way than the other confessions of the church. The synod, as a church meeting, accepts the Belhar Confession and calls on the General Synod of the Dutch Reformed Church to make the Belhar Confession in a church-orderly way part of the confessional base of the Dutch Reformed Church. (*Acta NGK Wes-Kaapland Sinode* 2011:77)[17]

The DRC Regional Synod consequently approved the motion the Belhar Confession. The synod decided the matter with close ballot papers – 544 for and 124 against, with papers spoilt. This meant that 80 percent of the counted vote was in favour of the Belhar Confession. The decision of the Regional Synod of the Western and Southern Cape was a small but significance step in the broader process of the acceptance of the Belhar Confession in the DRC.

Article 44 of the church order of the DRC General Synod stipulated the church-orderly process to be followed for amendments of the confessional basis of the DRC. According to Article 44.1, the confession could only be changed 'after each synod separately decides with a two-thirds majority in favour thereof.' This meant that a 100% affirmative vote of all ten regional synods of the DRC would have to be achieved before any amendments to the confessional basis could be tabled for adoption on General Synod level. In addition, two-thirds of all DRC church councils had to approve these amendments with a two-thirds majority *(Agenda Algemene Sinode NGK* 1998:424). The General Synod then had to approve the amendment (inclusion of the Belhar Confession in the confessional basis of the DRC) with a two-

---

[17] This proposal to the synod resulted from an in-depth discussion of the Belhar Confession at a meeting of the moderamen of the Western Cape Synod on 24 March 2009. See Hanekom (2014:10). Orginal wording: 'Die sinode is oortuig dat die Bybelse eis vir geregtigheid vir alle mense, versoening tussen alle mense en die eenheid van die kerk tot die kern van die evangelie behoort. Die Belydenis van Belhar verwoord hierdie evangeliese eis om geregtigheid, versoening en eenheid op 'n ander wyse as die ander belydenisskrifte van die kerk. Die sinode aanvaar as kerkvergadering die Belydenis van Belhar en daarom versoek hierdie vergadering die Algemene Sinode om die Belydenis van Belhar op 'n kerkordelike wyse deel van die Nederduitse Gereformeerde Kerk se belydenisgrondslag te maak.'

Acceptance, adoption, advocacy, reception and protestation

thirds majority. This amendment, approved in 2004, made it nearly impossible to change the confessional basis of the DRC. Most Reformed churches would change their confessional basis upon a two-third majority affirmative vote.

The DRC General Synod of 2011 expressed their commitment to the URCSA who professed that the Confession of Belhar was very important to them and that they wanted to make it part of the new denomination. The synod also acknowledged the DRCA and the RCA, who did not see their way clear to completely underwrite Belhar as a confession. The General Synod decided to make the Confession of Belhar a part of the confessional basis of the Dutch Reformed Church in a church-orderly way and tasked the moderamen to implement the necessary processes in this regard. The synod, furthermore, tasked the moderamen to conduct a thorough study of the historical, theological and contextual relevance of the Confession of Belhar so as to be in a position to advise the next General Synod and all church bodies. (*Agenda NGK Algemene Sinode* 2011:232-246; *Besluiteregister NGK Algemene Sinode* 2011:13). The synod acknowledged that there were many congregations, ministers and members in the church who were ready for a close unity and readily wanted to underwrite Belhar. However, there were many congregations, ministers and members who were ready for a close unity but for different reasons did not see their way open to underwrite Belhar as confession. The 2011 Synod was convinced that these different standpoints could be accommodated for in a 'spacious house', which would provide space for all (*Besluiteregister NGK Algemene Sinode* 2011:13).

The 2013 DRC Synod approved, with a huge majority, amendments to Article 1 of the church order to change the confessional basis of the DRC. The synod thereby proposed the inclusion of the Belhar as an optional confession within the confessional basis of the DRC. This was done in order to compromise the objective voices in the DRC. In doing so the DRC wanted to make room for those members of the church who would not subscribe to the confession. The following proposal regarding the inclusion of the Belhar Confession was sent to the ten regional synods of the DRC for their perusal, discussion and vote.

1. The Dutch Reformed Church is based on the Bible as the holy and infallible Word of God.

2.1 The doctrine which the Church confesses in agreement with the Word of God, is expressed in the ecumenical creeds, namely the Apostles' Creed, the Nicene Creed and the Creed of Athanasius; and the Three Forms of Unity, namely the Belgic Confession, the Heidelberg Catechism and the Canons of Dort.

2.2 The Belhar Confession is part of the confessional basis of the church, in a way that allow members, office-bearers and assemblies of the church to confess it as in agreement with the Word of God, as well as members, office-bearers and assemblies of the church that do not subscribe to it as a confession.

3. The Church accepts her calling to always confess her faith and that the expansion of her confessional basis should occur without force (*Besluiteregister NGK Algemene Sinode* 2013:173).[18]

The different regional synods voted as follows:[19]

Table 1.1: Regional Synod Reading the Belhar Confession as a historical text. voting on the amendment to the DRC confessional basis, 2013

No.	Synod	Yes-votes	No-Votes
1	Western and Southern Cape	73.3%	26.7%
2	Eastern	73.2%	26.8%
3	Eastern Cape	70%	30%
4	Namibia	58%	42%
5	Highveld	51.9%	49.1%
6	Kwazulu-Natal	52%	48%
7	Northern Synod	49%	51%
8	West Transvaal	42%	58%
9	Northern Cape	33%	67%
10	Free State	32%	68%

Only three of the ten synods of the DRC secured a two-thirds majority. The DRC Western and South Cape Synod of 2015 acknowledged that notwithstanding their 73.3% affirmative vote on the inclusion of the Belhar Confession in the confessional basis of the DRC, the General Synod of the DRC would not be able to change the confessional basis due to restrictions in the church order. They therefore requested

---

18 Kerkorde Artikel 1
   1. Die Nederduitse Gereformeerde Kerk is gegrond op die Bybel as die heilige en onfeilbare Woord van God.
   2.1 Die leer wat die Kerk in ooreenstemming met die Woord van God bely, word verwoord in
      2.1.1 die ekumeniese belydenisse, naamlik die Apostoliese Geloofsbelydenis, die Geloofsbelydenis van Nicea en die Geloofsbelydenis van Athanasius; en
      2.1.2 die Drie Formuliere van Eenheid, naamlik die Nederlandse Geloofsbelydenis, die Heidelbergse Kategismus en die Dordtse Leerreëls.
   2.2 Die Belydenis van Belhar is deel van die belydenisgrondslag van die Kerk, op so 'n wyse dat daar ruimte is vir lidmate, ampsdraers en vergaderinge wat dit as in ooreenstemming met die Woord van God bely, sowel as vir lidmate, ampsdraers en vergaderinge wat dit nie as 'n belydenisskrif onderskryf nie.
   3. Die Kerk aanvaar dat haar roeping om haar geloof te bely, altyd geld en dat 'n uitbreiding van haar belydenisgrondslag sonder dwang geskied.
19 Statistics of voting had been published in *Die Kerkbode*, 18 September 2015, p. 5.

the General Synod to amend Regulation 24 as well as Article 44.1 and 44.2 of the Order. They proposed the following:

- The General Synod amends the church order, Article 44.1 as follows [the formulation before the 2004 General Synod of the DRC]: Article 44.1 The amendment of the confession is possible only after each synod, with a two-thirds majority vote in favour of resolution. [The words 'as well as two-thirds of all church councils each with a two-thirds majority' is thus deleted.]
- The General Synod deletes Regulation 24 in its entirety (*Agenda NGK Algemene Sinode* 2015:435).

The Western and Southern Cape Synod also requested the DRC General Synod to amend Regulation 4 point 3.1 in such a way that made it possible for ministers of the Word, congregation members and church council meetings who wanted to accept the Belhar Confession to be able to do so. They proposed that the General Synod make it possible for synods to make other confessions that are not, part of their confessions, which is not contrary to Scripture, the three Formulas of Unity and the existing ecumenical creeds.

In addition, they proposed:
- The General Synod adds a new church order article at the end of Article 44 of the church order. The new article to read that synods may make other confessions part of their confessional basis, provided that the General Synod found that such confession is not contrary to Scripture, the three Creeds and existing ecumenical creeds. Such a decision is not being considered an amendment of the General Synod's confessions.

The General Synod grant permission to the Dutch Reformed Church in South Africa (Western and Southern Cape) and other synods who requested under [the new] Article 44.6 to make the Belhar Confession part of their confessional basis (*Agenda NGK Algemene Sinode* 2015:435).

The synod requested that the DRC and the URCSA develop a protocol to make provision for joint presbyteries to give greater expression of their unity. Lastly, the synod requested the General Synod to develop jointly with the URCSA a provisional church order which would enhance church reunification at large. The provisional order should allow that unity structures between congregations, presbyteries, synods and the General Synod of the Dutch Reformed family of churches come into existence without jeopardising the legal entity of the participating churches (*Agenda NGK Algemene Sinode* 2015:442).

The DRC Western and South Cape Synod, 2015 initiative gave new impetus to the church reunification talks. The four moderamen of the DRC family of churches met in Pretoria in May 2015 and decided to convene a special meeting on the prospects of a provisional church order or common set of rules. They also decided to invite representatives of the Protestant Church in the Netherlands (PCN) to this meeting in order that these representatives share with the DRC their vast knowledge of interim church orders, which they had gained during the 'Samen op Weg' process. A mandate was given to the DRC Southern and Western Cape to organise this meeting.

Delegates of the four churches met from the 11 to 13 July 2015 at the Volmoed Retreat and Conference Centre near Hermanus. The churches were represented by Mary-Anne Plaatjies-Van Huffel, Godfrey Betha and Leepo Modise from the URCSA, Tladi Pheko and Andries Hoffman from the DRCA, Victor Pillay of the RCA and Johann Ernst, Kobus Gerber and Gustav Claassen of the DRC. The DRC Western and Southern Cape, as hosts, was represented by Nelis Janse Van Rensburg, Quintus Heine and Charl Stander. Representatives of the URCSA Cape Regional Synod, namely Pieter Grove, Barnabas Ngqozela and David Carelse were also invited. Prof. Nelus Niemandt, the chairperson of the DRC, had to withdraw from the DRC General Synod delegation due to health issues. Dr Gustav Claassen substituted for him. Prof. Jerry Pillay, designated by the World Communion of Reformed Churches to facilitate the unification process, also had to withdraw due to other commitments. He was substituted by Rev. Peter Langerman, a minister of the Uniting Presbyterian Church in Southern Africa. Prof. Leo Koffeman and Evert Overeem of the PCN were invited. Nico Simpson from Bible-Media was also present and acted as summariser of the discussions. At the meeting between delegates of the four churches of the DRC family in Volmoed during 2015, the RCA was willing to accept the confession as a confession of a reunited church because it belonged to one of the churches, but provisions should be made to allow people the option of subscribing or not subscribing to the Belhar Confession. The delegates conveyed the commitment of the leadership of the Reformed Church in Africa to church reunification.

The meeting at Volmoed took cognisance that in 2012, the General Synod of the URCSA and the DRC Synod of 2013 had agreed on a Memorandum of Agreement and a Roadmap to Church Reunification (*Agenda Algemene Sinode NGK* 2015:240; *Report of a meeting between delegates of the four churches of the DRC family in South Africa* 2015:1-2).

The meeting at Volmoed decided that the provisional order would include a preamble that addressed the main items of history, justice and the confessional base (including the Belhar Confession and the Declaration of Laudium) and that highlighted the three or so main issues that should be addressed in the interim order. The moderamen of the four churches of the DRC family at their meeting of

25–26 May 2015 at Hatfield, Pretoria together envisaged the prospect of a provisional order that would afford them an opportunity to proceed towards church unity and establish a final church order. This provisional order was to be based on the confessional basis of the four churches (*Agenda Algemene Sinode NGK* 2015:208, 240; Report of a meeting between delegates of the four churches of the DRC family in South Africa 2015:16-17).

The 2015 General Synod of the DRC approved the provisional order and in doing so kindled the hope that church reunification could be attained based on the principles of the Belhar Confession (*Agenda Algemene Sinode NGK* 2015:208, 240). The following resolution was approved at the URCSA General Synod of October 2016:

1. The GS takes with appreciation note of the [indefatigable] efforts by the regional synods of the DRC to take up the Belhar Confession in the confessional basis of the DRC
2. The GS regretfully takes note of the [unsuccessful] efforts of the DRC General Synod regarding securing a [two-thirds] majority vote in every Regional Synod in order to include the Belhar Confession as a fully-fledged confession.
3. The GS affirms that we will still avail ourselves to accompany the DRC regarding the acceptance of the Belhar Confession.
4. The GS affirms that the acceptance of the Belhar Confession is being seen by URCSA as the acid test of the DRC's response to the challenge of becoming one, united and non-racial church with the other Dutch Reformed churches.
5. The GS states categorically that the Belhar Confession should be included as a [fully-fledged] confession in the confessional basis of the envisaged unified church. Optionality of the Belhar Confession is not an option for URCSA.
6. The GS approves the provisional church order as a way forward.
7. The GS requests the regional synods of the DRC who are willing to journey on [the] basis of the provisional church order to also indicate that they subscribe to the Memorandum of Agreement and the Roadmap to Church Reunification.
8. The GS assures the ministries, congregations, presbyteries and regional synods of the DRC who on [the] basis of the provincial church order want to unify with URCSA that the URCSA will embrace them with compassion and accompany them in their journey.
9. The GS requests the General Synod of the DRC to amend Regulation 24 as well as Article 44.1 and 44.2 of the church order of the General Synod of the DRC in totality in order to make church reunification possible.

10. The GS urges the DRC to confront recalcitrant members and congregations and regional synods of the DRC with the inescapable demand of the gospel that they should strive and indefatigably work towards the goal to become members of one non-racial reunited church.

11. The GS declares emphatically that restorative justice should shift hence on from the periphery to the axis of bilateral and multilateral talks of the DRC family. Justice does not pass over wrongs. Wrongs in church and society should be faced and addressed in a comprehensive manner. In doing so the DRC family will be able to overcome past divisions and find a new and richer unity. Without attending to the issue of restorative justice church reunification is not possible to ascertain.

12. The GS approves that the MOA is still the basis for our relationship with the DRC.

13. The GS approves that the joint projects of our churches: Season of Human Dignity and Churches Addressing Racism continue to assist in making unity a reality. *(Agenda General Synod URCSA 2016:111-112)*

The URCSA and the Belhar Confession

On the 14 April 1994, the DRMC and the DRCA unified in order to constitute the URCSA. At the Founding Synod, the URCSA approved the Belhar Confession as one of its four confessions (standards of unity), namely the Heidelberg Catechism (1563), the Belgic Confession (1561, revised 1619), the Canons of Dort (1618–1619) and the Confession of Belhar (*Skema Van Werksaamhede en HandelingeVGKSA* 1997:26, 504). In 1997, the URCSA requested Reformed churches around the world – by way of the WARC and the REC – to consider adopting the Belhar Confession so as to make it a part of the global Reformed confessional basis (*Skema Van Werksaamhede en HandelingeVGKSA* 1997:26, 504).

The consistent endeavours towards church reunification and the inclusion of the Belhar Confession in the envisaged unified church are reflected in the efforts of the moderamen of the URCSA regarding multi- and bilateral talks with the DRC family since 2001. Noteworthy are the Esselenpark Declaration (2006), the Bloemfontein Declaration (2006) and the Achterberg I and II declarations (2006 and 2007). The efforts at regional, presbytery and ministry levels are also recognised.

The URCSA General Synodical Commission (GSC) of 2004 regarded the DRC General Synod decision in 2004 concerning the notion of a 'spacious house' that would provide space for all as reprehensible. 'Such treatment of the confessional basis for a united church' is described as 'not helpful in the process of reuniting our divided family.' (Late report, *Minutes URCSA GSC* 2004:4). It was the contention of the moderamen spearheaded by Rev. James Buys as moderator of URCSA (who had tirelessly drafted most of the proposals on church reunification and the Belhar Confession during his tenure) that the decision of the DRC General Synod, 2004 did not represent a significant move in the process of church unity (*Minutes URCSA GSC* 2004:1). The contention of the URCSA was that the decision of the DRC Synod was fatally flawed in determining that the inclusion of the Confession of Belhar did not imply that congregants, church councils and ministers have to subscribe to this confession (*Minutes URCSA GSC* 2004:1). The implication of the decision of the DRC General Synod 2004 decision was that the Belhar Confession would have an optional status in the envisaged unified church. The moderamen of the URCSA considered the decision totally unacceptable as it

- denigrated the Confession of Belhar in relation to the other confessions;
- created a situation for doctrinal liberty;
- was unprecedented in the reformed tradition that certain confessions can merely be optional;
- undermined the legal requirements of common confessional basis as foundation for the formation of one denomination; and
- made a mockery of testing the church on a confession where the optional nature of such a confession makes testing a moot point (*Minutes URCSA GSC* 2004:1).

Regarding the decision of the DRC General Synod 2004, the General Synodical Commission of the URCSA in 2004 declared the following:

1. The GSC declares unambiguously its rejection of the inclusion of the Confession of Belhar as an optional confession. It rejects any notion of dealing with this confession in a context of doctrinal liberty.

2. We prayerfully request the DRC to urgently reconsider this part of her decision with the motivation given, because such treatment of the confessional basis for a united church is not helpful in the process of reuniting our divided family.

3. We request that the Confession of Belhar be treated no less and no more than the three formulas for unity which guide and guard our faith, life and work as members of the body of Christ.

4. The GSC recognises the principle of freedom of conscience and proposes that those parties unwilling to underwrite the confession be pastorally accompanied and encouraged to accept it and not be excluded from the new church.

5. The GSC rejects the notion of an 'urgent' unity based on unity structures that compromise any clear resolution of the confessional basis of a united church.

6. The GSC requests all church structures to evaluate the structures of co-operation and ensure that they express the message of the Confession of Belhar regarding the true unity, reconciliation with integrity and compassionate justice that empowers the poor.
7. The GSC decides that in all negotiations with the DRC on church unity, the agenda of negotiations should be based on the Confession of Belhar, its practical content, emotions and fears that exist, i.e. the historical baggage, the economic aspects, i.e. restitution and other factors that go with it.
8. The GSC appoints a task team to provide guidelines to the URCSA structures on the faith and conviction of the URCSA, as expressed in the Confession of Belhar as it impacts on the processes mentioned above. The task team provides these guidelines to the Executive Committee who will provide them to the church. The Executive Committee monitors and guides the reunification process with report to the General Synodical Commission or General Synod (*Minutes URCSA GSC* 2004:1).

The URCSA General Synod, 2005 affirmed that the Belhar Confession was non-negotiable in the church reunification process and that it was the omissible basis of a new, united church and hence not optional or unworthy of inclusion in the most intimate and sacral acts of worship. In their response to their criticism of the Belhar Confession and their convictions concerning the confession, the URCSA repeatedly stated that they had no desire to 'force' any church to accept the Belhar Confession (*Agenda General Synod URCSA* 2005:534). The URCSA General Synod, 2005 emphatically stated that the URCSA could never impose on other churches or require them to confess the same way, but that its deliberations with other churches were based on its confession with a view of reaching an eventual common understanding of the gospel. The 2005 General Synod, furthermore, approved the necessary church-orderly regulations, namely, the Reglement vir die Kombinasie Van Werksaamhede Van Gemeentes, Ringe en Sinodes uit Verskillende Kerkverbande to enable regional synods, presbyteries and local congregations who desired to do so on the basis of the acceptance of the Confession of Belhar, to unite with the DRC family to the fullest extent possible in ministry – even if structural unity, because of church-orderly impediments, was not yet possible (*Acts URCSA General Synod* 2005:137). The General Synod instructed the Permanent Judicial Commission to give urgent attention to the enabling legislation to make structural union possible. The URCSA premise was that this regulation would enable authentic unity structures, which would give expression to the URCSA's commitment to church reunification. The General Synod therefore, did not only condone such unions, it encouraged and supported them wholeheartedly (*Agenda General Synod URCSA* 2005:531-533).

During 2005, commissions, ministries as well as presbyteries of the DRC and the URCSA combined. The question concerning the confessional basis of such joint ventures surfaced. The URCSA asked for the 'unconditional acceptance of the Confession of Belhar as a requirement for the continuation of discussions on church unity' (*Agenda General Synod URCSA* 2008:533-534). URCSA's premise was that the Belhar Confession would be a full confession of the united church and that everyone would work together to help the church to grow to a full acceptance of the confession.

The URCSA General Synod of 2005 affirmed that the Belhar Confession was based upon, and was true to the Word of God and witnesses to the liberating acts of God in history and our own time; the Lordship of Jesus Christ over all areas of life and the empowering presence of the Holy Spirit in the life of those who believe. The synod affirmed that the confession has its historical roots in the Reformed tradition and had proved itself to be a worthy bearer of the historical continuation of the Reformed endeavour to be forever reforming in response to God's call in a changing world. The synod also affirmed that the historical context of Belhar represented the church with a moment of *kairos* in which the integrity of the gospel and the Reformed faith, the witness and very survival of the church was at stake. The Belhar Confession was a response of the church in faith at a time of tremendous challenge and adversity. This moment of *kairos* was a call to obedience in which the church rediscovered the faithfulness of God, the strength given by God's Holy Spirit in times of challenge and weakness, and the power of faithful witness to the powers of evil. The historical context, one of political and economic oppression, deep enmity and immeasurable suffering, however compelling, nonetheless, did not dictate the reaction of the church. Instead, the Holy Spirit enabled us to rise above political realities, economic hardship, social injustices and the denial of our very humanity, to rise above ourselves and affirm first and foremost, God as God of justice and reconciliation. In the Confession of Belhar, the first word is not to the desires of our own hearts, or the urgent voices of revenge and retribution, but to the reconciling Christ, who calls us to be agents of reconciliation and out of that reconciliation calls us to unity and justice. Hence the unity we seek is both demand and gift, which because of the Giver, though fraught with danger and pitfalls, becomes a burden that is light and a yoke that is easy. That in itself is a miracle of God's love, too precious to lose or give up or to subject to the casual carelessness of irreverent debate. Compromising on the Belhar Confession for the sake of the continuing weakness of some in the DRC is a betrayal not only of the URCSA, itself, but of the ecumenical Reformed family who have turned to the confession of Belhar for continued inspiration. The URCSA regard the Belhar Confession indispensable for the life of the new, united church, as non-negotiable in its power to reconcile, seek justice and address the wrongs done to the least of the family of Jesus (*Agenda General Synod URCSA* 2005:496).

At a meeting held at St RaphaelsRetreat House (Place of Worship) in Cape Town on 13 February 2006 the moderamen of the URCSA General Synod discussed the implications and interpretation of decisions of General Synod of 2005 regarding church unity and the acceptance of the Belhar Confession. After being requested by the Cape Regional moderamen to interpret the meaning of the words 'full acceptance of the Belhar Confession' in the decision that the synod had taken, the moderamen decided to clarify the decision as follows: That the expression 'full acceptance of Belhar Confession' does not mean that a DRC congregation is required to adopt Belhar as a formal fourth confession, which can only be done by the General Synod of the DRC after a prescribed legal procedure. What is meant here is that the Belhar Confession is an urgent and compelling message on unity, reconciliation and justice, which formulates not only what God gives us but also what God demands of us in serving the coming of God's reign in Southern Africa. The resolution of General Synod 2005 regarding joint ventures between the DRC and the URCSA is interpreted to require that a joint ministry between DRC and the URCSA bodies:

- should draw up a written agreement containing the terms of the collaboration, in which the Belhar Confession is mentioned by name as supplying the guiding principles and ethos for the joint ministry; and
- should require the participating body (church council, presbytery, Regional Synod) from the side of the DRC, to take one of the following steps: the DRC Church Council or relevant church body officially adopt the message of Belhar Confession; the DRC members or commission taking part in the joint committees or activities sign a document that they endorse the message of Belhar Confession (*General Synodical Commission* 2006:1).

On 20 June 2006, the DRC and the URCSA met at Esselenpark. They soon became aware of a new spirit of reconciliation and togetherness and a willingness to reach out to one another. They experienced that all were more willing to listen to one another and to assist one another on the road to reunification. In the opening session, the DRC leadership apologised once more for the pain and hurt that they had caused the URCSA and its members in the past. This confession was movingly accepted by the URCSA leadership, an act that set the tone for the whole meeting. On the final day, the URCSA leadership apologised in turn for the pain that the URCSA had caused the DRC. It was decided to enter into a covenant for unity. They choose the term 'covenant' because they want to bring themselves and the reunification process under the authority of the word of God and the will of Christ. The meeting envisaged a new organically united Reformed church, organised according to synodical-Presbyterian principles, which lives missional and is committed to the biblical demands of love, reconciliation, justice and peace. At the same time, they committed to non-racialism, inclusiveness and the acceptance and celebration of our multicultural composition. They agreed that the different languages in the churches would be treasured. The URCSA GSC then reconvened and made the following decision, which was hoped would take away the most difficult stumbling block.

> We accept the challenge to become one united church in three years' time. In this regard, the Confession of Belhar shall not function as a precondition for unity. Instead, the message of Belhar shall continue to be the inspiration and guide of both the process towards and the formation of the new church. In accordance with the decisions of both churches the Confession of Belhar shall function as a full confession in the new church and we shall work together to help the church as a whole grow towards its complete acceptance. We shall take this decision for full ratification to our next synod. (Covenanting for the Reunification of the Family of DRC family – Esselenpark Declaration 2006)

The URCSA and the DRC committed themselves at Esselenpark to church reunification within the next three years, where the Belhar was no longer a prerequisite for unity, but would function as a fully-fledged confession in the envisaged unified church.

The decision of the GSC of 2006 regarding the Belhar Confession caused a lot of confusion in the URCSA. Shortly after the GSC meeting, a memorandum was received from the presbytery of the SA Gestig, the oldest congregation of the URCSA, expressing their concern with the way in which the reunification process has been handled by the moderamen and the GSC. It alleged that the decision taken by the Esselenpark meeting of the GSC made the Belhar Confession into an 'optional' confession and therefore violated the decisions of the General Synod of 2005.

When discussing this memorandum by the SA Gestig presbytery, the GSC of 2007 expressed concern that the statement of the SA Gestig was first communicated to the press before the moderamen or the even the leadership in the Cape were notified. This led to the situation that the moderator, Prof. Thias Kgatla, was confronted by the press for a response before the moderamen even had knowledge of the statement. In response to the memorandum on the reunification process, the URCSA GSC decided as follows:

> We regret that the memorandum was presented to the media and that this happened before it was presented to the executive for their response.

> The negative language used in the memorandum was disturbing and did not communicate positively to the GSC.
>
> The GSC finds the procedure to come to the conclusion that the GSC violated the decisions of the General Synod instead of first to inquire for clarification, unhelpful. (*Minutes URCSA GSC* 2007:3)

The GSC, furthermore, affirmed that the words in the Esselenpark Declaration 'the Confession of Belhar shall not function as a precondition for unity' do not compromise the Confession of Belhar, for the following reasons:

1. The phrase was interpreted by the URCSA GSC at Esselenpark in June 2006 to mean: that the signing of the Confession of Belhar by all members of the sister churches in the DRC family shall not function as a precondition for unity, with the understanding that Belhar will be accepted as one of the four confessions of the foreseen united church. This position was the consensus of Actherberg 2 for the URCSA and the DRC. The RCA and the DRCA undertook to consider it.

2. Genuine confession of faith (with your lips) cannot be separated from 'believing with your heart' (see Rom 10:10). It can therefore not be forced or legislated. To expect every minister of another church to personally accept and sign Belhar will not be a meaningful unification strategy. The existing ministers and members of the DRCA were also not expected to sign Belhar in the process of the formation of the URCSA, which has Belhar as a fourth confession. The acceptance of Belhar as a fourth confession by the synods of the DRCA at the time was regarded as adequate. However, this does mean that all new ministers ('*proponente*') of the united church should affirm it when being licenced as ministers of the Word.

3. It is a fact that the URCSA consists of a diversity of people with a variety of languages, spiritualities and historical background. The DRC, DRCA and the RCA perhaps contain less internal diversity, but as part of the unification process, they add to the cultural, spiritual and ideological diversity of the DRC family. The only basis on which meaningful organic unity can be achieved among people of such diversity is if it becomes a home with enough space, with freedom for people to be different from one another, provided everyone eats from the same pot in the kitchen. The core teachings, values, processes and structures, therefore, need to be firmly established, while for the rest there should be freedom for people to express themselves in different ways.

4. There are two ways in which we could 'compromise' the Confession of Belhar. On the one hand, we could treat Belhar too lightly, lowering its value to a mere statement of faith that has no authority in a united church. That is unacceptable, and it is not what the GSC endorsed at Esselenpark or Achterberg. On the other hand, we could make too much of Belhar, making it into an imposition on the

members of sister churches. That would be in conflict with the nature of a confession as a voluntary, Spirit-induced stand that a person takes in the midst of a community of faith.

5. A confession is a compelling and transformative statement of truth, intended to direct and guide the lives of church members in a fundamental way. It should, therefore, find its echoes in the preaching, teaching, pastoral care, public witness, ministerial formation, etc., of the whole congregation. In this regard, it is a serious question whether the Belgic Confession and the Canons of Dordt are functioning as confessions in the URCSA or the rest of the DRC family. It is only the Heidelberg Catechism that functions to some extent in our family of DR churches. The 'acceptance' of Belhar should, therefore, mean living the vision expressed in it on a daily basis. And this means that there is still a huge amount that needs to be done in the URCSA, which has formally and officially accepted Belhar as a confession.

6. The URCSA premise is that the DRC should accept the Belhar Confession unconditionally as part of a reunited church's confessional basis. The church unification process between the DRC and the URCSA, therefore, came to a stalemate during 2005 after the DRC's General Synod 2004 had decided it will not be required of all members of a reunited church to endorse the confession. DRC believes that the differences over Belhar Confession are mainly about historical, emotional and symbolic factors rather than the material content itself (*Minutes URCSA GSC* 2007:4).

The Executive Committees of the DRCA, the URCSA, the RCA and the DRC met on 16 August 2006 in Bloemfontein to discuss church reunification and the confessional basis of the envisaged unified church. This was a breakthrough. The discussions were frank and open about the court cases between the URCSA and the DRCA, the synodical decisions of the four churches regarding church reunification and the confessional basis of the envisaged unified church as well as the way ahead. In the end, all four churches committed themselves to covenanting for unity. That paved the way for what was later to be known as the 'Achterbergh Declarations'.

From 6 to 8 November 2006, approximately 127 representatives of the DRC, DRCA, RCA and the URCSA met at Achterbergh near Krugersdorp to discuss the reunification of the family of DRC churches and how this can be realised. The meeting appointed ten task teams to work on the different aspects of reunification (Achterbergh Declaration I).

A second round of talks was held on 23 to 25 April 2007 between the churches at Achterbergh. The church model of the envisaged unified church, the confessional basis, reconciliation and joint ventures were thoroughly discussed at this consultation. Regarding the confessional basis of the envisaged unified church, the following were accepted as the first points of consensus between the four churches:

1. The Confession of Belhar should not be a precondition for church unity.
2. That we continue discussions between all four churches with the purpose of agreeing to the biblical content of the Confession of Belhar and writing a joint commentary on it. That will make it possible that in a new denominational tie (*kerkverband*) the biblical content of the Confession of Belhar can be preached, taught and used in ministry.
3. In the forming of a new denominational tie (*kerkverband*), the doctrinal basis must accommodate all four churches, synods and congregations without forcing anybody to accept or to abandon Belhar.
4. We respect the value that the Confession of Belhar as a confession has for the URCSA.

The following points reflect consensus between the URCSA and the DRC. The RCA and the DRCA were willing to consider it after taking part in the process agreed to in point 2.

- In a new denominational tie (kerkverband) the Confession of Belhar will be included in the confessional basis as a fourth confession, but it will not be expected of members and ministers who are not ready or willing to underwrite [accept] it as a confession.
- The growing towards full acceptance of the Confession of Belhar is an integral part of the processes of the new church union (Achterbergh Declaration II 2007:1).

Consensus could not be reached on the issue of reconciliation and this was referred to the interim committee for further refinement. The meeting also agreed that all the churches consult with their congregations on the consensus reached at this stage with the view of incorporating the views of congregations in the follow-up processes. The delegates left the Achterbergh II consultation with great optimism. They hoped that church reunification would be realised soon.

The DRC Synod of 2007, after testing their congregations on the Achterbergh Declaration II, realised that most DRC congregations were not ready to accept the proposals regarding the Belhar Confession. The synod stated:

1. In a new denominational relation ('*kerkverband*') the Confession of Belhar will be included in the confessional basis as a fourth confession, but it will not be expected of members and ministers who are not ready or willing to underwrite [accept] it as a confession.

2. The growing towards full acceptance of the Confession of Belhar is an integral part of the processes of the new church formation (*Achterbergh Declaration II 2007*:1; *Agenda NGK Algemene Sinode* 2007:393-396).

The 2007 Synod did not approve the proposals of Achterbergh II but rather decided to embark on a lengthy consultation process regarding them (*Besluiteregister NGK Algemene Sinode* 2007:12-14; *Notule NGK Algemene Sinode* 2007:1-3). The indecisiveness of the DRC on the Belhar Confession ultimately led to a declaration of a moratorium on unity talks by the URCSA General Synod 2008. After receiving feedback from their congregations, the DRC leadership retreated – even from the decisions of the General Synod in 2004. The Belhar Confession was once again drawn in as a bone of contention. Furthermore, on the issue of the model it, seems that there was a stronger movement towards a federal structure, moving away from the consensus met at Achterbergh II.

At a meeting in Hammanskraal (29 September to 5 October 2008), the General Synod of the URCSA affirmed:

1. The call for the unity of the church of Jesus Christ and especially at this time of the Dutch Reformed Church family as a call to obedience and a response to the prayer of Jesus Christ (Jn. 17) which the church desires to fulfil with all our heart.

2. This call to unity, reconciliation and justice as an inescapable gift and obligation laid upon us by the Confession of Belhar.

3. Our continuing commitment to this unity as expressed in the decisions and actions of successive synods of this church at both general and regional synodial level and as expressed also by the constant efforts towards unity at the level of presbyteries and commissions of the church and congregations on the basis of our common acceptance of the Confession of Belhar wherever possible.

4. Our desire that the unity of our churches of the Reformed family in South Africa should be expressed in organic unity reflective of the Presbyterial model and be structurally recognisable and spiritually strong.

5. Our firm conviction that the Confession of Belhar should be part of the confessional basis and identity of the newly formed denomination (*Acts General SynodURCSA* 2008:194-195).

The General Synod of the URCSA took cognisance of the reports emanating from the DRC General Synod of 2007 and of the resolutions of the moderamen (expanded) on Church Reunification (11–12 June 2008) where the view was expressed that while the Confession of Belhar 'has significant value and sentiment for the URCSA and some members of the DR Church', for the 'majority member and congregations of the Dutch Reformed Church the Confession of Belhar is not acceptable as fourth confession'. (see Addendum 9) The General Synod of the URCSA, 2008 expressed their disappointment at the DRC deviation from the consensus reached at the Achterbergh consultation and issued the following statement:

1. With deep distress that these latest decisions of the DRC represent a disturbing departure from our understanding reached at Esselenpark and the 'Points of Consensus' reached at the Achterberg consultations. These decisions renew the rejection of the Confession of Belhar as part of the confessional basis of the new united church to which we aspire.

2. With sadness that this remains the case even after the substantial concession on the manner in which the Confession of Belhar should be approached made by the URCSA General Synodical Commission at the Esselenpark meeting in 2006.

3. With deep disappointment that neither in the decisions of the DRC General Synod, nor in the most recent resolutions of the Expanded Moderamen has the 'Covenant Toward Church Unity' as formulated and accepted at Esselenpark, and put before, and accepted by the regional synods of the URCSA as a new, common theological basis for church union, featured in any recognisable way.

4. That by reintroducing the Confession of Belhar as a matter of political contention and the most visible and most objectionable barrier to church unification, the DRC is at significant variance with its own decision regarding the Confession of Belhar and the confessional basis of the new united church;

5. And that by this action the DRC has in effect turned away from the 'Covenant toward Church Unity' agreed upon at Esselenpark and has invalidated the grounds upon which the URCSA has taken its decision on Belhar as a gesture of reconciliation and obedience.

6. That the proposed model of unification, the so-called 'Joint General Synod' has nothing in common with the model of organic unity according to Presbyterian principles proposed by the URCSA and until now the model under discussion accepted by the DRC is, in fact, a revamped 'federal model' URCSA has consistently rejected over the years. It is a model that accepts, and reinforces the racially divided nature of our Dutch Reformed churches and represents a fundamental denial of what the URCSA stands for and is expressed in the Confession of Belhar and our understanding of Reformed Ecclesiology (*Acts General Synod URCSA* 2008:24-25).

Furthermore, the URSCA General Synod, 2007 decided to put a moratorium on the reunification talks between the URCSA and DRC until the DRC was seriously committed and ready for unity talks. The General Synod affirmed that the faith, courage and work of regional synods, presbyteries, commissions of the church and local congregations be respected and honoured by encouraging them. The synod further affirmed that

- where all efforts towards unification are done in faith and with integrity, in obedience to the call of Christ and on the basis of the acceptance of the Confession of Belhar, to continue with these efforts; and
- to thereby remain signs of hope, reconciliation and love to the fulfilment of justice, the edification and witness of the church and the glory of God (*Acts General Synod URCSA* 2008:24-25).

The General Synod, 2007 mandated the executive to invite the WARC to facilitate the process of reunification of the DRC family.

The General Synod 2007 then asked the moderamen to call for a public occasion where members and ministers of the DRC and the rest of the DRC family could publicly support, identify with and undersign the Confession of Belhar. The URCSA saw it as a meaningful way to make progress with regard to church unification and the commitment to the inclusion of the Belhar Confession in the envisaged unified church (*Acts General Synod URCSA* 2008:24-25). Mary-Anne Plaatjies-Van Huffel, Klippies Kritzinger, Nico Smith, Nico Botha and Daniël Kuys were appointed as a task team to execute the decision of the General Synod in this regard. The task team was unsuccessful in executing this decision.

In March 2009, at the invitation of the URCSA Africa and the DRC, the WARC undertook a mediation process to try to deal with the issues which had led to the breakdown of the reunification talks between the two. The WARC delegation consisted of Clifton Kirkpatrick, President of WARC, Setri Nyomi, General Secretary of WARC, Jerry Pillay, General Secretary of the Uniting Presbyterian Church in Southern Africa, Stephen Farris (Canada), Alexander Horsburgh (Scotland), Rommie Nauta (Netherlands), Egbert Rooze (Belgium) and Rev. Peggy Kabonde (Zambia).

In their report, the delegation expressed their support of the Belhar Confession as a common confession of the envisaged reunited church.[20] The WARC delegation urged the URCSA and the DRC to together engage in a serious study of the Belhar Confession, which should be accompanied by a study guide (Statement by the Delegation from the World Alliance of Reformed Churches 2009. See Addendum 10).

---

20 The URCSA delegation consisted of Prof. Thias Kgatla (moderator), Dr Mary-Anne Plaatjies-van Huffel, Rev. Godfrey Betha, Rev. Philemon Moloi, Rev. Reggie Nel, Dr Dawid Kuyler, Rev. Daniël Kuys, Rev. Jacob Nthakhe, Prof. Nico Smith, Dr Nico Botha (observer), Prof. Willem Saayman (observer), Rev. Awie Louw (observer). The DRC was represented by Prof. Piet Strauss, Mrs Rinel Hugo, Rev. Johan Pienaar, Dr Braam Hanekom, Rev. Pieter Raath, Dr Pieter van Jaarsveld, Prof. Piet Meiring, Dr Nelus Niemandt, Dr Kobus Gerber, Dr Nelis Janse van Rensburg, Dr Johan Ernst and Dr Elschè Buchner.

The study guide should clearly be supported by the leadership of both churches and designed jointly by leaders and adult education experts of both churches. The delegation found that the historical context of the confession needed to be unpacked, understood and researched together and suggested that the study guide should address questions directly. The delegation renewed the WARC's commitment to the process of pastoral accompaniment of the DRC Family. They committed themselves to a process of monitoring, facilitated by Dr Jerry Pillay. The WARC delegation was pleased to learn that the URCSA was more than willing to assist in this process but stressed the need for commitment to, and engagement in, the process. As a possible way forward in beginning this process the WARC task team recommended the appointment of a joint task team of five members from each denomination. This task team was to undertake the process of producing Bible study materials, finding internet information on the subject, observing and studying the responses of other churches and fostering dialogue and discussion within the DRC and the URCSA (Statement by the Delegation from the World Alliance of Reformed Churches 2009:1-3, see Addendum 10).

The General Synod of the URCSA 2012 expressed their appreciation for the breakthrough developments within the DRC General Synod of 2011 to start a process to accept the Belhar Confession in a church-orderly way (Minutes of the Sixth General Synod of URCSA 2012:14-15). The URCSA, therefore, revoked the 2008 decision on a moratorium on all three levels within the DRC Family of churches as the other two churches also showed their willingness to take part in the ongoing process of unity. The URSCA General Synod instructed all regional synods, presbyteries and congregations to engage their counterparts within the DRC, DRCA and RCA with sincerity but firmness as guided by the spirit of the Belhar Confession on all matters applying to the decision of the lifting of the moratorium. The URCSA reaffirmed that the Confession of Belhar should be taken up in the confessional basis of the reunited church and expressed understanding that the 2011 General Synod of the DRC decided to make the Confession of Belhar part of the confessional basis of the DRC in a church-orderly way (*Minutes of the Sixth General Synod of URCSA* 2012:14-15).

During bilateral talks on 25 and 26 July 2012, the executives of the URCSA and the DRC drafted a memorandum of agreement as a basis for the way forward under the guidance of the WCRC. The 2012 General Synod of the URCSA accepted the memorandum. The General Synod acknowledged with thanks the role played by the WCRC and especially the role of Dr Jerry Pillay in the journey of the churches (*Minutes of the Sixth General Synod of URCSA* 2012:11-13; Report of the Executive on Ecumenical Affairs to the General Synod 2012:37-41).

In 2013, the DRC General Synod also approved the Memorandum of Agreement. The URCSA and the DRC agreed to covenant together for unity. Furthermore, they agreed that the Belhar Confession would be part of the confessional basis of the reunited church. For two days (9 and 10 April 2013) at the Le Chateau Guest House in Kempton Park, the URCSA and the DRC discussed how they would continue on the journey ahead to grow together. They were, however, cautious not to create unrealistic expectations or quick fixes for the complex journey that lay ahead. In the light of this, the meeting drafted a 'Roadmap to Church Reunification' with ten steps (Addendum 12). The 'Roadmap' made provision that a 'Common Set of Rules' ('*Tussenorde*') for the churches be drawn up. The principles already agreed on in the Memorandum of Agreement were to be contained in the concept church order of the envisaged unified church (organic synodical-Presbyterian structure; missional structure; diversity of language and culture; unification of congregations, presbyteries and synods; the autonomy of the local congregation combined with the authority of the presbytery, synod and General Synod; and the inclusion of the Belhar Confession in the confessional basis) (Memorandum of Agreement 2012).

On the issue of restorative justice and reconciliation, the DRC and the URCSA acknowledged in the Memorandum of Agreement that church unity and the Belhar Confession urges the two churches to also speak about restorative justice and reconciliation. As churches they, therefore, decided to embrace the following:

1. Restorative justice should not be an end in itself but always lead to reconciliation. Reconciliation should be the restoration of communities at different levels of society: personal, social, political, denominational, economical, emotional and spiritual reconciliation between God and us.

2. We believe that restorative justice is a biblical imperative that restores life in its fullness. It restores imbalances of the past and imbalances in God's creation and glorifies God through our restored unity and reconciliation.

3. We accept that restorative justice is a complex process which will ask some sacrifices. We will, therefore, need good stewardship but also a clear vision on the possible outcomes of such a process.

Regarding reconciliation, the DRC and the URCSA agreed on the following statements:

1. We believe that true reconciliation is a deeply spiritual process. Christian principles like sacrifice and forgiveness should not be neglected. Without the necessary spiritual maturity, it could fail dismally.

2. We accept the reality that conflict, bitterness, hatred, racism, ethnicism, classism, sexism and a lot of emotional pain is still very much part of society. We must address some of the core reasons for conflict like misunderstandings and poor communication, bad and corrupt leadership, language, culture and religion,

ideologies and the greed for political power, injustices, personalities, scarce resources and imbalances in society (Memorandum of Agreement 2012:1-4).

The URCSA GSC of 2013, in session in Durban, took note of the decision of the DRC General Synod, 2013 regarding the Confession of Belhar: The GSC acknowledged the right of the DRC to formulate its own confessional basis, however, stated that the proposed wording of Article 1, clause 2.2 in the confessional basis of the DRC was not acceptable as it stood for a church order of a finally reunited church. The premise of the URCSA was that the DRC attempted to reconcile two contradictory confessional positions, and in the process created the danger of the authority of the confessions being challenged. The GSC understood the desire of the DRC to avoid division in the church; however, the Commission decided the following as a more adequate basis of dealing with the confession and church reunification:

1. The Confession of Belhar is recognised as the confession with the same authority as the formularies of unity.

2. The content of the Confession of Belhar, namely visible church unity, true reconciliation in Christ-overcoming racial divisions in Southern Africa and the world and God's preferential option for the poor is proposed for full subscription by every office in the new re-unified Church.

3. The content of the Confession of Belhar will be taught in catechism, preaching, theological education and embodied in a transforming Church.

4. Every minister/office in the Church is given time of one recess after reunification to consider and subscribe to the confession of Belhar formally.

5. Ministers that have an objection against the Confession on a particular point be allowed to submit a gravamen while they continue to be bound by their oath not to propagate their objections in any way.

6. Every new minister will be licenced only after subscribing to all four Confessions.

7. The GSC commits itself anew not to let go of the DRC, but to continue on the mutually critical and mutually affirmative journey on which we have embarked together, as spelled out in the Roadmap to church Re-Unification and the Memorandum of Agreement (*Minutes General Synodical Commission URCSA* 2013:1-2).

However, in the beginning of 2015, it seemed clear that the DRC would not be able to secure the approval from their regional in order to change their confessional basis. This created a huge strain on the bilateral talks between the DRC and the URCSA. On 24 April 2015, the moderamen commissioned the moderator of URCSA, Mary-Anne Plaatjies-Van Huffel, to draft a response on behalf of the URCSA regarding the failure of the different regional synods of the DRC to acceptance the Belhar Confession with a two-third majority vote. The statement reads as follows:

> The URCSA, however, want to emphasise that we applaud the efforts by the DRC on General Synod level, Regional Synod level as well as congregational level to take up the Belhar Confession in your confessional basis. We cherish your efforts. We affirm that we will still avail ourselves to accompany the DRC in this regard. We know that it could not have been an easy task to embark on this very difficult process to change the confessional basis of the DRC. We took cognisance that the current wording of the DRC's church order makes the change of the confessional basis of the DRC almost impossible (see Article 44.1 and 44.2). According to Article 44.1 the amendment of the Confession is only possible only after each Regional Synod of the DRC approved with a two-thirds majority and two-thirds of all church councils, each with a two-thirds majority in favour of the resolution. Article 44.2 states that Article 44.1 and 44.2 of the church order of the DRC is amended after each synod with a two-thirds majority voted in favour of the resolution, the General Synod then afterwards by a two-thirds majority vote in favour of it. (URCSA Executive Statement 2015:1; Addendum 13)

In discussions about church reunification, the URCSA had repeatedly stated that the Belhar Confession was non-negotiable in the envisaged reunified church. It seemed clear that without changes in the church order regulations of the DRC, namely, Articles 44.1 and 44.2, there would be no reunification of the church. Ironically, during 2015, two-thirds of the presbyteries of the PCUSA voted that the Belhar Confession could become part of the confessional basis of the PCUSA, while during the same year, the DRC, after years of multilateral talks, could not reach a two-thirds majority in order to make the Belhar Confession part of their confessional basis. Maybe the time had come to painfully admit to each other that Belhar was indeed 'a bridge too far' (Van der Merwe 2014:137-155).

As Jaap Durand, one of the drafters of the Belhar Confession rightly said:

> [T]he the division of the Dutch Reformed family of churches in South Africa into four different churches is neither the result of a schism on doctrinal issues, nor a schism caused by so-called non-theological factors, but the result of a deliberate 'missionary policy'. (Durand 1994:1)

According to Durand, this 'missionary policy' was basically and theologically flawed due its hidden racist agenda. In an effort to rationalise this hidden agenda, cultural and ethnic diversity was emphasised to such a degree that the idea of diversity was elevated to the level of an absolute; a biblical principle of equal value to that of unity. Durand than deduced that the difficulty in making any progress with unity talks between the DRC, the DRMC, the DRCA and the RCA lied in the implicit racism in the DRC's theological rationalisation of a divided DRC Church family. His notion was that the removal of a theological edifice meant that the foundation on which it was built still remained intact (Durand 1994:2). The question for Durand was that in its new theological appraisal and its evident willingness to change its stance on the question of diversity and the theological justification of separate churches, did the DRC address only the theological symptoms of a deep-seated racism, or was the cause itself eradicated? He writes:

> I am fully aware of everything the DRC has said about racism. I recognise the laudable way in which *Church and Society* 1990 rejects racism as a grievous sin which no person or church may defend or practice. But can we take these protestations seriously, if the one point where racism now clearly manifests itself is left intact? Why do the leadership and the decision-making bodies not combat racism in the church openly by confronting recalcitrant members and congregations with the inescapable demand of the gospel that they become members of one non-racial Dutch Reformed Church? (Durand 1994:3)

The question for Durand was whether overt or covert racism was implicitly condoned, not only by what a church is doing but also, more importantly, by what it is not doing. He deduced that this was going to be the acid test of whether the DRC had distanced itself from the racism of apartheid. He, furthermore, said that it becomes obvious if one asks the simple questions: What are the real reasons for the reluctance of the various DRC bodies to enter into a unification process in a meaningful way? What are the impediments? What is it that bothers them? According to Durand there was an underlying fear among a large number of rank-and-file members and ministers of the Word of the DRC that once the present structures were gone, they could be overrun by black people or forced into associations they did not desire. Durand rightly concluded that racism is not a sin exclusive to Afrikaners, or to white people for that matter. It lurks in the hearts of all of us (Durand 1994:3). The URCSA saw the acceptance of the Belhar Confession as the acid test of the DRC's response to the challenge of becoming one, united and non-racial church with the other Dutch Reformed churches and of whether the DRC had finally distanced itself from the racism of apartheid.

Unfinished business regarding the Belhar Confession and the issue of homosexuality

The URSCA General Synod of 2005 held in Pietermaritzburg took a decision (decision 90), which would be the interim guideline until the synods come to a final decision. The Interim Policy on Homosexuality of 2005 states, inter alia:

- Synod confirms that homosexual people are members of the church through faith in Jesus Christ.
- Synod rejects homophobia and any form of discrimination against homosexual persons.
- Synod appeals to the URCSA members to reach out with love and empathy to our homosexual brothers and sisters and embrace them as members of the body of Christ in our midst.
- Synod acknowledges the appropriate civil rights of homosexual persons (*Acts General Synod URCSA* 2005:209).

At the URSCA General Synod of 2008, the task team on homosexuality tabled a report with recommendations, which, after a robust debate, was referred to the regional synods for discussion and ratification. According to the task team, the Confession of Belhar brought with it a burden of responsibility the URCSA could not deny nor avoid regarding issues of diversity, dignity and humanity. The task team stated the following in this regard:

> Belhar disputes against an understanding of 'diversity' that is abused for reasons of negativity and rejection, instead of a diversity that celebrates the other and the richness of difference. The diversity that is absolutized is the diversity that seeks to find a negative 'otherness' that comes with enmity, distance, aversion, discrimination and degradation and in so doing eliminates dignity and the bond of humanity. The diversity that Belhar celebrates is the diversity that comes from celebrating both the richness of the creation of God and the dignity of the difference we see in the other. To 'absolutize' this diversity is to make it the foundation of the other's existence. The foundation of the other's existence is not the difference of skin colour, or gender, or culture, or sexual orientation. Rather it is their [humanness], their being created in the image of God, sharing humanity in all its fullness with us. We dignify both the difference and the togetherness with our respect and love and the embrace of our common creatureliness as image bearers of God. The dignity of difference is the dignity of personhood. This is what the church celebrates and embraces. Absolutizing this natural diversity which we should actually embrace and celebrate not only breaks the visible and active unity of the church, but accepts that the church must

live 'in despair of reconciliation'. This is an attitude Belhar utterly rejects. On the contrary, it is our calling, gift and obligation to live together as reconciled community. There is nothing that falls outside of this call and gift; nothing that makes us 'despair of reconciliation'. (*Acts General Synod URCSA* 2008:121; Report on Homosexuality)

The premise of the task team was that the rejection of the Belhar Confession regarding the exclusion of the other includes the protestation against the oppression, rejection and exploitation of gay persons as well as mentally and physically challenged people (whom we used to call 'disabled persons') and women. According to the synod:

> Belhar rejects the sinful absolutisation with a view to inferioritise, separate and discriminate, but expressly celebrates the diversity that affirms humanity and welcomes it as a gift from God for the richer life of the church. Belhar embraces that diversity as enriching and building the visible and active unity of the church. (*Acts General Synod URCSA* 2008:121)

According to the task team the whole of Article 4 of the confession, which deals with God as 'the One who wishes to bring about justice and true peace on earth', speaks of justice and inclusivity and, therefore, also speaks of the situation of gay persons and women. Their search for recognition and protection is a search for justice. 'In their woundedness, their vulnerability to the denial of their rights, the enmity of many in society and the church, and the rejection of their true and full humanity, homosexual persons have an inalienable right to call upon the God 'who in a special way (is) the God of the destitute, the poor and the wronged'. Their suffering is no less wrong than the suffering of the widows and the orphans and it is in regard to their right to justice that God 'wishes to teach the people of God to do what is good and to seek the right.' (Acts General Synod URCSA 2008:123; Report on Homosexuality). Therefore, the task team proposed that with regards to gay persons and women, in their struggle for the recognition of their rights to full humanity, the church also must learn 'to stand where God stands', to witness and strive against 'any form of injustice', so that also for those members of the body of Christ 'justice may roll down like waters, and righteousness like an ever-flowing stream'. (*Acts General Synod URCSA* 2008:123; Report on Homosexuality)

The view of the task team had been that in light of the Confession of Belhar the URCSA should accept and embrace homosexual persons in the fullest sense of the word. That means the church accepts

- that homosexual persons, on the basis of their faith in Jesus Christ as personal Saviour and Lord of their life and of the church, are therefore without any reservation full members of the church of Jesus Christ;

- that homosexual persons deserve therefore justice in the same way the church claims justice for the destitute and the wronged, both before and under the law, in civil society and in the church, and the church commits itself to actively seek that justice in all areas of life;
- that our commitment and calling to unity and reconciliation require that homosexual persons, as confessing members of the church, have access to all the offices of the church, including the office of minister of the Word; and
- that this access should, both in the interests of justice and pastoral concern, should not be prejudiced by demands for celibacy if the relationship is one of love, respect and real commitment (*Acts General Synod URCSA 2008*:125; Report on Homosexuality).

Among other issues, the task team acknowledged that the homosexual identity has very complex biological, psychological and sociological causes and that these are factors of which biblical writers in their times and circumstances had not been aware and saw no need to address. The synod affirmed:

- That Scripture's rejection is cantered upon gratuitous homosexual acts (homoeroticism) and was determined by conventions and norms current in the ancient contexts of the biblical authors, rather than the homosexual orientation and the desire of homosexual persons to enter into lasting, caring and loving relationships such as described above.
- That moreover the evidence of Scripture is overwhelmingly in favour of hospitality to those who are traditionally not welcomed, acceptance of those who are stigmatised, rejected and alienated, compassion towards those who endure anxiety, suffering and humiliation because of their identity, and solidarity with those who are marginalised and oppressed, justice to those who are wronged – in this case homosexual persons.
- That these principles constitute the heart of the ministry and Gospel of Jesus Christ as they are in equal measure found at the heart of the Confession of Belhar, and in this matter the church is once again called to 'stand where God stands'.
- That these considerations are essential to the unity of the church, the calling towards reconciliation placed upon the church by Jesus Christ, and the justice to which the church is obligated (*Acts General Synod URCSA 2008*:150-151; Report on Homosexuality).

The task team made the following recommendations to the General Synod:
- That our considerations entail that the same ethical directives that apply for heterosexual living in all its facets should also apply for homosexual living.

- Synod shall not require of them what it does not require of its heterosexual members.
- This means that homosexual persons express their intimate sexual relations within the context of the relationships accepted above, which for us means the context Christian marriage blessed by the church.
- In line with the provision made by law and the Constitution of South Africa, those who have conscientious objections to these unions shall not be obliged to officiate in them.
- Since homosexual couples cannot bring children into the world they should have the opportunity to adopt children and to participate in the Christian practice of hospitality to children and provide a safe home for them. The church offers the same covenantal support as it does heterosexual couples.
- As confessing members of the church of Christ homosexual Christians shall, on the basis of their faith in Jesus Christ have access to all the offices of the church, and upon fulfilment of all the academic requirements for the ministry, to the office of minister of the Word.
- Ongoing study and discussion in congregations of this report and these decisions are highly recommended and encouraged.
- In the ongoing process, Synod pleads for an ethic of love and graciousness, embrace and togetherness in the midst of differences that might still exist. Those who disagree with it shall not in any way be forced to accept it, while we hope that all will remain open to discussion and to the persuasion of the Holy Spirit of God (*Acts General Synod URCSA* 2008:151; Report on Homosexuality).

The URSCA have thus far failed to approve the above-mentioned recommendations. The General Synod of 2012, based on the principles of the Belhar Confession, affirmed the URCSA's long tradition of social justice founded on the fundamental human dignity of every individual, as well as its bearing on the controversial and emotional issues of gay rights. The General Synod, furthermore, called on all its members to exhibited concern over the protection of homosexuals from discriminatory practices. The General Synod also affirmed that the denial of human and civil rights to homosexuals was inconsistent with the biblical witness and Reformed theology.

Decisions of the issues concerning the theological and moral status of homosexual marriages, covenantal unions, the status of homosexuals as members of the church regarding baptism and the offices as church council members as well as the ordination of practicing homosexual persons in ministry are still outstanding (*Acts General Synod URCSA* 2005, 2008, 2012; Report on Homosexuality).

No consensus regarding the abovementioned report of the task team on homosexuality could be reached at regional synod level. However, taking into account the URCSA's understanding of the authority of Scripture as the norm for Christian faith and life, doctrine and ethics, other relevant scientific material on the subject of homosexuality and in light of Reformed theological perspectives and the perspectives offered to the URCSA regarding justice, diversity and inclusivity by the Confession of Belhar, the General Synod of the URCSA is obliged to formulate, before long, the URCSA official position regarding homosexuality and the Belhar Confession.

Conclusion

The Belhar Confession has an immense influence on the way that theology is practiced by the URSCA. The confession is about the integrity of the church in the public arena. The URCSA's premise is that the congregation's worship of God on Sunday continues and flows over into the worship of God during the week in the community, particularly by working with compassion, justice and reconciliation among people. The congregation serves God, who in a special way is the God of the suffering, the poor and those who are wronged (victimised), by supporting people in whatever form of suffering and need they may experience, by witnessing and fighting against all forms of injustice, by calling upon the government and the authorities to serve all the inhabitants of the country by allowing justice to prevail and by fighting against injustice. Article 4 of the Belhar Confession makes the bold claim that 'God is in a special way the God of the destitute, the poor, and the wronged and that that God calls the church to follow in this'.[21] In various ways over the years, the URCSA affirmed the importance and cardinal place of the Confession of Belhar for and in the life of the URCSA. There are new struggles the church has to address, such as restorative justice, hate speech, incitement, statelessness, atrocity crimes, human rights violations, state capture, land grabbing, gender justice, the neoliberal economic globalisation and eco-justice. The URCSA, as children of the Belhar and tomorrow's children,[22] are being challenged to take a public stand against the ills

---

21 Article 4 reads: We believe that God has revealed Godself as the One who wishes to bring about justice and true peace on earth; that in a world full of injustice and enmity God is in a special way the God of the destitute, the poor and the wronged and that God calls the church to follow in this; that God brings justice to the oppressed and gives bread to the hungry; that God frees the prisoner and restores sight to the blind; that God supports the downtrodden, protects the strangers, helps orphans and widows and blocks the path of the ungodly; that for God pure and undefiled religion is to visit the orphans and the widows in their suffering; that God wishes to teach the people of God to do what is good and to seek the right; that the church must therefore stand by people in any form of suffering and need, which implies, among other things, that the church must witness against and strive against any form of injustice, so that justice may roll down like waters, and righteousness like an ever-flowing stream.

22 See Alves (1972). The metaphor of 'dream' is also applied by Russel Botman (1994) in his dissertation.

in church and society. The URCSA should, therefore, engage actively in restorative justice issues and in so doing confess uncompromisingly God's sovereignty and God's justice for humanity and the earth.

Over the past three decades, the URCSA has tirelessly been unambiguous its rejection of the inclusion of the Confession of Belhar as an optional confession in the confessional basis of the envisaged unified church. It rejected vigorously any notion of dealing with the confession in a context of doctrinal liberty. The URCSA still upholds Karl Barth's notions on confessions. The URCSA, therefore, do not confess with an aim in view nor to effect and to carry out this or that with our confession. We are not in the business of marketing the Belhar. In our deliberations we, as Barth rightly once said, aim not at results and expect none – not from the DRC or any other church across the globe. The URCSA as children of the Belhar confess because God is God and does all things well, and because we know this, we cannot keep silence. As confessors, we are not concerned with any end but only with the honour of God (Barth 1969/1951:77-78). Confessions are not a mere human statement or an opinion or conviction. Confessions are an act of defiance and conflict as Barth (1969/1951:82) rightly conveyed. We embrace Barth's notion that confession is decisive action and not incidental reaction. (Barth 1969/1951/:80-81). Confessions are about making deliberate choices. Confession is a free action and is a response to a summons and rests ultimately on free choice. God compels us to confess. It proceeds from the Holy Spirit who breathes where He wills. Confessions are related to God's free grace. The URCSA, therefore, cannot demand confession from the DRC family or any other church, nor can one commission the DRC family or any other church to confess. We cannot persuade or force anyone to confess. We can and should only embody the Belhar Confession, namely, unity, justice and reconciliation, keeping in mind, however, that reconciliation without truth, justice and restoration is justice deferred.

Bibliography

Primary sources

Acta van die Nederduits Gereformeerde Kerk 1829.
Acta van die Nederduits Gereformeerde Kerk 1857.
Acta van die Algemene Sinode van die Nederduits Gereformeerde Kerk 1962.
Acta van die Algemene Sinode van die Nederduits Gereformeerde Kerk 1966.
Acta van die Algemene Sinode van die Nederduits Gereformeerde Sendingkerk 1950.
Acta an die Nederduits Gereformeerde Kerk in Afrika 1971.
Acta van die Nederduits Gereformeerde Kerk in Afrika 1983.
Acts of General Synod of the Uniting Reformed Church in Southern Africa 2001.
Acts of General Synod of the Uniting Reformed Church in Southern Africa 2005.

Acts General Synod Reformed Church in America. Report on Global Mission 2007.
Acts General Synod Reformed Church in America. Report on Global Mission 2008.
Acts and Proceedings General Synod Reformed Church in America 2009.
Acts and Proceedings General Synod Reformed Church in America 2010.
Acts Christian Reformed Church of North America Synod 1984. [Online] Available at http://www.crcna.org/ (Accessed 22 March 2015).
Acts Christian Reformed Church of North America Synod 1985. [Online] Available at http://www.crcna.org/ (Accessed 22 March 2015).
Acts Christian Reformed Church of North America Synod 1989. [Online] Available at http://www.crcna.org/ (Accessed 22 March 2015).
Acts Christian Reformed Church of North America Synod 1990. Grand Rapids: CRCNA. [Online] Available at http://www.crcna.org/pages/belhar.cfm (Accessed 22 March 2015).
Acts Christian Reformed Church of North America Synod 2007. [Online] Available at http://www.crcna.org/ (Accessed 22 March 2015).
Acts Synod Christian Reformed Church of North America Synod 2012. [Online] Available at http://www.crcna.org/ (Accessed 22 March 2015).
Acts Reformed Church in Africa 1986.
Acts Reformed Church in Africa 1990.
Acts Reformed Church in Africa 1998.
Agenda Algemene Sinode van die Nederduitse Gereformeerde Kerk 1966
Agenda Algemene Sinode van die Nederduitse Gereformeerde Kerk 1970.
Agenda Algemene Sinode van die Nederduitse Gereformeerde Kerk 1986.
Agenda Algemene Sinode van die Nederduitse Gereformeerde Kerk 1990.
Agenda Algemene Sinode van die Nederduitse Gereformeerde Kerk 1994.
Agenda Algemene Sinode van die Nederduitse Gereformeerde Kerk 1998.
Agenda Algemene Sinode van die Nederduitse Gereformeerde Kerk 2004.
Agenda Algemene Sinode van die Nederduitse Gereformeerde Kerk 2007.
Agenda Algemene Sinode van die Nederduitse Gereformeerde Kerk 2011.
Agenda Algemene Sinode van die Nederduitse Gereformeerde Kerk 2013.
Agenda Algemene Sinode van die Nederduitse Gereformeerde Kerk 2015.
Agenda en Acta Nederduits Gereformeerde Kerk Wes en Suid Kaap Sinode 2015.
Agenda en Handelinge Nederduits Gereformeerde Kerk in Afrika 1974.
Agenda en Handelinge Nederduits Gereformeerde Kerk in Afrika 1983.
Agenda en Handelinge Nederduits Gereformeerde Kerk in Afrika 1987.
Agenda en Handelinge Nederduits Gereformeerde Kerk in Afrika 1990.
Agenda en Handelinge Nederduits Gereformeerde Kerk in Afrika 2007.
Agenda en Handelinge Nederduits Gereformeerde Sendingkerk 1950.
Agenda en Handelinge Nederduits Gereformeerde Sendingkerk 1978.
Agenda en Handelinge Nederduits Gereformeerde Sendingkerk 1982.
Agenda en Handelinge Nederduits Gereformeerde Sendingkerk 1986.
Agenda en Handelinge Verenigende Gereformeerde Kerk in Suider Afrika 1997.
Agenda for Synod Christian Reformed Church of North America 1999. [Online] Available at http://www.crcna.org/ (Accessed 22 March 2015).
Agenda for Synod Christian Reformed Church of North America 2003. [Online] Available at http://www.crcna.org/ (Accessed 11 March 2015).

Agenda for Synod Christian Reformed Church of North America 2005. [Online] Available at http://www.crcna.org/ (Accessed 22 March 2015).
Agenda General Synod Uniting Reformed Church in Southern Africa 2005. Bloemfontein.
Agenda General Synod Uniting Reformed Church in Southern Africa 2008. Bloemfontein.
Agenda General Synod Uniting Reformed Church in Southern Africa 2012. Bloemfontein.
Agenda General Synod Uniting Reformed Church in Southern Africa 2016. Bloemfontein.
Agenda General Synodical Commission Uniting Reformed Church in Southern Africa. 2009. Bloemfontein.
Agenda Reformed Church in Africa.1990.
Acts General Synod Reformed Church in America.
Achterbergh Declaration 1 2006. Bloemfontein. [Online] Available at www.ngkok.co.za/achterberg2/default.htm (Accessed 22 March 2015).
Achterbergh Declaration II 2007. Bloemfontein. Available at www.ngkok.co.za/achterberg2/default.htm (Accessed 22 March 2015).
Acta Nederduits Gereformeerde Kerk Wes-Kaapland Sinode 2011.
Apartheid legislation 1850s–1970s. n.d. [Online] Available at http://www.sahistory.org.za/politics-and-society/apartheid-legislation-1850s-1970s (Accessed 11 March 2015).
Botha, J.G. & Naudé, P. 2006. *Belydenis van Belhar 1986: Teks en kommentaar.* 'n Publikasie van die Konvent vir Eenheid Kaapland.
Belhar Confession. 1986. The official English translation of the *Belhar Confession 1986* approved by the General Synod of 2008. Belhar: LUS Printers.
Beraad van Nederduitse Gereformeerde Kerke in SWA. Windhoek 1986.
Besluiteregister Algemene Sinode Nederduitse Gereformeerde Kerk 1990.
Besluiteregister Algemene Sinode Nederduitse Gereformeerde Kerk 1994
Besluiteregister Algemene Sinode Nederduitse Gereformeerde Kerk 1998
Besluiteregister Algemene Sinode Nederduitse Gereformeerde Kerk 2004.
Besluiteregister Algemene Sinode Nederduitse Gereformeerde Kerk 2007.
Besluiteregister Algemene Sinode Nederduitse Gereformeerde Kerk 2011.
Besluiteregister Algemene Sinode Nederduitse Gereformeerde Kerk 2013
Besluiteregister Algemene Sinode Nederduitse Gereformeerde Kerk 2015.
Covenanting for the reunification of the DRC family – Esselenpark Declaration 2006.
Christian Reformed Church. 2014. Consultation issues report on ecumenical faith declaration. [Online] Available at https://www.crcna.org/news-and-views/consultation-issues-report-ecumenical-faith-declaration (Accessed 11 March 2015).
Church Order and Regulations Regional Synod Cape 2004.
CRC Synod 2012 Advisory Committee 7 – Interdenominational Matters 2012.
Decisions of General Assembly of the UPCSA 2013.
Declaration of Laudium 1990.
Dutch Reformed Church Order 2007.
Handelinge Algemene Sinode van die Nederduitse Gereformeerde Kerk 1982.
Memorandum of Agreement between the URCSA and the DRC 2012 in *Agenda of the General Synod of URCSA*, October 2012.
Minutes of bilateral discussion with the Calvin Protestant Church held in Belhar 2006.
Minutes of the 3rd Annual SAARC Conference 1991.

Minutes of the meeting of the four moderamen of the DRC family 6–7 August 2014. Bloemfontein.
Minutes URCSA Executive Statement 2015. Bloemfontein.
Minutes URCSA General Synod 2012. Bloemfontein.
Minutes URCSA General Synodical Commission 2004. Bloemfontein.
Minutes URCSA General Synodical Commission 2006. Bloemfontein.
Minutes URCSA General Synodical Commission 2007. Bloemfontein.
Minutes URCSA General Synodical Commission 2013. Bloemfontein.
Minutes URCSA General Synodical Commission 2014. Bloemfontein.
Minutes URCSA General Synodical Commission 2015. Bloemfontein.
Notule NGK Algemene Sinode 2007. (pp. 1-5).
Notule ring van Wellington 1948. (pp. 1-2).
Notule ring van Wynberg 1948 (pp. 1-2).
Notule ring van Wynberg 1949 (pp. 1-2).
Notule van die Kerkraad van Swellendam. 4 Januarie 1845 (pp. 1-2).
Overture to the Synod of the Christian Reformed Church of North America 2009 (pp. 1-2).
Papers, Proceedings and Decisions for the 9th General Assembly of the UPCSA 2010.
Provisional Order with respect to the reunification of churches within the Dutch Reformed Church family. In *Agenda General Synod URCSA 2016.*
Presbyterian Church (USA) Minutes, Part 1, 2008.
Presbyterian Church (USA) (PCUSA). 2010. Proposed amendments to the Constitution, Part 2 of 3. Approved by the 219th General Assembly Office of the General Assembly.
Presbyterian Church (USA) (PCUSA). 2014. Report and recommendations from the General Assembly Special Committee on the Confession of Belhar to the 221st General Assembly of the Presbyterian Church (USA).
Report of a meeting between delegates of the four churches of the DRC family in South Africa, Volmoed, Hermanus, 13–15 July 2015. Bloemfontein.
Report of the Executive Committee on church unity to the Fifth General Synod of URCSA in session on 29 September to 5 October 2008. In *Agenda General Synod of the URCSA 2008.* Bloemfontein.
Report of the Executive on Ecumenical Affairs to the General Synod 2012. In *Agenda General Synod of the URCSA 2012.* Bloemfontein.
Report of the Executive of the URCSA. In *Agenda of the General Synodical Commission November 2015.* Bloemfontein.
Report on homosexuality to the General Synod of the Uniting Reformed Church in Southern Africa. In *Agenda General Synod of the URSCA 2008.* Bloemfontein.
Resolutions of the moderamen (expanded) of the DRC on church reunification 11–12 June 2008. Carmelite Retreat Centre.
Submission of the Uniting Reformed Church in Southern Africa to the Truth and Reconciliation Commission. 1997. Bloemfontein.
Skema van Werksaamhede en Handelinge, Tweede Algemene Sinode van die Verenigende Gereformeerde Kerk in Suider-Afrika. 1997. Bloemfontein.
Supplementary papers, Proceedings and Decisions for the Executive Commission of the UPCSA 2011.
Roadmap to church reunification. *In Agenda General Synod URCSA 2016.*

World Alliance of Reformed Churches (WARC). 1983a. *Proceedings of the 21st General Council of the World Alliance of Reformed Churches.* Geneva: WARC. [Online] Available at http://www.warc.ch/dcw/bs25/11.html. (Accessed 27 June 2015).
Verenigde Protestantse Kerk in België. 2015. Motivatie tot voorstel wijziging Constitutie Van de Verenigde Protestantse Kerk in België.In *Synode Report van de Verenigde Protestantse Kerk in België*, 2015.
World Alliance of Reformed Churches (WARC). 1983b. Resolution on racism and South Africa. In WARC, In *Proceedings of the 21st General Council of the World Alliance of Reformed Churches.* Geneva: WARC.
World Alliance of Reformed Churches (WARC). 1990. *Proceedings of the 22nd General Council of WARC (Seoul).* Geneva: WARC.
World Alliance of Reformed Churches (WARC). 1992. *Executive committee minutes.* Geneva: WARC.
World Alliance of Reformed Churches (WARC). 1997. Proceedings of the 23rd General Council of the World Alliance of Reformed Churches (Milan Opocenský, ed.). Geneva: WARC.
World Alliance of Reformed Churches (WARC). 1997a. *Executive committee minutes.* Geneva: WARC.
World Alliance of Reformed Churches (WARC). 1997b. *General Council Debrecen report of the executive committee on the relationship between the DRC and the Alliance.* Geneva: WARC.
World Alliance of Reformed Churches (WARC). 1997. *Proceedings of the 23rd General Council of the World Alliance of Reformed Churches* (Milan Opocenský, ed.). Geneva: WARC.

Apartheid laws

Aliens Control Act (No. 40 of 1973).
Aliens and Travellers Control Act (No. 29 of 1977).
Bantu Authorities Act (No. 68 of 1951).
Bantu Education Act (No. 47 of 19530.
Bantu Homelands Citizens Act (1970).
Bantu Homelands Citizenship Act (National States Citizenship Act) (No. 26 of 1970).
Bantu Homelands Constitution Act (National States Constitutional Act) (No. 21 of 1971).
Bantu/Native Building Workers Act (No. 27 of 1951).
Black Affairs Administration Act (No. 45 of 1971.
Black Labour Relations Regulation Amendment Act (No. 70 of 1973).
Black Labour (Settlement of Disputes) Amendment Act (No. 59 of 1955).
Black Laws Amendment Act (No. 7 of 1973).
Extension of University Education Act (No. 45 of 1959).
Group Areas Act (No. 41 of 1950).
Immorality Amendment Act (No. 21 of 1950).
Industrial Conciliation Amendment Act (1956).
Natives (Abolition of Passes and Co-ordination of Documents) Act (No. 67 of 1952).
Natives Labour (Settlement of Disputes) Act (1953)
Natives Laws Amendment Act (1952).
Natives (Prohibition of Interdicts) Act (No. 64 of 1956).

Natives Resettlement Act (No. 19 of 1954).
Promotion of Bantu Self-Government Act (1959).
Reservation of Separate Amenities Act (No. 49 of 1953)
Separate Representation of Voters Act (No. 46 of 1951).

Secondary sources

Adonis, J. 1982. *Die afgebreekte skeidsmuur weer opgebou: Die verstrengeling van die sendingbeleid van die Nederduitse Gereformeerde Kerk in Suid – Afrika met die praktyk en ideologie van die apartheid in historiese perspektief.* Amsterdam: Rodopi.

Algemene Sinodale Kommissie van die NGK. 1997. *Die verhaal van die Nederduitse Gereformeerde Kerk se reis met apartheid 1960–1994. 'n Getuienis en 'n belydenis.* Wellington: Hugenote Uitgewers.

Alves, R. 1972. *Tomorrow's child: Imagination, creativity and the rebirth of culture.* Eugene, OR: Wipf and Stock.

Barth, K. 1969/1951. *Church dogmatics* (Vol. 3, Part 4). Translated by G. Bromily & T.F. Torrance. Edinburgh: Bloomsbury T&T Clark.

Blei, K. 1994. South African 'apartheid' as a status confessionis'. In P. Reamonn, *Farewell to apartheid? Church relations in South Africa.* Geneva: WARC.

Boesak, A.A. 1984. *Black and reformed.* Bellville: Skotaville Publishers.

Boesak, A.A. 2008. To stand where God stands: Reflections on the Confession of Belhar after 25 years. *Studia Historiae Ecclesiasticae* 34(1):143-172.

Boesak, A.A., Weusmann, J. & Amjad-Ali, C. 2010. *Dreaming a different world globalisation and justice for humanity and the earth. The Challenge of the Accra Confession for the churches.* Stellenbosch: SUN PReSS.

Botha, J. 1991. Belhar: Yes or no? *Theological Forum* 19(2):2-10.

Botman, R. 1994. Discipleship as transformation? Towards a theology of transformation. A critical study of Dietrich Bonhoeffer's theology. PhD thesis, Stellenbosch University, Stellenbosch.

Botman, R. 1997. The Confession of Belhar and our common future. Address to the General Synod of the Reformed Church in America. [Online] Available at citeseerx.ist.psu.edu/viewdoc/download?doi=10.1.1.495.5869&rep=rep... PDF file (Accessed 27 June 2015).

Carstens, W.P. 1959. The Dutch Reformed Church militant. *Africa South* 3(2):48-53.

Cloete, G.D. & Smit, D.J. (eds). 1984. *A moment of truth. The confession of the Dutch Reformed Mission Church 1982.* Grand Rapids, MI: William B. Eerdmans.

Coertzen, P. 2010. Ontstaanskenmerke van die Stellenbosche Teologiese Seminarium. *Nederduitse Gereformeerde Teologiese Tydskrf* 51(1):41-55.

Cooper, J. 2010. Context and confusion: What does the Belhar confess? *Calvin Theological Seminary Forum*, Fall 2010:10-12.

Cooper, J. 2011a. Why the Belhar should not be a confession. *The Banner*, June 2011. [Online] Available at http://www.calvin.edu/library/database/crcpi/fulltext/banner/2011-0600-0037.pdf (Accessed 11 March 2015).

Cooper, J. 2011b. Affirm the Belhar? Yes, but not as a doctrinal standard. A contribution to the discussion in CRCNA. Calvin Theological Seminary. [Online] Available at www.calvinseminary.edu/wp.../Cooper.Belhar.Yesbutnotas%20Confession.11.pdf (Accessed 11 March 2015).

Douglass, J.D. & Opocensky, M. 1994. Open letter to the WARC member churches in South Africa. In P. Reamonn, *Farewell to apartheid? Church relations in South Africa*. Geneva: World Alliance of Reformed Churches.

Durand, J.F. 1994. Church unity and the Reformed churches in southern Africa. In P. Reamonn, *Farewell to apartheid? Church relations in South Africa*. Geneva: World Alliance of Reformed Churches.

Dutch Reformed Church (DRC). 1976. *Human relations and the South African scene in the light of the scripture.* (Official translation of the report 'Ras, volk en nasie en volkeverhoudinge in die lig van die Skrif'). Cape Town: Dutch Reformed Church Publishers.

General Synodal Commission of the Dutch Reformed Church. n.d. *The story of the Dutch Reformed Church's journey with apartheid 1960–1994. A testimony and a confession.* (English extract from the Afrikaans documens).

Fortein, E. 2016. *Allan Boesak en die Nederduitse Gereformeerde Sendingkerk: 'n teologies – historiese ondersoek.* PhD thesis, Universiteit Stellenbosch, Stellenbosch.

Geldenhuys, F.E. O'Brien. 1982. *In die stroomversnellings: Vyftig jaar van* die NG Kerk. Cape Town: Tafelberg.

Interchurch Relations Committee (IRC). 2009. The Belhar Confession: What the CRC can do with this gift. [Online] Available at www.gracegr.org/pdf/IRC_Belhar_Confession_Report.pdf (Accessed 11 March 2015).

Kriel, C.J. 1963. *Die geskiedenis van die Nederduitse Gereformeerde Sendingkerk in Suid-Afrika 1881–1956. 'n Historiese studie van die sendingwerk onder die kleurlingbevolking van Kaapland.* Paarl: Paarldrukpers.

Kritzinger, J.N.J. 2010. Celebrating communal authorship: The theological declaration of the Belydende Kring (1979) and the Belhar Confession. In honour of Simon Maimela and in memory of Chris Loff. *Studia Historiae Ecclesiasticae* 36(1):209-231.

Landman, C. 1991. The anthropology of apartheid according to official sources. *Journal of Theology for Southern Africa* 76:32-45.

Lenkabula, P. 2009. *Choose life, Act I, Hope.* Geneva: World Alliance of Reformed Churches.

Loff, C.J.A. 1998. *Bevryding tot eenwording. Die NG Sendmgkerk in Suid-Afrika 1881-1994.* Doktorale proefskrif, Teologiese Universiteit van die Gereformeerde Kerk in Nederland, Kampen.

Loff, C.J.A. 1981. *Dogter of verstoteling? Kantaantekeninge by die geskiedenis van die Ned. Geref. Sendingkerk in Suid-Afrika.* Cape Town: Maranatha.

Lombard, C. & Tjingaete, B. 1995. Wat het met EGKA gebeur?' In C. Lombard & J.H. Hunter (eds), *Kom ons word EEN*. Windhoek: EIN Publications.

Luke, S. & van Houten R.L. 1997. Racism. *Theological Forum* 25(4):4-6.

McGarrahan, E.T. 2008. *A study of the Belhar Confession and its accompanying letter.* Office of Theology and Worship General Assembly Council Presbyterian Church (USA). [Online] Available at https://www.pc-biz.org/Explorer.aspx?id=3353&promoID=17www.synatlantic.org/wp-content/uploads/2016/09/Belhar-study_guide.pdf (Accessed 11 March 2015).

Meiring, P. 1991. The Belhar Confession 1986: A Dutch Reformed perspective. *Theological Forum* 19(1):18-23.

Morkel, A.T.& Thebus, M. 2011. Reverend I.D. Morkel church founder and activist.

Nederduitse Gereformeerde Kerk (NGK) Algemene Sinode. 1975. *Ras, volk en nasie en volkereverhoudinge in die lig van die Skrifbeleidstuk*. Goedgekeur deur die Algemene Sinode van die Ned Geref Kerk. Kaapstad: NG Kerk-Uitgewers.

Nederduitse Gereformeerde Kerk (NGK), Algemene Sinode 1986. *Kerk en Samelewing 1990, 'n getuienis van die Nederduitse Gereformeerde Kerk soos aanvaar deur die Algemene Sinode van die Ned Geref Kerk*. Bloemfontein: NG Sendingpers.

Parsons, G. 2015. Confession of Belhar approved by presbyteries. [Online] Available at http://pres-outlook.org/2015/04/confession-of-belhar-approved-by-presbyteries/ (Accessed 11 March 2015).

Plaatjies-Van Huffel, M-A. 2009. Die doleansie kerkreg en kerkregering van die Nederduitse Gereformeerde sendingkerke en die VGKSA. PhD thesis, University of Pretoria, Pretoria. [Online] Available at http://upetd.up.ac.za/thesis/available/etd-04022009-190218/ (Accessed 11 March 2015).

Plaatjies-Van Huffel, M-A. 2011. Dirk Smith – An apologist for confession. In L. Hansen, N. Koopman & R. Vosloo (eds), *Living theology*. Wellington: Bybel-Media.

Plaatjies-Van Huffel, M-A. 2013a.The Belhar Confession: Born in the struggle against apartheid in southern Africa, guiding light today. *Studia Historicae Ecclesiasticae* 39(1):185-203.

Plaatjies-Van Huffel M-A. 2013b. Reading the Belhar Confession as a historical text. In M.A. Plaatjies-Van Huffel & R.R. Vosloo, *Reformed churches in South Africa and the struggle for justice – Remembering 1960–1990*. Stellenbosch: SUN PReSS. https://doi.org/10.18820/9781920689117

Plaatjies-Van Huffel, M-A. 2014. The Belhar Confession in its historical context. *Nederduitse Gereformeerde Teologiese Tydskrif* 55(1/2):308-309. https://doi.org/10.5952/55-1-2-527

Reamonn, P. 1994. *Farewell to apartheid? Church relations in South Africa*. Geneva: World Alliance of Reformed Churches.

Schrotenboer, P.G. 1991. The Belhar Confession 1986. *Theological Forum* 19(2):1.

Smit, D.J. 1984. What does *status confessionis* mean? In G. Cloete & D. Smit (eds), *A moment of truth: The confession of the Dutch Reformed Mission Church*. Grand Rapids, MI: William B. Eerdmans.

The Cottesloe Declaration, 1960. [Online] Available at http://www.kerkargief.co.za/doks/bely/DF_Cottesloe.pdf (Accessed 11 March 2015).

Van der Borght, E.A.J.G. 2012. Belhar revisited. The unity of the church and socio-cultural identities within the Reformed tradition *Nederduitse Gereformeerde Teologiese Tydskrif* 53, Supp. 2:75-88.

Van der Merwe, J. 1990. Ras, volk en nasie en kerk en samelewing as beleidstukke van die Ned. Geref. Kerk – 'n kerkhistoriese studie. Unpublished dissertation, University of Pretroria, Pretoria.

Van der Merwe, J. 2010. Cottesloe 50 years later: Did the Dutch Reformed Church answer to the call? *Nederduitse Gereformeerde Teologiese Tydskrif* 51:154-162.

Van der Merwe, J. 2013. The Dutch Reformed Church from ras, volk en nasie to kerk en samelewing: The struggle goes on. In M.A. Plaatjies-Van Huffel & R.R. Vosloo, *Reformed churches in South Africa and the struggle for justice – Remembering 1960–1990*. Stellenbosch: SUN PReSS.

Van der Merwe. J. 2014. From 'Blood River' to 'Belhar': A bridge too far? *Studia Historiae Ecclesiasticae* 40(1):137-155.

Van der Watt, P.B. (1977). *Die Nederduitse Gereformeerde Kerk*, Drie dele. Pretoria: NGK Boekhandel.

Van Houten, R.L. 1997. Introduction. *Theological Forum* 25(4):1-3.

Van Schalwyk, A. 1950. Beleidsrigtings t.o.v. die naturelle vraagstuk in Suid-Afrika. Referate gelewer op die Kerklike Kongres, Bloemfontein, 4–6 April 1950. Bloemfontein: NG Sendingspers.

Vellem, V.S. 2013. The 'native experiment': The formation of the Bantu Presbyterian Church and the defects of faith transplanted on African soil. *Missionalia* 41(2). *[Online] Available at* http://www.scielo.org.za/scielo.php?pid=S0256-95072013000800005&script=sci_arttext&tlng=es. (Accessed 27 June 2015).

THE MISSION OF THE DUTCH REFORMED CHURCH

as mission for colonisation and division of the Reformed Church in South Africa (1652–1982)

Sipho Mahokoto[1]

Introduction

The arrival of the Dutch in the Cape in 1652 heralded the start of the Reform faith in South Africa. The first decades that followed were characterised by joint worship for white and 'coloured' people, although the coloured people often had reserved seats in the church. In time, however, the inclusion of non-white Christians in the church services of the Dutch Reformed Church (DRC) raised concerns and led to uneasiness among many white people. This influenced the rejection of Christian inclusivity in order to fuel white superiority, racial discrimination, inequality and social division within society. However, the aim of this essay is not to cover all these fundamental historical events that maintained division among Christians during the missionary work of the DRC.[2] This essay will mainly discuss certain events in the history of the church, especially, in the DRC, that perpetuated and emphasised the inequalities among Christians and dominance of a certain racial group over the others. One can further argue that the question of inequality, racism and injustices that emanated from mission, especially within the DRC illuminated and raised serious concerns within the South African context.

This essay focuses on how divisions and racial prejudice came into being since the birth of Christianity in South Africa in 1652. Among other things, one can mention the forceful removal of the Khoikhoi and many other black people from their own land by the white settlers. This essay also relates how the sacraments of Baptism and Holy Communion were used as tools for maintaining inequalities, divisions and injustices among Christians, which also led to deliberate racial discrimination. This essay also briefly discusses two important DRC Synod decisions, namely, the decision taken at the 1829 Synod, where it was agreed that the Holy Communion

---

1 Dr. Sipho Mahokoto is a minister of the Word of the URCSA at Kayamandi congregation and is also the senior programme coordinator at the EFSA Institute, Stellenbosch.
2 For a more comprehensive history on the historical background of the Belhar Confession please read the following essay in this publication: 'Acceptance, Adoption, Advocacy, Reception and Protestation: A Chronology of the Belhar Confession' by Mary-Anne Plaatjies-Van Huffel.

should be served to all members of the church simultaneously and that all should worship together as a symbol of church unity. A second important decision taken at the 1857 Synod separated the worship services (including Holy Communion) along racial lines. In this essay, I argue that this decision of 1857 had serious implications for the division within the Dutch Reformed family of churches on racial lines for decades until this day.

This essay unfolds by exploring the establishment of separate Dutch Reformed churches for coloured, black and Indian people and the rise of the apartheid policy in South Africa, which was legitimised by the DRC. It must be noted that racial segregation comes a long way and can be traced back to the birth of Christianity in South Africa. The current church unity discussions do not occur in a historical vacuum; they originate from within a specific historical context marked by division, oppression, and inequality among believers. Among other scholars, this essay draws on the work of Adonis (1982), Elphick (2012), Loff (1981) and Giliomee (2003).

The year 1652: Christianity and the colonisation of South Africa

The South African Reformed Church historian Johannes Adonis observes that the birth of Christianity in South Africa following the arrival of Jan van Riebeeck in the Cape in 1652 will always mark the beginning of the period of colonisation of South Africa. For Adonis, the beginning of the Christian religion in South Africa defined the very beginning of the time of colonialism. He also regards the planting and the carrying over of the Christian faith to the southern point of Africa as a new product of colonialism politics of the Vereenigde Oost-Indische Compagnie (VOC) (United East India Company, or Dutch East Indian Company) (Adonis 1982:28-29). Another church historian, Richard Elphick, in line with Adonis, notes that the DRC, the spiritual home of most Dutch-speaking settlers, pioneered the practice of segregated churches, and in the twentieth century, decisively shaped apartheid theory. Elphick further states that there was severe tension between two of the DRC's fervently-held commitments, namely, to evangelise people of colour and to preserve white supremacy (Elphick 2012:39). This clearly underlines the mission of colonisation and the preservation of white power over other racial groups. And all this came at a high cost as many black people lost almost everything to white people.

Adonis argues that the VOC had a purely commercial motive for establishing a presence in the Cape. They wanted to gain a monopoly of the valuable trade and thus exclude all competitors (Adonis 1982:2). However, it can be argued that the VOC had a double agenda. This becomes clear when Adonis records that the VOC gave Van Riebeeck the responsibility of keeping good and friendly relations with the

Khoikhoi³, who were the providers of necessary fresh meat for those for the visiting ships of the VOC. Jonathan Gerstner, in line with Adonis, points out the VOC at first intended simply to provide a port of call for Dutch ships to pick up fresh supplies. However, he adds that as early as 1657, the company allowed some of its former employees to settle and farm. In later decades, immigration added to their ranks (Gerstner1997:16) As a result of the influx of immigrants coming to the shores of Cape Town to work for the VOC and to farm, some tensions between the indigenous people and the white people started to develop.

Gerstner states that the DRC as the established church exercised a virtual monopoly of Christian expression in the new colony. He further indicates that the life and theology of the Reformed church played a formative role in the development of South African culture. This contributed particularly to the creation of a distinctive identity among the white settlers and to their conviction of their superiority over the indigenous peoples and slaves (Gerstner 1997:16). The inequalities between the Khoikhoi people and the white people resulted not only in a loss of materialistic things but also to the loss of the Khoikhoi people's identity and dignity. Elphick sheds light in this regard when he argues that after decades of work on white-owned farms, Khoi people were no longer an independent people in language, dress and social attitudes. Their traditional political structures had long ago collapsed. To Elphick, it was clear that the roots of inequalities between the white and the Khoisan people were very deep and caused a lot of pain and tension between these racial groups (Elphick 2012:28).

Among other questionable practices in the history of church planting and Christianising of the Khoikhoi people, was the seizure of their land by the Dutch settlers. Gerstner states that settlers received land grants for farms close to the Cape fort, and with rapid demographic growth, the colony expanded. This growth was accompanied by the subjugation of the indigenous Khoikhoi by the settlers and the seizure of their land and livestock (Gerstner 1997:16). The unjust seizing of land by the settlers resulted in slavery. The late South African Reformed Church historian Chris Loff asserts that during the course of the years the free Burgers and later the Trekboers identified more land, which they took for themselves. This resulted in less grazing for the Khoikhoi's cattle and in certain instances, these indigenous people were forced to move deeper into the hinterland, otherwise, they would lose their livestock (Loff 1981:15).

---

3   They were later called 'coloureds' during the apartheid regime. According to Adonis, it was only in the 19th century that the term 'coloured' was used. According to him, Troup, he quotes, 'Was under the impression that, the 'Cape Coloureds' are derived from a basic mixture of Khoikhoi, San and Malay slave, with a strong infusion of the blood of the black African and of the White master'. See Adonis (1982:9).

In line with Loff on the matter of land acquisition, Adonis argues that the Khoikhoi complained about the way they were removed from their land. They publicly claimed that the land belonged to them, that they have a right to it and that they would never allow Hollanders to acquire it Adonis 1982:7). The forceful removal of the Khoikhoi people from their own land was unjust and caused violence and resentment between them and the white settlers. I argue that what started as mission, church planting and evangelisation of the Khoikhoi people resulted in clear injustice that could not be tolerated. However, In 1661, the VOC suggested that in future the company must buy the land from the Khoikhoi communities. Subsequently, in 1672, the company bought a huge portion of land from them. Adonis (1982:7-8) believes that following this development, the position of the Khoikhoi people became worse.

The Khoikhoi realised that more livestock for Hollanders meant less land for them. Clearly, they were alienated from their ownership of land and livestock. This contributed negatively to the Khoikhoi people's social life as they continued to suffer under slavery. The hardships that many black people suffered all over South Africa started with the forced removal from their land. Land was important for the Khoikhoi. It can be said that land meant life and that in an unjust way, this source of life was seized from them and many other black people in South Africa. Hence, many black people still suffer and struggle for survival today as 'life' has been taken away from them. Today in South Africa, the land restitution and land redistribution issue is not only an issue of justice but also a call for reconciliation. The question of land reform cannot be ignored in South Africa as many white DRC members still enjoy the privileges of owning huge hectares of land taken forcefully from the indigenous people.

The South African Reformed ethicist Welile Mazamisa correctly says that the land problem in South Africa is not only a political, economic and emotional reality, it is also an ethical issue of significance (Mazamisa 1994:210).[4] Mazamisa strongly argues that there can be no political, economic and racial solution in South Africa unless the land problem tackled. For Mazamisa, land is particularly important for those who have lost it through colonialism and resettlement programmes. He emphatically says that we cannot allow the current land distribution between black and white people to remain unchallenged (Mazamisa 1994:210). In South Africa, land

---

4   Mazamisa articulates the importance of land by using Walter Brueggemann's words, saying: 'The sense of being lost, displaced, and homeless is pervasive in contemporary culture. Brueggemann goes on to say the yearning to belong somewhere; to have a home; to be in a safe place is a deep and moving pursuit. Loss of place and yearning for place are dominant images.' Mazamisa further explains that this yearning and despair, which I believe also is the same yearning of the Khoisan people is subtly expressed in the pathos of freedom songs like '*Sikhalela umhlaba wethu owathathwa ngabelungu*' (We cry for our land that was taken by the white people). The dominant image among black people is one of rootlessness.

reform is still highly contested and it creates tensions between black people and white farm owners. As a result of the removals from their land, many black people became economically weak and poor and to become slaves of the white farmers. A friend of mine, Pastor Xola Skosana of the Way of Life Church in Khayelitsha calls this suffering of black people due to these injustices in South Africa a 'black pain'.

I maintain that we cannot speak of church unity, especially for the South African situation, without dealing with the question of justice pertaining to land restitution and land distribution. It is clear that the question of land and land reform is not just an issue of livelihood, but it is also an issue of economic justice. Hence, in many areas in South Africa, mainly in black settlements, people suffer from poverty and poor living conditions. For many South Africans, the government, and given its close relationship with the government, the DRC, are to be blamed for all types of injustices against black people in this country ever since the time of Jan van Riebeeck.

Now a question can be asked as to whether the unity of the DR family of churches can play a significant role in restoring justice to those who have suffered. With regard to the land that was taken forcefully from many black people by the white people who belonged to the DRC, what will be the cost of the unity of this family of churches? Can unity work among black and white members of this family of churches without correcting these injustices, especially regarding the land issue as an economic issue which has led to poverty and suffering among many black people? It becomes evident that there is a need for collaborative efforts in healing these divisions. Even though the unity of the DRC family of churches is an interesting point of focus, the question of justice regarding land reform and land restitution will remain the biggest challenge and a threat to this unity.

The South African historian, Hermann Giliomee points out that although the British government was not a social revolutionary, it was firmer than the VOC regarding the land issue. The Khoikhoi had recourse to the courts and the right to own land. However, Giliomee asserts that these rights were not effective, given that most of the Khoikhoi were not Christians and as such, could not swear an oath. For this reason, Giliomee argues, almost no Khoikhoi owned land, for without an oath, their evidence of land ownership counted very little and soon all the richer people were white and almost all the very poor people were black or coloured. This makes it clearer as to why many Khoikhoi people were kept as slaves and farm workers and not converted to Christianity (Giliomee 2003:217). If Khoikhoi people became Christians, they would have the same status and rights as the whites. Mazamisa notes that large tracts of South African land were historically reserved for white ownership with less than one percent of land owned by black people. In his opinion, this has resulted in far-reaching implications for the political economy and human relations in the country. As Mazamisa puts it:

> The exclusion of blacks from land ownership has been undergirded by the Afrikaner land theology which has preached racial hegemony over land. Afrikaner land theology does not question the legitimacy of white land ownership, because God himself gave the land to his chosen people. (Mazamisa 1994:213)

It is on these grounds that racial division and inequality of believers was maintained by whites in order to preserve their white supremacy and oppression over other racial groups.

Regarding the land issue and reconciliation, Ernst Conradie, in his article titled 'Reconciliation as One Guiding Vision for South Africa? Conceptual Analysis and Theological Reflection', notes that the Kairos Document of 1985 'denounced the prioritising of reconciliation as 'church theology'. Conradie states that it famously maintained that 'it would be totally unchristian to plead for reconciliation and peace before the present injustices have been removed.' Conradie goes on to say: 'Any such plea plays into the hands of the oppressor, by trying to persuade those of us who are oppressed to accept our oppression and to become reconciled to the intolerance crimes that are committed against us' (Conradie 2013:14).

For Conradie, this' is not Christian reconciliation, it is sin '(Conradie 2013:14). He notes that black theologians, such as Itumeleng Mosala and Tinyiko Maluleke, have argued that the primary need is not for reconciliation between black people and white people in South Africa. Conradie refers to Maluleke, who argues:

> Our alienation is not alienation from white people first and foremost. Our alienation is from our land, our cattle, our labour which is objectified in industrial machines and technological instrumentation. Our reconciliation with white people will follow from our reconciliation with our fundamental means of livelihood. (cited in Conradie 2013:15)

In line with Mosala and Maluleke, I must emphasise that reconciliation in South Africa is impossible without justice. Reconciliation will only be possible if the indigenous people of South Africa get their relinquished land back. Reconciliation begins when injustices are corrected and the wronged are reinstated their dignity, in this case, especially regarding their land.

The forced removal of Khoikhoi people from their land created so much tension between them and whites that around 1658, Jan van Riebeeck found it very difficult hard to use them to work for him. He, therefore, encouraged the settlers to acquire slaves for labour. Christoff Pauw underlines that the VOC imported slaves from the Dutch colonies in the East. As the Khoi became incorporated into colonial society they lost their self-sufficiency and started to work as slaves (Pauw 2007:55-97). It can be argued that the mission of the DRC on church planting and evangelisation among Khoikhoi people was a 'mission possible' for colonisation and for maintaining inequality and racial division.

The South African church historian J.W. Hofmeyr notes that the first DRC congregation was established in Cape Town in 1665. Hofmeyr maintains that although a number of Khoikhoi people became economically involved in the establishment of the Cape of Good Hope refreshment station in the Cape (Giliomee:215),[5] they initially had little interest in the religion of the white settlers (Hofmeyr 1994:11). The first Khoikhoi male was only baptised in 1662, and only three women had been baptised by then. Jonathan Gerstner recalls that the first child recorded as baptised at the Cape was the son of Willem Barentsz Wylant, 'the first-born Christian who was born in this fortress'. Gerstner also states that there were only four converts to Christianity from the Khoikhoi in the seventeenth century, and all four eventually renounced the Christian life. Most importantly, Gerstner underlines that Christian status and European descent became increasingly identified in people's minds, as did 'heathen' status and indigenous or slave descent (Gerstner 1997:24-25).

During this period, the question of the baptism of slaves' children was a serious debate. Elphick underscores that the Dutch Reformed sacraments of Baptism and Holy Communion provided a social boundary that reinforced the emerging identity of white settlers as 'Christians' and excluded most 'heathen' slaves, Khoisan, and free people of colour (Elphick 2012:39). Gerstner also affirms this by stating that distinctions were made among baptised members and that there were two lists with 'names of Christian children' and 'Slave children of the Honourable Company.' (Gerstner 1997:25). It is evident that the sacraments and mixed marriages between black and white people were strictly prohibited, as these would result in the reinforcement of social equality. Perhaps it can be said that this situation was the root cause of church division, segregation and later the apartheid system. Elphick also states that the Graaff-Reinet settlers denounced the missionaries for putting Khoisan and Xhosa people 'on an equal footing with the Christians,' that is, with the white people (Elphick 2012:27). Both the sacraments of Baptism and of Holy

---

5   Hermann Giliomee points out that 'The Cape of Good Hope's administration which was under the control of the Dutch East India Company (DEIC) was mostly based on status distinctions of which that between burghers and company servants, and burghers and slaves were the most important.' However, Giliomee also highlights that, within the European context, the higher officials of the Company and rich burghers acquired more power and status, but the further these burghers moved into the inside the less these distinctions within a white society counted.

Communion were, for decades, used as means of maintaining division without even recognising the socio-ethical implications of these sacraments.

As mentioned, in 1665 the congregation of Cape Town was established. This was followed in 1686 by the Stellenbosch congregation, the Drakenstein (Paarl) congregation in 1691, the Rhoodezand (Tulbagh) congregation in 1743, and the Swartland (Malmesbury) congregation in 1745 (Hofmeyr 1994:20). At the time, attempts were made by some DRC ministers to have slaves baptised as well. Giliomee affirms that these attempts, made by Reverend M.C. Vos and H.R. Van Lier, to influence slaveholders to let their slaves be baptised were largely unsuccessful. As Giliomee puts it: 'As a result of the resolution of the Synod of Dort of 1618–1619, as well as some ambiguous government proclamations, slaveholders had concluded that they would be forced to free baptised slaves' (Giliomee 2003:216; see also *Acta van die NGK* 1857:59-60).[6]

Gerstner, in line with Giliomee, states that the Synod of Dort had addressed the question of the baptism of slave children held by Christian owners, concluding that slaves were part of the household of the slaveholder, following the practice of Abraham. Gerstner states that theologians favoured delaying baptism until a slave was converted and eventually all agreed that Christian slaves could not be sold out of the spiritual household in which they were born (Gerstner 1997:18). In a sense, baptism was the key to unlocking the chains of slavery and bringing about equal social status and this was refused by their white bosses, hence the slaves were not baptised.

Giliomee asserts that the main reason for the gap between master and slave was because the church had to be mindful of the key concern of its members, to prevent '*gelykstelling*', or 'social levelling', which he calls 'The flip side of white egalitarianism' (Giliomee 2003:216).[7] Richard Elphick too states that many Dutch-speaking white people feared that missions would lead to '*gelykstelling*', that is,

---

[6] Giliomee reckons that the slaveholders had a belief that Christianity narrowed the gap between master and slave, and that to have them baptised was detrimental to investment. He argues that, as elsewhere, masters at the Cape followed the market and they were aware that slaves who were not baptised were more marketable.

[7] Giliomee points out clearly that opposition to this social levelling manifested itself in response to any action that violated the social conventions that underpinned the status and class hierarchy. In his words, he argues: 'The company's status hierarchy, which formally was carried over to the British period, burghers with property enjoyed high status outside the ranks of government, and those without property somewhat less and a white '*knecht*' and a free black considerably less.' However, even lower down were Khoisan servants, while slaves were at the very last level down of the social ladder. He states that they were in fact condemned to a form of social death, a stigma often carried over to their descendants.

to equalisation among races. This fear came from eighteenth-century colonists' belief that civil rights derived from one's status as a Christian, and from the consequent fear of slaveholders that their slaves, if baptised, would thereupon be free (Elphick 2012:42-43).

The prevention of equality became evident in many respects in church circles. This caused great tension in many congregations and there were clear indications that the 'heathens' (non-whites) were not welcome in the church where white members worship the Lord. This manifested itself in the congregation of Graaff-Reinet where the so-called 'heathen Hottentots' were regarded as enemies of the Lord. According to Elphick, on the 9th of July 1801, a band of colonists arrived to demand that Khoisan people should be barred from the church, and 'that the seats should be washed, the pavement broken up, the pulpit covered with black cloth, as a demonstration of mourning.' (Elphick 2012:26). This was racism at its extreme and a clear sign of racial division. This act did not only affect the church, it also affected other social structures.

Loff critically argues that it is not really true that all baptised slaves were freed or that freed slaves were baptised. Loff states that in the beginning, the slaves used to be freed after their baptism. He maintains that according to an investigation made on earlier registers, it shows that most of the slaves who were baptised belonged to the company, and most of the freed slaves were slaves of private people (Loff 1981:16). In support of his argument on the question of freed slaves after baptism, Loff considers the case of Bentura Visser (after baptism known as Bentura Johannes), the so-called 'bastaard' who was baptised on 26 October 1828, just before the 1829 Synod of the DRC. Although Bentura was baptised and confirmed as a member of the congregation, some white members were unhappy with him partaking in Holy Communion services simultaneously with them. Rev. J. Spijker stood by Bentura's side and maintained that he (Bentura) was baptised and confirmed in front of the congregation and, therefore, there is was no reason why he should enjoy Communion separately (Loff 1983:11-15). In Bentura's case, it became clear that the white congregants had serious problems with him; not necessarily for his baptism, but for sharing Holy Communion together with them.

The DRC Synod of 1829

The tension caused by racial division and the striving for equality became a long struggle in the church among Christians. Elphick states that the Dutch Reformed missionaries were faced with a problem of how to integrate their black converts into long-established white congregations, for whom the church buildings, its worship, and sacraments were the focus of white peoples' community life and their group identity. Elphick points out that there were bitter disputes in many Western Cape congregations over whether black Christians could take Communion with white people or even be allowed into the church (Elphick 2012:43). This resulted in many Dutch settlers leaving the colony. The so-called 'Great Trek' was partly because of disputes over race in the local congregations.

In 1829, some rural Dutch congregations asked for separate facilities and services for black converts. Elphick, in line with Pauw, states that the 1829 DRC Synod was engaged in a debate as to whether persons of colour admitted as members of the church should be served Holy Communion equally with born Christians (Elphick 2012:43). Pauw points out that the matter attracted much debate and it was brought to the attention of the 1829 Synod, who discussed the following proposal: 'To have the Sacrament of the Lord's Supper dispensed at the same time to all members of the church without distinction.' Pauw further states that during the deliberations the official representative of the state at the synod (known as the commissioner-politics) interrupted and said that it was 'derogatory for the dignity of the Christian religion' to discuss such a matter (Pauw 2007:67-71). The synod appoved aproposal for the simultaneous taking of Holy Communion by the congregants nothwitstanding race, colour of background (*Acta NGK* 1829:63, 71; Loff 1998:87).

According to Loff, the minutes show that this matter was not debated by the synod. Loff further emphasised that what we do know is that it was 'advised' that, accordance with the Bible teaching and the spirit of Christianity, the church was forced to make no exceptions in this regard; people should take Holy Communion together. Furthermore, the role of the commissioner-politics in this case was clearly that of a civil servant who used his authority to prevent a question that was humiliating for the church from being discussed. The commissioner-politics believed that it ought to be an accepted and irrefutable principle that there could be no discrimination at Communion (Loff 1983:15-16).

In line with Loff, Johan Botha underlines that the government official present at the synod meeting in 1829 advised the DRC that the mere discussion of the possible creation of separate occasions and locations for sharing in the Lord's Supper for church members from various race and population groups discredited the dignity of the gospel. The synod decided that all confirmed members should partake equally and jointly in the Lord's Supper (Botha 2002:52). The Swedish theologian, Lennart Henriksson alludes to this by saying that it was impossible for the split of the Holy Communion service as the British government then kept an eye on the church and, moreover, had the last say on all church decisions. According to Ordinance

50, all free people were considered equal before the law (Henriksson 2010:51-52).[8] Loff notes that neither the presbytery nor the synod meetings directly referred to Ordinance 50 (Loff 1983:17).

The South African theologian Charles Villa-Vicencio also affirms that there was initially a measure of church integration in the major centres of the Western Cape. When rural and frontier congregations began to demand separate facilities and services for black converts, theological tradition initially prevailed and baptism was affirmed as the sole theological qualification for church membership. Villa-Vicencio states that the social discrimination between slaves and slave owners, frontier farmers and the indigenous population and generally, between black and white people, gained the upper hand (Villa-Vicencio 1988:26). Even though the 1829 DRC Synod formally rejected discrimination on racial lines, it never meant that in practice coloured people were not discriminated against at church services and at the Table of the Holy Communion.

The DRC Synod of 1857

The decision of the 1857 DRC Synod eventually opened the door to the splitting of worship services for white and coloured Christians.

The decision of the synod reads as follows:
> The Synod considers it desirable and according to the Holy Scripture that our heathen members (non-whites) be accepted and initiated into our congregations wherever it is possible; but where this measure, as a result of the weakness of some, would stand in the way of promoting the work of Christ among the heathen people, then congregations set up among the heathen, or still to be set up, should enjoy their Christian privileges in a separate building or institution. (*Acta NGK* 1857:59-60)[9]

The tension of serving Holy Communion to persons of colour simultaneously with the born Christians intensified over decades. This also opened the door to the split of worship services between the Khoikhoi people and the white congregants.

---

8   In 1828, the Cape Parliament promulgated Ordinance 50, which aimed at ensuring equality before the law of 'every free inhabitant in the Colony'. Effectively the ordinance curtailed the power that an employer had over his employees.

9   Original wording: '*De Synode beschouwt het wenschlijk en schrifmatig dat onze ledematen uit de Heidenen, in onze bestaande gemeenten opgenomen en ingelljfd worden, overall waar zulks geschieden kan; maar waar deze maatregel, ten gevolge van de zwakheid van sommigen de bevordering van de zaak van Christus onder de Heidenen, in de weg zoude staan, de gemeenten uit de Heidenen opgerigt, of nog op te rigten, hare Christelijke voorregten in een afzonderlijk gebouw of gesticht genieten zal.*'

The reality is that the decision of the DRC Synod of 1857 applied to an already existing separation of facilities and services for black converts. The South African Missionary Society and its associates refused to be absorbed by the DRC, in which that would determine sacrificing their autonomy and parting with those members who were Lutherans (Giliomee 2003:218)[10] Adonis states that already in 1824, the South African Missionary Society had built their own church building for the black Christians in Stellenbosch and in 1829 P.D Lückhoff of the Rhenish Mission worked there. Adonis claims that in a white congregation of Durbanville, the church council in 1839 decided that the freed slave men must sit on the gallery in the church, while the women sit under the gallery. There were reserved places for the non-white people in the church (Adonis 1982:52).

It must be noted that black converts were separated from their families during church services. Black men and women congregants had to sit separately from their white counterparts who sat together with their families. There is no reason given for this sitting arrangement. Perhaps it was that the black converts were not regarded as officially married Christian couples, as the white families were. Although this style of seating in church can still be noticed, even in the Orthodox tradition, in the case of the DRC it seems to have been done to prevent non-white men and women from occupying the same seating areas in the church. What was the practice of the DRC in the early years with regard to the seating arrangement in the church still exists among black congregations in the 21st century.

Adonis mentions that even before the Synod of 1857 some white congregations of the DRC sat in the same service as the black converts. But this practice became a problem to various other white congregations In Calvinia for instance, white congregants protested against the black congregants who were using their church building (Adonis 1982:52-53). On 4 January 1845, a number of white congregants confronted the church council of Swellendam with a request to not share the same Table of Holy Communion with the black congregants (Adonis 1982:53; *Notule van die Kerkraad van Swellendam* 4 Januarie 1845:1-2;). However, the church council was disappointed by this request.

---

10 The South African Missionary Society and its associates refused to be absorbed by the DRC, in which that would determine sacrificing their autonomy and parting with those members who were Lutherans. Giliomee asserts that the DRC was not hostile to the missionary work, however, it wanted to bring missionary work done by its members under its own control, especially since they dominated the ranks of the *Zuid – Afrikaansche Zending Genootschap* (ZAZG) and its affiliated local bodies. This is the reason why this body (the ZAZG) did not want to be absorbed and being under the control of the DRC supremacy.

Many white church members in the DRC rejected the idea of separate church services, especially on racial lines. However, this protest simply introduced the roots of racism very strongly. According to Stephen Fowl and Gregory Jones, in their book titled *Reading in Communion: Scripture and Ethics in Christian Life,* the structures of apartheid were already deeply embedded in the practice and characters of the majority of the DRC members. For them, Scripture was invoked after the fact to support that which was already in place. Fowl and Jones further state that in the early days, the DRC in principle maintained a doctrine of church unity, but in practice, manifested the sorts of class, cultural and educational divisions typical of other churches in the seventeenth and eighteenth centuries. This became evident in cases where black people were evangelised and began to enter the DRC. In principle, they were eligible to share in the Lord's Supper with their white fellow Christians. However, this clearly angered some white DRC members who argued their black fellow Christians should have separate services (Fowl & Jones 1991:96).

In this regard, we could ask: What does it mean to refuse to share the Holy Communion with other people from different racial groups? Does exclusion not reflect the opposite of the meaning of the Lord's Supper? Fowl and Jones state that there were several courageous pastors who recognised the sin of excluding fellow Christians from the Lord's Table on the basis of race (Fowl & Jones 1991:96-97). It can be said that the request by the congregants was a protest against the unity of the church and the quest for reconciliation and justice.

Henrikson notes that in 1843, long after the 1829 Synod of the DRC (in which the British government had a final say on church decisions), an important prerequisite came about in when the government lifted its heavy overcoat from the shoulders of the church and the church became free to take its own decisions (Henrikson 2010:53). However, by 1847, the case was not yet resolved and some white congregants emphasised that the black congregants must worship in a separate building of their own.

Contrary to the DRC Synod decision in 1857, Robert Vosloo, in his article 'The Welcoming Table? The Lord's Supper, Exclusion, and the Reformed Tradition' observes the Lord's Supper in another interesting angle when he strongly argues that the Lord's Table is not a table of separation and exclusion, but it can be described as 'the welcoming table'. (Vosloo 2012:483-484). His perspective on the Lord's Table as a welcoming table strongly criticises the infamous decision of the 1857 DRC Synod, as well as the whole idea of racial discrimination and separation of worship services. In fact, in many, ways this proposition of Vosloo supports the 1829 Synod decision. Vosloo uses the words 'unconditional acceptance of all participants' at the Lord's Supper in affirmation of the visible unity of Christ's body and the grace of the Host to show that exclusion has no place at the Lord's Table. He, therefore, concludes that the Lord's Supper is inextricably linked to hospitality, as well as the need to challenge certain reductive practices of exclusion and restricted access (Vosloo 2012:484). According to Elphick, the DRC leaders' support for the 1857 Synod decision simply recognised that because of 'the weakness of some' [white people], racial prejudice would not disappear rapidly. They gave priority to their principal goal of Christianising heathens and preventing *'gelykstelling'*, or 'racial equalisation' (Elphick 2012:43-44). Loff also emphasises this point that the separate congregations challenge was more than just a problem of 'colour difference', but colour prejudice, in other words, racism. For Loff, the synod accepted that there was such a strong colour prejudice among the white people that they refused to tolerate the black people in their midst, especially with regard to Holy Communion (Loff 1983:19-20). The 1857 Synod's conclusion was that the most sensible practice would be to start teaching people from the indigenous groupings on premises geographically apart from those of the Dutch people. It is evident that the separation of the races in the church of God has perpetuated the motivation for the racial apartheid ideology, which led to different racial laws in South Africa. The church division, or perhaps the disunity among Christians, had a negative impact on the South African context.

Elphick affirms that in retrospect, the 1857 synodical resolution may seem a portentous precedent of the DRC's later advocacy of apartheid. Yet, it merely gave official sanction to arrangements already in practice (Elphick 2012:44). This separation process within the Dutch Reformed family of churches became common practice and eventually determined the structure and order of the church and that of South African society. According to Pieter Coertzen, up until the end of the 18th century, the DRC had no specific missionary policy, and that converts and children out of the heathendom were taken up into existing Dutch Reformed congregations. Then at the end of the 18th century, missionary societies started working in South Africa. These societies started to separate meetings for converts from the heathen and this eventually led to separate congregations. As Coertzen puts it: 'After 1857 the mission congregations became mere annexures, copies of the white congregations without any representation on the church council, presbyteries, and synod or with any form of official connection between them' (Coertzen 2000:181).

It must be noted that even before and after the 1857 Synod, there were schisms in the DRC and the new churches like the Volkskerk, the Nederduitsch Hervormde Kerk van Afrika (NHK), and the Gereformeerde Kerk (GK) emerged (Elphick 2012:44-51) It can be stated that the DRC 1857 Synod decision became a decisive factor for church division on racial lines. Elphick highlights that S.P. Engelbrecht believed that the root cause of the founding of the NHK was the hostility of the Voortrekkers' to *'gelykstelling'*, or racial equalising, especially in the Cape church (Engelbrecht 2012:46.).

Racial segregation of worship services and the rise of apartheid policy

Vosloo states that the 1857 Synod decision played at least some role in paving the way for the establishment of separate Dutch Reformed churches along racial lines and that the mission policy of this church continued to play a major role in providing the moral underpinnings for the theological legitimisation of the policy of apartheid (Vosloo 2012:486-487). In 1880, the DRC Synod decided to make it possible for its mission parishes to join a segregated new order. In 1881, a separate Dutch Reformed Mission Church (DRMC) was established for 'coloured' people. Several other ethnic churches followed. In 1951, the Dutch Reformed Church in Africa (DRCA) for black people was established in the Eastern Cape. In 1968 the Indian Reformed Church, better known as Reformed Church in Africa (RCA), was established in Natal for Indian people.

Adonis points out that despite being organised into separate ethnic churches there was no difference between the coloured DRMC and the white DRC congregants in terms of the confession, church governing, administration or language (Adonis 1982:60). This racial segregation of worship services was the result of the missionary work of the DRC. This move was seen to be one of 'weakness', rather than something that could in principle, be justified. Pauw notes that the DRC's missionary policy of separate denominations for different ethnic groups fitted the apartheid model of separate development (Pauw 2007:58).

It should be noted that the apartheid was already at work in a silent way when these churches were established. Charles Villa-Vicencio states that Allan Boesak observed that the DRC must assume special responsibility for the prevailing apartheid policy of South Africa. Apartheid had been born in the womb of the DRC. Details of the policy were worked out by that church and it had provided moral and theological justification for apartheid. According to Villa-Vicencio, shortly after the election of the National Party to power in 1948, *Die Kerkbode*, the official newspaper of the NGK, noted with pride: 'As a church we have always worked purposefully for the separation of the races. In this regard apartheid can rightfully be called a church policy' (Villa-Vicencio 1983:59). The separation of worship services was clearly racism at its highest function. All the signs of racial prejudices and all other forms of injustice that arose from the church affected the community and social structures tremendously. Suffice to say that the 'new' democratic South Africa still suffers from these injustices. In fact, the 1857 Synod decision was not only executed in the church set up and structures, but it was also directly applied in society. The South African society, in the long run, was structured exactly in the same way that the DRC had structured itself. This church division and its legitimisation of apartheid harmed the society.

Some decades after this synod decision, the reality of division expanded within the DRC and the idea of separate worship services was gradually introduced and executed in many DRC congregations. The Canadian peace researcher and expert on security and disarmament Ernie Regehr asserts that the moderator of the DRC, Dr J.D. Vorster, emphatically rejected the idea of mixed worship and, according to Regehr, he once publicly said a speech: 'We must create separate facilities for blacks in their own areas, and if there is no alternative, we must give them Sundays off so that they can stay in their own houses and worship in their own churches' (cited in Regehr 1979:216-217).

The separation of church worship services led to the separation of many other structures in society, including schools and universities. Eugene Klaaren shed light on this matter, especially in his chapter titled 'Creation and Apartheid: South African Theology since 1948', where he underlines that in 1957, at a decisive point in the history of higher education in South Africa, Hendrik G. Stoker, the South African neo-Calvinist philosopher, advocated separate universities for Africans, whites, and coloured people (Klaaren 1997:372). The idea behind this was a well-structured apartheid policy that prevented any chances of unity in diversity in church and society. Klaaren states that at this crossroads of policy and theory, Hendrik Stoker strongly urged the extension of apartheid education, which he took to be firmly supported in the comprehensive philosophy of lawful creation that he developed. Klaaren further says the neo-Calvinist line of thought also affirmed distinctly sovereign social spheres such as family, school, church, and state, each under the absolute sovereignty of the Creator. This teaching was often used to support apartheid (Klaaren 1997:373).

We could ask whether the structuring of the DR family of churches on racial order had any positive contribution to the church's involvement on issues of justice and reconciliation. In its witness to the world and as a social ethic, what did the DRC do to preserve the unity of the church, and to be the bearers of reconciliation between the racial groups that belonged to it? Instead, the DRC opted for racial prejudice and preached the gospel of apartheid as the way of life in church and society.

In his book, *The Church Struggle in South Africa*, John de Gruchy writes:
> We have seen enough already to know that racism in South Africa did not arrive when the National Party (NP) came to power in 1948 with its clarion call to apartheid. But 1948 is symbolic of a dramatic change in the meaning of racism for South Africans. (De Gruchy 1986:53)[11]

---

11 It is quite interesting to see how the churches engaged the government on the apartheid policy; they were never silent in opposing the policy.

De Gruchy further notes that racial discrimination was entrenched in the Union Constitution and determined much of the legislation between the year 1910 and 1948, but it did not have the rigid, ideological character that it began to assume under the apartheid slogan. Churches have been dealing with the question of racism in South Africa for a very long time. Statements were issued in opposition to the situation and the spreading of racism all over South African society, including the church. Racism became a major concern, as it not only affected the life of the church but also caused a great harm to the life of the broader South African society. It can be said that racism, especially being driven by the church, became an ethical concern and a crime against humanity.

De Gruchy recalls that already in November 1948, the Episcopal Synod of the Church of the Province issued a lengthy statement on the race issue. The bishops agreed with the resolution of the Lambeth Conference earlier that year, which had declared that 'discrimination between men on the grounds of race alone is inconsistent with the principles of the Christian religion' (De Gruchy 1986:55). The implications of church division accumulated further and affected the whole South African context including churches who were not even affiliates of the DR family of churches.

In the past, many churches in South Africa were divided along racial lines, and as a result of racism, the South African society was structured in the same way. Coertzen alludes to this when he states that cultural segregation became race segregation and this eventually led to apartheid as a policy. Coertzen cites Kinghorn, who described apartheid policy as a norm in the country that affected everything; the justice system, the social interaction between people, sport, the workplace and also the church itself (cited in Coertzen 2000:182). The apartheid policy destroyed all the possible relations between black and white people; and any bond of unity among South Africans. This situation also had an impact on church and society. The seriousness of the apartheid policy could no longer be tolerated and some action to prevent further destruction of South African society by apartheid was the only route to be followed.

In opposition to the Afrikaner theology of creation that perpetuated injustices and gave rise to apartheid, a South African black theology emerged. This was a theology of struggle against injustices in township, church and university. Klaaren reckons that black theology, in its forceful opposition to Afrikaner law-and-order creationism responded with a liberating theology of creation (Klaaren 1997:377). A number of black South African theologians, such as Desmond Tutu, Manas Buthelezi, Allan Boesak, Russel Botman, Takatso Mofokeng, Buti Tlhagale and Ilumeleng Mosala, to mention but a few, in favour of the black theology of liberation were vocal in opposing apartheid in South Africa.

In May 1968, numerous churches in South Africa combined under the umbrella body of the inter-denominational South African Council of Churches (SACC) and fought against racism and apartheid. As Dolamo puts it: 'The testimony of the churches in the South African struggle through the SACC against oppression, domination and liberation, has been that of prophecy to protest to resistance' (Dolamo 2000:225.) According to Dolamo, the prophetic function of the church is basic to all the other functions and it includes all of them. The type of prophecy that Dolamo suggests is an ability to read a situation correctly by doing social analysis and suggesting solutions to the problems. In this case, the problem of apartheid as racism and heresy was tackled and apartheid was, therefore, condemned on ethical grounds. The South African society suffered the consequences of the apartheid system. The consequences of apartheid and racism in South Africa are much more serious than the problem itself, which could have been solved a long time ago. Division is always costly and it always carries negative outcomes for church and society. On the one hand, the voices of the churches and political organisations against racism grew, while on the other hand, the government maintained the status quo on apartheid and racism. This situation did not only affect the Christians in South Africa, but it seriously contaminated the South African society.

At the 1978 Synod, the DRMC declared that the ideology of apartheid was in conflict with the teaching of the gospel on unity and on reconciliation. The World Alliance of Reformed Churches (WARC) – later known as the World Communion of Reformed Churches (WCRC) – in 1982 in Ottawa, declared apartheid as heresy and sin and a *status confessionis* was declared. After this WARC gathering the DRMC at its 1982 Synod strongly opposed the ideology of apartheid and through the drafting of the Belhar Confession, affirmed the equal status of people of God, the unity of the church, the work of Christ's reconciliation and the justice of God through the formulation and the draft of the Belhar Confession (Addendum 1 WARC Resolution on racism and South Africa). The Belhar Confession confessed God as the God of unity, of reconciliation and justice. The WARC gathering played a crucial role in the struggle against apartheid in South Africa and led to the Belhar Confession and its unequivocally denouncement of the unethical apartheid policy on biblical grounds.

Conclusion

The mission work resulted in the colonisation of South Africa and church divisions that impacted negatively in society. Until this day, these divisions pose a serious threat to the life of the church and its witness to issues of justice, peace and reconciliation in society. It can be concluded that the seriousness of the segregation policy in the form of racial prejudice or racism gave birth to the apartheid policy in South Africa. The DRC entertained the segregation policy within church circles and later legitimised the apartheid policy of the white government in South Africa. What started as a challenge on sharing the Holy Communion simultaneously gradually became a racial challenge that opened the door to separate church building and later it developed to the policy apartheid. Richard Elphick alludes to this fact when he states that in the nineteenth century, the DRC, the spiritual home of most Dutch-speaking settlers, pioneered the practice of segregated churches, and in the twentieth century, decisively shaped apartheid theory (Elphick 2012:39).

This paper radically challenges this idea and practice of the DRC regarding Baptism and Holy Communion. It pleads for unity in diversity and that such unity must express itself in society in terms of our witnessing together on issues of justice.

The Belhar Confession pleads for meaningful church unity, which is not disconnected to justice and reconciliation within the church and society. The question of equality (over against the idea of *'geen gelykstelling'*) remains the biggest challenge for the church in South Africa today, especially regarding church unity and the response of the church to socio-economic and other ethical challenges that are a threat to unity. The divisions of the DRC family of churches on racial grounds remained a challenge that existed for decades. This also challenges the existing internal unity of the Uniting Reformed Church in Southern Africa, which seems to keep this status quo of being a united but racially divided church. Divisions in South Africa, including church divisions, will only come to an end if issues of unity, social justice and reconciliation are taken seriously and implemented in a meaningful way.

Bibliography

Primary sources
Acta van die Nederduits Gereformeerde Kerk 1829.
Acta van die Nederduits Gereformeerde Kerk 1857.

Secondary sources
Adonis, J. 1982. *Die afgebreekte skeidsmuur weer opgebou*. Amsterdam: Rodopi.
Belhar Confession, 1986. The official English translation of the *Belhar Confession* approved by the General Synod of 2008. Belhar: LUS Printers.
Botha, J. 2002. Accounting for the hope that is in us of embodied unity, true reconciliation and compassionate justice: Our story is part of the bigger story. In P. Coertzen (ed.), *350 jaar Gereformeerd*. Bloemfontein: CLF.
Coertzen, P. 2000. The unity of the family of Dutch Reformed churches in South Africa: Then and now – prospects and frustrations – A Dutch Reformed perspective. *Nederduitse Gereformeerde Teologiese Tydskrf* 41. (3/4):181-190.

Conradie, E. 2013. Reconciliation as one guiding vision for South Africa? Conceptual analysis and theological reflection: In P. Conradie (ed.), *Reconciliation: A guiding vision for South Africa*? Stellenbosch: SUN PReSS. https://doi.org/10.18820/9781920689094

de Gruchy, J. 1986. *The church struggle in South Africa* (2nd edition). Grand Rapids, MI: William B. Eerdmans.

Dolamo, R.T.H. 2000. The South African church struggle against apartheid (1948–1990): A theological-ethical critique. *Dutch Reformed Theological Journal* XXXXI(3/4):255-260.

Elphick, R. 2012. *The equality of believers: Protestant missionaries and the racial politics of South Africa*. Pietermaritzburg, South Africa: University of KwaZulu-Natal Press.

Fowl, S.E. & Jones, L.G. 1991. *Reading in Communion: Scripture and ethics in Christian life*. Grand Rapids, MI: William B. Eerdmans.

Gerstner, J. 1997. A Christian monopoly: The Reformed Church and colonial society under Dutch rule. In R. Elphick & R. Davenport (eds), *Christianity in South Africa: A political, social, and cultural history*. Claremont: David Philip Publishers.

Giliomee, H. 2003. 'The weakness of some': The Dutch Reformed Church and white supremacy. *Scriptura* 83:212-244. https://doi.org/10.7833/83-0-880

Henriksson, L. 2010. *A journey with a status confessionis: Analysis of an apartheid related conflict between the Dutch Reformed Church in South Africa and the World Alliance of the Reformed Churches, 1982–1998*. Uppsala, Sweden: Swedish Institute of Missionary Research.

Hofmeyr, J.W. 1994. Christianity in the period of Dutch colonisation. In W. Hofmeyr & G.J. Pillay (eds), *A history of Christianity in South Africa* (Vol. 1). Pretoria: HAUM Tertiary.

Klaaren, E.M. 1997. Creation and apartheid: South African theology since 1948 In R. Elphick & R. Davenport (eds), *Christianity in South Africa: A political, social, and cultural history*. Claremont: David Philip Publishers.

Loff, C. 1981. *Dogter of verstoteling? Kantaantekeninge by die geskiedenis van die Nederduitse Gereformeerde Sendingkerk in Suid-Afrika*. Cape Town. Predikante Broederkring.

Loff, C. 1983. The history of a heresy. In J. de Gruchy & C. Villa-Vicencio (eds), *Apartheid is a heresy*. Claremont: David Philip Publishers.

Loff, C. 1998. *Bevryding tot eenwording: Die Nederduitse Gereformeerde Sendingkerk in Suid-Afrika 1881–1994*. DTh. thesis, Theologische Universiteit Kampen, Kampen.

Mazamisa, W. 1994. Reparation and land: In C. Villa-Vicencio & J. de Gruchy (eds), *Doing ethics in context: South African perspectives. Theology and praxis*, Volume II. Claremont: David Philip Publishers.

Pauw, C. 2007. *Anti-partheid theology in the Dutch Reformed family of churches. A depth-hermeneutical analysis*. Amsterdam: Vrije Universiteit.

Plaatjies-Van Huffel, M-A. 2008. *Die doleansie kerkreg en kerkregering van die Nederduitse Gereformeerde sendingkerke en die VGKSA*. Pretoria: University of Pretoria. [Online] Available at http://upetd.up.ac.za/thesis/available/etd-04022009-190218/ (Accessed 11 March 2015).

Plaatjies-Van Huffel, M-A. 2011. Dirk Smith – An apologist for confession. In L. Hansen, N. Koopman & R. Vosloo (eds), *Living theology*. Wellington, South Africas: Bybel-Media.

Plaatjies-Van Huffel, M-A. 2013a. Reading the Belhar Confession as a historical text. In M.A. Plaatjies-Van Huffel and R.R. Vosloo (eds), *Reformed churches in South Africa and the struggle for justice – Remembering 1960–1990*. Stellenbosch: SUN PReSS. https://doi.org/10.18820/9781920689117

Plaatjies-Van Huffel, M-A. 2013b. The Belhar Confession: Born in the struggle against apartheid in southern Africa, guiding light today. *Studia Historicae Ecclesiasticae* 39(1):185-203.

Plaatjies-Van Huffel, M-A. 2014. The Belhar Confession in its historical context. *Nederduitse Gereformeerde Teologiese Tydskrif* 55(1/2):308-309. https://doi.org/10.5952/55-1-2-527

Regehr, E. 1979. *Perceptions of apartheid*. Scottdale, PA: Herald Press.

Villa-Vicencio, C. 1983. An all-pervading heresy: Racism and the English-speaking churches. In J. de Gruchy & C. Villa-Vicencio (eds), *Apartheid is a heresy*. Claremont: David Philip Publishers.

Villa-Vicencio, C. 1988. *Trapped in apartheid*. Maryknoll, NY: Orbis.

Vosloo, R. 2012. The Welcoming Table? The Lord's Supper, exclusion, and the Reformed tradition. In: E. van der Borght and P. van Geest (eds), *Strangers and pilgrims on earth: Essays in honour of Abraham van de Beek*. Leiden: BRILL.

UNITY AND DIVERSITY

An overview of the URCSA decisions on church unity since 1994

Willem Saayman[1]

Introduction

This chapter is taken from a paper delivered at the General Synod of URCSA on October 2008 and gives an overview of decisions taken by various organs of the Uniting Reformed Church of SA (URCSA) about unification with the Dutch Reformed Church (DRC) since 1994. As the debate about unity, unification and/or reunification in the family of Dutch Reformed churches has been vigorously pursued since before 1994, however, the chapter also briefly sketches the historical background and context of this debate in general. Finally, the chapter gives an assessment of the state of the debate in July 2008.

A historical overview

The early years

The DRC Synod of 1857 reiterated the point of view expressed by all synods of the church since the first synod in 1829, namely that the unity of Christian believers was the scriptural imperative.[2] Yet the synod also took the first decision to justify and allow racial separation in ecclesial practice through racially separated communion services for white and black DRC members. The application of this decision in local congregations gradually led to communities of white and black members of the DRC growing further apart, ending in the constitution of racially separated congregations. Twenty-four years later, and without taking any synodical decision to the contrary to gainsay the decisions of the synods from 1829 until 1857, the Dutch Reformed Mission Church (DRMC) for coloured members was constituted on the advice of the missionaries and the Interior Mission Commission (*'Binnelandse*

---

[1] Professor Emeritus, Department of Missiology, Unisa and URCSA member, Eersterust/Melodi ya Tshwane.
[2] For a more comprehensive history on the historical background of the Belhar Confession please read the following essay in this publication: 'Acceptance, Adoption, Advocacy, Reception and Protestation: A Chronology of the Belhar Confession' by Mary-Anne Plaatjies-Van Huffel.

Sendingkommissie') of the church (Smith 1980:84). The first racially separated 'daughter church' of the DRC thus came into being in an attempt to improve co-ordination in mission within the Cape, and as recognition of the reality that the separate celebration of the sacraments (supposed to be a practical aid to speed the evangelisation of 'the heathen') had grown, for all practical purposes, into parallel racially separated congregations in many locations (Smith 1980:85). Another important observation that must be made is that all black converts (coloured as well as black African) became members of the one Mission Church. What happened in the Cape became the blueprint for Dutch Reformed churches in the Free State, Transvaal and Natal.[3] None of these synods had any extended theological debates about unity and diversity. The practical consequence of the mission policy applied in all the various DRC synods was that racially separated congregations came into existence. In most cases the synodical mission commissions (and not the synods themselves) took the final decision to constitute a racially separated synod in the province for black converts (later called the Dutch Reformed Church in Africa).

The first slight diversion to the pattern came with the constitution of the Dutch Reformed Bantu Church in SA (in the Cape Province) in 1951. Until the 1920s, the DRC in the Cape had not undertaken any specific, organised mission work among Africans. The mission work was mainly concentrated on coloured people (who lived in far greater numbers in the south-western Cape than Africans), but it was not closed to African participation, so there were indeed African converts who became members of the DRMC. In 1924, however, the Cape Synod of the DRC decided to start concentrated, organised mission work among 'natives' (Africans), especially in the Transkei area (Smith 1980:102). So, we have this uniform development in DRC church planting in all the regional synods until the 1950s. As a result of the consistent racially separated church practice and mission work, racially separated mission churches (which accommodated both coloured and African converts) came into being. It is important to note that from 1881 until 1951 no ethnic differentiation was made in the DRC Mission churches in the various provinces between coloured and African members. Even in the inland provinces (Free State, Transvaal and Natal), where there were more African than coloured members in the DRC Mission churches, coloured and African members belonged to the same congregations and one synod in one church. Ethnic differentiation only came into being when the (white) Cape Synod decided to put its work in the Transkei on a separate footing, leading to the formation of the DRC Bantu Church in 1951. Between 1881 and 1951, therefore, separate DRC Mission churches were formed along practical and geographical lines, separating white DRC members from their black counterparts. Ethnicity did not

---

3   At that stage, the DRC existed as four provincial synods; a united national General Synod had not been formed.

enter the picture at all before 1951, neither was there any theological debate about racially separated churches at a synodical level. The decision to institute separate congregations and churches was taken by functionaries at a local level. In the mid-fifties, things began to change, though, in the sense that separation was introduced at synodical, church political level between coloured and African. I argue that this was indeed part of a wider change in DRC mission, which was largely spurred on by the findings and recommendations of the Tomlinson Report (Saayman 2007:69-78). I now turn my attention to my motivation for this argument.

The shift from the practical to the theological-political

The shift from the practical to the theological-political did not start only in the 1940 and 1950s. In 1929, the Cape and Free State synods of the Mission Church held a joint conference for their moderature. Their proposal for the formation of an Advisory Council for Mission churches (at that stage consisting only in the Cape and Free State synods) was accepted by the respective mother churches. The Transvaal Mission Church joined this council upon its own formation in 1932. For some reason, the Cape Mission Church decided in 1950 to withdraw from the council. Then in 1951, the DRC Bantu Church in SA was constituted by the Cape Synod to accommodate the growing number of African converts from the rural areas and the Transkei. At this stage, concludes Smith, the formation of a separate Bantu church was still the spontaneous response to the practical developments – in line with developments since 1857 (Smith 1980:104-105). The Bantu members were concentrated in the Transkei, used Xhosa and not Afrikaans in their services, and it therefore made sense to constitute a separate church for them.

The withdrawal of the Cape DRC Mission Church left the Advisory Council with mainly African churches as members, and in 1955 the various white DRC synods decided to form the Federal Council of Dutch Reformed Mission Churches to bring together coloured and African synods as well as the foreign daughter churches (Crafford 1982:563). There thus seemed to be centrifugal as well as centripetal forces at work in the various DRC Mission churches (mainly constituted on a geographical, non-ethnic and non-tribal basis at this stage) in the early 1950s. The new Mission churches were mainly African (simply organised on a provincial basis), while the existing (Cape) Coloured Mission Church was beginning to consider an existence on its own. Whatever the case might have been there does not (yet) seem to have been strong pressure to organise on the basis of ethnicity, although the pressure was building. Bosch (1984:28) concludes that the exclusivist Afrikaner (ethnic) mobilisation started in the 1930s, on the basis laid by S.J. du Toit already early in the twentieth century.[4] This early foundation was laid especially on impulses generated by Reformed evangelicalism and the Dutch Calvinist Revival under Groen van Prinsterer (Bosch:25-29), later reinforced by Kuyperian Christian nationalism. Deist (1990:129) clearly indicates the combination of urbanisation, poverty and unemployment that enabled Kuyperian Christian nationalism to flourish in this situation and set the stage for Afrikaner ethnocentricity. It received a vitalising impulse from German neo-Fichtean romantic nationalism introduced into the Afrikaner community by outstanding young students such as N.J. Diederichs, P.J. Meyer, HF Verwoerd and others who studied in Germany during the 1930s. They introduced especially the Fichtean idea of 'the organic unity of language, culture, and political self-determination' (Bosch 1984:29). As one of them, Diederichs would later formulate it, 'a person is first of all a member of the nation [*volk*]' (Bosch 1984:30). For this reason, 'Service to my nation is service to God, *for love of my nation is part of my love to God*' (Bosch 1984:30, emphasis added).

Into this context the Tomlinson Report was introduced in 1955 – which would prove to have far-reaching consequences for DRC mission work (Saayman 2007:69-99, 2008). The Tomlinson Commission was the first to replace the term 'native' for indigenous African people with the more ethnically charged term 'Bantu' (Tomlinson Report 1955:1-2). The report concluded that the African ('Bantu') Society of South Africa consisted of four distinct cultural/ethnic units: the Nguni, Sotho-Tswana, Venda and Shangaan-Tsonga (Tomlinson Report 1955:1). The important elements that determined one's national (ethnic) identity were culture and language (Ashforth 1990:161; Saayman 2008:12-13;). Whether African people were born in one of the core areas of the four groups or in a 'white' city, or whether urban African people still felt or indeed ever had felt any affinity for such a core area, they could claim a national identity only in terms of language and culture, which bound them to a specific ethnic group. The Tomlinson Report was not simply some dry and dusty government research report destined to gather dust and nothing more. It was rather the determined response of the newly-elected National Party government to prove that their apartheid policy was not simply some airy-fairy ideological construct, but rather a hard-nosed and idealistic political programme that could once and for all solve South Africa's central political problem: the 'Native question' (Saayman 2008:1-2). In this conviction, they were strongly supported by the DRC, whose request to government indeed contributed to the appointment of the commission (Saayman 2008:5). It was no surprise, therefore, that the publication of the report immediately reflected itself in the DRC debate on mission policy (Saayman 2008:13-15 for examples). My contention is that the debate and eventual decisions on the creation

---

4   I fully agree with Bosch's analysis – see Saayman (2008:3-4).

of ethnically based, racially separated autogenous churches was an area where the Tomlinson Report had significant influence.

In 1957, the all-white Council of Dutch Reformed Churches (consisting of the four provincial synods) issued a policy statement to confirm and emphasise the importance of the formation and development of autonomous, autogenous churches in order to evangelise the indigenous South African people (Van der Walt 1963:443). The Council concluded that the formation of such churches was what Scripture required (without referring to or rescinding the 1857 decision, which still stood unchallenged). No mention was made of the established policy of constituting separate churches on the basis of historical practice – now it was supposedly based on theological and Scriptural requirements. An important shift had indeed taken place. Van der Walt (1963:466) concludes that the main principle of the formation of autogenous churches has now been established (and has indeed been the leading principle since 1881): the existence of a national character (*volksaard*) and national identity (*volkseie*) as ordinations of God's creation which should be respected. Indeed, Council considered identity and intimacy based on natural relationship and collective culture to be important determinants in the visible revelation of the Church of Christ (Durand 1961:120).[5]

I cannot agree with Van der Walt that it was a seamless progression since 1881 (also Smith 1980 for a similar objection). Early separation in the church was the practical result of the social and racial institution of Afrikaner, and indeed South African, life. As Smith points out, until the end of the nineteenth century there was indeed little evidence of any theological motivation for racial separation in the DRC. It was only later in the twentieth century that the DRC started providing theological justification for racially separated churches (Smith 1980:312). Indeed, Van Schalkwyk described the process thus in 1952:

> Under the present circumstances we are strong proponents of the policy of apartheid ... Apartheid has become part of our view of life. To scientifically justify such a view – and we need such justification – we are now looking for a scientific basis for our arguments in favour of the policy of apartheid. (cited in Deist 1990:136)[6]

---

5   Note the obvious similarities with the Tomlinson Report.
6   Van Schalkwyk actually wrote this in an attempt to make his colleagues realise to what extent the apartheid context was determining their theological thinking. His main argument was that for precisely the same contextual reasons a later generation of Afrikaner theologians might come to an opposite conclusion about the so-called 'biblical justification' of apartheid – prophetic words indeed!

It is my contention that for the first half of the twentieth century indeed the generally accepted missiological thinking on autonomous indigenous younger churches as expressed especially in Anglo-American missiology (with its emphasis on administrative and organisational categories) was considered adequate. By the mid-fifties of the twentieth century, though, the justification has adopted a clear ethno-theological nature (Cloete & Smit 1984:312). It seems quite clear to me that an important shift in theological thinking about the continued as well as the future existence of separate churches had therefore taken place.

This would be confirmed by developments subsequent to the formation of the General Synod of the Dutch Reformed Church in Africa in 1963. Originally the synod consisted of the various provincial DR Mission Church synods (in other words, with separation simply along practical and geographical lines). This soon started to change. In 1966, the Cape Synod of the DRCA was divided through the secession of the Regional Synod of Phororo (the Northern Cape). This sudden secession had a historical and contextual basis. It had already been reported to the Cape Synod in 1953 that the mission work in the Northern Cape (later Phororo) was progressing well, but that because of ethnic considerations (the converts were mainly Tswana speaking) the converts should rather be incorporated into the DRC Mission Church in the Western Transvaal (also Tswana speaking). At the time, nothing was done about this suggestion. When the Cape Synod of the DRCA decided in 1963 to recommend the secession of the Northern Cape, the justification was that 'the Tswana form a discrete ethnic group and are treated as such by the state' (*DRCA Synod* 1953:117). For the first time, ethnicity became the principle for separation within the DRCA – and my contention is that this is to a large degree a direct result of the findings and recommendations of the Tomlinson Report and the significant influence it had on DRC mission. There is indeed a sense in which one can argue that the Tomlinson Report provided the theological/philosophical capstone for the evolution of racist practice and thinking present in the (evolving) Afrikaner community and DRC since 1652. What started out as the practical everyday consequence of an inclination the colonists brought with them from Europe had now evolved into acceptance of the ethnical structuring of church membership as final solution. The church had an essential share in the development of this thinking and it could be expected that the DRC would eventually feel obliged to develop the ethno-theology required to justify racial separation in its churches.

The black churches' response since 1987

The meeting of the General Synod of the DRCA in 1987 took a major step forward. It signified a complete changing of the guard at the level of the moderature, with Rev. S. Buti elected as moderator, Rev. M. Maphoto as assessor, Dr N. Smith as actuarius, and Dr S. Pitikoe as scribe. Synod decided that the acceptance of the

Belhar Confession would not be a condition for unifying with the DRMC (or other DR churches). Yet the DRMC decisions at their 1986 synod in favour of unity of all four churches were confirmed. Immediately at the first meeting of the new moderature Dr Smith proposed that a letter be written to the moderamen of the DRC, DRMC and the RCA to invite them to a discussion of the possible unification of the racially separated DR churches. The DRC responded that they were not interested in such discussions, as they felt that unity was expressed adequately in the form of the Federal Mission Council of the DRC. The RCA responded that they would only take part in such discussions if the DRC also took part. The DRMC, however, responded positively and very enthusiastically that it would welcome such talks.

Eventually, the moderamen of the DRCA and the DRMC decided at the beginning of 1994 that the two churches would convene separate synod meetings at the same time in Cape Town during the year. There the final decisions about unification would be taken, after which the two synods would meet for the actual unification of the two churches. There were a few further hiccups (which would later prove to have serious consequences in the Free State and Phororo regional synods of the DRCA), but eventually, in April 1994, the Uniting Reformed Church of Southern Africa came into being.

Important decisions and milestones since 1994

Practical co-operation: The Commission for Witness and Service

The first URCSA Synod decided that the General Commission for Witness should continue efforts to coordinate and unify witness actions of the URCSA, DRC and the RCA. This decision was based on a consensus reached at the Vereeniging Consultation in March 1989 (Addendum 6) by the whole DRC family, which stated: 'We solemnly promise to work towards becoming one united, non-racial Reformed Church in Southern and Central Africa'. The latter decision was also received positively by the synods of the DRC and the RCA, so that at the 1997 synod of the URCSA the formation of a General Commission for Witness Action consisting of representatives of all three churches could be confirmed and written into the church Polity and Regulations of the URCSA (*Handelinge VGKSA Algemene Sinode* 1997:677-686).

Practical co-operation thus took place right from the start. Although the problems around the DRCA in the Free State and Phororo and the court cases in this regard led to stresses and strains, these were overcome. The 2005 General Synod could, therefore, deal positively with a decision taken by the URCSA, DRC and RCA to group together the various commissions dealing with witness and service in the three churches (*Acta URCSA General Synod* 2005:148). A united ministry group for Witness and Service consisting of representatives of the URCSA, DRC and the RCA formed and the DRCA was constituted in September 2006. Practical cooperation takes place at the local level in many areas, and at the national level in terms of theological education at Stellenbosch and Pretoria. This seems to be an area where a positive report can be issued on the 1994-2008 period. (For specific examples of practical co-operation, see Nel & Du Toit 2007:116-134)

Matters dealing with theology, faith and church polity

The URSCA General Synodical Committee (GSC) of Goudini in 1996 decided that the DRC should first adopt the Confession of Belhar before further discussions about unification could take place. This decision contradicted decisions taken by the synods of the DRCA and the DRMC before unification. This caused renewed strain in the talks with the DRC, RCA and the DRCA. However, the 2001 Synod of the URCSA repudiated the GSC and re-affirmed the pre-1994 decisions that Belhar would not be a condition before unification (*Acts URCSA General Synod* 2001:120). It took some time before a relationship of trust was re-established between the dialogue partners, but the organs of the URCSA tried by various means to undo the damage.

A totally new spirit was at work at the joint meeting of the General Synodical Commission of the URCSA and the moderamen of the General Synod of the DRC (extended executive committees at Esselenpark in June 2006 (Addendum 4). As a result, the two commissions consented to a covenant for church unification. Belhar would not be a condition for the continuation of the process and, according to Botha, it was decided that the national leadership of the relevant churches would meet at Achterberg (outside Krugersdorp) in November 2006 (cited in Nel & Du Toit, 2007:28). This meeting obviously did not have the church-political ('*kerkregtelike*') status of an official organ of any of the churches, but since the wider leadership of the URCSA, DRC, RCA as well as the DRCA were represented, it still carried great weight. A solemn decision was taken to pursue the road to unity jointly, despite future problems and obstacles. According to Botha, representatives of the URCSA who were present (and who had been involved in unity talks since 1994) describe this meeting as a complete sea change, a real *metanoia* for all concerned (cited in Nel & Du Toit 2007:25-30). It seemed as if at last the theological distrust was overcome through the deep realisation that 'we are brother and sisters for Jesus's sake'. There are clearly still outstanding issues such as the name of the envisaged unified church, the church-political position of local congregations in the same locality, etc. But it seems as if the theological foundation had been properly laid.

During the first half of 2008 new obstacles seem to have arisen. My report and interpretation here rest on oral information I have been given. According to this information, there is strong resistance among (some) local DRC congregations to organic unity with the URCSA (at least in some regional synods of the DRC). It is not clear whether this resistance is motivated by rejection of Belhar, but it is strong enough for the DRC to advise slowing down the process, and concentrating on practical co-operation at a local level.

Timeline

The debate about racial separation in the DRC goes back a long way. It is very necessary to keep this historical context in mind when taking any new decisions. A brief timeline will be helpful in respecting the historical context:

1. Racially separated Dutch Reformed churches came into being as a result of the racial prejudice of the early Dutch colonists and their descendants (the well-known weakness of some of the 1857 decision). This resulted in church ministry and practice which had the unintended consequence of bringing into being racially separated local congregations and eventually racially separated churches since 1881.

2. This remained the case until the 1940s-1950s, when ethno-theological arguments were introduced to justify not only racial separation, but also ethnic separation.

3. The black Dutch Reformed churches started responding to this racial separation in the DRC especially since the mid-1980s. The DRCA and the DRMC, in their debates about the relationship between racially separated Dutch Reformed churches, expressed a desire for unity straightaway.

4. The debate intensified around the adoption of the Confession of Belhar by the DRMC in 1986. After the General Synod of the DRCA in 1987, the DRCA issued an invitation to all four Dutch Reformed churches to participate in talks about unification. Only the DRMC responded positively to this invitation.

5. With the unification of the DRCA and the DRMC in 1994, the newly-constituted church expressed in its very name the desire that all other Dutch Reformed churches in southern Africa would join in the process of unification.

6. Since that time, the URCSA has steadfastly attempted to take the debate further and reach some fruitful conclusion. The DRC, RCA and the DRCA were all involved in the process and expressed a desire for greater unity. The Achterberg consultation seemed to provide a decisive breakthrough.

7. At the moment there appears to be some confusion about the immediate way ahead.

Possible scenarios

I prefer to give my personal assessment of the state of the debate in the form of possible scenarios:

The best-case scenario

The reality is that the debate about unity between racially separated DR churches has been going on for decades, and the specific debate between the URCSA and the DRC (later joined by the RCA and DRCA) from 1994 until 2008. During the course of this debate all fundamental theological issues have been dealt with to such an extent that a solemn decision to unite has been taken at Achterberg. This leads to the logical next step. The four churches take the necessary preliminary decisions in their respective synods, and set the date for a convent of unity ('*eenheidskonvent*'). Important outstanding issues, such as the name for the united church and language use, are deferred to the convent. Organic church unity takes place in the firm knowledge that no natural organism comes into life fully grown: a healthy adulthood presupposes a period of growth (sometimes through stormy adolescence and teen-age).

The worst-case scenario

A grim determination not to 'surrender', but rather to 'fight to the bitter end' (for 'the truth once given to the saints'?), wins the day. 'No further concessions!', becomes the slogan, and church unity discussions come to a shuddering halt in 'the 1857 cul-de-sac'. Family relations of more than 350 years and an imperfect but proud mission record count for nothing and what follows is a sad commentary on the teaching of the New Testament that no member of the body of Christ can tell any other member: 'I don't need you!'.

The in-between scenario

Despite the good progress made on matters of theology, church polity, practical co-operation, etc., another 'time-out' is called (in response to the inability of the DRC to move ahead). The growing weariness with the incredibly laborious pace of unity discussions, noticeable in places in the URCSA, brings the URCSA to decide to call a moratorium (temporary halt) on church unity discussions with the DRC (and probably the RCA and the DRCA, as they seem to choose to go at the DRC's pace). Instead, the church starts serious unity discussions with other members of the Reformed, Presbyterian, Congregational and other families of believers. The URCSA and the DRC in the Western Cape, equally tired by the slow progress, decide to go ahead and unite (probably as regional synods). The result is that we now have another new member of the DRC family, so if the talks start again (as they will have to – Jesus is still praying that we be one as he and the father are one – John 17:20-21), it will be between the URCSA, DRC, RCA, the DRCA and 'United Reformed Church Western Cape' (for lack of a better name). Who knows how this will influence the situation? Only a very brave person will try to predict.

Conclusion

I never meant to hide behind the smokescreen of 'possible scenarios'. Allow me a personal word, therefore, in conclusion. The scriptural imperative for the unity of Christ's followers across racial divides has been recognised by official DRC formations since its first synod in 1829. This imperative has not been gainsaid by the DRC, URCSA, RCA or the DRCA in a period of intense discussions since (at least) 1987. Various minutes of general synods of the URCSA over the years express appreciation for the positive approach to church unity in the other churches (*Acts General Synod URCSA* 2001:123). It seems that even the most apparent stumbling block, the Confession of Belhar, does not present insurmountable confessional or theological problems, as the General Synod of the DRC decided already in 1994 that Belhar was not in opposition with the Three Formularies of Unity. This decision was confirmed in 1998 (*Acts General Synod URCSA* 2001:120). It was against this background that the General Synod decided in 2005 that, since there seem to be no confessional impediments or differences between the four churches, to pursue unity on an organic basis (*Acts General Synod URCSA* 2005:136).

This positive approach and spirit can also be noticed in practical joint projects, co-operative church ministries, etc. The URCSA noted these instances of practical co-operation (e.g., see *Acts URCSA General Synod* 2001:123, 2005:148). If one then adds to this the positive evaluations of the Esselenpark and Achterberg meetings (Addendum 4), it seems as if issues around faith, spirituality and practical action have been successfully resolved. All that is lacking is the practical execution in church judicial terms of a decision to unite organically. Another delay will truly serve no purpose and can only be termed escapist. Outstanding issues, such as the name of the church and the language issue, are indeed important in themselves, but they are not issues of faith! and all four churches involved in the unity discussions state categorically that faith in the Lord Jesus Christ is the only decisive condition for membership of the church.

Any piecemeal unification, such as the possible unity of the two Western Cape regional synods, cannot really solve the problem and may indeed have a negative effect. The struggle to stabilise theological education in the Northern synods many years after Stellenbosch and Bellville united should serve as a warning sign. My own conclusion, therefore, is a passionate call to the relevant church structures:

Please face the consequences of your own theological statements (because nobody gainsays the necessity of one united church) and, with the courage of your convictions, take the logical next step: unite organically.

Bibliography

Primary sources

Skema van Werksaamhede en Handelinge, Tweede Algemene Sinode van die Verenigende Gereformeerde Kerk in Suider-Afrika. 1997. Bloemfontein.

Agenda General Synod Uniting Reformed Church in Southern Africa. Upington, 1–7 October 2001. Bloemfontein.

Acts of General Synod of the Uniting Reformed Church in Southern Africa 2005 (26 September–2 October, Pietermaritzburg).

Secondary sources

Ashforth, A. 1990. *The politics of official discourse in twentieth-century South Africa.* Oxford: Clarendon Press.

Belhar Confession. 1986. The official English translation of the *Belhar Confession 1986* approved by the General Synod of 2008. Belhar: LUS Printers.

Bosch, D.J. 1984. The roots and fruits of Afrikaner civil religion. In J.W. Hofmeyr & W.S. Vorster (eds), *New faces of Africa.* Pretoria: University of South Africa Press.

Crafford, D. 1982. *Aan God die dank. Geskiedenis van die sending van die Ned. Geref. Kerk binne die Republiek van Suid-Afrika en enkele aangrensende buurstate*, Deel I. Pretoria: NG Kerk Boekhandel.

Deist, F.E. 1990. Notes on the context and hermeneutic of Afrikaner civil religion, in Krtizinger J.N.J. & W Saayman (eds), *Mission in creative tension. A dialogue with David Bosch.*

Durand, J.J.F. 1961. *Una Sancta Catholica in sendingperspektief. 'n analise van die probleme rondom kerklike pluriformiteit en ekumenisiteit in die sending.* Amsterdam: Ten Have.

Hofmeyr, J.W. & Vorster W.S. (eds). 1984. *New faces of Africa. Essays in honour of Ben (Barend Jacobus) Marais.* Pretoria: University of South Africa Press.

Kamfer, P.P.A. 1955. *Die volksorganiese sendingmetode by Bruno Gutmann.* Amsterdam: Swets & Zeitlinger.

Krige, W.A. 1954. *Die probleem van eiesoortige kerkvorming by Christian Keysser.* Franeker: Wever.

Nel, R. & Du Toit J. (eds). 2007. *Ons pelgrimstog na eenheid/Our pilgrimage to unity: Conversations on healing and reconciliation within the Duthd Reformed Church family.* University of Pretoria, Department of Church History.

Saayman, W. 2007. *Being missionary, being human. An overview of Dutch Reformed Church Mission.* Pietermaritzburg: Cluster Publications.

Saayman, W. 2008. The Tomlinson Report and the third Wave of Dutch Reformed mission: Context and content. *Nederduitse Gereformeerde Teologiese Tydskrif* 49(3/4):240-253.

Smith, N.J. 1980. *Elkeen in sy eie taal. Die planting van afsonderlike kerke vir die nie-blanke bevolkingsgroepe deur die Nederduitse Gereformeerde Kerk in Suid-Afrika: 'n teologiese beoordeling*, 2e Uitgawe. Pretoria: NG Kerk Boekhandel.

Tomlinson Report. 1955. *Samevatting van die verslag van die Kommissie vir die Sosio-ekonomiese Ontwikkeling van die Bantoegebiede binne die Unie van Suid-Afrika.* Pretoria: Government Printer.

Van der Walt, I.J. 1963. *Eiesoortigheid en die sending: eiesoortige kerkvorming as missiologiese probleem met besondere verwysing na Suid-Afrika.* Potchefstroom: Pro Rege Pers.

SECTION TWO

Theological and ethical themes regarding the Belhar Confession

THE UNIFICATION PROCESS IN THE DUTCH REFORMED CHURCH FAMILY AND THE UNITING REFORMED CHURCH IN SOUTHERN AFRICA

The confessional basis and Confession of Belhar

Leepo Modise[1]

Introduction

Church unity is a matter of the utmost priority. It is a holy matter of the Holy Spirit. The church is Christ's body and He is the head of His unique creation which was bought by His blood. What the members of the church do with His church must take place under the guidance of the Holy Spirit and according to the living Word of Christ. Christ has only one body and desires the unity of His church in fellowship, in service, in love and in suffering. Church unity is not a question of choice – the people of God are sure that it is God's will according to his Word. The time when unity should be achieved is not the people's choice either, as people are divided and separated because of sin. Consequently, the day of salvation is now – unity must come as quickly as possible. This chapter discusses the concept of church unity, and its surrounding problems, such as acceptance of the Belhar Confession as the confession of a united church.

Church unity

One should distinguish between church unity and the unification of the church. Church unity is a given; the unification of the church, or rather of churches, is something we should work towards achieving. The Confession of Belhar (1986) states:

> [Church] unity is, therefore, both a gift and an obligation for the church of Jesus Christ; that through the working of God's Spirit it is a binding force, yet simultaneously a reality which must be earnestly pursued and sought: one which the people of God must continually be built up to attain; that this unity must become visible so that the world may believe that separation, enmity and hatred between people and groups is sin which Christ has

---

[1] Prof. Leepo Modise is attached to the Department of Philosophy, Practical and. Systematic Theology, University of South Africa. Prof. Leepo was elected as the actuarius of the General Synod (church law expert) at the General Synod 2012 and is currently the moderator of the Southern Regional Synod.

already conquered, and accordingly that anything which threatens this unity may have no place in the church and must be resisted.[2]

Church unity is a given, as a fruit of the cross of Christ. The twofold unity has been affected: between God and human beings and between Jews and Gentiles (these two groups representing believers from every nation). The relevance of the Belhar Confession is not confined to southern Africa. It addresses three key issues of concern to all Reformed and global churches: unity of the church and unity among all people; reconciliation within the church and society; and God's justice. In a certain sense, this unity is already unification because God and humanity, and human beings among themselves and even humanity and nature, started out in close fellowship. Gaillardetz (2008:85) postulates that this unity is based on the doctrine of the Trinity. The doctrine of the Trinity describes how God is one and illustrates to us that God's unity is a relational, differentiated and fecund unity (it is able to support the growth of other healthy forms of unity). By analogy, it is the same with the church (body of Christ). If the oneness of the church emphasises the church's deep spiritual unity as the one people of God and the body of Christ, the unity of the church highlights the relational, differentiated and fecund character of the unity of the church. The catholicity of the church reminds Christians that the unity of the church is, following the analogy of the triune life of God, a differentiated and relational unity (Gaillardetz 2008:85). Hence, the Belhar Confession begins with the triune life of God, which is able to support the growth of healthy church unity.[3]

It is safe to say that most of the sixteenth-century reformers were no longer persuaded by the ability of any set of ecclesiastical structures, in and of themselves, to preserve church unity. The church must be sought not in any single institutional structure, but in the one faith in Christ offered in response to the Word of God (Gaillardetz 2008:102). It is argued that the unity of Christians cannot be fostered otherwise than by promoting the return of the dissidents to the one true Church of Christ, which in the past they so unfortunately abandoned. Return, we say, to the one true Church of Christ, which by the will of the founder forever remains what Christ himself destined the church to be for the common salvation of the human race (Neuner & Dupuis 1982:376). The argument is that the church needs to be united around Christ and the Holy Communion.

---

[2] All extracts from the Confession of Belhar in this chapter are taken from the English translation at Addendum 15, The Confession of Belhar. Also available at http://urcsa.net/wp-content/uploads/2016/02/Belhar-Confession.pdf

[3] Belhar Confession, articles 1 and 2: 'We believe in the triune God, Father, Son and Holy Spirit, who gathers, protects and cares for the church through Word and Spirit. This, God has done since the beginning of the world and will do to the end. We believe in one holy, universal Christian Church, the communion of saints called from the entire human family.'

When dealing with church unity and the triune life of God as the supporter of the growth of a healthy church unity, one needs to borrow the concept of *'ujamaa'* from the African philosophical theory of togetherness. The Swahili term *'ujamaa'* has a rich and broad semantic field of meaning, suggesting the notion of extended family in the service of Julius Nyerere's programme of African socialism. African theologians have appreciated the term as denoting church unity (Gaillardetz 2008:127). This term denotes the togetherness of the people of God as called by God from all racial groups, reconciled by Christ through his blood and renewed by the spirit of God.

Onwubiko (2001:36) explains that the concept of *'ujamaa'*, properly understood as 'togetherness', 'familyhood', does not depend on consanguinity. It depicts a 'community spirit' of togetherness, which regards all people as 'brothers and sisters'. This community spirit in turn shapes distinctive African understandings of personhood. In most African societies, there is a very limited sense of individual autonomy. Hence, the Uniting Reformed Church in Southern Africa (URCSA) as a Reformed and African church confesses and confirms this oneness or togetherness through its Confession of Belhar and church order, as is stated in Article 4.3 of the church order, which reads:

> The believers accept mutual responsibility for one another in their spiritual and physical needs. The congregation lives as a family of God where they are inextricably bound to one another and where they mutually share joy and sorrow. Each considers the other higher than him/herself and no one only cares about his/her own needs, but also about the needs of others. In this way, they share one another's burdens and fulfil the law of Christ. (URCSA Church Order 2013, Art. 4.3)

One is human because of others, with others, and for others (*motho ke motho ka batho bang*): 'I am because we are, and since we are therefore we are, and since we are therefore I am.' 'I belong, therefore I am.' In an African context, the social aspect in this regard predominates over the individualistic aspect. A human being exists as a person, naturally and necessarily enmeshed in a web of relationships. Human beings' very existence, their human reality, is bound up in those relationships. These relationships provide the most prolific, the most profound and the most intense source of motivation for living and for action (Gaillardetz 2008:127).

In this sense, the term *'ujamaa'* is highly suggestive as a way of describing the church as the family of God. It is not surprising, then, that this metaphor is used in this chapter to denote the unity of the church in the URCSA as a Reformed and African church. The church family has its origin in the blessed Trinity in the depths of which the Holy Spirit is the bond of communion. Imagining the church as family offers a helpful path for relating the relationality of family life to the trinitarian foundations of the church. Hence, the Confession of Belhar opens with the unity of God, then moves to the unity of human beings (church and society) and ends with the unity of God, which is the circle that cannot be broken by any forces of evil.

In an African perspective, the church is seen as a distinctive form of family, which clearly reflects the sense of reciprocal responsibilities and overarching interdependence that must exist among all church members. Given the traditional African emphasis on the extended family as a place of belonging and a context for a deeper experience of solidarity and care for others, the church as a family provides an apt starting point for African ecclesial reflection (Gaillardetz 2008:128). Hence, the URCSA as a Reformed and African church issued the following church order (Art. 4):

> The congregation forms a community of believers in a particular place to serve God, one another and the world. The service of God has a bearing on the whole life of the congregation and therefore includes service to one another and the world. The essence of this service of God is found where the congregation meets round the Word of God and the sacraments. There God is worshipped and praised; his Word listened to, the sacraments received, and all needs brought before him in order to strengthen the believers in their faith and to prepare them for their service to one another and the world. The believers accept mutual responsibility for one another in their spiritual and physical needs. The congregation lives as a family of God where they are inextricably bound to one another and where they mutually share joy and sorrow. Each considers the other higher than him/herself and no one only cares about his/her own needs, but also about the needs of others. In this way, they share one another's burdens and fulfil the law of Christ. The congregation's service to humankind and the world consists in proclaiming God's reconciling and liberating acts in and for the world, living out Christ's love, calling humankind to reconciliation with God and reconciliation and peace amongst one another. The congregation serves God, who in a special way, is the God of the suffering, the poor and those who are wronged (victimised), by supporting people in whatever form of suffering and need they may experience, by witnessing and fighting against all forms of injustice; by calling upon the government and the authorities to serve all the inhabitants of the country by allowing justice to prevail and by fighting against injustice. The congregation serves God by witnessing against all rulers and those who are privileged who out of selfishness seek their own interest and who have power over others and who do them wrong. (URCSA Church Order 2013, Art. 4)

This 'family' concept of the church in southern Africa is not actualised beyond congregational borders, and it has not been a reality in South African Christians' experience in the church of Christ, or in the so-called DRC family.[4] The service of God, service to one another and service to the world has not been a reality because of enmity and hatred between whites and blacks, divisions within the church along racial lines, and in terms of class and gender, which are sins that Christ overcame on the cross.

This unity (family) was destroyed by sin and had to be restored by the reconciliatory work of Christ on the cross; in this sense unity is given through faith in Christ. This church unity is like a reconciliatory (saving) act of God, in fact, as part of a reconciliatory act of God, this church unity is achieved on the cross and is afterwards to be applied by the Holy Spirit in the lives of the people of God. This is the process of unification. The proclamation of the Confession of Belhar that reconciliation is possible in Christ and that cultural and other 'natural' differences are gifts for the building up of the church and society should be heard loudly and clearly across South Africa and the whole of Africa.

Comprehensive reconciliation is only possible through Christ, His sacrifice on the cross and His Holy Spirit. This is so because our sin, our wrong acts and practices are part of our history in our practical situation. These historical sins have been deposited in our personal lives and in our relationships, as well as in our patterns of behaviour and in the consequent structures which we have created. These sins have been cemented into the basic fabric of our lives and our relationships. What is even more alarming is that we as Christians remain sinners until the end of our lives, albeit saved sinners. This means that the possibility of sin, of falling short, of rebellion against God's ways and of lovelessness is a permanent situation in which we not only personally find ourselves, but in which we live, in relationships and structures. Consequently, we must guard and pray continuously against all possible aberrations from the Gospel in society and in reformed practice. In view of the above, the statement now becomes relevant that reconciliation is only possible through the cross of Christ. Our sin and failures and their reflections in our personal, relationships and structural lives cannot be rectified merely by change, by better behaviour or by new approaches. Our sin has to be wiped out, removed, destroyed and forgotten. How is that possible? Through confession of our sins to Christ, faith

---

4   The DRC family, namely the Dutch Reformed Church (whites), the Dutch Reformed Church in Africa (blacks) and the Reformed Church in Africa (Indians). They are a family because they share the same identity in terms of racial division and confessions of faith. While the URCSA is an independent family, which is identified by the Confession of Belhar and which rejects divisions among people based on race, colour, gender or class. Hence, we speak of unification of the DRC family and the URCSA in the title of the chapter.

in him to remove, destroy and wipe them from God's memory, as well as by the realisation that they have also been wiped out from our memory. This is a deep cleansing experience in our personal and national lives (Meyer 1991:9).

Furthermore, Koopman postulates that, in the three articles of the Belhar Confession the people who confess Belhar Confession, confessed that separating, dividing and alienating the diversity of people in South African churches and society was not God's plan or solution for South Africa, because God is the God who brings unity among his diversity of people (Koopman 2007:96-97). In a context where the pseudo-gospel that the death and resurrection of Jesus Christ was not strong enough to reconcile people was proclaimed, the faith of Belhar protested: God is the God who reconciles humans with Himself, humans with each other and with the rest of creation, and in the context of justice that wanted people to doubt whether they are fully human and whether they are fully children of God, the Belhar Confession states that God is the God of justice who identifies in a special way with the suffering, the poor and the wronged in an action of injustice.

The unification process within the DRC family and the URCSA

The process of unification needs to start somewhere when a split in the church has occurred. There is no church unification process without the first stage, which is a split or division. Therefore, it is important to briefly sketch the background to the split in the church in general and the DRC family. A further church unification process is of paramount importance, since the Belhar Confession emphasises that church unity is a gift and it is also an obligation that the people of God need to pursue. Hence, the point of departure lies in tracing the footprint of the split in the church in general and the DRC in particular.

Church divisions have taken place throughout the history of religion; and the longer the history continued the worse things became. For many reasons, Protestantism became the prime example of a faith that give rise to the forming of separate churches. It appears that the Reformation never developed an ecclesiology compatible with its soteriology. Reformed theology and Western theology have developed in such a way that ecclesiology is commonly stated in the ideal mode. It airily evokes what the church is in the purpose of God, but disdains the messy human reality. So often ecclesiology offers a 'God's eye view' but turns a blind eye to the human aspect (Avis 2006:204). Hence the Reformation has never developed an ecclesiology compatible with its soteriology, because soteriology is found in the cross through the reconciling act of Christ where people from the messy human reality are reconciled with God and with their fellow human beings to make this gift

(Unity) a reality for the world. Once the human reality is not taken into consideration, then ecclesiology stands alone without soteriology. This results in divisions.

The diversity of Christian communities reflected in the Scriptures was to increase in the following centuries. The history of many of these divisions has been written by the victors, and so we researchers and Christians tend to look back on early Christianity from the perspective of an orthodoxy challenged by different heretical and schismatic movements. The irony is that such an approach is old-fashioned and fails to take account of the ways in which many of these movements that were later viewed as heretical or schismatic assumed that they were in fact authentically Christian (Ehrman 2003).

Gaillardetz (2008:90) argues that, as Christianity took root in the Mediterranean, it was inevitable that it would be influenced by larger cultural contexts. Beyond the distinctions in Christian traditions of the fifth century, a more sweeping division in Christianity began to develop in the third and fourth centuries; this corresponded to the two dominant cultures of the time. The eventual schism between the Christian churches associated with these two cultures is often dated to 1054, but they began drifting apart much earlier. This progressive drift was the result of a volatile confluence of political, social, economic and theological factors. As early as the third century, one can detect subtle but growing theological differences between the Eastern and Western traditions. The Western theological trajectory was more practical, the Eastern more speculative. The longer the history continued the worse the split or divisions became. One can go on and on regarding this division of the church in history. One needs to consider the South African historical context of the Dutch Reformed Church in South Africa.

In South Africa, the DRC became the best-known example of splitting the church on racial grounds. This chapter is all about the process of reuniting the racially divided DRC family. It is importance to give a brief historical background on how this division began in the DRC. In 1652, the Dutch established a settlement at the Cape and introduced Reformed theology to South Africa. Up to 1857, people of mixed descent as well as people of African heritage were accepted as fully-fledged members of the DRC in South Africa. On 29 April 1829, the DRC Synod dealt with an enquiry by the Somerset West congregation regarding separate facilities and services for congregants of mixed descent. The infamous DRC Synod of 1857 approved separate services for 'coloured' members of the church (Plaatjies-Van Huffel 2011, 2013a, 2013b, 2014).

Various foreign mission organisations started working in South Africa, which led to the formation of several denominations among the indigenous people of South Africa who would otherwise have been excluded from the main churches. This process motivated the DRC in South Africa to start its own independent mission work. In 1857, the DRC Synod decided to have separate services for its coloured members.[5] The origin of the URCSA lies in the DRC mission work through the establishment of the Dutch Reformed Mission Church (DRMC) and the Dutch Reformed Church in Africa (DRCA), which united on 14 April 1994 to form the URCSA. There were, and are, both black and white churches in the Dutch Reformed block, as described below:

- The DRC, with two-and-half million white members, was the largest of the three. This was, in fact, the oldest autonomous denomination in South Africa, having become independent of its mother church in the Netherlands in 1824. It began mission work among the indigenous peoples of South Africa in 1826 and among the black people of South Africa in 1826, as a result of which the three black churches of this block were created.
- A separate church, the (DRMC) was formed in 1881. This comprised people of mixed race, known both officially and popularly as 'coloureds'. The church had a membership of 573 400 in 1970.
- The DRCA for African people was founded in 1963 as an offshoot of the DRMC with a membership of 924 000. In 1994, these two churches tried to reunite as the URCSA.
- The Reformed Church in Africa for Indian people, founded in 1968. Its membership totalled only a few thousand (Best 2002: xxii-xxiii).

From 1957 onwards, these churches were linked in a Federal Council of Dutch Reformed Churches, the member churches of which met for consultation every four years. In 1982, this body was transformed into a General Synod, which had a certain amount of jurisdiction and which, from then on, met every two years. As will be seen, its member churches were separated on ethnic lines. This of course was very much in line with the doctrine of apartheid, although these ethnic divisions were also in line with the strand of thinking in the international missionary movement, which favoured the creation of three independent churches. Still, although they were born of apartheid thinking, in time, the black Dutch Reformed churches were to reject apartheid decisively. This was expressed in the 1994 formation of the URCSA, which brought the DRMC and DRCA together in a single united body. However, before this, these churches had made their rejection of apartheid clear by moving into membership with the South African Council of Churches (SACC). They were to play a crucial role in forcing the abandonment of apartheid in both church and state in the last two decades of the twentieth century (Best 2002: xxii–xxiii).

---

5   For a more comprehensive history on the historical background of the Belhar Confession please read the essay in this publication, 'Acceptance, Adoption, Advocacy, Reception and Protestation: A Chronology of the Belhar Confession' by Mary-Anne Plaatjies-Van Huffel.

The URCSA consists of approximately 1 230 000 members, of whom about 500 000 are confessing members (excluding all those who are only baptised) and 683 congregations. Its name (which is in the continuous tense) and its logo (which is an incomplete circle) reflect the church's emphasis on unity and its hope for even greater church unification within the family of God. The church consists of hundreds of congregations. These congregations belong to the regional presbytery and a particular number of presbyteries form a synod. The URSCA consists of seven regional synods, namely Namibia, Northern Transvaal, Southern Transvaal, Phororo (Northern Cape), Cape, KwaZulu-Natal, Free State and Lesotho.

If unity is indeed a fruit of the reconciliatory work of Christ on the cross, reuniting the DRC family and the URCSA are of paramount importance, because it is a biblical and a confessional imperative. The process of unifying these churches is as important as calling people to faith in Christ or as important as the Eucharist and the Word of God. When the people of God are gathered at the Table of the Lord to partake of the Lord's Supper, they believe that this action does not only draw them into saving communion with God in Christ, but also constitutes them as Christ's body, the church. The metaphor of 'the body of Christ' has a standing history, with a rich breadth of meaning. The body of Christ could refer to:

- the Word made flesh;
- the Eucharistic body; and
- the body of Christ, the church.

De Lubac (1949) argues that, although it is true that the church constituted the Eucharist, it was equally true that the Eucharist established the church. The fluidity of the meaning of the metaphor of the body of Christ helped to preserve the importance of the connections between sacramental theology and ecclesiology. Consider the following passage from a famous sermon by St. Augustine: 'Since you are the body of Christ and his members, it is your mystery that is placed on the Lord's Table, it is your mystery that you receive ... be what you see, and receive what you are (Hill 1993:300-301).

Consider also the following quote from Gaillardetz:
> For what is the bread? It is the body of Christ. And what do those who receive it become? The body of Christ, is not many bodies but one body. Or as bread is completely one, although made of up many grains of wheat, and these, albeit unseen, nonetheless remain present, in such a way that their difference is not apparent since they have been made a perfect whole, so too are we mutually joined to one another and together united with Christ. (Gaillardetz 2008:87)

In fact, the unity of the church is indeed directly related to the world's coming to faith in Christ (John 17:20ff).

At this stage, it has become clear that the unification of the church is by no means an easy task and this is not only true of the process taking place in the DRC family and the URCSA. There are many reasons, such as vested interests and ideologically supported suspicions. Several non-theological obstacles have already been dealt with in the journey to reunification.

Theologically, it should be kept in mind that the division of the church in general and in the DRC family and the URCSA is a form of a sin and the reunification of the church is part of reconciliation/redemption, which means a fight against sin and is part of the process of overcoming the effects of sin. If one takes into account the power of sin and the fact that sin creates structures of its own that resist dismantling; if one further remember that the divisions in the DRC family are part of the inclusive blueprint of apartheid that created extraordinarily strong structures that the people of God will wrestle with for decades to come, even in the democratic South Africa where apartheid has theoretically been dismantled but internally exists as internalised oppression and internalised domination, then one would understand the resistance against the process of reunification a little better. In one way or the other communities grow, develop and pass through certain stages. Ultimately the entire society also grows and develops towards a particular point of transition (Bandura 1997.23).

The view that black people are inherently inferior to white people has been referred to as 'old-fashioned' racism. Old-fashioned racism was both blatant and explicit. Until 1994, apartheid was legalised in South Africa and this legalised system provided an extreme example of structural racism. This brand of racism involved behaviours, practices and attitudes that overtly defined black people as inferior to white people and less powerful. These behaviours, practices and attitudes have caused a serious division in society and have left the entire South African society in a state of disintegration.

This resistance is a modern form of racism (Batts 1989:18). It is helpful to distinguish between old-fashioned racism and modern racism since it is useful to recognise and acknowledge the way in which racism has changed. This form of racism has created a sophisticated division among the people of God. Modern racism involves the giving of non-race-related reasons for behaviours that continue to exclude and discriminate against other people. It is important to think of modern racism as internalised dominance; attitudes that are so deeply entrenched that they exist at a subconscious level. While modern racism is often not intentionally malicious, it is still based on the assumption that black people are inferior to white people. As a result, this subtler form of racism continues to deny access to black people. The negative feelings that are attached to this belief do not change or disappear just because of changes in laws and practices. Instead, the feelings must be submerged and hidden because of the changes in what is viewed as legal and politically correct in our society.

The reference in the negotiations to culture and language (like Afrikaans) is an example of non-theological obstacles and is quite comprehensible. The DRC was seen for so many years as the last bulwark for Afrikaners that it is no surprise that cultural arguments against unification should be brought into play. It is very interesting that the ballgame has now changed from non-theological to more theological in nature, namely the acceptance and the optionality of the Belhar Confession as obstacles to the process of unification of the DRC family and the URCSA. Prof. Piet Strauss, the then moderator of the General Synod of the DRC, said the following in his greeting to the General Synod of URCSA at Hammanskraal in 2008:

> It has, however, been said that we (DRC) are excluding the Confession of Belhar from the confessions of the new denomination planned and that we departed from the decision taken in this regard at Hartenbos in 2004. What we said is that there [is] strong resistance in the DRC against Belhar as a confession, but that we propose that there should be room for those in favour of and against Belhar. In essence, this is still Hartenbos 2004. I also noted in the letter of the Synodical Commission of your [URCSA] Cape Synod to our [DRC] Synod in the Western Cape that this 'DRC-view' as endorsed by our [DRC] Western Cape Moderature was not acceptable to URCSA. In the same letter we are accused of 'shifting the goalposts' around [the] Belhar Confession. (*Acts General Synod URCSA* 2008:137)

The Confession of Belhar has always been a stumbling block in the unity process, with the DRC hitherto being unwilling to adopt this document as a confession. The URCSA, for its part, have said that they are not willing to negotiate the exclusion of this confession from a new, united church. The compromise the DRC is opting for is willingness to negotiate ways in which the Belhar Confession could form part of the confessional basis of a new, united church, on the condition that it must not be compulsory for all members of the new church to subscribe to the Confession (*Die Ligdraer*, 8 November 1998, p. 1).

The Confession of Belhar in relation to church unity

The Confession of Belhar seems to have become one of the stumbling blocks in the process, despite the finding of the General Synod of the DRC of 1990 that the

Belhar Confession was not inherently in conflict with its present articles of faith. In fact, there are remarkable agreements between the Belhar Confession and the two versions of *Church and Society* of the DRC (*Die Kerkbode* 27 January 1995). These agreements do not concern side issues, but central ones related to the rejection of apartheid and they represent a clear development in the thinking of the DRC. The above point is confirmed by the Rustenburg Declaration of November 1990, point 2.2, which reads as follows:

> As representatives of the Christian Church in South Africa, we recognise that the South African situation owes much to the content of western colonialism, to the stifling of conscience by inherited social attitudes which blind communities to the wrong they reflect and to a weakness common to the worldwide church in dealing with social evil. Now, however, we confess our sin and acknowledge our heretical part in the policy of apartheid which has led to such extreme suffering for so many in our land. We denounce apartheid, in its intention, its implementation and its consequences, as an evil policy. The practice and defence of apartheid as though it were biblically and theologically legitimated is an act of disobedience to God, a denial of the Gospel of Jesus Christ and a sin against our unity in the Holy Spirit. (Rustenburg Declaration of November 1990:1)

Kerk en Samelewing (*Church and Society*) is a witness document accepted as a policy guideline for the DRC at the General Synod held in Cape Town in October 1986. Naude argues that on the surface there is a strong convergence in the content of the Confession of Belhar and *Church and Society* (1986) (Naude 2012:148). It is important to note that DRC Synod members view the Belhar Confession as being on the same level as the two versions of *Church and Society*, however, he document was never declared a 'confession'. Furthermore, there was no *status confessionis* that led to the drafting of *Church and Society*; therefore, the argument does not hold up. In that sense, the way these two churches viewed *Church and Society* and the Belhar Confession became a stumbling block in the way of unification in the 1990s and early 2000s.

The DRC accepting but not accepting the Belhar Confession

The wave of acceptance of the Belhar Confession moved into the Dutch Reformed Church. In May 2011, the DRC Regional Synod of the Southern and Western Cape accepted the Belhar Confession as a confession of faith based on Scripture and Reformed traditions. The decision of the synod reads as follows:

> The synod is convinced that the biblical call for justice for all people, reconciliation between people, and the unity of the church are at the heart of the gospel. The Belhar Confession gives expression to the call of the gospel

in a different way than the other confessions of the church. The synod, as a church meeting, accepts the Belhar Confession and calls on the General Synod of the Dutch Reformed Church to make the Belhar Confession in a church-orderly way part of the confessional base of the Dutch Reformed Church. (*Acta NGK Wes-Kaapland Sinode* 2011:77)[6]

The decision of the regional Southern and Western Cape Synod was a huge step towards the acceptance of Belhar Confession by the General Synod of the DRC in October 2011. Dr Braam Hanekom and Rev. Nelis van Rensburg came to the session and pleaded that the General Synod should take a decision on Belhar as was done at the Cape Synod and then asked that the formal route be followed. They explained the process that they followed at the Cape where the Belhar Confession was accepted by the Regional Synod. Dr Hanekom and Rev. Van Rensburg at the table closed the debate with arguments why Belhar should be accepted. Rev. Van Rensburg showed how Belhar fitted all the general requirements of a confession. This argument illustrated how the decision of the Cape Synod had an impact on the decision of the DRC General Synod to accept Belhar Confession (URCSA pastoral letter of 14 October 2011).

The other wave of acceptance was seen as a miracle on the 13 October 2011 when the DRC General Synod accepted Belhar Confession with more than two-thirds majority (90% votes). This was another step that led to the acceptance of the Belhar Confession by other regions, presbyteries and church councils. Kuyler, in a URSCA pastoral letter to congregation writes:

> By this time all of you [URCSA members] have heard that the General Synod of the Dutch Reformed Church has accepted the Belhar Confession on 13 October 2011 with a majority of more than 90%. This event was attended by the moderator, Prof. Thias Kgatla, and the scribe, Dr Dawid Kuyler as fraternal delegates to the meeting. The Dutch Reformed Church took the first step in accepting Belhar by showing the way to regional synods, presbyteries and congregations. According to their church order, Article 44, they will now start the process of taking Belhar back to the congregations and guiding them to come to the same position as what the General Synod took. Their leadership has committed themselves to assist and gave us [URCSA representatives]

---

6 Translation: 'Die sinode is oortuig dat die Bybelse eis vir geregtigheid vir alle mense, versoening tussen alle mense en die eenheid van die kerk tot die kern van die evangelie behoort. Die Belydenis van Belhar verwoord hierdie evangeliese eis om geregtigheid, versoening en eenheid op 'n ander wyse as die ander belydenisskrifte van die kerk. Die sinode aanvaar as kerkvergadering die Belydenis van Belhar en daarom versoek hierdie vergadering die Algemene Sinode om die Belydenis van Belhar op 'n kerkordelike wyse deel van die Nederduitse Gereformeerde Kerk se belydenisgrondslag te maak.'

the assurance that they will ask URCSA to be part of this journey. (URCSA pastoral letter of 14 October 2011)

The Belhar Confession is relevant to all Christian churches today because it addresses critical issues emphasised in Scripture – unity among the people of God, reconciliation within the church and society, injustices of all kinds, and God's bias on behalf of those who have been wronged. There was a great hope from the URCSA after the 2011 DRC General Synod when the synod started the process to accept the Belhar Confession to the local congregations, presbyteries and the regional synods. This was a great breakthrough in the DRC, but at the same time there was a stumbling block concerning the inclusion of the confession in the DRC's church order in Article 1. The problem lay in Article 44, which states that all regional synods should obtain two-thirds majority for the church order article to be changed. In the process of accepting Belhar Confession, out of ten regional synods, six convened and out of these six, three (Free State, Namibia and Northern Cape) voted 'No' to the inclusion of the Confession to Article 1. Highfield did not reach a two-thirds majority and only two agreed to the inclusion of Belhar Confession into their church order.

Taking these statistics and Article 44.1[7] of the DRC into consideration it stands to reason that the Belhar Confession could not be included into the confessional basis of the DRC in Article 1. The church order is written in such a way that church unity in relation to the Belhar Confession should be very difficult. One needs to look how the DRC plays with words within Article 44[8] in terms of the amendments of Article 44.1 and 44.2. All other articles can be amended by two-third majority of the General Synod while 44.1 and 44.2 can only be amended after all regional synods approve with two-third majority, then the General Synod with two third majority. The DRC uses the church order Article 44 as a gatekeeper to prevent the Belhar Confession from entering into its confessional basis We have learned from the apartheid era that if one needs or wants to keep people separate one must have many acts and regulations; this is the same situation in the DRC now. The Belhar Confession is part of the package of the church unification together with church unity and restorative justice. If one may use the metaphor of the three-legged pot for the united church, without the Belhar Confession this church will not stand. These three points are

---

7   Article 44.1 states that amendment of the confessional basis is possible only after it has been approved by a two-thirds majority of each synod and two-thirds of all the church councils, each supporting it with a two-thirds majority.
8   44.2. Article 44.1 and 44.2 of the church order are amended after each synod has approved it with a two-thirds majority and General Synod thereafter approves it with a two-thirds majority.
    44.3. General Synod may, with the exception of Article 44.1 and 44.2, amend or augment the church order with a two-thirds majority.

the points of reference in the Memorandum of Agreement between URCSA and DRC (Addendum 11).

It is interesting to note that issues of church divisions, poverty, classism, oppression, social injustice and hatred were seen as pertaining exclusively to the DRMC. The acceptance of the Belhar Confession by other Reformed churches in the world proved that the DRC were not serious and genuine about their claims that the Belhar Confession dealt exclusively with DRMC issues. The relevance of the confession is not confined to southern Africa or its religious context. It addresses three key issues of concern to all churches: unity of the church and unity among all people, reconciliation within the church and society, and God's justice. The Belhar Confession as a Reformed confession has been carried by URCSA on behalf of all Reformed churches. The words of Barth justify this:

> A reformed creed is the statement, spontaneously and publicly formulated by a Christian community within a geographically limited area, which, until further action, defines its character to outsiders, and which, until further action, gives guidance for its own doctrine and life; it is a formulation of the insight currently given to the whole Christian Church by the revelation of God in Jesus Christ by the Holy Scripture alone. (Barth 1962:112)

In line with Barth, the URCSA General Synod of 2005 confirmed that the Belhar Confession, although written and accepted by the church at a specific time and place, is a living confession inspiring the church worldwide, and is not aimed against certain groups and not confined by political or geographical boundaries. It is made by the members of the URCSA, which is not a church with a confession whose value lies in the mindless repetition of words, but a confessing church, on whom the obligation rests to allow the confession to become a way of life, utterly convincing in its love, utterly compelling in its call. The way in which the Confession of Belhar has reached far beyond URCSA and South Africa to constantly inspire the churches of our reformed family and the broader ecumenical movement is a source of humble rejoicing and deep gratitude for which the URCSA praises God (Acts General Synod URCSA 2005:152). The act of acceptance of the Belhar Confession nullifies the false claims of the DRC that this confession is exclusively a DRMC confession that addresses DRMC issues.

Furthermore, the Belhar Confession has become such a symbol of the faith and perseverance of suppressed and oppressed people in a situation of a 'total onslaught' on their human dignity, heritage and history (to mention only what the Truth and Reconciliation Commission has revealed so clearly about the gross injustices of this system supported by the DRC) that a 'No' by the DRC to Belhar as a fourth confession can only strengthen the existing impression that the DRC has shown very few signs of remorse for its support of apartheid, both structurally and at grassroots level. The failure to accept Belhar as the fourth confession will be interpreted as a sign of the utmost insensitivity.

This is even more so as the confession of the DRC that apartheid is a sin, and its confession of the role it played in establishing and upholding apartheid has not achieved any sort of credibility with those who were on the receiving side. The few very carefully formulated sentences penned during a few synodical meetings were not very credible. This impression of a very faint and softly spoken confession was strengthened by the fact that virtually no public and symbolic acts followed – acts like confessing at the synodical meetings of the other family members or asking them to co-operate in a few big worship services where public confession could be made to those who suffered, or even organising services of confession at the local level. The DRC appears to think it may just possibly, here and there, incidentally and unintentionally, have hurt a few people, and that a few rather unemotional words can easily rectify the situation.

The Uniting Reformed Church in Southern Africa on the Belhar Confession

There is, however, another way of looking at it. If church unity is a given, a fruit of the redemption wrought on the cross, is it not true that the people of God should accept one another unconditionally? Is this not what God does, not justifying the righteous, but the godless? Is agreement on the articles of faith or cross of Christ the basis for unity? Should churches (re-) unite because they agree with each other or should they (re-) unite because they are one in Christ, and afterwards grow closer to each other in their faith while they live in mutual fellowship? What is the best situation for agreement: living at a distance and bargaining in a negotiation process, or living in fellowship in which we share something of our life experience? Is not one of the grave problems of the DRC from grassroots up to the level of the local church council and minister that these whites have had virtually no exposure to the atrocities of the apartheid era – in state, society and church – and that the only hope of their ever having such exposure may be in living in the same local church as those Christians who have experienced apartheid directly? Does not the name Uniting Reformed Church invite this church to go into a unification process with the DRC without the condition of prior acceptance of the Belhar Confession? The position of the URCSA is very clear in terms of the Belhar Confession in the new unified church: that Belhar Confession is a 'must' confession in the new united church if it can be attained, because Belhar Confession is a staff that needs to lead the DRC family and URCSA towards unity, reconciliation and restorative justice.

Conclusion

I would like to conclude this chapter with the decision of the General Synod 2005 with regard to the Belhar Confession:

We are called to strengthen our confessional commitment NOT dilute it. Compromising on the Confession of Belhar for the sake of the continuing weakness of some in the DRC, is betrayal of only of the URCSA, itself, but of the ecumenical Reformed family who have turned to the Confession of Belhar for continued inspiration. These are reasons why Belhar is precious to the URCSA. It is for these reasons we regard it as indispensable for the life of the new, united church, as non-negotiable in its power to reconcile, seek justice and address the wrongs done to the least of the family of Jesus. It is for these reasons that we so passionately protect it from wilful misinterpretation, deliberate mudslinging, and mischievous political manipulation. (Acts General Synod URCSA 2005:152-153)

Bibliography

Primary sources

Acts General Synod Uniting Reformed Church in Southern Africa 2005.
Acta Nederduits Gereformeerde Kerk Wes-Kaapland Sinode 2011.
Rustenburg Declaration of November 1990. [Online] Available at http://kerkargief.co.za/doks/bely/DF_Rustenburg.pdf (Accessed 1 May 2015).
URCSA General Synod Church Order 2013.

Secondary sources

Avis, P. 2006. *Beyond the Reformation? Authority, primacy and unity in the conciliar tradition.* London: T&T Clark.
Bandura, A. 1997. *Self-efficacy in changing society.* Cambridge, UK: Cambridge University Press.
Barth, K. 1969/1951. *Church dogmatics* (Vol. 3, Part 4). Translated by G. Bromily & T.F. Torrance. Edinburgh: Bloomsbury T&T Clark.
Barth, K. 2004/1958. *Church dogmatics* (Vol. 4, Part 2). Translated by G. Bromily & T.F. Torrance. Edinburgh: Bloomsbury T&T Clark.
Belhar Confession, 1986. The official English translation of the *Belhar Confession 1986* approved by the General Synod of 2008. Belhar: LUS Printers.
Best, T.D. 2002. *Christ divided: Liberation, ecumenism and race in South Africa.* Pretoria: University of South Africa Press.
De Lubac, H. 1949. *Corpus Mysticum: L' ecucharistie et l' Eglise au Moyen Age: Etude Historique.* Paris: Aubier.
Ehrman, B. 2003. *Lost Christianities: The battles for Scripture and the faiths we never knew.* New York: Oxford University Press.

Gaillardetz, R.R. 2008. *Ecclesiology for a global church: A people called and sent.* New York: Orbis Books.

Hill, E. (ed.). 1993. *Sermons of St Augustine* (Vol. III/7). Hyde Park, NY: New City Press.

Neuner, J. & Dupuis, J. 1982 T*he Christian faith in the doctrinal documents of the Catholic Church.* New York: Alba House.

Onwubiko, OA. 2001. *The church in mission in the light of ecclessia in Africa,* Nairobi, Kenya: Pauline Publications Africa.

Plaatjies-Van Huffel, M-A. 2013a. Reading the Belhar Confession as a historical text. In M.A. Plaatjies-Van Huffel and R.R. Vosloo (eds), *Reformed churches in South Africa and the struggle for justice – Remembering 1960–1990.* Stellenbosch: SUN PReSS. https://doi.org/10.18820/9781920689117

Plaatjies-Van Huffel, M-A. 2013b. The Belhar Confession: Born in the struggle against apartheid in southern Africa. *Studia Historicae Ecclesiasticae* 39(1):185-203.

Plaatjies-Van Huffel M-A. 2014. The Belhar Confession in its historical context. *Nederduitse Gereformeerde Teologiese Tydskrif* 55(1/2):308-309. https://doi.org/10.5952/55-1-2-527

Saayman, W. 2007. *Being missionary, being human: An overview of Dutch Reformed mission history.* Pietermaritzburg: Cluster Publications.

Tingle, R. 1992. *Revolution or reconciliation? The struggle in the church in South Africa.* London: Christian Studies Centre.

CONVERSION TOWARDS RADICAL INCLUSIVITY

Ernst Conradie[1]

Inclusivity in the Belhar Confession

The word 'inclusive' is not used in the Belhar Confession. One may argue that it is implied, for example, in the calling of the church 'from the entire human family' and the denial that 'descent or any other human or social factor should be a consideration in determining membership of the church' (Art. 2). Inclusivity is also implied in the critique of situations where 'the enforced separation of people on a racial basis promotes and perpetuates alienation, hatred and enmity' (Art. 3). Finally, the Belhar Confession holds that God is 'in a special way the God of the destitute, the poor and the wronged and that he calls His church to follow him in this' (Art. 4)[2]. Inclusivity, one may say, is indeed integral to all three of the core themes of the Belhar Confession, namely, unity, reconciliation and justice.

This emphasis on inclusivity is of course not unique to the Belhar Confession. It is found in the Freedom Charter's emphasis that South Africa belongs to its entire people. On this basis, the option for an inclusive democracy has become the cornerstone of the South African constitution. Such a shared emphasis on inclusivity may be attractive for the sake of a public way of doing theology. However, it also harbours the danger of weakening the core content of a Christian understanding of unity, reconciliation and justice. Something similar has happened with concepts such as human dignity, equality, vision and mission. Often these words have been taken over within a secular context and reimported in ecclesial language but with its secularised connotations. For example, every institution nowadays finds it necessary

---

1 Ernst Conradie (1962–) is senior professor in the Department of Religion and Theology at the University of the Western Cape (UWC) where he teaches systematic theology and ethics. He joined the staff of the UWC in 1993. He served as chairperson of the Department of Religion and Theology for three terms (2000–2001, 2006–2007, 2012–), as chairperson of the Arts Postgraduate Board of Studies (2000–2007) and of the Arts Research Committee (2010–) and as acting deputy dean for research and postgraduate studies in the Faculty of Arts (September 2011–June 2012, July–August 2013). He is the convener of the steering committee for an international research project entitled 'Christian Faith and the Earth' (2007–2013). He is a co-editor of the journal *Scriptura* and the secretary of the editorial board of the series *Studies in Ethics and Theology* (published by Bible-Media). He is also the current conference secretary of the Theological Society of South Africa.

2 All extracts from the Confession of Belhar in this chapter are taken from the English translation at Addendum 15, The Confession of Belhar. Also available at http://urcsa.net/wp-content/uploads/2016/02/Belhar-Confession.pdf

to adopt a vision and mission statement. This strategy is adopted by congregations on good grounds but often in such a way that the managerial connotations of the world of business are also adopted in the process.

In this contribution, I will seek to recover the evangelical roots of the notion of inclusivity in the ministry of Jesus of Nazareth. I will develop the thesis that a radical sense of inclusivity lies at the very core of Jesus' ministry and that this impulse has sustained the subsequent Christian tradition in ever-changing and expanding contexts. I cannot support this thesis with detailed exegetical and historical evidence here – so it would have to suffice to articulate the thesis as clearly as possible in order to allow others to test and (if it can be sustained) to develop that further.

Inclusivity in the ministry of Jesus of Nazareth

According to the Markan version of the gospel, Jesus' ministry could be captured in the words, 'The time has come, and the kingdom of God has come near; repent, and believe the good news' (Mark1:14, New Revised Standard Version).[3] The gospels make it clear what that means by tracing Jesus engagements with the people of Galilee (mainly): the sick, the lame, the blind, the deaf, the mentally disturbed, prostitutes, lepers, tax collectors, Pharisees, Samaritans, Roman officials and indeed 'the crowds'. Why did Jesus call these people, most of whom were marginalised by society in one way or another, to conversion? Likewise, the ministry of John the Baptist (working in the Jordan valley) was one of 'proclaiming a baptism of repentance for the forgiveness of sins' (Mark 1:4).

Why would one call the marginalised, the victims of history to conversion? This is a tricky question! In classic evangelical theology, the assumed answer is the universality of sin: all people have sinned before God and are called to repentance. Inclusivity is here understood in terms of the equalising implications of the forgiveness of sins. We are all sinners and in need of God's forgiveness. As forgiven sinners, no one has a higher status before God than anyone else. This ministry may commence anywhere and has to be extended everywhere. In contemporary contextual theologies, instead, the tendency is to draw a sharp distinction between perpetrators and victims so that the victims would be affirmed as recipients of God's inclusive grace, while prophetic critique (and the call to conversion) is mainly addressed at perpetrators (speaking truth to the principalities and powers). These intuitions are at odds with each other but are brought together in a remarkable way in the Belhar Confession.

---

3   Scriptural quotations in the chapter follow the New Revised Standard Version (NRSV).

Perhaps the clue to this perplexing question lies in recognising that Galilee was the breeding ground for political resistance against the Roman occupation, anxiously awaiting the coming Messiah who would liberate them from imperial oppression. In 6 CE, Judas of Galilee led an armed revolt against the Roman occupation, following the census imposed for Roman tax purposes by Quirinius – a revolt which was crushed brutally by the Romans. The Zealots, the revolutionary party at that time, had their stronghold in Galilee. Jesus' disciples included Simon the Zealot, John and James (nicknamed 'sons of the thunder') and Judas Iscariot who betrayed him. The term 'Iscariot' may refer to his carrying a dagger which would imply that he may be counted among the revolutionaries. Perhaps Judas became dissatisfied with Jesus' peaceful tactics to liberate Israel from the Roman occupation? There can be little doubt that Jesus was regarded by the authorities in Jerusalem as a political threat given the Messianic expectations surrounding him and his ability to draw crowds. What was he doing with several thousand men in desolate places in Galilee?

On this basis, one may observe that the widespread assumption among the people of Galilee was that their main problems were related to the imperial Roman occupation. If only the Roman yoke could be removed, things would be better. There would have been differences of opinion as to when it would be best to liberate Israel from the Romans and whether the political compromise should prevail a bit longer (from which the temple establishment in Jerusalem clearly benefited), but not whether the Roman occupation is desirable. In short, the diagnosis was that the main problem lies on the outside, not on the inside.

I would suggest that Jesus' ministry was based on the opposite intuition, namely that the effects of the Roman occupation were exacerbated by a lack of social solidarity from the inside. This was evident from the ways in which various groups were marginalised in Galilee – those people on whom Jesus focussed in his ministry of healing and compassion. Yet he called those very people to conversion. Why? It may not be so difficult to understand. The sick, lame and blind would have welcomed Jesus' healing ministry for obvious reasons. But would they have welcomed Jesus' scandalising inclusion of women and even prostitutes in his circle of disciples as appropriate? The prostitutes may have welcomed such social acceptance bestowed on them, but they would have been disgusted by Jesus' contact with lepers, again for obvious reasons. Would the lepers have welcomed the mentally disturbed with whom they shared hiding places away from the towns? The hungry would be grateful for some bread and may have been willing to share that with others, even with beggars, but what would they have thought about the rumours that Jesus was a glutton and a drunkard? Likewise, the Zealots among the disciples of Jesus would undoubtedly have frowned upon his table fellowship with tax collectors who were collaborators with the imperial occupation. None of the people of Galilee would have appreciated Jesus' engagements with the despised Samaritans or with Roman officials, or his occasional contact with Gentiles.

In short, it is one thing to be included as a previously marginalised recipient of God's grace, to experience God's acceptance and pardon through Jesus' notorious table fellowship, but it is another to accept the inclusion of other marginalised groups. That required a call for conversion. The call to conversion was only possible on the basis of repentance, namely, the recognition that the problem does not merely lie on the outside, but also in the hearts and minds of those who received the proclamation of a new dispensation. The key to such conversion was entertaining the vision of God's coming reign. No one definition of what God's reign means would suffice, but it clearly includes the connotation of a dispensation where those who were previously excluded are now being included as recipients of God's grace. This implies the need for solidarity among those who were marginalised. This is incredibly difficult given the temptation to claim God's favour exclusively for one group. Jesus, therefore, had to explain this vision of the reign of God in numerous parables. At the core of this vision lies an understanding of the heart of God, whom Jesus called in intimate household imagery to be his loving Father. It is only when one gathers something of the magnanimous grace and inclusive hospitality of the Father that one can share in God's reign.

It is clear from the gospel accounts that many groups in Galilee, Samaria and Judea rejected this vision of the reign of God and its implications for social solidarity. Jesus himself was rejected in his home town of Nazareth as a troublemaker. One may say that many rejected the radical inclusivity of Jesus' ministry. This poses a complex paradox of inclusion and (self-) exclusion. One may wish to be included, but this can only be sustained if one is prepared not to exclude others who are also included in this way. In the name of radical inclusivity some would, therefore, need to be excluded, at least temporarily, because they insist on excluding others, even if such exclusion goes against the very grain of the spirit of inclusivity. It is little wonder that this vision has proved to be so elusive. The paradox can hardly be sustained and appears to be contradictory. The execution of Jesus in Jerusalem implies a clear rejection of this as an appropriate vision. It was rejected both by those who allowed no compromise with imperial powers (Judas?) and by those who favoured such a compromise. In the end, Jesus' own closest followers rejected it, such as Peter, the rock on whom the church would subsequently be built. It appears only a few women among his followers remained behind, albeit somewhat at a distance.

Inclusivity in the apostolic ministries

Jesus drew inspiration from the Hebrew Scriptures that tell the story of God's elective grace, of choosing a band of runaway slaves to exemplify who God's people were. This is a complex narrative in which Israel repeatedly made exclusivist claims to regard themselves as the chosen people of the Creator of the whole world. Only gradually and with much agony were they able to understand the identity and character of this God, a God of mercy and justice, a God of the underdogs who realises that those who were marginalised may easily come to marginalise others if they secure positions of relative power. If Jerusalem was the centripetal focus of the history of salvation, God's grace extends centrifugally to all the nations. It brings good news for the whole earth.

After the death and resurrection of Jesus as the Christ, his disciples realised that the inclusive message of Jesus was not restricted to Galilee. They discovered its significance also for Judea (where it was scarcely understood) and Samaria and for those in the Jewish diaspora towards the ends of the earth. One may say that this implied the inclusion of those who were previously excluded (in marginalised minorities) as recipients of grace. It also meant the inclusion of such people in the early Christian communities – with all the complexities that this entailed.

A major further shift occurred in the ministry of Peter and especially of Paul to the Gentiles. As a staunch Pharisee, Paul's inclination was to purify the remnant of those who remained faithful (the Hasidim) to God's law – to secure God's favour and to prevent further catastrophes like the Babylonian exile. His conversion implied a shift from logic of exclusion to one of receiving God's inclusive grace. Moreover, he had to discover that the logic of inclusivity was not only relevant for Jews in Galilee but extended to Gentiles throughout the known world of that time. This was the radical implication of the recognition that the main problem was not only imperial oppression but a lack of solidarity among the victims of history. In his letters, Paul followed Jesus' example in using household imagery to explain the inclusive grace of the Father. The whole household of God extends throughout the *Oekumene* (the whole inhabited world) and includes Gentiles as adopted children and as heirs of God's family (Eph. 2:19), in anticipation of the coming reign of God. Paul's letters reveal the difficulties that this posed in early Christian communities. There were numerous practical problems associated with the inclusion of women (as equal members of the household), of Gentiles, of the poor in general and especially of slaves. Again, and again, Paul had to call Christians to conversion, to comprehend the scope of God's inclusive grace. In all his letters, he spelled out some household rules for communities that now included those who were previously excluded.

A contentious example may be found in the first letter to Timothy, probably written by a disciple of Paul towards the end of the first century CE in an era of relative stability where the main concern shifted towards institution-building in Christian communities. Like Paul, the author of the letter emphasises the radical inclusivity of God's grace. This extends to all people (see 1 Tim. 2:1, 4, 6). However, the rest of the letter shows how difficult it was to sustain this logic in a context of striving for public honour and 'consumerist' greed (1 Tim. 6:5-10). Some contemporary critics would say that this disciple of Paul himself did not sustain the radical logic of inclusivity and accepted too many compromises, especially regarding the place of women (1 Tim. 2:8-15) and of slaves (1 Tim. 6:1-2) in such communities.

Inclusivity in the South African context

The subsequent history of Christianity tells multiple stories of how this message of God's inclusive grace was proclaimed and rediscovered in new contexts and later in new continents. It is a message that is often embraced by the victims of history (by slaves, by prisoners, by refugees, by the victims of imperialism and colonialism, by Dalits, the untouchables amongst the lowest castes, by the poor and by women in general) – for obvious reasons given the exclusion of such victims wherever the find themselves. However, these victims of history typically had to be called to conversion to realise that they may easily become part of the problem too. These stories all too often also show how those in positions of political, economic and ecclesial power claimed the message for themselves exclusively or claimed to be the true carriers of this message. They even enforced the message upon others and in this way demonstrated how they failed to understand its logic.

Admittedly, rich people were also included in the early Christian communities, as were people in positions of civil responsibility and the educated elite. Their inclusion in such communities meant that they had to realise that they need to use their talents and their influence for the sake of the community and for the whole of society. They could not continue to adopt logic of exclusion or elitism based on wealth, social status, education or military power. Throughout history, many influential Christians tried to make compromises in this regard and harmonised the gospel message to fit their cultural identities, status and needs.

In the South African context, those who were victims of imperial, colonial and patriarchal oppression embraced the message even though it was carried by messengers who claimed to understand it best and who also claimed it for themselves exclusively. The messengers seemed to think that this message of inclusivity is compatible with erecting boundaries between people based on race, presumably for the sake of survival, and to maintain their 'civilised' culture, but, to protect privileges associated with political power, cheap labour, education and class differentiation.

There were occasional prophets who warned that this logic of exclusion is not compatible with the gospel. Already in the 1950s, Ben Marais reminded Christians of the need to retrieve a *'Christelike broederskapsleer'* (a Christian brotherhood, but what then about sisterhood?). By the early 1980s, the declaration of a *status confessionis* became necessary to protect the integrity of the radical inclusivity of the Christian message. The Belhar Confession spelled out the implications of that message for church unity, reconciliation and justice in the South African context.

Since 1986, many Christians in South Africa and elsewhere in the world have been called to discover the implications of the logic of inclusion amid new challenges. In each case, that called for conversion to see that God's grace extends to those who are excluded within current constellations of power. The implications of the logic of inclusion in the whole household of God are being discovered with respect to those who are HIV-positive (the church has Aids), those with a homosexual orientation, those who are migrants and refugees (for example, from elsewhere in Africa), the unemployed and frustrated youth, criminals, gangsters, sex workers, beggars and homeless people. In each case, such inclusion threatens to divide the church. Others realised that the household of God also includes pets, domesticated animals (those who are slaughtered for human consumption), wild animals, birds (the swallows of Psalm 84), insects, tree, plants and bacteria. In each case those who are being included are called to conversion. In each case, the powerful have to discover that it is not they (the powerful) who are called to include others on their own terms (for the sake of charity), but that they themselves are being included by God's grace in God's household. Indeed, as Jesus' encounter with the rich young man shows (see Mark 10), the conversion of the powerful has always been even more complex than the conversion of the marginalised.

Conclusion: Exclusion on the basis of the logic of inclusion?

The gospel's logic of inclusive grace poses not only practical problems but also logical problems. What is to be done when those who are included wish to exclude others? Surely, one cannot include those who insist on excluding others? Should people with such exclusivist claims not then be excluded themselves? Surely the harsh condemnations found in the gospel narratives (aimed especially at the Pharisees and the Sadducees) show that Jesus recognised the need to exclude some people where necessary? Should we not follow Jesus' example in this regard? Should we not exercise the Petrine duty to carry the keys to the kingdom of God? What about church discipline?

Let me make this more personal and practical. There are quite a few groups of people whom I would like to see publicly condemned and excluded as members of God's household. These include (!) fundamentalists, creationists, AWB militarists, racists, rapists, anti-gay lobbyists, Zuma-'*imbongis*', wealthy prosperity preachers, paedophiles, climate denialists – and, to be honest, many of those beggars who pester me when I am in a hurry. Perhaps I can find place in my heart for fundamentalists but not for racists? Does God's grace also include such people?

Or is this perhaps a matter of self-isolation and self-exclusion? The logic of apartheid exemplifies such self-isolation, setting oneself apart from others. Often this is done in the name of purity, being distinct from the rest of the society as God's holy people, the communion of the saints. However, as the ongoing debates on the Belhar Confession illustrate, it is not always clear who is including or excluding whom and from what people are being excluded.

No wonder that it is much easier to adopt group formation based on shared identities. It is much easier to understand narrow group identities, from the inside and from the outside. No wonder that the people of Galilee in the end rejected Jesus' message. It was much easier to locate their main problem as lying on the outside, with the Roman occupation, rather than on the inside, in their own hearts and minds.

Bibliography

Belhar Confession, 1986. The official English translation of the *Belhar Confession 1986* approved by the General Synod of 2008. Belhar: LUS Printers.

Marais, B. 1946. Die Christelike broederskapsleer en sy toepassing in die kerk van die eerste drie eeue. Unpublished DPhil thesis, Stellenbosch University, Stellenbosch.

Marais, B. 1972. Real brotherhood in South Africa. Report of SPROCAS: The church and apartheid. *Pro Veritate*, 15 February.

YEARNING FOR A JUST AND INCLUSIVE SOCIETY

David Peter Carelse[1]

Introduction

This chapter is taken from a paper presented at the 3rd International Conference on Minority Issues and Mission, held in Japan at the Korean Youth Ministry Centre in Tokyo, 18 to 21 November 2015.[2]

In a sermon at the 25th celebrations of the Confession of Belhar, Dirkie Smit articulated the following regarding the delegates of the Dutch Reformed Mission Church (DRMC) Synod where the draft confession was adopted:

> They remembered that evening these words from 1 Peter 3. In many ways, they recognised themselves in the people to whom Peter is writing – in the same way that the church has done this so often, again and again, in so many historical situations. Peter writes to 'aliens' and 'exiles,' believers, who feel marginalised and insignificant, excluded and threatened, minorities without respect, victims of ridicule, having to deal with hardships and suffering – who therefore consider giving up their faith, losing their hope, failing the love to which they were called. Peter pleads with them, reminding them of who they are, of the hope they have inherited ... They remembered that evening the long tradition in which they stood and the worldwide community to which they belong. (Smit 2011:1)

---

1. David Peter Carelse is a minister of the Word in the Uniting Reformed Church in Southern Africa (URCSA) and Actuarius of its Cape Regional Synod BA BTh LicTh (Western Cape), MTh *cum laude* (Stellenbosch), BProc Cert. Management Principles for Church Leaders (South Africa), Cert. Legal Practice PhD Law Candidate (Cape Town).
2. The theme of the paper was 'Together Towards a Just and Inclusive Society in Japan and the World.' The conference was hosted by the Korean Christian Church in Japan with support of the World Council of Churches (WCC) and churches in Korea, Japan, Taiwan, Canada, USA, Germany, Australia.

What he said in the sermon must be understood within the historical context in which the confession was adopted by the then DRMC.³ The above quote reflects their experiences of suffering, despair and humiliation during the apartheid era. That evening in 1982 the opening words of the report from the commission who had been appointed to draft a confession were 'In fulfilling its task, your Commission took 1 Peter 3:15-16 as guideline.' Why this Scripture reading? Because the DRMC recognised their painful experiences and cries in the painful experiences and cries of the people of Asia Minor to whom Peter is writing: experiences of exclusion, of being regarded as aliens and exiles, marginalised, insignificant, excluded and threatened, minorities without respect, victims of ridicule, hardships, suffering. The believers of 1982 linked their desire for recognition and their yearning for a just and inclusive society with the living hope proclaimed by Peter. The hope lived within them; the hope was in their minds and hearts (Smit 2006:2). But isn't this also true of the Korean Christian Church in Japan?

When the members of the Korean Christian Church in Japan celebrated their 60th anniversary in 1968 under the Theme: 'Forward, Following Jesus Christ into the World', they surely remembered the Korean students who started to worship together in Japan in 1908 under difficult circumstances; they surely remembered pastor Han Sok-Po and his missionary work since 1909; they remembered the migration of mothers and fathers because of political and economic reasons and how these founding members fought for recognition. They remembered how those heroes of faith spoke the Word without fear because the life, death, resurrection and promised coming of Jesus gave them hope. The histories of God's people across the globe affirms that they have a common memory of suffering, exclusion and the denial of basic human rights. This suffering compels us to reflect on the imaginative possibilities of God's liberating, healing love for the broken realities of our lives. The world is full of people with cries in their hearts of minorities seeking grace amid their trauma.

---

3   The Dutch Reformed Church decided in 1857 that separate worship services must be held for non-whites because of the weakness of some of its members. The next logical step was the formation of a separate church. In 1881 representatives of five mission congregations assembled in Wellington near Cape Town to form a Church for the 'coloureds.' It was named the Dutch Reformed Mission Church (DRMC). A similar Church was formed for the 'blacks/bantu' in 1910. Years later a similar church was formed for those from 'Indian' and 'Muslim' descent – the Reformed Church in Africa (1968). In 1974, the DRCA decided in favour of church unity. In 1978, the DRMC decided likewise. After 16 years of discussions between the DRMC and the DRCA the new church was born on 14 April 1994 and given the name the Uniting Reformed Church in Southern Africa (URCSA). The word 'Uniting' was chosen to indicate the longing to unify with the DRC and the RCA and other Reformed churches in southern Africa.

This chapter first addresses inequality. Secondly, it focuses on racism and its impact on people's human dignity. The chapter also reflects on the efforts of the joint ministry of the Dutch Reformed Church (DRC) and the URCSA to address racism. The chapter then explores the effects of hate speech on the wellbeing of minorities, and considers the jurisprudential treatment of hate speech in South Africa. Finally, the chapter argues that the metaphors of dream, liturgy and solidarity (within the Confession of Belhar) are tools which churches across the Globe can use effectively to fight their respective struggles for just and inclusive societies. I now turn to the South African landscape of inequality.

Economic inequality

Since 1994, the church in South Africa has been part of a democratic society. The Preamble to the Constitution states that the people of South Africa recognise the injustices of their past and commit themselves to improve the quality of life of all citizens; to free the potential of each person living here; and to heal the divisions of the past. Section 9 of the Constitution contains the equality provision clause. Equality is formulated as both a value and a right and means that everyone is equal before the law. Equality includes the full and equal enjoyment of all rights and freedoms. The state must not discriminate unfairly against anyone and no person may unfairly discriminate against anyone. Twenty-one years after the reconstitution of the South African legal order the people can look back and be proud of many achievements. The country, however, still faces serious injustices of which inequality is but one. I will describe briefly the nature of this injustice and the reasons why the church should care about inequality.

Inequality and the reasons to care about it

Stan du Plessis, professor in economics at Stellenbosch University believes that talking about inequality is not so easy. According to him, people or communities can be unequal along many different dimensions: income, consumption, assets, opportunities, education, influence and abilities (Du Plessis 2015:3). Based on these dimensions, economists tend to operate with four concepts aof inequality. We can measure (or try to measure):

- the gaps between the top and bottom;
- the entire distribution;
- just sensitive parts of the distribution; or
- the persistence of the distribution over time.

He continues by asking: Why should the church care about inequality? There are normative reasons why the Church should care. Inequality may reduce happiness; it keeps people from living a quality life. The absence of resources to live a quality life is morally objectionable and in conflict with the values of a just and inclusive society. In addition, economists and theologians often focus just on market inequality and not on the inequality that arises from exploitation of the other (Du Plessis 2015:3). The church must also consider the positive reasons why she should care about inequality. Where inequality is a major challenge it may undermine social stability in the society and/or encourage leisure as opposed to work; it may lower economic growth; it is always the cause of persistent poverty; and lastly, it may distort the political system through special interest politics and the creation of oligarchy (Du Plessis 2015:5). I do however submit that the church also has ethical and theological reasons to care about inequality. The prophets Amos, Micah, Isaiah and Jeremiah spoke out loudly against corruption, maladministration, misgovernment, economic malpractices of wealth, and unjust laws and oppressive decrees that do not afford everybody equal chances to be elected to economic decision-making bodies or as court staff. The Jubilee and other measures are pronounced as God's dream to restore and to redistribute; and to protect the widow and the poor, the orphan and the foreigner. Let me continue with a glimpse into the situation in South Africa.

A glimpse into the situation in South Africa

The inequality that caused massive poverty in the apartheid era did not disappear. Sampie Terreblanche, in his fascinating study, *A History of Inequality in South Africa*, argues that the overall situation, since the dawn of democracy, has not changed significantly, especially for the poorest of the poor. This economist refers to the 2001 Annual Report of Statistics South Africa (SSA), which states that the top 20 percent of households (approximate 17 percent of the population) received more than 70 percent of the national income. The improvement in the quality of life of the poor did not improve meaningfully because in 1996 at least 41.4 percent of all households lived in poverty, in other words, they had to live on a monthly income of between R601 and R1 000 (Terreblanche 2005:132). In the previous year (1995), statistics show that 65 percent of black people between the ages of 16 and 24, especially in rural areas, were unemployed (Terreblanche 2005:133). The economic liberation of black people is limited to a new, growing, black elite. The gap between the rich white and the poor white, the rich black and the poor black is increasing. In South Africa, at least, this amounts to an infringement of the poor's constitutionally guaranteed rights.

Terreblanche puts some blame for this unacceptable economic situation on the economic premise that a high growth rate will automatically lead to massive employment and eradication of poverty, and the failure of the Truth and

Reconciliation Commission (TRC).[4] His criticism is that the TRC refused to face the consequences of the pre-1994 economic policies and is, therefore, in a manner guilty of deliberately 'bringing about and sustaining, white wealth and white privileges on the one hand, and black poverty, black deprivation and black humiliation on the other' (Terreblanche 2005). The premise of growth is for him a myth and naïve optimism. Other causes mentioned for this inequality in South Africa and in Africa are toxic leadership instead of life-giving leadership (Kretzschmar 2010:59; see also De Wet 2014),[5] the legacies of colonialism (Naude 2010:57; Thompson 1997:45), the too often silence and hesitance of the churches to address issues of human sexuality and dignity, the absence of a theology of justice (Oduyoye), the legacies of legal injustice over decades (Lebacqs 1987:75), and modernism – separation of life from morality (Smit 2007:84-85) In his presentation for the 13th Annual Nelson Mandela Lecture for 2015, the French economist Thomas Piketty (2014) gave the audience a clear understanding of the inequality in South Africa (see also Ostry et al. 2015; *The Sunday Independent*, 4 October 2015, p. 6). The top 10 percent in the country currently earn two-thirds of the total income, with 80 percent of them being white. This scenario is far worse than that of Brazil, where it is closer to 55 percent or in Europe where the percentage is around 30 to 35 percent. South Africa has many structural inequities. The inequality resulted in an unsatisfactory education system. The very rich continue to rise to a higher income level because of a lack of transparency of who owns what; this retards growth and development. There is a close link between inequality and racism and it is now time to engage with racism.

Racism

In the book *Nairobi to Vancouver*, Phillip Potter writes that the Programme to Combat Racism goes as far back as 1969 when the Central Committee of the World Council of Churches (WCC) decided that 'any form of segregation based on race, colour or ethnic origin is contrary the Gospel' (Potter 1983:1). The WCC took a clear stand that racism does not only challenge the integrity of the church but it also violates the wholeness and credibility of the Christian faith. In 1971 the WCC Central

---

4   The Truth and Reconciliation Commission was set up in terms of the Promotion of National Unity and Reconciliation Act (No. 34 of 1995) and was based in Cape Town. The hearings started in 1996. The mandate and purpose of the TRC was political. It had to promote national unity. The practical ways towards this unity was to foster reconciliation by revealing the truth about gross human rights violations between March 1960 and May 1994. The commission was also to assist with reparation, rehabilitation and to grant amnesty.
5   Louise Kretzschmar describes toxic leaders as those who are corrupt. An example of a life-giving leader, she says, is Albert Luthuli, a former president of the African National Congress and also winner of the Nobel Prize for Peace.

Committee approved a 'Special Fund', to be used to combat racism: The mandate given was as follows:

1. That proceeds from the Special Fund be used to support organizations that 'combat racism, rather than welfare organizations that alleviate the effects of racism'.

2. That the grants raise the level of awareness and strengthen the organizational capacity of racially oppressed peoples, without the manner in which they are spent being controlled.

3. That southern Africa be a priority 'due to the overt and intensive nature of white racism and the increasing awareness on the part of the oppressed in their struggle for liberation'. (Minutes of WCC Central Committee 1971:41-42)

In the light of this broad programme of the WCC, it is impossible to discuss the nature, origin, manifestations and presence of racism in South Africa in depth in one paper. Nor is it possible to find one definition of racism that can capture adequately the personal and structural hurt, alienation and disadvantage caused to millions of victims over decades. I dare, however, to elaborate on the nature, manifestations and presence of racism.

The nature, manifestations and presence of racism

In a well-argued contribution titled *Racism in Post-apartheid South Africa*, Nico Koopman, professor in ethics at the Faculty of Theology at Stellenbosch University maintains that any definition or description of racism must 'sufficiently describe the pain and destruction racism causes to so many people and societies.' (Koopman 1998:153). He continues by saying that any definition or description runs the risk 'of underestimating the magnitude and the mystery of the suffering this evil has had on millions all over the world'. According to him a conceptualisation of racism must take the various elements, such as ethnic, religious, political, cultural, biological, educational, economic and social difference into consideration. Koopman concurs with the definition of racism as understood by two Dutch scholars, Hans Opschoor and Theo Witvliet, who say that racism is the 'specific ideology, which organizes and regulates the exploitation and dependence of a specific race on the basis of the assumed cultural and/or biological inferiority of the race' (Koopman 1998:155).

Koopman argues further that racism is not only a matter of political governance. It also influences our interpretation of God's Word, how we think and how we construct our worldview.

Racism is not only attitudinal, but also structural. It is not merely a vague feeling of racial superiority, but a system of domination, furnished with social, political and economic structures of domination. To put it in another way, racism excludes groups on the basis of race or colour. People with more or less the same physical and biological features and attributes and the same cultural affiliation view society in a way that implies that the group to which they belong is superior to other groups and that society must be structured in terms of this perceived superiority and inferiority. One should also not forget that economic power is a tool used to maintain this ideology. When an ideology is perceived to be the genuine interpretation of the characteristics of the church as *una sancta catholica*, it becomes a pseudo-religion and a 'gospel' opposing the very nature of the Gospel of Jesus Christ. For South Africans, racism as a combination of institutional power plus racial prejudice is a legacy of apartheid.

Racism as a legacy of apartheid

The question whether the adoption of the Constitution and the hearings of the TRC brought an end to all racial disharmony in our country is answered differently by academics. Jakes Gerwel, the well-known education academic and former rector of the University of the Western Cape, made his views known in a chapter 'National Reconciliation: Holy Grail or Secular Pact' in Villa-Vilencio's book, *Looking Back, Reaching Forward*. According to Gerwel, ten years after the starting of negotiations for a new political order South Africa was a nation in relatively good health. We must avoid, Gerwel argues, to confuse politics and theology because then we will fail to see 'a united South African nationhood'. Gerwel states emphatically that South Africa is not an unreconciled nation (Gerwel 2000:279). It has been argued by some academics and ordinary citizens at conferences and in newspapers that racial incidents that are currently occurring at schools, universities, on the roads and in other public buildings cannot be attributed to apartheid.

As a survivor of the vicious apartheid onslaught, I humbly submit that the legacy of apartheid cannot be denied. The levels of racism as an apartheid legacy are still very high. Despite progress in this regard racism between black and white is still prevalent on both subtle and explicit levels. The history of racism in South Africa has not been just personal. Racism in the past and up to now is also a system of advantage and not just a matter of social choice. The legal and political system had cut people off from other human beings and divided them in schools, universities, other public buildings, and Sunday worship.

The destructive nature of racism

The divisive nature of racism is always the result of a destructive social ethics and of sin as the failure to worship God as God (Niebuhr 1967:121). The type of faith underlying such racism is a natural faith. It is also a national faith that has as purpose the protection of national interest. This faith determines the boundaries between love and hate, between friend and foe. The selfish heart, which is driven by relative values, divides people within themselves and from others. Its theology is directed at self-defensiveness because it becomes a weapon in the struggle for self-defence and hence also for the 'Gods' to whom this theology swears allegiance. The society becomes a closed society with relative values such as money, self-interests, the nation, the cultural group, pleasures, or the glorification of national heroes as if they are absolute. The URCSA and the DRC have signed a Memorandum of Agreement to heal the divisions of the past, to forgive, to strive for reunification, to engage in constructive ethics, to acknowledge the need for restorative justice, and to serve the Lord in joint synodical ministries. (Addendum 11). An example of such ministries is the joint initiative to address racism.

The joint URCSA and DRC initiative to address racism

The World Communion of Reformed Churches (WCRC) called the executive of the URCSA to a consultation of what communion means. The consultation took place in Grand Rapids, USA from 4 to 7 February 2014. One of the issues that hamper communion in and between churches that was raised at the consultation was racism. In consultation with the president of WCRC and member churches, the URCSA and the DRC embarked on a joint research project to address racism constructively in all its manifestations in church and in all structures of society through academic, theological and other programmes. The aim is to assist and empower churches to restore people's human dignity and bring about healing and reconciliation. The two churches declared that racism on various levels, personal and institutional, is toxic to interpersonal relations and to society. It destroys the core of communion in the church among God's people and in society. Racism operates with the assumption that certain persons or groups of people are superior to others. These assumptions determine our thinking, our attitudes and our actions towards others. Racism prevents people to contribute to one another so that we all may benefit in the fullness of life.[6] Racism perpetuates itself within society, and if left unchallenged, it cripples society. The DRC and the URCSA are convinced that if there is an Institution in society that still has the credibility and the trust from citizens to engage in public affairs, then it is the church as a faith community. There are various reasons why

---

6 The URCSA and the DRC based the contents of their proposal on the following decision of the WCC 2010: 'Racism, caste-based discrimination, and other exclusionary practices are inherently sinful because, on several levels, they subvert the double commandment: 'to love God and our neighbour as ourselves' (Mt. 20:37-39 NRSV).

the church in South Africa should be part of the solution to foster human dignity by addressing racism in a constructive way, namely:

- In South Africa churches have been directly and indirectly involved in the establishment of racism and racist attitudes and behaviour. Churches provided a theological basis for race discrimination. The churches, especially the DRC, owe it to themselves and to society to embark on a journey to undo their legacy.
- The church is witness to the Gospel of Jesus Christ that brought salvation to all humankind. In Christ, all is restored in their human dignity.
- According to the Gospel, Christ has broken down the walls that separated people.
- The church has the ministry of reconciliation and healing.
- The church has the ministry of justice.
- The church is strategically placed in society by having congregations everywhere and is therefore able to reach people from all walks of life at grassroots level.

Hate speech

The transition from apartheid to democracy

The political change of South Africa in 1994 from a racist oligarchy to an open and democratic society brought about an evolution in almost all the legal arrangements. The final Constitution adopted by the Constitutional Assembly in 1996[7] brought about a permanent new legal and political order. The Republic of South Africa became a sovereign, democratic state founded on the values of non-racialism and non-sexism, the rule of law, advancement of human rights and freedoms, human dignity, and the achievement of equality (s.1). Parliamentary sovereignty of the British colonial era and the apartheid era was replaced by constitutional sovereignty. The legal implication hereof is that the Constitution (and not the parliament anymore) is the supreme law of the Republic. The Constitution now reigns supreme, and is the measure against which all other law (e.g. customary law, common law) is tested by the courts (s. 2). The Constitution contains a Bill of Rights that sets out a list of civil, political, and socio-economic rights. The right to freedom of speech (or expression) is a political right. Hate speech is regulated together with the right to freedom of speech.

The history of pre-1994 South Africa is filled with painful incidents of the brutal suppression of citizens and the Press/Media to speak freely. Before the promulgation

---

7   The Constitution is available at http://www.gov.za/sites/www.gov.za/files/images/a108-96.pdf

of the Interim Constitution in 1993[8], freedom of expression was a residual common law or Roman-Dutch law freedom (De Waal 1998). The right to freedom of speech and the description of hate speech is contained in Section 16 of the 1996 Constitution, as follows:

'Freedom of expression. – (1) Everyone has the right to freedom of expression, which includes –

(a) freedom of the press and other media;

(b freedom to receive or impart information or ideas;

(c) freedom of artistic activity;

(d) academic freedom and freedom of scientific research.

The right in subsection (1) does not extend to –

(a) propaganda for war;

(b) incitement of imminent violence; or

(c) advocacy of hatred that is based on race, ethnicity, gender or religion, and that constitutes incitement to cause harm.'

A number of international human rights documents recognise the need to restrict the scope of freedom of expression. The formulation of section 16(2)(c) reminds of article 20(2) of the International Convention on Civil and Political Rights, 1996: 'Any advocacy of national, racial or religious hatred that constitutes incitement to discrimination, hostility or violence shall be prohibited by law.' Like any other constitutional right, the right to freedom of expression is not absolute. It is limited by the rights of others and by the legitimate needs of public society. This constitutional principle was accepted as in *De Reuck v. Director Public Prosecutions (Witwatersrand Local Division) and Others* 2003(3) SA 389 (W) 425G:

> I reiterate that the rights contained in the Bill of Rights are not absolute. Rights have to be exercised with due regard and respect for the rights of others. Organised society can only operate on the basis of rights being exercised harmoniously with the rights of others. Of course, the rights exercised by an individual may come into conflict with the rights exercised by another, and where rights come into conflict, a balancing is required.

In the light of South Africa's history of the brutal abuses of human rights it is recognised that safety, public order, health and democratic values justify the imposition of limitations on the exercise of all fundamental rights (De Vos &

---

8 Promugated in Constitution of the Republic of South Africa Act (No. 200 of 1993).

Freedman 2014:347). Therefore, freedom of expression too may be limited by complying with the provisions of the general limitation clause in section 36 (Basson 1994:50). Section 16(2) cited previously is regarded as an internal limitation of the right to freedom of speech and it operates independently of Section 36.[9] The scope of section 16(1), right to freedom of speech, is circumscribed by section 16(2), which means that the right to freedom of expression or speech does not extend to the three actions listed in section 16(2)(a)–(c). Christa van Wyk, professor in comparative law at the University of South Africa, argues that this internal limitation signals a clear message to all citizens and all others living in South Africa that hate speech will not be tolerated (Van Wyk 2002:4). According to her, hate speech is of nature degrading, insulting and of low value. Hate speech, which is often regarded as synonymous with expressions of racism and racial hatred, also has a destabilising and divisive effect on society. It encourages discrimination between groups, which may lead to violence and a breakdown in public order. Hate speech amounts not so much to hostility between individuals but rather involves groups, or the individual's membership of an ethnic, gender, racial, or religious group (Van Wyk 2002). Hate speech can consists of words, songs or any other expression that amount to incitement, encouragement or indoctrination of a group and that may cause harm to the targeted group. Harm must be interpreted broadly and includes financial, physical or emotional harm. Hate speech has an impact on the human dignity, self-worth and need for acceptance of the individual or his/her group. To strengthen the advocacy of hatred from constitutional protection, South Africa has created other measures which can also deal with hate speech. These measures are:

The South African Human Rights Commission (SAHRC) (s. 181(1)(b))

The Equality Court

Section 9(4) of the Constitution provides that 'National legislation must be enacted to prevent or prohibit unfair discrimination'. This section authorised the birth of the Promotion of Equality and Prevention of Unfair Discrimination Act (also called PEPUDA) (No. 4 of 2000). This act established the Equality Courts (which began operating in 2003). A general prohibition on hate speech was enacted in section 10 of this Act (read with section 12) and does place limits on several kinds of speech. From the criteria and list of grounds it is clear that the prohibition on hate speech

---

9   Limitation of rights
    (1) The rights in the Bill of Rights may be limited only in terms of law of general application to the extent that the limitation is reasonable and justifiable in an open and democratic society based on human dignity, equality and freedom, taking into account all relevant factors.

in PEPUDA is more far-reaching than the description of hate speech in section 16(2)(c) of the Constitution (De Vos 2014:545). Section 10 of PEPUDA provides:

Prohibition of hate speech. (1) No person may publish, propagate, advocate or communicate words based on one or more of the prohibited grounds,[10] against any person, that could reasonably be construed to demonstrate a clear intention to:

(a) be hurtful;

(b) be harmful or to incite harm; or

(c) promote or propagate hatred.

The constitutional treatment of hate speech

Here I will deal with the cases of Bongani Masuku, Julius Malema and others.[11] The matter of Bongani Masuku of COSATU (Congress of South African Trade Unions) is an interesting case that was decided on the issue of hate speech. He was investigated by the South African Human Rights Commission (SAHRC) for a complaint of hate speech lodged by the South African Jewish Board of Deputies. The complaint was lodged on 26th March 2009 against numerous anti-Semitic utterances made by Masuku at a rally held by the Palestinian Solidarity Committee at the Wits University campus on 5th March 2009. During his speech at the rally, Mr Masuku's remarks were seen to have incited violence and hatred among the students present. These are some of those remarks:

COSATU has got members here even on this campus; we can make sure that for that side it will be hell.

> COSATU is with you, we will do everything to make sure that whether it's at Wits University, whether it's at Orange Grove, anyone who does not support equality and dignity, who does not support the rights of other people must face the consequences even if it means that we will do something that may necessarily cause what is regarded as harm.

---

10 Section 1 of the Promotion of Equality Act lists the following grounds: 'race, gender, sex, pregnancy, marital status, ethnic or social origin, colour, sexual orientation, age, disability, religion, conscience, belief, culture, language and birth.' The Preamble to this Act provides that it 'endeavours to facilitate the transition to a democratic society, united in its diversity, marked by human relations that are caring and compassionate, and guided by the principles of equality, fairness, equity, social progress, justice, human dignity and freedom.'

11 Incidents of hate speech (or racism) are often visible on media like Facebook and Twitter. Incidents of alleged hate speech (or racism) at schools is regularly reported to the South African Human Rights Commission.

The following things are going to apply: any South African family who sends its son or daughter to be part of the Israeli Defence Force must not blame us if something happens to them with immediate effect.

The Jewish Board also complained about comments made by Mr Masuku on the internet. The SAHRC interpreted the verbal and written remarks/statements in the light of section 16 of the Constitution, section 10 of the Equality Act, and judgements (*Freedom Front v. SAHRC* 2003 (11) BCLR 1283; also the finding in *South African National Defence Force Union v. Minister of Defence* 1999 (4) SA 469.) It argued that implicit in provisions 16 and 10 is an acknowledgement that certain expressions do not deserve constitutional protection because, among other things, it has the potential to impinge adversely on the dignity of others and cause harm. The Constitution is founded on the principles of dignity, equal worth and freedom and these objectives should be carried out in practice. Two elements must be present before an expression can be considered hate speech. Firstly, the expression must constitute advocacy of hatred on one of the listed grounds; and secondly, the advocacy must constitute incitement to cause harm. Although freedom of expression is one of the foundations of any democratic society, section 10(2) defines a boundary beyond which the right of expression does not go. The commission argued that the words 'it will be hell' and 'we will do something that may necessarily cause what is regarded as harm' for any group of students, taken in its proper context are threatening. The words were conveyed as a warning to the effect that, should one support Israel, one would suffer harm. The other comments and statements made are also of an extreme nature that advocate and imply that the Jewish and Israeli community are to be despised, scorned and ridiculed, thus subjecting them to ill-treatment based on their religious affiliation. A *prima facie* case of hate speech was clearly established as the statements and comments by Mr Masuku were seen as being offensive and unpalatable to society. Considering the above, the commission found that the statements made by Mr Bongani Masuku amounted to hate speech.

The Equality Court had to consider whether Mr Julius Malema[12] had engaged in hate speech when he sang the song, '*Awudubula (i) bhulu ... Dubula amabhunu baya raypha*' (Shoot the Boer/farmer ... Shoot the Boers/farmers they are rapists/robbers) In his interpretation and application of the relevant provisions, Judge Lamont relied on international law and foreign law, the court's duty to protect minorities, and a jurisprudence of '*Ubuntu*'.

---

12 (20968/2010) [2011] ZAEQC 2; 20111 (6) SA 240 (EqC); [2011] 4All SA 293 (EqC); 2011 (12) BCLR 1289 (EqC) (12 September 2011).

Judge Lamont ruled that it must not be forgotten that minority groups are particularly vulnerable. It is precisely the individuals who are members of such minorities who are vulnerable to discriminatory treatment and who in a very special sense must look to the Bill of Rights for protection. The judge went on to say that the court has a clear duty to assist such affected people. He continued to rule that minorities are not to be denied the right in community with other members of their group, to enjoy their own culture, to profess and practice their own religion, or to use their own language. Minorities have no legislative or executive powers and are compelled to approach the court to protect their rights. They are particularly at risk due to the expense involved in such approaches. That they are minorities and experience such difficulties often results in them being driven to protect their identity by invoking and enforcing within their group, customs practices and conventions believed to be appropriate. In addition, they are fragile in that they are readily assumed by the mass and lose their identity. In the judgement in *Freedom Front v South African Human Rights Commission*,[13] Judge Lamont argued that a court that hears a matter must, while balancing the rights in question, take account of the construction of what hate speech is; that it is directed at a minority.

'*Ubuntu*' is a concept of African philosophy that has received a wide range of recognition and application in theology and law. It is described as a sense of belonging, the wholeness of joy, being allowed to be truly human (Mazamisa 1994:210). *Ubuntu* is also a vital metaphor for the people of South Africa because it calls us, as a dialogical discipleship, into a community structure. *Ubuntu* fosters dialogue. Therefore, it is *Ubuntu* to love and care for others, to be kindly towards others. It is *Ubuntu* to be just and fair, to be compassionate and to help others in distress. It is *Ubuntu* to be the church in Africa (Botman 1995:169). *Ubuntu* further designates the authenticity and credibility of the church. For the URCSA, the context – our habitus – is important as it influences the way we theologise (see Maluleke 1996:3-19). Much appreciated therefore is the systematic approach to define wellbeing and wellness of humans in terms of an African-Christian approach and the interconnectedness of God-human-and-world.

Ubuntu has even received meaningful attention in the field of law. The epilogue to the Interim Constitution recognised the concept of *Ubuntu*. This concept was not repeated in the final Constitution. Despite this, there have been many *Ubuntu*-

---

13   2000 (11) BCLR 1283 (SAHRC) at 1296.

based judgements.[14] Judge Lamont followed these judgements and applied *Ubuntu* to make his ruling on the Malema issue. Lamont interprets *'Ubuntu'* as a concept which dictates that a high value be placed on the life of a human being. He maintains that *Ubuntu* is inextricably linked to the values of (and places a high premium on) dignity, compassion, humaneness and respect for humanity of another. In addition, it dictates good attitudes and shared concern, and favours civility and civilised dialogue premised on mutual tolerance. Judge Lamont accordingly found that Mr Malema had indeed engaged in hate speech. He further ordered that both Mr Malema and the African National Congress be interdicted and restrained from singing the song known as *'Dubula Ibhunu'* at any public or private meeting held or conducted by them. This ruling confirms a ruling of the Constitutional Court that the state has an obligation to regulate hate speech, since hate speech may pose harm to the constitutionally mandated objective of building a non-racial and non-sexist society based on human dignity and the achievement of equality.

I now turn to the question how the church should influence society and liberate her members from racism, hate speech and inequality. Injustices take place in all daily life. The Uniting Reformed Church in Southern Africa (URCSA) has used metaphors in the Confession of Belhar as a liberating tool to inform its members, to form compassion, love and hope, and to transform unjust structures (social, political, educational, and legal).

Prophetic imagination dreaming God's shalom

George Hunsberger, ordained minister in the Presbyterian Church (USA) and professor of missiology at Western Theological Seminary in Holland Michigan. In a provocative chapter, 'Missional Vocation: Called and Sent to Represent the Reign of God', in the book, *Missional Church. A Vision for the Sending of the church in North America*, he is concerned about how the church can be faithful to its missional mandate. According to him, it is the church's calling to embody the Gospel's 'challenging relevance' (Hunsberger 1998:79). The missional mandate is sometimes perceived as a crisis. He mentions that the Chinese character for signifying the idea of 'crisis' combines two other characters; the one for 'danger' and the other for 'opportunity'.

---

14 S v Makwanyane and Another 1995 (3) SA 191 (CC) (para [131], [225], [250], [307]); Port Elizabeth Municipality v Various Occupiers 2005 (1) SA 517 (CC) at para [37]; Dikoko v Mokatla 2006 (6) SA 235 (CC) at paras [68]-[69], [112] and [115]-[116]; Masethla v President of RSA 2008 (1) SA 566 (CC) at para [238]. See also Union of Refugee Women v Private Security Industry Regulatory Authority 2007 (4) SA 395 (CC); Hoffmann v South African Airways 2001 (1) SA 1 (CC) (para [38]); Du Plooy v. Minister of Correctional Services & Others (2004) 3 ALL SA 613 (T); Bhe and Others v Magistrate Khayelitsha and Others 2005 (1) SA 580 (CC) at paras [45] and [163]; Department of Land Affairs & Others v. Goedgelegen Tropical Fruits (Pty) Ltd 2007 (6) SA 199 (CC).

A crisis is made of both. I humbly submit that the Confession of Belhar does not only describe the dangers (injustices) but it also points to opportunities. In Article 3, Belhar confesses clearly:

> That God by his life-giving Word and Spirit has conquered the powers of sin and death, and therefore also of irreconciliation and hatred, bitterness and enmity; that God, by His life-giving Word and Spirit will enable His people to live in a new obedience which can open new possibilities of life for society and the world; that the credibility of this message is seriously affected and its beneficial work obstructed when it is proclaimed in a land which professes to be Christian, but in which the enforced separation of people on a racial basis promotes and perpetuates alienation, hatred and enmity.[15]

The adoption of the Accra Confession and the Confession of Belhar is for him a 'recommitment to this dream and vision' of Jesus. Smit too, while emphasising the importance of vision and dream in the search for a good society, declares that this confession is not just an ordinary dream (Cloete & Smit 1984:68. To be able to imagine God's dream the ecumenical church has to see things differently. We first have to see the context as it is and commit ourselves to change it in accordance with God's dream! (Botman 2001:69-81). Dreams and visions must be rooted in inherited faith identity, or they become mere wishes, fads, and daydreams. We have to become humble and concerned about other's need in order to see things from a totally different perspective that is the perspective of God's gracious reign over the whole of reality.

Hauerwas too puts much emphasis on how we must envision the Just and Inclusive. The secret, he says, is 'seeing correctly' or 'looking in the right direction' (cited in Smit 2007:368). Through seeing we attain the ability to influence society. The vocabulary of the church, he says, is itself already an argument just to the extent that its descriptions and re-descriptions cannot help but challenge our normal way of seeing the World. Seeing must lead us to action. One important aspect of intercultural encounters is that they help us to develop respect for the cultural and racial 'Other' and in this way come to know and evaluate our own cultural presuppositions and blind spots.

Seeing is also the ability to engage in transcultural ethical discourses. In his *Exclusion and Embrace*, Miroslav Volf (1996:40ff) refers to the exclusion Abraham experienced as a foreigner when he left his own family and culture to follow the calling of God.

---

15 Extracts from the Confession of Belhar in this chapter are taken from the English translation at Addendum 15, The Confession of Belhar. Also available at http://urcsa.net/wp-content/uploads/2016/02/Belhar-Confession.pdf

Volf argues that we only take people's suffering serious if, after careful listening to their cries, we are willing to say to the oppressor that we do not agree with him/her; that he/she according to our best insights speaks ideas and walks paths that are both false and harmful – false in as far as their view of God is concerned, and harmful for creation, for the vulnerable members of society and for the flourishing of true humanity (Volf 1996:40ff). But how do we learn to see in the right direction, to see differently and to help those guilty of racism and hate speech to see their fellow brother/sister differently, to see them created in the image of God? We learn this ability in the worship, in a liturgy that is connected to public life.

A liturgy connected to public life

Article 2 of the Confession of Belhar connects the Sunday worship to the public life:

> That we share one faith, have one calling, are of one soul and one mind; have one God and father, are filled with one Spirit, are baptised with one baptism, eat of one bread and drink of one cup, confess one Name, are obedient to one Lord, work with one cause, and share one hope; ... that we need one another and up build one another, admonishing and comforting one another; that we suffer with one another for the sake of righteousness; pray together; together serve God in this world; and together fight against all which may threaten or hinder this unity.

The pray together; one baptism, eat of one bread, drink of one cup, confess one Name, portrays the Sunday worship. The Confession of Belhar understands Christianity as a 'world-formative Christianity' (Wolterstorff 1994:48, 2011:57). The whole service (Sunday liturgy) must be directed at strengthening the faith of the worshippers for their obedient living from Monday to Saturday (public liturgy). Worship is thus the liturgy for the public liturgy outside (Berger 1985:425-432). The bread, cup and prayers are food for the pilgrims for their journey into the world to create that desired good, just society; food for their pilgrimage of justice, peace and human dignity. In the worship, the proclamation of the Word reminds us of our calling, of our *vocatio* to do what is good and to seek the right. From the liturgy, the people depart with a renewed vision of the value-patterns of God's kingdom (Wainwright 1980:8). When we have communion with the Lord and one another like the disciples on the road to Emmaus then our eyes open ... And then we see! (Bria 1996:45). Authentic liturgy opens the heart and eyes! Authentic liturgy develops a spirituality which grows out of the lived experience of the minorities. It ensures a conversion from self-complacency and self-sufficiency to that of community with the wounded. Worship is the centre of the whole life of the church; it is the true act of its up building (Barth 1958:695-710, 1960:90). We pray (*lex orandi*) what we believe (*lex credendi*) and we then act/live (*lex vivendi*) what we believe. It is in liturgy that the church becomes what it theologically is – the earthly-historical form of existence of our Risen Lord and Saviour. In liturgy, Christocracy becomes living reality: Christ is the Lord of the Church and the public world! (as proclaimed in Art. 5 of the Confession of Belhar). Even the church polity and church order that directs the church Mission in the world must have has its origin in the worship and liturgy. Church polity can therefore be nothing else than liturgical church polity (Barth 1958:695-710; Koffeman 2014:84-96). There must be a direct link between the Sunday worship and our action in the world. In the liturgy, the worshippers must be equipped spiritually, morally and intellectually to do justice, to heal, to respect the human dignity of others, to live a holy life. The relationship of liturgy, holiness and justice is a preoccupation of the Sunday service. God's justice is a manifestation of his holiness and our justice is a reflection of God's holiness (Wolterstorff, 1991:29). It is however important that the language of the liturgy and worship reflects an image of God as One Who understands the woundedness of minorities. In her book, *Mother, Mourner and Midwife. Re-imagining God's Delivering Presence in the Old Testament*, the South African feminist theologian Julia Claassen speaks of feminine images of God. These images, she says, offer the potential to speak to people who are dealing with deep-seated experiences of pain. She encourages the church to search for a new language to speak about God. Not patriarchal and paternalistic, but compassionate; a language that pictures God as always being concerned about our woundability (Claassen 2012:34). The Worship service sends us out into the world fully equipped with this language, fully touched by God's love for the World, wholly anointed with new eyes to embrace the downtrodden and the excluded, by practising liberative solidarity.

Liberative solidarity

The Confession of Belhar (Art. 4) calls on the church across the globe to embody the type of solidarity that God has shown:

> We believe that God has revealed himself as the One who wishes to bring about justice and true peace among men; that in a world full of injustice and enmity He is in a special way the God of the destitute, the poor and the wronged and that He calls his church to follow Him in this.

Is solidarity possible without prayer? Can we protect the stranger without prayer? A good society, a just and inclusive society is a society that reflects the justice, peace, compassion, friendship, love of the kingdom of God. We can work for the dawn of the kingdom only if we regular pray in expectation: Let thy kingdom come! This prayer is the struggle for human righteousness (Barth 1981:205). Prayer is a fundamental ethical activity in the battle for renewal. Prayer is the first step in accepting responsibility for the doing of righteousness; prayer is commitment to transform our societies to become Just and Inclusive even if it demands of us to swim ever against the stream.

Conclusion

The chapter endeavoured to explore how certain injustices have a negative impact on the establishment of a just and inclusive society in South Africa. The purpose was also to demonstrate that the church is called by her Lord to be a caring, liberating, healing, listening empowering space where people can flourish to their maximum potential – spiritually, economically, socially and emotionally. I have opted for an interdisciplinary approach of theology and law. I concluded with the proposal that the Confession of Belhar could serve as a hermeneutical tool for the broader church, especially because the global context is 'a system of apartheid.' And furthermore, the economic empire against which this confession and the Accra Declaration direct themselves, is an obstacle for the global church. I have also argued that the South African jurisprudence has transformative potential; but law has it shortcomings, its limits (see Davis 2006:301-327; Dugard 2006:261-282). The Constitution has more than once been described as a transformative Constitution. (See Davis & Klare 2010:403-509; De Vos & Freedman 2014:26-30; Klare 1998:146-188).

Transformation, as I have indicated, is also a key term in theology. On the issue of transformation, as well as on issues like *Ubuntu*, promoting of human rights and morality, the disciplines of law and theology have a common agenda. A partnership with the church is therefore not only needed but is an utmost necessity. In South Africa, Japan and the rest of the world, the church has a responsibility to become involved in writing of government policies, as well as commentary on drafts for national, provincial and local legislation. The nature of this partnership, I believe, should not be critical solidarity, but rather prophetic faithfulness (Vellem 2013:176-178). In South Africa, our distinguished and learned chief judge, the honourable Justice Mogoeng W.A. Mogoeng, in the keynote address at the Second Annual Law and Religion Conference in Stellenbosch on 27 May 2014, makes this meaningful remark regarding such a partnership:

> I believe that we can only become a better people if religion is allowed to influence laws that govern our daily lives starting with the Constitution of any country. I hope to support this conclusion with particular reference to principles drawn from the Christian faith ... The levels of maladministration, crime and corruption ... that have permeated all facets of society, price-fixing and fronting included, would in my view be effectively turned around significantly, if religion were to be factored in the law-making process. (Mogoeng 2014)

I end with a statement of Dirk Smit from one of his many thought-provoking articles that combines an ethic of being (good character/virtue ethics) with an ethic of doing (the right action/duty ethics) and the wise (situation ethics).

It is obvious that civil societies, that democratic societies, that good societies, that just societies, need more than constitutions, laws, structures, institutions and systems. A democratic, good, just society needs good people, responsible citizens of character and virtue, just people who practice justice themselves. A just society needs more than a prophetic, speaking church. It needs a worshipping church, subverting the everyday realities, reminding people, giving people hope, forming people, calling people to responsible and moral life, a life of justice, teaching people to practice justice, to accept one another and to live in community, in solidarity, in care of the marginalised and the suffering, to give people their due. (Smit 2007:391)

Bibliography

Primary sources

Minutes World Council of Churches Central Committee Addis Ababa. 1971

Secondary sources

Barth, K. 2004/1958. *Church dogmatics* (Vol. 4, Part 2). Translated by G. Bromily & T.F. Torrance. Edinburgh: Bloomsbury T&T Clark.
Barth, K. 1960. *The Humanity of God*. Richmond, KY: John Knox Press.
Basson, D. 1994. *South Africa's interim Constitution. Text and notes:* Kenwyn, South Africa: Juta & Co.
Boesak, A.A. 1984. *Black and reformed: Apartheid, liberation and the Calvinist tradition.* Stellenbosch: SUN PReSS.
Boesak, A.A. 2005. *The tenderness of conscience*. Stellenbosch: SUN PReSS.
Bosch, D.J. 1991. *Transforming missions*. Maryknoll, NY: Orbis Books.
Bosch, D.J. 1995. *Believing in the future: Towards a missiology of Western culture*. Harrisburg, PA: Trinity Press International.
Botman, H.R.1993. *Discipleship as Transformation? Towards a theology of transformation*. Unpublished PhD Thesis. University of Stellenbosch.
Botman, H.R. 1995. Dealing with diversity. In D. Buchanan & J. Hendriks (eds), *Meeting the future: Christian leadership in South Africa*. Randburg, Souith Africa: Knowledge Resources.
Botman, H.R. 2001. Hope as the coming reign of God. In W. Brueggemann (ed.), *Hope for the world. Mission in a global context.* Louisvilly, KY: Westminster Knox Press.
Botman, H.R. 2002. The end of hope or a new horizon of hope? An autreach to those in Africa who dare hope. *Nederduitse Gereformeerde Teologiese Tydskrif* 43(1/2):22-31. Inaugural lecture as professor in Missiology at Stellenbosch University.

Botman, H.R. 2013. Dread, hope and the African dream: An ecumenical collage. Lecture presented upon receipt of the Princeton Theological Seminary's Abraham Kuyper Prize for Excellence in Reformed Theology and Public Life, Princeton Theological Seminary, Princeton, NJ (18 April 2013).

Bria, I. 1996. *The liturgy after the liturgy. Mission and witness from the Orthodox perspective.* Geneva: WCC Publications.

Buchanan, D & Hendriks, J. (eds). 1995. *Meeting the future. Christian leadership in South Africa.* Pretoria: Knowledge Resources.

Cloete, G.D. & Smit, D.J. (eds). 1984. *A moment of truth.* Cape Town: Tafelberg Publishers.

Coertzen, P., Green M.C. & Hansen, L. (eds). 2015. *Law and religion in Africa. The quest for the common good in pluralistic societies.* Stellenbosch: SUN PReSS. https://doi.org/10.18820/9781928314004

Conradie, E.M. (ed.). 2013. *South African perspectives on notions and forms of ecumenicity.* Stellenbosch: SUN PReSS.

Davis, D.M. 2006. Adjudicating the socio-economic rights in the South African Constitution: Towards 'deference lite'? *South African Journal on Human Rights* 22(2):301-327).

Davis, D.M. & Klare, K. 2010. Transformative constitutionalism and the common law and customary law. *South African Journal on Human Rights* 26(3):403-509).

Davis, D., Richter, A. & Saunders, C. (eds). 2015. *An inquiry into the existence of global values: Through the lens of comparative constitutional law.* Oxford, UK and Portland, OR: Hart Publishing.

de Gruchy, J.W. 1986. *Cry justice!* London: Collins Liturgical Publications.

de Gruchy, J.W. 1991. *Liberating reformed theology.* Claremont: David Philip Publishers.

de Gruchy, J.W. 1995. *Christianity and democracy.* Cambridge: Cambridge University Press. https://doi.org/10.1017/CBO9780511627927

de Gruchy, J.W. 2000. *Seeing things differently.* Cape Town: Mercer Books.

du Plessis, L.M 1973. The juridical relevance of Christian justice. PhD thesis, Potchefstroom University for Higher Christian Education.

de Vos, P. & Freedman, W. (eds). 2014. *South African constitutional law in context.* Cape Town: ABC Press.

de Waal, J., Currie, I & Erasmus, G. 1998. *The Bill of Rights handbook.* Kenwyn, South Africa: Juta & Co.

de Wet, F.W. 2014. The role of prophetic action in public theology: The implications for addressing corruption in a context of sustainable development. *Die Skriflig* 48(1) Art. 171. https://doi.org/10.4102/ids.v48i1.1718

Dugard, J. 2006. Court of first instance? Towards a pro-poor jurisdiction for the South African Constitutional Court? *South African Journal on Human Rights* 22(2):261-282.

du Plessis, S. 2015. Economic inequality in South Africa. Paper delivered at the Winter Week Conference on Faithful Discipleship: Changing the World, Stellenbosch University, Stellenbosch (4-8 June).

Ellis, N.C. 1988. *Congregations: Their power to form and transform.* Louisville, KY: Westminster Knox Press.

Gerwell, J. 2000. National reconciliation: Holy grail or secular pact? In C. Villa-Vicencio & W. Verwoerd (eds), *Looking back reaching forward: Reflections on the Truth and Reconciliation Commission of South Africa.* Cape Town: University of Cape Town Press.

Guder, D.L. (ed.). 1998. *Missional Church: A vision for the sending of the church in North America*. Grand Rapids, MI: William B. Eerdmans.

Gutiérrez, G. 1990. *The truth shall make you free*. Maryknoll, NY: Orbis Books.

Huber, W. 1988. *Kirche*. München: Chr. Kaiser Verlag.

Hunsberger, G. 1998. Missional vocation: Called and sent to represent the reign of God. In D.L. Guder (ed.), *Missional church. A vision for the sending of the church in North America*. Grand Rapids, MI: William B. Eerdmans.

International Convention on Civil and Political Rights 1996. [Online] Available at www.cirp.org/library/ethics/UN-covenant (Accessed 21 February 2021)

Klare, K. 1998. Legal culture and transformative constitutionalism. *South African Journal on Human Rights* 14:146-188.

Koffeman, L.J. 2014. *In order to serve. An ecumenical introduction to church polity*. Zürich: Lit Verlag.

Koopman, N. 1998. Racism in post-apartheid South Africa. In L. Kretzschmar & L. Hulley (eds), *Questions about life and morality: Christian ethics in South Africa today*. Pretoria: Van Schaik Publishers.

Koopman, N. 2003. Trinitarian anthropology, ubuntu and human rights. In H.R. Botman & K. Spörre (eds), *Building a human rights culture. South African and Swedish perspectives*. Falun: Stralins.

Koopman, N. 2005. Bonhoeffer's anthropology and the anthropology of ubuntu. *Nederlands Theological Journal*, July:195-206.

Kretzschmar, L. & Bentley, W. (eds). 2010. *What is a good life. An introduction to Christian ethics in the 21st Century*: Kempton Park, South Africa: AcadSA.

Kretzschmar, L. & Hulley, L. (eds). 2013. *Life Morality. Christian Ethics in South Africa Today*. Pretoria: Van Schaik Publishers.

Lebacqz, K. 1987. *Justice in and unjust world. Foundations for a Christian approach to justice*. Minneapolis, MN: Augsburg.

Leith J.H. 1988. *The Reformed imperative. What the church has to say that no one else can say*. Philadelphia, PA: Westminster Press.

le Roux, W. & van Marle, K. 2007. *Post-apartheid fragments. Law, politics and critique*. Pretoria: University of South Africa Press.

Maluleke, T. 1996. Black and African theologies in the new world order: A time to drink from our own wells. *Journal of Theology for Southern Africa* 96:3-19.

Mazamisa, W. 1994. Reparation and land: In C. Villa-Vicencio & J. de Gruchy (eds), *Doing ethics in context: South African perspectives. Theology and praxis* (Vol. II). Claremont: David Philip Publishers.

Mogoeng, M.W.A. 2014. 'Fornication' and 'sanctity of the family'. Keynote address at the Second Annual Law and Religion Conference, Law and Religion in Africa: The Quest for the Common Good in Pluralistic Societies, Stellenbosch University, Stellenbosch (26-28 May).

Modise, L.J. 2016. Well-being and wellness in the twenty-first century: A theanthropocosmic approach. *Journal of Religion and Health* 55(6):1876–1890. https://doi.org/10.1007/s10943-015-0140-4

Mouton, A.E.J. 1995. *Reading a New Testament document ethically: Towards an accountable use of Scripture in Christian ethics, through analysing the transformative potential of the Ephesians Epistle*. PhD thesis, University of the Western Cape, Bellville, South Africa.

Niebuhr, H.R. 1967. *The meaning of revelation*. New York: MacMillan.

Opschoor, H. & Witvliet, T. 1983. De onderschatting van het racisme. *Wending* 38(9):554-565

Piketty, T. 2014. *Capital in the twenty-first century*. Translated by A. Goldhammer. Cambridge, MA: Belknap Press of Harvard University Press. https://doi.org/10.4159/9780674369542

Plaatjies-Van Huffel, M-A. 2013a. Reading the Belhar Confession as a historical text. In M.A. Plaatjies-Van Huffel and R.R. Vosloo (eds), *Reformed churches in South Africa and the struggle for justice – Remembering 1960–1990*. Stellenbosch: SUN PReSS. https://doi.org/10.18820/9781920689117

Plaatjies-Van Huffel, M-A. 2013b. The Belhar Confession: Born in the struggle against apartheid in southern Africa. *Studia Historicae Ecclesiasticae* 39(1):185-203.

Plaatjies-Van Huffel, M-A. 2014. The Belhar Confession in its historical context. *Nederduitse Gereformeerde Teologiese Tydskrif* 55(1/2):308-309. https://doi.org/10.5952/55-1-2-527

Potter, P. 1983. *Nairobi to Vancouver, 1983*. Report of the Central Committee to the Six Assembly of the World Council of Churches, 1975–1983. Geneva: WCC Press.

Saayman, W. & Kritzinger. K. (eds). 2013. *Mission in bold humility: David Bosch's work considered*. Eugene, OR: Wipf and Stock.

Smit, D.J. 2007. *Essays in public theology. Collected essays 1*. Stellenbosch: SUN PReSS.

Terreblanche, S.J. 1990. *Political economy and social wealth: With a focus on South Africa*. Pretoria: Van Schaik Publishers.

Terreblanche, S.J. 2005. *A history of inequality in South Africa, 1652–2002*. Pietermaritzburg: KMM Review Publishing.

Thompson, J.M. 1997. *Justice and peace: A Christian primer*. Maryknoll, NY: Orbis.

Acts of General Synod of the Uniting Reformed Church in Southern Africa 2008. Fifth General Synod held at Hammanskraal, 29–5 October 2008.

URCSA. 2012. *Church Order and Regulations of the General Synod of the Uniting Reformed Church in Southern Africa*

van Wyk, C. 2002. *The constitutional treatment of hate speech in South Africa*. Paper delivered at the XVIth Congress of the International Academy of Comparative Law, Brisbane, Australia (14–20 July).

Villa-Vicencio, C. & de Gruchy, J.W. 1994. *Doing ethics in theology*. Claremont: David Philip Publishers.

Villa-Vicencio, C. & Verwoerd, H. 2000. *Looking back, reaching forward. Reflections on the Truth and Reconciliation Commission of South Africa*. Cape Town: University of Cape Town Press.

Volf, M. 1996. *Exclusion and embrace: A theological exploration of identity, otherness, and reconciliation*. Nashville, TN: Abingdon Press.

Wolterstorff, N. 1991. Justice as condition for authentic liturgy. *Theology Today* 48(1):6-21. https://doi.org/10.1177/004057369104800102

Wolterstorff, N. 1994. *Until justice and peace embrace* (2nd edition). Grand Rapids, MI: William B. Eerdmans.

Wolterstorff, N. 2011 *Hearing the call: Liturgy, justice, church and world*. Grand Rapids, MI: William B. Eerdmans.

BELHAR AS A THERAPEUTIC RESOURCE TO THE DUTCH REFORMED CHURCH FAMILY

Eugene Baron[1]

Introduction

Rightfully so, the Confession of Belhar[2] was never intended to be a '*stok om mee te slaan*' (a stick to beat with) (Smit 2009b:299), as it is often perceived. This sentiment prevails due to the association of the Confession to the 'work of Boesak' or 'liberation theology' (see Kritzinger 2010). It became to many a 'stumbling block' because they argue that the confession has 'strong political connotations' and 'the potential to divide the DRC' (see Botman 2006:243). Along these lines, the Belhar Confession has a very negative connotation among DRC family members. I might not be fully able to turn the negative connotations around, but this small contribution is intended to look for a means in which this confessional document can minimise the negative connotations attached to it, like the references made to the document mentioned earlier, but also to rightfully ask the question, how can this confessional document,[3] Belhar, be a therapeutic resource for the DRC family during the current reunification process, as well reaching the moment we all hope for, becoming a united church? How can this confessional document serve as 'a stick to walk with'? (Smit 2009b:299). Smit contends that confessions are not only written for liturgical purposes, as it is commonly perceived. Confessions fulfil many purposes:

- They provide the church with a language to proclaim God's praise, both in liturgy and ordinary life.
- They become hermeneutical lenses by which to read the Scriptures.
- They express identity and thereby contribute to the sense of belonging.

---

1 Eugene Baron is a lecturer in the Department Christian Spirituality, Church History, and Missiology at the University of South Africa, and also a minister at the Uniting Reformed Church in South Africa, Toekomsrus congregation.
2 The author will hereafter in most cases refer to the Belhar Confession as simply 'Belhar'.
3 Recently the idea of a 'document' or literary text playing a key role in healing was also emphasised by Chris van der Merwe and Pumla Gobodo-Madikizela in their book '*Narrating our Healing: Perspectives on Working Through Trauma*'. More recently the 2012 contribution of Vosloo on the role of haling through literary texts in his article entitled, 'Traumatic Memory, Representation and Forgiveness: Some Remarks in Conversation with Antjie Krog's *Country of My Skull*' is also noted. In his contribution, Vosloo argues that literature has the power to express and represent traumatic memory and that it can play an important role in 'narrating our healing'.

- They assist in instructing and forming new believers.
- They help the church to distinguish truth from falsehood.
- They serve as forms of public witness to Jesus Christ the Lord as the gospel (Smit 2009b:302).

Although Smit refers to certain functions or purposes that confessions can serve, they are indeed important for the healing of members in our church from both sides of the divide in the DRC family.[4] The contextual embeddedness of the Belhar Confession, imbued with rich contextual meaning, may serve as a therapeutic document for the DRC family, but also for those who want to get involved in the implicit realities that the Confession up until now confronts.

A confession is not drafted to become an ornament; it is useful not only for the moment but also for future moments to reflect upon. Smit proposes that confessions exist to become 'interpretive statements of the meaning of the biblical message' for the church and for their time, to 'form of a concrete embodiment' of the church's convictions in 'everyday actions, including, cultural, social, political and economic activities' (Smit 2009b:295).

Smit argues that although Reformed confessions have authority because it is 'subjected to the sole and final authority of the Word of God' and 'represents how earlier generations have understood the Word of God' this authority remains relative. It is relative in the sense that it is always 'historical (contextual) in nature and the products of human beings' (Smit 2009b:298). Smit urges, therefore, that the historical, social, cultural and contextual nature of confessions is always respected, taken seriously, and that the church should be sensitive to the grammatical and conceptual instrumentation that were available to the original authors. He unequivocally argues that confessional documents should never be treated as 'historical documents with timeless and eternal propositions' (Smit 2009b:299). The Confession of Belhar was also not different.

Victor Frankl

Victor Frankl was a Viennese psychiatrist, and one of the foremost representatives (other exponents of existential psychology are among others Rollo May and Paul Tillich) of existential psychology. He was born in 1905 and died in 1997. Frankl's therapy emerged as a result of the foundational theory of existentialism that

---

4   Here I refer to the Uniting Reformed Church and the rest of the DRC family (DRC, DRCA and RCA) who are currently in the process of reunification.

became known as logotherapy[5]. Many clinics were established in South Africa and elsewhere around the world. (Meyer et al. 2008:437) Frankl was a student of Sigmund Freud and Alfred Adler, who both focussed on the inner driving forces of human behaviour. Freud who placed emphasis on the will to pleasure and Adler the will to power were according to Frankl a one-sided approach to human nature and the motivation of behaviour. Frankl argued that the overriding and primary motive of human motivation is the will to meaning.

One of the important experiences in the life of Frankl was his experience as a victim and survivor of the Holocaust. Frankl's work was developed at a time when he was an influential psychiatrist but at the same time also a Jewish prisoner number 199 104 during the time of Nazi Germany. During these times, he and others were subjected to very crude circumstances, when they were often deprived of the necessities of life, and this contributed to their psychological well-being, their dignity and worth. While these almost unbearable circumstances are enough to lose one's sense of joy and meaning in life, Frankl indeed argued otherwise. He argued that these most adverse circumstances play a significant role in forming values in people's lives. Just to have the idea that you live for 'something' (despite the suffering) is what makes it worthwhile to endure. (Meyer et al. 2008:437).

Frankl's contribution to the existentialism approach

The focus of Frankl's his work is constituted in his book, *Man's Search for Meaning*. In this book, he explains the existential approach as he presented in his Oskar Pfister Award lecture at the 1985 Annual Meeting of the American Psychiatric Association in Dallas, Texas. From the opening stance, it is important to note that for Frankl, human beings are at the core of their selves' religious beings (Frankl 1948:152). Frankl's view of human nature goes beyond the explanation of Sigmund Freud who focuses on the intra-psychic conflict and the Adlerian school of thought. Frankl argues that Freud

> does not pay sufficient tribute to self-transcendence. It mainly considers man a being that is out to overcome a certain inner condition, namely the feeling of inferiority which he tries to get rid of by developing the striving of superiority. (Frankl 1948:138)

In the lecture, Frankl contends that it was, in fact, Oskar Pfister who pointed out that complimentary to depth psychology (Freudians and Adlerians) is the 'recognition

---

5 Logotherapy is also referred to as 'existential therapy'. In the process of therapy the therapists are merely 'fellow travellers' (see Corey 2013:145). *Logos*, which denotes *meaning*, is therapy which focused by the search for meaning. Clients themselves construct, their own particular meaning, not the therapist providing them with answers.

of that spiritual height of our nature', which Frankl himself refer to as the 'will to meaning'.

Frankl believes that meaning is probed when situations in life, not only confront us but place a demand on us; 'presents a question to us – a question to which we have to answer by doing something in that given situation'. He further elaborates that meaning could be defined as 'suddenly becoming aware of a possibility against the background of reality'. This possibility or opportunity to create meaning makes sense and cannot be offered by a psychiatric or psychologist. However, what they can do is to show people 'that life never ceases to offer us meaning up to its last moment, up to our last breath' (Frankl 1948:141).

Frankl believes that there are 'down to earth' as well as 'up to heaven' meanings. With reference to the former (down to earth meanings), he explains three avenues that lead up to meaning fulfilment, namely, 'doing a deed or creating a work, experiencing something or encountering someone', and when faced with 'a fate we cannot change' and a situation where people are called upon to make the best of it by rising and growing above themselves, in a quest to change themselves (Frankl 1948:141-143). Frankl argues that these three avenues,

> equally holds for the three components of the tragic triad – pain, guilt, and death – in as much we may turn suffering into a human achievement and accomplishment; derive from guilt the opportunity to change for the better, and see in life transitoriness an incentive to take responsible action. (Frankl 1948:142)

Now to turn to what Frankl refers to 'up in heaven' or ultimate meaning (Frankl 1948:143). It is the kind of meaning that speak to 'the whole, of the universe or at least a meaning of one's life as a whole; at any rate, a long-range meaning'. It refers to the end of life, in metaphorical terms, the 'close of the curtain', when the 'last piece of the puzzle' completes the whole. Ultimate meaning is not easy to articulate or to construct, but Frankl, says there exists a gap between the known and unknown and the use of 'symbols' is a way and serves as a means to construct meaning in a moment of meaninglessness. He argues people do it in fact when they refer to God. 'By and large, the divine, too, is symbolized by what it is not. God's attributes are human properties. God is portrayed in anthropomorphic ways' (Frankl 1948:148).

Belhar as a meaningful document

In order to find meaning, the historical context of the Belhar Confession is important. In her research, Plaatjies-Van Huffel did exactly this. She investigated the origin of the confession when she asked the following pertinent questions: What is the context? What is the setting? Where and why was it written? Who is the author and what is his or her place, position, role, reputation, status in society, what kind of document is it? What point is the author trying to make? What is the motive (purpose) of the author(s) in preparing it? Who was it written for? What is known about the audience? What is the argument and strategy utilised by the authors to achieve their goals? (Plaatjies-Van Huffel 2014:302).

In answering the question of the time in which the Belhar Confession was written Plaatjies-Van Huffel (2014:303) refers to the struggle against apartheid in South Africa (see also Botman 2006:241). The DRC was pressured by the ecumenical movement in South Africa, the South African Council of Churches (SACC) as well as the motion tabled by Allan Boesak at the WARC General Assembly in Ottawa, Canada in August 1982 to declare apartheid a heresy. Plaatjies-Van Huffel also refers to the establishment of a separate congregation for the natives, and the decision in some DRC congregations that other races (non-whites) can join the white church (DRC) but on condition that there be separate seats made available for the so-called 'heathen'. She also records that the DRC in Ceres constructed a separate building for the teaching of catechism classes and for the ministering of Holy Communion to the 'heathen' (Plaatjies-Van Huffel 2014:306).

The first racially segregated church, the Dutch Reformed Mission Church (DRMC) was established in 1881.[6] According to Plaatjies-Van Huffel (2014:308), this marked the time when 'church apartheid was officially introduced into the Dutch Reformed Church'. Plaatjies-Van Huffel also discusses the pivotal role that the DRC played with the promulgation and endorsement of the apartheid laws, namely, the Immorality Amendment Act (No. 21 of 1950), the Group Areas Act (No. 41 of 1950) and the Population Registration Act (No 30 of 1950) (Plaatjies-Van Huffel 2014:309). This was the context that gave rise to the decision of the DRMC Synod in 1982 to decide to draft the Confession of Belhar. Though much more can be said about the historical context and the socio-political realities that were the impetus behind the emergence of the Belhar Confession, it suffices to say that the confession itself is embedded in a very sad space of the history of South Africa, but in particular within the DRC family.

The contribution of Johan Botha (2010:37) is also of important when he refers to the 'difficult times', with reference to the birthing of the Belhar Confession. The difficult times were characterised by the conflict of words, and later with guns. It started with war on the borders of the country when children fought and murdered each other.

---

[6] For a more comprehensive history on the historical background of the Belhar Confession please read the following essay in this publication; *Acceptance, Adoption, Advocacy, Reception and Protestation: A Chronology of the Belhar Confession* by Mary-Anne Plaatjies-Van Huffel.

It brings our attention to June 1976 when the conflict came to the nearby street, not only on the borders anymore. The birthing of Belhar was also during a time when schooling was often interrupted and when people came in direct confrontation with the apartheid government of the day. Heavily armed military vehicles and armed soldiers patrolled through the townships. Botha describes the suffering: 'in baie Van ons se huise (in many of our homes) en die hele gemeenskap is uiteindelik geraak' (and the whole community was affected) (Botha 2010:37).

Durand, in reference to the context of Belhar, shares his own story of the emergence of Belhar. Durand expressed his deep-seated disappointment in the apartheid policy at the time, which he said started to gain momentum during his years as a student at the Vrije Universiteit in Amsterdam, in the Netherlands. He explains the Sharpeville massacre, when he and his wife was still in the Netherlands and how he felt so powerless about the fact that he was not able to intervene in the state of affairs of the country at the time. He articulates his sense of anxiety, at the time, for the future of South Africa (cited in Du Toit 2014:3).

The Sharpeville massacre was a concern not only nationally, but internationally, and because most churches were members of the World Council of Churches, there was a special conference arranged in Cottesloe, Johannesburg in December 1960 to discuss the events of Sharpeville. Durand refers to the strong critique during the conference on the position of the DRC with reference the situation in the country, and that in their (DRC) own congregations, members were divided on the basis of race (cited in Du Toit 2014:9).

The Cottesloe 'critique' was one of the main points on the agenda at the Theological Day at Stellenbosch University[7] and Durand recalls a specific situation where his doctoral thesis was mentioned. During the unfolding of events, Prof. J.C.G. Kotze of the University of Stellenbosch said, 'Hierdie proefskrif bevestig elke woord wat in die Cottesloe-verklaring opgeneem is' (This dissertation proved everything that was taken up in the Cottesloe Declaration). According to Prof. Kotze, what inspired the Cottesloe meeting in Johannesburg was indeed the fact that the DRC was based on racial segregation. His own literary contribution, his dissertation was on 'die eenheid van die kerk binne 'n sendingsperspektief' (the unity of the church from a missionary perspective). His experience includes also of being associated with communism. Durand recalls the words of Prof. Koot Vorster referred to in *Die Burger*, in which he refers to those who studied outside the borders of South Africa (which Durand believed was in a sense a message personally also directed to him) as one

---

7   At Stellenbosch University there were at the beginning of every year a theological day, where the Faculty of Theology focused on a theme and students as well as staff, and ministers of the DRC participated.

that came back to South Africa with *'vuil naels'* (dirty nails). In his article, Vorster referred to those people as communists (cited in Du Toit 2014:9).

What is also quite striking in Durand's personal account of the road to Belhar is his own story as a white missionary reverend in Port Elizabeth, and how he, in his eight years of being a minister in the DRMC, was exposed to and able to learn through first-hand experience the dire need in which blacks in South Africa suffered. At one time, he recalls how he asked himself during the apartheid times: 'Hoe kan aan mense dinge gedoen word, dinge wat ten hemele skree vanwee die onreg daarvan?' (How can things be done to people, things that cry to the heavens because of the injustice?) (Du Toit 2014:17).

Durand also refers to his own involvement in the DRC Synod in 1974 in Cape Town where he presented the synod with his research on the blacks in the cities, and which turned out to be a humiliating occasion because of the way they dealt with his report. He said the report that was tabled did indeed criticise the theological justification of apartheid and pointed out that there were no grounds in Scripture to substantiate such an 'apartheid' theology. Rev. Attie van Wyk, presented the report to the synod, and then as Durand recalls, the synod rejected the section compiled by Durand. He mentions the *'skynheiligheid'* (hypocrisy), which was the most striking thing about how the synod went about in their discussion about the report. His report. Which also mentions the dire situation that blacks in the cities were experiencing as a result of apartheid, was rejected, and as he notes, was seen as a 'Marxist' analysis of the situation in South Africa.

Durand also described his life at the University of the Western Cape as a lecturer and his conversations with theological students of the DRMC. He mentions the tensions that existed on campus, the riots and also refers to the detainment of most of the theological students by the security police. He an occasion when a student was supposed to deliver his *'proefpreek'* (trail sermon); how they waited for the appearance of the student, only to be informed later that the student had been detained. Finally, he recalls his 'divorce' from the DRC when he finally wrote a letter to the DRC in which he stated that he is no longer *'beroepbaar'* (available for a call) in the DRC.

Plaatjies-Van Huffel (2014:31), Botha (2010:37) and Durand (cited in Du Toit 2014:3-39) all give socio-historical contributions in which they unpack the 'forces' that led to the decision by the Dutch Reformed Mission Church's Synod in 1982 to draft the Belhar Confession. My argument that Belhar has meaning supports these types of analyses. However, my argument stretches beyond this in that I attempt to weigh the socio-historical context against the Words and Witness of God in the Bible, through the person of Jesus Christ to makes sense of the suffering of the members who belong to the DRC family during the apartheid milieu.

Smit helps us to bring the contextual realities during the time of apartheid and the emergence of the confession in good dialogue. Smit engages with Barth's *Church Dogmatics*, Volume 4, which specifically deals with Christology (Smit (2009a:337). In his argument uses Barth's treatise on Christology to substantiate why God is the 'God of the poor' and the destitute by. Barth argues that Jesus (as the royal man) is 'a reflection of God in correspondence with God's own purpose and work and attitude of God' (Smit 2009a:342).

In his treatise, Barth shows how God through Jesus is deduced from four observations in the New Testament Scriptures, In terms of Jesus as the 'Royal man', Barth argues that Jesus

> shares as such the strange destiny which falls on God and His people in the world – to be the One who is forgotten and despised and discounted by men ... He (Jesus) ignored all those who are high and mighty and wealthy in the world in favour of the weak and meek and lowly. (cited in Smit 2009a:342)

Smit reflects on Barth's exposition of the miracles of Jesus in the New Testament. Barth reflected God, through Jesus in different ways. He maintains that God turns to 'the man with whom things are going badly; who is needy and frightened and harassed'. The miracles of Jesus showcase his response to 'human misery' and the physical suffering of people. This reflects a God who is 'directly interested in the humanity and His creatures, beyond or above or through his sin He is interested in man himself'. Also, 'God self-evidently places himself at the side of humanity, makes their suffering His own, and takes up their struggle against the hostile powers' (cited in Smit 2009a:348). Barth argues, 'it is the free grace that is active in the miracles' (cited in Smit 2009a:349), and this, acclaims Barth, is where Protestantism failed – to show, 'That the message of the Kingdom, symbolically enacted in the miracles of Jesus, is the message of the omnipotence of mercy and unconditionally complete liberation from the destructive powers of evil' (cited in Smit 2009a:349).

Smit concludes that Protestantism orientated itself to a particular bias and view humanity as sinful, not as humanity in misery and suffering. Smit sums up the work of Barth and how the miracles of Jesus help us to see God as the 'God of the poor' and the destitute:

> [T]he miracles help us to understand God's grace in its radicality and unconditionality, addressed to humanity in sloth and misery – not only to sinners, but to God's creatures, the partners in the covenant, in sin and in suffering as a result of the power of evil. In the act of reconciliation in Christ,

God overcomes all these barriers in his free grace and his omnipotent mercy. That is the message and reality of the Kingdom, the heart of the gospel, the content of all theology, and the reason for abundant joy. (Smita 2009:350)

Smit believes that Barth challenges the DRC family to exchange the particularised and often mutually exclusive 'paradigms of salvation' for a more inclusive 'paradigm of grace in Jesus Christ' (Smit 2009a:358). Smit argues that [especially] Protestants and the DRC family should make room, create spaces for seeing God as the God of the poor and destitute – as portrayed in the miracles of Jesus. He brings. Therefore. the implicit experiences and contextual realities during the time of the emergence of the Belhar Confession in conversation with the portrayal of God in the New Testament.

The 'no' of Belhar as a way to search for meaning

Plaatjies-Van Huffel (2014:302) refers to the reasons why the DRMC declared a *status confessionis* – apartheid. But why was apartheid so wrong that a confession was needed? Botman (2006:241) contends that though the word 'apartheid' was not used in the document, the Confession of Belhar does speak of racism. He refers to the discussion of the DRMC Synod in 1982, which he argues was a confession against false doctrine instead of a political system. He does not ignore the political system prevailing at the time, and points out that there was such a political situation in South Africa that endorsed apartheid. However, the synod agreed that the document should not be 'overtly political'. Boltman confirms this when he states in his comparative analysis between the Barmen Declaration and the Belhar Confession that both emanated as a result of political situations. He points out that though the political situation of South Africa is not explicitly mentioned in the confession, it can be resolved when those who read the confession and declaration (Belhar and Barmen) today are prepared to do the social analysis that precedes the lives of those confessions. Though I agree with Botman not to be overtly political in the confessions, I believe that the 'no's (injustice, division or separate development, the irreconcilability of people) implicitly embedded in the Confession, which would have overtly rejected the political context of South Africa at the time, should have been more strongly voiced in the commentaries of the time, and even in the present. During discussions on the aftermath of apartheid, I came across one such commentary by Piet Naudé. I will now briefly refer to his contribution.

Naudé in his 2010 book *Neither Calendar nor Clock, Perspectives on the Belhar Confession* makes sense of the confession by shedding more light in his contribution on the 'no's of Belhar: 'The church confesses spiritual but also physically and social unity of the church' (Naudé 2010:46). Naudé refers to the DRC Synod of 1857 when he discusses the 'no' of Belhar for separate development within the DRC family.

> The weaknesses of some not to receive Holy Communion with new converts from a different background, language and culture, as well as the missiological practice and method of converting people as an ethic entity, became the principle used to justify separate church formation. Once this ethic or cultural principle comes to determine actual membership of the church, a false requirement beyond faith in Christ is set down. This doctrine is to be rejected as a false vision of the church in which human and social factors supersede our being in Christ. (Naudé 2010:46)

Belhar confess reconciliation. The harsh reality of the ideology of the DRC at the time of apartheid supported the view that people of different races were irreconcilable. The underlying experiences of suffering that were caused by the 'forced separation on racial grounds' in South African society (Naudé, 2010:46) led to Belhar saying 'no' to this ideology. Naudé (2010:46) argues that a teaching which professes that people from different racial backgrounds are in principle irreconcilable and should be physically and spatially separated should be rejected. Therefore, the Belhar confessed in the positive – the reconciliation of people.

In the context of injustices (justice) Naudé (2010:47) argues that Belhar 'addresses the specific situation of South Africa in the 1980s. He declares that 'It was in a time when the '*Afrikaner volk*', (who also remembers a time when they were classified as the poor and downtrodden under British rule)', became oppressors themselves when the United Nations (UN) and the rest of the free world accepted the Universal Declaration of Human Rights (UDHR). Despite the positive development within the structure and policies of the UN, the project of apartheid was endorsed. The '*Afrikaner volk*' ushered in the injustices of apartheid, and the DRC, consisting mainly of Afrikaners at the time, also endorsed it as 'the will of God'. This became known as the apartheid ideology, fostered, and espoused by the Dutch Reformed Church.

Belhar as a therapeutic document

This section briefly considers the existential approach of Victor Frankl and explains why the Confession of Belhar is a therapeutic document. The section refers to the DRC family, as the Uniting Reformed Church (URCSA) and the DRC are historically bound to each other.

The experiences of Frankl and his own life story speak to the heart of the matter of 'meaning'. Frankl points to his own experience as a Holocaust victim and survivor and the dire circumstances he had to face in Nazi Germany. Belhar, to be a therapeutic document, should reflect the suffering, the crude and unbearable circumstances of the past. Frankl maintains that if Belhar can sufficiently tell the story of human beings who were faced with situations in life, that 'confronted them, that placed a demand on them, presented a question to them, which they had to answer by doing something in that given situation', then it will have meaning (Frankl 1948:141).

Belhar meets the criteria of 'down to earth meanings' due to the encompassing 'experiences of something' (apartheid), the encountering of someone (the oppressors and supporters of an ideology of apartheid) (Frankl 1948:141-143). Belhar is written because of the tragic stories of human beings on South African soil. Belhar, as the forerunner of stories of suffering, division, injustice and the irreconcilability of people, placed a demand on the DRMC to answer by doing something; by drafting the Belhar Confession in the apartheid situation to create and construct meaning(s). This is 'unearthed' by the analysis of Smit in which he comments on Belhar's reference to the God of the poor and the destitute through his analysis of Barth's Christology. In his analysis, he points out the association of God, reflected in the Bible, with the needy, the frightened, and the harassed. He argues that humans should be viewed not only in terms of their sinful nature but as 'humanity in misery and suffering' (Smit 2009a:348). Through his analysis, Smit demonstrates how Belhar can be a resource for the church to shed light on the implicit experiences and contextual realities during the time of the emergence of the Belhar Confession in conversation with the portrayal of God in the New Testament.

Attempts such as the work done by Smit are aimed at creating meaning as spiritual beings. Deep reflections of the suffering and period of apartheid will bring members within the DRC family, not only to a point of consciousness but despite the suffering and the past painful experiences to reach a point where you 'just to have the idea that you live for 'something' (despite the suffering and make life worthwhile to endure. (Meyer et al. 2008:437). As spiritual beings[8] we can quest for more than this by recognising the 'spiritual height of our nature' – our will to ultimate meaning, and be open to the possibility to see God in the 'whole' picture (Frankl 1948:152). We do not have to only look into ourselves (depth psychology) but must look outside ourselves, and 'look up' for the meaning of our painful past of the DRC family. The room and space are created also for people's particular experiences of suffering, which Frankl (1948:141) notes, is not determined and cannot be offered by a psychiatrist or psychologist.

The Belhar Confession has three positive articles in which it confesses unity, reconciliation and justice – to point out how God is reflected through the life of

---

8   Frankl argues that human beings are at the core religious beings.

Jesus Christ in the gospels, and where he stands (with the poor and destitute). But it is in the historical realities in apartheid South Africa and through the context of Belhar through which we are able to pick up the painful experience of people, where we come to understand the real, but also the complexities under which people suffered. The brutal way in which the church that was supposed to be a therapeutic space, the 'balm of Gilead', endorsed the apartheid laws of the time.

The oppressors, as well as the oppressed, were affected by the socio-political and historical realities during the time and before the drafting of Belhar, either by the suffering under the apartheid system, the painful experiences caused by the church, or simply by being confronted with the complicit action of the DRC with the apartheid laws of the time, and their treatment of other races (blacks, coloured, Indians) within the DRC family. If one can fully engage with the pain, the struggle and the negative bitter experiences of the past, and by focusing on the 'no's of Belhar that are implicitly part of the confession, I argue that the DRC family will then be able to adequately create meaning (s) out of their respective experiences. The confession is adequate as it stands. In fact, it is more than what it is – to 'confess'; it can assist the DRC family to understand who God is.[9] This is important for Frankl also in his account of ultimate meaning. We create meaning out of suffering when we try to make sense of the context, not only referring to the context. We create meaning when we put our experience in light of God's words and work in the life of Jesus Christ for our 'down to earth meanings' but we also the see the bigger 'up to heaven' meaning of the suffering and painful past. We make sense of our suffering when we read it from the negative side (Belhar's implicit 'no's); what Kritzinger refers to as that which we are 'testifying against' or 'the teachings and practices that threaten it' (Kritzinger 2010:13). We make sense of Belhar when we discuss and articulate the full impact and experiences that Belhar implicitly confesses in conversation with what is reflected through the life and words of God through Jesus Christ.

Implications for the DRC family

The Belhar Confession has created much tension between the URCSA, the DRC and other churches within the DRC family. One of the arguments is that the confession is written within a context of apartheid, and was seen as a political document. Much of the resistance within the DRC church is based on the struggle to accept the document, perhaps not solely because of the reasoning that Belhar is not aligned with the Bible, but rather that it is not meant, relevant, or appropriate for this 'new dispensation'. They would argue, let us not be caught up in the memory of the past.

---

9   Not that we are adequately able to understand God, but we can create meaning through symbols, metaphors and his Words and works through the Life of Jesus.

This new season in the country calls for an approach that would not 'further divide the flock of God', but that would rather bring the church together without delving too much into the past. As I have reasoned previously in an article concerning the outcome of the TRC process in South Africa, that as much as it was a process of reconciliation and forgiveness and striving towards national unity, the issues of remorse and repentance that should have been part of the process were not included. This would have demanded an inquiry of the past, and for the betterment, a reconciliation process (See Baron 2015). We will always be haunted by the past if we do not deal with the past.

Inasmuch as Smit and Naude (2010:1) speak of confessions as historical in nature, with emphasis on Belhar, I see a rigorous analysis of the Belhar against the backdrop of the political (which Smit argues in his forward to the book of Naude) circumstances, and the 'no's' of Belhar (division and unity; fragmentation and reconciliation, injustice and justice) fully examined. An important question that needs attention is how valuable will this confession be in a united church? Members of the rest of the DRC family and URCSA are bound to each other in history. This can be for both (the URCSA and the rest of the DRC family) either a document that can serve as a means of reflection on the past in the quest for meaning, or it can be as referred to as a stumbling block that could hamper all future efforts of unity. One way of dealing with this confession is to obliterate the past, which is impossible, or try to run away from it and allow the pain and suffering of the past to haunt the DRC. We could also accept that Belhar can allow the DRC family to reflect together for purpose and ultimate meaning in relation to the suffering and painful past experiences and place it within the 'bigger picture' of the purpose of God for the DRC family.

Conclusion

During the times of apartheid, Durand conducted interviews with black people in the cities and held group discussions to describe and understand the dire situation in which they lived (cited in Du Toit 2014:18). However, we were only able to do a little of that in this chapter where the focus is on the emergence of Belhar in the context of the suffering and painful past that members of the DRC family faced in South Africa. Durand tells of his reflection and empathy towards the suffering and eventually shares his experience and the suffering of people during the time of Belhar. Plaatjies-Van Huffel and Botha did the same when they share the socio-historical circumstance as a prelude to Belhar, as did Naude in his contribution to 'unearth' the no's of Belhar. We are, therefore, challenged by Belhar to place the suffering and painful past in the light of the Bible, which the Belhar Confession embodies. Frankl declares that it is when we try to make sense of our past that we begin to regain hope; when we read it through the confession and God's ultimate plan for His people. The Belhar takes these experiences seriously and brings new meaning to them when put into God's light (the Bible).

Bibliography

Belhar Confession, 1986. The official English translation of the *Belhar Confession 1986* approved by the General Synod of 2008. Belhar: LUS Printers.

Baron, E. 2015. Remorse and repentance stripped of its validity. Amnesty granted by the Truth and Reconciliation Commission of South Africa. *Studia Historiae Ecclesiasticae* 41(1):168-184.

Botha, J. 2010. Belhar – waarvandaan? In J. Botha & P. Naude, *Goeie nuus om te bely. Die belydenis van Belhar en die pad van aanvaarding*. Wellington: Bybel-Media.

Botman, H.R. 2006. Barmen to Belhar: A contemporary confessing journey. *Nederduitse Gereformeerde Teologiese Tydskrif* 47(1/2):240-249.

Corey, G. 2013. *Theory and practice of counselling and psychotherapy* (9th edition). Belmont, CA: Brooks/Cole.

du Toit, D. (ed.). 2014. *Jaap Durand praat oor eenheid, versoening en geregtigheid*. Wellington: Bybelkor.

Frankl, V.E. 1948. *Man's search for ultimate meaning*. USA: Perseus Publishing.

Kritzinger, J.N.J. 2010. Celebrating communal authorship: The theological declaration of the Belydende Kring (1979) and the Belhar Confession. In honour of Simon Maimela and in memory of Chris Loff. *Studia Historiae Ecclesiasticae* 36(1):209-231.

Lubbe, J. 2013. Die Belydenis van Belhar – getuienis, stok en staf, credo? [Online] Available at http://belydenisvanbelhar.co.za/ander-bydraes/die-belydenis Van-belhar-getuienis-stok-staf-credo/ (Accessed 21 February 2015)

Meyer, W., Moore, C, & Viljoen, H. 2008. *Personology. From individual to ecosystem* (4th edition). Johannesburg: Heinemann Publishers.

Naudé, P.J. 2010. *Neither calender nor clock. Perspectives on the Belhar Confession*. Cambridge, UK: William B. Eerdmans.

Plaatjies-Van Huffel, M-A. 2014. The Belhar Confession in its historical context. *Nederduitse Gereformeerde Teologiese Tydskrif* 55(1/2):308-309. https://doi.org/10.5952/55-1-2-527

Smit, D.J. 2009a. Confessing as gathering the fragments? In R. Vosloo (ed.), *Essays on being reformed. Collected essays 3*. Stellenbosch: SUN PReSS.

Smit, D.J. 2009b. Paradigms of radical grace. In R. Vosloo (ed.), *Essays on being reformed. Collected essays 3*. Stellenbosch: SUN PReSS.

van der Merwe, C. & Gobodo-Madikizela, P. 2009. *Narrating our healing: Perspectives on working through trauma*. Newcastle, UK: Cambridge Scholars Publishing.

Vosloo, R.R. 2012. Traumatic memory, representations and forgiveness: Some remarks in conversation with Antjie Krog's *Country of My Skull. In die Skriflig* 46(1):1-7. https://doi.org/10.4102/ids.v46i1.53

THE BELHAR CONFESSION OF FAITH
A spirituality sense-making confession

Leepo Modise

Introduction

Over the years, the Uniting Reformed Church in Southern Africa (URCSA) has affirmed the extremely important and cardinal place of the Belhar Confession for and in the life of the church in various ways. The unconditional acceptance of the Confession of Belhar as a requirement for the continuation of the discussions on church unity has, for a long time, been a bone of contention. The URSCA has anticipated the acceptance of Belhar by the Dutch Reformed Church (DRC) with a deep longing, and is praying for the day when the DRC will walk the road of the church union with the URCSA's 'obedience to the Lord of the church' by accepting this confession, which we regard as founded in the Scriptures. In this paper, I discuss the spirituality aspect of the Belhar Confession of faith as opposed to the religious aspect[1] seen by other church members.

Background

The Belhar Confession has its roots in the struggle against apartheid in southern Africa. In its response to apartheid, the World Alliance of Reformed Churches (WARC) states:

> The white Afrikaans Reformed Churches through the years have worked out in considerable detail both the policy itself and the theological and moral justification for the system. Apartheid is therefore, a pseudo-religious ideology as well as a political policy. It depends to a large extent on this moral and theological justification. The division of the Reformed churches in South Africa on the basis of race and colour is being defended as a faithful interpretation of the will of God and of Reformed understanding of the church in the world. (Addendum 1, WARC Resolution on Racism and South Africa)

---

1   The distinction between religion and spirituality will be explained later in the chapter.

The WARC declared that the situation in South Africa constituted a *status confessionis*, which means that the WARC regard this an issue on which it is impossible to differ without seriously jeopardising the integrity of our common confession as Reformed churches. Based on this situation, the WARC made the following declaration:

> We declare with the black Reformed Christians of South Africa that apartheid (separate development) is a sin and that the moral and theological justification of it is a travesty of the Gospel and, in its persistent disobedience to the Word of God, a theological heresy. (Addendum 1, WARC Resolution on Racism and South Africa)

At its synod later that year, the Dutch Reformed Mission Church (DRMC) followed in the footsteps of the WARC and declared a *status confessionis* (*Agenda en Handelinge NGSK* 1982:439). The church realised that in a situation like this the church must confess anew to the truths of the Bible in the light of the pseudo-gospel. The DRMC decided to draw up a confession. This 'outcry of faith' and 'call for faithfulness and repentance' was first drafted in 1982 by the commission of four theologians (Prof. D.J. Smit, J.J.F. du Rand, G. Bam and Dr A.A Boesak) within DRMC under the leadership of Dirkie Smit as the main drafter of the text, which was later accepted by the synod as the Belhar Confession.

This was a confession in draft form, which was distributed to the whole DRMC for comment and was to be finalised at the next synod in 1986. The 1986 DRMC Synod accepted the confession. In this confession, the rejection of apartheid was made an article of faith (De Gruchy 1994:166). The name 'Belhar' in the Confession refers to the suburb of Belhar in the Western Cape where the synod met. The Confession was also adopted by the Dutch Reformed Church in Africa (DRCA) when the DRMC and the DRCA unified in 1994 to form a new church, namely the URCSA and this confession became part of the confessional basis of the URCSA. It is now one of the 'standards of unity' of the URCSA. In his address to the URCSA General Synod of 2005, Setri Nyomi said that the Belhar confession can be described as a modern-day standard of Christian unity. It sees unity as a gift of God and obligation, both a binding force and a reality to be earnestly pursued. Originating from a people who were oppressed and who were living expressions of the evils of apartheid, it is remarkable that the Confession was set in a call for unity and reconciliation. It described any enmity between people and people groups as sinful and called for unity to be visible. Such unity must be active in sharing and can only be established under freedom (*Acts of the URCSA General Synod* 2005:225).

The Belhar Confession has been a burning issue in the process of church unity and the unity talks between the URCSA and other DRC family members – an issue that drives these members away from achieving organic of unity. It has been an issue because some members perceived this confession as a political/ideological document and not a spiritual confession of faith from the heart. Even on the 13 of October 2011, some members of DRC opposed to the Belhar Confession still raised objections, such as, it is liberation or black theology, not a confession, politically motivated, and unbiblical. People were warned that congregations would break away if the confession was accepted. One minister said that during a vote in his church council of 144 members, 141 voted against Belhar (URCSA pastoral letter of 14 October 2011).

The Confession is based on Scripture as the word of God and is a witness to the liberating acts of God in history and our own time, the lordship of Jesus Christ over all areas of life, and the empowering presence of the Holy Spirit in the life of those who believe (Acts of General Synod URCSA 2005:151). At the DRC General Synod meeting on the 13 October 2011, members in favour of Belhar confession also presented their cases with passion and mentioned that they need this confession because it spoke about unity, reconciliation and justice in a unique biblical and reformed way and that it addressed the South African context (URCSA pastoral letter of 14 October 2011).

The Belhar Confession has its historical and theological roots in the Reformed tradition and has proved itself to be a worthy bearer of the historical continuation of the reformed endeavour to be forever reforming in response to God's call in a changing world. The confession's relevance is not confined to southern Africa or its religious context. It addresses three key issues of concern in all churches: unity of the church and unity among all people, reconciliation within the church and society, and God's justice. The Belhar Confession of faith as a Reformed confession is carried by the URCSA on behalf of all reformed churches. This is justified by the words of Barth:

> A reformed creed is the statement, spontaneously and publicly formulated by a Christian community within a geographically limited area, which, until further action, defines its character to outsiders, and which, until further action, gives guidance for its own doctrine and life; it is a formulation of the insight currently given to the whole Christian Church by the revelation of God in Jesus Christ by the Holy Scripture alone. (Barth 1962:112)

In line with Barth (1962) the URCSA General Synod of 2005 confirmed that the Belhar Confession, although written and accepted by the church at a specific time and place, is a living confession inspiring the church worldwide. It is not aimed against certain groups and is not confined by political or geographical boundaries. The confession confirms that the URCSA not a church with a confession whose value lies in the mindless repetitions of words. It is rather a confessing church – one on which rests the obligation to allow the Confession to become a way of life, utterly convincing in its love, utterly compelling in its call. The way in which the Confession of Belhar has reached far beyond URCSA and South Africa to constantly inspire the churches of our Reformed family and the broader ecumenical movement is a source of humble rejoicing and deep gratitude for which the members of the URCSA praise God (*Acts of the General Synod URCSA* 2005:152).

The Belhar Confession is relevant to all Christian churches because it addresses critical issues emphasised in Scripture: unity among the people of God, reconciliation within the church and society, injustices of all kinds, and God's bias on behalf of those who have been wronged (Plaatjies-Van Huffel 2014:308-309).

The Belhar Confession addresses spirituality issues and questions. As Wright (2005:2) argues, everybody seeks meaning, purpose, direction and connection in life. All human beings, at some point, ask questions such as 'Who am I?'; Why am I here?'; 'Where am I going?'; and 'How do I get there?' We all pursue relationships, work and activities that nurture and feel right to us. The Belhar Confession of faith as a spirituality confession rather than a religious document tries to answer these questions.

Distinction between spirituality and religion in relation to the Belhar Confession

Considering the Belhar Confession, one might see spirituality as an engine of human life; a power that gives a person life during difficult, challenging and uncomfortable conditions. The Confession was a response of the church in faith at a time of tremendous challenge and adversity. This moment of *kairos* was a call to obedience in which the church rediscovered the faithfulness of God, the strength given by God's Holy Spirit in times of challenge and weakness, and the power of faithful witness to the powers of evil. The Confession of Belhar, does not refer to the desires of our own heart, or the urgent voices of revenge and retribution, but to the reconciling Christ, who calls us to be agents of reconciliation and out of that reconciliation calls us to unity and justice (*Acts of the General Synod URCSA* 2005:151).

In the Belhar Confession, the lives of the people in relation to triune God are of paramount importance. The historical context (the political and economic oppression, deep enmity and immeasurable suffering), however compelling, did not dictate the reaction of the church. Instead the Holy Spirit enabled human beings to rise above political realities, economic hardship, social injustices and denial of human's very humanity; to rise above human-self and affirm first and foremost, God as God of Justice and reconciliation. This section focuses on the reflection of spirituality in the broader sense within the content of the Belhar Confession against its religious limitations.

A distinction can be made between Christian spirituality and spirituality in general. Thus, when people use the word 'spirituality' they may mean very different things. Spirituality is an awareness or consciousness of another Being or Force other than the human spirit or physical reality. It is a conviction that what is real is not restricted to what our five senses can perceive, but that an entire spiritual world exists that is both separate from human and physical reality and interacts with human and physical reality. According to Thomas, 'spirituality' is best defined as the sum of all the uniquely human capacities and functions: self-awareness, self-transcendence, memory, anticipation, rationality (in the broadest sense), creativity, plus the moral, intellectual, social, political, aesthetic and religious capacities, all understood as embodied. This means that spirituality is universal, essentially linked to humanity, and certainly not optional. Even though all people are spiritual, spirituality can be either 'good or bad, life-enhancing or life-destructive' (Thomas 2000:268).

Spirituality is the solid centre in the lives of the people that enables them to express themselves in the world and to cope with all complexities and conflicts of being alive. The absence of spirituality brings the feeling of being adrift, rootless, despairing and aimless (Wright 2005:7). Therefore, spirituality is the very root of our being — who we think we are, why we are here, and what we should do with our lives. Spirituality is the search for wholeness, meaning, purpose, connection and the resolution of those great existential questions we face in life. If spirituality means anything, it means a sense of connection with oneself, each other, work, home and church as well as that which is beyond the self. Spirituality is thus fundamental to the right relationships with ourselves, others and beyond. Pera and Van Tonder (2005:18) posit that human spirituality is that part of the person most deeply concerned with feelings, with the need for meaning in life, with convictions, belief systems, values, dreams, interpersonal relationships, the relationship with God and the physical-organic environment.

Spirituality has to do with depth value, relatedness, the heart, and personal substance and is not an object of religious belief or something that concerns immortality. In this view, spirituality engages all the elements needed for caring and relatedness of human beings as well as with God (Pera & Van Tonder 2005:18). The Belhar Confession reflects spirituality rather than religion.

Spirituality is all about a theanthropocosmic[2] sense-making approach, the relationship with us, others, God and the physical-organic environment. Wright confirms: 'Indeed, if spirituality concerns right relationship, relationship that has meaning and nurturance for us with ourselves, each other, the world and perhaps our God, and which as acted out in compassionate ways in the world' (Wright 2005:7).

Spirituality can go beyond the limitations of the human mind, soul and body. It assures human beings that they are not alone, that they do not have to be in control of other human beings. This allows them to trust, to be honest and therefore vulnerable, and to live in acceptance of human-self and other human beings and faith in a power greater than human-self. Article 4 of the Belhar Confession states:

> We believe that God has revealed Godself as the One who wishes to bring about justice and true peace on earth; that in a world full of injustice and enmity God is in a special way the God of the destitute, the poor and wronged and that God calls the church to follow in this; that God brings justice to the oppressed and gives bread to the hungry; that God frees the prisoner and restores sight to the blind; that God supports the downtrodden, protects the strangers, helps orphans and widows and blocks the path of the ungodly; that for God pure and undefiled religion is to visit the orphans and the widows in their suffering; that God wishes to teach the people of God to do what is good and seek the right. That the church must therefore stand by people in any form of suffering and need, which implies, among other things, that the church must witness against and strive against any form of injustice, so that justice may roll down like waters and righteousness like an ever-flowing stream; that the church belonging to God, should stand where God stands, namely against injustice and with the wronged ... in the name of the gospel.[3]

Spirituality is that tendency that moves the individual towards hope, transcendence, connectedness, compassion, wellness, and wholeness. Spirituality includes one's capacity for creativity, growth, and the development of a value system. Spirituality can be seen as an activity that inspires in one the desire to transcend the realm of the material; spirituality is seen as the inward activity of growth and maturation that happens in each human being. Spirituality is not just a theory, it is praxis. Spirituality is about personal, individual, intense, and often secret experiences of the presence of God. There is always confusion about spirituality and religion, which

---

2 'Theanthropocosmic' refers to theos – God; 'anthropos' to human being and cosmos – physical-organic environment.

3 Extracts from the Confession of Belhar in this chapter are taken from the English translation at Addendum 15, The Confession of Belhar. Also available at http://urcsa.net/wp-content/uploads/2016/02/Belhar-Confession.pdf

is why most of the opponents of the Belhar Confession of faith when approaching or studying this confession find themselves trapped in the religious realm rather than in the spirituality realm. Hence it is important to give a brief description of religion.

Religion is institutional activity that brings forth spirituality. Wright (2005:3) suggests that religion can be seen as ritual, liturgy, dogma and the various practices that human beings collectively bring to human spiritual life to codify and unify it with others. Religion offers a channel for the expression of a human being's spirituality. It concerns rules and regulations, systems and hierarchies, the order of succession and perpetuation of the religious institution — it is about power. Religion as power-play can manipulate people. Religious people can be motivated by religious reasons and systems (Kemeny 2007). Tshaka (2010:23) alludes that theology does not start from a religious experience as the form whose content is revelation. Religion is not the object of theological reflection. It is not the concrete reality from which theological concepts are derived. The object of theological reflection is not the relationship of humanity to God in religious experience, but that of God to humanity in Jesus Christ.

Spirituality is an inward activity. Religion, on the other hand, is the outward form, the container, especially the liturgy and all acts of worship that teach, praise, and give thanks to God. Religion is empty without a spirituality content. Religion and spirituality are thus intertwined; religion provides a focus for spirituality expression and creates the context for spirituality to emerge. At some point, most religions sought to suppress any individual expression of spirituality that challenges accepted dogma.

Religion has more to do with conformity of individuals to a religious group that accepts a certain doctrine or dogma, while spirituality is about the individual choice of what will inwardly inspire the desire to be part of the religious group. Religion is overpowering individual thinking through social construction and conformity to the group, while spirituality is empowering individual thinking through social deconstruction[4]. Van der Walt (2001:3), citing Karl Marx, states that religion can have no positive influence on society or societal structures like schools, churches and business. It may offer rewards in the life hereafter, but in fact intends to keep the oppressed quiet in the here and now, and the powerful in society uses it to maintain the status quo. Religion does not influence society but rather societal structures. The socio-economic-political circumstances in society determine the religion of that society. According to Van der Walt (2001), religion is indeed influenced by the

---

4 Social deconstruction is the reverse process to undo the socially constructed ideology or system within the society.

socio-economic-political context. It can even function as an ideology that supports and condones the present order to be sacrosanct. Depending on the aspects of focus, it is even possible that faith can be both a supporter as well as a critic of the existing order in society. This is the situation within the members of the DRC family regarding the social order before the democratic era, when the DRMC consciously drafted and adopted the Belhar Confession of faith.

In fact, there is no special religious dimension, because God is directly involved in every field of experience as the Spirit of God or the Holy Spirit. We can explain this metaphorically in terms of the engine of a motor car. Every field of experience has its own spark plug, the nucleus or core of the field of experience where the Spirit of God is continually sparking and fusing, connecting God, being human and the physical-organic environment in a pattern of experience (Van Niekerk 2008:69). The idea of a religious dimension among various human dimensions of experience in our lives creates the impression that God hovers outside non-religious 'ordinary' human dimensions, and is allowed to enter our lives only through a so-called religious and supernatural faith dimension. In the traditional sense, religious faith plays a basic role among the multiplicity of fields and modes of experience of our created existence, but does not form intrinsically and initially part of human experience. One of the basic premises is that one can only speak of faith as faith-experience in a similar way as thought experience, experience of emotions and experiential apportioning of justness (Modise 2009:23).

Spirituality is a broader and more inclusive term than religion. Spirituality retains its broad meaning, linked to the totality of human understanding and experience, also linked to both religion and culture. Spirituality is not a narrow separate compartment of religion; it is an essential part of our humanity and world. Hence the author sees the Belhar Confession as spirituality – a confession of faith, not in a religious sense – that is supposed to become a power-play tool or something that manipulates people to accept a certain reality in life or is used to push people to unity in the church and society. Its intention is that human beings may live as God intends them to live – to have peace, justice, love and reconciliation among the whole human race.

The Belhar Confession in relation to spirituality

It is argued that spirituality is the search for wholeness, meaning, purpose, connection and resolution of those great existential questions that human beings are faced with in life. The Belhar Confession as a product of active faith addresses the existential questions that affect humanity. Spirituality has come out of the closet of ignorance. The Belhar Confession was born out of a long period of ignorance of the DRC family about the lives of people in South Africa under the pretext of religious doctrines and systems that supported the apartheid regime. Melanie Verwoerd (1997:54), in addressing a symposium in Johannesburg between members of the African National Congress Commission for Religious Affairs and the Christian Democratic Party of the Netherlands, said that the relationship between the DRC and the previous regime had been well documented and needed not be repeated here. Suffice to say that it is well known (although not widely accepted by the DRC) that for many years the DRC played a crucial role in supplying a theological justification of apartheid to the state. This is clear proof of how the DRC chose to be ignorant about the situation in that time. This ended when the Spirit of God inspired the DRMC in 1982 to bring the church and society to its consciousness about the situation in South Africa through Belhar Confession.

The opening sentence of the letter that accompanies the Confession states that: 'we are deeply conscious that moments of such seriousness can arise in the life of the Church that it may feel the need to confess its faith anew in the light of a specific situation'. (Appendix 15, Accompanying Letter) This statement illustrates that the URCSA (Formally the DRCA and the DRMC) had been ignorant of the situation and now the spirit of God had inspired the church to confess anew. Therefore, this confession is not a religious document that needs to be debated, but is a spirituality confession that emerged from within individual believer and needed individuals to embrace it with love, passion and hope.

The connectedness of the triune God in the Belhar Confession

Article 1 of the Belhar Confession declares that unity is important for the existence of the Godhead. This section deals with the intra-relationship and wholeness of the triune God who gathers, protects and cares for his people. That God gathers his people shows the importance of human race unity. The providence of God (protection and caring) to his people is an act of the theanthropocosmic connectedness. It is an illustration that God cannot distance himself from his people, hence the protection and caring of his people. In this perspective, the Belhar Confession teaches the human race how God is connected to his people, as is stated in Article 4 of the confession (See earlier).

In terms of spirituality, intra-connectedness and interconnectedness are important components from the point of view that the intra- and interconnectedness of the triune God with the human race through God's providence as to in the Belhar Confession serves as a prototype for the human race to have such interconnectedness. Jesus Christ as the head of the church in his priestly prayer prayed for the unity of the church – that all believers in him may be one, just like him and the Father are one, him in the Father and the Father in him, and believers may also be in them so that they may be brought to complete unity (John 17:21-22. New Revises Standard Version).[5]

The connectedness of the human being in the Belhar Confession

Article 2 of the Belhar Confession emphasises the interrelationship and wholeness of the human race. The article states: 'We believe in one holy, universal Christian Church, the communion of saints called from the entire human family.' Hence, the Belhar Confession of faith is spirituality because it deals with the right relationship of the human race, and right relationship with God, thus, the fundamental characteristics of spirituality as stated in Article 3. In this article, the church confesses it is spirituality (relational, connected and united) and calls that Christians do likewise through confessing and moving towards unity of the entire human race. The church sees beyond materialism and materialistic sense-making; it does not see colour of the other human being, nationality, ethnic or status, but it sees the communion of saints. The church sees the connectedness of the human race. Furthermore, when the church confesses, it does not see any colour, nationality, ethnic, language or status but a communion of saints.

The URCSA and other reformed churches that have adopted this confession of faith confess in this way:' Christ's work of reconciliation is made manifest in the church as the community of believers who have been reconciled with God and with one another ... in that we love one another'. Hence this confession is spirituality. Wright (2005:7) contends that spirituality is concerned about the right relationship, a relationship that has meaning and nurturance for the human race with us, each other, the world and perhaps our God, and that is acted out in compassionate ways in the world.

For people in volatile situations, the development of relationships that carry the notions of positive belonging and bonding, particularly those who had poor interpersonal relationships in the past, help, support and contribute to troubled people's experience. As Stone affirms:

> A solid supportive relationship does not only serve to help troubled people to feel comfortable, but also becomes the means through which the minister can move them from catharsis (the release of emotions) to action. The relationship is not the goal of crisis intervention, but the basis upon which the care process grows towards crisis resolution. (Stone 1993:39)

---

5 Scriptural quotations in this chapter follow the New Revised Standard Version (NRSV)

In relationships, people learn to know each other better. They share their experiences of handling crises to a greater extent while supporting each other to healthier and sound relationships. Van Niekerk (1989:31) and Van den Heever (1989:13) share the same sentiments and agree that close relationships with friends or family have a positive impact on the wellbeing levels of a human being and the processes of nation-healing. James and Gilliland (2005:495) assert that social support systems are important to avoid a burnout syndrome. Support systems act as the boosters of the individual and assist in maintaining psychological and physical wellbeing over time.

The notion that James et al. (2005) call 'social support systems' are simply relationships that comprise the multiplicity of relationships in one person's life-world referred to earlier. They try to demonstrate how one person comes to know other persons in various relationships, simultaneously starting to learn to assist these persons and to be assisted by them. In the processes of establishing these relationships, coping mechanisms, stress-related experiences naturally forming part of these relationships, emerge. The Belhar Confession of faith challenges the Christians in South Africa and the entire Christian community in the Reformed tradition worldwide to explore this theanthropocosmic relationship, which includes a multiplicity of relationships in one person's life-world. The lack of this loving connection to another human being and God made it easy to disconnect, dehumanise and see other human beings as 'it' or a resource (tool).

The URCSA as the church that confesses the Belhar Confession would like to demonstrate love, peace, reconciliation and unity to all within the entire universe. The URCSA, by confessing the Belhar Confession, illustrates the love and care for and about other human beings not because they are different from us, or separated from us, but because they are us. By this confession, the URCSA relates and connects to others because it shares a common humanity; in the other are us, in us is the other. What this church does to them, it does to us. Such caring love for another is an act of spirituality; a sacred thing. Article 2 of the Confession emphasises this caring love for another. Hence the Belhar Confession is a confession that reflects spirituality or the connectedness of God, and all humanity.

Reconciliation as binding factor for connectedness/unity

Article 3 of the Belhar Confession reinforces the interconnectedness and wholeness of the human race that need to reconcile with God and other human beings. This reinforcement is the message of reconciliation entrusted to the church by God through Christ. Barth writes:

> The God who acts as Reconciler in Jesus Christ is one God, and so too is the man reconciled with Him in God. Similarly, the work of atonement which is His action is one. But the forms in which He and His act are revealed to us, the problems that have to be weighed and unfolded in Dogmatics, cannot be treated at a single glance without violence, abbreviation and distortion. (Barth 1958:3)

The Belhar Confession as spirituality encourages the church to preach and practice the message of reconciliation, the message of peace and justice. This message is necessary for the people of South Africa and other parts of the world where there is hatred, war and injustice.

Suggit (1994:113) states that reconciliation is the responsibility of God to restore to humankind the freedom which they were created to enjoy. In addition, he proposes that the word 'redemption' means buying back or ransoming and is a useful term to describe the overcoming of the broken relationship that separates the human race from one another, from God the source of life, and from the physical-organic environment. Article 3 of the Belhar Confession of faith states:

> We believe that God has entrusted to the church with the message of reconciliation in and through Jesus Christ; that the church is called to be the salt of the earth and the light of the world and that the church is called blessed because it is a peacemaker, that the church is witness both by word and by deed to the new heaven and the new earth in which righteousness dwells; that God's s life-giving Word and Spirit has conquered the powers of sin and death, and therefore also of irreconciliation and hatred, bitterness and enmity; that God's life-giving Word and Spirit will enable the church to live in new obedience, which can open new possibilities of life for society and the world.

For that matter, the Confession of Belhar is against all actions that lead to injustice, separation and hatred; it urges all who confess this confession to strive for peace, love, justice, compassion and reconciliation throughout the ages and under all circumstances. All that is mentioned in this confession strive for reconciliation and connectedness/unity, which are the characteristics of spirituality; hence I perceive Belhar Confession more as a spirituality (broader sense) confession of faith. To confirm the connotation between the Belhar Confession and spirituality, Landman

(2007) states that spirituality is a tendency that moves individuals towards knowledge, love, meaning, peace, hope, transcendence, connectedness, compassion, wellness and wholeness. These characteristics of spirituality are the same characteristics that reflect within the Belhar Confession of faith, hence perceived by the author as spirituality rather than a religious declaration.

The Belhar articles discussed above illustrate that the intra-connectedness of the Godhead and the interconnectedness of God and human races as well as the interconnectedness among the human race are pivotal within the Belhar Confession of faith. The centre that holds this connectedness in spirituality is a caring spirit of God to human beings and human beings to other human beings. Article 4 of the Belhar Confession addresses or confesses compassionate care. De Gruchy contends:

Thus the Belhar Confession states that the church must stand by people in any form of suffering and need, which implies, among other things, that the church must witness against and strive against any form of injustice ... that the church as the possession of God must stand where He (God) stands, namely against injustice and with the wronged; that in following Christ the church must witness against all the powerful and privileged who selfishly seek their own interests and thus control and harm others. (De Gruchy 1994:167)

Here the Confession urges the members of the confessing church to show compassionate care to the human race irrespective of race, colour, creed and class. This compassionate care should be demonstrated towards everybody, especially the poor, orphans, widows, wronged, oppressed, prisoners, downtrodden and strangers.

The Confession emphasises that in caring for other, we care for us. Yet, it is this quality of non-judgemental caring, whether explicit or not, that has underpinned caring ideals for centuries. Such caring love for another is an act of spirituality, a sacred action in itself. Wright (2005:7) ponders that the love known as 'agape' enables human beings to bridge the gap of disconnectedness to make that connection. To be available with caring compassion for other human beings is achievable because we do not see them as 'other', but as us. Caring for our neighbours no matter how we perceive them to be or what they have done, can be accomplished with equity and equanimity. When we see ourselves mirrored in the other, we are no longer separate but connected.

Article 4 of the confession states that the church is called to stand by the people in any form of suffering and need, which implies, among other things, that the church must witness against any form of injustices, so that justice may roll down like waters, and righteousness like an ever-flowing stream, because in a special way God is the God of the destitute, the poor and the wronged ... and that the church as

God's possession is called to stand where God stands, namely against injustice and with the wronged.

Article 5 of the confession gives a plan of action to vitalise the words in the four articles discussed above. It stresses the words and deeds. It deals with the notion of 'confess what you practice' or 'practice what you confess'. The article stresses the words and deeds of the people of God, thus the URCSA confesses that we believe that in obedience to Jesus Christ, the only head of the church, the church is called to confess and to do all these things, even though the authorities and human laws might forbid them, punishment and suffering be the consequence. We confess Jesus is Lord. From this chapter, we are convinced that this confession is spirituality, because spirituality is not just a theory but praxis. It is about personal, individual, intense, and often secret experiences of the presence of God.

Conclusion

On a concluding note, the Belhar Confession of faith as spirituality goes beyond the limitation of religious ritual, liturgy, dogma and various practices that we collectively bring to our spirituality life to codify and unify our spiritual life with others. Hence some Christians within the DRC family may equate it to the DRC documents such as *Church and Society* when addressing theological students at Stellenbosch on church unity. The Belhar Confession of faith assures Christians that they are not alone, that they do not have control of others, thereby allowing themselves to trust, to be honest and therefore vulnerable, and to live in acceptance of themselves (URCSA members) and others (DRCA, DRC, RCA and the entire world) as well as possessing a faith in power greater than themselves. Hence, the Belhar Confession of faith is spirituality rather than religious by nature, because religion can be seen as the ritual, church orders, liturgy, dogma and various practices that the human race collectively brings to its spiritual life to codify and unify their spiritual life with others. Religion has more to do with the conformity of individuals with the religious group that accepts certain doctrine or dogma. In this sense, the doctrine or dogma in most cases separates the human race from one another. The Belhar Confession of faith provides a spiritual map and compass for Reformed churches to sail through the stormy waters in the right direction of life.

Bibliography

Primary sources

Agenda en Handelinge Nederduits Gereformeerde Sendingkerk 1982.

Secondary sources

Barth, K. 2004/1955. *Church dogmatics* (Vol. 4, Part 2). Translated by G. Bromily & T.F. Torrance. Edinburgh: Bloomsbury T&T Clark.

Belhar Confession, 1986. The official English translation of the *Belhar Confession 1986* approved by the General Synod of 2008. Belhar: LUS Printers.

James, R.K. & Gilliland, B.E. 2005. *Crisis intervention strategies.* Belmont. CA: Thomson/Brooks Cole.

Kemeny, PC. 2007. *Church, state and public justice.* Downers Grove, IL: Intervarsity Press.

Landman, C. 2007. Doing narrative counselling in the context of township spirituality. DTh thesis, University of South Africa, Pretoria.

Modise, L.J. 2009. Reflections on the well-being levels of professionals in rural and semi-rural areas – A faith theoretical perspective. DTh thesis University of South Africa, Pretoria.

Pera, S.A. & van Tonder S. 2005. *Religious and cultural forces in the transcultural nursing.* In S.A. Pera & S. van Tonder (eds), *Ethics in health care* (2nd edition). Cape Town: Juta & Co.

Plaatjies-Van Huffel, M-A. 2014. The Belhar Confession in its historical context. *Nederduitse Gereformeerde Teologiese Tydskrif* 55(1/2):308-309. https://doi.org/10.5952/55-1-2-527

Stone, H.W. 1993. *Crisis counselling.* Minneapolis, MN: Augsburg Fortress.

Suggit, J. 1994. *Redemption: Freedom regained.* In J.W. de Gruchy & C. Villa-Vicencio (eds), *Doing theology in context. South African perspectives* (Vol. 1). Claremont: David Philip Publishers.

Thomas, O. 2000. Some problems in contemporary Christian spirituality. *Anglican Theological Review* 82(2):267-287.

Tshaka, R.S. 2010. *Confessional theology? A critical analysis of the theology of Karl Barth and its significance for the Belhar Confession.* Newcastle, UK: Cambridge Scholars Publishing.

van den Heever, GA. 1989. Neighbourliness and the alleviation of stress- perspective from the New Testament. In P.G.R. de Villiers (ed.), *The Bible and stress.* Pretoria: University of South Africa.

van der Walt, BJ. 2001. *Transformed by renewing of your mind: Shaping a biblical worldview and a Christian perspective on scholarship.* Potchefstroom: The Institute for Contemporary Christians in Africa.

van Niekerk, E. 2008. *Faith, philosophy and science,* TL 501/2008. Pretoria: University of South Africa.

van Niekerk, E. 2009. *Faith, philosophy and Science* TL 501/2009. Pretoria: University of South Africa.

van Niekerk, E. 1989. Religion as neighbourliness? The phenomenon of stress in framework of human meaning and goals. In P.G.R. de Villiers (ed.), *The Bible and stress.* Pretoria: University of South Africa.

Verwoerd, M. 1997. *Public values and cultural diversity.* Johannesburg: Salty Print.

Wright, S. 2005. *Reflections on spirituality and health*. Philadelphia, PA: Whurr Publishers. https://doi.org/10.1002/9780470777923

Zodhiates, S. 1992. *The complete word study dictionary New Testament Scripture reference index*. Chattanooga, TN: AMG Publishers.

THE BELHAR CONFESSION
Addressing racism in church and society

Dawid Kuyler[1]

Peter Lodberg (1996:177) shows clearly the relationship between ethics and ecclesiology within the church and apartheid. The theological justification of apartheid called for a confessional and ethical response. Just like the current upsurge of racism in post-apartheid South Africa is calling of a response from the churches. Therefore, I would like to show the link between ecclesiology and ethics and show how the Belhar Confession can be utilised in addressing racism.[2] In 1948, the nationalist party released the following statement:

> There are two sections of thought in South Africa in regard to the policy affecting the non-European community. On the one hand, there is the policy of equality, which advocates equal rights within the same political structure for all civilised and educated persons, irrespective of race or colour, and the gradual granting of the franchise to non-Europeans as they become qualified to make use of democratic rights. On the other hand, there is the policy of separation (apartheid) which has grown from the experience of the established European population of the country, and which is based on the Christian principles of Justice and reasonableness. (Statement by the National Party of South Africa, 29 March 1948)

Through the years, the white Afrikaans Reformed churches of South Africa have worked out in considerable detail both the apartheid policy itself and the theological and moral justification for the system. Apartheid ('separate development') is, therefore, seen as a pseudo-religious ideology as well as a political policy. (Addendum 1, WARC Resolution on Racism and South Africa, Called to Witness 1983:26-30; Ottawa

---

[1] In December 1984, candidate of ministry Dawid Kuyler, a white member of the DRC, was called to a DRCM congregation on the wine farms near Stellenbosch. As an ordained minister of the DRMC he attended the historic 1986 Synod of the DRMC and in so doing became one of the first co-signatures of the Confession of Belhar. In 1994, he got a call to become a chaplain in the Department of Correctional Services. He served in this position until 2015. He had been a co-pastor in numerous congregations of URCSA. Since 2008, he has been the scribe of the General Synod of URCSA.

[2] This lecture was given at the Western Theological Seminary in October 2013.

Proceedings; WARC Ottawa Proceedings 1983:176-180).[3] Apartheid depended to a large extent on this moral and theological justification of apartheid. The DRC defended the division of Reformed churches in South Africa on the basis of race and colour as a faithful interpretation of the will of God and of the Reformed understanding of the church in the world. This led to the division of Christians at the Table of the Lord as a matter of practice and policy. This situation presented a challenge to the World Alliance of Reformed Churches (WARC) (WARC Called to Witness 1983:26-30; WARC Ottawa Proceedings 1983:176-180). Already in 1964, the General Council of the WARC, meeting in Frankfurt, declared that racism is nothing less than a betrayal of the gospel:

> The unity in Christ of members, not only of different confessions and denominations but of different nations and races, points to the fullness of the unity of all in God's coming kingdom. Therefore, the exclusion of any person on grounds of race, colour or nationality, from any congregation and part of the life of the church contradicts the very nature of the church. In such a case, the gospel is actually obscured from the world and the witness of the churches made ineffective. (WARC Called to Witness 1983:26)

In 1970, the General Council held in Nairobi confirmed this stance:

> The church must recognise racism for the idolatry it is ... The church that by doctrine and/or practice affirms segregation of peoples (e.g. racial segregation) as a law for its life cannot be regarded as an authentic member of the body of Christ. (Addendum 1, WARC Resolution on Racism and South Africa; WARC Called to Witness 1983:26-30; WARC Ottawa Proceedings 1983:176-180)

The DRC and the Nederduitse Hervormde Kerk did not take heed of the WARC declaration on racism. The WARC states clearly that the DRC and the Nederduitse Hervormde Kerk, in not only accepting, but actively justifying the apartheid system by misusing the gospel and the Reformed confession, contradict in doctrine and in action the promise which they profess to believe (Addendum 1; WARC Called to Witness 1983:26-30; WARC Ottawa Proceedings 1983:176-180). The WARC General Council 1982 affirmed earlier statements on the issue of racism and apartheid in 1964 and 1970, and reiterated its firm conviction that apartheid was sinful and incompatible with the gospel as (a) It is based on a fundamental irreconcilability of human beings, thus rendering ineffective the reconciling and uniting power of our Lord Jesus Christ; (b) In its application to racist structures it has led to exclusive

---

[3] For a more comprehensive history on the historical background of the Belhar Confession see the essay in this publication 'Acceptance, Adoption, Advocacy, Reception and Protestation: A Chronology of the Belhar Confession' by Mary-Anne Plaatjies-Van Huffel.

privileges for the white section of the population at the expense of the blacks; and (c) It has created a situation of injustice and oppression, large-scale deportation causing havoc to family life, and suffering to millions. Apartheid ought thus to be recognised as incurring the anger and sorrow of the God in whose image all human beings are created (WARC Ottawa Proceedings 1983:176-180).

The ecumenical church equally responded to the claim of the theological justification of apartheid by the white Afrikaans Reformed churches. Resolution 43 of the 1948 Lambeth Conference of Anglican Bishops states:

> The Conference is convinced that discrimination between men on the grounds of race alone is inconsistent with the principles of Christ's religion. We urge that, in every land-men of every race should be encouraged to develop in accordance with their abilities; and that this involves fairness of opportunity in trades and professions, in facilities for travelling and in the provision of housing, in education at all stages, and in schemes of social welfare. Every churchman should be assured of a cordial welcome in any church of our Communion, and no one should be ineligible for any position in the church by reason of his race or colour (The Lambeth Conference:13, Resolution 43).

According to Trevor Huddleston, racialism in any form is an 'inherent blasphemy against the nature of God who has created man in his own image, saying also that 'the Calvinism of the Afrikaner' like all heresies and deviations from Catholic truth ... is sub-Christian' (Huddleston 1956:180).

In 1960, after the Sharpeville massacre, delegates from the World Council of Churches (WCC) member churches in South Africa, representatives of the WCC from outside the country, and ecumenical institutions including the WCC, the LWF and the WARC met at the Cottesloe hostel of the University of the Witwatersrand in Johannesburg to discuss the situation in South Africa. In the statement, issued after the meeting one can clearly see how ecclesiology and ethics are being linked. At this meeting (the 'Cottesloe Consultation'), the role of the church regarding racism had been interrogated by delegates. The Cottesloe Declaration reads as follows:

> The Church of Jesus Christ, by its nature and calling, is deeply concerned with the welfare of all people, both as individuals and as members of social groups. It is called to minister to human need in whatever circumstances and forms it appears, and to insist that all be done with justice. In its social witness, the church must take cognisance of all attitudes, forces, policies and laws which affect the life of a people; but the church must proclaim that the final criterion of all social and political action is the principles of Scripture regarding the realisation of all men of a life worthy of their

God-given vocation. We make bold therefore to address this appeal to our churches and to all Christians, calling on them to consider every point where they may unite their ministry on behalf of a human being in the spirit of equity. (Cottesloe Declaration, Part 1)

The synods of the Afrikaans-speaking churches held in 1960 rejected the recommendations of the Consultation. The DRC and the Nederduitsch Hervormde Kerk van Afrika decided to resign from the WCC.

In 1969, the WCC launched the Programme to Combat Racism in response to a 1968 mandate from the council's Fourth Assembly in Uppsala, Sweden (WCC n.d). At their Sixth Assembly, held in Dar es Salaam, Tanzania from 13 to 25 June 1977, The Lutheran World Federation (LWF) issued a statement on the situation in South Africa namely 'Southern Africa: Confessional Integrity' (LWF n.d.). In the statement, the LWF declared that the racial segregation and the theological justification thereof by the reformed churches constitute a *status confessionis* (a basis in faith for churches to reject apartheid publicly and unequivocally). In 1982, the WARC declared apartheid a heresy and called for a *status confessionis* for the South African situation:

> Therefore, the General Council declares that this situation constitutes a *status confessionis* for our churches, which means that we regard this as an issue on which it is not possible to differ without seriously jeopardising the integrity of our common confession as Reformed churches. We declare, with black Reformed Christians of South Africa that apartheid ('separate development') is a sin, and that the moral and theological justification of it is a travesty of the gospel, and in its persistent disobedience to the word of God, a theological heresy. (WARC Called to Witness 1983:26-30; WARC Ottawa Proceedings 1983:176-180)

Alfred Rauhaus (2009:628-633) rightly argues that the *status confessionis* was indeed an ethical issue.

Ecclesiology and ethics in the Belhar Confession

In 1982, the WARC stated clearly that the gospel of Jesus Christ demands a community of believers that transcends all barriers of race – a community in which the love for Christ and for one another has overcome the divisions of race and colour. The gospel confronts racism, which is in its very essence a form of idolatry. Racism fosters a false sense of supremacy, it denies the common humanity of believers, and it denies Christ's reconciling, humanising work. It systematises oppression, domination and injustice. As such the struggle against racism, wherever it is found, in overt and covert forms, is a responsibility laid upon the church by the gospel of Jesus Christ in every country and society Addendum 1; WARC Called to Witness 1983:26-30; WARC Ottawa Proceedings 1983:176-180). God wants to unite his church and breaks the human-made walls of separations and create one united church. He wants to reconcile those who were estranged from one another and are living in bitterness and separation. The Confession *of* Belhar is anchored on three pillars: unity, reconciliation and justice. Article 1 of the Belhar Confession begins with the words: 'We believe in the triune God, Father, Son and Holy Spirit, who through Word and Spirit gathers, protects and cares for his church from the beginning of the world and will do to the end'.[4]

The church, therefore, has an ethical responsibility towards members of the ecclesiological community as well as towards the world. We should accept each another as created in God`s image. God in Jesus Christ has affirmed human dignity.

Article 2 of the Belhar Confession states how the relationship with other members of the church is based on the reconciliatory work of Christ.

> That Christ's work of reconciliation is made manifest in the church as the community of believers who have been reconciled with God and with one another; that unity is, therefore, both a gift and an obligation for the church of Jesus Christ; that through the working of God's Spirit it is a binding force, yet simultaneously a reality which must be earnestly pursued and sought: one which the people of God must continually be built up to attain.

Article 2 of the confession clearly spells out the relationship between members of the churches and the ethical way they should relate with one another:

> Together are built up to the stature of Christ, to the new humanity; together know and bear one another's burdens, thereby fulfilling the law of Christ that we need one another and up build one another, admonishing and comforting one another; that we suffer with one another for the sake of righteousness; pray together; together serve God in this world; and together fight against all which may threaten or hinder this unity; that this unity can be established only in freedom and not under constraint.

We are ethically bound to resist anything that can threaten this community. Members of the church are therefore compelled to uphold the rich diversity of language, culture, etc., within the church. The church as an ethical community created by God

---

4   All extracts from the Confession of Belhar in this chapter are taken from the English translation at Addendum 15, The Confession of Belhar. Also available at http://urcsa.net/wp-content/uploads/2016/02/Belhar-Confession.pdf

also needs to be clear which behaviour among members of the church is unethical and should be rejected. Article 1 of the confession affirms this and declares

> that the variety of spiritual gifts, opportunities, backgrounds, convictions, as well as the various languages and cultures, are, by virtue of the reconciliation in Christ, opportunities for mutual service and enrichment within the one visible people of God.

Article 2 continues:

> Therefore we reject any doctrine which absolutises either natural diversity or the sinful separation of people in such a way that this absolutisation hinders or breaks the visible and active unity of the church, or even leads to the establishment of a separate church formation; which professes that this spiritual unity is truly being maintained in the bond of peace while believers of the same confession are in effect alienated from one another for the sake of diversity and in despair of reconciliation; which denies that a refusal earnestly to pursue this visible unity as a priceless gift is sin; which explicitly or implicitly maintains that descent or any other human or social factor should be a consideration in determining membership of the church.

Constructive engagement with racism

During February 2014, on behalf of the URCSA, I attended a consultation of the World Communion of Reformed Churches (WCRC) in Grand Rapids, Michigan regarding the meaning of communion. The consultation considered, among other issues, the obstacles in relations between the member churches, such as, the immense financial barriers and unjust economic structures that dominate the community; the long-standing geographical obstacles, especially those caused by colonialism; and racial challenges, including the resurgence of racial economic patriarchal challenges that continue to come up, and discriminatory practices. Racism was seen as one of the important issues that hampered communion in and between churches.

The URCSA as faith community engages with the issue of racism on different levels. On my return to South Africa, the executive of the URCSA commissioned me to draft a proposal (later known as 'Churches Addressing Racism in Southern Africa') suggesting how the URCSA jointly with other churches may address the problem of racism in post-apartheid South Africa in a constructive manner. During April 2014, the executive of the URCSA approved the Churches Addressing Racism in Southern Africa programme in principle since it would support the strategic objective regarding internal unity in the strategic plan of the URCSA and could also be of assistance regarding the reunification process between the URCSA and the DRC (*Minutes Executive General Synod URCSA* 2014). In 2014, the General Synodical Commission

approved the Churches Addressing Racism in Southern Africa programme. The General Synod of the URCSA acknowledged
- that racism is prevailing on various levels, personal and institutional, and is toxic to interpersonal relations and to society;
- that racism destroys the core of communion in the church among God's people and in society;
- that racism operates with the assumption that certain persons or groups of people are superior to others;
- that these assumptions determine our thinking, or attitudes and our actions towards others;
- that racism prevents people from contributing to one another so that all may benefit in the fullness of life;
- that because racism perpetuates itself within society if left unchallenged, it cripples society; and
- that racism scares people, harms people and society and destroys people and society (Churches Addressing Racism in South Africa 2014:7).

In order to foster human dignity by addressing racism in a constructive way, the URCSA made the following statement:
- In South Africa churches have been directly and indirectly involved in the establishment of racism and racist attitudes and behaviour. Churches provided a theological basis for race discrimination. The churches owe it to themselves and to society to embark on a journey to undo their legacy.
- The church is witness to the Gospel of Jesus Christ that brought salvation to all humankind. In Christ, all is restored in their human dignity.
- According to Ephesians, Christ has broken down the walls that separated people.
- The church has the ministry of reconciliation.
- The church has the ministry of justice.

The church is strategically placed in society by having congregations everywhere and is therefore able to reach people from all walks of life at the grassroots level (Churches Addressing Racism in South Africa 2014:7).

The 'Churches Addressing Racism in Southern Africa' programme aims to address racism in church and society. With this programme the URCSA wants to bring

dignity and healing in church and society. The programme follows a hermeneutical approach in order to enhance the understanding of people with regard to:
- the dynamics of society and church that created and perpetuate racism;
- the teachings of Scripture about human dignity;
- the teachings of Christ who came to be our peace and to destroy the barriers between people; and
- the role of the church as a healing community in society.

The programme will do this through academic and theological modules at universities and seminaries; research and publications on the topic; short courses, workshops and retreats for ministers and other church leaders; and developing and proving teaching material for children and adults (Churches Addressing Racism in Southern Africa 2014:5).

The URCSA with the DRC, the DRCA and the Reformed Church in Africa approved a 'Season of Human Dignity' to attend to the issue of human dignity. The goal of the 'Season of Human Dignity' is to testify to the new life in Christ in which the intrinsic value that God gives to each person is guaranteed. The 'Season of Human Dignity' is a space in which reflections and dialogue about human dignity is promoted and will span over several years. The DRC family hope to later include other churches and start a national movement for human dignity. (Season of Human Dignity)

The URCSA also initiated a programme to address racism. At a meeting of the leadership of the URCSA and the DRC in February 2014, racism was identified as a serious stumbling block on the way to unity, reconciliation and justice. The following statement was issued after the meeting:

> Recognising the destructive power of racism so embedded in all our communities, we resolve to jointly develop and implement a programme for our churches to help us all to address this challenge in a way that will bring us closer together and enhance the healing we so long for. (Minutes of the meeting of the four moderamen of the DRC family 2014:1-4)

The URCSA took cognisance of the declaration by the WCC Conference on Racism in 2010 and made the following statement:

> Racism, caste-based discrimination, and other exclusionary practices are inherently sinful because, on several levels, they subvert the double commandment: 'to love God and our neighbour as ourselves (Matthew 20:37-39)'. These exclusionary practices are expressions of self-deification on the part of those who practice them and, thereby, violate the First Commandment (Exodus 20:3) that states that we can have no other gods

before the One True God, who creates, redeems, and sustains all, including us and those we consider as 'them'. These forms of discrimination deny the biblical witness of Genesis 1:26-27, which affirms that the human being is created in the image of God. These harmful exclusionary practices belie the reality that the socially constructed divisions we devise to separate ourselves from each other have no place in Christ (Galatians 3:28). Racism, caste-based discrimination, and other forms of discrimination foster hatred and violence – the very antithesis of the fruit of the Spirit (Galatians 5:22), and a negation of our faith in God who gave us life and sent his son to ensure life for all, in all its abundance (John 10:10). These sinful practices of dehumanising exclusion are governed by a denial of the blessedness of the rich diversity within the creation itself, where each kind of living thing was named and pronounced 'good' (Genesis 1). Diversity within the good creation is a reflection of the value of diversity within the very life of the triune God, who creates, preserves, and loves in freedom and abundance. The biblical witness enjoins us to celebrate the blessedness of diversity as a gift (Romans 12) designed to bless the churches and the communities which they serve. Wherever and whenever we reject these instances of God's fecundity and abundance, we deny the very nature of the God we claim to profess. (WCC Statement on Racism 2010)

The WCC Conference on Racism in 2010 also declared the following regarding the church's role:

We note and celebrate the various ways in which some of our churches have been working diligently not only to challenge diverse forms of discrimination but have also initiated programmes designed to promote greater understanding and acceptance across multicultural and religious lines. However, the churches have not done as much as they should in addressing racial and other exclusionary practices within their own ranks. This is a state of affairs which cannot continue if the churches are to have any credibility in their claim to be the body of Christ. Because the very nature of racial and other forms of discrimination entails levels of economic, social, and political marginalisation which create profound suffering and life-long hardship, our local and national churches cannot continue to ignore this nightmarish reality in which men, women, and children of God are condemned to live. The entire body of Christ has a prophetic task to denounce by word and deed all forms and expressions of existence which constrain the reality of the abundant life which God offered to us in Jesus Christ. Our failure to do so constitutes disobedience to the God we endeavour to serve through faithful discipleship. (WCC Statement on Racism 2010)

The above declaration of the WCC indicates clearly that the church is one of the institutions in society which should address racism. During November 2015, the Nelson Mandela Foundation and the Achmat Kathrada Foundation launched the Anti-Racism Network of South Africa (ARNSA). At the launch, Dr Dawid Kuyler, scribe of the General Synod of the URCSA represented the URCSA. The week of 14 to 21 March 2016 was identified as the first 'Anti-Racism Week' in South Africa. The moderamen urged local congregations to take the lead in sharing our hurtful stories as well as stories of hope. Congregations were urged to embody reconciliation and justice by arranging marches and events to show that we are part of the solution and by bringing people of races together in worship services to celebrate our common human dignity (Pastoral letter regarding racism 2016).

Dealing with racism in church and society

As children of the Belhar Confession, the URCSA are, therefore, obliged to denounce the sin of racism emerging in post-apartheid South Africa. But how do we combat racism in our society? Racism is no longer institutionalised in the laws, policies, but is still embedded in the structures of the nation. Notwithstanding the resolutions on *status confessionis* and the drafting and acceptance of the Belhar Confession, racism still has a bearing on church and society in post-apartheid South Africa. On 22 January 2016, the moderamen of the URCSA, Prof. Mary-Anne Plaatjies-Van Huffel (moderator), Rev. Motlalentwa Betha (vice-moderator), Dr Dawid Kuyler (scribe), Prof. Leepo Modise (church law expert), Rev. Colin Goeiman (representative of the Northern Synod), Rev. Thamsanqa Ngema (representative of the Kwazulu-Natal Synod), and Rev. W. Julius (representative of the Namibia Synod) issued a pastoral letter regarding the upsurge of racism in post-apartheid South Africa. In this document, the moderamen gave guidance to the URCSA of how to address racism in church and society. The response of the URCSA to racism, however, is not the first or the last word by the URCSA on this burning issue. From 1978, the DRMC and the URCSA issued numerous resolutions and statements on racism (Addendum 13; *Acts DRMC* 1978, 1982, 1986; *Acts General Synod URCSA* 1990, 1994; Statement of the URCSA on Xenophobia 2016). During 2004, the URCSA called on all her members to act towards the issue of xenophobia in the spirit of Article 4 of the Belhar Confession:

> The Uniting Reformed Church in Southern Africa condemns the xenophobic attacks against a defenceless people in the strongest possible terms...We call on Christians in general, but on members of URCSA, in particular, to remember that our Lord and Saviour Jesus Christ was once a refugee, who fled with his parents from the land of His birth. Anyone who follows and believes in this Christ will treat refugees with the utmost respect and dignity. As Christ became stateless and homeless, so did the refugees in our midst. We must have compassion with them, as Christ had compassion on us. When

they suffer their pain, bewilderment and uncertainty it must also touch our own lives. We are bound together in a common humanity. We call on all our members to act on this matter in the spirit of our Belhar Confession. God sides with the poor and the oppressed and the church must stand where God stands. As a church, we have no choice, but compelled by our faith, especially our faith expressed in our Belhar Confession, we must stand where God stands, against the injustices and with those who have been wronged. We call on all our members and Congregations in the areas where these attacks on refugees occur to act in the spirit of the Belhar Confession. (Press statement, URCSA on the xenophobic attacks, 20 May 2008)

In 2015, the moderamen of the General Synod of URCSA commissioned the moderator of the General Synod of the URCSA, Prof. Mary-Anne Plaatjies-Van Huffel, to draft a press statement regarding the upsurge of xenophobia in the country. This statement was issued on 16 April 2015 (Addendum 14). The statement is published in German as '*Wie wir auf Fremde in unserer Mitte reagieren, das berührt das Herz der kirchlichen Lehre in Für das Recht streiten. 30 Jahre Bekenntnis*' (2016).

> The premise of the URCSA is that racism is sin and we, as church, are not safeguard from this sin in any way. The URCSA struggles with the legacy of racism and is in some cases perpetuating racism prejudices and practices and, therefore, as church the URCSA cannot point fingers to others in society when it comes to racism. (Pastoral letter regarding racism 2016)

In order to address racism in society, the URCSA acknowledged and confessed in the pastoral letter that the URCSA, which consist of differences races, cultures and language groups, is not an example of a non-racist church. The fact that at some places people of races are worshipping together does not mean that the URCSA is a truly multicultural church. In a multicultural society, every member feels worthy to be part of the community. According to Degenaar (2000:156), multiculturalism does not represent a means to an equal society, but an alternative to one where equality has given way to the toleration of difference and of inequality. From the standpoint of multiculturalism, however, differences are welcomed as expressions of cultural diversity and equality. The 2016 pastoral letter regarding racism states:

> The reality is that we are part of a race divided society in Southern Africa in which racism is well and alive. We have to confess that we are not doing enough to address racism constructively and that we do not help one another to combat this destructive sin. The only way to address a problem is first to acknowledge the problem. (Pastoral letter regarding racism 2016)

Article 2 of the Belhar Confession challenges us to embody unity and reconciliation:

> [T]hat unity is, therefore, both a gift and an obligation for the church of Jesus Christ; that through the working of God's Spirit it is a binding force, yet simultaneously a reality which must be earnestly pursued and sought: one which the people of God must continually be built up to attain; that this unity must become visible so that the world may believe that separation, enmity and hatred between people and groups is sin which Christ has already conquered, and accordingly that anything which threatens this unity may have no place in the church and must be resisted.

The church, as an ethical community, should embody the message of reconciliation. As stated in Article 3 of the confession:

> We believe that God has entrusted the church with the message of reconciliation in and through Jesus Christ; that the church is called to be the salt of the earth and the light of the world; that the church is called blessed because it is a peacemaker; that the church is a witness both by word and by deed to the new heaven and the new earth in which righteousness dwells ... Therefore, we reject any doctrine, which, in such a situation sanctions in the name of the gospel or of the will of God the forced separation of people on the grounds of race and colour and thereby in advance obstructs and weakens the ministry and experience of reconciliation in Christ.

God has entrusted us with the message of reconciliation. Genesis 1 states that we are all made in the image of God. Throughout history, different groups developed along culture, political and language lines. In Ephesians 2:15 and 19-22 (NIV) we read that we are a new creation through Christ. The triune God in his grace made us part of this new creation. Our departure in addressing racism is not in the differences of people and races, but in being us part of this new creation of God. We should, therefore, intentionally address the issue of multicultural in the URCSA. According to Degenaar (2000:166), to ignore differences among cultures and differences within cultures is a refusal to admit that each cultural group has its own history and that justice demands that each should be treated accordingly. Multiculturalism refers not only to the coexistence of various cultures but also to cultural differences running across various cultures and being inherent in any distinct cultures (Degenaar 2000:168). We still have a long way to go before we will truly be a multicultural church. For Degenaar (2000:169), to be human is to affirm one's humanity by recognising the humanity of others in its infinite variety of content and form. If we take this prescription seriously, then we can view the multicultural diversity in South Africa as a wonderful opportunity to discover our humanness.

Article 3 of the Belhar Confession reminds us that credibility of the message of reconciliation is seriously jeopardised and its beneficial work obstructed if we do not, for example, address issues such as racism appropriately. Racism should never be overlooked or negated by a cheap reconciliation. Reconciliation is never cheap. God takes the initiative in bringing about justice. Article 4 of the confession confirms this when it declares:

> We believe that God has revealed himself as the One who wishes to bring about justice and true peace among men; that in a world full of injustice and enmity He is in a special way the God of the destitute, the poor and the wronged and that He calls his church to follow Him in this.

Racism functions at various levels. It can be on a personal level but it can also be institutionalised and entrenched in systems. As children of God, we do not have the luxury to choose whether we would like to engage in the struggle against racism. The Belhar Confession spells out the basic points of departure from which we should get involved. It challenges us to set an example or to embody how a non-racist society should look like. Obedience to Jesus Christ is the bottom-line. Not obedience to my own race, culture, language or social economic position. Jesus Christ the only head of the church called us to confess and to do all these things. Article 5 of the confession states, 'even though the authorities and human laws might forbid them and punishment and suffering be the consequence'.

Conclusion

People act unethically when they do not follow their principles and when they capitulate to influences and powers in the community. Article 5 of the Belhar Confession clearly states that what we confess in Articles 1 to 4 needs to be put into practice at all costs. 'We believe that, in obedience to Jesus Christ, its only head, the church is called to confess ... even though the authorities and human laws might forbid them.' This is the cost of discipleship. As Dietrich Bonhoeffer wrote in his famous book, *The Cost of Discipleship*:

> As we embark upon discipleship we surrender ourselves to Christ in union with his death – we give over our lives to death. Thus, it begins; the cross is not the terrible end to an otherwise god-fearing and happy life, but it meets us at the beginning of our communion with Christ. When Christ calls a man, he bids him come and die. (Bonhoeffer 1948:44)

Looking at the Belhar Confession through the lens of ecclesiology and ethics opens a new dimension in reading the confession. It also challenges the church as an institution and individual members to ask questions about our own ecclesiology and our ethics. We need to ask the many questions but I would just like to mention two:

- How ethical are we as the URCSA in our dealing with one another at all levels of being a church?
- Are we ethical in principle, but not in praxis?

The URCSA envisaged to address racism constructively in all its forms in church and society through academic, theological and other programmes, such as Churches Addressing Racism in Southern Africa, to assist and empower churches to restore people's human dignity and bring about healing.

Bibliography

Primary sources

Churches addressing racism in southern Africa *In Minutes Executive General Synod URCSA* 2014.

The Cottesloe Declaration, 1960. [Online] Available at http://www.kerkargief.co.za/doks/bely/DF_Cottesloe.pdf (Accessed 11 March 2015).

Lutheran World Federation (LWF). n.d. Sixth Assembly in Dar es Salaam, Tanzania, 13–25 June 1977, A statement on Southern Africa: Confessional Integrity. [Online] Available at http://www.lwf-assembly2003.org/lwf-assembly/htdocs/history.html#1977%20%E2%80%93%20Dar-es-Salaam,%20Tanzania (Accessed 3 September 2015).

Minutes Executive General Synod URCSA April 2014.

Minutes of the meeting of the four moderamen of the DRC family 6–7 August 2014. Bloemfontein.

Pastoral Letter of URCSA regarding racism, 2016.

Season of Human Dignity. [Online] Available at http://www.humandignity.co.za or http://www.menswaardigheid.co.za (Accessed 3 September 2015).

The Lambeth Conference: Resolutions Archive from 1948. [Online] Available at http://www.anglicancommunion.org/media/127737/1948.pdf?language=English (Accessed 3 September 2015).

World Alliance of Reformed Churches, 1983. *Called to Witness to the Gospel Today, Studies from the World Alliance of Reformed Churches*,No 1. Geneva: WARC, 1983:26-30.

World Alliance of Reformed Churches, 1983. *Proceedings of the 21st General Council of the World Alliance of Reformed Churches.* Geneva: WARC. [Online] Available at http://www.warc.ch/dcw/bs25/11.html. (Accessed 27 June 2015) pp. 176-180.

World Council of Churches (WCC). n.d. World Council of Churches Programme to Combat Racism. [Online] Available at https://www.aluka.org/struggles/collection/WCC (Accessed 3 September 2015).

World Council of Churches (WCC). 2010. Statement from the WCC Conference on Racism Today. [Online] Available at http://www.oikoumene.org/en/resources/documents/wcc-programmes/unity-mission-evangelism-and-spirituality/just-and-inclusive-communities/racism/statement-from-the-wcc-conference-on-racism-today (Accessed 3 September 2015).

Secondary sources

Belhar Confession, 1986. The official English translation of the *Belhar Confession 1986* approved by the General Synod of 2008. Belhar:LUS Printers.

Bonhoeffer, D. 1948. *The cost of discipleship*. London: SCM Press.

Degenaar, J. 2000. Multiculturalism: How can the human world live its difference? In E. van Vugt & D. Cloete (eds), *Race and reconciliation in South Africa: A multicultural dialogue in comparative perspective*. New York: Lexington books.

Graff, G. 2011. Everything has changed, but nothing has changed: Shame, racism, and a dream deferred. *The Journal of Psychohistory* 38(4):346-358.

Huddleston, T. 1956. *Naught for your comfort*. New York: Doubleday.

Lodberg, P. 1996. Apartheid as a church-dividing ethical issue. *The Ecumenical Review* 48(2):173-177. https://doi.org/10.1111/j.1758-6623.1996.tb03462.x

Mufamadi, T.D.2011. The World Council of Churches and its Programme to Combat Racism: The evolution and development of their fight against apartheid, 1969–1994. PhD thesis, University of South Africa, Pretoria.

Nail, P.R., Harton, H. & Barnes, A. 2008. A test of Dovidio and Gaertner's integrated model of racism. *North American Journal of Psychology* 10(1):197-220

Plaatjies-Van Huffel, M-A. 2014. The Belhar Confession in its historical context. *Nederduitse Gereformeerde Teologiese Tydskrif* 55(1/2):308-309. https://doi.org/10.5952/55-1-2-527

Punt, J. 2009. Post-apartheid racism in South Africa: The Bible, social identity and stereotyping. *Religion and Theology* 16(3):246-272. https://doi.org/10.1163/102308009X12561890523672

Rauhaus, A. 2009. Is an ethical status confessionis possible? *HTS Teologiese Studies/Theological Studies* 65(1):6 pages.

Walker, M. 2005: Race is nowhere and race is everywhere: narratives from black and white South African university students in post-apartheid South Africa. *British Journal of Sociology of Education* 26(1):41-54. https://doi.org/10.1080/0142569042000292707

WARC (World Alliance of Reformed Churches). 1983. *Called to witness to the Gospel today, studies from the World Alliance of Reformed Churches*, No1. Geneva: WARC.

THE BELHAR CONFESSION AND THE ESTABLISHMENT OF A THEOLOGY OF DEVELOPMENT

Jacques Walter Beukes[1]

Introduction

This chapter is mostly taken from an unpublished PhD thesis by Jacques Beukes (Beukes 2014). It contains a practical theological reflection on the meaning of Article 4 of the Confession of Belhar as a basis for the establishment of a theology of development in the Uniting Reformed Church in Southern Africa (URCSA). The Confession of Belhar came about following the social injustices of the past that resulted from the policy of apartheid. However, since the democratic transition in 1994, remarkable and fundamental political changes in South African society occurred. The unjust system of apartheid was replaced by a democratic system of government in which all South Africans could enjoy a new constitution that protect and recognised everyone's freedom and dignity (Pieterse 2001:75) There were political as well as economic expectations by many South Africans – especially by the previously disadvantaged people, that the democratisation would result in a better life for all, especially since the ANCs 1994 'A Better Life for all' campaign promised this better future for all South African citizens. However, more than twenty years after democracy, the current South African context shows that increasing widespread inconsistency, poverty and social problems in the country still exist (Beukes 2014).

This chapter aims to make a theological contribution to effectively address the poverty situation in South Africa by being faithful to the biblical command of a just society, and also by being faithful to the Confession of Belhar, more predominantly Article 4, which supports the establishment of a theology of development. Also, because of the magnitude of the human need, inequality, widespread poverty and social problems in our country, the church is challenged to engage in a mode of development. The post-apartheid context requires effective involvement of the

---

1 Dr Jacques Beukes is a lecturer/assessor and moderator Theology and Ministry; student chaplain and programme developer of theology courses of the Hugenote College – Wellington from 2014. He specialises in theology of development. His dissertation is titled 'A Practical Theological Reflection on the Meaning of Article 4 of the Belhar Confession as Basis for the Establishment of a Theology of Development within the Uniting Reformed Church of Southern Africa (URCSA)'.

church. Being the church of necessity involves engaging in the wider social world (De Gruchy & Ellis 2008:2-3). The church has great potential to be an effective role-player in development in the South African context given its good infrastructure and human resources (Koegelenberg 1992:6). Faith communities and their networks have essential roles to play in shaping social values, such as honesty, compassion and solidarity with the weak and the poor (Swart 2006:7). Therefore, I would go even further by suggesting that the URCSA, based on its biblical and confessional foundation, is required to effectively engage in the fight against poverty, social injustice and oppression.

The Confession of Belhar, which originated in the apartheid regime and which expressed and addressed injustices, is still relevant in a post-apartheid context of increasing poverty and inequality. During the apartheid regime, Christians and church leaders fought together against the biggest social and political problems of the day. This can be because members of this church were predominantly black and therefore victims of apartheid. Today, the situation is similar in that most of the members of this church are poor and so represent a similar pastoral and prophetic context for the church (De Gruchy & Ellis 2008:3). While the church's role during the apartheid era was that of resistance, the role should change in a post-apartheid South African context to one of reconstruction and assistance.

It is against this background that Article 4 of the Confession of Belhar serves as a motivation for the establishment of a 'theology of development' to address systemic poverty and oppression in a post-apartheid South African context. This chapter firstly focuses on church involvement as a biblical-theological obligation. Secondly an exploration and investigation of the meaning of a theology of development and a definition will be put forward. The third part of this chapter gives a brief overview on Articles 1 to 3 and 5 of the confession. This is followed by an in-depth discussion on the meaning of Article 4 of the confession as a basis for the establishment of a theology of development in the URCSA.

Church involvement: A biblical-theological obligation

Poverty is not just out in the community or just within the Christian community, but it is a common reality. The church, therefore, lives in and with poverty (De Bruyn & Pauw 2004:207). Economic issues are an integral part of the mission of the church (Nürnberger 1994:118-121). However, it is not wise to focus only on economic and political issues in the church as the church will not be fulfilling its calling holistically. The non-economic aspects of development strategies, for example, social values, relationships and the promotion of social capital, also plays an important role and the church should be aware of these. A positive moral and ethical basis is essential for economic success (Swart & Venter 2001:485). The church is, therefore, challenged to play a vital role in the moral development and revival in our country. Moral education can be seen as one of the main focuses of the church on the grounds of the church in being. Various sources, such as, business, government, academia and churches, are calling for moral communities that can and must serve as a safety net. This is a serious cry for a changing society. This plea asks the church to help form a society with better discipline, acceptable behaviour, more obedience, and a greater emphasis on the expression of values. Churches are, therefore, well positioned as religious communities of the triune God, and who may serve as moral communities in our country that could promote justice in society (Cloete 2007:66-6; Van der Ven, Dreyer & Pieterse 2002:1097).

Poverty deprives people of their dignity, threatens their security and often leads to stigmatisation. The church can and should play a major role in the confirmation of people's self-esteem and self-respect. How we think and talk about the poor is very important. That people are poor and often do not have jobs does not mean they are less human than those who have more. Neither does it mean that these people do not have potential or ability to do anything about their circumstances (Cloete 2007:67). The presence of God creates a space where people can be more and go beyond their circumstances and the perceptions of society (Odendaal 2004:298-299). The assumption underlying theological reflection on development is that the church should do well to those who are poor, oppressed and marginalised. We seem to forget this in the process the faith and works of the poor. It is simply wrong to assume that poor people do not have the ability to also 'do'. Poor people are always involved in strategies to survive. The Bible also calls the poor to do good works. The following statement by Myers confirms the importance of works or action for the establishment of identity:

> When the poor accept their marred identity and their distorted sense of vocation as normative and immutable, their poverty is complete. It is also permanent unless this issue is addressed and they are helped to recover their identity as children of God, made in God's image and their true vocation as productive stewards in the world God made for them. Who we are is a question of both being and doing. I believe that poverty mars both parts of the identity of the poor. The result is that people who are poor no longer know who they are neither (being) nor do they believe that they have a vocation of any value (doing). (Myers (1999:76)

When the church becomes involved in development and the handling of poverty, it is of the utmost importance to remember that even the poor are created in the image of God. They also receive talents to be co-workers of God, which implies that the poor are not simply the passive object of good works (De Gruchy 2003:22-24). The church has a huge role to play in restoring people's dignity as God created beings and as workers in his plan of salvation on earth, however, one of the most pressing questions is how this goal will be achieved in a society that is so prevalent characterised by the motif of economic profit? In his article titled 'Human Dignity and Economic Globalization', Botman asked the question of how the restoration of human dignity as one of the objectives of the Constitution is to be achieved in a South Africa also characterised by economic globalisation? He then referred to the work of Zygmunt Bauman, a political sociologist, on the effects of economic globalisation (Botman 2004:318). According to Bauman, economic globalisation is aimed at the tourist's dreams and desires rather than to the local poor. In South Africa, we sit with the dilemma that although the Constitution gives very clear goals on how the lives of South Africans can be improved, the situation in our country is not favourable for them. Thousands of South Africans are still without jobs, housing and education. Human dignity, equality and freedom can only be obtained if socio-economic conditions change drastically. According to Botman (2004:320), South Africa has passed transformation in general, but this initial transformation must now be followed up by a deeper transformation. In South Africa, the economic environment is not conducive to the achievement of objectives stated in the Constitution. Rather, the economic situation in our country contrasts many respects to these objectives. Economic globalisation creates a definite form of freedom, but not necessarily the freedom that promises a better future for all. Botman express the ethical dilemma created by this situation as follows:

> In the context of globalisation the 'ethic of dignity', the orientation favoured by a strong social ethics, and the 'ethics of interest', the orientation favoured by the current global economic reality, come into conflict and this requires a fundamental moral choice from individuals, communities and society at large. (Botman 2004:323)

Considering these evil consequences of economic globalisation, it is essential that the economic life of our country is evaluated on the basis of the following questions: What does the economy do for the poor? What does it do to people in general? How do people take part in the economy? The economy is a human reality – people working together to support the creation of God. This work should promote the material and spiritual wellbeing of people. The economy affects people's hopes and expectations for themselves and for their fellow man. It affects people's faith in God (Lutz 1987:75). Every economic decision and institution will have to be evaluated based on the question of whether it protects or undermines the dignity of people. Human dignity is a divine gift, and a country's economic system should respect and confirm it. Economic issues are never neutral but can serve or endangered a community and the commitment to the common good (Sedgwick 1999:225).

Considering all the urgent and complex challenges associated with poverty there is the need for the church in a very special way to become involved in civil society. A specific contribution as formulated many years ago by the first president and father of Tanzanian independence, Julius Nyerere, is certainly relevant for the church in South Africa today:

> [U]nless we participate actively in the rebellion against those social structures and economic organisations which condemn people to poverty, humiliation and degradation, the church will become irrelevant to people, and the Christian religion will degenerate into a set of superstitions accepted by the fearful. Unless the church, its members and its organisations, express God's love for people by involvement and leadership in constructive protest against the present conditions of humankind, then it will become identified with injustice and persecution. If this happens, it will die, and humanly speaking deserves to die. (Nyerere 1972:1)

The ethical dilemma is caused by the current economic market-orientated paradigm should certainly be high on the agenda of the church. The voice of the oppressed and the poor is difficult to hear in such a system, if heard at all. As already pointed out, the system serves the exclusion of people best.

Thus, in arguing so far for the involvement of the church as a biblical obligation based on the socio-economic challenges the church faces, the critical question regarding the mode of church involvement remains. According to Swart (2006:14), the response of churches in poverty, can be described as charity. He further points out that church involvement in poverty is eminently a theological matter. The profound issue is whether churches remain faithful to the Gospel – a commitment, which unquestionably implies participation in the change of the social conditions of the poor. Santa Ana and Barreiro express their views on the real contribution of the church in this regard:

> The proclamation of the good news must be rooted in practical action to secure a transformation of the structures which presuppose the existence of poverty and indeed tend to create poverty. The proclamation of the message of Jesus requires the church to engage in action to promote justice at the social level (both institutional and structural) and not simply at the level of the individual. (Santa Ana & Barreiro 1980:182)

Swart offers a three-pronged explanation of charity that is characteristic of the current limited church involvement in poverty. First, it refers to a first phase of awareness of the social and economic problems that arose with the industrial revolution and colonial expansion. Second, it refers to the social involvement of the church sector to charity. Churches often do not have the capacity for a truly critical socio-theoretical concept that the sector can help to rise above such a limited way of thinking and action. Finally, this way of social engagement represents a kind of paternalism, which historically results in almost total alienation between Christian churches on the one hand and the poor and the working class on the other (Swart 2006:20-28).

It is not just the poor who live in poverty; the church also consists of those who struggle economically to survive as well as those that thrive. This important point is underlined by Le Bruyns and Pauw (2004:207) as they believe that churches for the most part are constantly busy with their own things, services and ministry and not consciously and constructively involved in the public domain – particularly as part of their witness and proclamation ('*kerygma*'). This frequent one-way focus is, therefore, strategic to tackling poverty among the members of the church, because as members they can relate to, and be part of the society. If the church in general realises that poverty and the poor is part of its faith and life, this will be a small yet profound step in the right direction. (Le Bruyns & Pauw 2004:207).

Until now, I have argued that the church is a central institution and place of the particularly marginalised in society. The church is perfectly positioned when it comes to the development of the marginalised and the restoring and healing of the community. Therefore, it is the role of the church to address the problem of poverty and restore hope and dignity theologically but holistically. The church is supposed to be characterised by commitment, love, sharing in vulnerability, communion, integrity, humility, righteousness and the promotion of justice. These characteristics should be the message that the church offers society and the world. The church, which was founded by Jesus Christ, lives by the proclamation of the apostolic message and is alive by continuing acts of God in the sacraments and carrying out its mission of worship, witness and service in the world. This is a church that was sent by Christ to live through its ongoing innovative presence in their midst. God's vision for His church is that it is a church of teaching, a church of community and caring, a church that worships, as well as a church that preaches the gospel, and to live accordingly (a biblical obligation).

A theology of development

This part of the chapter explores a theology of development on the basis of the development discourse (Abrecht & Land 1969; Alszeghy & Flick 1971; Dunne 1969; Gern 1999; Myers 2011; Rendtorff 1969, 1971; Swart 2010). Development is aimed at improving people's lives and is the heart of all social and economic injustices involving people. From the background of church involvement, this section now examines how the Confession of Belhar contributes to the establishment of a theology of development in the URCSA. The need to place people central to development is crucial in this discussion. However, the critical question is still: How can the Confession of Belhar establish a new-found motivation in the URCSA and its members of active involvement in the current South African context? However, it is first necessary to define 'theology of development'. With the church that is constantly challenged by various social problems, the broader church became aware that they could not continue to give priority to their own identity without being involved in the development of the world (Gern 1999:441). This involvement of the church in development has brought a new approach, namely a theology of development.

A 'theology of development' refers to a theological perspective that developed in ecumenical circles and which is motivated by the desire of Christians to creatively and wholehearted be involved in the search for solutions to human, social and political problems in the contemporary world (Dunne 1969:i). A theology of development focuses, from a practical theological perspective, on the holistic people-centred development approach (Yoms 2013). Even Myers (2011:47) considers that any involvement of churches and Christians in development can be seen in this context as an approach that is theologically motivated and therefore, according to my understanding, also implies a theology of development. A theology of development should be grounded in the declaration that God and humanity are connected because of the cross (Moltmann 1969:96). Swart (2010:211) explains that a theology of development is a theology with a task to empower the church as an effective role player within development.

Considering the previous argument, I suggest the following definition of a theology of development:

> A theology of development includes a theological, ecclesiastical, Christian, biblical and confessional foundation and perspective as motivation to Christian active involvement and participation of churches, NGOs, CBOs, FBOs and Christians as agents of change and representatives of God in the socio-economic problems of society. Furthermore, a theology of development implies a spiritual and physical transformation and change and improvement in the lives of individuals, communities and contexts as a developmental approach with God's restoration in the world as a result.

The Confession of Belhar as a church-theological response

Article 4 of the Belhar Confession [2] deals with God as the one who brings justice and true peace to the earth and further declares the responsibilities of the church. (Boesak 2008:8). Faith in the triune God (Article 1), the unity of the church (Article 2), reconciliation in the church and society (Article 3) are all very closely linked to Article 4 on justice and peace (Botha & Naudé 2010:183). Article 4 confesses firstly about God in whom righteousness dwells, then about the church that should live this justice – just like God, in a practical way in the world (Botha & Naudé 2006:13).

The main theme of Article 4 is justice. The article is also connected to service (serving) on the basis of the testimony of God. Words such as 'service', 'aid' and 'sorrow' are reminiscent of the general wording of Belhar. It is clear the article encourages members of the congregation to take responsibility for each other in terms of spiritual and material needs (Van Rooi 2007:806). Therefore, just as the church seeks to be in the fight to follow Christ to justice for the poor and those who are discriminated against, so the church must follow Christ in this case. (Boesak 2008:9; Smit 2011:9). Therefore, it is necessary to motivate the need for a theology of development from Belhar for the URCSA. The church belongs to God and thus called to stand where God stands. This means that the church will testify against injustice and against all the powerful who selfishly seeks only their own interests. This also means that the church will learn to discern the 'when' and 'how' it is necessary to fight against injustice but also to learn to distinguish 'when' and 'how' it is necessary to argue for justice.

In a world full of injustice and enmity, the biblical God is the help of the helpless and in a special way the God of the destitute, the poor and the downtrodden (Smit 2011:9). Within this, the church praises God because God is revealed as such a God. To confess about justice, the drafters of the confession had to find new words. (Botha & Naudé 2010:66). For a long time, the synod had not debated as much on justice as on unity and reconciliation. However, even after the years of rejection and violence that they had to endure, the people in South Africa maintained their faith in God. Faith in and the hope of compassion, mercy and justice of God deepened and lived in the heart of the members of the Dutch Reformed Mission Church (DRMC).

It is clear that the drafters of Belhar were led by the Holy Spirit in the light of the Word of God. As a reader and believer of the Confession, one is indeed affected by the succession of biblical phrases in the formulation of Article 4. The Bible speaks the exact language we hear in Belhar. This article also deals with God's image as

---

2 The Confession of Belhar consists of five articles namely, Introduction (triune God), unity, reconciliation, justice and a conclusion. However, this chapter focuses only be on Article 4.

it confesses that he is the God who cares for all in need. There can be no doubt that God is compassionate (Botha & Naudé 2010:67). Boesak supports this idea and implies that the Confession arose from the ranks of the poor and oppressed, the despised and the voiceless, the discouraged and downtrodden. For Boesak, this is probably the most sublime and attacking characteristic of the Confession as he argues:

> In other words, and in the unguarded, heated moments of debate we see this emerging more and more, the real reason for the rejection of Belhar is the fact that it is the voice of those who had no voice, who, in fact, had no right to speak; the least of those whom God should have chosen to speak prophetically to the powerful. (Boesak 2008:9)

Precisely herein are we as God's church called us to follow him. This is what Botha and Naudé emphasise in their contribution as they argue that God's followers do good in seeking justice for those in need. Therefore, the church is called to assist people in need and suffering and to testify and to fight against any form of injustice. It is, therefore, non-negotiable that the church must be where God is, and ought to stand where God stands, namely against injustice and with the downtrodden regardless of race, class or culture (Boesak 2008; Botha & Naudé 2010:67).

For the URCSA, the need for a theology of development to be established from Article 4 of the Confession of Belhar stems from the argument that God's compassionate justice is particularly relevant to us in South Africa, where socio-economic and other forms of injustices are to some very favourable, but to others very detrimental. The confession gives clear guidance from the Scriptures: The Church must make a choice to stand where God stands. Because God is the source of justice, he stands in situations of injustice with the victims. As followers of Jesus, as people in the service of God, the church is called to the grace year, the year of restoration, to help and to deliver. The church must witness against injustice. This includes – as the Bible illustrates with Amos, Hosea, Jeremiah, Jesus and James – a clear testimony against people with power to determine their own interest to the disadvantage of others. The church must support and give practical assistance to people who are suffering – no matter what form this suffering is and regardless of who is suffering (Botha & Naudé 2010:186, 2012:19). Boesak defends this point in a clarification of his theological (and not socio-economic or political) approach as he also believes that the church is called to stand where God stands. Boesak writes:

> [Jesus'] birthplace was not the palaces of the privileged or the high-steepled stain glass-windowed sanctuaries of white power. It gave voice to the voiceless and power to the powerless. Nor was it the child of esoteric academic debate; it emerged from the struggles of ordinary people living in the presence of evil and with the promises of God and it spoke with the

eloquence of faith. It was not commissioned by the powerful to legitimise earthly power. It places earthly power under the critique of heaven and earth: of the outraged God and the suffering people. In its words pulsates a life, lived not under the protection of the throne but in the shadow of the cross. In it one will not find the arrogance of certitude; it is the trembling steadfastness of those who walk by faith, not by sight. In essence, this is what those who embrace the Confession of Belhar embrace, and this is what they share with those who accept the confession as their own. (Boesak 2008:9)

Who God is and stands for can be found in a poignant description of how God stands for justice in Article 4 of the Confession of Belhar:

[That] God brings justice to the oppressed and gives bread to the hungry; that God frees the prisoner and restores sight to the blind; that God supports the downtrodden, protects the strangers, helps orphans and widows and blocks the path of the ungodly; that for God pure and undefiled religion is to visit the orphans and the widows in their suffering; that God wishes to teach the people of God to do what is good and to seek the right; that the church, therefore must therefore stand by people in any form of suffering and need, which implies, among other things, that the church must witness against and strive against any form of injustice, so that justice roll down like waters, and righteousness like an ever-flowing stream.[3]

Also from Article 4:

[T]hat the church belonging to God, should stand where God stands, namely against injustice and with the wronged; that in following Christ the church must witness against all the powerful and privileged who selfishly seek their own interests and and thus control and harm others.

These confessions from Article 4 should be embodied by all believers who believe in the Confession of Belhar.

Article 4 also declares and confesses that 'God is in a special way the God of the destitute, the poor and the wronged and that God calls the church is called to follow in this'. For most, especially in DRC circles, this is the most controversial part

---

3   Extracts from the Confession of Belhar in this chapter are taken from the English translation at Addendum 15, The Confession of Belhar. Also available at http://urcsa.net/wp-content/uploads/2016/02/Belhar-Confession.pdf

of the Confession (Clark 2001:8). This is supported and confirmed by Naudé when he argues:

> This has been the most contentious article of the Belhar Confession and has been and is still today being used to discredit the Confession as 'liberation theology' built on the notion of a Marxist class struggle. (Naudé 2012:150)

Smit (2011:9) explains that during the 1982 Synod it was proposed that the expression in Article 4, 'God of the destitute, the poor and the wronged', be amended in order to use the language of liberation theology that God is the 'God of the poor', or 'to the side of the poor' (Botha & Naudé 2010:66-67). The synod explicitly and deliberately turned down the amendment as it would sound as if God are in a socio-economic class struggle in society on the part of some and against others. Also, the faith of the members would not be articulated properly (Botha & Naudé 2010:66-67; Smit 2011:9). Furthermore, if the synod approved the amendments synod would not have been expressing the faith in the hearts of their DRMC members, but rather the slogans of our time (Botha & Naudé 2010:66-67).

The expression 'in a special way' is of key importance. Smit (1998:10) clarifies that this expression infers that God loves all people, but that the Bible testifies that God is really in a special way concerned and compassioned about those in need, the weak, the victims, the suffering, the widows and orphans, the poor and the marginalised, the oppressed and hungry, the bowed and sorrowful, the deaf and the blind and the wronged. He further and states that the terms 'needy, poor and disadvantaged' and later 'people in any form of suffering and distress' attempt to remain faithful to the richness and fullness of the biblical testimony to this merciful God and does not limit everything to a socio-economic term 'poor'. Equally Botha and Naude (2010:67) believe that when Belhar uses the term 'in a special way', then it stays true to the richness and fullness of the Bible that endless testifies about the mercy of God. Likewise, for Boesak (2008:9) this expression should rather be approached theologically and not socio-economic nor political. God's justice in the Bible is a saving justice and a compassionate justice, which freed from distress and give justice to those who are victimised. This is the biblical God's faithfulness to his covenant, to his promises and his eternal love (Smit 2011:9-10). According to the biblical tradition, God hears the prayers of those in need, God see the plight of those who are enslaved by sin and suffering, and God cares, intervene, just and holy, forgive and accept, help and comfort, through compassionate justice. For Smit (2011:9) this explanation distinguishes the biblical view of justice from that of philosophical theories of justice.

In dealing with poverty, justice and reconciliation follows very strongly and it is precisely for this reason that poverty alone cannot be addressed by the poor. Poverty must be addressed by the larger society, by believers collectively. The motivation behind this is a theological understanding of the church which cares for each other and accordingly Belhar addresses the systems that maintain poverty. Smit (2011) is convinced that God is on the side of the poor in the fight against injustice.

The following question is asked regularly: Is it true that Belhar covers liberation theology that teaches that God is especially on the side of the poor? In his doctoral thesis, De Beer validates that it was striking that in the debate on Belhar in the *Kerkbode* of June 1998, relatively there was little debate on the content of the Confession. For him, this indicates that the content is not the main problem for critics of Belhar, but rather the events, people and issues that were associated with Belhar. However, the objection on contents to the confession related specifically to Article 4 – the righteousness and justice of God. The part that causes the greatest obstacle were the expressions in the Confession that

> God has revealed Godself as the One who wishes to bring about justice and true peace on earth; that in a world full of injustice and enmity God is in a special way the God of the destitute, the poor and the wronged and that God calls the church to follow in this. (Clark 2001:8; De Beer 2008:129; Naudé 2012:150)

De Beer asks the question that many critics have asked in the past. He asks whether the phrase 'in a special way the God of the destitute' is not susceptible to misunderstanding, as it might sound like liberation theology.

Smit (2009) also supports Botha and Naudé's rejection to the liberation theology question and explained that the reference to God, and that of the destitute, poor and disadvantaged, are not to be explained from liberation theology, but from the Bible. The message of the Belhar Confession is that you cannot separate between outreach and care (De Beer 2008:200). People should be able to see the love of your words. The Confession of Belhar confesses that God calls the church and the faithful to follow him through a series of biblical associations reminiscent of that perpetual biblical motif.

Critics of the confession still link Article 4 of the Confession to 'liberation theology' to oppose and reject the confession as a whole (Naudé 2010:16). Such a rejection firstly does not fully consider Scripture's constant witness to God's law and for being with those without rights. This is made clear from the quoted scriptures in the Confession of Belhar. Secondly, criticisms of this wording do not consider that the Confession itself testifies on God's 'distinctiveness' in the context of a world full of injustice and enmity (Naudé 2010:16-17). God does not stand by the poor because they are poor or because he was in a special way the God of the poor (Botha & Naudé 2010:184-1; Naudé 2010:16-17, 85).

The phrase 'in a special way' is really the deciding factor in this debate. It is like a parent with two children, of whom one is born with a disability and has special needs. In this situation, the parent is involved in a special r way with care and love for this child because of the child's special needs. This does not mean that the parent gives less love or care to her child. It cannot be assumed that the parent deliberately favours the vulnerable. The same applies to the Belhar Confession. This is why it is rather a biblical witness of the true character of God. It is also unfair to dismiss the whole Confession as liberation theology because of this part of Article 4.

Article 4 and the theological connectedness and guidelines for a theology of development

While studying the Belhar Confession, both Tshaka and Smit raised important critical questions regarding the church's involvement in the world. Tshaka asks: 'What are the challenges that face the URCSA in South Africa in its current changed and changing context? Is the URCSA doing enough to deal with the realisation of issues such as unity, reconciliation and justice?' (Tshaka 2005:262). Smit asks the question: 'What would this truly mean in our world, our societies, today – to be a church [that] embody the claims and convictions of our own confession?' (Smit 2006:299). Smit (2006:9) is adamant when he says that on the one hand, the need for reformed confession arises from moral or ethical crises and challenges. On the other hand, any such act of confession calls to embodiment, the living, the application and the doing of the gospel as it is expressed in the confessional language.

God reveals himself as the one whose works are perfect, and all his ways are just. He is a faithful God who does no wrong. God is working to bring about a creation order based on justice and peace when it comes to the management of human affairs (Myers 1999:29). When dealing with poverty, aspects of justice and reconciliation of the Confession of Belhar strongly emerges. Poverty can not only be addressed by the poor, but the poor should be assisted by the larger society and by the believers collectively. God is in a special way the God of the destitute, the poor and the wronged (Botha & Naudé 2006:13). God is in a very special way the God of the poor and the wronged. This might have been a thorny issue when it comes to debates about issues of justice in the church, and has also been a stumbling block for unity, but the poor, the socially and economically weak and threatened, will always be the object of the church's primary and particular concern, and it will always insist on the state's special responsibility for these weaker members of society.

'God calls the church to follow him in this.' This biblical claim is unequivocally stated in Article 4, 'that the church should stand where God stands' (Boesak 2008:9).

Churches that confess a confession such as the Confession of Belhar are indeed called to stand where God stands.

God brings justice to the oppressed and gives bread to the hungry. It is clear that God has a special soft spot for those without rights as widows, orphans and strangers (Botha & Naudé 2010:185). The Belhar Confession was not only formulated through a hermeneutic 'view from below', but also existentially in line with the experience of oppression and the oppressed and marginalised people themselves (Tshaka 2005:256). Within this, the experience of the church in her being is such that she cannot help but to assist the wronged and to seek justice. The church as an agent of change are taught by God and called to be actively involved. De Gruchy shares the same view, but put it differently when saying: 'It takes the church as given, one social institution among many – albeit a very important one – and seeks to shift its resources, activities, and ideological power, to the side of the poor and the oppressed (De Gruchy 2007:358). He also mentions that we are a divided church precisely because not all the members of our churches have taken sides against oppression. In other words, not all Christians have united themselves with God who is always on the side of the oppressed. There can be no abandoning of the public sphere (De Gruchy 2007:363).

The people of God are called to repentance and confession of sin so that God can teach them, as he stands for justice and peace. The church must, therefore, stand by people in any form of suffering and need. The church must make a choice to stand where God stands: Because he is the source of justice, he stands in situations of injustice with the victims.

As mentioned before, the church must witness against all the powerful and privileged, against injustice and for justice and give support and practical assistance to people who are suffering. Based on the above argument I proposed that the URCSA, in her quest to tackle the problem of poverty among its members effectively, and in the light of its historical vocation and identity, are called anew to take the Belhar Confession Article 4 as a fundamental starting point. Article 4 motivates the URCSA to be, in a new way, empowered to effectively combat poverty by being involved in a theology of development. A theology of development will make a special contribution in respect of the recent concern precisely raised by the URCSA's 2012 General Synod in Okahandja as it was realised that the URCSA's voice has been silent despite various injustices which occur in society (*Acta General Synod URCSA* 2012:28). The following table gives a theological comparison of between Article 4 of the Confession of Belhar and a theology of development pertaining to that specific part of the article:

Theological comparisons between Article 4 of the Confession of Belhar and a theology of development[4]

Article 4 of the Confession of Belhar confesses that:	A theology of development implies that:
God has revealed himself as the one who wishes to bring about justice and true peace among people.	It is an approach that makes God's restoration of the world as an important priority (Myers 1999:42).
In a world full of injustice and enmity, God is in a special way the God of the destitute, the poor and the wronged and calls the church to follow in this.	Christ's love and hope are demonstrated to the destitute, the poor and wronged regardless of race, culture or background (Moltmann 1969:96).
God brings justice to the oppressed and gives bread to the hungry; God frees the prisoner and restores sight to the blind; God supports the downtrodden, protects the strangers, helps orphans and widows and blocks the path of the ungodly; for God, pure and undefiled religion is to visit the orphans and the widows in their suffering.	The church is empowered to play an effective role in development (August 2010:50; Korten 1990:118; Swart 2006:3).
God wishes to teach the people of God to do what is good and to seek the right.	God is actively working in the world to realise its goals. For this reason, God is deeply involved in the work of the church in the world and also in transformative development (Myers 1999:20).
The church must therefore stand by people in any form of suffering and need.	The church is focused on man (people-centred) (Korten 1990:115-123; Speckman 2007:35; Swart 2008:122-123).
The church must witness against and strive against any form of injustice, so that justice may roll down like waters, and righteousness like an ever-flowing stream.	The church is creative and wholeheartedly engaged in the problems of the world (Dunne 1969:i).
The church belonging to God, should stand where God stands, namely against injustice and with the wronged.	A preference is made – God to stand by the poor, the needy and victims (Swart 2010:211).
In following Christ, the church must witness against all the powerful and privileged who selfishly seek their own interests and thus control and harm others.	The church empowers members and clergy as well as people outside the church to address all forms of injustice (Jenkins 1969:53).

---

4   This table consists only of a few of the theological comparisons between Article 4 and a theology of development. More comparisons can be added.

Conclusion

Considering the argument in the chapter and the comparisons given in the above table, I am convinced that the Confession of Belhar can make a significant contribution to a theology of development that can motivate a renewed and constructive engagement and momentum within the church, especially the URCSA. This engagement should focus on the public role of the church in development, particularly in the empowerment of individuals and communities, but should also to recognise the powerlessThe role of the URCSA in development is non-negotiable because of biblical claims and confessional convictions with specific reference to Article 4 of the Confession of Belhar. The confession affirms the calling of God to be agents of change in this world, therefore, the URCSA is encouraged to wholeheartedly embrace a theology of development.

Bibliography

Primary sources

Acts of General Synod of the Uniting Reformed Church in Southern Africa 2012.

Secondary sources

Abrecht, P. & Land, P. 1969. Common Christian convictions about development. In D. Munby (ed.), *World development: Challenge to the churches*. Washington, DC: Corpus Books.

Alszeghy, Z. & Flick, M. 1971. Theology of development: A quest of method. In P. Land (ed.), *Theology meets progress: Human implications of development*. Rome: Gregorian University Press.

August, K.T. 1999. A curriculum for community development in practical theology. MPA thesis, University of Stellenbosch, Stellenbosch.

August, K.T. 2010. *Equipping the saints: God's measure for development*. Bellville, South Africa: The Print-Man.

Belhar Confession. 1986. Belhar: LUS Printers.

Beukes, J.W. 2014. 'n Prakties-teologiese besinning oor die betekenis van Artikel 4 van die Belydenis van Belhar as grondslag vir die vestiging van 'n teologie van ontwikkeling in die Verenigende Gereformeerde Kerk in Suider-Afrika (VGKSA). PhD thesis. University of Stellenbosch, Stellenbosch.

Boesak, A.A. 2008. To stand where God stands: Reflections on the Confession of Belhar after 25 years. *Studia Historiae Ecclesiasticae* 34(1):143-172.

Botha, J.G. & Naudé, P. 2006. *Belydenis van Belhar 1986: Teks en kommentaar*. 'n publikasie van die Konvent vir Eenheid, Kaapland.

Botha, J.G. & Naudé, P. 2010. *Goeie nuus om te bely: Die Belydenis van Belhar en die pad van aanvaarding*. Wellington: Bybel-Media.

Botman, H.R. 2004. Human dignity and economic globalisation. *Nederduitse Gereformeerde Teologiese Tydskrif* 45(2):317-327.

Clark, A. 2001. Die debat in *Die Kerkbode* oor die Belhar-Belydenis en die invloed wat dit het op kerkvereniging. MDiv dissertation, Stellenbosch University, Stellenbosch.
Cloete, A. 2007. Geloofsgebaseerde organisasies en werkloosheid: 'n Empiriese ondersoek binne die Paarl-Wellington-gemeenskap. PhD thesis, University of South Africa, Pretoria.
de Beer, J.M. 2008. Die missionêre waarde van die Belhar-Belydenis vir die NG Kerk: Instrument tot eenwording. PhD thesis, University of Pretoria, Pretoria.
de Gruchy, S.M. 2003. Of agency, assets and appreciation: Seeking some commonalities between theology and development. *Journal of Theology for Southern Africa* 117:20-39.
de Gruchy, S.M. 2007. On not abandoning church theology: Dirk Smit on church and politics. *Nederduitse Gereformeerde Teologiese Tydskrif* 48(1):356-365.
de Gruchy, S.M. & Ellis, W. 2008. Christian leadership in another country: Contributing to an ethical development agenda in South Africa. In S.M. de Gruchy, N. Koopman & S. Strijbos (eds), *From our side: Emerging perspectives in development and ethics*. Leiden BRILL.
Dunne, G.H. (ed.). 1969. In search of a theology of development. Geneva Sodepax Report. Geneva: Committee on Society, Development and Peace (The Ecumenical Centre). Geneva: WCC Publications.
Gern, W. 1999. Christian development services. In E. Fahlbusch et al. (eds), *The Encyclopedia of Christianity*. Grand Rapids, MI: William B. Eerdmans.
Jenkins, D. 1969. The power of the powerless. In G.H. Dunne (ed.), *In search of a theology of development*. Geneva: Sodepax Report.
Koegelenberg, R.A. (ed.). 1992. *Church and development: An interdisciplinary approach*. Bellville, South Africa: Ecumenical Foundation of Southern Africa (EFSA).
Korten, D.C. 1990. *Getting to the 21st century: Voluntary action and the global agenda*. West Hartford, CT: Kumarian Press.
le Bruyns, C. & Pauw, C. 2004. Looking in two ways: Poverty in South Africa and its ecclesiological implications. *Nederduitse Gereformeerde Teologiese Tydskrif* 45(2):202-213.
Lutz, C.P. 1987. *God, goods and the common good*. Minneapolis, MN: Augsburg.
Moltmann, J. 1969. The Christian theology of hope and its bearing on development. In G.H. Dunne, G.H. (ed.), *In search of a theology of development*. Geneva: Sodepax Report.
Myers, B.L. 1999. *Walking with the poor: Principles and practices of transformational development*. Maryknoll, NY: Orbis.
Myers, B.L. 2011. *Walking with the poor: Principles and practices of transformational development* (3rd edition). Maryknoll, NY: Orbis.
Naudé, P. 2010. *Neither calender nor clock: Perspectives on the Belhar Confession*. Grand Rapids, MI: William B. Eerdmans.
Naudé, P. 2012. The Belhar Confession and church and society: A comparative reading in five statements. *Acta Theologica* 32(2):147-161.
Nürnberger, K. 1994. The task of the church concerning the economy in a post-apartheid South Africa. *Missionalia* 22(2):118-146.
Nyerere, J. 1972. *Poverty, Christianity and revolution*. Ottawa: Canadian Catholic Conference.
Odendaal, M. 2004. Meditating on poverty: Seeking guidance from the Psalms. *Nederduitse Gereformeerde Teologiese Tydskrif* 45(2):293-299.

Pieterse, H.J.C. 2001. The human face of God for the poor. *Praktiese Teologie in Suid-Afrika*, 16(1):75-104.

Plaatjies-Van Huffel, M-A. 2008. Die doleansie kerkreg en kerkregering van die Nederduitse Gereformeerde sendingkerke en die VGKSA. [online] Available at http://upetd.up.ac.za/thesis/available/etd-04022009-190218/ (Accessed 21 March 2015).

Plaatjies-Van Huffel, M-A. 2013a. Reading the Belhar Confession as a historical text. In M.A. Plaatjies-Van Huffel and R.R. Vosloo (eds), *Reformed churches in South Africa and the struggle for justice – Remembering 1960–1990*. Stellenbosch: SUN PReSS. https://doi.org/10.18820/9781920689117

Plaatjies-Van Huffel, M-A. 2013b. The Belhar Confession: Born in the struggle against apartheid in southern Africa. *Studia Historicae Ecclesiasticae* 39(1):185-203.

Plaatjies-Van Huffel, M-A. 2014. The Belhar Confession: in its historical context. *Nederduitse Gereformeerde Teologiese Tydskrif* 55(1):308-309. https://doi.org/10.5952/55-1-2-527

Rendtorff, T. 1969. A theology of development? In search of a theology of development. Papers from a consultation on Theology and Development held by Sodepax in Cartigny, Switzerland, November 1969. Geneva: Sodepax.

Rendtorff, T. 1971. Christian foundation of worldly commitment. In P. Land (ed.), *Theology meets progress: Human implications of development*. Rome: Gregorian University Press.

Santa Ana, J. de & Barreiro, J. 1980. *Separation without hope: The church and the poor during the industrial revolution and colonial expansion*. Maryknoll, NY: Orbis.

Sedgwick, P.H. 1999. *The market economy and Christian ethics*. Cambridge, UK: Cambridge University Press. https://doi.org/10.1017/CBO9780511488368

Smit, D.J. 1984a. Wat beteken *status confessionis*? In G. Cloete & D. Smit(eds), *'n Oomblik van waarheid: Opstelle rondom die NG Sendingkerk se afkondiging van 'n status confessionis en die opstel van 'n konsepbelydenis*. Cape Town: Tafelberg.

Smit, D.J. 1984b. Op 'n besonderse wyse die God van die noodlydende, die arme en die verontregte. In G. Cloete & D. Smit(eds), *'n Oomblik van waarheid: Opstelle rondom die NG Sendingkerk se afkondiging van 'n status confessionis en die opstel van 'n konsepbelydenis*. Cape Town: Tafelberg.

Smit, D.J. 1998. Wat beteken 'gereformeerd'? In W.A. Boesak & P.J.A. Fourie (eds), *Vraagtekens oor gereformeerd*. Belhar, Cape Town: LUS Printers.

Smit, D.J. 2000. Versoening – en Belhar. *Gereformeerd Theologisch Tijdschrift*, 100(4):159-172.

Smit, D.J. 2002. Deel van kerk deur die eeue – die werklike kerk op soek na die ware kerk. In C. Burger & I. Nell (eds), *Draers van die waarheid: Nuwe-Testamentiese visies vir die gemeente*. Stellenbosch: Buvton.

Smit, D.J. 2004. Oor die kerk en maatskaplike uitdagings in ons land. *Nederduitse Gereformeerde Teologiese Tydskrif* 45(2):350-362.

Smit, D.J. 2006. Barmen and Belhar in conversation – a South African perspective. *Nederduitse Gereformeerde Teologiese Tydskrif* 47(1/2):291-301.

Smit D.J. 2006. Die Gereformeerde siening van belydenis? Enkele algemene gedagtes. [Online] Available at http://www.ngkok.co.za/KonventAlgemeen/OpmerkingsOorBelydenis_ Smit DJ_2006.pdf (Accesed 10 July 2008).

Smit, D.J. 2008. *Geloof en openbare lewe: Versamelde opstelle 2*. Stellenbosch: SUN PReSS.

Smit, D.J. 2011. 'n Blik op eenheid, versoening en geregtigheid 1986 en 2011: Oor die teologiese inhoud van die Belydenis van Belhar. Lecture given at the Faculty of Theology, University of the Free State, Bloemfontein (31 Oktober).

Smit, D.J. 2012. Oor die teologiese inhoud van die Belydenis van Belhar. *Acta Theologica*, 32(2):184-202.

Speckman, M.T. 2007. *A biblical vision for Africa's development.* Pietermaritzburg: Cluster.

Swart, I. 2006. 'Transforming social welfare? The religious discourse on social development in post-apartheid South Africa'. Paper presented at the First Conference of the South African Swedish-Research Links Project, Welfare and Religion in a Global Perspective: Theoretical and Methodological Exchange across the North-South Divide (WRIGP), Stellenbosch (6–8 December).

Swart, I. 2008. Market economy development, local economic experience and the Christian movement towards alternatives in a South African city region. In S. de Gruchy, N. Koopman & S. Strijbos (eds), *From our side: Emerging perspectives in development and ethics.* Leiden: BRILL.

Swart, I. 2010. The third public: Hermeneutical key to the theological debate on church and development? In I. Swart, H. Rocher, S. Green & J. Erasmus (eds), *Religion and social development in post-apartheid South Africa: Perspectives for critical engagement.* Stellenbosch: SUN PReSS.

Swart, I. & Venter, D. 2001. NGO's and churches: Civil society actors and the promise of fourth generation development in South Africa. In J. Coetzee, J. Graaff, F. Hendricks & G. Wood (eds), *Development: Theory, policy and practice* Cape Town: Oxford University Press.

Tshaka, R.S. 2005. Confessional theology? A critical analysis of the theology of Karl Barth and its significance for the Belhar Confession. DTh thesis, University of Stellenbosch, Stellenbsch.

van Rooi, L.B. 2007. Bevry om te bely en te beliggaam: 'n Ekklesiologiese besinning oor die kerkorde van die VGKSA. *Nederduitse Gereformeerde Teologiese Tydskrif* 48(3/4):799-810.

van der Ven, J.A., Dreyer, J. & Pieterse, H.J.C. 2002. The formation of churches as moral communities. *Practical Theology in South Africa* 17(1):102-110.

BELHAR CONFESSION, CHILDREN AND THE EUCHARIST

Towards restoration of broken relationships

Tipi Jacob Nthakhe[1]

Abstract

This chapter reflects on the participation of children in the Eucharist as an indicative and imperative of the Belhar Confession. In some churches, children are often made invisible through neglect and exclusion from church activities, such as partaking of the Eucharist. This chapter rejects any doctrine or practice that excludes children from joining in the covenant meal because it is a meal which marks communion with Christ and with one another.

Belhar is not only a confession that is recited during worship services but a way of life towards the restoration of broken relationships. Like all other Reformation confessions through which the church confessed its faith within a specific context, so was Belhar a confession that the church adopted to confess its faith within the context of apartheid in South Africa. It was in this context that the church felt challenged to formulate a confession that would not only capture the spirit of the time but also challenge the people of South Africa and the world to live and act towards the restoration of broken relationships. Apartheid had not only managed to separate people from one another based on the colour of their skin but it also managed to break down relationships that existed between them as image-bearers of God.

In the midst of the brokenness in church and society, Belhar brought a message of hope and restoration calling upon the church and society by hearing, trusting and obeying Jesus Christ in every aspect of its life. It called on the church and society not only to confess but to stand where God stands; for unity, justice and reconciliation in all circumstances where deceit, enmity and exclusion are taking place. It is in such situations that the church needs to proclaim in fresh ways what it believes, especially when it feels that the gospel of Jesus Christ is under threat.

---

1 Dr Tipi Jacob Nthakhe serves in Melodi ya Tshwane (MYT) as a full-time minister. Melodi ya Tshwane is a multicultural congregation in the city centre of Pretoria.

Wherever and whenever the truth is threatened, the church is left with no option but to act through word and deed.

Introduction

Belhar is one of the most significant confessions to have ever come from the African soil. It was born during the apartheid crisis that befell South Africa over a period of more than three and a half centuries. It called upon the church to assess its role, impact and relevance in a country that was at war with itself because the struggle against apartheid was waged by South Africans against other South Africans. In other instances, it was waged by Christians against other Christians and at the same time, as the struggle against apartheid, oppression and dehumanisation continued in the broader South African communities, a subtle exploitation, rejection and exclusion of children on the basis of age was equally taking place in the church when the Eucharist was celebrated.

Just as the struggle against apartheid was a justice issue, this chapter moves from the premise that the exclusion of children from partaking of the Eucharist is also a justice issue because the Eucharist is a covenantal meal that should be shared by all God's people in remembrance of God's saving act in the life, death and resurrection of Jesus Christ. Every time Christians come together to partake of the covenant meal, not only do they remember the Lord who died but they also deepen fellowship with him and with one another (NGK 2012:113). With his body that was broken, Christians are reminded that Christ brought peace by making Jews and Gentiles one people (Eph. 2:14, New Revised Standard Version).[2] With his body that is shared, they are reminded that Christ broke down the walls of partition that separated those who were once enemies. Indeed, with his body that is celebrated, Christians in South Africa in particular, are reminded that Christ has removed all kinds of barriers that separated black, white, Indian and coloured, rich, poor, male, female, young and old.

The admission of children to the Eucharist should be based on a deepened understanding and practice of community which the church shares with Christ and with one another. The admission or exclusion of children to the Eucharist carries implications for the understanding of the nature of the church. It means that the church is either an open or welcoming or a closed and unwelcoming church. To this

---

2   Scriptural quotations in this chapter follow the New Revised Standard Version (NRSV).

effect, Muller-Fharenholz gives a fine description of what the church is and how it should be like:

> The Church is seen as the community which reflects God's determination to gather people from all cultures, races, classes and ages. The community which God wills is inclusive, and by its very nature, it transcends human barriers. Therefore, the admission of children is not simply a marginal change in the worship life of the church. It poses a far-reaching question to the churches as they exist today: Are you as inclusive and comprehensive as you are called to be? (Muller-Fharenholz 1982:9)

The Eucharist is central to the being and worship of the church. It is a memorial meal that reminds the church that everything that has been broken is restored in Christ and everything that has been divided is reunited and reconciled in Christ. By eating the bread and drinking from the cup, the church calls to mind how God restored the broken relationship between God and humanity. By eating the bread and drinking from the cup, the church reaffirms that the reconciliation and salvation that God granted to humanity and the whole of creation was not for sale but for free. It was not for certain people or groups of people but for the whole creation. This gift from God is meant to redeem and restore the whole of creation, including people, relationships and institutions. Macy sums it up by saying:

> The Eucharist is first and foremost a ritual meal, a sharing in the life, death and resurrection of Jesus the Christ by the community founded in his name. It is something one does, not something about which one talks. No more important statement can be made about the Lord's Supper. It is a celebration, a way of life; a celebration of a way of life. (Macy 1992:15)

Since the Eucharist reminds us of all these truths, it would be wrong to see the Eucharist as a private or personal affair. By its nature, the Eucharist offers an open invitation to the whole church that is united in love as members of one body around the Table. It has never been, and should never be an 'adults only' affair but a meal for the 'whole church' gathered, protected and cared for by God around the Table. It is there around the Table, where unity among all members of the body of Christ including children must become visible. Article 2 of the Belhar Confession states that the unity of the church 'must become visible so that the world may believe that separation, enmity and hatred between people and groups is sin which Christ has already conquered'.[3] Indeed, Christ has conquered separation of people on the basis of race, culture, religion or age. This means that Christ has also conquered

---

3 Extracts from the Confession of Belhar in this chapter are taken from the English translation at Addendum 15, The Confession of Belhar. Also available at http://urcsa.net/wp-content/uploads/2016/02/Belhar-Confession.pdf

the exclusion of children from the inclusive covenant meal that the whole people of God are invited to partake of freely. It is undisputable that Belhar is against any form of oppression and exclusion of any of God's people by other people of God. It is also undisputable that any form of oppression and exclusion is a sin that Christ has already overcome. Therefore, children, as part of God's people, should neither be oppressed nor excluded from any church activity including participation in the Eucharist. The exclusion of children as God's people from sharing with other God's people what Christ commanded is a justice issue that needs to be defended at all costs. Once children are not taken seriously, protected and cared for, the likelihood is great that injustice will be done to them.

Belhar is very emphatic on the point that where injustice is done, there is a demand for justice.; where relations are broken, there is a demand for restoration; where people have been separated from one another because of human or artificial reasons, there is a demand for reconciliation; and where people are excluded, there is a demand for inclusion. Therefore, in any community of believers that becomes contaminated with separation of people from one another because of human or artificial reasons, there is a demand for reconciliation. In any congregation that excludes its children (women, the poor and the downtrodden), there is a need for inclusivity for the sake of unity in the body of Christ.

Belhar as proclamation

The message of Belhar came as 'good news' (euangelion-εὐαγγέλιον) and 'proclamation' (kerugma-κήρυγμα) at a very critical time in the history of South Africa. Borrowing from Lombard (2009:15), and accepting it as proclamation, we may as well regard 'Belhar as public theology.' It was imposible for Belhar to be kept hidden from the URCSA, South Africa, and the ecumenical world. As a demonstration of the Christian faith expressed from the dungeons of oppression, one cannot help but agree with Lombard that the Christian faith is always intended to be a 'public faith', a faith whose light is not to be hidden under the bed or behind a bushel; whose salt is intended to be mixed into the broth of real life, to flavour it and bring it to its full aroma (Lombard 2009:95). Belhar came as prophetic at a time when the truth of the gospel was at stake; a time when the preaching of the gospel was facing unprecedented challenges. Describing those challenges, Nolan writes:

> In South Africa today, the preaching of the gospel is facing an unprecedented challenge. Our country has been experiencing a serious political crisis for some time and now the crisis has reached a breaking-point. This alone presents those who believe in the gospel of Jesus Christ with a challenge. How does one preach the gospel in our present circumstances of conflict and crisis? But what makes the challenge urgent and demanding is the

simple fact that the gospel has been, and still is, associated with a political system that is now regarded by almost the whole world as a crime against humanity. (Nolan 1988:5)

In the same vein, the Kairos Document described the challenges facing South Africa in its own unique way:

> The time has come. The moment of truth has arrived. South Africa has been plunged into a crisis that is shaking the foundations and there is every indication that the crisis has only just begun and that it will deepen and become even more threatening in the months to come. It is the Kairos or moment of truth not only for apartheid but also for the church. (Kairos Theologians 1985:11)

Definitely, it was the *kairos*[4] or moment of truth not only for apartheid but also for the church. The *kairos* moment says it was not easy for ministers and preachers of the gospel at that time because the challenge facing them was how to preach the gospel in a situation of a crisis. Obviously, there was uncertainty as to how to rebuke the perpetrators of apartheid and how to encourage and bring hope to the oppressed at the same time. It was either that the preacher was on the side of the oppressor or on the side of the oppressed. The situation did not allow any neutrality.

Indeed, there was no room for neutrality or cover-up because the moment of truth had arrived as the Kairos Document shows. It was the right moment for the truth to be told as the church in South Africa was exposed for what it really was. One of the truths that were exposed was that the preaching of the gospel in the country had never been racially, politically, economically and culturally neutral. It had struggled to be a pure proclamation of the gospel of Jesus Christ, the Son of God who came as a sacrifice to restore broken relationships. Since the coming of the colonisers and missionaries to the shores of South Africa, it had struggled, and most of the time failed, to reunite those who were separated by the system of apartheid around the Eucharist Table. According to Nolan (1988:1), 'it justified and legitimised colonialism, imperialism and European superiority.' It was at the Eucharist Table that things went wrong for 'black and coloured' people. It was at the Eucharist Table where God's people were supposed to be united but, unfortunately, it was there where they were separated.[5] In retrospection, it could, therefore, be said that the gospel that came

---

4 '*Kairos*' is an ancient Greek word meaning the right or opportune moment/the supreme moment. The ancient Greeks had two words for time, '*chronos*' and '*kairos*'. While the former refers to chronological or sequential time, the latter signifies a time lapse, a moment of indeterminate time in which everything happens.

5 For a detailed discussion of the birth of apartheid around the Eucharist see Loff (1983:17-22).

to the shores of this country with colonialists and missionaries was a gospel that justified and legitimised division between people according to culture, race and status. Nolan declares:

> Despite their barbaric methods and attitudes, the colonisers believed that what they were bringing to this part of the world was 'civilisation' and that the basis of this 'civilisation' was the message of Jesus Christ. The British never doubted that they were living and acting according to the gospel of Jesus Christ. (Nolan 1988:1)

Saayman adds to this by saying that 'real Christianisation would take place only if the hold of the traditional African system could be broken' (Saayman 1991:32) In this way, the gospel of the colonisers became so entangled with the practice and policy of apartheid that it became difficult to draw a line between church and politics; gospel and apartheid. In 1945, the Nationalist Party accepted apartheid as its official racial policy and the Dutch Reformed Church (DRC) provided a theological justification. As a result, the gospel that was preached evolved into a proclamation of the gospel that promoted and protected apartheid and that drove people apart from one another in church and society on many grounds. It promoted and protected the separation of people on the basis of the colour of their skin, cultural background, language and behavioural differences (Smith 2004:71). In the midst of this 'pseudo-gospel' of separation and division, Belhar came as a proclamation of the 'good news' in the same way as Isaiah 6:5-10 was proclaimed redemption to the sins of Israel.

In a country like South Africa that needed healing, Belhar came as prophetic proclamation denouncing apartheid as sin, heresy and mockery of the gospel (Nolan 1988:2). Looking at all the social ills caused by the oppression and suffering of black people; it all came down to the fact that the country needed healing. Taking into consideration the healing that was to take place, Belhar came not only to condemn the status quo but to promote unity, reconciliation and justice. It was unbelievable to see that the oppressed were the ones who offered the olive branch in search of healing of the church and country. This is clearly expressed in Article 3 of the confession:

> We believe that God has entrusted to his Church the message of reconciliation in and through Jesus Christ; that the church is called to be the salt of the earth and the light of the world that the church is called blessed because it is a peacemaker, that the church is witness both by word and by deed to the new heaven and the new earth in which righteousness dwells.

This Belhar message of unity, reconciliation and justice came at the right moment (*kairos*) as proclamation against oppression and injustice in church and society. It came as a challenge to citizens of the country, especially Christians, to stand up and take action for the common good of the South African society. It came as a challenge to those who found themselves on the side of the oppressor and those sitting on the fence to cross over to the other side and be united in faith and action with the oppressed. The dividing line was clear. It was either being an oppressor or the oppressed. In such a situation, the church took a definite stance of where it stood. It was either on the side of the oppressor or on the side of the oppressed. The church could not sit on the fence and claim to be neutral.

This was the reality. It was a moment of truth for the church and the country. It was unfortunate that at that time the church (both black and white and especially the DRC) was deeply involved in political affairs to such an extent that it made the Bible part of the problem rather than the solution. Voster gives an example of what Prof. E.P. Groenewald once said in justification of apartheid: 'God consciously divided man into races, peoples and tongues; that apartheid is the will of God and that it leads to national, social and religious apartheid.' He went further to say that 'race policy of the Afrikaner gives proof of their fear of God' (Voster 1983:96).

On the other hand, the oppressed used the Bible as a tool of liberation. They used it to fight against apartheid and its theological justification. Speaking from the side of the oppressed, Article 4 uses among other verses, John 14:27, Ephesians 2:14 and Isaiah 1:16-17 to say that God is the one who brings true justice and peace in a world full of injustice and enmity. God is in a special way a God of the destitute, the poor and the wronged. It is for this reason that in Article 3 of the confession, the oppressed Christians confess that:

> God's life-giving Word and Spirit has conquered the powers of sin and death, and therefore also of irreconciliation and hatred, bitterness and enmity; that God's life-giving Word and Spirit will enable the church to live in a new obedience which can open new possibilities of life for society and the world. (Bierma 2007:3)

In the context of deceit, hopelessness and uncertainty, Belhar brought a message of truth, hope and courage. Besides rejecting apartheid, which set people apart from one another and excluded others, it emphasised the credibility of the gospel. It highlighted the wrongs which the church entertained. It spoke strongly against the church, which shared the same baptism and celebrated the same Eucharist and yet closed its ears to the good news. Adding to this prophetic message of Belhar, the Kairos Document (Kairos Theologians 1985:11) spoke strongly against God's people attending and worshipping in church buildings, while in the townships fellow brothers and sisters in the police and military services were beating, torturing and killing fellow brothers and sisters.

This proclamation to which Belhar added its voice came from prophetic figures like Allan Boesak, Desmond Tutu and Trevor Huddleston; as well as from bodies like the South African Council of Churches, the World Council of Churches, and the Institute of Contextual Theology. All these made prophetic statements and declarations denouncing apartheid and its brutal effects on black, Indian, coloured, women and children. Those who felt the pain at most were young people and children. Many of them were injured during the riots and others lost their lives. Those who survived the bullets ended in police cells while others skipped the country. Those who stayed in the country continued the struggle as young activists. They joined their brothers and sisters in protest marches singing liberation songs while chanting the slogan of the moment '*A luta continua*'.[6] This slogan was a kind of energy booster to the crowds as it demonstrated a point of no-return to those who stood up and fought for their rights. As things were heating up in the country, the World Alliance of Reformed Churches (WARC) declared apartheid sinful and any theological and moral justification of it a heresy (Addendum 1 WARC Resolution on racism and South Africa). This ecumenical body further suspended the membership of the DRC and Nederduitsche Hervormde Kerk (NHK) for their justification and practice of apartheid. It further called for a status confessionis,[7] a decision endorsed by the DRMC Synod in 1982 leading to the birth of the Belhar Confession.

Now, after almost thirty years of the Belhar Confession's existence, the URCSA can look back with gratitude to the Almighty for the confession that brought hope to the people of South Africa and the world. People of faith can also give thanks for the crisis that provided a fertile confessional occasion for the church to confess and reaffirm its faith.

It was not by mistake that this confession was born at that time. It was also not by mistake that it was born out of the hearts of the faithful who chose to stand where stands. Indeed, it was not by mistake that it was born in a situation of a crisis when the truth of the gospel was at stake. Such times call for brave men and women to stand up and fight for the truth. Hence, we could safely say that the Belhar Confession was born out the hearts of people who were guided and empowered by the Holy Spirit to stand up against all forms of oppression, suffering and injustice

---

6   This phrase was commonly used in political gatherings and rallies to pump up the masses in their defiance of the police and security service. Its correct wording is actually '*A luta continua, vitória é certa*' which means: 'The struggle continues, – victory is certain.' However, the phrase has been corrupted over the years and is more likely to be written '*Aluta Continua, Victoria Acerta*'.

7   A *status confessionis* refers to a historical period during which the church sees a need to confess anew. In 1982 the then DRMC felt a need to confess in the midst of pain and suffering caused by the minority of white people over the majority of black people in South Africa. The then DRMC called for a *status confessionis* by adopting the Belhar Confession which rejected apartheid as indicated in its three core pillars of justice, reconciliation and justice. (see Loff 1983:176).

inflicted by one group of people over the others. This was a positive response of obedience, readiness and willingness from the church to bring good news to the country that was in a crisis through its confession.

In the midst of the brokenness in church and society, Belhar brought a message of hope and restoration calling upon both the church and society to a new way of life by hearing, trusting and obeying Jesus Christ in every aspect of its life. By so doing, the church reasserted its integrity, identity and faithfulness by responding to God's calling in the same way that Isaiah did in 6:5-10. It was out of humility and not arrogance; out of truth and not deceit that the DRMC through Belhar presented itself as a tool in God's hand to be used by the Spirit to repair the brokenness in church and society. In the same way as Isaiah did, the DRMC pitied itself as a church of people with unclean lips living among people of unclean lips and yet its eyes had seen the Lord (Isa. 6:5). Knowing that it was a church 'in' but not 'of' this world, the DRMC through Belhar, availed itself to be used by God. It gave South Africa and the world a unique, special and relevant confession that spoke to a situation in life of the time. The DRMC did this, not regarding itself as a fixer of the status quo. It did this without any intention to produce a political document or a theological declaration but out of an openness to the Spirit to lead it to produce a confession that the church, society and the ecumenical world needed at a critical time.

Tshaka (2005:101) captures the mood of Reformed confessions coming out of a *status confessionis* by saying that a Reformed confession is not something that elevates the group that promulgates it above those who are making a mockery out of the gospel. Instead it is made with a deepest conviction that the church cannot do anything else in a *status confessionis* but confess. It was in the same vein that the authors of the Belhar Confession put together this confession with a deep theological conviction that from time to time God through the Spirit calls the church to say what it believes. They did this by producing the first confession from the African soil; not as something to brag about or use as a stick to hit others with but as an additional confession to the three others from the Reformed tradition (Belgic Confession, Heidelberg Catechism and the Canons of Dort) which are deeply rooted in the Word of God and forms the confessional basis of the URCSA.

Belhar and children

This section considers what Belhar says about children in general and in particular their participation in the Eucharist. This statement is deliberately formulated as such because it is a given that Belhar does not speak directly about children but this does not mean it is silent as far as they are concerned. The question of whether children are members of the church and should, therefore, be allowed to partake of the Eucharist is the same as many other questions asked about them.

Just as Belhar, the Bible does not give a clear-cut answer as to whether children may or may not be allowed to partake of the Eucharist (I mean a definite 'yes' or 'no' answer) but there are implications that sway in the direction of the 'yes they may'. What needs to be kept in mind when dealing with this issue is God's special relationship with believers and their children, which is rooted in the covenant with Abraham in Genesis:

> I will make you very fruitful; I will make nations of you, and kings will come from you. I will establish my covenant as an everlasting covenant between me and you and your descendants after you for the generations to come, to be your God and the God of your descendants after you. (Gen. 17:6-7)

A good theological interpretation and understanding of this covenant relationship forms the basis for understanding the place and role of children in the Bible. Bierma maintains:

> There is one community of God throughout all redemptive history, and children are full members of that community. As we say in the form for the baptism of children, 'God graciously includes our children in his covenant, and all his promises are for them as well as for us'. (Bierma 2007:3)

On the basis of the covenant that God established with Abraham, the father of all nations, children of believers received the sacrament of initiation (circumcision) into that covenant community (Gen. 17:10-14). In the same way, children of believers today must receive the sacrament of initiation (Baptism) that has replaced circumcision. In relation to the Eucharist, Bierma (2007:3) asks this very critical question: Why, then, would the same not apply to the sacrament of nurture? If in the Old Testament covenant children participated in the household and communal celebrations of the Passover (Ex. 12:3-4, 21-26) and other sacred meals of remembrance (Deut. 12:6-7), they should also be welcome at the New Testament counterpart to these feasts: The Lord's Supper. Members of the Old Covenant community were 'all baptised into Moses in the cloud and in the sea,' and they 'all ate the same spiritual food and drank the same spiritual drink' from Christ (1 Cor. 10:1-4).

The Bible is clear on the participation of children in both household and communal sacred meals. To start anywhere else when dealing with children other than in the in the Bible, culture, tradition and confessions may lead to a misconstrued understanding and interpretation of their place and role in the church. Starting other than in places mentioned above may also lead to misconstrued understanding and interpretation of what the church is and who belongs to it. It is for this reason that Article 1 of Belhar states that 'the triune God ... gathers, protects and cares for the church from the beginning of the world and will do so to the end'. Already here, a question may be asked as to whether children are not part of these people gathered, protected and cared for by God?

A similar question could be asked in relation to Article 2 of whether children do not belong to the one holy, universal Christian Church, the communion of saints called from the entire human family. Belhar is clear on the composition of the church and calls for this composition not to be tempered with. All members belonging to this church must be united because they are bound by God's Spirit. It goes further to say that this composition of a united membership must not only be maintained but pursued and sought. If this is what the church believes, then the church must do all it can to have children as part and parcel of those who 'share one faith, have one calling, are of one soul and one mind; have one God and Father, are filled with one Spirit, are baptised with one baptism, eat of one bread and drink of one cup'.

As much as children are part of the community of saints that share one baptism, so are they part of the community that is gathered around the Eucharist Table. Macy agrees to this by saying that Eucharist is 'first and foremost a ritual meal, a sharing in the life, death and resurrection of Jesus Christ by the community founded in his name. It is something one does, not something about which one talks' (Macy 1992:200). This means that we cannot only say we are going to church to partake of the Eucharist but we have to do it. Our 'we' should be a genuine 'we,' inclusive and not exclusive since the Eucharist is an inclusive meal that should be celebrated by the entire communion of saints.

The celebration of the Eucharist is different from a celebration of any other party like a wedding or a birthday party but it is a special type of party, which Macy (1992:200) refers to as: 'a celebration, a way of life; a celebration of a way of life'. This means that Eucharist is a way of life and every time the church celebrates it, it lives out the promise contained in it. Every time the church eats and drinks, it proclaims the death of the Lord until he comes. Living out the promise contained in the Eucharist entails the whole unity that is a human being.

Therefore, children are part of the church formed out of a people who celebrate a way of life. A people who form a community of faith called from the entire humanity to live out the promise contained in Baptism and the Eucharist. They are to partake of the Eucharist and live out the promise contained in it by worshipping God through word and deed. They are part of the '*koinonia*'[8] of which membership is not self-determined but decided by Christ, the initiator and giver of Eucharist. Therefore, their exclusion from this *koinonia* amounts to the incompleteness of the *koinonia*.

---

8   *Koinonia* is a Greek word that denotes the idealised state of fellowship and unity that should exist within the Christian church, the Body of Christ.

It is for this reason that Jesus strongly warns his disciples in Mark 10:14 'Let the children come to me, do not hinder them for the kingdom of God is of such.'

Jesus' invitation to children supports some theological principles that inform the composition of the church as his body. Firstly, the invitation highlights the importance that Jesus places on children. He had a special place for them in his life, ministry and the kingdom of God hence he rebuked his disciples' attempts to prevent them from accessing him. His treatment of children shows that children are fully human, worthy of respect, dignity and human rights like any other person. They need to be looked at in the light of Genesis 1:27 as image-bearers of God with inherent value.

Secondly, Jesus' invitation to children came as a break away from the stereotypes of his time. The ancient Greco-Roman society viewed children as being on par with animals, quite a far throw from fully human image-bearers. They were considered more as young animals to be trained than human beings to be guided in a learning process (Stonehouse & May 2010:12). Jesus' break from tradition brought in a new dispensation that accommodated societal outcasts (children and women) and in so doing, mended broken relationships.

In his busy schedule, Jesus made time for children and women. He held children in his arms (Mark 10:16) and healed them (Mark 5:21-24, 35-43, 7:24-30). He associated with the Samaritan woman and asked water from her (John 4:7-10); allowed a sinful woman to anoint his feet (Luke 7:36-50). After engaging children, they would no longer be ignored as marginal members of the kingdom of God just tagging along with their parents, waiting to grow up and become real members. Stonehouse and May (2010:14). correctly point out that 'children are models in the kingdom of God, showing adults how to enter'.

Jesus' invitation also communicated a sense of belonging to children. It showed that discipleship is inclusive and participatory. Stonehouse (1998:40) adds that 'the sense of belonging grows as one participates'. Belonging and participating in kingdom issues calls for all God's people and not just those who are grown up or those who are intellectually mature.

Jesus' invitation demonstrates that the kingdom of God is not for a special group of people but it is open for all who come in the offering of praise and thanks to God. Belonging and participation go far beyond the intellectual capacity of people but extends to include the heart and will. It takes the 'whole' person who belongs to participate freely and fully. In a congregation, the persons who may be the most free and most whole participants are the children. When children say 'Thank you,

God,' they say it freely and fully. Their vital participation in the community's worship helps all who are present to participate freely and fully.

Summing up Jesus' invitation to children to come to him, he wanted to demonstrate the inclusive nature of God's people gathered around him. Not only the disciples or the multitudes were allowed in his company but the children as well. The invitation further demonstrated the inclusive nature of those gathered around the audible word, meaning that children are also allowed to hear the good news as taught and preached.

Finally, the invitation to children shows that just as they are allowed to gather around the audible word (sermon) so must they be allowed to gather around the visible word (Eucharist). The privilege that Jesus granted to children to come to him should never be compromised for anything else. It is for this reason that in its rejections, Article 2 of Belhar rejects any practice or doctrine which:

> absolutises either natural diversity or the sinful separation of people in such a way that this absolutisation hinders or breaks the visible and active unity of the church, or even leads to the establishment of a separate church formation; which professes that this spiritual unity is truly being maintained in the bond of peace while believers of the same confession are in effect alienated from one another for the sake of diversity and in despair of reconciliation; which denies that a refusal earnestly to pursue this visible unity as a priceless gift is sin; which explicitly or implicitly maintains that descent or any other human or social factor should be a consideration in determining membership of the church.

Belhar reiterates and emphasises the inclusiveness of God's people that must be manifested and made active in how Christians love one another, practice and pursue community with one another. As God's people, they are obliged to give themselves willingly and joyfully to be of benefit and blessing to one another. They need to share one faith, have one calling, be of one soul and one mind; have one God and Father and be filled with one Spirit.

All God's people (including children) are baptised with one baptism and must, therefore, eat of one bread and drink of one cup, confess one Name, be obedient to one Lord, work for one cause, and share one hope. Together they come to know the height and the breadth and the depth of the love of Christ and share all these with the rest of humanity so that the triune God be known throughout the universe (Addendum 15, Confession of Belhar).

Belhar and children's spirituality

The earlier section on Belhar and children focused more on the place and role of children in the community of faith. The reason for starting with allocating them within the community of faith was to avoid a situation where we talk about them as if they are just 'extras' and not full members of this community and part the body of Christ. So far it is evident that because they have one calling, are of one soul and mind, have one God, are filled with one Spirit and are baptised with one baptism, they should, therefore, eat one bread and drink from one cup with other members of the church.

This section focuses on how children's spirituality is informed by Belhar. We should take extra caution when dealing with children's spirituality. According to Nye (2009:7) 'we tend to think about spirituality in ways that depend on having adult capacities, thereby excluding children or indeed others with little (religious) knowledge, or limited intellectual capacities (e.g. people with brain damage or dementia).' This shows the importance of dealing with spirituality in a fair and inclusive manner so that at the end other people are not left out.

Stonehouse (1998:21) also shares the same sentiment as Nye, namely that many scholars who write about spiritual formation do so as if it applies exclusively to adults or older teenagers. The question flowing from this allegation is whether one needs to grow up first before one's spiritual life can be formed? The fact is that personality starts forming at a very early age when children develop different elements of their personhood with which they will relate to God. Young as they are, they come to know and experience God in their own ways.

> They are becoming persons who will be inclined toward faith or persons who will find it hard to trust, persons who take the initiative, can stick with a task, and are ready to serve others or persons who do not believe they can make a difference in their own lives or the life of anyone else. (Stonehouse 1998:21)

I agree with Stonehouse that the 'spiritual life of the child is forming at a deep level. Healthy personality development prepares children for openness to God.' Already as young children, they are growing up becoming persons who are and will be inclined towards faith while others grow up not believing. This is because children are different, just as adults are different. Because all people are different, Stonehouse (1998:21) warns that 'To not be concerned about spiritual formation during childhood is to ignore the very foundations of the spiritual life.'

Today one often hears adults complaining that children are different from what they (adults) used to be as they were growing up. There is a bit of truth in what they say because times have changed, circumstances have changed and as a result, there is no way that things can stay the same. In the African culture, a child does not only belong to his or her biological parents but belongs to the whole community and the upbringing is the responsibility of that community in which the child grows up.

In this way, there is no uncertainty as to whose responsibility it is to bring up that child. The most important thing is to bring the child up in as proper and humanly a way as possible. It is for this reason that the Setswana proverb says: '*lore lo ojwa lo sa le metsi*' (you bend a stick while it is still 'wet' and flexible otherwise when it hardens it breaks when you try to bend it).

If spirituality can be given the attention it deserves, then vital and positive contributions can be made in children's lives. As Stonehouse (1998:22) avers: 'spiritual formation is a process for all life including childhood'. Emphasising this, Nye maintains: 'If our practices and thinking about children do not take this into account, we run the risk of making significant mistakes, even of damaging their spiritual lives' (Nye 2009:xi).

For the sake of unity in the church, there needs to be freedom of association, co-operation, openness and acceptance of all members without any constraint. Article 2 of Belhar states that this unity of the people of God (adults and children) must be

> manifested and be active in a variety of ways: that we love one another; that we experience, practice and pursue community with one another; that we are obligated to give ourselves willingly and joyfully to be of benefit and blessing to one another.

By so doing, all members of the body of Christ will not only be serving God in this world but will be serving their brothers and sisters for the sake of unity, justice and reconciliation.

United in Christ, all members are to stand together and fight against all which may threaten or hinder the unity of members. Since the exclusion of children from partaking of the Eucharist amounts to exclusion from the table of fellowship, Article 2 of Belhar addresses this kind of exclusion in its rejections. It prescribes how to fight against all that hinders and threatens the unity of members by rejecting any practice or doctrine

> which absolutises either natural diversity or the sinful separation of people in such a way that this absolutisation hinders or breaks the visible and active unity of the church, or even leads to the establishment of a separate church formation.

Belhar and the Eucharist

As already mentioned, the Eucharist is a covenantal meal that is shared by all God's people in remembrance of God's saving act in the life, death and resurrection of Jesus Christ. It is a celebration of communion with the living Lord and with one another. When the congregation comes together around the Table, not only does it remember the Lord who died for their sins but it shows a close relationship with him and a close relationship that exists among those who are gathered around that Table.

Macy (1992:53) states that through the Holy Spirit Christ, 'the presence of the risen Lord exists not only in the bread but in the community itself.' By the same Spirit, the community that is gathered around the Table is united as members of one body in true brotherly and sisterly love as written in 1 Corinthians 10:17: 'Because there is one loaf of bread, all of us, though many, are one body, for we all share the same loaf.'

Article 2 of Belhar describes the nature of the community that gathers around the Eucharist table as 'a community of believers who have been reconciled with God and with one another.' The unity of this community is 'both a gift and an obligation for the Church ... which must be earnestly pursued and sought: one which people of God must continually be built up to attain.' Speaking about unity, Van der Zee (2004:199) offers that it starts at the celebration of the Eucharist and must be seen and understood as a chance for a close encounter with God. Through the bread and wine, God comes to nourish, to heal and to dress our deep wounds. It is an encounter with Jesus Christ who brings us into a special communion with himself, the Father, the Holy Spirit and with each other so that his life and saving power nourishes our bodies and souls.

As we come together with our children to celebrate the Eucharist, we must insist that through the sacrament we are actually united with the very Son of God in his glorified humanity. All this is accomplished through the Holy Spirit, who is the bond between us and our ascended Lord. The celebration of the Eucharist is much more than just members of the church coming together to share the bread and wine as part of the church practice or tradition, it is what Van der Zee (2004:202) calls the divine human-ward movement and the human-God ward movement of worship which culminates in Christ. This divine human-ward movement is the movement of incarnation; of God becoming human in Christ's total identification with fallen human beings. The 'human-God ward movement' does not refer to human attempts to please or even worship God but rather to their sharing in Christ's response of obedient love and worship as their faithful high priest.

Sharing the same sentiment, Witherington (2007:134) argues that the Eucharist should be seen as a chance for a close encounter with Jesus, a chance for a moment of clarity and recognition in one's life that Christ comes to meet us, bless us, forgive us, over and over again, and that we can and must actively participate in this joyful event. As the true destiny of humankind, Jesus Christ is not only the mediator but the centre and content of the Eucharist. Through faith, he meets believers at and in the Eucharist. It is for this reason that the Eucharist should be an open meal to which access is free and unconditional. It should be an open invitation to everyone as in the words of the 'Hosanna Hymn': '*Hee, ba nyorilweng, tloo le tle metsing, Sedibeng sa bophelo bo sa feleng, moya phutheho, di tlatsana di re, motho mang le mang, a tle*' (You, who are thirsty, come, come to the water, to the well of everlasting life; the spirit and congregation agree together by saying; everybody, everybody, please come.)

This openness and accessibility of the Eucharist as portrayed in the invitation of this song and others similar, brings us to these critical questions: Is the Eucharist only for the righteous? Is the Eucharist only for adults? These types of questions prompt us to look at the character of those who joined in the last supper with Christ. On that night, there 'were certainly Jews', some better Jews than others. There was Judas who betrayed Jesus (Matt. 26:14-16), Simon Peter who denied Jesus (Matt. 26:31-36), and disciples who could not keep watch with Jesus for only one hour but fell asleep during difficult times when his soul was overwhelmed by sorrow to the point of death (Matt. 26:38-41).

From the examples above, it is clear that Eucharist and other meals that Jesus taught about in Luke 14:1-24 are supposed to be open and welcoming to all. Jesus set an example by allowing and welcoming his disciples (different as they were) at the Eucharist. He even went further to share a meal with men travelling on the road to Emmaus. In their discussion, it was clear that they had given up on him being the one to redeem Israel. They were so disappointed in him that they were oblivious to the fact that it was Jesus himself walking with them. When he was at the table with them, he took bread, gave thanks, broke it and began to give it to them. Their eyes were opened and they recognised him, and he disappeared from their sight. It was only after he had disappeared that their eyes were opened and they realised that he was the risen Son of God (Luke 24:30-32).

Based on the character of the Emmaus sojourners who were oblivious as to who Jesus was, as well as the character of the disciples who celebrated the last supper with Christ, it is clear that this meal is a meal of grace given freely by Christ for a certain purpose. It is a meal of Godly love that is not dependent on any condition of the receiver but on Christ as the provider and the giver of life (John 6:35). Referring to himself as the bread of life, in John 6:35-50, Jesus made it clear to those around him that everyone who comes to him as the provider and giver of life shall never go hungry or thirsty. By this, he wanted them to know and believe that he was sent by God to give life freely to those who believed in him: 'I am the bread of life. Your ancestors ate the manna in the wilderness, yet they died. But here is the bread that comes down from heaven, which anyone may eat and not die (John 6:48-50).

Belhar as a call to action

A careful reading of Belhar is enough to convince one that this confession is a call to action. It challenges an individual, groups of people and institutions to stand up and fight against any form of injustice. It says categorically that the message of the church must be reflected in the form of the church. In Article 3 we read that God has entrusted to the church the message of reconciliation in and through Jesus Christ. This means that the gospel of Jesus Christ must be displayed in the lives of members of the church. As followers of Jesus Christ, they are called to be the salt of the earth and the light of the world.

De Gruchy and Villa-Vicencio (1983:158) declare that people should be able to see the Gospel of Christ in the life of the church. They should be able to see in the church an inclusive fellowship and a freedom of association in the Christian brotherhood and sisterhood. They should be able to see the power of God at work in the church changing hostility into love. Their positive influence should infiltrate the world that is full of enmity, separation and exclusion because they are called to stand where God stands (Psalm 103:6).

The changing of hostility into love of the other is not and has never been an easy exercise. History shows that in South Africa separation and domination by one group over the other, which led to all forms of exclusion of others, started around the Eucharist Table when white members of the DRC refused to break bread and drink from the same cup with non-white members of the same church. Boesak says that 'this sinful attitude was not only tolerated in the church of the nineteenth century but in 1857 became a law for the life of the church, even when the church knew that it was contrary to the gospel' (Boesak 1983:xi). The evolution of apartheid took place within the framework of the 1857[9] decision of the DRC Synod and became the

---

9   The DRC synodical decision of 1857, which gave birth to racially divided churches of the DRC family read as follows: 'The Synod considers it desirable and according to the Holy Scripture that our heathen members be accepted and initiated into our congregations wherever it is possible; but where this measure, as a result of the weakness of some, would stand in the way of promoting the work of Christ among the heathen people, then congregations set up among the heathen, or still to be set up, should enjoy their Christian privileges in a separate building or institution' (see Loff 1983:19).

way of life for the church and the whole South African community. The outcomes of this synod's decision were separate churches and separate ministries for whites and blacks; a separation which has been controversial for the past three hundred and fifty years.

Since the time of the separating of the church on racial grounds, a separation which led to a way of life in church and society, the struggle to reconciliation has been very intensive, difficult and painful. Dealing with apartheid meant dealing with a way of life that kept on rebuilding the walls of divisions that were broken down at Golgotha. Dealing with apartheid was a call to action not only to change but to destroy a way of life that encouraged separation and enmity between people who were supposed to live together as a community of God. Dealing with apartheid was a call to action to destroy the systematised old way of life that threatened the integrity of the gospel and the new way of life that calls Christians to work for the restoration of broken relationships because God is a God of relationships.

As a response to the call to action, Belhar generally challenges Christians to work for the expression of God's reconciliation. Everywhere in the community or in the life of the church where there is conformity to the doctrine and practices of racial separation, oppression and exclusion, the measure of this conformity is the measure of the church's deviation from the purpose of Christ. Critiquing this deviation, Belhar (Art. 3) states that

> any teaching which attempts to legitimate such forced separation by appeal to the gospel, and is not prepared to venture on the road of obedience and reconciliation, but rather, out of prejudice, fear, selfishness and unbelief, denies in advance the reconciling power of the gospel, must be considered ideology and false doctrine.

If one was to try to sum up the message of Belhar, one would side with Durand (2009:128), who avers that its inclusiveness and deep concern with all forms of marginalisation and exclusion present a powerful hermeneutic of equality and justice for all God's children. This is the call to all Christians to join in all efforts aimed at achieving a just society by not dwelling inside the comfortable walls of the church but by stepping out courageously into the streets of our towns, cities and villages with open arms to accommodate those at the periphery of our societies.

Conclusion

Belhar is deeply embedded on the principles of unity, reconciliation and justice and calls for all Christians to join in the struggle for the liberation of all the oppressed, excluded and the creation of a just society. The challenge to renewal and action that is set out in this wonderful confession is addressed to the church to stand where God stands and give support and love to those on the fringes of church and society. The church is challenged to stretch out welcoming hands and embrace them into the community of God's people so that together, they can enjoy abundant life provided by Christ. Children have always been part of the community of faith, from the time God established an everlasting covenant with Abraham. Since then, they participated in the household and community sacred meals and feasts like the Passover and others. The community of faith must, therefore, create an atmosphere in which all members including children know that they belong. They must enjoy being part of this family and share in the fellowship that reminds them always that they belong to each other because they are all family. Members of the family should never feel lonely, neglected or unwanted. In many parts of the world, the church is set against a dark scenario of exclusion and oppression of the weak by the powerful; exclusion and oppression of the poor by the rich; of female by the male counterparts and of children by the grown-ups. All these forms of exclusion and oppression should constantly challenge the church about its understanding and affirmation that every human being – including the children – are of infinite value as image-bearers of God. Therefore, based on Belhar's three principles of unity, reconciliation and justice, one could ask the following questions: If the church confesses to being one, are children not part of this unity? If God entrusted upon the church the message of reconciliation, can't it reconcile with its children? If God brings justice by supporting the downtrodden, protecting the strangers and helping the orphans and widows, can't the church do the same by standing where God stands?

Bibliography

Belhar Confession, 1986. The official English translation of the *Belhar Confession 1986* approved by the General Synod of 2008. Belhar:LUS Printers.

Bierma, L.D. 2007. Children at the Lord's Supper and Reformed theology. *Forum* 14(2):3-4.

Boesak, A.A. 1983. He made us all, but... In J. D. de Gruchy & C. Villa-Vicencio (ds), *Apartheid is a heresy*. Claremont: David Philip Publishers.

Nederduitse Gereformeerde Kerk (NGK), Algemene Kommissie vir die Erediens. 2012. *Handleiding vir die Erediens van die Nederduitse Gereformeerde Kerk*. Wellington: Bybel-Media.

Kairos Theologians (Group). 1985. *Challenge to the church: A theological comment on the political crisis in South Africa*. The Kairos Document. Geneva: WCC.

Lake, S. 2006. *Let the children come to communion*. Gosport, UK: Ashford Colour Press.

Loff, C. 1983. The history of a heresy. In J.D. de Gruchy & C. Villa-Vicencio (eds), *Apartheid is a heresy*. Claremont: David Philip Publishers.

Lombard, C. 2009. Belhar as Public Theology- Honouring Jaap Durand. In E. Conradie & C. Lombard (eds), *Discerning God's justice in Church, Society and Academy*, (pp. 93-129). Stellenbosch: SUN PReSS.

Macy G. 1992. *The banquet's wisdom: A short history of the theologies of the Lord's Supper*. Mahwah, NJ: Paulist Press.

Muller-Fahrenholz, G. (ed.). 1980. *...and do not hinder them: An ecumenical plea for the admission of children to the Eucharist*. Geneva: WCC.

Nolan, A. 1988. *God in South Africa: The challenge of the gospel*. Claremont: David Philip Publishers.

Nye, R. 2009. *Children's spirituality: What is it and why it matters*. London: Church House Publishers.

Plaatjies-Van Huffel, Mary-Anne. 2013a. Reading the Belhar Confession – as historical text. In *Reformed churches in South Africa and the struggle for justice – Remembering 1960-1990* (Editors M.A. Plaatjies-Van Huffel and R.R. Vosloo), Stellenbosch: SUN PReSS. https://doi.org/10.18820/9781920689117

Plaatjies-Van Huffel, M-A. 2013b. The Belhar Confession: Born in the struggle against apartheid in southern Africa. *Studia Historicae Ecclesiasticae* 39(1):185-203.

Saayman, W. 1991. *Christian mission in South Africa*. Pretoria: University of South Africa Press.

Smith, N. 2004. A church as the captive of an ideology. In W. Weisse & C. Anthonissen (eds), *Maintaining apartheid or promoting change? The role of the Dutch Reformed Church in a phase of increasing conflict in South Africa*. New York: Waxman Munster.

Stonehouse, C. 1998. *Join children on the spiritual journey: Nurturing a life of faith*. Grand Rapids, MI: Baker Books.

Stonehouse, C. & May, S. 2010. *Listening to children on the spiritual journey*. Grand Rapids: Baker Academic.

Tshaka, R. 2005. Confessional theology? A critical analysis of the theology of Karl Barth and its significance for the Belhar Confession. PhD thesis, University of Stellenbosch, Stellenbosch.

van der Zee, J. 2004. *Christ, Baptism and the Lord's Supper*. Downers Grove, IL: Intervarsity Press.

Voster, W. 1983. The Bible and apartheid 1. In J.D. de Gruchy & C. Villa-Vicencio (eds), *Apartheid is a heresy*. Claremont: David Philip Publishers.

Wallis, J. 2013. *On God's side: What religion forgets and politics hasn't learned about serving the common good*. Grand Rapids, MI: Brazos Press.

Whitherington, B. 2007. *Making a meal of it: Rethinking theology of the Lord's Supper*. Waco, TX: Baylor University Press.

STANDING WHERE GOD STANDS (OUTSIDE THE GATE, WITH CHRIST)

The Belhar Confession as a call for public pastoral care

Llewellyn L.M. MacMaster[1]

This chapter begins by briefly discussing the main elements of the Belhar Confession as the source for a reflection on the call for public pastoral care. Recognising the importance of context, it will then revisit the socio-economic situation in the 1980s and draw some lines to the present situation in South Africa. The reference to Christ's suffering 'outside the gate' or 'outside the camp' in Hebrews 13 forms a strong argument for the view that pastoral care should be public and not confined to the comfort and safety of our religious spaces. The Synoptic discussion of Hebrews 13:1-13 will take us to the final section on the call for public pastoral care as a faithful response to the Belhar Confession.

The text of the Belhar Confession

This section considers the text of the Belhar Confession and shows how it shifted the understanding of community beyond human-made confines and restrictions towards a broader and more open view of community. The opening statement of the confession reads as follows:

> We believe in the triune God, Father, Son and Holy Spirit, who through Word and Spirit gathers, protects and cares for the church from the beginning of the world and will do to the end.[2]

Already in this opening paragraph of the confession, with its reference to the triune God's gathering, protection and care for the church 'from the beginning of the world', we are made aware that God is the Subject, the Initiator, and Creator of the church. The entire confession is founded in and 'encircled' by our faith in the triune God (Naudé 2010:6).

---

[1] Dr L.M.L. Macmaster is a research fellow of Stellenbosch University in the Department Practical Theology and Missiology and the manager of Civil Society Relations, Division for Social Impact at Stellenbosch University

[2] All extracts from the Confession of Belhar in this chapter are taken from the English translation at Addendum 15, The Confession of Belhar. Also available at http://urcsa.net/wp-content/uploads/2016/02/Belhar-Confession.pdf

This is a powerful opening statement that does not always get the attention due to it because of the focus on the three articles that form the main body of the confession, namely, unity, reconciliation and justice. The triune God is the beginning and the end, and is active from the very beginning – gathering, protecting and caring for the church. The act of gathering started outside a clearly defined community. The community of believers, the covenant community, is a result of the gathering. Adam and Eve are created as co-creators and caregivers of the created world, the *kosmos*. Abraham is called and covenanted not for himself and his descendants, but ultimately to be the father of 'many nations' (Gen. 17:3, New Revised Standard Version).[3] In Deuteronomy 7, Israel is reminded that Godself decided to choose Israel, and not because of Israel's strength. Israel and the church were chosen or elected by God without merit.

Our Lord Jesus Christ was sent to the world because of God's love for the world. His teachings, life and ministry clearly show that God's plan of salvation transcended humanly determined borders and divisions. He responded to pleas for healing from a wide variety of people and was not afraid to put people before the Sabbath (law). His eating and drinking with people drew criticism from the religious leaders of his time and he was called a 'gluttonous man, and a winebibber, a friend of publicans and sinners' (Luke 7:34). Jesus, however, was very clear about his mission and the purpose of his ministry and was prepared to die carrying out the mandate of his Father. In the same manner, he called his followers to this same obedience, reminding them that the servant is not greater than his or her lord (John 15:20). His so-called high-priestly prayer (John 17) gives us a clear indication of our calling as church. Jesus is not praying for his followers to be taken out of the world, but for his Father to keep them from evil (John 17:15). He continues, 'As thou hast sent me into the world, even so I have also sent them into the world' (John 17:18).

Empowered by the Holy Spirit, the apostles set out to proclaim the message of salvation beyond their immediate and known contexts. The Greek word for church, *ekklēsía* means 'called from and into' – the believers were called out of the world and into the kingdom of God to be Church. Peter reminds the church of her identity and calling: 'But ye are a chosen generation, a royal priesthood, a holy nation, a peculiar people, that ye should show forth the praises of him who hath called you out of darkness into his marvellous light' (1 Peter 2:9).

The 'revival or renaissance in trinitarian theology' (Vosloo 2004:72) has brought new emphasis on 'the notion of relationality and interdependence in God,' which in turn 'paves the way for the understanding of human beings as relational and

---

3   Scriptural quotations in this chapter follow the New Revised Standard Version (NRSV).

interdependent creatures' (Koopman 2003:197) and 'calling us to share in their loving communion' (Pembroke 2006:1). The opening reference to the triune God is 'ultimately a practical doctrine with radical consequences for Christian life' (LaCugna 1991:1). It is a reminder to us, every time we confess that God reaches out to the world in Christ and through the power and presence of the Spirit, inviting us to participate in the event of the divine relations (Pembroke 2006:13) as the communion of saints. Christians are called into communion with each other because they bear the image of the triune God.

Article 2 of the confession starts with this sentence: 'We believe in one holy, universal Christian Church, the communion of saints called from the entire human family.' The 'Constantine' institutionalisation of the church that led to a situation of institutionalism, and a subsequent move away from 'going out' or 'sending', has resulted in a narrow and inward focus. Instead of following the missional mandate, the church has too often followed and aligned itself to cultural, socio-political or economic ideologies, systems and powers. This has influenced not only the demographic composition of churches, denominations and congregations, but also the mission, diaconate and pastorate of the church. To be the holy, universal (Catholic) church in the true sense of the word inevitably would lead to tension and conflict, with a tendency to ethnicity, racially or culturally segregated churches and communities with all sorts of exclusionary criteria for membership, and 'door-keeping' to ensure the protection of own interests. The Belhar Confession, based on sound biblical teaching, rightfully rejects any doctrine. It is sad that the unification process between the Uniting Reformed Church in Southern Africa (URCSA) and the rest of the Dutch Reformed Church (DRC) family has been derailed so many times that people on both sides of the spectrum are seriously doubting whether unity will ever be achieved. There is a strong temptation to give up, to accept that it was never meant to be, to continue to use all sorts of arguments to justify our separateness. In this regard, we are reminded of the prayer contained in the accompanying letter to the draft confession (1982), namely 'that this act of confession will not place false stumbling blocks in the way and thereby cause and foster false divisions, but rather that it will be reconciling and uniting' (Cloete & Smit 1984:6). But, as Smit points out, church unity is 'not simply a well-sounding slogan that can be bandied about'. Smit draws a sharp link between unity and justice and rightfully states that 'on the way to effective unity the pain of unrighteousness will be exposed in a thousand ways,' and that this will not be easy for anyone. He then raises an extremely important question that cuts right across and deep into the heart of the intentions of those involved in unity talks and those who stand watching and commenting from their respective 'camps': Those who oppose church unity for fear of what it might imply in practice have possibly understood the tight connection between unity and justice in an intuitive way better than those who romantically advocate it (Smit 1984:55).

As we continue to work towards unity between the URCSA and the rest of the DRC family, we are reminded of the accompanying letter's reference to 'growing pains' as we 'struggle to conquer alienation, bitterness, irreconciliation, and fear' (Cloete & Smit, 1984:6). But we will continue, because unity is 'both a gift and an obligation for the Church of Jesus Christ,' and through our disunity we are failing not only our country, but also the kingdom of God (Jaap Durand, cited in Du Toit 2014:55). Or, as Piet Naudé (2010:8) puts it, '[A] dis-united church is in conflict with what God intended the church to be'. This separation leads to the 'othering' (Narrowe 2003:164)[4] of people and perpetuates prejudice, fear, selfishness, alienation, hatred and enmity. This, in turn, makes it easier to discriminate against 'others' and to strip people of their God-given humanity and dignity. The ministry and experience of reconciliation in Christ have indeed been obstructed and weakened. Despite the realities of the past that separated us and left us with deep resentment and suspicion, we are called to a ministry of reconciliation.

Reconciliation is more than a wish and a prayer that hopefully will 'happen' without our involvement and some sacrifice from all of us. It means standing where God stands, within the worldly realities. 'Reconciliation,' says Villa-Vicencio (discussing political reconciliation in Africa), 'is both process and goal'. As process, it is

> inevitably uneven … it requires restraint, generosity of spirit, empathy, and perseverance. It is about exploring ways of gaining a deeper and more inclusive understanding of the problems that are at the root of conflict … Above all, it is about finding ways to connect people across what are often historic and entrenched barriers of suspicion, prejudice, and inequality. (Villa-Vicencio 2009:170)

According to Villa-Vicencio, the goal of reconciliation

> at the level of *having* is the creation of a socio-economic situation in which people have equal access to essential social services and basic material necessities. At the level of belonging, it involves the transcending of identity barriers where entrenched privilege subordinates or excludes others. Put differently, reconciliation is about the sharing the resources of life that are available in a given place at a given time. (Villa-Vicencio 2009:17)

These are important aspects of reconciliation that are easily forgotten when reconciliation is sugar-coated by focusing only on the 'feel-good' element, with no regard for the strong connection between reconciliation and justice. The Institute

---

4 'Othering' in the general discourse is portrayed as the sometimes conscious tactic of the power holders to keep or make the powerless, and is often seen as undemocratic, imperialist and quite wrong'.

for Justice and Reconciliation (IJR) points out that how we remember the violent and divisive nature of apartheid matters for reconciliation (Wale 2014:29).

There will always be an element of 'confrontation' inherent in the ministry of reconciliation. We all should be confronted with our sin, sinful tendencies and our stubbornness and unwillingness to commit to and work towards reconciliation with God and with the other.

Initially, Article 4 was one of the main bones of contention and reason for the DRC rejecting the Belhar Confession. Even in the initial discussion of the draft confession at the 1982 Synod of the Dutch Reformed Mission Church (DRMC), several speakers voiced their reservations about the idea that God is 'the God of the poor,' or that he would be 'on the side of the poor'. However, the commission responsible for the formulation pointed out that those expressions were 'simply the basic, historic biblical and Christian conviction that God is the help of the helpless' (Smit 1984:59). The issue of justice will always be controversial in situations of inequality, exploitation, marginalisation and oppression of people. Despite the biblical evidence, people with power and privilege will not be comfortable with statements that, 'in a world full of injustice and enmity,' God is 'in a special way the God of the destitute, the poor and the wronged and that God calls the church to follow in this'. However, the sovereign God can never be bought over, claimed exclusively or coerced into worldly schemes and systems that exclude the poor, powerless, marginalised and oppressed.

Article 4 of the confession – on justice and injustice – provides the main argument for the thesis of this chapter, namely that the Belhar Confession is a call for public pastoral care. The article continues,

> that God brings justice to the oppressed and gives bread to the hungry; that God frees the prisoner and restores sight to the blind; that God supports the downtrodden, protects the strangers, helps orphans and widows and blocks the path of the ungodly; that for God pure and undefiled religion is to visit the orphans and the widows in their suffering; that God wishes to teach the people of God to do what is good and to seek the right; that the church must therefore stand by people in any form of suffering and need, which implies, among other things, that the church must witness against and strive against any form of injustice, so that justice may roll down like waters, and righteousness like an ever-flowing stream; that the church belonging to God, should stand where God stands, namely against injustice and with the wronged; that in following Christ the church must witness against all the powerful and privileged who selfishly seek their own interests and thus control and harm others.

This article has so many elements of pastoral care written all over it, and one can see a very strong link between justice and pastoral care. It is important to 'contextualise' the Belhar Confession, specifically regarding the kind of society the church found itself in then and now. Piet Naudé (2010:185-200), for example, correctly expands the focus of this reconciliation from 'the enforced separation of people on a racial basis' to include sexism and gender discrimination or divisions, as well as the marginalisation of people living with HIV and Aids – issues that were not even part of the dominant public or theological discourse at the time. It is important to consider the wider socio-economic context within which the Belhar Confession came into being in the 1980s, and to briefly discuss the current context in South Africa.

The socio-economic context of the Belhar Confession – then and now

When the DRMC adopted the Belhar Confession in the 1980s, first as a draft Confession in 1982 and then as a full confession in 1986, South Africa was governed by the National Party (NP) with its apartheid policies. Apartheid was more than just a political system; it was a massive programme of social engineering, aimed at keeping black South Africans disorganised and economically dependent. Apartheid policies resulted in economic inequality, social exclusion, deprivation, dehumanisation and all kinds of hardships for people of colour. Apartheid was not just about political power; it was also about the control of the economy to the benefit of the minority white population at the expense of the majority of black people. Poverty is a social, economic and political problem of enormous proportions and complexity, and children are its most vulnerable victims (Carder, cited in Couture 2000:11). The SA Statistics' extended definition of poverty declares that poverty is 'the denial of opportunities and choices most basic to human development to lead a long, healthy, creative life and to enjoy a decent standard of living, freedom, dignity, self-esteem and respect' (cited in Western Cape Youth Commission 2008:17).

In South Africa, poverty exists because of a deliberate policy, and material poverty was reinforced by racist policies that were (and are) an assault on people's humanity (Wilson & Ramphele 1989:4). The unemployment problem has deep roots in the apartheid era maldistribution of access to assets and skills (Butler 2004:72). It is important to note that a 'plethora of legislation' (Salo 2004:74) was promulgated as part of British colonial rule to ensure that racial segregation was maintained and the economic interests of the minority protected, even before the NP took power. By 1948, South Africa was 'already a comprehensively racialized, segregated state', and this segregation 'served the interests of major sectors of white society, especially agriculture, mining and labour' (Welsh 2009:47).

Under apartheid, state spending was racially skewed and opportunities for social upliftment for black people were extremely limited. There were 'pitifully few legal avenues to financial success open to Africans' (Schärf 1990:233). Government spending on education was a good indication of systemic and structural injustice that entrenched and perpetuated inequality. Just after the NP came into power in 1948, the unequal per capita funding was reflected in that for every R10 spent on a white pupil, R1 was spent on a black child. By 1976, the ratio was 14:1, despite huge investments in black education (Bloch 2009:45). Mamphela Ramphele correctly says that 'the markedly inferior education imposed on African children from the 1950s has had a devastating and lasting impact on the capacity of the majority population to free themselves from the shackles of the apartheid past' (Ramphele 2008:171). Bernard Magubane refers to the 'perverted logic of apartheid' as a policy of 'naked exploitation allied with dishonesty' (Magubane 1979:149, 159). He continues:

> It is a distorted love of one's own people based on hatred, fear, and contempt for others. It misdirects the service to one's own people into the subjugation and exploitation of all other peoples. It is a nationalism that is opposed to a free and independent growth of other nationalities. It spiritualises the national sentiment into crass economic gains. (Magubane 1979:248)

Dutch, English and Afrikaner rule had the net effect that the indigenous peoples of this country were robbed of the wealth, of the land, and of their human dignity. The white settlers made sure that they, and not the African minority, would remain in control of the economy, as Allan Boesak points out:

> The common thread, as in the beginning of the colonial project, was the need for white solidarity to secure white supremacy ... It is important to remember that white, racial solidarity guaranteed white political hegemony, which in turn guaranteed white economic superiority. That early creation of a platform of wealth remains one of the most potent factors preventing genuine black economic empowerment even today. (Boesak 2005:13)

When apartheid officially came to an end in 1994, it left in its wake a population with vast inequalities across racial groups. The country also inherited vast inequalities in education, health and basic infrastructure, such as access to safe water, sanitation and housing (Hoogeveen & Özler 2006:59). Our broad unemployment rate stays one of the highest in the world. Villa-Vicencio reminds us that 'democracy and access to resources go hand in hand'. He continues:

> These are essential ingredients of social justice and political polarisation in countries struggling to transcend long periods of conflict and autocratic rule. Countries such as South Africa have attained an important level of political democracy by conducting free and fair elections. The struggle for economic justice is more elusive. (Villa-Vicencio 2009:28)

Today, South Africa is still one of the most unequal countries in the world. Some commentators believe that the gap between the rich and the poor in South African has widened and that township residents have become increasingly impoverished. Poverty is a complex phenomenon. It is 'not self-eliminating, but rather has a built-in self-perpetuating tendency' (Hofmeyer & Nyoka 2013:16). Service delivery protests across the country indicate that too many people and communities are still not experiencing the 'better life for all' that has been promised by politicians. Villa-Vicencio points out that part of the negotiated settlement was to recognise that white South Africans, who controlled the economy, needed to be drawn into the new political dispensation – to enable them to experience the kind of belonging and well-being that provided a vested interest in the future of the nation. But it was equally important that black entrepreneurs be drawn into the centre of the economy through broad-based black economic empowerment. Villa-Vicenzio avers that it was

> even more important to ensure the poor, who can realistically only look longingly at the privilege of those (both black and white) who benefit from the wealth of the nation, have reason to believe that their material needs and aspirations can be met within the emerging economy. (Villa-Vicencio 2009:28)

Villa-Vicencio sounded this warning more than a decade ago in stating that 'patience and national unity in time give way to impatience and social unrest in the face of the grim reality of continuing social exclusion (and material deprivation), although the language of exclusion changes in post-independent states' (Villa-Vicencio (2009:59). We will have to continuously ask 'the awkward questions about social inequality' and how 'the playing fields are going to be levelled' (Alexander 2013:62). 'If we continue to ignore these questions,' warns Neville Alexander (2013:62), 'this inequality will wreck the entire country sooner rather than later'. He continues, 'Our society time and again sees the warning signs in the many protests and 'riots' about service delivery, financial exclusions and other manifestations of abhorrent social inequality'.

The increase in social ills such as alcoholism, drug abuse, gangsterism, abuse of women and children, violent crime and other forms of violence are clear indications that all is not well with our nation. Demombynes and Özler (2006:289) point to some arguments regarding the link between the local distribution of economic welfare and the prevalence of crime. Criminals are more likely to come from the bottom end of the wage distribution. The lack of social capital and the lack of upward mobility may also be linked with the prevalence of crime. Seekings and Nattrass (2006:299), however, state that 'there is no evidence that the unemployed are any more likely to engage in acts of crime or violence than anyone else'. Clearly, we need to guard against over-generalising the link between poverty and crime, but at the same time we should acknowledge that poverty and economic deprivation create a situation of vulnerability for many people and communities. The expansion of opportunities at the top in the two decades following the end of apartheid did not necessarily bring significant improvement for most people at the bottom (Seekings & Nattrass 2006:301).

Discussing the 'criminal economy' on the Cape Flats, André Standing (2003) gives three reasons for community support for gangs and gangsterism, namely by providing income, via community governance and via acts of philanthropy. The income from the criminal economy 'represents a rational response to an economic crisis,' cushioning the effects of poverty (Standing 2003:6). Although this may be a question of survival for many poverty-stricken people, Standing rightfully points out that 'the dynamics of the illicit economy undermines and exacerbates the social and economic condition of the Cape Flats,' perpetuating gross inequalities and restricting mobility. The other reason for community support for gang and drug lords stems from the criminal elite's disposition for acts of philanthropy. Residents turn to gang bosses for money to help them with their day-to-day costs of living. Gang bosses are reported to have assisted churches with projects; they sponsor many local football teams, as well as teams competing in the Coon Carnival. The ecumenical secretary of the Western Cape Provincial Council of Churches (WCPCC) articulates the frustration of religious leaders with this situation in the communities: 'The church has responded to the economic and social crises of the Cape Flats emotionally, whereas, the criminal elite have responded materially by providing the rudiments of an alternative welfare system' (Standing 2003:9).

All the factors discussed above have resulted in many persons and communities suffering multiple cases of traumatisation and marginalisation on a continuous basis. The idea of 'continuous' traumatic stress (CTS), in contradistinction to the 'post' in post-traumatic stress disorder (PTSD), was originally generated among a group of anti-apartheid mental health activists in the context of the political violence and state oppression in South Africa in the 1980s by Gill Straker and the Sanctuaries Counselling Team (Eagle & Kaminer 2013:85; Straker 2013:209). The CTS is focused primarily on the present and future exposure to trauma, rather than on that which has already taken place. The reference here is to prolonged traumatisation that is 'characteristic of many economically disadvantaged communities' with 'repeated exposure to community violence on a daily basis' (Kaminer & Eagle 2010:48). This socio-economic and political situation provide the context for the thesis that the Belhar Confession is a call for public pastoral care. It is a call for faith communities to stand where God stands and to go 'outside the gate' in terms of Hebrews 13.

Standing where God stands – with Christ outside the gate

Hebrews 13:11 'For when the blood of animals is brought into the sanctuary by the high priest as a sacrifice for sin, the victims' bodies are burned outside the limits of the camp [Lev.16:27]. (v. 12) Therefore, Jesus also suffered and died outside the [city's] gate in order that He might purify and consecrate the people through [the shedding of] His own blood and set them apart as holy [for God]. (v. 13) Let us the go forth [from all that would prevent us] to Him outside the camp [at Calvary], bearing the contempt and abuse and shame with Him [Lev. 16:27].

The Belhar Confession proclaims that the church as the possession of God 'must stand where He stands, namely against injustice and with the wronged'. The discussion on Hebrews 13, with its imperative of going forth 'to Him outside the camp', reminds us of Jesus' teaching about the last judgement in Matthew 25:31-46.

Even before we read verse 13 (the call to join Christ outside the gate), it will be very helpful to highlight a few other verses preceding it regarding their relevance to our discussion of public pastoral care. I concur with DeSilva that the first six verses in Hebrews 13 are not loosely placed verses with no relation to the rest of the epistle, but contain 'exhortations of primary importance' for the author's solution 'to the pastoral needs of his hearers' (DeSilva 2000:485; also O'Brien 2010:502). These verses are about wholehearted service to God in very practical terms – true service to God involves serving his people. DeSilva also sees a strong link between the topics addressed in these verses and the issue of justice. In verse 1 the readers are encouraged to continue in mutual love, with love being the foundation of Christian faith and service. By the blood of Christ, they have become brothers and sisters, and their relationships should be marked by the love that characterises siblings (*phil-adelphia*). Mutual support, solidarity and aid within the fellowship of believers should be characteristic of the family of God. Hospitality to strangers (*philo-xenia*, v. 2) has become a very important theological discussion in recent years. 'Hospitality is a concrete and personal expression of Christian love, intended to include strangers in a circle of care' (O'Brien 2010:506); it is to remain 'the hallmark of this community' (DeSilva 2000:487). The exhortation here is bolstered by a form of the Golden Rule (Matt. 7:12) – 'as though you [were] bound together ('*Syndein*') with them' and 'as though you were in the same body with them' (i.e. those who are being tortured). Here we have the notion of intense identification with those who are suffering. The reference to faithfulness in their marriages (v. 4) is a reminder to the listeners, that they were called to holy living as sanctified people. Guarding against the love of money (vv. 5-6) is an appropriate message for every age, and a reminder that we cannot serve two gods, God and Mammon, at the same time. The believers should never doubt the age-old promise by God that he would never leave or forsake them, and that the Lord was and is their helper.

The social location of the listeners is linked to and intertwined with those who laid and formed the foundations of the faith community, the now-deceased leaders. They should therefore remember their leaders; 'those who spoke the word of God to you' (v. 7). Every time they remember their leaders, they recall and retell their stories and, in so doing, they also re-member them – i.e. make them members again, and keep them a part of the community's story. The listeners are furthermore encouraged to 'consider the outcome of their conduct' and to 'imitate their faith'. Remembering their former leaders would help them to deal with their own challenges, would encourage them not to give up their faith. But, they had more than the examples of faithful, dedicated discipleship to hold up before themselves – they had THE example of the faithful Servant who chose the way of suffering beyond the comfort and protection of religious safety zones.

Jesus Christ himself suffered outside the gate, 'outside those places in which we find comfort and security' (Long 2011:234). There is a sense that Jesus, by suffering outside the city gate, 'desacralized the earth and its creatures and re-stressed the sanctity of human and divine life together, in fellowship with one another' (Witherington III 2007:362). The Hebrews author's major stress, according to Witherington III (2007:362), is 'that Christians come out in the open, be prepared to own their faith in public and be prepared to suffer abuse for Jesus ... even by spending time with those who have been shamed – namely prisoners.' according to Wolfram Kistner, the author's reference is to the hill on which Jesus was crucified (Boesak & Kistner 1985:79). It was the place where people who had been excluded from the community of the people of God were put to death. Kistner is unambiguous in his interpretation of Hebrews 13:13:

> The author's message is a straightforward one. Whoever wants to live in community with Christ, sustained by his power in this world, can do so only by going outside the gate and becoming one of those people who have nothing to rely on but God's unmerited love and forgiveness. (Boesak & Kistner 1985:79)

Even though their former leaders were no longer available to guide and help them, Jesus Christ was always available, unchanging from day to day, from year to year (Heb. 13:8).

According to O'Brien:
> The Christological confession would remind them that the same Christ, who was real to them at the beginning, when their former leaders were with them, is seated at the right hand in heaven and rules continually. Their circumstances and perspective may change, but Jesus Christ and his gospel do not. (O'Brien 2010:517)

'Outside the gate' and 'outside the camp' are not merely geographical terms. They describe, according to Kistner, the context to which our Lord invites us to experience his presence and power(Boesak & Kistner 1985:79). Jesus' own life and ministry attest to a ministry and service to the marginalised, the powerless and the voiceless. If we think we will find him only in our church buildings and religious sanctuaries, we may completely miss him. 'I was hungry and you gave me food, I was thirsty and you gave me drink, I was a stranger and you welcomed me. I was naked and you clothed me, I was sick and you visited me' (Matt. 25:35).

Their leaders 'who spoke the word of God to them' led by example, because they had their own faith firmly rooted and grounded in the unchanging Christ, the Son and key figure in God's saving plan, through whom God spoke 'in these last days' (Heb. 1:2). Indeed, the leaders' firmness was made possible by 'the unwavering reliability of the object of their trust, Jesus' (DeSilva 2000:494). The conviction that 'Jesus Christ is the same yesterday and today and forever' (Heb.13:8) therefore provides the 'bedrock of trust' of the departed leaders, as well as the trust that the addressees are called to exhibit if they are to attain the 'preservation of their souls' (Heb. 10:39). The constancy, the reliability of Jesus Christ, therefore, should also inspire and motivate the readers today to follow and imitate their leaders who followed Jesus – even to suffering outside the gate, outside the camp.

A call for public pastoral care

The socio-economic situation in South Africa, with specific reference to the high levels of unemployment, poverty and inequality, as well as the range of social ills manifesting themselves in communities, present the church with no choice but to be engaged in public pastoral care. Furthermore, serious questions are being raised regarding the continuing legacy of colonialism and apartheid and the struggle to overcome racism, even among the younger generation of South Africans. Has the church as a collective done enough to contribute meaningfully to national reconciliation and nation-building? In the accompanying letter to the draft confession (1982), the then DRMC stated, 'We are only too well aware that this confession calls for the dismantling of structures and thought, of church, and of society which have developed over the years' (Cloete & Smit 1984:6). This is something that we are still grappling with seriously. Many, if not most, of the structures and systems that kept colonialism and apartheid in place are pretty much still intact. In many cases, these have become the source of a neo-apartheid in the form of classism, as some black people are now in a position to move up the socio-economic ladder, while the poorer and poorest are left behind. We see this even in instances where and when the African National Congress (ANC) government uses the same legislation and methods to supress opposition and protests. The result of all this is that people still suffer today because of structural and systemic injustices. A caring church should therefore confess her faith with open eyes and an awareness of the needs of people and the people in need. This seems to be the general response of people when there is a reference to public pastoral care. It is true, on the one hand, that the public theology agenda has been dominated up to now by the contributions of ethicists and systematic theologians. The question is: 'Can there ever really be a total separation of theology into watertight divisions?' Specialisation in particular fields should never have resulted in a fragmentation of theology. Experience in practical ministry has taught us that life is one whole, and that dealing with a single life issue needs knowledge of all theological disciplines. On the other hand, it also is true that pastoral care has been dominated for many years by the so-called clinical pastoral paradigm (Patton 1993:4; Ramsay 2004:1), or what Daniël Louw (1998:27) calls 'the so-called client-centred or empirical model'.

Two new paradigms emerged towards the end of the twentieth century that are gradually eclipsing the clinical pastoral paradigm, namely the 'communal contextual' and 'intercultural paradigms' (Patton 1993:4; Ramsay 2004:1). The communal contextual paradigm draws on the ecological metaphor of a web to describe tensively held dual foci – the first being the ecclesial contexts that sustain and strengthen community practices of care; the second being the widened horizons of the fields that conceive care as including the public, structural and political dimensions of individual and relational experience (Ramsay 2004:1). Charles Gerkin (1986) is credited for the way in which he has turned our attention beyond the intrapsychic 'therapeutic metaphor' to the social context of the work of pastoral care. We must listen at many levels. If we attend to the social context, we are likely to discover that the practice of pastoral theology cannot avoid wider public implications. Individual healing does not happen apart from social remedies. According to Bonnie J. Miller-McLemore (2004:45), Anton Boisen's metaphor from the 1950s of the 'living human document' as a prime text has mutated into the 'living human web'. She continues:

> Problems previously defined along private lines as signs of personal weakness and moral turpitude such as drugs, alcoholism, depression, poor academic performance, and even failed marriages or delinquent children, are redefined in broader public and political terms as a result of unjust patriarchal social structures and racist ideologies. Recent feminist, poststructuralist, and postmodernist theory take the premise that the 'personal is political' to a new level: The personal is not only political, it is socially constructed. That is, power relationships in history and society construct the self. (Miller-McLemore 2004:50)

Thus, the image or metaphor of the web brings into focus public issues that determine the health of the web as equally important as issues of individual emotional wellbeing. The result is that other social sciences, such as economics or political science, together with psychology, become powerful tools of interpretation. In a time of radical transition, those who engage in pastoral care not only need to sustain persons and communities through conflict and upheaval; they also need to engage in efforts towards social transformation (Miller-McLemore & Anderson 1995:99-113). Pastoral theologians and counsellors today are more accountable in study and in practice to the political and social factors that impinge on people's lives on the local and global levels than previous definitions of the field have acknowledged and allowed.

The trauma and pain that resulted from the effects of the oppressive apartheid policies in the lives of millions of people in South Africa can never really be measured or adequately expressed in words. In so many cases, the scars and open wounds stay evident and manifest in some of the social ills that black communities are still facing and struggling to overcome. But, according to President Zuma, it is not just ordinary citizens who are affected by the culture of disrespect, dehumanisation and violence. In his Freedom Day speech on 27 April 2015, he referred to the unruly conduct of parliamentarians as

> a glaring example of the nature of apartheid culture of violence that is left with us. It's not just with ordinary people, it's even in Parliament. We need to be cured. We're sick. We have a problem which we need to address. All of us.[5]

Interestingly, two months prior to the president's reference to the nation being sick, the Leader of the Opposition in Parliament, Mr Mmusi Maimane, in response to the president's State of the Nation Address, accused President Zuma of being 'a broken man, presiding over a broken society ... willing to break every democratic institution to try and fix the legal predicament you find yourself in'.[6] Clearly, there is acknowledgement, albeit for different reasons and from different perspectives,

---

5   Available at: https://www.enca.com/south-africa/sa-sick-nation-needs-be-cured-zuma; http://www.iol.co.za/news/politics/apartheid-left-sa-a-sick-nation-zuma-1.1850779#.VeuAGLRjOfQ (Accessed 5 September 2015).
6   Available at: http://www.timeslive.co.za/politics/2015/02/17/mmusi-maimane-s-sona-debate-speech-a-broken-man-presiding-over-a-broken-society (Accessed 5 September 2015).

that our country and nation are in need of healing.⁷ One can state that the deeper problem of the challenge is not (just) political or socio-economic, but spiritual. This reminds us of Allan Boesak's appeal for a 'tenderness of conscience' when he argues:

> (T)he impetus for transformation in South Africa and the shaping of our democratic identity cannot be the enormous amount of discussion, debates and sloganeering that our democratic efforts, or Thabo Mbeki's dream of an African renaissance, have generated during the last decade. It is my view that that impetus lies in the restoration of the tenderness of conscience, of the refusal to live with injustice, poverty and inhumanity, of the political articulation of the conviction, in the face of injustice, that 'this must not be', grounded in the spirituality that has always been the life-giving source of meaningful African existence. (Boesak 2005:214)

Interestingly, former president Thabo Mbeki, in his 2006 Nelson Mandela lecture, shifted from his 'predominantly negative and dismissive attitude to religion during his vice-presidency and the early years of his presidency to the public embrace of religion, particularly the Bible' (West 2010:43). Mbeki (2006:1-2) turned to the Bible to interpret the concept of 'ubuntu', stating that The Book of Proverbs (3:27-31) in the Holy Bible contains some injunctions that capture a number of elements of what I believe constitute important features of the Spirit of Ubuntu, which we should strive to implant in the very bosom of the new South Africa that is being born – the food of the soul that would inspire all our people to say that they are proud to be South African! Mbeki also engages with Proverbs 6:6-11, as well as Genesis 3:19, John 1:1 and Matthew 4:4/Luke 4:4, acknowledging that the 'scepticism of our age has dulled our collective and individual sensitivity to the messages of this Book of Faith and all the messages that it seeks to convey to all of us' (Mbeki 2006:7). He, however, believes that Proverbs 'raise important issues that bear on what our nation is trying to do to define the soul of the new South Africa' (Mbeki 2006:7). Mbeki argues that talking about a better life for all within 'the context of a shared sense of national unity and national reconciliation' means that we 'must look beyond the undoubtedly correct

---

7   On two separate occasions in 2014, President Zuma called on clergy to pray for the speedy return of Jesus in order to cleanse us, before His final return, 'because we have caused more damage than before. He must just come for a few years to help us so that we are ready for when he finally comes' (September 2014). In the second instance, in December 2014, he said the following, 'The sins we have today are more than those that Jesus came to salvage. I ask the priests to ask God to send His son to come back again to cleanse our sins' Available at: http://www.news24.com/Archives/City-Press/Jesus-must-return-to-cleanse-our-sins-Jacob-Zuma-20150429 (Accessed 5 September 2015) and http://www.news24.com/SouthAfrica/News/Zuma-calls-for-a-speedy-Second-Coming-20141228 (Accessed 5 September 2015).

economic objectives our nation has set itself' (Mbeki 2006:9) as we pursue and work towards Mandela's RDP of the soul.

The ANC policy document, The RDP of the Soul produced by the ANC Commission on Religious Affairs and tabled at the 2007 Polokwane Conference at which Jacob Zuma was chosen as president of the ANC, links with and builds on Mbeki's Nelson Mandela lecture. The document argues for a 'secular spirituality' that 'extends spiritual understanding from the religious world to the secular creation'. It views ubuntu as the 'spiritual truth of all humanity' to be taken into all progressive religious, political and economic institutions. 'Ubuntu rules,' it declared (ANC 2007:6). The document is characterised by compassion, co-operation and commitment, which are the 'fruit of secular spirituality, the heartbeat of ubuntu, the essence of 'The RDP of the Soul'. The document does not deny the important role of traditional religion practices:

> None of this denies the positive role that religion can play: the value of sacraments, the message of theology, the empowering experience of communities of faith, the role of history, the proclamation of the prophets, the lives of the saints: all feed the spirituality of the human world, the secular reality in which the soul of humanity has its being. (ANC 2007:6)

This document, therefore, argues that a RDP of the soul is necessary because of the damage inflicted historically, institutionally and physically by Western forms of knowledge and practice (West 2010:48).

The important role played by faith communities in the past in helping people cope with the damage and trauma of displacement, and to create spaces of safety and affinity in the new townships to which they were moved, where they were virtual strangers to one another, needs to be recognised (MacMaster 2010:96). Besides caring for members and non-members, faith communities in black townships also had the extremely difficult task of re-aligning and re-inventing themselves in the light of the new challenges brought about by the forced removals and other forms of apartheid legislation, while working with very limited resources. In this regard, these faith communities, despite their own brokenness and fragility, have been crucial in taking care of people through a ministry of presence, showing remarkable resilience. The work and ministry of many non-prominent leaders and caregivers cannot be appreciated too much, and should be honoured. They were the ones in the trenches of many struggles, who were prepared to go where most would not and were not willing to go – even to the point of laying down their own lives in some cases. They did not always have the 'proper' theological or pastoral training, did not always follow the prescribed pastoral processes, and did not have the correct theoretical and methodological frameworks. However, their sense of calling, their love for people, and their refusal to give up on God's promises of a better life kept them going. We should always show gratitude to these men and women for sowing the seeds that allowed the church to continue to grow and the faith communities to keep on playing a significant role in communities across South Africa.

These remarkable people of faith have shown us the way to practise public pastoral care. They understood very clearly that the prophetic and priestly or pastoral aspects of our being church or believers cannot, and should not, be separated for the sake of academic disciplines. They might not have been able to formulate a practical-theological ecclesiology, but they understood what it meant to wrestle continuously with the following questions: What does it mean to be the church of God in the world at a point in time and in a particular context? What is the calling or task of the church when presented with challenges of racism, discrimination, inequality, exploitation and other forms of injustice?

The Belhar Confession reminds us that theology is not only about God, about the church, and about Scripture, but that it is also about a context, or contextual situation, about interpreting the situation, about a vision and a strategy (Hendriks 2001:6-16). This implies a shift from an ontological paradigm in the direction of a hermeneutical paradigm (Louw 1992:122). It means a move away from a one-dimensional, rational, subject-object approach, which leads to a deductive style and a positivistic, even triumphalist attitude in doing theology (Hendriks 2001:2). In a hermeneutical paradigm, we focus on an understanding and interpretation of God's acts of salvation in history with the aim of helping people find meaning in their lives and lived experiences through faith. It is about the praxis of God in the world – it is about function, action, praxis and operationalisation, without abandoning the theological character of the church (Louw 1992:125). It will require that we make use of social and cultural sciences, starting with interpretation (therefore hermeneutics). Such a practical-theological ecclesiology wants to focus on the life and function of the congregation (church, faith community), bringing the theological and empirical views of the congregation into creative tension with each other.

Jesus' own words and teaching provide the basis for a public pastoral care paradigm, imbedded within a missional ecclesiology. In his high-priestly prayer in John 17, he prays to his Father not to take the disciples out of the world, but for their protection from the evil one and their sanctification by the truth. They are to be sent into the world, as he was sent by the Father into the world. Jesus' depiction of his disciples, the church, as 'the salt of the earth' and 'the light of the world' (Matt. 5:13-16), has through the ages become a powerful symbol of the church's self-understanding of her relationship to, as well as her calling in, the world – as a missional church (Hendriks 2004:70) – 'being, not just doing mission' (Keifert 2006:28). A missional ecclesiology calls us to active participate in God's redemptive will in this world, 'to participate obediently' in God's missional praxis (Hendriks 2004:24). The church is in essence and by nature, a 'sent people' and can never become so self-focussed that it closes its eyes and ears to the joys and pains, the positive and negative developments in the world.

Public pastoral care presents a holistic view of human beings in which the public and private aspects of their lives cannot be separated without distortion (Wimberley 2006). According to Wimberley, the pastoral counsellor becomes 'a public theologian and social critic who offers alternative visions of human worth and value in public discussions that challenge market-driven and commodity-oriented images of self-worth' (Wimberley 2006:130).

Public pastoral care is not and cannot just be the work of ordained pastors. It functions within a communal contextual paradigm that emphasises the caring community and various contexts of care (Patton 1993:5). The communal contextual model 'reacts against the clericalization, clinicalization and individualization of pastoral care and pastoral theology' (Lartey 2006:123). This approach wants to re-emphasise the biblical fact that the church is a relational and corporate community, and that this community is both the base and the agent of pastoral care. It is 'contextual' because it pays much more attention to the historical, social and cultural contexts of the community that mediate pastoral care. 'It argues that attention needs to be paid to the wider social environment for effective care of persons to occur' (Lartey 2006:124). 'Care' and 'community' are related, but 'it is memory that brings them fully into relationship' (Patton 1993:27). For Patton, remembered means 'to re-member'. He continues,

> The opposite of remember is not to forget, but to dis-member ... Because I remember I can care. Because I remember, I can experience community in celebrating a God who remembers. Moreover, in the strength of knowing that I am remembered I can express care for others through hearing and remembering them ... We remember because God remembers ... As a community of anamnesis, of remembering, the church is challenged to remember as an act of caring. (Patton 1993:27-30)

One of the biggest mistakes that we can make is to treat these stories with disrespect, to regard them as not important, to reduce these communities and people to objects of our theology, mission, evangelism, or even care. We care as we remember and enable others to remember and 'connect' their stories to the larger one. The most useful, though it is not necessarily the most efficient, memory device is learning to hear hurts that need healing as part of a story. A good pastoral carer listens for 'the times, places, and particularities that give a person's story meaning and allow it to be held respectfully in memory' (Patton

1993:36). Edward Wimberly also emphasises the narrative approach as central to pastoral care within the African-American context. From a narrative perspective, 'pastoral care' can be defined as bringing all the resources of the faith story into the context of caring relationships, to bear upon the lives of people as they face life struggles that are personal, interpersonal, and emotional (Wimberly 1991:18). Wimberly adds that 'story-listening', that is, 'emphatically hearing the story of the person involved in life struggles,' is also an important dimension of African American pastoral care, 'to avoid the trap of shifting the focus from the needs of the person facing life struggles' (Wimberly 1991:18-19). Listening and remembering is a form of validation and affirmation for all people in general, but, in particular, for persons and groups of people who have suffered for so long, and who still feel and experience dehumanisation as a result of poverty, marginalisation and exploitation – despite political freedom. The CTS experienced by many communities because of systemic and structural deprivation and marginalisation needs to be recognised and addressed by public pastoral carers. Without a deeper listening, re-membering and empathetic understanding, our care becomes superficial and ineffective, and only adds to the continuing dehumanisation and objectification of poor and suffering people.

Allan Boesak echoes the spirit, intention and message of the Belhar Confession when he poignantly reminds us that:

> Walking with God is walking with Jesus, restoring life to the bodies of children and thereby restoring life to the hearts of their parents. It is walking with Jesus, making the wounded whole, healing the sick, liberating those in prison, touching the untouchables and overturning the thrones of the Untouchables ... Walking with God is to stand where God stands, and to fight for whom God fights: the poor, the weak, the powerless and the defenceless. It is to have the courage to know that trepidation before the might of the powerful is overturned by the fear of the LORD. (Boesak 2005:234)

Public pastoral care is care that operates on several levels with multiple skills and that recognises the complexities and intersectionalities of human life and the lived experiences of people, especially the poor, vulnerable, marginalised and voiceless in society. Public pastoral care entails an awareness of the need for the 'continual conversion' of the church 'as the congregation hears, responds to and obeys the gospel of Jesus Christ in ever new and more comprehensive ways' (Guder 2000:150). It implies that we 'participate obediently' in God's missional praxis (Hendriks 2004:24).

Clearly, this understanding of pastoral care cannot be confined to the safe spaces of our comfort zones where we gather to worship God (which will always be an important and integral part of our faith!). It will necessarily take us 'outside the gate' and 'outside the camp' – to the 'koppie' at Marikana, into the street alongside the victims of xenophobia, in the waiting rooms of health institutions where the poor wait for hours to be treated, in the mud schools where educators and learners try to bring hope through education, in the flooded streets and shacks during rainy seasons, at the bedside of Aids patients, in the lonely corners where victims of abuse and violence are crying and nursing their wounds and scars. It may ask of us a willingness and preparedness to bear contempt and abuse and shame with him, to suffer with him. It calls on us to have the ears, eyes, hearts and hands of Christ – to live and walk with eyes wide open.

Bibliography

Primary sources

African National Congress (ANC). 2007. Section 7: RDP of the Soul. Umrabulo. Special series on the ANC 52nd National Conference 2007: Policy discussion documents. [Online] Available at: http://www.anc.org.za/ancdocs/policy/2007/discussion/rdp.html (Accessed 6 September 2015).

Statement by the National Party of South Africa, 29 March 1948)). [Online] Available at http://www.sahistory.org.za/archive/statement-national-party-south-africa. (12 September 2015).

Secondary sources

Alexander, N. 2013. *Thoughts on the New South Africa*. Auckland Park, South Africa: Jacana Media.

Belhar Confession. 1986. The official English translation of the *Belhar Confession 1986* approved by the General Synod of 2008. Belhar: LUS Printers.

Bloch, G. 2009. *The toxic mix. What's wrong with South Africa's schools andhHow to fix it*. Cape Town: Tafelberg.

Boesak, A. & Kistner, W. 1985. Proclamation and protest: The lost sons, and outside the gate. In C. Villa-Vicencio & J.W. de Gruchy (eds), *Resistance and hope. South African essays in honour of Beyers Naudé*. Claremont: David Philip Publishers.

Boesak, A. 2005. *The Tenderness of conscience. African renaissance and the pirituality of politics*. Stellenbosch: SUN PReSS.

Gerkin, C. 1984. *The living human document: Revisioning pastoral counselling in a hermeneutical mode*. Nashville, TN: Abingdon Press.

Gerkin, C. 1986. *Widening the horizons: Pastoral responses to a fragmented society*. Philadelphia, PA: Westminster John Knox Press.

Butler, A. 2004. *Contemporary South Africa*. New York: Palgrave Macmillan.

Cloete, G.D. & Smit, D.J. (eds). 1984. *A moment of truth. The confession of the Dutch Reformed Mission Church 1982*. Grand Rapids, MI: William B. Eerdmans.

Couture, P.D. 2000. *Seeing children, seeing God. A practical theology for children and poverty*. Nashville, TN: Abingdon Press.

Demombynes, G. & Özler, B. 2006. Crime and local inequality in South Africa. In H. Bhorat & R. Kanbur (eds), *Poverty and policy in post-apartheid South Africa*. Cape Town: HSRC Press.

DeSilva, D.A. 2000. *Perseverance in gratitude. A socio-rhetorical commentary on the Epistle 'to the Hebrews'*. Grand Rapids, MI: William B. Eerdmans.

du Toit, D. (ed.). 2014. *Jaap Durand praat oor eenheid, versoening en geregtigheid*. Wellington: Bybel-Media.

Eagle, G. & Kaminer, D. 2013. Continuous traumatic stress: Expanding the lexicon of traumatic stress. *Peace and Conflict: Journal of Peace Psychology* 19(2):85-99. https://doi.org/10.1037/a0032485

Guder, D.L. 2000. *The continuing conversion of the church*. The Gospel and our Culture Series). Grand Rapids, MI: William B. Eerdmans.

Hendricks, H.J. 2001. Developing a contextual, missional ecclesiology in a congregation using practical theological methodology. *Practical Theology in South Africa* 16(1):1-18.

Hendriks, H.J. 2004. *Studying congregations in Africa*. Wellington: Lux Verbi.

Hofmeyer, J. & Nyoka, A. 2013. *Confronting exclusion. Transformation audit*. Cape Town: Institute for Justice and Reconciliation.

Hoogeveen, J.G. & Özler, B. 2006. Poverty and inequality in post-apartheid South Africa: 1995-2000. In H. Bhorat & R. Kanbur (eds), *Poverty and policy in post-apartheid South Africa*. Cape Town: HSRC Press.

Kaminer, D. & Eagle, G. 2010. *Traumatic stress in South Africa*. Johannesburg: Wits University Press. https://doi.org/10.26530/OAPEN_626383

Keifert, P.R. 2006. *We are here now: A new missional era, a missional journey of spiritual discovery*. Eagle, ID: Allelon Publishing.

Koopman, N.N. 2006. Curing or caring? Some theological comments about healing. *Religion and Theology* 13:38-53. https://doi.org/10.1163/157430106778007716

LaCugna, C.M. 1991. *God for us. The Trinity and Christian life*. New York: HarperCollins.

Lartey, E.Y. 2006. *Pastoral theology in an intercultural world*. Peterborough, UK: Epworth.

Long, D.S. 2011. *Hebrews*. Louisville, KY: Westminster John Knox Press.

Louw, D.J. 1998 *A pastoral hermeneutics of care and encounter. A theological design for a basic theory, anthropology, method and therapy*. Wellington: Lux Verbi.

MacMaster, L.L.M. 2010. In search of a family: The challenge of gangsterism to faith communities on the Cape Flats. DTh thesis, Stellenbosch University, Stellenbosch.

Magubane, B.M. 1979. *The political economy of race and class in South Africa*. New York: Monthly Review Press.

Mbeki, T. 2006. 4th Annual Nelson Mandela lecture. Presented at the University of Witwatersrand, Johannesburg (29 July). [Online] Available at http://www.info.gov.za/speeches/2006/06073111151005.htm (Accessed 5 September 2015).

Miller-McLemore, B.J. 2004. Pastoral theology as public theology: Revolutions in the 'fourth area'. In N.J. Ramsay (ed.), *Pastoral care and counselling. Redefining the paradigms*. Nashville, TN: Abingdon Press.

Miller-McLemore, B.J. & Anderson. H. 1995. Gender and pastoral care. In P.D. Couture & R.J. Hunter (eds), *Pastoral care and social conflict*. Nashville, TN: Abingdon Press.

Narrowe, J. 2003. Othering from within – Sometimes other, sometimes not. On being a Young Turk in Sweden. In K. Sporre & H.R. Botman (eds), *Building a human rights culture. South African and Swedish perspectives*. Falun, Sweden: Högskolan Dalarna.

Naudé, P.J. 2010. *Neither calendar nor clock. Perspectives on the Belhar Confession*. Grand Rapids, MI: William B. Eerdmans.

O'Brien, P.T. 2010. *The Letter to the Hebrews*. Grand Rapids, MI: William B. Eerdmans.

Patton, J. 1993 *Pastoral care in context. An introduction to pastoral care*. Louisville, KY: Westminster John Knox Press.

Pembroke, N. 2006. *Renewing pastoral practice: Trinitarian perspectives on pastoral care and counselling*. Aldershot, UK: Ashgate Publishing.

Ramphele, R. 2008. *Laying ghosts to rest. Dilemmas of the transformation in South Africa*. Cape Town: Tafelberg.

Ramsay, N.J. 2004. A time of ferment and redefinition. In N.J. Ramsay (ed.), *Pastoral care and counselling. Redefining the paradigms*. Nashville, TN: Abingdon Press.

Salo, E.R. 2004. Respectable mothers, tough men and good daughters producing persons in Manenberg township in South Africa. DPhil dissertation, Emory University, Atlanta, GA.

Seekings, J & Nattrass, N. 2006. *Class, race, and inequality in South Africa*. Scottsville, South Africa: University of Kwa-Zulu Natal Press.

Smit, D.J. 1984. In a special way the God of the destitute, the poor, and the wronged. In G.D. Cloete & D.J. Smit (eds), *A moment of truth. The confession of the Dutch Reformed Mission Church 1982*. Grand Rapids, MI: William B. Eerdmans.

Standing, A. 2003. The social contradictions of organised crime on the Cape Flats. Occasional Paper 74, Institute of Security Studies. [Online] Available at http://www.iss.org.za (Accessed 4 April 2016).

Straker, G. 2013. Continuous traumatic stress: Personal reflections 25 years on. *Peace and Conflict: Journal of Peace Psychology* 19(2):209-217. https://doi.org/10.1037/a0032532

Villa-Vicencio, C. 2009. *Walk with us and listen. Political reconciliation in Africa*. Cape Town: University of Cape Town Press.

Vosloo, R.R. 2004. Identity, otherness and the triune God: Theological groundwork for a Christian ethic of hospitality. *Journal of Theology for Southern Africa* 119:69-89.

Wale, K. 2014. *SA reconciliation barometer 2014*. Cape Town: Institute for Justice and Reconciliation.

Welsh, D. 2009. *The Rise and fall of apartheid*. Johannesburg & Cape Town: Jonathan Ball Publishers.

West, G. 2010. Jesus, Jacob Zuma, and the New Jerusalem: Religion in the public realm between Polokwane and the Presidency. *Journal for the Study of Religion* 23(1/2):43-70.

Wilson, F. & Ramphele, M. 1989. *Uprooting poverty: The South African challenge*. Claremont: David Philip Publishers.

Wimberly, E.P. 1991. *African American pastoral Care*. Nashville, TN: Abingdon Press.

Wimberly, E.P. 2006. *African American Pastoral Care and Counselling: The Politics of Oppression and Empowerment*. Nashville, KY: Abingdon Press.

Witherington III, B. 2007. *Letters and homilies for Jewish Christians. A socio-rhetorical commentary on Hebrews, James and Jude*. Downers Grove, Il: IVP Academic.

THE BELHAR CONFESSION AND COMPASSIONATE JUSTICE

Henry Gerhardus Platt[1]

Introduction

Compelled by our confessional foundation and guidance (i.e. Apostolicum, Heidelberg Confession, Belhar Confession) the Uniting Reformed Church in Southern Africa (URCSA) engages in the public sphere, which includes the involvement with the work of orphans and vulnerable children. The latter are children whose mother, father or both parents have died; are affected by the human immunodeficiency virus infection and acquired immune deficiency syndrome (HIV and Aids); and need of care, including those advantaged, in conflict with the law, or subject to abuse and violence (Namibia Department of Welfare. 2nd National Conference *2002*:7). Vulnerable children, including orphans, abandoned children, unaccompanied minors, separated children and child-headed households, tend to be at high risk of statelessness. The main reason for their risk of becoming stateless is their lack of identity documentation; the lack of documentary proof of their citizenship.

Numerous projects in the URCSA give emotional, spiritual and material assistance to orphans and vulnerable children. Article 4 of the Belhar Confession states clearly that the church should stands alongside God who is in a special way

> the God of the destitute, the poor and the wronged and that God calls the church to follow him in this … that God helps orphans and widows and blocks the path of the ungodly; that for God pure and undefiled religion is to visit the orphans and the widows in their suffering; that God wishes to teach the people of God to do what is good and to seek the right; that the church must therefore stand by people in any form of suffering and need, which implies, among other things, that the church must witness against

---

[1] The Doctor of Philosophy was awarded to Hendrik Gert Platt on 2 June 1989 by the Hebrew Union College, Jewish Institute of Religion in Ohio. The title of his dissertation is *Divine rule and political aggression: A study of first millennium cuneiform inscriptions*. Dr Henry Platt, executive director of the faith-based organisation, the church Alliance for Orphans and vulnerable children (CAFO). The CAFO's interfaith membership, present in 68 towns and villages throughout Namibia's 13 provinces, has reached more than 8 000 orphans and vulnerable.

and strive against any form of injustice, so that justice may roll down like waters, and righteousness like an ever-flowing stream.[2]

God is the protector of the downtrodden. The URCSA is therefore compelled to show compassionate justice to the most vulnerable among us.

The root of the URCSA understanding of compassion lies within the understanding of the nature of God. The god of the Bible is a compassionate God (Smit 2006:457). Throughout the Old and New Testaments, God's compassionate character is revealed through his acts of kindness and concern for human suffering (i.e. Ex. 15:13; 20:6, 22:21-23, 23:9, 33:19, 34:6; Lev. 19:9-18; Deut.10:18; Ps. 72:12-14, 11:7, 86:15, 103:8, 118:1-3, 116:5; Prov.19:17, 21:10; Isa. 1:17; Hos. 1:7; Joel 2:13; Mic. 6:8; Zech. 7:9; Matt. 5:43-48, 9:35-36, 15:22; Mark 8:2; Luke 4:18, 6:36, 10:30-37; 1 John 4:9,10; 2 Cor. 1:3-5; 1 Eph. 4:32; Col. 1:19; James 2:1-13, 5:1, etc., New Revised Standard version).[3] According to the Bible, God's justice is saving justice, caring justice, merciful justice (Smit 2006:457). In the Hebrew Scriptures, God is spoken of as El Rachum – God the compassionate (Deut. 4:31). The compassionate God (El Malai Rachamim) is also full of mercy:

> How can I give you up, O Ephraim? How can I hand you over, O Israel? How can I make you like Admah? How can I treat you like Zeboiim? My heart recoils within me; my compassion grows warm and tender. (Hos. 11:8)

God cares, saves, forgives, accepts, justifies, renews, liberates and set free, heals and comforts – all out of compassion. The New Testament builds on the Old Testament understanding of God's compassion, for example, from Luke 6:36: 'Be merciful, just as your Father is merciful.' And from Ephesians 4:32: 'Be kind to one another, tender-hearted, forgiving each other, just as God in Christ also has forgiven you.'

The triune God of compassionate justice calls the church to follow him in bestowing mercy to the most vulnerable among us: 'Be compassionate as God is compassionate' (Luke 6:36). As Smit, one of the drafters of the Belhar Confession rightly said: 'God calls the church to follow in the same compassionate justice, to practice compassionate justice, to embody compassionate justice' (Smit 2006:457). Compassion constitutes a fundamental attribute of the character of God. Compassion is much more than sympathy. It involves an experience of intimacy by which one participates in another's life. The Latin word *Misericordia* expresses the basic idea: The compassionate person has a heart for those in misery (National Conference of Catholic Bishops 1989:1). Compassion, therefore, is not simply the desire to be

---

[2] Extracts from the Confession of Belhar in this chapter are taken from the English translation at Addendum 15, The Confession of Belhar. Also available at www.vgksa.org.za/documents/The%20 Belhar%20Confession.pdf

[3] Scriptural quotations in this chapter follow the New Revised Standard Version (NRSV).

kind to orphans and vulnerable children. Compassionate justice means to cross borders between rich and poor, cultures, races, religions, gender and generations, the powerful and the vulnerable. In Article 4 of the Belhar Confession, the triune God calls the church to practice, live, and embody compassionate justice.

Scope of the orphans and vulnerable children crisis

Creating a viable future for orphans and vulnerable children is a daunting task, one in which we all must actively take part. The traditional African extended family can no longer accommodate all the orphans in its social welfare network; there are increasing numbers of children living alone, caring for younger siblings, hungry and unable to attend school. The pressures associated with the high cost of living have forced many of these children to leave school as they worry more about where to get their next meal. Most orphans and vulnerable children (OVC) being looked after by their siblings, as well as poor households, are at risk of exposure to violence and abuse. The URCSA is being invited to strengthen our awareness of and increase commitment to action for justice regarding the OVC. HIV/Aids and poverty threaten the safety and survival of millions of children across sub-Saharan Africa (Olson, Knight & Foster 2006:1-15). It is a crisis as never seen before. Extended families die, leaving children with limited survival networks. This tragedy is further intensified by poverty and unemployment. It is estimated that more than 13 million children under the age of 15 have already lost one or both parents to HIV and Aids. Worldwide in 2007, an estimated 15 million children lost one or both parents due to Aids, including nearly 12 million children in sub-Saharan Africa (UNICEF Children and Aids 2008:21). By 2010, this number rose to more than 25 million. It is estimated that there are more that 34 million orphans in sub-Saharan Africa, with 11 million orphaned because of HIV and Aids in the family. (UNICEF Children and Aids 2008:5). Sue Perry rightly maintains that HIV has forced us back to re-look at our core value system and our faith mandate. (Perry 2008:8). She recommends on HIV competence, what is lacking, and the challenge to develop competence. The UN Children's Fund (UNICEF) reports that there are 3.7 million orphans in South Africa. According to Chitando, African churches need friendly feet to journey with individuals and communities living with HIV and Aids, warm hearts to show compassion, and anointed hands to effect healing (Chitando 2007:2). At the same time, it should be said that some churches have done such a great deal in trying to address the situation. However, it is indeed true that most of the churches are not responding effectively to these escalating needs of orphans and vulnerable children, as their interventions are sporadic and non-mobilised for impact.

Today, the church is called upon to respond as a matter of urgency, and with an effective strategy. Churches must, therefore, capacitate themselves as best they can to effectively respond to the OVC crisis through effective tools. Churches are best placed. It is estimated that in Africa there are more than two million churches, mosques, and other institutions of faith. In 2001, the United Nations declared the following regarding the global HIV/Aids pandemic:

> Deeply concerned that the global HIV/Aids epidemic, through its devastating scale and impact, constitutes a global emergency and one of the most formidable challenges to human life and dignity, as well as to the effective enjoyment of human rights, which undermines social and economic development throughout the world and affects all levels of society – national, community, family and individual. (United NationsGeneral Assembly, 2001. Declaration of Commitment on HIV/Aids Special session on Aids, 25-27 June 2001)

The church should highlight the theological, ethical and pastoral approaches to the problem. Churches have always been strong in their approach to *'Ubuntu'* and its emphasis on the extended family, where one forms part of the other. The church is characterised by its approach to stand together and to care for one another. It means that a child is everybody's child. This will become even more important as the burden to care increases; as more caregivers die. Families cannot cope alone, as they are stretched to breaking point. And it is a serious problem, as extended families care for over 90% of orphaned children in sub-Saharan Africa.

Furthermore, in the light of poverty and escalating number of orphans and vulnerable children, it is important that the church ensures that the safety net for children is in place. Statistics are staggering: 'The number of children living with HIV per year globally has increased eight-fold since 1990. An estimated 2 million children were living with HIV in 2007, 90% of them in sub-Saharan Africa (Richter 2008:1-14). And '370 000 children were newly infected with HIV in 2007, representing 17% of all new HIV infections globally' (Richter 2008:14; UNAids 2008:1). Furthermore, nearly 25 million people have died from Aids, and 33 million people worldwide are living with HIV. Chitando rightly comments that 'HIV/Aids is a threat to the security and well-being of millions of children across the world. The impacts of the pandemic on children, families, communities and wider society are multi-faceted and wide-reaching' (UNICEF Addressing the Needs of Children 2006:5). This needs nothing less than action of national and global significance. The pace of action must increase more intensely in order to make impact.

How serious do we take this situation and what on actions do we want to take as a response? The Aids pandemic presents one of the most significant challenges of our times. The orphans and vulnerable children picture is gloomy: 'At the end of 2007, 2.1 million (1.9 million to 2.4 million) children younger than 15 years were estimated to be living with HIV and 420 000 were newly infected, with well over 90% infected through mother-to-child-transmission' (UNAids Towards Universal Access 2008:7). In this report, South Africa is rated highest (of 20 countries) with the largest estimated number of pregnant women (220 000) and 15% of the total number of pregnant women living with HIV in a low- and middle-income countries (2007). Also, South Africa is rated higher with 57% deaths among children younger than five years attributed to HIV. And day by day this trend continues as Aids kills 8 500 people every day. It is estimated that there will be 20 million Aids orphans by 2010, and nine out of ten people carrying the virus do not know they have it (UNAids Towards Universal Access 2008:8). The question is: Do we stand by those who suffer, by the victims, the weak, the abused and the powerless?

A church-based approach to orphans and vulnerable children

The church, belonging to the compassionate God, is called to stand where God stands, namely with the most vulnerable among us. The URCSA, therefore, attended a conference held on 25 September to 1 October 2004 in Nairobi, Kenya on the issue of the churches response to HIV/Aids and orphans and vulnerable children. The URCSA sees the orphans and vulnerable children crisis as an opportune time to live, practice and embody the Belhar Confession. The goal of the conference was to provide a forum for Presbyterian and Reformed churches from Africa to share challenges and build strategies that position the church to lead the fight against the spread of HIV and Aids and engage in compassionate care for those affected and infected. Among the issues discussed were:

- Best practices of churches on HIV/Aids;
- Issues related to HIV/Aids that people see happening in their congregations but are reluctant to talk about;
- Significant issues commonly raised by women within our churches;
- Spirituality and Christian discipleship in the context of HIV/Aids;
- Church behaviour, spirituality, culture and tradition that impede the church from moving forward on HIV/Aids strategies;
- Foundational beliefs of confession, repentance, forgiveness and restoration as they relate to HIV/Aids from an individual and congregational perspective;
- Issues that are related to culture and tradition and the spiritual belief systems that conflict with Christian beliefs and that perpetuate the spread of HIV/Aids;
- Awareness of the impact of conflict in the different countries on the spread of HIV/Aids; and
- Building and support networks among churches and related organisations.

A committee was set up to facilitate joint projects and South Africa. A possible joint venture between the URCSA and the UPCSA on the issues of HIV and Aids and Women as well as Orphaned and Vulnerable Children were discussed (*Agenda General Synod URCSA* 2005:116).

During 2005, the Support Ministry of Service and Witness signed a Memorandum of Agreement with the Christian Aids Bureau (CABSA). The mission of CABSA is to guide and support Christian communities to understand their calling and become HIV competent, through advocacy, providing information, mobilising and networking. The church is ideally positioned to be HIV competent and caring Christian communities, addressing the challenges of HIV and Aids and ministering reconciliation and hope in a world with HIV/Aids. The synod challenged congregations to be more proactive in their outreach to the poor and persons affected and infected by HIV/Aids and called on members to be more involved in programmes and issues such as World Aids Day, home-based healthcare, orphans and vulnerable children, job creation and early childhood development. (*Agenda General Synod URCSA* 2005:205-206). The synod mandated the General Synodical Commission for Diaconal Services to work in conjunction with the regional synodical commissions for Diaconal Services to produce the necessary HIV/Aids material on the basis of the HIV/Aids statement in partnership with relevant structures like CABSA. Dr H.G. Platt was tasked to draw up an effective orphans and vulnerable children programme in congregations. Every congregation must form an active Aids Action Group. Synod recommended that regional synod's Ministries for Service and Witness conduct audits in all its presbyteries and congregations on the actions and processes regarding the pandemic of HIV/Aids and orphans and vulnerable children programmes in congregations. The synod requested the regional synods to make the results of the audits available to all the URCSAs congregations as a means of enabling and empowering congregations to network with each other in their regions and to have a unified approach in terms of formulating an HIV/Aids strategy and programme of action on this issue The synod, furthermore, tasked the Support Ministry for Service And Witness to devise a mechanism to help identify child-headed households and to develop ways the church can support these households, source government funding to support them and provide homes for them. Synod called on congregations to make their buildings available as one-stop health centres where professionals and volunteers could offer a variety of services, especially in the fight against HIV/Aids (Report of Service and Witness Ministry 2006:4-5).

Since 2005, Sunday of Compassion has become a joint project for the DRC family (the DRC, URCSA, DRCA and the RCA) and is managed by the United Service and Witness Ministry (General Synod). The URCSA usually celebrates a month of compassion in August with a special service on the last Sunday of the month. The purpose of the occasion is generally to remind members and congregations about the Lord's calling to the church to be compassionate and to create opportunities to inform congregations where and how they can become involved in the ministry of compassion.

In 2008, the General Synod of the URCSA encouraged its ministers and members to actively join in community and development structures in their fight against poverty or any other form of economic injustice (*Acts General Synod URCSA* 2008:73). Without the proper support structures, orphans and other vulnerable children are at risk. The church needs an informed approach for best-practice future intervention. Caring for orphans and vulnerable children must be holistic The URCSA should offer love, care, truth and compassionate justice to the orphans and vulnerable children. As in Article 4 of the confession, the URCSA should stand where God stands, namely against injustice and with the wronged; that in following Christ the church must witness against all the powerful and privileged who selfishly seek their own interests and thus control and harm others. Based on their understanding of the Belhar Confession. the URCSA should

- extend support and services to all children in need, including, but not limited to, children who have lost parents;
- build policies and programmes that support extended family and community networks in caring for children; and
- tackle poverty and gender inequality, which strongly influence child outcomes and amplify the impact of HIV and Aids on children.

The church is uniquely placed to combat HIV and Aids and to protect the marginalised and most vulnerable in society. People living and dying with Aids have medical needs as well as spiritual and emotional needs. The church should respond appropriately to the need for pastoral care, education for prevention and social ministry. Pastoral care encompasses all the actions the church undertakes in relation to the spiritual, physical, social, economic, and political needs of the affected individual. The church should reach out with compassion to those exposed to or experiencing this disease and must stand in solidarity with them and their families. The church can bring healing, hope and accompaniment to all people affected by HIV and Aids. Awareness raising (advocacy) and mobilisation of the community about the needs of orphans and vulnerable children is essential. The question is whether the church is equipped and mobilised to efficiently address the pandemic. The church should accompany those affected by Aids and condemn all forms of stigmatisation in their approach to orphans and vulnerable children. The Jesus we are following is the compassionate one who leads us to the world with all its needs.

Conclusion

The URCSA enters the conversation about HIV/Aids and the response to the orphans and vulnerable children crisis in the conviction that God makes a preferential option for the most vulnerable among us. The URCSA's responses to orphans and vulnerable children are therefore based on the confessional basis of the church. For the past two decades, the URCSA has called the local congregations to engage in compassionate justice and non-judgemental care and to respond to those living with HIV and Aids with respect, support and compassion. Compassion is a word of action. Discrimination or stigmatisation of any human being is against God's will. I believe that the lessons learned from the struggle against apartheid and the drafting, adopting and worldwide reception of the Belhar Confession can serve as encouragement to us, with the same prophetic commitment, to address the major challenges of the HIV/Aids pandemic. The church, motivated by its Belhar Confession that seeks to portray a loving God that stands at the side of the poor, the needy and the vulnerable is in the best position to face and address the problem. The most vulnerable among us should see in our lives and actions and in our being the face of the triune God of compassionate justice. The URCSA should, in obedience to the call of Christ, attend efficiently to the orphans and vulnerable children problem. This will be a sign of hope, reconciliation and love to the most vulnerable among us. In doing so, the URCSA will invite people to life in fullness in Christ, promote healing and wholeness for all of life, engage in prophetic dialogue with others on societal matters, embody, model and promote moral values of Scripture and the Belhar Confession and will seek and advocate justice for all.

Bibliography

Primary sources

Agenda General Synod Uniting Reformed Church in Southern Africa 2005. Bloemfontein.
Namibia Department of Welfare. 2002. *2nd National Conference on Orphans and Other Vulnerable Children Namibia Department of Welfare* 2002
National Conference of Catholic Bishops. 1989. *Called to compassion and responsibility A response to the HIV/AIDS crisis.* Washington, DC: United States Catholic Conference.
Report of Service and Witness Ministry. 2006. In *Agenda of the URCSA General Synod Commission.* Esselenpark, Johannesburg, 19–20 June 2006.
UNAids, 2008. *Towards Universal Access. Scaling up HIV services for women and children in the health sector. Progress Report 2008,* UNAids.
UNICEF. 2006. *Children and aids 2008.* Third stocktaking report. Geneva: UNICEF.
UNICEF. 2006. *Addressing the needs of children orphaned and made vulnerable by HIV/Aids: The Experiences of UNICEF in Tanzania, Rwanda and Swaziland.* 2006.
United Nations. 2001. Declaration of Commitment on HIV/Aids. United Nations General Assembly Special session on Aids, 25–27 June 2001. [Online] Available at www.un.org/ga/aids/coverage/FinalDeclarationHIVAIDS.htm (Accessed 11 March 2015)

Secondary sources

Belhar Confession. 1986. The official English translation of the *Belhar Confession 1986* approved by the General Synod of 2008. Belhar: LUS Printers.

Chitando, E. 2007. *Acting in hope. African churches and HIV/Aids.* Geneva: WCC Publications.

Olson, K., Knight, Z.S. & Foster, G. 2006. From faith to action: Strengthening family and community care for orphans and vulnerable children in sub-Saharan Africa. [Online] Available at http://bettercarenetwork.org/library/the-continuum-of-care/community-based-care-mechanisms/from-faith-to-action-strengthening-family-and-community-care-options-for-orphans-and-vulnerable (Accessed 1 April 2015).

Perry, S. 2008. *Beacons of hope. HIV competent churches: A framework for Action.* Geneva: WCC Publications.

Richter, L. 2008. No small issue: Children and families. Plenary presentation at the 17th International Aids Conference, Universal Action Now, Mexico City, Mexico (3–8 August).

Smit, D. 2006. Compassionate justice? In *Handelinge van die VGKSA Sinode Kaapland.* Wellington: Bybel-Media.

THE BELHAR CONFESSION AND INTERNAL UNITY

'[A]nd together fight against everything that may threaten or hinder this unity.' (Belhar Confession)

Daniël Kuys

Introduction

As we mark the 30th anniversary of the adoption of the Belhar Confession, it gives us an opportunity to evaluate the state of our internal unity. We need to do this, not for historical reasons only, but to discern for ourselves how we have progressed and grown in the embodiment of what we believe a united church should be. Since this is a matter of faith, we must do this evaluation honestly. We should ask and answer certain questions: Have we allowed the faith we confess in the unity of the church to change and transform racially divided churches of the past to a church united in it? Or have we resisted and neglected the force of the truth of unity in the life of the Uniting Reformed Church of South Africa (URCSA)? As a church, we must always be aware that what we believe as a community of faith, we must pursue in the life of the church.

Real internal unity has been a continual challenge since the inception of the URCSA. This should be of serious concern to the URCSA, especially for our leadership. Our internal unity is an important marker and example for the ongoing unification process with the Dutch Reformed Church in South Africa (DRC), the Dutch Reformed Church in Africa (DRCA) and the Reformed Church in Africa (RCA). Our internal unity must serve as an example of the possibility for us to live together as a people of faith, despite our somewhat turbulent political history and coming from different, races, cultures and traditions. We, as the current formation in the unification process, must, therefore, make sure that we get it right. It is important for us and for those with whom we still intend to unite.

If, however, we fail in this current endeavour to build a truly uniting it will be more difficult to achieve this, especially regarding any unity with the DRC, which, given our history, poses unique challenges.

The Belhar Confession on unity

This section considers what the Belhar Confession says about unity. The Belhar Confession does not only speak of a past practice of racially divide churches, condemning it as contrary to the Word of God, but it also gives direction in practical terms of how a united church should look like in reality. In that sense, it gives us guidelines for the life of the church in this regard. Article 1 of the Belhar Confession says the following about unity:

> We believe ... that unity is, therefore, both a gift and obligation for the church of Jesus Christ; that through the working of God's Spirit it is a binding force, yet simultaneously a reality which must be earnestly pursued and sought: one which the people of God must continually be built up to attain; that this unity must become visible so that the world may believe that separation, enmity and hatred between people and groups is sin which Christ has already conquered, and accordingly that anything which threatens this unity may have no place in the church and must be resisted; that this unity of the people of God must be manifested and be active in a variety of ways: in that we love one another; that we experience, practice and pursue community with one another; that we are obligated to give ourselves willingly and joyfully to be of benefit and blessing to one another; that we share one faith, have one calling, are of one soul and one mind; have one God and Father, are filled with one Spirit, are baptised with one baptism, eat of one bread and drink of one cup, confess one Name, are obedient to one Lord, work for one cause, and share one hope; together come to know the height and the breadth and the depth of the love of Christ; together are built up to the stature of Christ, to the new humanity; together know and bear one another's burdens, thereby fulfilling the law of Christ that we need one another and upbuild one another, admonishing and comforting one another; that we suffer with one another for the sake of righteousness; pray together; together serve God in this world; and together fight against everything that may threaten or hinder this unity; that this unity can be established only in freedom and not under constraint; that the variety of spiritual gifts, opportunities, backgrounds, convictions, as well as the diversity of languages and cultures, are by virtue of the reconciliation in Christ, opportunities for mutual service and enrichment within the one visible people of God.[1]

---

1   Extracts from the Confession of Belhar in this chapter are taken from the English translation at Addendum 15, The Confession of Belhar. Also available at www.vgksa.org.za/documents/The%20 Belhar%20Confession.pdf

The following are some key phrases in the article on unity from the confession, which should give clarity on what the Belhar Confession specifically and practically asks of us:

'... a gift and an obligation'

'... through the working of the God's Spirit it is a binding force'

'... a reality which we must be earnestly pursued and sought'

'... one which the people of God must continually be build up to attain'

'... that this unity must become visible'

'... that this unity of the people of God must be manifested and be active in a variety of ways: in that we love one another; that we experience, practice and pursue community with one another'

'... together are built up to the stature of Christ, to the new humanity; together know and bear one another's burdens'

'... together fight against everything that may threaten or hinder this unity'

Against the background of the above key issues in the Belhar Confession, we must evaluate ourselves as a denomination, with regards to our structures, decisions, policy positions, and even the spirit within URCSA, and whether in the way we are a church, we are threatening or hindering internal unity.

Schism within the URCSA

On 14 April 1994, the Dutch Reformed Mission Church (DRMC) and the DRCA unified to constitute the URCSA (*Acta VGKSA Algemene Sinode* 1994:290). However, this unification did initially occur without problems. The internal unity in URCSA was at stake in the early stages of its existence. Right from the start, at their first meeting, the moderamen took note of the complaints of the DRCA regional synods of the Free State and Phororo regarding the church unification (*Skema Algemene Sinode VGKSA* 1997:20). The developments in these two regional synods presented the URCSA with serious problems and challenges. This was a major setback and the URCSA was to be severely shaken and tested. The unification process followed between the DRMC and the DRCA was legally challenged. In the end, the South African Appeals Court on 27 November 1998 judged in favour of those in the DRCA in the Free State and Phororo who challenged the legality of the unification. With this judgement, the Appeal Court declared that despite the unification between the DRMC and the DRCA the DRCA in the Free State and Phororo still exists (*Nederduitse Gereformeerde Kerk (OVS), Nederduitse Gereformeerde Kerk in Afrika; Phororo en die Verenigende Gereformeerde Kerk in Suider-Afrika saaknommer* 536/96). This was a major blow, not only to the unification process that had led to the unification of the two churches but also for the internal unity, because some of those who left the URCSA were also delegates at the Founding Synod. What happened here was a schism in the newly founded denomination.

Children of apartheid

I think the main challenge to unify the URCSA internally was that the process leading to the unification failed to adequately take into account our divided history in South Africa – our shared and horrific, racist apartheid history of separation. This history would prove to be a division to break down in our midst. The apartheid theology and ideology engineered our minds, attitudes and thoughts, to conform to what the apartheid system wanted us to be and to believe about ourselves and other people. We must acknowledge that the indoctrination of the apartheid system and the apartheid theology had a deep-seated impact in our lives and behaviour. In a sense, the system was successfully implemented in many ways in our lives. We have internalised this life of separation and disunity.

One thing that we must acknowledge and confess to ourselves is that all of us in the URCSA are victims of that system and that we in some shape or form, unknowingly act out that indoctrination. Given this, we must also acknowledge that after a lifetime of this system we need a process of debriefing on the impact this system had or has on us and our behaviour. We must acknowledge and begin a process of dealing with this so that we can put it behind us so as to become a truly unified church. The thoughts and actions of superiority, inferiority, and prejudice were part of the South African way of living under apartheid. We were divided by race and forced to live apart. In our separateness, we conjure up images of one another, fed by what the system of apartheid ideology and theology indoctrinated us with. We who became the URCSA did not escape the negative impact and social engineering that this division had on us. If we want to build a church that is truly unified internally, we must recognise our apartheid history and the impact it has in pursuing and building internal unity.

Dr Beyers Naudé eloquently writes of the truth of our apartheid past and the challenge it poses for unity and internal. In a very insightful observation, Naudé says,

> The unification between the NGSK and the NGKA will undoubtedly bring forward serious, yet unresolved differences of language, culture, history, theological training, diaconal services, traditional, cultural attitudes which form part of the history of each one of the communities that we represent. We must also not forget that the establishment and ruthless implementation of apartheid over more than half a century has left a deeply engrained attitude of racism and paternalism in the hearts of all South Africans- including

'coloured', Indian and black. These scars in our thinking and attitude will take very long to disappear or to be removed. (Beyers Naudé 1993:1)

In this article, Dr Naudé further contends that because of this historical reality the URCSA will find itself in a position where there will be from time to time serious differences of opinion. He proposes a way forward to deal with these historical issues:

It will require an ongoing process of biblical education, of theological re-thinking, of deliberate efforts at helping our people to accept one another in trust, to help one another in our need, and to build together this Unifying Church in Southern Africa. (Beyers Naudé 1993)

We need to take seriously consider what Naudé says as a guiding principle dealing with the reality of our internal unity. In 1997, I reflected on this issue when I wrote the following:

It must never be forgotten that the URCSA comes from a past of deep division and alienation. Church unity (internal) does not happen overnight. It is a process of sacrifices, of hard and difficult work. It is not good enough that in essence we simply be still the former churches that we were. (*Die Ligdraer* 1997:1)

Considering the realities mentioned above and that these realities were not given enough thought in the process to unification, it must be concluded that we have operated with a very limited focus and vision. We had only our focus and vision of when the unification would take place. All our discernment and negotiations went into that process. We have not cast our focus and vision backwards into history and forward into the future beyond the point of forming the new church. We did not adequately strategically plan for the kind of church we want to be and the possible challenges we were about to face. Our focus and vision for the URCSA should have been much broader, wider and further into the future, using our past to create that unified church.

Are we perhaps threatening or hindering internal unity?

It seems that in what we do and how we structure the URCSA, we tend to separate the church more than bring the church together in one body. I want to refer to some issues within the URCSA that divide the church more than unite it.

Theological training

The Founding Synod in 1994 accepted the ideal of one training for all the theology students and future ministers of URCSA. For the interim period, the then Faculty of

Theology at the University of the Western Cape (UWC) was accepted as the southern part of the country. Since the synod was not ready at the time to determine a northern part of the country, it was decided that a final decision was to be made at a later stage. It was decided that Turfloop would be the northern part of the country training centre. In the meantime, the training centre in the south moved from the UWC to join the Faculty of Theology at Stellenbosch University (US).

The issue of theological training developed in quite a different direction than that of the unity ideal. The URCSA continued to add theological training centres to the existing ones. At the 2008 Synod, the application of the Regional Synod of the Free State and Lesotho for a ministerial formation centre at the University of the Free State was approved. This also serves the Regional Synod of Phororo. A combined Curatorium between these regional synods were formed for this purpose. The 2008 Synod decided to accept in principle that ministerial formation centres be decentralised and that the formation centres be established closer to members (*Acts General Synod URCSA* 2008:74). The 2008 General Synod entrenched this fragmentation of theological training in the URCSA with a policy decision on theological training: 'When a Regional Ministerial Formation Task team wishes to establish a centre for ministerial formation or make significant changes to an existing centre, it submits an application to the Ministerial Formation Task Team of the General Synod' (*Acts General Synod URCSA* 2012:47). The ideal of the Founding Synod of the URCSA was forgotten and in the end abandoned!

A theological training centre at one of the universities in South Africa, where all the ministers of URCSA could be trained, could have been a powerful instrument to help achieve internal unity. It could have started a process of internal unity on a particular level of the work of the URCSA, which could have positively influenced and greatly enhanced the process of internal unity. We must recognise that theological training can and must contribute to internal unity. We have a chance to bridge the divide of the past by training all the URCSA ministers together in one place. To create a true internal unity, we must deliver ministers to the church that can serve in any congregation throughout the URCSA, not only in the former churches and language groups they originate from. Failing this, we will remain in our separate apartheid corners and just come together in presbytery and synod meetings. This is not the unity the Belhar Confession speaks of. To achieve this ideal, not only one location for theological training is needed, but also fundamental changes and additions should be made to the curriculum of ministers in training. It should become compulsory for theology students to learn a language spoken in the URCSA other than their mother tongue. Cultural studies should be added, especially the issue of cultural sensitivity and awareness of different cultural traditions and respect for them. Students should have a programme of contact with communities other than the ones they come from in order to increase their knowledge of these different communities in the URCSA. When we train ministers in this way, we will go a long way in entrenching internal unity. The URCSA General Synod of 2008 decided to change the regulations regarding theological formation. This was done to ensure that a minister of the Word or candidate for ministry from any language or cultural group could be called to any congregation in URCSA.

The 2008 General Synod made the following changes concerning theological training:
- Language proficiency: At least one year in an indigenous African language other than the student's mother tongue. This should enable a student to achieve a basic conversational competence in that language.
- Practical ministry experience: From the first year of study, all students are expected to be involved in various forms of ministry in congregations of the URCSA who have been orientated in the programme, at a level of responsibility in keeping with their level of studies. This experience of ministry, under the supervision of a URCSA minister as a mentor, should include exposure to a variety of urban and rural ministry contexts, ecumenical service agencies or NGOs, and congregations of other language or cultural groups.

My premise is that one church having different theological training centres does not help internal unity. It rather obstructs it.

Old divisions and attitudes entrenched

That our internal unity is a neglected project means that we are still strangers to one another; we still have difficulty in trusting and accepting one another. We still look at each other with the eyes of our historical apartheid past. This becomes even more evident when we have to elect leaders. In some cases, these kinds of divisions are even written into church law, as in the case of the church order of the Regional Synod of the Cape. The regulation that legislates the election of office-bearers for the Christian Women Ministry, reads: 'an equal number of Afrikaans and Xhosa speaking members must be included.' This in itself is not wrong. We are and must be a church that accommodates the diverse cultures in the URCSA. However, it is of concern when we see the reaction and emotions that are generated when one language group has been chosen and the fear expressed that the other might be overlooked. It is worrying to witness the agitation and very vocal reminder of protest this election sometimes causes. It shows that we in the URCSA really do not trust one another and that we are not comfortable with one another. It also shows that we have not yet accepted one another. We are not together in this church. We still languish in our former corners of existence. We still have the notion of 'they' and 'us'. We are, even in some cases, provincial or regional in our attitudes and approaches to issues in the church. The divisional mindset of the apartheid indoctrination is still part of the make-up of some of us and our being, whether we want to acknowledge it or not. On a human, person-to-person level we have not yet succeeded to come together as one united church.

Singing from separate hymn sheets

One of the clear signs that we are not a church internally united is our worship services. Walk into an isiXhosa- or Sotho-speaking congregation on a Sunday morning and you will find the congregation singing from the 'Hosanna' hymnal. Walk into an Afrikaans-speaking congregation and the congregation sings from the 'Sionsgesange' hymnal. To have one hymnbook and to be able to sing together is another way that can unite us in faith and as people. This is a serious issue of exclusion that happens in the church. How divided are we, even in praising the Lord! We should develop a hymnbook for the URCSA from which we all can sing in our different tongues. The Founding General Synod in 1994 decided that both the 'Hosanna' and the new 'Sionsgesange' would be used in the URCSA until the synod decides otherwise. Twenty years later, we still sing from different hymnbooks, which perpetuates the notion of separateness and contradicts internal unity. Bringing these two hymnbooks together in one hymnal will surely strengthen internal unity. Let us sing from the same hymn sheet – rather sooner than later.

Concern for internal unity

On several occasions, concern over the state of the internal unity has been expressed within the URCSA. These concerns go back as early as the second General Synod of the URCSA in 1997 in Bloemfontein. Dr Daniël Maluleke touched on the issue during a Bible study on unity when he said:

> We must pro-actively encourage our local congregations to celebrate our unification. How many ministers in the Uniting Reformed Church in Southern Africa have ever exchanged pulpits? When last have you met as ministers to discuss the experience of our unification process? The process of unification needs to be pro-actively promoted so that the world may believe. Therefore, the visible unity among us is of vital importance. We are happy with the event which took place at Belhar on the 14 April, but we do not continue with the process of our local congregations. (*Skema van Werksaamhede VGKSA* 1997:582)

The same concern was expressed at the third General Synod in Upington in 2001 where questions were raised about the effectiveness of unity within the URCSA. It was said that we are structurally one, but practically separated. The feeling at that synod was that we often fail to practice what we confess in the Belhar Confession that unity is a gift and an obligation for the church of Jesus Christ and that through the working of God's Spirit it is a binding force. This synod adopted a decision on the intention of internal unity, which was a restatement of the Belhar Confession, namely:

> We in the URCSA strive and work for what Belhar (Confession) calls us to do, namely, to visible unity [sic], among all the people in the URCSA and that this should become reality in a variety of ways. (*Acts General Synod URCSA* 2001:45)

The concerns about the lack of internal unity grew from synod to synod, but without a proper reaction or plans to address that concern.

Good intentions without proper action

Between 2001 and 2008, the challenge of internal unity was not discussed. The importance of internal unity was put again on the agenda of the 2008 General Synod. The synod approved, as a matter of priority, to task the executive to appoint a task team to provide the URCSA with a strategic plan regarding the process of internal unity. Such a plan should have included clear guidelines to all decision-making structures of the URCSA as well as the ministries of the URCSA. The General Synod tasked the Financial Administration Ministry to secure financial support for the implementation of the decision on internal unity. The General Synodical Commission of 2009 appointed a task team consisting of Dr Daniël Maluleke, Rev. Reggie Nel and the late Prof. Welile Mazamisa to drive the process of internal church unity.

The General Synodical Commission reported to the 2012 Synod on this endeavour, as follows: 'Unfortunately this important task was not fulfilled; however, the issue was taken up in the strategic plan and will, therefore, be on the agenda for the future' (*Agenda General Synod URCSA* 2012:111). The Draft Strategic Plan of the URCSA of 2012, which synod had adopted, was not clear on the strategic objectives or activities regarding internal church unity. The plan failed to address the issue. Although the vision of the URCSA in the Draft Strategic Plan states clearly that the URCSA is a committed and united church in service of unity, no reference to internal unity was made in the five strategic goals of the plan. The Draft Strategic Plan of 2012 only refers to unity in the strategic goals in a general sense as 'promotion and extension of church unity.' (Draft Strategic Plan of URCSA 2012:1-22) General Synod 2012 approved the following recommendation regarding internal church unity: 'The General Synod 2012 requested the newly elected executive to see to it that a task team be elected and to continue the task given in 2008' (*Acts General Synod URCSA* 2012:3) The General Synodical Commission of November 2013 requested the regional moderamen to nominate people to serve on the task team as follows: 'The GSC request the task team to provide a report as soon as possible' (*General Synodical Commission* 2013:16). During the recess, numerous consultations on General Synodical level regarding revisiting the strategic objectives of the Draft Strategic Plan 2012 took place. The General Synodical Commission of 2015 approved the Strategic Plan 2016–2024. This will be tabled for final approval by the General Synod 2016.

The new Strategic Plan 2016–2024 addresses internal church unity, multi-culturalism and transculturalism as strategic objectives of the URCSA. Strategic activities mentioned in the plan include the following:
- Supports efforts to develop congregations that will reflect the transculturalism make-up of the society;
- Addresses unity, reconciliation and justice in preaching, publications, discussion groups, conferences, ministries, and at congregational, Presbytery and Regional Synod level;
- The Core Ministry Public Witness arranges conferences unity, reconciliation and justice, multiculturalism and transculturalism;
- The Support Ministry of Publication Communication and Archives issues regular circulars with suggested solutions of how to embrace unity, reconciliation and justice, multi-culturalism and transculturalism;
- The Core Ministry Public Witness develops programmes to promote an ethos of unity, reconciliation and justice, multiculturalism and transculturalism in the URCSA and tables reports to the General Synod;
- Encourages partnership between congregations from different cultural or ethnic backgrounds, holds joint services regularly, shares and exchange pulpits, and shares resources (Strategic Plan URCSA 2016–2024:1-40).

The envisaged outcomes of the strategic objectives include the following:
- Will improve relations between different racial and cultural groups in the URCSA.
- Will effectively address internal church unity, multi and transculturalism in the URCSA.
- Will enhance transformation of the URCSA to a truly transcultural church in a Reformed African context.
- Will enhance the establishment of transculturalism congregations in the URCSA.
- Regional synods will submit reports on internal unity/ multiculturalism and transculturalism on an annual basis to the General Synodical Commission (GSC).

- Will enhance love, understanding, relationships and the importance of working together in the URCSA.
- Will enhance the spirit of Ubuntu in the URCSA. (Strategic Plan URCSA 2016–2024:1-40)

The issue of internal unity, which is vital for the URCSA identity as a united church, had been delayed and postponed from synod to synod without proper action or a proper plan. Whether the commitments in the Strategic Plan 2016–2024 regarding internal unity are embraced wholeheartedly by the URCSA at large will only be known after the General Synod in 2016.

Conclusion

The situation in the URCSA regarding internal unity is indeed of deep concern. If one looks back at the 22 years of the existence of the URSCA, one can conclude that the church lacks a serious commitment to the issue of internal unity. This is not regarded as a pressing issue in URCSA and, therefore, we do not seem very concerned that the URCSA remains largely the DRMC and the DRCA, which is a serious indictment of the state our unification project. The identity of the URCSA has not been changed and no serious attempts are being made to change it. We cannot remain as we are and call ourselves the Uniting Reformed Church. 'Uniting' means, a process, a movement of being a church united. In uniting, the URCSA must take into consideration where we come from, our history, and determine how we are going to merge everything that we are into a new identity as a church. In the beginning of this chapter, I suggested that we should evaluate ourselves as a denomination in light of our structures, decisions, policy positions and even the spirit within the URCSA; whether we are 'threatening or hindering' internal unity.

We must evaluate ourselves against the spirit and letter of the Belhar Confession on the key issues of unity and ask ourselves, how do we fare in terms of these issues?

Internal unity as:
    'A gift and obligation'.
    'Through the working of the Spirit it's a binding force'.
    'A reality which must be earnestly pursued and sought'.
    'One which the people of God, must continually be build up to attain'.
    In addition,
    'This unity must be visible'.

'This unity of the people of God must be manifested and be active in a variety of ways: Love one another; that we experience and pursue community with one another'.

'Together are built up to the stature of Christ; to the new humanity; together know and bear one another's burdens'.

'Together fight against everything that may hinder this unity'.

With regards to the Belhar Confession, our faith, we are supposed to mirror our confession when it comes to unity within ourselves as a church. Internal unity evaded us for 22 years through our own acts of commission and omission. Through our decisions, policies and structures or lack of them, we have failed to live up to the call of the Belhar Confession to be a truly united church. As such, we ourselves are a 'threat and a hinder,' to our internal unity. Indeed, the Belhar Confession must not only guide us in terms of addressing the threat and hindering of that unity within the apartheid context, it is a neglected truth that we must pursue in living faith, with regards to our internal unity in URCSA.

We confess in the Belhar Confession our strong commitment to unity, also internal unity: 'and together fight against everything that may threaten or hinder this unity.' There are many things, practices, decisions, etc., that threaten and hinders our internal unity. Together we must fight against these in order to visibly realise our faith in the Belhar Confession – Unity – Internal Unity.

Bibliography

Primary sources

Acts of General Synod of the Uniting Reformed Church in Southern Africa 2001 (1–7 October, Upington).

Acts of General Synod of the Uniting Reformed Church in Southern Africa 2005 (26 September–2 October, Pietermaritzburg).

Acts of General Synod of the Uniting Reformed Church in Southern Africa (29 September–5 October 2008, Hammanskraal.

Acts of General Synod of the Uniting Reformed Church in Southern Africa 2012 (1–7 October, Okahandja, Namibia).

Agenda General Synod of the Uniting Reformed Church in Southern Africa 1994 (14–17 April 1994, Belhar.

Agenda General Synod of the Uniting Reformed Church in Southern Africa 2001 (1–7 October 2001, Upington).

Agenda General Synod of the Uniting Reformed Church in Southern Africa 2005 (26 September–2 October 2005, Pietermaritzburg).

Agenda General Synod of the Uniting Reformed Church in Southern Africa 2008 (29 September–5 October 2008, Hammanskraal).

Agenda General Synod of the Uniting Reformed Church in Southern Africa 2012 (1–7 October 2012, Okahandja, Namibia).
General Synodical Commission. 2009. *Minutes of General Synodical Commission of the Uniting Reformed Church in Southern Africa 2009.*
General Synodical Commission. 2013. *Minutes of the General Synodical Commission of the Uniting Reformed Church in Southern Africa 2013.*
Kerkorde en Algemene Bepalinge, Streeksinodale Bepalinge en Reglemente van die Streeksinode Kaapland van die VGKSA, 2010.
Skema van werksaamhede en Handelinge Algemene Sinode VGKSA 14–17 April 1994, Belhar.
Skema van werksaamhede en Handelinge Algemene Sinode VGKSA 14–20 April 1997, Bloemfontein.
Uniting Reformed Church in Southern Africa. 2012. *Strategic plan 2012 of the Uniting Reformed Church in Southern Africa.* Bloemfontein.
Uniting Reformed Church in Southern Africa. 2012. *Strategic plan 2016–2024 of the Uniting Reformed Church in Southern Africa.* Bloemfontein.
Uniting Reformed Church in Southern Africa. 2012. *Draft strategic plan 2012 of the Uniting Reformed Church in Southern Africa.* Bloemfontein.

Secondary sources

Belhar Confession. 1986. The official English translation of the *Belhar Confession 1986* approved by the General Synod of 2008. Belhar: LUS Printers.
Beyers Naudé. CF. 1993. *The unification between the NGSK and the NGKA.* Die Ligdraer Vol 4. 1993:1.
Kuys, D. 1997. Editorial article in *Die Ligdraer.*
Plaatjies-Van Huffel, M-A. 2008. Die doleansie kerkreg en kerkregering van die Nederduitse Gereformeerde sendingkerke en die VGKSA. [Online] Available at http://upetd.up.ac.za/thesis/available/etd-04022009-190218/ (Accessed 21 March 2015).

FROM A RACIALLY-SEGREGATED CONGREGATION TOWARDS A MULTI-ETHNIC, MULTICULTURAL CONGREGATION

Dawid Johannes Van Huffel

Introduction

This chapter is taken from a paper presented at Stellenbosch University during the Winter School, 2-4 June 2011.[1]

We live in a diverse country with various cultures, but unfortunately, on local congregational level the URCSA does not reflect this diversity. The Uniting Reformed Church in Southern Africa (URCSA) consists of all eleven cultural groups and languages in South Africa, namely, English, Afrikaans, Ndebele, Sepedi, Xhosa, Venda, Tswana, Southern Sotho, Zulu, Swazi or SiSwati and Tsonga, as well he eleven cultural and languages groups in Namibia, namely, English, Afrikaans, Rukwangali, Silozi, Setswana, Damara/Nama, Herero and Oshiwambo. Twenty years after unification, The URCSA still struggles with internal unity due to haphazard approach to the managing of diversity and multiculturalism in the church. Most congregations or even some of the synods of the URCSA are largely homogenous with the majority culture group influencing the decision making, liturgy and ministries. Luckily, due to demographic changes the makeup of some congregations in the URCSA is changing. For example, in squatter camps, informal settlements, new human settlements (the human settlement programme of the government) and in the inner-city, people from different cultural and ethnic groups are forced to live next to each other. Large groups of people from the townships are now moving to the inner-city (Saayman 2010:135-145). The changes in the demographics in post-apartheid South Africa gave the church an opportunity to expand multicultural churches.

---

[1] Reverend Dawid van Huffel presented this paper at Stellenbosch University during the Winter School, 2-4 June 2011, 'Changing the world? An invitation to faithful discipleship and responsible citizenship'. He was assisted in his presentation with members of the ward namely Tebogo Mahelie, a Sotho-speaking member of the URCSA Scottsdene, and Piet van Rooi, an Afrikaans-speaking church council member of the URCSA Scottsdene.

The Scottsdene URCSA: Becoming a multi-ethnic-multicultural church

The Scottsdene URCSA is one of the few congregations in the URCSA who are making a concerted effort to become a multi-ethnic and a multicultural church and in doing so embrace diversity and experience the rich value thereof. Article 2 of the Belhar Confession states clearly that

> unity is, therefore, both a gift and an obligation for the church of Jesus Christ; that through the working of God's Spirit it is a binding force, yet simultaneously a reality, which must be earnestly pursued and sought: one which the people of God must continually be built up to attain. [2]

Before 2004, the membership of the URCSA Scottsdene consisted of people of mixed decent, primarily Afrikaans-speaking congregants. Sunday morning is still the most racial segregated hour in South Africa as Eddy Van der Borght (2009:4-29) righty deduced in his inaugural lecture delivered on accepting the position of Vrije University Amsterdam Desmond Tutu Chair holder in the areas of Youth, Sports and Reconciliation, at the Faculty of Theology of Vrije University Amsterdam on 7 October 2009. According to Van der Borght (2009:4) theological uncertainty contributes to the ongoing racially segregated religious practice.

The demographics of post-apartheid South Africa did not change much and could be blamed for the fact that Sunday morning is still the most racial segregated hour in South Africa. South Africans at large still live in racial demarcated areas created by the apartheid government. The apartheid laws, *inter alia*, the Group Areas Act (No. 41 of 1950), the Prevention of Illegal Squatting Act, (No. 52 of 1951), the Bantu Authorities Act (No. 68 of 1951), the Native Laws Amendment Act of 1952, the Promotion of Bantu Self-government Act (No. 46 of 1959), the Urban Bantu Councils Act (No. 79 of 1961), the Bantu Homelands Citizens Act of 1970, the Natives Land Act (No. 27 of 1913), the Natives (Urban Areas) Act of 1923, the Group Areas Act (No. 41 of 1950), and the Prevention of Illegal Squatting Act (No. 52 of 1951), forced people to live racial segregated area. Article 2 of the Belhar Confession, however, states that

> the unity of the people of God must be manifested and be active in a variety of ways: in that we love one another; that we experience, practice and pursue community with one another; that we are obligated to give ourselves willingly and joyfully to be of benefit and blessing to one another.

---

2   Extracts from the Confession of Belhar in this chapter are taken from the English translation at Addendum 15, The Confession of Belhar. Also available at http://urcsa.net/wp-content/uploads/2016/02/Belhar-Confession.pdf

Since 2004, people from different cultural backgrounds become members of the Scottsdene congregation in Kraaifontein, an Afrikaans-speaking congregation of URCSA. Demographical changes played a major role in the changes of the denominational profile. In 1997, the church council of Scottsdene had erected a makeshift building in Wallacedene, an informal settlement in Kraaifontein, where their members staying in Wallacedene could attend church services. Rev. Dawid Van Huffel, the minister of the URCSA Scottsdene, attended to the pastoral needs of the congregants of the URCSA Scottsdene residing in Wallacedene. Meanwhile isiXhosa-speaking members from the Langa URCSA congregation, 30 kilometres from Scottsdene, moved into Wallacedene, living near to the Afrikaans-speaking members of the Scottsdene URCSA. Langa is a suburb in Cape Town, established in 1927 in terms of the 1923 Urban Areas Act. It is one of the many areas in South Africa that were designated for black Africans before the apartheid era. While residential areas like Scottsdene, Scottsville, Northpine and Bernadino Heights had been erected in Kraaifontein by the apartheid government for people of mixed decent. The Group Areas Act of 1950 gave the government power to demarcate where each racial group could live and own property. This meant that from 1927, Xhosa people lived in Langa, while residential areas in Kraaifontein, namely Scottsdene, Scottsville, Northpine and Bernadino Heights, were restricted for people from mixed decent.

Prof. Welile Llewellyn Mazamiza of Langa URCSA attended to the pastoral needs of the isiXhosa-speaking members of the Langa URCSA residing in Wallacedene. In Wallacedene, both Afrikaans- and isiXhosa-speaking people was forced to live next to each other and shared the same space. Ten years after the unification of the Dutch Reformed Church in Africa (DRCA) and the Dutch Reformed Mission Church (DRMC), the isiXhosa-speaking members of URCSA residing in the Wallacedene settlement still had to travel weekly to the Langa Township, mostly by public transport, to attend church services, while there had been an URCSA congregation close by. The members of the Langa URCSA encountered numerous challenges. Firstly, the distance that they had to travel from Wallacedene to Langa to attend church services, funeral services or ministry activities became a costly endeavour. Secondly, it became difficult for the church council and minister of the Word of Langa URCSA to attend to the pastoral needs members of the Langa congregation living in Wallacedene. The Wallacedene members of the church applied in vain to become an autonomous URCSA congregation in Wallacedene (Potwana 2015:38-55).

During 2005, the members of the Langa URCSA resided in Wallacedene requested Rev. Dawid Van Huffel to conduct the Eucharist and Baptism during the Easter weekend (Minutes Church Council URCSA Scottsdene 2006). Afterwards the members of the ward approached Rev. Van Huffel in order to transfer their membership to the URCSA Scottsdene. This was done to comply to the church order regulations of the

URCSA which clearly says the following with regard to the transferal of certificates of membership:

> Members moving to other congregations need to obtain their membership certificates within six months of their departure and submit these to the church council under whose care they now live; once that has happened they will be acknowledged as members of the new congregation and their names entered into the register. Membership certificates will be issued to new members on request. Membership certificates are issued free of charge, except in cases where members resign from the church, in which case the church council has the right to charge a fee. (Church Order General Synod URCSA 2012, Article 71.2)

The URCSA Scottsdene, therefore, officially requested the Langa URCSA to transfer the members to URCSA Scottsdene.

During 2006, the church council of the Langa URCSA, under the leadership of Prof. Mazamisa approved the transfer of the members of the Langa congregation living in Wallacedene to Scottsdene URCSA. Prof. Mazamisa believed that the walls of separation brought on by the former racially-segregated churches in South Africa and discrimination based on race and colour should be eradicated. His premise was that the URCSA should embrace diversity at all levels, reflect diversity in worship, in the ministry, be able to share power in the leadership of the ministries and host strangers and aliens notwithstanding race, culture or class, language or gender. Therefore, he was very agreeable to transferring the members of Langa residing in Wallacedene to Scottsdene URCSA. On 14 May 2006, during a Sunday morning service in Scottsdene URCSA the offical transfer of membership took place (Minutes Church Council URCSA Scottsdene 2006). From then on, those isiXhosa-speaking congregants living in Wallacedene had access to a place of worship in their neighbourhood. The URCSA Scottsdene became one of the few multiracial congregations of the URCSA in the Regional Synod of the Cape.

Many challenges laid ahead of the congregation on their road of becoming a multi-ethnic-multicultural congregation. Problems arose regarding language, cultural praxes, liturgy, ministerial needs. The church council of Scottsdene and the members of the ward jointly attended to the challenges (*Minutes Church Council URCSA Scottsdene* 2006–2015; *Minutes of CWM URCSA Scottsdene* 2006–2014.). The first step of becoming a multicultural congregation was to change to homogenous worship services. In order to accommodate both language and cultural groups, the church council approved that one combined service on a monthly basis would took place in the makeshift building and that both the Xhosa 'Hosanna' hymnal and the Afrikaans '*Nuwe Sions*' hymnal should be used. The sermons would also be interpreted into the two languages. Evangelist Dipilo was appointed on a contractual basis by the church council of Scottsdene URCSA to attend to the pastoral needs of the isiXhosa-speaking members in the ward.

In 2008, The church council of the URCSA Scottsdene called an isiXhosa-speaking minister of the Word to the congregation, namely Prof. Dawid Xolile Simon (*Minutes Church Council URCSA Scottsdene* 2006). Prof. Simon is a full-time lecturer in Missiology at the University Stellenbosch, but agreed to minister on a part-time basis in the multi-ethnic-multicultural ward of the congregation. Currently, the Scottsdene URCSA has four ministers, namely, Rev. Dawid Van Huffel, Rev. Clive Rademeyer, Prof. Dawid Xolile Simon and Prof. Mary-Anne Plaatjies-Van Huffel. This multi-ethnic-multicultural pastoral team has a positive influence in the ward, especially regarding the enhancing of dialogue between the different language and cultural groups. All the ministers of the congregation are involved in the programmatic work of the ministries, namely, the Christian Youth Ministry (CYM), the Christian Men Ministry (CMM), the Christian Woman Ministry (CWM) and the congregation at large. Currently, the ward has two joint worship services a month, in which English, Afrikaans and isiXhosa are used. (*Minutes Church Council URCSA Scottsdene* 2006–2015; *Minutes of CWM URCSA Scottsdene* 2006–2014.). Congregants of both racial groups are comfortable to worship in one place as one congregation as part of the body of Christ despite their different backgrounds, culture or ethnicity. In doing so they are making unity visible in the URCSA.

The URCSA Scottsdene soon realised that the pluralist model, which allows the congregations of URCSA to retain their cultural identities and express them, seemed to represent a pragmatic answer to ethnic identities and was not conducive for churches to evolve in multi-ethnic- multicultural churches. The pluralist model assumes equal access to the decision-making structure on, for example, congregational, ministry presbytery or synodical level. However, in reality, that access and power were unevenly distributed in the ministries, resulting in tension, for example, in the Christian Women Ministry. Often CWM members from the different cultural groups would defend their own interests, or try to preserve their cultural identity.

The USRSCA has given much attention to conflict resolution. Without a definite blueprint, the URCSA Scottsdene searched for novel approaches to manage ethnic diversity on local congregational level.

What does a multicultural church look like?

In their search for a new approach, the URSCA Scottsdene encountered questions such as What is culture? Why is it important to take account of culture important in a multicultural ministry? Numerous scholars address the issue of multiculturalism, pluralism, cross-cultural conflict and multicultural ministry. According to Kraft, the term 'culture' is the label anthropologists give to the structured customs and underlying worldview assumptions which people govern their lives (Kraft 1996:385). According to missiologist Paul Hiebert, 'culture' is the integrated system of ideas, feelings, and values and their associated patterns of behaviour and products shared by a group of people who organise and regulate what they think, feel and do (Hiebert 1985:30). From 2004, the Scottsdene URCSA were challenged on their integrated system of ideas, feelings, and values and their associated patterns of behaviour and products in their journey from a mono-cultural context to a contested multi-religious and multicultural context in plural society. According to anthropologist Clifford Geertz, 'culture' denotes a historically transmitted pattern of meanings embodied in symbols; a system of inherited conceptions expressed in symbolic forms by means of which men communicate, perpetuate, and develop their knowledge about and attitudes towards life (Geertz 1993:89). Shortly after the transfer of members, the URCSA Scottsdene realised that cultures are more than mere expressions of meaning systems; that most of what people convey as being cultural is not always rational and that cultures offer conflicting patterns of interaction. In the process, the URCSA Scottsdene learned to move away from generalisations of a culture as a whole.

The Scottsdene URCSA soon realised that to achieve greater racial and cultural integration in the congregation they should focus on issues of racial diversity. The congregation had mostly been dominated by one culture. The church council affirmed the value of diverse cultures coexisting creatively in one congregation. Twenty years after unification, most of the URCSA's congregations are still mono-ethnic. According to (Yang 2012:18) a mono-ethnic church model implies separate churches of separate language and cultural groups.

The Scottsdene URCSA moved from being a mono-ethnic congregation to what Yang would call a multi-ethnic or integrated congregational model (Yang 2012:20): Yang defines the a 'mono-cultural model' as a congregational church that is homogeneous in language, ethnicity and culture (Yang 2012:24) a 'multi-ethnic congregation' is a multiracial congregation that is made up of diverse ethnic groups and cultures, and worships different languages. The URCSA Scottsdene intentionally utilised English, Afrikaans and isiXhosa in the Wallacedene's worship services. In the beginning, the church council did not address the ways in which such a congregation's structures and practices could reflect cultural diversity. For example, in the Afrikaans-speaking CWM and the isiXhosa-speaking CWM the leadership processes follow one particular culture's way of doing things. The church council realised more should be done to fully integrate the two groups. The pastors address the topic of racial divisions in their preaching and the discussions of the ministries, for example, the CWM and CMM and catechism. As a multi-ethnic-multicultural church, the URCSA Scottsdene intentionally draws different cultural perspectives into the life and leadership processes of the congregation. As Geertz rightly says:

> Religion is a system of symbols which acts to establish powerful, pervasive, and long-lasting moods and motivations in men by formulating conceptions of a general order of existence and clothing these conceptions with such an aura of factuality that the moods and motivations seem uniquely realistic. (Geertz 1993:90)

The URCSA Scottsdene realised that a multi-ethnic-multicultural church is all about accepting and embracing a diversity of peoples; it is about drawing diverse cultural voices into the decision-making structures of the congregation.

Article 2 of the Belhar Confession Article 2 states clearly that we reject any doctrine which absolutises either natural diversity or the sinful separation of people in such a way that this absolutisation hinders or breaks the visible and active unity of the church, or even leads to the establishment of a separate church formation. The URCSA should, therefore, take account of the Bennett scale in order to address cultural sensitivity in a holistic way. Milton Bennettdeveloped the Bennett scale, also called the Developmental Model of Intercultural Sensitivity which describes the different ways in which people can become more cultural sensitive, *inter alia*, denial, defence, minimisation, acceptance, adaptation and integration (Bennett 1986:179-196, 1993:109-135; Bennett & Bennett 2004:147-165).

Denial of cultural difference

Denial of cultural difference is the situation where one's own cultural perspective is viewed as the only real one. The dominant groups usually say to the minor groups: You should do it like us – for example, sing like us, dress like us. The discourse is usually about us and them. As Kraft (1996:387) rightly says, in cross-cultural ministry, the problems that arise from differences in worldview are the most difficult to deal with.

Defence

One's own culture is viewed as the best or the most evolved form of civilisation. This notion is surfacing in discourses, especially at synodical level and ministries concerning who should be chosen to positions of power. It is usually about one language and one cultural group versus the others. It also surfaces in unspoken assumptions that one's own culture and/or racial group is superior and, therefore, better equipped to lead the ministry, the commission, or task groups than other cultural or racial groups. Sometimes it can be portrayed as 'reversal', namely when an individual portrays a negative view of his or her own culture and a high regard of other cultures.

Minimisation

Minimisation of cultural difference is the stage when people will say: 'We are all basically alike. I don't see any real differences, we are all human beings.' In this case, differences between cultural and language groups are minimised.

Acceptance

Acceptance of cultural difference is present when one's own culture is experienced as just one of many equally complex worldviews. According to Kraft, 'worldview', the deep level of culture, is the culturally structured set of assumptions (including values and commitments/allegiances) underlying how a people perceive and respond to reality. Worldview is not separate from culture (Kraft 1996:385). In this case, congregants should be self-reflective on their experiences of other cultures and should be able to acknowledge others as different from themselves, but equally as members of the body of Christ. In the Wallacedene ward, the commonalities between the different cultural and language groups are being embraced, differences are being acknowledged and respect for other perspectives is being expressed. Members of the ministry became wary of imposing their way of doing things on others and in so doing they embraced The Belhar Confession Article 2, which states that

> this unity can be established only in freedom and not under constraint; that the variety of spiritual gifts, opportunities, backgrounds, convictions, as well as the diversity of languages and cultures, are by virtue of the reconciliation in Christ, opportunities for mutual service and enrichment within the one visible people of God.

Adaptation

Adaption to cultural difference is the state in which experience in another culture leads to changes in perception and behaviour. Adaptation, however, is not assimilation. As Kraft rightly cautions, even good changes, if they are introduced in the wrong way, can lead to cultural disequilibrium and demoralisation (Kraft 1996:388). After ten years experiencing each other's culture, the members of the Scottsdene URCSA are slowly but surely adapting. A multicultural ministry takes a lot of listening. While serving as an Afrikaans-speaking minister in the multicultural ward of my congregation in Wallacedene, consisting of both Afrikaans- and isiXhosa-speaking congregants, I realised that what I was saying and what they were hearing were quite different. I realised that I should communicate properly. There has been a shifting of frames of reference and behaviours to be able to think and act from the perspective of the other culture. For example, at a congregational meeting where the way forward had been discussed, the isiXhosa-speaking members of the ward in Wallacedene said: 'We live amongst Afrikaans-speaking people, our children is going to the same schools. We do not have any problem with church services where both Afrikaans and Xhosa hymnals are being used and simultaneous translation of the sermon is being done.' After twelve years, cross-cultural relationships of transparency and trust are growing. As in Article 2 of the confession, we should, therefore, as children of the Belhar Confession,

> reject any doctrine which absolutises either natural diversity or the sinful separation of people in such a way that this absolutisation hinders or breaks the visible and active unity of the church, or even leads to the establishment of a separate church formation.

Integration

The integration stage is often accompanied by a sense of disorientation and alienation.

What is a multi-ethnic-multicultural church?

Article 2 of the Belhar Confession states clearly that this unity

> must become visible so that the world may believe that separation, enmity and hatred between people and groups is sin which Christ has already conquered, and accordingly that anything which threatens this unity may have no place in the church and must be resisted.

I believe the best definition was offered by the late missiologist Paul Hiebert, who said, a multi-ethnic church is

> a church in which there is an attitude and practice of accepting people of all ethnic, class and national origins as equal and fully participating members and ministers in the fellowship of the church; the manifestation of this attitude and practice by the involvement of people from different ethnic, social and national communities as members in the church. (Hiebert 1985:3)

To have members of other language, race or cultural groups in the URCSA as a denomination or local congregation does mean that the URCSA is a multi-ethnic church. Multicultural churches and multiracial churches are not the same thing. A congregation of the URCSA can be multiracial if persons of other languages or cultural groups simply attend the services. Being a multi-ethnic congregation has nothing to do about size. It rather has to do with an attitude and practice of accepting people of all ethnic groups and nationalities as fully-fledged members of the body of Christ. It is about the intentional engagement of cultures. A multicultural church will not simply have people who are from different language and cultural groups. It will rather engage in other cultural contexts. It, however, becomes clear to us that in places where culture is already blended, it is easier to be racially diverse. Members of the congregation who already eat, work, shop and share common public spaces (schools, public transport, residential areas) and then come to church together to worship are already adapted to a prevalent culture. However, the older generation find it more difficult to adapt.

Conclusion

I concur with Kraft that if we are to reach people for Christ and see them gathered into Christ-honouring and culture-affirming churches, we will have to deal with them within their culture and in terms of their worldview (Kraft 1996:388). Our calling as children of the Belhar Confession is to build relationships across cultural, language and ethnic boundaries. Unity is indeed both a gift and an obligation for the church of Jesus Christ. We, as children of the Belhar Confession, should shrine away from anything that absolutises natural diversity, culture, language or praxis or the sinful separation of people in such a way that hinders or breaks the visible and active unity of the church.

Bibliography

Primary sources

Minutes Church Council of the Uniting Reformed Church in Southern Africa, Scottsdene 2006-2014.
Minutes of Christian Women Ministries of the Uniting Reformed Church in Southern Africa, Scottsdene 2006-2014.
URCSA. 2012. *Church Order and Regulations of the General Synod of the Uniting Reformed Church in Southern Africa*.

Secondary sources

Belhar Confession. 1986. Belhar: LUS Printers.
Bennett, M. J. 1993. Cultural marginality: Identity issues in intercultural training. In R.M. Paige (ed.), *Education for the intercultural experience* (2nd edition). Yarmouth, ME: Intercultural Press.
Bennett, M. J. 2004. Becoming intercultural competent. In J. Wurzel (ed.), *Towards multiculturalism: a reader in multicultural education* (2nd ed). Newton, MA: Intercultural Resource Corporation.

Bennett, Milton J. 1977. *Developmental model of intercultural sensitivity* (DMIS). Minneapolis, MN: University of Minnesota. https://doi.org/10.1016/0147-1767(86)90005-2

Bennett, Milton J. (1986). A developmental approach to training for intercultural sensitivity. *International Journal of Intercultural Relations* 10(2):179-196.

Elmer, D. 2006. *Cross-cultural conflict: building relationships for effective ministry*. Downers Grove, IL: Intervarsity Press.

Geertz, C. 1993. *The interpretation of cultures: Selected essays*. Waukegan, Il: Fontana Press.

Hiebert, P.G. 1985. *Anthropological insights for missionaries*. Grand Rapids, MI: Baker Publishing.

Kraft, C.H. 1996. *Anthropology for Christian witness*. Maryknoll, NY: Orbis.

Kymlicka, W. 2003. Multicultural state and intercultural citizen. *Theory and Research in Education* 1:147-16. https://doi.org/10.1177/1477878503001002001

Perkins, J. 1993. *Beyond charity: The call to Christian community development*. Grand Rapids, MI: Baker Books.

Potwana, S. 2015. A church judicial research on multiculturalism in URCSA. MDiv thesis, University of Stellenbosch, Stellenbosch.

Saayman, W. 2010. The beautiful birdsong of Tshwane: Preliminary reflections on the beginnings of the Uniting Reformed Church of Southern Africa (URCSA) congregation Melodi ya Tshwane. *Studia Historiae Ecclesiasticae* 36(2):135-145.

Sheffield, D. 2005. The multicultural leader: Developing a Catholic personality. Jacksonville Beach, FL: Clements Publishing.

van der Borght, E.A.J.G. 2009. *Sunday morning – The most segregated hour: On racial reconciliation as unfinished business for theology in South Africa and beyond*. Amsterdam: Faculty of Theology, VU University Amsterdam.

Yang, M. 2012 Ways of being a multicultural church: An evaluation of multicultural church models in the Baptist Union of Victoria. MA thesis, the University of Divinity, Melbourne, Australia.

LIVING BELHAR

Enhancing the reception of Belhar in congregations

J.N.J. (Klippies) Kritzinger[1]

Introduction

If the Confession of Belhar is to function credibly as a 'confessional standard' in the Uniting Reformed Church in Southern Africa (URCSA), it needs to become thoroughly integrated into the daily life of its congregations – informing and transforming worship, instruction, care, witness and service (URCSA 2012b:9-10).[2] Unfortunately, the reality in many URCSA congregations is quite different. One example will suffice: When the Assessment Committee of the Ministerial Formation Task Team (Curatorium) of the Northern and Southern synods interview new applicants for ministry studies, one of the questions asked of the applicants is whether they know the Confession of Belhar and what they think of it. Some applicants have never heard of Belhar, while others say: 'We recite it sometimes in church on Sundays.' Very few applicants have a copy of the full confession, but occasionally there is an applicant who has studied it and can discuss it.

This ignorance is in sharp contrast with the official view of the URCSA General Synod, which has repeatedly affirmed that Belhar should be an essential part of the confessional basis of a united church in the DRC family. One example (among many) of this commitment to Belhar is the statement of the 2008 General Synod:

> That the Confession of Belhar is not just of 'sentimental value' but is an irreplaceable gift to the church of Jesus Christ in the country and abroad as well as an authentic expression of Reformed theology for our times and contexts and as such honoured and accepted by churches in the Reformed family across the world. (*Agenda General Synod URCSA* 2008:31)

Belhar expresses 'our deepest held convictions on the call of the Gospel with regard to the unity of the church and our faith' (*Agenda General Synod URCSA*:

---

1. Prof Klippies Kritzinger lectured at Department of Church History, Christian Spirituality and Missiology, University of South Africa, Pretoria, South Africa. His is a co-pastor of Melodi ya Tshwane.
2. These five dimensions are identified in Article 5 of the URCSA church order as essential dimensions (called 'universal services') of a congregation.

31). The discrepancy between this official position of the church and the lack of knowledge of Belhar in many URCSA congregations constitutes a credibility crisis. Many reasons could be adduced for this disappointing situation, however, that is not the purpose of this paper. Instead, I reflect on how the 'reception' of Belhar in the URCSA congregations can be enhanced through the development of appropriate group study material that can help members to live – and love – the Confession of Belhar.[3] I do this by discussing a study guide, *Living Belhar 2014: A Workbook for Wards in Melodi ya Tshwane* (MyT 2014), which was prepared under the auspices of the Melodi ya Tshwane (MyT) church council to enable adult URCSA members to understand and embody this confession.[4] To place the study guide in its proper context, this chapter discusses the background and purpose of *Living Belhar*, its structureand the group process. The chapter closes with a theological reflection and conclusion.

Background of *Living Belhar*

The origin of the study guide (and the learning-doing group process it facilitates) goes back to the decision of the 2008 General Synod at Hammanskraal 'to put a moratorium on the reunification talks between the URCSA and the DRC until the DRC is seriously committed and ready for unity talks' (*Acts General Synod URCSA* 2008:31). One of the reasons for that decision was that the DRC General Synod was not prepared to support a model of full organic church unity or to make the Belhar Confession an integral part of its confessional basis. This disappointment in the DRC's official position was exacerbated by the way in which Prof. P.J. Strauss, then moderator of the DRC General Synod, conveyed the greetings of his church to the synod (*Acts General Synod URCSA* 2008:29-33). As a follow-up to the moratorium decision, the following resolution was adopted:

> The Synod requests the Moderamen to call for a public occasion where members and ministers of the DRC and the rest of the DRC family can publicly support, identify with and undersign the Confession of Belhar. We propose this as a way to continue meaningful progress with regard to church

---

3   Deeper reflection is necessary on the ongoing process of internal 'reception' of Belhar in the URCSA, particularly in the congregations that belonged to the DRCA before the formation of the URCSA. All the ministers, church council members and members of the former DRCA were not required to personally endorse Belhar with their signatures in the unification process. As a result, the confession did not receive the prominence it deserved in those sectors on the URCSA. The helpful comments of Naudé (2010:132-135) on the 'reception' of confessions need to be further developed and focussed on this particular issue.

4   Melodi ya Tshwane was established in 1992 as a congregation of the DRCA and became part of the URCSA in 1994. It originated as a congregation of predominantly domestic workers but its membership has expanded to include families of professionals and students who live in the former 'white' suburbs of the City of Tshwane (see Saayman 2010).

unification as URCSA understand it. This will open new possibilities for our walking this road together. (*Acts General Synod URCSA* 2008:32)

The decision was intended to express recognition that not all DRC members were opposed to the Belhar Confession or to organic unity with the URCSA. The synod resolution wanted to give those DRC members the opportunity to express their public support for Belhar. To implement this resolution of General Synod, the General Synodical Commission (GSC) of 2009 took the following decision:

> The meeting decides to: Request Dr Mary-Anne Plaatjies-Van Huffel (as convenor) to liaise with Prof Klippies Kritzinger, Dr Nico Smith and Rev Daniël Kuys to arrange a launch of the project in the Western Cape on 16 December 2008 [sic].[5] They are requested to include prominent members of the DRC who accept the Belhar Confession and other member churches in SA to take part in this public event. The public event should be attended by the Moderamen and from there a roll-out should take place in Regional synods, presbyteries and congregations.
>
> An article for URCSA News and a circular to the congregations, explaining the event and process, should be prepared by the Scribe and (he) be assisted by Dr Henry Platt, Rev. Colin Goeiman and Rev. Daniël l Kuys. (*Agenda General Synod URCSA* 2012:32)

This committee never had a face-to-face meeting, but corresponded by email. During those email discussions, some differences emerged between the committee members, which eventually derailed the whole process. Instead of analysing the process, let me state my approach to carrying out the General Synod resolution. I was uncomfortable with a scenario where the URCSA would invite the DRC members to come to a public venue and queue up to sign the Confession of Belhar, while the URCSA members looked on. To me that smacked of an 'us-them' mentality: 'We have the truth; they must come and get it from us.' For me that disagreed with the content and purpose of the Confession of Belhar. I therefore proposed a preparatory process through which small groups (consisting of equal numbers of the URCSA and the DRC members) throughout southern Africa would study Belhar together and then convene in a number of decentralised public places to commit themselves jointly to embody its message. For that purpose, I started developing a study guide for use by small groups of URCSA and DRC members, helping them to discover each other while discovering the message of Belhar together. While drawing up that guide, I spoke with Dr Frederick Marais and Dr Chris van Wyk of the DRC and adopted some

---

5   Since this decision was taken during the 2009 GSC meeting, which took place on 26–29 October 2009, the target date of 16 December 2008 for this decision should probably read 16 December 2009 (or 2010).

good ideas from them on how to structure helpful processes for group discussion. I owe the idea of a '5x5 journey' and the sequence: 'embrace-discover-commit' for each group session to their creative input.

When the ad hoc commission of the URCSA General Synod stopped functioning, I left the half-completed booklet hanging in the air. A few years later, however, I mentioned it to Rev. Cobus van Wyngaard during a conversation on church unity and the role of Belhar and sent him a copy of the draft. He thought that it was worth trying out the material with a group of URCSA and DRC ministers in Pretoria. Consequently, a group of five URCSA and five DRC ministers embarked on a '5x5 journey' together during April to September 2013 to test the viability of the material.[6] The positive experience of the process convinced the participants of the potential of the process, and a group of four colleagues[7] reworked the booklet for ongoing use, believing that it could have a wider impact. When the DRC compiled a digital package of study material on Belhar during 2013 to be sent out to all DRC congregations, *Living Belhar* (Kritzinger et al. 2013a) was included. It was also translated into Afrikaans as *Leef Belhar* (Kritzinger et al. 2013b). I am not sure how many DRC or joint DRC-URCSA groups used that booklet in group discussions, but the lack of knowledge of Belhar in our congregation (Melodi ya Tshwane) convinced me that it was necessary to adapt the booklet for group study within a URCSA congregation. This gave rise to *Living Belhar 2014: A Workbook for Wards in Melodi ya Tshwane* (MyT 2014), which consisted of ten chapters, thus giving groups two sessions to explore each article of Belhar. The full English translation of Belhar and its accompanying letter[8] were included as an addendum, since only selected extracts from the confession were quoted in the chapters (see *Agenda General Synod URCSA* 2008:522-524).

The Melodi ya Tshwane church council released the booklet for use by the wards of the congregation during Easter 2014, with the prayer 'that the power of Christ's resurrection will transform our hands into instruments of hope, unity, reconciliation, justice and obedience' (MyT 2014:3).

The purpose of the booklet is expressed in its preface, which is entitled 'Invitation to a journey':

> This booklet presents the Confession of Belhar as a way of life. It is designed to help a group of URCSA members to embrace one another as fellow

---

6   The notion of a '5x5 journey' implies that five URCSA members and five DRC members pledge to meet for five weeks as a group to work through the study material. I adopted this creative format on the advice of Frederick Marais and Chris van Wyk.
7   The group consisted of Dr T.J. Nthakhe, Rev. P.M. Maruping, Rev. C. van Wyngaard and myself.
8   The English translation used in the booklet was the one authorised by the 2008 General Synod, which contains gender inclusive language.

believers, discover more clearly what Belhar says, and commit themselves to daily habits and projects that embody the message of this confession. This is a journey of ten sessions for a group of URCSA members to discover Belhar together. Each chapter will take no more than an hour and a half (90 minutes) to complete. The purpose of this booklet is therefore not to convince anyone of the truth or value of Belhar. It is designed for a group of people who already accept its message and want to understand it better in order to put it into practice. It is an invitation to live Belhar, by starting a joint movement for hope, unity, reconciliation, justice and obedience in South African society at large. It is based on the understanding that the Confession of Belhar requires from us a conversion towards each other. (MyT 2014:3)

The purpose of the booklet is not apologetic or persuasive in the sense of trying to convince a sceptical member to adopt the vision of Belhar; instead it assumes a basic allegiance to the confession and helps a group of URCSA members to embrace its message, while embracing each other.

Structure of *Living Belhar*

The structure of the study guide flowed from the need to find an acronym that expresses the message of Belhar in a way that can be easily remembered by church members, including children. It could be argued that a confession has not been adequately 'received' in a church unless its children are able to understand it and begin to put it into practice, even if in a rudimentary way. I was looking for an acronym that conveys the message of Belhar in the way that the acronym 'TULIP'[9] conveys the message of the Canons of Dordt. After considering a few alternatives, I settled for the acronym 'HANDS', based on the following catchphrases:

---

9 TULIP summarises the message of the five Canons as Total depravity, Unconditional election, Limited atonement, Irresistible grace, and Preservation of the saints. One weakness of TULIP is that it mainly emphasises what God does, and that it does so by using abstract nouns (election, atonement, grace, preservation), with the result that it fails to inspire or attract. One could argue, however, that it is faithful in capturing the doctrinal (or doctrinaire) intent of the Canons of Dordt. Another weakness of TULIP as an acronym is that there is no integral link between the flower image (tulip) and the content of the Canons; the only connection seems to be their common Dutch origin.

Hope in God's faithfulness (Article 1)
Accept one another (Article 2)
Nurture reconciliation (Article 3)
Do justice (Article 4)
Serve one Lord (Article 5)

The preface of the booklet explains the acronym like this:

Taken together, the first letters of these phrases produce the acronym HANDS. We believe that this is an apt expression of the message of Belhar, since it is a call to action as much as an exposition of Christian truth. In each chapter, a specific use of our hands expresses the particular way of life envisaged in Belhar. (MyT 2014:3)

The acronym HANDS, based on these five catchphrases, is not the only (or even the most obvious) way to capture the message of Belhar. These catchphrases are imperatives (calls to action), rather than indicatives that only affirm God's action: Belhar *calls* us to hope, to accept, to nurture, to do, and to serve – and it does so on the basis of God's prevenient and ongoing work of grace, through Word and Spirit. In each chapter, these two lines (grace and gratitude; God's initiative and human response) are stressed, to avoid a moralistic reading of Belhar as merely 'what we must do.' But I nevertheless decided to pitch the catchphrases in the form of imperatives, as challenges to action.

It is necessary to explain briefly why I chose these catchphrases, so that my interpretation of the confession may become clear.

Hope in God's faithfulness

Article 1 of the Belhar Confession expresses hope in God's faithfulness.

> We believe in the triune God, Father, Son and Holy Spirit, who through Word and Spirit gathers, protects and cares for the church from the beginning of the world and will do to the end.[10]

Numerous options are available for characterising the main thrust of this article. Its emphasis on the gracious initiative of the triune God to call the church into being and to preserve it throughout history calls forth a response of grateful wonder; it also elicits an openness to be further gathered, fed and protected by God's Word and Spirit. But the more I meditated on this rich sentence, the more I became

---

10 Extracts from the Confession of Belhar in this chapter are taken from the English translation at Addendum 15, The Confession of Belhar. Also available at http://urcsa.net/wp-content/uploads/2016/02/Belhar-Confession.pdf

convinced that the 'sting' of Article 1 is in its 'tail' – that the last six words ('and will do to the end') presents the punchline. And that brought me to the theme of 'hope': God's faithful gathering and feeding of the church calls forth gratitude and obedience but above all its calls forth hope in God's ongoing faithfulness – 'to the end.' This led me to make 'Hope in God's faithfulness' the catchphrase for Article 1.[11]

Accept one another

This catchphrase for Article 2 of Belhar – 'Accept one another' – is rather predictable and not likely to be controversial. The only criticism that one could level against it is that it does not emphasise God's initiative as highlighted in Article 2, namely that unity is both a gift and an obligation. A catchphrase like 'Accept one another as God's children' or 'Become God's one church' would perhaps do greater justice to the content of Article 2, but such phrases lose some their catchiness.

Nurture reconciliation

The essence of Article 3, which deals with reconciliation, could be captured in action phrases like 'Reconcile with one another' or 'Be reconciled to one another', but I wanted to emphasise the delicateness and provisionality of the reconciliation journey and chose the verb 'nurture' instead. The expression 'prepared to venture on the road of obedience and reconciliation' in Article 3 suggests that reconciliation is a nurturing journey together, during which broken relationships are gradually restored, deep disappointments are slowly overcome, and trust is nurtured one step at a time.

Do justice and serve one Lord

The catchphrase for the last two articles – 'Do justice and serve one Lord' – is also straightforward, with the understanding that the words do not capture everything contained in those articles but are meant to attract attention to the main challenges embodied in them.

---

11 While writing this chapter, I discovered that the RCA study guide also identifies hope as the key emphasis of Article 1. See Session 8: The Belhar as an affirmation of hope (RCA 2006:47-50).

Different hand gestures

To establish an integral link between the HANDS acronym and the macro-structure of the booklet, I connected each article of Belhar with a specific hand gesture or action.

Hope in God's faithfulness – with empty hands
Accept one another – with open hands
Nurture reconciliation – wash your hands
Do justice – work with your hands (or get your hands dirty)
Serve one Lord – walk hand-in-hand

My intention with this aspect of the design was not to over-elaborate or allegorise the 'hands' image, but to underline the concrete and bodily nature of the challenge presented to us by the gospel, as articulated in the Confession of Belhar. These hand gestures represent life postures and are used particularly in the ritual (Sending out) sections at the end of each group session, as explained later.

The group process of *Living Belhar*

In addition to the five-fold macro-structure of the booklet, the micro-structure of each group session also moves through five consecutive phases: Welcoming, Embracing, Discovering, Committing and Sending out. It is possible to depict the overall framework of the booklet as follows:

	H	A	N	D	S
Belhar article	1	2	3	4	5
Catchphrase	Hope in God's faithfulness	Accept one another	Nurture reconciliation	Do Justice	Serve one Lord
Hand gesture	With empty hands	With open hands	Wash your hands	Work with your hands	Walk hand-in-hand
Group session process	Welcoming	Welcoming	Welcoming	Welcoming	Welcoming
	Embracing	Embracing	Embracing	Embracing	Embracing
	Discovering	Discovering	Discovering	Discovering	Discovering
	Committing	Committing	Committing	Committing	Committing
	Sending out	Sending out	Sending out	Sending out	Sending out

The Introduction to the booklet describes the group facilitation process (MyT 2014:4-5).

You will notice that the *Living Belhar* chapters discussed here are not written in a question-and-answer style. Rather, each *Living Belhar* meeting consist of five 'movements', which draw the group closer together and open up a space where members can share their thoughts. The task of a facilitator is to help the group to 'walk through' these five movements. The following overview will help you to understand the nature of these movements.

1. Welcoming

The way in which we welcome each other into the meeting sets the tone for how our discussions will proceed. The facilitator needs to make sure that the group members sit in such a way that everyone can join in freely. If one person is left out of the group by the seating arrangement, change that before going on. Make sure that the meeting starts on time, so that you do not exceed an hour and a half. Open with a short prayer in which the group acknowledges that it is God who has gathered them together.

2. Embracing

Belhar emphasises that Christians from all backgrounds are one in Christ, and that they, therefore, need to work towards reconciled relationships among themselves. In South Africa generally, and also in our churches, we often continue to live in separate worlds. To overcome this separation in some way, begin each meeting by allowing time for group members to share something about themselves to embrace each other through careful listening. This movement is often the space where the group grows the most. The facilitator needs to be sensitive to what is happening and discern when it is wise to allow the sharing to continue and when the group needs to be moved along, since this movement can easily take up too much time.

3. Discovering

In this 'discovering' movement we turn our attention to the Confession of Belhar. Each week a section of Belhar and one passage from the Bible are read out loud in the group. We encourage all the group members to prepare for the meeting by reading the Bible passage and the section from Belhar before the meeting. Each chapter contains open-ended questions which the facilitator can use to draw members into the discussion. These questions do not aim at 'final' answers from the group, but are rather meant to stimulate a joint discovery of Belhar in the light of Scripture.

4. Committing

Learning to live the Belhar Confession is a life-long journey of discipleship. Each week we commit ourselves to continue our shared journey. The first aspect of this commitment is towards each other, and you will find very practical suggestions about the shape that this commitment could take, but it involves meeting other group members in different ways during the week to deepen the impact of our shared journey on our lives. The other aspect of commitment is to look at our society with different eyes: each week we commit ourselves to learn to live more actively for hope, unity, reconciliation, justice and obedience.

5. Sending Out

We start each meeting with prayer to express that it is God who gathers us together. Likewise, we close with a prayer to acknowledge that God is sending us out into the community to live the message of Belhar. When we pray we stand in a position that reminds us of the specific article from Belhar that we discussed. For example, we face east after discussing our hope in God's faithfulness and we stand in a circle facing outwards after reflecting on how to do justice.

This five-fold process, and the sequence in which it unfolds, begins with relational and interpersonal domain (welcoming and embracing), moves to cognitive and volitional domains (discovering and committing) and culminates in a faith ritual (sending out). An unexpected insight that dawned on the group while reviewing the booklet was that a kind of resonance had developed between the micro-structure within each session and the macro-structure (or flow of thought) within Belhar itself:

Macro-structure of Belhar session		Micro-structure of each group
Art. 1	God gathers the church	Welcoming (receive each other as gifts from God)
Art. 2	Unity as gift and obligation	Embracing (get to know one another better)
Art. 3	Reconciliation	Discovering (discuss truth, debate, see agreement)
Art. 4	Justice	Committing (take a concrete stand, make decisions)
Art. 5	Obey Jesus as Lord	Sending out (entrust each other to the care of God)

These movements are clearly not identical; they are parallel embodiments of a covenantal encounter between the living God and God's people. It is part of the genius of the Confession of Belhar that it charts this covenantal logic in the sequence of its five articles. The group who revised the *Living Belhar* booklet wondered whether some form of this five-step sequence could be developed into a liturgical framework for the worship services of a Reformed congregation. We wondered whether there was a better way for a church to be faithful to its confessional basis than to embody its 'logic' every Sunday in the flow and patterning of its worship.

Theological reflection

The Bible passages used in each of the group sessions to illumine the five articles of Belhar are:

Article 1	Ezekiel 36:24-28 and Romans 13:11-14
Article 2	Ephesians 4:1-6, 14-16 and 1 Corinthians 12:12-26
Article 3	Matthew 5:21-24 and Acts 6:1-6
Article 4	Isaiah 58:1-10 and Matthew 25:31-40
Article 5	Acts 5:27-32 and Philippians 1:27-30

Not all of these passages are referred to in Belhar as justification for its views; they were selected for the clear way in which they express the challenges contained in Belhar. At the end of the *Living Belhar 2014* booklet, there is a brief reflection on the underlying theological assumptions that informed it.[12] I reproduce that whole section (MyT 2014:24-25) here, with a few editorial changes.

The booklet does not try to be an in-depth discussion concerning the theology of Belhar, but we do think that a number of points are important enough that something need to be said about them. To assist group members to understand the theological thinking that informs this booklet, we offer the following five points of explanation:

All five articles of Belhar are equally important

It has become customary to say that the message of the Confession of Belhar has to do with Unity (Art. 2), Reconciliation (Art. 3) and Justice (Art. 4). By doing so, the importance of Article 1 (Hope) and Article 5 (Obedience) are downplayed or ignored. These then become mere 'book stops' around the 'real confession'. The integrity of the confession is damaged by doing that. Belhar does not incite us to 'man-made' activism; it invites us to become part of God's nurturing, uniting, reconciling,

---

12 I acknowledge the contribution of the group of the URCSA and the DRC ministers who participated in the 2013 group process in Pretoria, particularly Dr I.J. Nthakhe, Rev. P.M. Maruping and Rev. C. van Wyngaard, who collaborated with me in revising the booklet after our group experience. Their creative insights are incorporated in this section of the booklet.

transforming and sanctifying mission in society. Our work for unity, reconciliation and justice must be embedded in the faithfulness of the triune God (Art. 1) and in our obedience to Jesus Christ as Lord (Art. 5). It is also important to remember that none of the middle three articles more important than the others. Even if we feel personally called to work for the unity of the church, Belhar reminds us that we cannot separate this from reconciliation in society and standing against injustice. In this way, we are drawn beyond our personal interests and into an integrated participation in God's transformation of the world. We hope that this booklet will draw participants into a Belhar spirituality of hopeful trust in God's faithfulness (Art. 1) and resolute commitment to serve nobody and nothing else (Art. 5).

Truth needs to be done

The understanding or truth expressed in the Confession of Belhar is not one of abstract ideas or doctrines that hang in the air. It expresses the biblical notion that the truth of God is transformative: it sets us free (John 8:32, New International Version)[13] and therefore we need to do (or practice) the truth (1 John 1:6). There is a close relationship between what God has done (and keeps on doing) and what we need to do. Because we believe that through the work of God's Spirit the church is made one, we practice and pursue community with one another. Because we believe in the message of reconciliation in and through Christ, we seek to live in obedience as peacemakers. Because we believe that God stands against injustice and with the wronged, we witness against those who selfishly seek to control and harm others. The truth of God is concrete: it needs to be lived from day to day. We hope that this booklet will help individuals and group to *do* the *living* truth of Belhar.

Spiritual and material

The Confession of Belhar presents a holistic and integrated view of human life. It does not separate sacred from secular, soul from body, Sunday from weekday, or church from world. It does not construct a divide between 'the bad world here below' and 'the ideal world in heaven above'. It is shaped by the vision of the coming Reign (kingdom) of God, which is about resurrection, peace, justice and joy. It therefore calls believers to move hopefully into that promised future, because the decisive battle over sin, death and evil has taken place already in the cross and resurrection of Christ. Bodies are therefore just as important as souls. The Spirit of God creates wholeness in us and togetherness among us. Often our theologies try to clearly separate that which is holy from that which is not, making it difficult for us to relate our faith to life. Belhar calls us into the messiness of life, and we hope

---

13 Scriptural quotations in this chapter follow the New International Version (NIV).

that life in all its messiness will be at the heart of the discussions of groups using this booklet.

Knowing together, growing together

The process of learning and interaction in this booklet is based on the insight that Christians cannot understand the will of God by themselves, in isolation from others. It is only 'together with all the saints' (Eph. 3:18) that one can begin to understand the full extent of Christ's love. We have therefore written the booklet in such a way that it would be impossible to work through it alone. Our hope is that people from different backgrounds, churches and communities will come together to seek the will of God, and to discern what *living* Belhar would mean today.

Accompanying letter

The motivation behind the drafting of the Confession of Belhar – and the purpose for which it was written – is clearly explained in the accompanying letter, which is attached to this booklet as part of Addendum 15. In the same way that Belhar cannot be understood without Articles 1 and 5, it should also not be read in isolation from its accompanying letter. We hope that participants will all read it together with the confession.

Six different uses of a confession

A confession like Belhar has at least six different functions in the life of a congregation (Smit 2009b:302):

- It provides members with a language and vocabulary to praise God.
- It gives them a distinctly Reformed way of reading the Bible.
- It provides them with a theological identity and a sense of belonging.
- It is used to instruct new believers in the faith, especially through catechism classes.
- It guides the church to discern the will of God by distinguishing truth from falsehood.
- It is a form of public witness to the truth of the gospel.

If the Confession of Belhar is to play any of these six roles in a congregation, all its members need to know it well and grow in living its message from day to day. The purpose of this booklet is to contribute towards that goal.

Conclusion: Living Belhar – Loving Belhar

On the front cover of the *Living Belhar 2014* booklet, the following graphic expresses the centrality of 'hands' in the treatment of the confession (MyT 2014:1). I designed it as an additional aid to reinforce the HANDS acronym

After producing this graphic in 2013, I discovered that the Reformed Church in America (RCA) also uses 'hands' symbolism to explain the message of Belhar to their members.[14] The RCA graphic is very like mine, but it does not seem as if they arrived at it via a HANDS acronym for the content of the confession as I did. The two projects arrived at a remarkably similar 'hands' symbolism, even though there was no contact between them. This is probably because truth – as articulated by Belhar – is not merely a matter of intellectual affirmation or emotional identification, but also of action: something to be *done* with your *hands*. In addition, the image of diverse people reaching out to each other is a predictable image for the message of unity and reconciliation in the Confession of Belhar. The real challenge, however, is not to create good symbols but to make them become a reality, so that this liberating 'hands-on' Christianity may become deeply entrenched in the lives of all the congregations, ministries, families and members of the URCSA. For this mammoth task, three dimensions will be critical:

1. The urgent development and wide distribution of a range of age-appropriate and ministry-appropriate study booklets to help the URCSA members learn how to love and live Belhar. This will have to begin in a well-designed Sunday school and catechism curriculum, followed by attractive and challenging youth study materials, and finally a series of booklets (similar to *Living Belhar*) for use by church councils, ministries, wards and cell groups.

2. The creation of songs, rituals and liturgical forms to entrench the message of Belhar in the weekly worship services of the URCSA congregations. This should

---

14 In 2006, the Reformed Church in America published *Unity, Reconciliation and Justice. A Study Guide for the Belhar Confession* (RCA 2006).

include much more than the recitation of a liturgical summary of Belhar in worship service (see e.g. Kritzinger 2014).

3. The application of Belhar to challenges that have emerged in the past 30 years and that were not explicitly envisaged in the initial formulation of the confession. The following areas, in no particular order of importance, suggest themselves for priority attention, each requiring study materials for group discussions and action:
   - Belhar and xenophobia (Addendum 14);
   - Belhar and discrimination against LGBTI communities;
   - Belhar and globalisation;
   - Belhar and relations with people of other faiths;
   - Belhar and the stigmatisation of people living with HIV and Aids;
   - Belhar and child abuse/trafficking;
   - Belhar and violence against women
   - Belhar and orphans;
   - Belhar and people with disabilities; and
   - Belhar and Palestine.

The Confession of Belhar clearly does not 'have all the answers' to these complex challenges facing congregations today, but it is certainly one of the important resources that the URCSA must use in addressing these issues.

In conclusion, let me refer to the 2008 General Synod resolution to invite DRC members to identify themselves publicly with Belhar, in which the *Living Belhar* booklet had its origin. After the disappointment with the DRC's recent attempt to amend Article 1 of its church order to include Belhar in some way, the 2008 the URCSA proposal has gained new relevance. Perhaps the time has now come for all the DRC members who identify with Belhar to be challenged to stand up and say so publicly. But perhaps the time has also come for all the URCSA members who love and live Belhar to do the same – and to do so publicly together with all members of the DRC family who are prepared to join them. I propose that public gatherings be arranged during September 2016 (exactly 30 years after the adoption of Belhar as a confession) in as many venues as possible across southern Africa, to show that we are a church that confesses our faith (and not merely a church that has four confessions somewhere on a bookshelf). In those gatherings, all the members of the DRC family should be invited to stand up and affirm their allegiance to the dynamic truth of Scripture, as articulated in the Confession of

Belhar. At those occasions, we should also launch (or advertise) all the actions and projects through which we are using our hands to embody Belhar, particularly in relation to the challenges listed earlier. For such a process to be meaningful, thorough preparation and intense engagement within and between congregations of the four DRC churches at ground level will be necessary. In that process, the *Living Belhar* booklet could play a constructive role, not only in its own right as an entry-level study guide, but perhaps also as a prototype for the parallel booklets that need to be developed to foster this process.

Bibliography

Primary sources

Acts of General Synod of the Uniting Reformed Church in Southern Africa. 2008. (29 September–5 October 2008, Hammanskraal). Bloemfontein.

Agenda General Synod Uniting Reformed Church in Southern Africa. 2008. (29 September–5 October 2008, Hammanskraal). Bloemfontein.

Agenda General Synod Uniting Reformed Church in Southern Africa. 2012. Bloemfontein. (1–7 October 2012, Okahandja, Namibia. Bloemfontein.

Church Order and Regulations of the General Synod of the Uniting Reformed Church in Southern Africa 2012. Bloemfontein.

Reformed Church in America (RCA). 2006. *Unity, reconciliation and justice. A study guide for the Belhar Confession.* Faith Alive Christian Resources, Reformed Church Press.

Secondary sources

Kritzinger, J.N.J. 2014. Concrete spirituality. *HTS Teologiese Studies/Theological Studies* 70(3), Art. #2782, 12 pages. https://doi.org/10.4102/hts.v70i3.2782

Kritzinger, J.N.J., Nthakhe, J., Maruping, P. & van Wyngaard, C. 2013a. *Living Belhar: Embrace, discover, commit. Invitation to a journey.* Wellington: Bible-Media.

Kritzinger, J.N.J., Nthakhe, J., Maruping, P. & van Wyngaard, C. 2013b. *Leef Belhar: Verwelkom, ontdek, verbind. Uitnodiging tot 'n reis.* Wellington: Bybel-Media.

MyT (Melodi ya Tshwane). 2014. Living Belhar 2014: A workbook for wards in Melodi ya Tshwane (unpublished photocopied booklet).

Naudé, P.J. 2010. *Neither calendar nor clock. Perspectives on the Belhar Confession.* Grand Rapids, MI: William B. Eerdmans.

Saayman, W.A. 2010. The beautiful birdsong of Tshwane: Preliminary reflections on the beginnings of the Uniting Reformed Church in Southern Africa (URCSA) congregation Melodi ya Tshwane. *Studia Historiae Ecclesiasticae* 36(2):135-145.

Smit, D.J. 2009. *Essays on being Reformed, Collected essays 3.* Stellenbosch: SUN PReSS.

UNWRAPPING THE GIFT OF THE BELHAR CONFESSION

Motlalentwa Godfrey Betha[1]

Introduction

Time and again we hear statements and comments that the Belhar Confession is an obstacle to true reunification within the Dutch Reformed Church (DRC) family, that it is outdated and irrelevant to present day South Africa, and that it reminds people of emotional, historical, and symbolic events of the past. Some are even going to an extent of questioning whether we are trying to correct the past with a confession. There is sheer ignorance about the role the Belhar Confession has played, is playing, and will play in the future within the DRC family and the Reformed world as a whole. In some instances, the comments are shrouded with racism and indignation because the confession did not originate from the dominant community, that is, those who are reputed to be sent by God to bring civilisation and progress to the world. But it originated from the underside of history and mainly people of colour. The Belhar Confession is a homegrown statement of Reformed faith that emerged from African soil and context. Instead of building on our experiences as guided by God through the Belhar Confession, we find ourselves going backwards and forwards to make ourselves clear to those who do not want to accept this reality.

We are aware that some find it difficult to comprehend issues raised in the Belhar Confession. We will continue clarifying these issues with love and compassion until these people too understand the spirit of the Belhar Confession – assuredly believe, regardless of what others may believe and regardless of the opposition, rejection, or persecution that may come to us for taking the stand we are taking. Christians are, by definition, people who make their own confession known: 'Jesus is Lord' (Rom. 10:9-10, New Revised Standard Version).[2] The Christian Church, called and held together by Jesus Christ himself, lives only through the continual renewal of this fundamental confession of faith. A 'confession of faith' may thus be defined more precisely as a public declaration before God and the world of what a church believes. It is an officially adopted statement.

---

1 Motlalentwa Godfrey Betha is the vice-chairperson of the Uniting Reformed Church in Southern Africa. Rev. Betha presented a paper on the Belhar Confession at the General Synod of the Reformed Church in America, 2009 (*Acts and Proceedings General Synod Reformed Church in America 250-255*).
2 Scriptural quotations in this chapter follow the New Revised Standard Version (NRSV).

The 'Belydende Kring' Declaration and the drafting of the Belhar Confession

From time to time there are controversies surrounding the question of who really wrote (or did not write) the Belhar Confession, and all sorts of conclusions are drawn from this. According to Prof. J.N.J. (Klippies) Kritzinger in his unpublished article titled 'To Stand Where God Stands: Nurturing Justice and Solidarity through Liturgy,' what has not been highlighted yet in these debates is the role of the 1979 Theological Declaration of the 'Broederkring', later renamed 'Belydende Kring' (literally 'Confessing Circle'). According to Plaatjies-Van Huffel (2014:314), the 'Broederkring van NG Kerke' was established in 1974 in Bloemfontein by about 60 ministers and evangelists from the DRCA and the DRMC. This declaration was published in 1982 in a collection of contemporary Reformed confessions entitled *Reformed Witness Today* (Vischer 1982:22). It is clear that this declaration was used by the authors of Belhar, since certain of its phrases have been incorporated almost verbatim into Belhar, particularly the words: 'As God's property the church must be busy standing where God stands, namely, against injustice and with those who are denied justice' (Vischer 1982:22). Various other phrases from the Belydende Kring Declaration have also been incorporated in Belhar, to the extent that one could almost regard it as a prototype of Belhar, even though Belhar is much longer and developed the theological ideas of the Belydende Kring Declaration in various ways. The other significant difference is that the Belydende Kring Declaration did not address reconciliation at all; it limited itself to unity and justice.

Many ministers and theologians played a role in the shaping of Belhar and its prototype, the Belydende Kring Declaration. At the Hammanskraal Belydende Kring Conference in august 1979 where the Belydende Kring Declaration was drafted, ministers from all three black Reformed churches in South Africa were present. Kritzinger (2010:209-231) highlights the role which the theological declaration of the Belydende Kring played as one of the significant documents used by the authors while formulating the Belhar Confession. Smit admits the role of Beyers Naudé, the Christian Institute, the South African Council of Churches, the broader ecumenical movement, the Belydende Kring, the ABRECSA, as well as a whole generation of theologians and church leaders, such as Daan Cloete, Chris Loff, Shun Govender, Hannes Adonis, Johan Botha, Welile Mazamisa, Takatso Mofokeng and many of their contemporaries ultimately played in the conceptualising of the confession. Smit also refers to the contributions of students and younger ministers, like Russel Botman, James Buys and Leonardo Appies (Smit 2006:293).

The confession only put into words the observation of black people about the situation in South Africa. According to Kritzinger, the first and clearest influence of the Belydende Kring Declaration on the Belhar Confession is the one found in article 4 of the Belhar Confession. For example: 'As God's property the church must be busy standing where God stands, viz. against injustice and with those who are denied justice' (Belydende Kring Declaration), versus 'We believe: that the church, belonging to God, should stand where God stands, namely against injustice and with the wronged'.[3] During the 1979 'Belydende Kring' consultation, Rev. Chris Loff, as coordinator of the drafting team of the Belydende Kring, presented a draft declaration to the plenary of the 'Belydende Kring'. The Belhar Confession is therefore not the brainchild of two or three authors of the Dutch Reformed Mission Church (DRMC). There seems to be a popular perception in the DRC that Belhar was conceptualised by Allan Boesak and is influenced by liberation theology.

During the consultation of the 'Belydende Kring', where the draft declaration was tabled, Allan Boesak questioned the phrase 'to stand where God stands' since it was, to his mind, not dynamic enough. He suggested something like 'to move where God moves,' but Dr Loff insisted that the declaration should read as proposed – and the meeting agreed with him. It is indeed with fear and trembling that we go to stand out there, outside the gate, to bear the shame of Christ where he stands among the abused little girls, the raped women, the evicted farm workers, the HIV-positive youth, the Aids orphans, the fearful and the confused. Plaatjies-Van Huffel (2014:320) notes the following: 'The Belhar Confession is a product of a communal society which was composed during the height of resistance against apartheid in South Africa.'

Belhar in the wider discourse about confessions

According to Botman, the Barmen Declaration (1934) and the Confession of Belhar (1986) have played formative roles in the making and unmaking of ecclesial and political life in Germany and South Africa (Botman 2006:240). The Belhar's theological significance does not only lie in its contextual association with apartheid (a word which is not mentioned in the text), but in its insistence that the question of ethics is also central to confession. Belhar consists of five clauses embedded in its confessional struggle against apartheid (Botman 2006:240). Throughout the history of the Christian era, churches have written confessions of faith because they were compelled to do so, not just because they thought it would be a good idea, or acceptable to the world. But they did so fully aware that the world would most probably hate and persecute them precisely because of the stand they were taking. In some instances, confessions of faith resulted from a sense of urgent

---

3   Extracts from the Confession of Belhar in this chapter are taken from the English translation at Addendum 15, The Confession of Belhar. Also available at http://urcsa.net/wp-content/uploads/2016/02/Belhar-Confession.pdf

need to correct some distortion of the truth and certain claims on the gospel that threatened the integrity of the church's faith and life within it (the church). The confession might result from some political or cultural movement outside the church that openly attacks or subtly seeks to compromise the church's commitment to the gospel. Sometimes the urgency to confess came from the church's conviction that it has a great insight into the promises and demands of the gospel that is desperately needed by both the church and the world.

Both Barmen and Belhar responded to specific, and in some ways similar, historical challenges, but both regarded these as symptoms of deeper, more fundamental theological and ecclesiological problems and temptations, that had been growing over a long period of time, and that can again in history manifest itself in perhaps different symptoms. Both confessions wanted to affirm positively, against this fundamental but hidden false understanding of gospel and church, the wonderful news of the living, Triune God (Smit 2006:293).

In the case of the Belhar Confession, all three scenarios played a crucial role in its genesis. On one hand, there was a sense of urgent need to correct some distortion of the truth and the claim of the gospel that threatened the integrity of the church's faith and life. Apartheid ideology was eroding the fundamental truth of the gospel. On the other hand, it had been defended and justified by the church that brought the gospel to South Africa. South Africans, particularly people of colour, were on the verge of forsaking and rejecting the gospel because of what was being done to them. The white churches were involved in practising heresy because of their theological justification of the system. The Confession of Belhar corrects the wrong teaching of the DRC but also to provides authentic Christian witness to the world.

The Belhar Confession: Correcting URCSA's life and conduct

The Belhar Confession offered the church new hope and understanding of their social conditions in the light of God's revelatory word. The Confession of Belhar ushered us into a new common human good that is warm, rich, and self-correcting despite the pain we had to endure. The Confession gives us a new understanding of who we are and recognises ourselves and each other in our common history, hoping, grappling with our collective pasts, struggling creatively for freedom, working, celebrating, worshipping, and welcoming all in our midst including those who benefited from our oppression, without any hint of bitterness and arrogance.

The Belhar Confession revives our old memories lest we forget them. Already in 1978, the Dutch Reformed Mission Church (DRMC) Synod declared that apartheid and the moral and theological justification of it ridiculed the gospel and was a theological heresy (*Agenda en Handelinge NGSK* 1978:2, 21). It is these memories and scars we carry in our souls that keep reminding us that we were oppressed and we should never dare to oppress others. We are constantly reminded never to adopt a stance towards the future in which we place and interpret ourselves, our desires, our choices, and our actions as the central subjects in the creation and destiny of a new united church. The confession reminds us never to use our memories to retaliate, or to ground our grudges or use them to promote our selfish agendas and subjugate the aspirations of others.

We are constantly reminded to be vigilant against any in-creeping ideology that feeds on racial prejudices. Already in the 1980s, the World Alliance of Reformed Churches (WARC) declared that the moral and theological justification of apartheid (racism) is a travesty of the gospel, and in its persistent disobedience to the word of God, a theological heresy (WARC 1983:177f., 1990:173-175, 279-281).[4] We are called by the Belhar Confession to see in others the image of the liberating God who seeks to liberate others through us. We are petitioned with the prayerful petition of the Lord's Day 49 in the Belgic Confession: 'your kingdom come, your will be done, on earth as in heaven.' The Belhar Confession reminds us that God's kingdom is founded on the conviction that the God in whom we trust is not indifferent to human history. He is immediately and imminently interested and is able, through his grace, wisdom, and power, to intervene and transform our world. He demonstrated this when the Word of God was incarnated and assumed human nature.

The Belhar Confession keeps on prompting us to ask, what sort of church are we? What sort of church must we become? It keeps reminding us to live authentically – that is, attentively, intelligently, reasonably, responsibly – under the dictates of the reign of God and to guard against falling into the distortion and deformation of other people. It calls us to be a united Uniting Reformed Church for we cannot be a uniting church without first becoming united ourselves. The Belhar Confession energises us to pray to the Lord of hosts to purge all disunity, strife and tensions that may arise among ourselves. We are a uniting church that strives for reconciliation and justice within the Reformed family of churches. It is in our discovery of our purpose that we will be a revitalised and rejuvenated uniting church. We can become a hope to those who do not have hope. We know that if the purpose for which we exist is well articulated among our members it builds morale among our members and those who rub their shoulders with us. Our purpose helps us to focus and have greater impact on what we do. This is a new fertile ground we are challenged to explore as a uniting church. En route to reunification of the DRC family in southern Africa, the Belhar Confession remains our guiding resource for co-operation,

---

4   For a more comprehensive history on the historical background of the Belhar Confession please read the following essay in this publication 'Acceptance, Adoption, Advocacy, Reception and Protestation – A Chronology of the Belhar Confession' by Mary-Anne Plaatjies-Van Huffel.

restoration, revitalisation, and reconciliation. Therefore, the Belhar Confession can never become irrelevant to our existential issues. (Addendum 11, Memorandum of Agreement between the DRC and URCSA; Addendum 12, The Roadmap to Church Reunification: DRC and URCSA; Addendum 13, Response of the URCSA with regard to the acceptance/ (non) acceptance of the Belhar Confession in the DRC)

It takes us along the path of rethinking ways of being a Christian Church by constantly taking up a place before the cross of Jesus of Nazareth. It is at the cross where we grasp the enormity of the human suffering and oppression of the poor, exploited and marginalised of our society. We are constantly reminded to confess and repent of our ethnocentricity, sexism, cultural superiority and marginalisation of others. The Belhar Confession we are cautioned never to embrace tendencies that lead to utopian or romantic schemes. We are reminded to recognise ourselves and one another in our past, our hopes, and to grapple with our collective efforts and struggle creatively for a common future which can be celebrated together. Never must we indulge in a selective interest that hides our evil intentions and presents us a picture of black or white innocence before one another. Our Christian journey remains a sterile and routine gesture unless we continually expose ourselves to the searching light of the gospel of Jesus of Nazareth, where our racism, sexism, cultural superiority, and marginalisation of others are revealed and condemned (Landman 2006:283-290).

The Belhar Confession cautions us never to be agents of any other force – including the state – despite how convinced we might be of its programmes. As Botman states, the Uniting Reformed Church in Southern Africa is merely the present trustee of this great confessional treasure which is relevant to the neo-capitalist global economy' (Botman 2006:5). We should rather grasp opportunities to cross all barriers to proclaim the gospel of Jesus of Nazareth to all the people. The Belhar Confession reminds us of the enormity of the true suffering of Jesus Christ and orientates us to commitment of emancipating ourselves to become agents of transformation. We should never entertain the temptation of distorting our experiences of the way Jesus taught us to love others as we love ourselves. We are obliged to become a uniting church that is purpose-driven according to biblical perspectives.

Conclusion

The Belhar Confession was an appropriate response within the DRC family in South Africa. It brought necessary clarification to hard and pressing theological questions of the time. The apartheid ideology and the role the white church played called for an urgent public witness. Something had to be done to correct the perceptions and refute the liars. It was in this milieu, when there was lots of confusion, that God intervened and blessed the church with a gift of a confession that will remain a guiding light forever. The confession was not their invasion but their verbalisation of what God was leading them to say. The church confessed what it confessed out of gratitude and humility, not out of arrogance, blame-portioning, condemnation, self-exaltation, holier-than-thou-attitude, or self-gratification, but out of hope for all (black and white) in the country. The starting point in our mission is: Why do we exist? What is the purpose of our life? What is God's purpose for our lives? The Belhar Confession helps us to answer these questions.

Bibliography

Primary sources

Acts and proceedings General Synod Reformed Church in America 2009.
Agenda en Handelinge Nederduits Gereformeerde Sendingkerk 1978.
World Alliance of Reformed Churces (WARC). 1983. *Proceedings of the 21st General Council of the World Alliance of Reformed Churches.* [Online] Available at http://www.warc.ch/dcw/bs25/11.html (Accessed 27 June 2015).
World Alliance of Reformed Churces (WARC). 1990. *Proceedings of the 22nd General Council of WARC in Seoul.* Geneva: WARC.
Memorandum of Agreement between the URCSA and the DRC 2012 in *Agenda of the General Synod of URCSA*, October 2012
Roadmap to church reunification. *In Agenda General Synod URCSA* 2016.

Secondary sources

Boesak, A.A. 2008. To stand where God stands: Reflections on the Confession of Belhar after 25 years. *Studia Historiae Ecclesiasticae* 34(1):143-172.
Botman, H.R. 2006. Barmen to Belhar: A contemporary confessing journey. *Nederduitse Gereformeerde Teologiese Tydskrif* 47(1/2):240-249.
Kritzinger, J.N.J. 2010. Celebrating communal authorship: The theological declaration of the Belydende Kring (1979) and the Belhar Confession. In honour of Simon Maimela and in memory of Chris Loff. *Studia Historiae Ecclesiasticae* 36(1):209-231.
Landman, C. 2006. Can justice be embodied in sexist language? A challenge to the Confession of Belhar. *Nederduitse Gereformeerde Teologiese Tydskrif* 47(1/2):283-290.
Plaatjies-Van Huffel, M-A. 2014. The Belhar Confession in its historical context. *Nederduitse Gereformeerde Teologiese Tydskrif* 55(1/2):308-309. https://doi.org/10.5952/55-1-2-527
Smit, D.J. 2006. Barmen and Belhar in conversation – a South African perspective. *Nederduitse Gereformeerde Teologiese Tydskrif* 47(1/2):291-301.
Vischer, L. (ed.) 1982. *Reformed witness today: A collection of confessions and statements of faith issued by Reformed churches.* Bern: Evangelische Arbeitstelle Oekumene Schweiz.

THE HISTORY OF BELHAR

Johannes Cornelius Adonis[1]

Abstract

This chapter tells the story of the Confession of Belhar. It traces its origin and describes the events that led up to the confession. The chapter considers the important role played by students, various church leaders, church communities and church meetings. The chapter also describes the way that the apartheid policy in South Africa constituted a *status confessionis* for the churches. The chapter chronicles the development of the concept-confession and the final acceptance of the Confession of Belhar in 1986. The story of the Confession of Belhar is placed within the context of the broader challenge of church unity and unification. The last section outlines the current status of the Confession of Belhar within the family of Dutch Reformed churches. The chapter emphasises that Belhar challenges Christians and churches to live out that which they believe and confess.

Introduction

The chapter is taken from a paper read at the Barmen/Belhar Consultation, Belhar, 18 October 2004 and an article published in the *Nederduitse Gereformeerd Teologiese Tydskrif* of March/June 2006 (Adonis 2006).

Belhar has continually challenged us to live out that which we believe and confess and, when I say 'we' I do not mean only the family of Dutch Reformed churches. If I understand the message of Belhar correctly, then I am thinking of the church in its broadest sense, as well as of our society and the world in which we live. What Christians in the church confess in the words of Belhar indeed has meaning for the world in which we live. As far as I am concerned, Barmen and Belhar have much in common with one another and both have over the years inspired many Christians.

The origins of Belhar

The origins of Belhar are in a certain sense very closely connected to the apartheid policy of the National Party (NP). Already in 1950, the former Wynberg presbytery

---

[1] Professor Johannes Adonis taught Ecclesiology and Church Law at the Faculty of Theology of both the University of the Western Cape and Stellenbosch University.

of the Dutch Reformed Mission Church in South Africa (DRMC) became directly involved with the policies of apartheid (Loff 1998:248). By then, the NP of Dr Malan had already won its political victory and implemented its apartheid policy. Already in the *Die Kerkbode* of 22 September 1948, the policy of apartheid was called a 'church policy' (Loff 1998:233).

In 1950, a certain Mr. J. Abrahamse sent a letter on behalf of 116 church members belonging to 27 congregations of the former Dutch Reformed Mission Church (DRMC) to its moderamen in which it was declared that the apartheid policy was unchristian and therefore, must be rejected and not be applied in the church nor in rest of the country. The leadership of both the Dutch Reformed Church (DRC) and DRMC did not support these members. At their 1950 Synod, the former DRMC had already decided that they would neither reject nor approve a political policy. It appears, therefore, that this decision of the DRMC Synod was not consistently followed.

Over time the former DRMC would condemn more and more aspects of the apartheid policy. In the 1970s, the church was requested to evaluate it theologically. This request came from the Theological School of the DRMC, which at that time was already a faculty of the University of the Western Cape (UWC). Prof. J.J.F. Durand and the theology students played an important role in this theological evaluation of the apartheid. The students concluded that the forced separation of people contradicted the gospel of reconciliation and expressed the wish that the DRMC should officially endorse this position (Loff 1998:251). Three ministers, reverends J.J.F. Mettler, I.J. Mentor and R.J. Stevens, presented this position to the DRMC Synod. The central aspect of this position was that the apartheid policy of the government was contradictory to the gospel of Jesus Christ and should, therefore, be rejected (Loff 1998:252). The synod discussed this position and after several amendments it was accepted. This decision was an important milestone for the synod. At the same time, the mission policy of the DRC was also rejected. With its rejection of the policy of apartheid, the DRMC made a very clear decision in favour of the (re-)unification of the family of DR churches. The decision that the policy of apartheid is contrary to the gospel also strengthened the desire for structural church unification (Loff 1998:253).

The *status confessionis*

In 1982, the World Alliance of Reformed Churches (WARC) held its General Assembly in Ottawa, Canada. The member churches of the family of DR churches were all members of the World Alliance. At the meeting, Dr Allan Boesak of the DRMC was chosen as president of the WARC (Loff 1998:261). The WARC discussed the political situation in South Africa and concluded that '[t]he promises of God for this world and for his church are in direct contradiction to apartheid ideals and practices'

(Loff 1998:261). This statement is in fact a restatement of the 1978 declaration by the DRMC that 'the apartheid policy is in contradiction to the gospel'. The WARC went further and stated that the churches who accepted and defended apartheid 'contradict in doctrine and in action the promise which they profess to believe' (Loff 1998:261). The two member churches that were guilty of this charge were the DRC and the Nederduitse Hervormde Kerk (Dutch Reformed Church in Africa). The World Alliance concluded 'that this situation constitutes a *status confessionis* for our churches, which means that we regard this as an issue on which it is not possible to differ without seriously jeopardizing the integrity of our common confession as Reformed churches' (Loff 1998:151).

The WARC also declared that the political policy of apartheid was considered a sin and that its moral and theological justification was 'a travesty of the gospel, and its persistent disobedience to the Word of God, a theological heresy' (Loff 1998:261). The result of all of this was that the World Alliance acted against the two offending South African churches by deciding to suspend their membership of the organisation until they distanced themselves from the ideology and policy of apartheid.

The action by the WARC against the two Reformed churches came before the DRMC Synod in 1982 via its Commission for Ecumenical Matters (*Acta NGSK* 1982). On Friday 1 October 1982, the synod discussed this crucial matter at length. That the synod spent the whole Friday and the morning session of the Saturday (2 October) discussing the report was an indication of its significance for the synod (Loff 1998:262). The synod first had to decide on the following proposal: 'because the secular gospel of Apartheid profoundly endangers the confession of reconciliation in Jesus Christ and the unity of the Church of Jesus Christ in its very essence, the DR Mission Church declares that it presents a *status confessionis* for the Church of Jesus Christ' (Loff 1998:262). The synod accepted this proposal. However, there were 29 ministers and 12 elders who gave notice that they did not support this decision. The second proposal that the synod had to consider read as follows: 'We declare that apartheid [separate development] is a sin, that its moral and theological justification makes a travesty of the gospel and that its continued disobedience to the Word of God is a theological heresy' (Loff 1998:262). The synod also accepted this second proposal.

The implications of the *status confessionis*

When the synod finally brought the entire proposal of the Commission for Ecumenical Matters to the vote it was accepted by the majority. The question that now arose was: What were the implications of this *status confessionis* for the church? Prof. Gustav Bam, professor in practical theology at UWC, then delivered an important address. In it he particularly emphasised the implications of the announcement of the *status confessionis* for the church and said: 'The faith is clearly confessed and the false teaching that is in contradiction with this is clearly rejected' (Loff 1998:162). Following this, he requested the synod, in light of the preceding events, to name an ad hoc committee who would write a confession to present to the synod for its approval (Loff 1998:263, fn. 163). However, 51 members of the synod pointed out that they had voted against the declaration of a *status confessionis* (Loff 1998:263). After this, two ministers, Revs Jaco Coetzee and A.B. Van Wyk, proposed that the synod constitute an ad hoc commission to prepare a confession following the *status confessionis* against apartheid and to present it to this same synod (Loff 1998:264, fn. 165). This proposal was accepted without opposition and the moderator appointed the ad hoc commission consisting of Rev. I.J. Mentor (moderator), Dr A.A. Boesak (assessor), Dr D.J. Smit, Dr J.J.F. Durand and Dr G. Bam (chairperson). The synod was also requested to respond to a report by the Commission for Ecumenical Matters on the following matter:

> It is the conviction of the Synod that the Dutch Reformed Church believes in the gospel of apartheid, which is in direct contradiction to the Gospel message of reconciliation and the visible unity of the church. For this reason, the Mission Church brings the decision of 1978 on that it cannot but with the greatest regret accuse the DR Church of theological heresy and idolatry, given her theologically formulated position and the implementation thereof in practice. The DR Mission Church makes this call in deep humility and introspection so that we not, 'while preaching for others, be rejectable ourselves' (1 Cor. 9:27). (Loff 1998:264, fn. 168)

This proposal was somewhat amended and was approved by the synod. Eighty-five members voted against the inclusion of the word 'idolatry' in the proposal (Loff 1998:264 fn. 170). The synod then made it clear that despite its decisions against the DR Church, it wished to retain its ties with the DRC. It was furthermore decided that the decision on the *status confessionis* and the 1978 decisions on apartheid would be presented to the General Synod of the DRC (Loff 1998:fn. 171). This was to be handed 'personally' to the General Synod that would meet later that year. The intention for taking this course of action was to persuade the DRC and to give it the opportunity to distance itself from the apartheid policy. The DRMC Synod also expressed its appreciation to those members within the DRC who delivered a prophetic witness with regard to apartheid and church unity (Loff 1998:265, fn. 173). Finally, the synod expressed its gratitude and great appreciation for the work of the Temporary Commission for Ecumenical Matters for their work in this regard (Loff 1998:fn. 174).

The draft confession of Belhar

The commission that had the task of drawing up a confession promptly reported to the synod. The synod had suggested a procedure that would assign the status of confession to the draft confession (Loff 1998:265, fn. 175). It was also decided that lesser church bodies would also be given the opportunity to evaluate the confession. After this preceding process was completed, the synod accepted the draft confession. The draft confession was also sent to the congregations and presbyteries of the church so that these lesser bodies could also express their opinion on the matter. Dr Loff mentions in his outstanding study that by 26 November 1985, only 161 of the 267 congregations had not yet reported back. Of the 32 presbyteries, only 11 did not respond (Loff 1998:265). During the 1986 Synod, it was clear that since 1982 there had been no objections against or amendments suggested to the proposed confession, except an objection against the formulation in paragraph 4 of the draft confession, namely that God is 'in a special way the God of the destitute, the poor and the wronged' (Loff 1998:266, fn. 183).

During the DRMC Synod on 26 September 1986, the moment arrived when the new confession would be accepted. These events took place amid great public interest. The report on the draft confession was discussed. Professors Bam and Smit strongly argued for the approval of the confession. It was a remarkable moment when 400 delegates gave their approval of the confession while 71 gave note that they could not accept it (Loff 1998:fn. 185). Thus, the Confession of Belhar was accepted with great joy and gratitude by the majority of delegates. One day after its acceptance great interest was taken in the fact that various delegates, who originally opposed the confession, afterwards did sign it. After this, the synod took numerous decisions to help people in the practical implementation of the Confession of Belhar. Pastoral measures were undertaken to provide for the needs of ministers who had originally not seen their way open to sign the confession. This also applied to lesser church bodies that still had objections against specific aspects of the confession. The synod continually emphasised that the motive of unity in the confession ought to receive priority. This idea became an important objective in the period that followed.

The unity of the church and church unification

It is interesting to note that church unification within the family of DR churches was already discussed at a much earlier stage. However, it is also true that not everyone within the family of DR churches felt the same about the matter. In 1978, the former DRMC had already decided to structurally unite with other churches in the family. In 1986, the DRMC took note that very little progress had been made on this important matter. The discussion on unity with the DRC mostly dealt with the declaration of the *status confessionis* and the acceptance of the draft confession by the former DRMC in 1982 (*Acta NGSK* 1986:15-19; Loff 1998:268).

After the acceptance of the Confession of Belhar, the DRMC once again continued the discussions about church unification with the other members of the family of DR churches. The Reformed Church in Africa and the DRC were for various reasons, not very optimistic about this. However, the DR Church in Africa (DRCA) did indicate its willingness to begin discussions on unification with the DRMC. Thus, it happened that these two churches formed a discussion commission that negotiated this important matter from 9 September 1987. The DRC and the Reformed Church in Africa were continually and openly invited to these discussions. However, the RCA never responded to the invitations and the type of discussions between the DRC and the DRMC did not produce the hoped-for results – even after the intervention of the Reformed Ecumenical Synod in March 1989. The discussions on church unification between the DRCA and the DRMC were more successful. In 1990, the DRCA and the DRMC held a convent in Belhar (Cape Town) that would eventually result in church unification between the two churches in 1994. The original aim was for the two churches unite in 1990, however, this could not take place yet since the DRCA had not yet accepted the Confession of Belhar. The alternative was that the DRMC give up the Confession, which did not happen as the DRCA finally accepted the Belhar Confession.

> The church unification that was to take place in 1990 was finally celebrated with great joy and excitement on 14 April 1994. This important event took place in the same church building where the Confession of Belhar was officially accepted in 1986. At the DRMC Synod of 1994 a 'unification clause' was drawn up to ensure that the unification process would take place well and justly. There were about 45 ministers in the former DRMC who gave the impression that they were a 'pressure group against church unification' (Loff 1998:273). The Synod of the DRMC appointed an 'ad hoc commission for pastoral discussions' to openly assist persons in congregations in their 'problems, fears, doubts and uncertainties' regarding the issue. This commission also proposed that such members be treated as members of the DRMC and after unification as members of the URCSA. In Bloemfontein in 1997, the Evangelical Reformed Church in Africa (ERCA) joined the URCSA. The ERCA was a Reformed church established in Namibia by the DRC in 1975. (*Acta VGKSA* 1997:427-428)

What is the position of the Confession of Belhar within the family of DR churches?

The DRMC and the DRCA accepted the Confession of Belhar as their confession in 1994 when they united to form the URCSA. No other Reformed church in this family has done the same. With the formation of the URCSA in 1994, part of the DRCA (Free State and Phororo synods) did not see their way open to accept the confession. The General Synod of the DRC in 1998 accepted, as it stated in *Die Kerkbode* of 8 October 2004, the essential content (*'wesenlike inhoud'*) of the Confession of Belhar for the sake of the unification process, but wished to 'not at the moment recommend it as a fourth confession'.

The General Synod of the DRC in 2002 stated that provision must be made for the acceptance of the Confession of Belhar as confession for the new church, but in such a way that it serves the unification process in a positive way. This last phrase wanted to ensure that the confession not be enforced on its members. Even if accepted as confession, no church member or congregation must be forced to sign it.

The decision of the General Synod of the DRC in 2004 with regards to church unity reads as follows:

> The DRC reaffirms its serious and clear commitment to the restoration of one church denomination with the other three churches in the DRC family, namely the URC, RCA and DRCA. The DRC decides that:
> - The Confession of Belhar be included in a restored church denomination.
> - The decision be left to members, church councils and ministers to decide whether they want to accept the Confession of Belhar.
> - We are convinced that the differences on the Confession of Belhar have to do with historical, emotional and symbolic factors.

The synod proposed that the following will occur:
- A process of consultation with regional synods and church councils be started to talk about the unification process.
- The process of consultation must be finalised by January 2006.
- The result of the process of consultation be processed by a task team and used in the discussion with the DR Church family (General Synod of the DRC, Information brochure, October 2004).

Conclusion

Since the 1970s, the synods of the former DRMC continually discussed the policy of apartheid or aspects thereof. Originally the DRMC only condemned aspects of the policy that it saw as contrary to Scripture. In 1982, the DRMC again came to the conclusion that the theological justification of apartheid is contrary to the gospel and formulated the Confession of Belhar in reaction to it. On the basis of this new confession, the DRCM entered into discussions with the DRCA and the ERCA aimed at the unification of the three churches. While the latter discussions were successful, similar discussions with other members of the same church family continues till today and its success is eagerly hoped for and greatly anticipated.

Bibliography

Primary sources

Agenda en Handelinge Nederduits Gereformeerde Sendingkerk 1986 (Belhar).
Die Kerkbode. 2004. Editorial, 8 October.
General Synod of the DRC, 2004. General Synod of the DR, Information brochure, October 2004.
Skema van werksaamhede en Handelinge, Tweede Algemene Sinode van die Verenigende Gereformeerde Kerk in Suider-Afrika 1997 (Bloemfontein).

Secondary sources

Adonis, J.C. 2006. The history of Belhar. *Nederduitse Gereformeerde Teologiese Tydskrif* 7(1/2):234-239.
Loff, C.J.A. 1998. Bevryding tot eenwording. Die Nederduitse Gereformeerde Sendingkerk in Suid-Afrika 1881–1994. PhD thesis, Theologische Universiteit Kampen, Kampen.

CAN JUSTICE BE EMBODIED IN SEXIST LANGUAGE?

A challenge to the Confession of Belhar

Christina Landman[1]

Abstract

This chapter is taken from an article published in the *Nederduitse Gereformeerd Teologiese Tydskrif* (Landman 2006). It poses the question of why the Confession of Belhar was not written in inclusive language, since it was accepted at the 1986 Synod of the Dutch Reformed Mission Church (DRMC), which is after the 1982 Synod where women were restored to the office of minister. It argues that the concept of justice is presented at an advanced level in the Confession of Belhar; however, it is regrettable that, in this confession, justice is embodied in sexist language. The article suggests certain changes in the language of the Confession of Belhar in order to include women. Furthermore, it explores possible ways in which a confession with healthy insights into justice, such as the Confession of Belhar, can enhance the political and social wellbeing of women by reflecting the interconnectedness of people in its use of inclusive language.

Introduction

The Confession of Belhar was formally accepted in 1986 by the DRMC (at the time) as an authority of faith. The political events leading to the formulation and acceptance of this confession are well known. The Confession of Belhar is one of several documents of faith which were formulated when ecclesiastical voices of protest burst into the open after the Sharpeville massacre and Cottesloe Church Conference of the 1960s (Jonker 1993:443). The Confession of Belhar confessed its

---

1 Prof. Christina Landman a National Research Foundation (NRF) C2-rated researcher in history/religion. She was the first South African-born woman to become a professor of theology at a South African university and has been a lecturer and researcher at Unisa for the past 35 years. Prof. Landman is the editor of *Studia Historiae Ecclesiasticae* (an accredited journal) and the *Oral History Journal of South Africa*. She is a member of the Executive of the Oral History Society of South Africa and the Church History Society of Southern Africa. She has published extensively in the fields of oral history and gender studies. She also serves on the Advisory Board of the National Orders that advises President Zuma on the awarding of National Orders.

belief in justice as opposed to the practice of apartheid which was theologically supported by the white Dutch Reformed Church (DRC).

The Confession of Belhar remained loyal to the ecumenical movement confessing opposition to apartheid, which started in the 1960s. However, one may ask whether it stayed loyal to the liberation of women – a 'movement' started by the DRMC itself in 1982. In that year, the DRMC was the first of the Dutch Reformed family of churches in South Africa to restore women to the office of minister. What had begun at the 1982 Synod does not seem to have been upheld by the next synod in 1986 when the Confession of Belhar, couched in sexist language, was accepted.

Since 1982, almost a quarter of a century ago, only four women have been ordained as ministers in the Uniting Reformed Church in South Africa (URCSA), as the DRMC is now known after its amalgamation with the Dutch Reformed Church in Africa (DRCA). In fact, for ten years after the synod's decision on women's ordination, no woman was ordained at all. It was only in 1992 that Mary-Anne Plaatjies was ordained as minister in Robertson in the Cape Province (Landman 1998:126).

It seems that the church was not ready for the ordination of women in 1982 when one considers that, in 1986, a confession was formally accepted in the same church, which is formulated in language insensitive towards and exclusive of women. One cannot argue that inclusive language was unknown to the ecclesiastical sodality at that time. In Europe and the USA, the issue of language was at the height of both academic and ecclesiastical discussion. A revised edition of an inclusive language lectionary, which was prepared by the National Council of the Churches of Christ in the USA, had already been published in 1986 (National Council of the Churches of Christ in the United States of America 1986).

John de Gruchy (1991:174) affirms that the Confession of Belhar is now to be accepted by all who are ordained in the URCSA, giving rise to the ironical situation that, at ordination, women candidates have to confess their faith in justice and equality in sexist language.

If the church was not ready to ordain women in practice in 1982, and to confess its faith in inclusive language in 1986, we are constrained to ask whether the church is ready now, and of what benefit the use of inclusive language will be to the spiritual wellbeing of women in the church.

This chapter argues that the Confession of Belhar is advanced in its vision of justice. It puts forward the ensuing argument that, to be true to its own insight into justice, the Confession of Belhar should embody justice in language which does justice to justice – that is, an inclusive language which embodies the interconnectedness between people.

The call for a just language has been at the core of women's theologies for a long time. This chapter starts by dealing with women's call for justice and for the embodiment of justice in a language of interconnectedness. The chapter then considers the embodiment of justice in the Confession of Belhar. Next, the chapter gives some suggestions to promote inclusivity and interconnectedness and discusses practical implications of an inclusive confession.

The embodiment of justice in women's theologies

With the commencement of the modern feminist movement in the 1970s, the aims of women's liberation were set out clearly. According to the branch of feminism which concerns us here, theological feminism, justice will be done to women when

- the stereotyping of women has been shifted, and women have been empowered against their identities of failure (social justice);
- women's political powerlessness has been overturned and women have been empowered as moral agents (political justice); and
- women's exploitation as workers has been converted into equal job opportunities (economic justice), and women have access to the symbols, the language and the confessions of the church (spiritual justice) (see Meyer-Wilmes 1995:165-166).

The embodiment of justice has been an insight of theological feminism since the commencement of its justice talk. 'Embodiment' is used with two references in theological feminism:

- Women's physical bodies are the sites where justice is to be practised, that is, embodied. We experience [in]justice with our bodies when we are raped and assaulted, or treated with respect and care (Gilson 1996:82). Justice is also embodied in language, which constitutes our experiences.
- Language not only shows us how we are perceived; language not only enables us to hear each other speak; language not only breaks the silence (Isherwood & McEwan 2001:118). Language indeed creates us. Language makes us what we are. Language embodies us. Language is the flesh made word.

With the power of language thus established, the importance of a language of interconnectedness for expressions of faith, such as a confession, becomes apparent. Women need a religious language that not only reflects our process of becoming (Isherwood & McEwan 2001:118), but embodies a new way of life for women of faith.

In short, we need a language that embodies the justice towards women, which is still sorely lacking in the ecclesiastical arena.

The embodiment of justice in the Confession of Belhar

This section starts by considering some secondary sources dealing with the embodiment of justice in the confession.

Secondary sources

Much has been written about the way in which the Confession of Belhar deals with justice, albeit lacking focus on justice towards women. The Confession of Belhar favours an image of God that honours God as the God of justice. Russel Botman sees in this an explicit call on the church to discipleship: 'God is revealed in a special way as the God of justice ... and God calls the church to stand where God is standing' (Botman 2000:210). That, for Botman, is praxeology, which in Belhar has received confessional status within the church.

For Willie Jonker (with reference to Dirkie Smit) (1993:452,) the Belhar image of the just God not only calls the church, but the whole of society, to duty. During a time when almost no distinction was made between church and state, Jonker (and Smit) confessed in sympathy with the Confession of Belhar that political and social life should be critically tested against the biblical and Belhar presentation of God as just, and God's world as one called to justice.

De Gruchy (1991:174) views this call to justice as a call for unity. The church is to unite in its commitment to the struggle against all forms of social injustice. As such, then, Belhar is an invitation to the white DRC to join in this confession of justice, commitment and unity.

Meyer (2000:117) investigates the claims of the previously mentioned authors that Belhar's image of God as a God of justice is a biblical image. Through an exciting reading of Luke, Meyer explores the dialogical spaces between the awesome God and the merciful God, and finds the biblical God of justice to be the One in whom resistance against social injustice blends with compassion. In this lies the example for the church to follow.

Finally, Koos Vorster expresses his concern about the image of God as the God who sides with the destitute and the poor. According to Vorster, this image of God is not in accordance with the Reformed confessional tradition, nor is it in line with the Bible. In the Bible, Vorster finds God to be the God of all, the God who has chosen Abraham as the father of all the faithful, Abraham being a rich and affluent person (Vorster 1998:478).

Is the God of justice 'in a special way the God of the destitute, the poor and the wronged' as confessed in Belhar? And what should be the church's response to this? These are the questions posed by the commentators on Belhar as explained in the above paragraphs. I consider these questions in the following subsection by referring back to the text of the Confession of Belhar.

The Belhar text as a primary source

It is my conviction that Belhar's confession of justice is much broader than just the image of God as a God of justice, and a call on the church to commit itself to opposing injustice. I shall briefly explore two concepts of justice in Belhar, which I find to be specifically relevant to the issue of justice towards women.

Moral agency

Belhar confesses moral agency. Moral agency entails more than commitment to resisting injustice. Moral agency includes initiating, planning and executing moral action in an unjust society and a divided church. Article 4 of the confession, which is replete with verbs, describes moral agency in biblical terms. Moral agency is bringing justice, giving bread, setting free, supporting, protecting, helping, blocking.

However, since Belhar describes these powerful acts of justice in sexist language, one may indeed wonder whether women are included here as moral agents for justice, or whether they are simply seen as the victims of injustice. The very first sentence of Article 4 raises this concern: 'We believe that God has revealed Godself as the One who wishes to bring about justice and true peace on earth'. The only reference in Article 4 to women is to the widows, who are destitute because they do not have men to care for them. The danger of sexist language, then, becomes apparent. The use of sexist language here robs women of their status and potency as moral agents in the church and in society.

Shifting of dualisms

Belhar, furthermore, confesses the shifting of dualisms. In confessing unity, Article 2 of Belhar explores the dialogical spaces between love and hate, friendship and enmity, my faith and your faith, my Spirit and your Spirit, my Lord and your Lord, my hope and your hope, my prayer and your prayer, my race and your race. However, when again this unity is described in sexist terms, one needs to ask whether Belhar is not still upholding the dualism between male and female, that is, the hierarchy between men and women. Belhar confesses that we are one because we 'have one God and Father', yet the urgent question arises as to whether the unity shared by men and women can be on an equal basis when it is presided over by the maleness of God. When the reconciliation between believers and God is taken as the basis for unity, but God is described as a man ('Father') and in male terms, one cannot help but suspect that, here, women are not confessed to be believers in equal terms. So, in this instance too, the use of sexist language deprives women of their equal status as believers, and hijacks the just God to belong to a specific gender.

In short, while Belhar does justice to the concept of justice, its language does not. While Belhar confesses moral agency and unity of belief, sexist language itself undermines these concepts of justice, and ultimately diminishes women's role as moral agents and equal believers in church and society.

Suggestions promoting inclusivity and interconnectedness

To include women as moral agents and deconstruct the hierarchy of men over women based on the image of God as male, the Confession of Belhar, then, needs to strengthen itself through empowering language which embodies women's experiences. Since the concepts of justice in Belhar are strong and healthy, only a few changes in language are necessary to achieve the aim of inclusivity.

References to believers should be inclusive. In the English text only one case of exclusivity appears, that is in Article 4, which confesses that God wishes to bring peace 'among men'. [2] In the Afrikaans text reference is here made to *'mense'* (people), the usage of which may solve the problem in the English.

References to the maleness of God should be excluded. Pronouns which make God male can be replaced by the repetition of 'God'. Although this may appear clumsy at first sight, it reflects a sound theology of interconnectedness. The first part of Article 4, then, may read as follows:

> We believe that God has revealed Godself as the One who wishes to bring about justice and true peace among people; that in a world full of injustice and enmity God is in a special way the God of the destitute, the poor and the wronged and that God calls God's Church to follow God in this.

It will be much more difficult to change the male images which refer to God in the Confession of Belhar. At the beginning and at the end of this confession, God is referred to as 'Father, Son and Holy Spirit'. Since women theologians argue that male images of God support an unhealthy hierarchy of men over women, the confession

---

2   The Synod of the former Dutch Reformed Mission Church (DRMC) adopted the draft Confession of Belhar in 1982 with an accompanying letter drafted in Afrikaans. Earlier English versions of the Belhar Confession utilised patriarchal language. The 2008 General Synod of the Uniting Reformed Church in Southern Africa (URCSA) adopted a gender-neutral English translation (see Addendum 15).

obviously needs to change this image to one of inclusivity and interconnectedness. Mary Grey (2001:9) points out that more than 30 years have elapsed since Mary Daly in 1973 wrote *Beyond God the Father*. Since then women have struggled to include female imagery to describe the divine and, as far as Belhar is concerned, with little success. Grey (2001:53) is convinced that we cannot talk about God as a God of justice while describing God as a patriarchal lord and judge. As power-in-relation, God empowers us to make justice; as power-in-relation, God empowers us with sensitivity, compassion, empathy, affiliation and bonding.

As far as Belhar is concerned, I would suggest that, in Article 1 of the confession, God be confessed not as 'Father, Son' but as 'Caretaker, Saviour', since that is exactly how God is described and confessed in the rest of the sentence. Article 1 will then read:

> We believe in the triune God, Caretaker, Saviour and Holy Spirit, who gathers, protects and cares for God's Church by God's Word and God's Spirit, as God has done since the beginning of the world and will do to the end.

The confession will then also end by confessing our belief in God as 'Caretaker and Saviour'. The Afrikaans text, I suppose, may use the designations '*Versorger*' and '*Verlosser*'. Again, it needs to be said that these are images that are not foreign to either the Reformed faith, or to the confession itself, which expressed its belief in God's care of the world and God's saving activity throughout.

Practical implications of an inclusive confession

One can indeed ask whether, in practice, women in the church will benefit from an inclusive language of interconnectedness. Is language that important, and is it important at grassroots level, or is inclusive language simply academics at play? Throughout this chapter, a social constructionist point of view has been maintained; a view that language constitutes people. Social construction theory believes that people's thinking and doing are controlled by social discourses. Discourses are grand narratives constructed as knowledge and truth by the powerful in society. Social construction theory, furthermore, believes that social construction itself takes place through language (Landman 2005:32). If language, then, is the instrument through which women have been socially constructed in the church, the issue of sexist language is indeed an important one. Sexist language constructs passive women who are powerless in the face of social injustices such as domestic violence, rape and the spreading of the HI-virus.

At the beginning and ending of their book, *Introducing Feminist Theology*, Lisa Isherwood and Dorothea McEwan (2001:9, 151) describe the achievements of women theologians worldwide during the past 30 years. Using their insights, I shall now ask, in the next six points, whether women of faith in South Africa have made similar gains in the face of the historical injustices committed against them. Proposals will be made on how the Confession of Belhar can empower South African women of faith through its concepts of justice when women are constituted through an inclusive language of interconnectedness.

1. Women's theologies worldwide empower women to become part of practical solutions to the ethical problem of injustice (Isherwood & McEwan 2001:9). Of course, to do this, women need a political voice from within the church. In South Africa, the political voice of women of faith is indeed soft, if not silent. In awarding a political role to the church, the Confession of Belhar can empower women of faith to voice themselves in favour of justice in dialogue between church and state.

2. Women's theologies worldwide empower women to 'connect individual to societal demands', thus placing the private sphere on the agenda of the combatting of injustice (Isherwood & McEwan 2001:9). While South African women do hold important positions in (secular) politics, women locally do not hold positions of equality in the private sphere of their intimate relationships, where domestic violence and the HIV infection reign. However, the Confession of Belhar confesses to the church's obligation to combat injustice in private spheres, and is therefore excellently placed to empower women of faith in this regard.

3. Women's theologies worldwide empower women and men 'to form relationships built on mutuality' (Isherwood & McEwan 2001:9) thereby making justice a relational issue in the workplace, friendships, intimacy and church. Having been moulded by patriarchal stereotyping, women of faith have had little opportunity till now to give themselves new names. By using inclusive language, the Confession of Belhar can assist in this by means of its insistence on people being equal before God. Belhar insists that people should be freed of human stereotyping in terms of race. Gender needs to be added to this insight.

4. Women's theologies worldwide 'empower women and men to grow into a mutual relationship with the divine' (Isherwood & McEwan 2001:9). Everybody is thus acknowledged as a moral agent for justice. In South Africa, women are finding their voice and expanding their roles as moral agents, vis-a-vis rape and domestic violence. The Confession of Belhar can enhance these roles by describing women's needs with more insights than only those that of 'widows'.

5. Women's theologies worldwide empower women to develop hermeneutical principles to read the Bible from a justice point of view (Isherwood & McEwan 2001:151). In South Africa, this has been set in action by women theologians such

as Madipoane Masenya, and the women theologians who participated locally in the *Leefstyl-Bybel vir Vroue* (Lifestyle Bible for Women) (Landman 2003). The Confession of Belhar uses the Bible as an inter-text in its cry for justice and, as such, can empower women to do the same for the sake of women's liberation.

6. If the Confession of Belhar were to include women through inclusive language and symbols, and embodied women's experiences in confessional language, empowered women of faith might engage in the following (see Isherwood & McEwan 2001:151):
    - Belhar, hopefully, will encourage women to rewrite their own histories as histories of moral agency and the distribution of justice in society.
    - Belhar will energise women to join other women in their justified struggle for ordination.
    - Belhar will encourage inclusive liturgies and spiritualities.
    - Belhar will encourage women to become engaged in eco-theology and the fight for a mutual relationship between people and nature. On the agenda to be challenged are nuclear warfare, globalisation and sex tourism.
    - Belhar will help women of faith towards positive embodiment, that is, to come to a sense of the goodness of the body. South African women have been stylised by pietistic discourses on the sinfulness of the body, and especially the female body, which kept them from enjoying and celebrating their bodies as women of faith.

Conclusion

In 1984, at a conference held at the University of Washington in Seattle to celebrate half a century after the Barmen Confession was issued against the injustices of the Nazi regime in Germany, the German woman theologian, Dorothee Sölle, read a paper entitled 'Justice is the true name of peace, and resistance is the true name of faith' (Sölle 1986:303-334). In this paper, she criticised neo-conservative readings of the Barmen Declaration, readings which propagate the complete separation of church and state. No, says Sölle, the church must remain radically, and with great resistance, involved in politics. The church should resist things like nuclear politics, and the way in which society blames everything from inflation to job losses to the disintegration of the 'traditional family'.

Sölle here identifies two tendencies in modern-day Germany, which are also prevalent in the South Africa of today, and which concern women and the formation of a confession of faith. The first is the separation between church and state, which in South Africa effectively means that the church may not intervene in state affairs, but that the state can regulate belief. This is foreign to the cultures of the South

African people, both black and white, who prefer an integrated worldview. It also robs women of faith of their political voice.

In the second place, Sölle refers to the backlash against empowered women, blaming them not only for the disintegration of the traditional family, but also for all societal evils as if the latter can be traced back to this disintegration. In South Africa, too, a return to the traditional family is propagated from ecclesiastical platforms. This type of talk is strengthened by the HIV epidemic, which is blamed on the lack of traditional values in society today – including women's liberation. However, local women theologians like myself blame HIV, partly at least, on the patriarchal family itself and on male power in general, which forces women to have unsafe sex. These women theologians do think that the values of the family should be upheld but that, in families, men and women should have mutual power. Research has shown that families are the happiest, and healthiest, when power is shared. It is not the family which should be undermined, but the patriarchal family. It is not the values of loyalty and faithfulness which should be resisted, but the patriarchal values of unequal power.

The Confession of Belhar already confesses the political voice of the church. What still needs to be done is to include women of faith in both the church's own politics and its political call for justice and to embody this commitment in the inclusive language of interconnectedness.

Bibliography

Belhar Confession, 1986. The official English translation of the *Belhar Confession 1986* approved by the General Synod of 2008. Belhar:LUS Printers.
Botman, R. 2000. Discipleship and practical theology: The case of South Africa. *International Journal of Practical Theology* 4:201-212. https://doi.org/10.1515/ijpt.2000.4.2.201
de Gruchy, J.W. 1991. The church always reforming. *The Princeton Seminary Bulletin* 12(2):154-185.
Gilson, A.B. 1996. Embodiment. In L Russell & J.S. Clarkson (eds), *Dictionary of feminist theologies*. Louisville, KY: Westminster John Knox Press.
Grey, M. 2001. *Introducing feminist images of God*. Sheffield: Sheffield Academic Press.
Isherwood, L & McEwan, D. 2001. *Introducing feminist theology* (2nd edition). Sheffield: Sheffield Academic Press.
Jonker, W.D. 1993. Die moderne belydenisbeweging in Suid-Afrika – en Calvyn. *In die Skriflig* 27(4):443-461. https://doi.org/10.4102/ids.v27i4.1472
Landman, C. 1998. Gereformeerde vroue – verenig en hervorm? In W.A. Boesak & P.J.A. Fourie, *Vraagtekens oor Gereformeerdheid*. Belhar: LUS Printers.
Landman, C. 2003. *Leefstyl-Bybel vir vroue*. Cape Town: Lux Verbi-BM.
Landman, C. 2005. Religion as a healing discourse. Pastoral counselling in a township setting. Uncompleted DTh dissertation, University of South Africa, Pretoria.

Landman, C. 2006. Can justice be embodied in sexist language? A challenge to the Confession of Belhar. *Nederduitse Gereformeerde Teologiese Tydskrif* 47(1/2):283-290.

Meyer, E.E. 2000. Interpreting Luke with the Confession of Belhar. *Scriptura* 72:113-120.

Meyer-Wilmes, H. 1995. *Rebellion on the borders (Rebellion auf der Grenze)*. Kampen, Nethjerlands: Kok Pharos.

National Council of the Churches of Christ in the United States of America. (1986). *An Inclusive-language lectionary*. Atlanta, GA: Published for the Cooperative Publication Association by John Knox Press.

Sölle, D. 1986. Justice is the true name of peace, and resistance is the true name of faith. In H.G. Locke (ed.), *The Barmen Confession: Papers from The Seattle Assembly*. Lewiston, NY: The Edwin Mellen Press.

Vorster, J.M. 1998. Die belydenis van Belhar in dogma-historiese perspektief. *In die Skriflig* 32(4):469-485. https://doi.org/10.4102/ids.v32i4.1658

BARMEN TO BELHAR

A contemporary confessing journey

Hayman Russel Botman[1]

Abstract

This chapter is taken from an article published in the *Nederduitse Gereformeerde Teologiese Tydskrif* (Botman 2006). The Barmen Declaration (1934) and the Confession of Belhar (1986) played formative roles in the making and unmaking of ecclesial and political life in Germany and South Africa. Their continuing relevance as contemporary confessions has been seen in the many studies conducted on them internationally and in the fact that churches in other countries have decided to include them in their confessional heritage. This chapter pays tribute to these two landmark confessions. I start with a narrative of the emergence of the idea that apartheid is a heresy. This is followed by a discussion of the relationship between Barmen and Belhar. Thereafter, I turn to the question of why the white Dutch Reformed Church (DRC) cannot yet accept the Confession of Belhar. In conclusion, I share some views on the future relevance of the Confession of Belhar.

The narrative of Belhar's emergence

As a student of Professor Jaap Durand in 1978, I was challenged, together with the rest of the class, to come to a theological evaluation of the problem of apartheid. He refused to accept our usual legal ('apartheid is a crime against humanity'), political ('apartheid is undemocratic') and economic ('apartheid is an exploitation of human and natural resources') condemnations of apartheid. Together we revisited Karl Barth's theology. Eventually our class arrived at the idea that apartheid takes its point of departure in the irreconcilability of people. That represented the theological centre of the problem of apartheid.

---

[1] Prof. Hayman Russel Botman was first appointed in 2007, and reappointed for a second term in 2011 as, rector and vice-chancellor of Stellenbosch University (SU), he was a director and executive committee member of Higher Education South Africa (Hesa), and served as Chair of the Higher Education Quality Committee's audit of the University of the Witwatersrand. At continental level, he was vice-president of the Association for African Universities (AAU), as well as a member of the international board of trustees of the African Institute for Mathematical Sciences (Aims).

This theological discovery was communicated to the Dutch Reformed Mission Church (DRMC) Synod in October of that year. Synod then adopted the notion and opened the way for further reflection in local congregations. The most important consequence of this theological discovery was the declaration of a *status confessionis*[2] on the theological justification of apartheid by the World Alliance of Reformed Churches (WARC) in Ottawa in 1982 and by the DRMC synod, meeting in Belhar that year. The Confession of Belhar was drafted in 1982 and, after ratification by most of the congregations, formally adopted by the DRMC Synod in 1986.

The Uniting Reformed Church in Southern Africa (URCSA),[3] which emerged from the struggle against the heresy of apartheid made a renewed commitment to the Confession of Belhar.[4] Before unification on 14 April 1994, two very important discussions took place: first, by which name shall the church be known, and second, on which confessional basis should it be established? After lengthy debate, it was decided to dispose of the word 'Dutch' in the name of the church, thereby giving more prominence to the post-colonial African identity of the church. The URCSA then went further in adopting the Confession of Belhar as of the same status as the Belgic Confession, the Canons of Dordt and the Heidelberg Catechism. As a direct result of the confessional position on church unity and reconciliation, the URCSA calls itself the 'uniting' church in order to secure an open door to other Reformed churches in southern Africa, and specifically the white DRC and the Indian Reformed Church in Africa.

Belhar and Barmen

Belhar and Barmen have become symbols of liberation[5] in two different contexts where Christians had to respond to a *status confessionis*. Despite their symbolic congruence, the Declaration of Barmen and the Confession of Belhar differ in many ways. Barmen presents itself as a theological declaration true to the Word of God, while Belhar considers itself a confession. The Barmen Declaration is a text with six theses on 'evangelical truths' central to the situation of its time in the Nazi regime,

---

2   See Smit (1984:7-32) for the meaning and history of the term in his article entitled 'What Does Status Confessionis Mean?' in *A Moment of Truth: The Confession of the Dutch Reformed Mission Church 1982.*

3   The Dutch Reformed Mission Church and the Dutch Reformed Church in Africa unified in April 1994 to form the Uniting Reformed Church in Southern Africa

4   The story about this struggle can be found in *A Moment of Truth: The Confession of the Dutch Reformed Mission Church 1982* (Cloete & Smit 1984); and more recently in *Vraagtekens oor Gereformeerdheid?* (Boesak & Fourie 1998).

5   The phrase 'symbol of liberation' was used by De Gruchy (1984a:59-71) with reference to the Declaration of Barmen.

and Belhar consists of five clauses embedded in its confessional struggle against apartheid.[6]

Much has been said about the lack of direct reference to the Jewish problem in Barmen and a clearer political statement.[7] Belhar, on the other hand was formulated, not only hermeneutically with a 'view from below', but existentially in accordance with the experience of oppression and by oppressed and marginalised people themselves. The Confession of Belhar speaks of racism, but does not mention apartheid as a political system. There was an explicit discussion in the 1982 Synod about this matter and it was deliberately resolved to confess against a false doctrine rather than a political system. Therefore, it is also possible to read Belhar as a confession that is not overtly political. However, we have seen that church unity (Clause 2 of Barmen) is as political in South Africa as civil disobedience (Clause 5). The matter of political content can only be resolved if those of us who read these confessions today are prepared to do the social analysis that precedes the lives of these confessions.

I have argued the point about the relationship between Belhar and black theology as well as African theology in an article entitled 'Discipleship and Practical Theology: The Case of South Africa', published in the *International Journal of Practical Theology* (2000a:231-242). The direct relationship between black theology and the quest of a *status confessionis* in the South African context relates to the theological leadership of Manas Buthelezi (in the Lutheran World Federation) and Allan Boesak (in the WARC).

Edmund Arens (1989) proposed a useful model of five categories to study and compare different confessions. Huber further developed his thoughts and typified the following categories: the baptismal creed, the confession of guilt, the doxology, the doctrinal confession and the situative confession Huber (1991:48-60). According to this model one can say that the Confession of Belhar and the Barmen Declaration are both confessional statements of the situational type, but with Barmen using doctrinal language Huber (1991:48-60) and Belhar using ethical language (De Gruchy 1990:13-14). As such they both form 'symbols of liberation' that seek to redefine the relations between the Christian confession and the political reality. Both these

---

6   Reflections on the relationship between Barmen and Belhar have been ongoing. See for example, Horn (1984:34-66, 1988:105-120). There are other scholars, such as D.J. Smit, who prefer to speak of three clauses with a preamble and a conclusion.
7   Huber (1991:54-56) referred to the lack of direct reference to the Jewish problem with reference to Karl Barth's letter to Eberhard Bethge after he read the Bonhoeffer bibliography in 1967. Horn (1988:112) refers to the political content of Barmen and argues that regardless of the doctrinal nature of its language, Barmen are as political as the early church's confession: 'Jesus is Lord'.

confessions arose from a context of a concrete heresy and attempted to understand the theological problem in biblical terms. What is 'biblical' is interpreted as Christological. Their doctrinal (Barmen) and ethical (Belhar) content, therefore, bears a very specific Christological form. This results in different presentations of their Christology. While the Christology of Barmen essentially combats natural theology in a doctrinal fashion, the Christology of Belhar is rooted in social ethics. Belhar's theological significance does not only lie in its contextual association with apartheid (a word which is not mentioned in the text), but in its insistence that the question of ethics is also central to confession.

This characteristic Christology of Belhar consequentially focuses strongly on discipleship. This means that its five confessional clauses must be read as practices which the church is called to do in its calling to discipleship ('*imitatio Christi*'). Just like Barmen, it first confesses faith in the Triune God. However, it goes further in identifying the practices of such a God: 'who collects, defends and cares for his Church by his Word and Spirit'. Secondly, Belhar speaks about the unity of the church in Jesus Christ which means that believers should 'experience, practice and pursue community with one another' in freedom and not under constraint. Thirdly, it says what the people believe regarding reconciliation and connects it to the responsibility of the church to act in reconciliation. The fourth clause centralises the focus of justice expressed as discipleship. The fifth section refers to costly practices of absolute obedience to God.

The story of the heresy of apartheid is never complete without a reference to its impact on the white DRC. This story is also the story of a racially divided church and a racial theology (Smit 1992:88-110). As such, the story cannot really be complete without a reflection on the impact the Confession of Belhar has had on the white DRC.

The DRC also had to ask how apartheid relates to the Christian faith. In 1974, the DRC proposed a theology of racial separation in their policy document 'Human Relations and the South African Scene in the Light of Scripture'. The declaration claimed to be an attempt by the church to listen anew to 'what the Word of God had to say on race relations in a plural society.

Theologically, however, their understanding was determined more by the additional source of a natural theology. To understand how the DRC arrived at its theological justification of apartheid one has to look at the strenuous debate between the senior theologians who followed the neo-Calvinist theology of the Dutch theologian, Abraham Kuyper, and the young theologians who followed Karl Barth's dialectical theology (see Botman 2000b:342-361; Durand 1988:121-138). The senior theologians regarded Barth as suspect because they disagreed with his views on Scripture and regarded his views on the authority and inspiration of scripture as less than orthodox. The seniors defended creation theology and the idea of the orders of creation.

By 1974, the majority opinion of the DRC confirmed that creation theology as it relates to the biblical narrative of the tower of Babel in Genesis 11 would serve as adequate cornerstone of a theology of race. Jaap Durand, the professor who invited my class to study Karl Barth's theology in order to come to an understanding of the theological centre of the problem of apartheid, makes the following poignant statement regarding the eventual result of the power struggle between the senior Kuyperians and the young Barthians in the DRC:

> Unfortunately, Barth's theological influence ... was negative as far as the three most crucial decades in the development of Afrikaner Reformed theology are concerned. During this period, from the beginning of the 1930's to the end of the 1950's, Barthian theology had such a formidable opponent in Kuyperianism that it was never able to obtain a firm foothold in the field of Afrikaner theological thinking ... It was only as late as the 1960's, and particularly the early 1970's, that the Barthian resistance to a creation theology began to take hold among young Afrikaner theologians and new thoughts with a definite Barthian flavour made significant inroads into the debates on church and society. (Durand 1988:122)

The real root of the DRC's apartheid thinking, however, goes further back to the DRC's mission policy already established in 1935. Here the DRC developed its understanding of church planting in a racist form. Theologically, the DRC's official position was based on an interpretation of Abraham Kuyper's neo-Calvinist theology (De Gruchy 1984b, 1991; Strauss 1995:4-27). The DRC started by taking Kuyper's creation theology and developing it into a grand natural theological foundation for racial separation and the racial separation of churches.

According to Durand, a Barthian resistance began to take hold among young Afrikaner theologians in the early 1970s. Their foothold was unfortunately not strong enough in the DRC in 1974 to resist the acceptance of the theological justification of apartheid. Neither has it been strong enough to this day to lead the DRC to accept the Confession of Belhar, despite its clear Barthian features.

The DRC has, to this date not been able to accept the Confession of Belhar. The DRC decided at its General Synodical Committee (GSC) of 1996 that the Confession of Belhar constitutes 'a stumbling block to some of our (its) members' (DRC 1996). because it has a strong political connotation and is regarded as the fruit of a theology of liberation. Although there was no unanimous agreement on the latter, the GSC declared that the Confession of Belhar has the potential to divide the DRC.

Therefore, the meeting resolved that acceptance of the Confession of Belhar was at that stage not an option for the DRC. The GSC drew attention to the 1990 resolution of the General Synod. This resolution stated that the Belhar Confession as such was not in conflict with the three doctrinal standards of Reformed confessions, namely the Belgic Confession, the Heidelberg Catechism and the Canons of Dordt, and that it need not cause estrangement between the churches. In addition, it compromised by saying:

> The GSC ... is of the opinion that the Confession of Belhar cannot simply be brushed off as 'liberation theology'. It has to be seen against the background of the suffering and need of believing and devout members whose faith is stranded in a crisis as a result of the system of apartheid. The GSC is of the opinion that the 'unconditional acceptance' of the Confession of Belhar as a fourth confession additional to the three doctrinal standards will presently cause so much disunity in the DRC that at the moment it is no option. (DRC 1996:12)

What are the conditions set by the DRC for the acceptance of the Confession of Belhar? First, a revision of the belief that God is a God of justice who, in a situation of injustice and enmity is revealed in a special way as the God of the oppressed and the destitute (Confession of Belhar, 1986, Art. 4). The DRC maintains that certain statements could have been formulated differently, among others, article 4 of the Belhar Confession. (DRC 1990).

Centrally the DRC stands against the Confession of Belhar because it refuses to reflect on the confession from the theological framework of a biblical understanding of reconciliation. Instead, the church narrowly judged apartheid from the ethical framework of the second table of the law, namely, a sin against fellow human beings. I have argued this point in an article entitled 'Gereformeerdheid en die Belydenis van Belhar' (Botman 1986). Perhaps, the DRC should begin a reflection on Barmen to take itself towards a firmer understanding of the theology of Belhar.

Whatever the DRC may do eventually, the URCSA and Christians who regard the Confession of Belhar as an expression of its own faith must face a more urgent question: What is the relevance of the Confession of Belhar after apartheid? I am aware that it is possible to ask: 'Whereto after Belhar?' However, I think it is the wrong question. Instead, we should continue the search for the relevance of Belhar in the current context.

As I have said, the Confession of Belhar has five sections. First, it confesses faith in the Triune God. Then it speaks about the unity of the church in Jesus Christ. Thirdly, it says what the people believe regarding reconciliation. The fifth section refers to the absolute obedience to God. The fourth point states the justice question:

> We believe that God revealed himself as the One who wishes to bring about justice and true peace on earth; that in a world full of injustice and enmity God is in a special way the God of the destitute, the poor and the wronged and that God calls the church to follow in this; that God brings justice to the oppressed and gives bread to the hungry; that God frees the prisoner and restores sight to the blind; that God supports the downtrodden, protects the strangers, helps orphans and widows and blocks the path of the ungodly; that for God pure and undefiled religion is to visit the orphans and the widows in their suffering; that God wishes to teach the people of God to do what is good and to seek the right ; that the church must therefore stand by people in any form of suffering and need, which means, among other things, that the church must witness against and strive against any form of injustice, so that justice may roll down like waters and righteousness like an ever-flowing stream; that the church belonging to God, should stand where God stands, namely against injustice and with the wronged; that in following Christ the church must witness against all the powerful and privileged who seek selfishly their own interests and thus control and harm others. Therefore, we reject any ideology which would legitimate forms of injustice and any doctrine which is unwilling to resist such an ideology in the name of the gospel.[8]

The justice question is here also at heart a confessional concern for economic justice. The Confession of Belhar is a testimony to the liberating activity of God in history and context, including that of a global economic reality. It challenges the church as a community to follow God in God's liberating actions. The poor and oppressed are identified as the prime interlocutors of such actions. God is a God of justice seeking and acting for justice in a world of enmity and suffering.

Finding a way between an uncritical progressive understanding of God as 'a God of the poor' or an equally uncritical conservative view of God as 'a God of compassion', Belhar has opted for the Barthian description of this relationship.[9] God has been

---

8 Extracts from the Confession of Belhar in this chapter are taken from the English translation at Addendum 15, The Confession of Belhar. Also available at http://urcsa.net/wp-content/uploads/2016/02/Belhar-Confession.pdf

9 Barth clearly understood that the church must side with the poor, oppressed and exploited people. His discussion of the mercy and righteousness of God in *Church Dogmatics* II/1 reveals this: 'God always takes his stand unconditionally and passionately on this side and on this side alone: against the lofty and on behalf of the lowly; against those who already enjoy right and privilege and on behalf of those who are denied it and deprived of it' (Barth 2003/1940:386).

revealed, it says, as One who wishes to bring about justice and true peace among people. This revelation is embedded in a contextual understanding of how God acts. In a world full of injustice and enmity, God is in a special way the God of the destitute, the poor and the wronged. This is then extended ecclesiological. It means that the church is called, in these actions, to follow God, standing by people in any form of suffering and need, which means, among other things, that the church shall witness against and strive against any form of injustice, so that 'justice may roll down like waters, and righteousness like an ever-flowing stream'. Standing with God impels the church, as God's possession in this world, to stand where God stands, namely against injustice and with the wronged. Barth's strong call for focusing on the historical-theological meaning of discipleship, in the form of Dietrich Bonhoeffer's argument, is then retrieved (Barth 1958:533-553). In following Christ, the church must witness against all the powerful and privileged 'who seek selfishly their own interests and thus control and harm others.' In a world of enmity, a world of the powerful over against the powerless and where the privileged seek selfishly their own interest and control over others, the Word of God calls us to revisit our discipleship in light of the challenges of the global economy.

During the time of Barmen and Belhar the central institutional question revolved around the church and the nation state. In the current context, the market economy is the primary authority with its own secular, neo-capitalist ideology. We are all subjected, no longer so much to religious institutions or states, with their accountability to God or people respectively, but this time to unaccountable financial transactions which operate around the world anonymously and with impunity. Bob Goudzwaard correctly concludes that 'in this time of globalization it is not the presence of church and state, but far more their absence or end which sets the tone of the debate' (Goudzwaard 1998:10). This point of departure of economic globalisation is not as important to the existence of the church itself as it is to the socio-economic meaning of its confessions.

I chaired a historic consultation of African scholars on the issue: 'How our faith is being challenged by economic globalisation' in Kitwe, Zambia in 1996 where a new groundbreaking theological awareness arose. This consultation proposed that Africa is faced with a *status confessionis* in the light of the exclusionary nature of economic globalisation. This matter was referred to the executive of the WARC for ecumenical evaluation and action. A discussion ensued between me and Ulrich Möller, ecumenical secretary of the Lippische Kirche, after which we decided to disagree about a definition of a *status confessionis* and agree on a request for a *processus confessionis* on economic injustice. (*Reformed World* 2004:202-212).

Urged by the Southern African Alliance of Reformed Churches (SAARC), of which I was the moderator at the time, the executive of WARC allowed time for a special forum of churches from the South which was to be sponsored by the SAARC on 13 August 1997. An interesting flow of events led to a situation where I was instructed to lead the forum and present to them a paper defending the issue of a *processus confessionis* on economic globalisation. In addition, I had the responsibility to prepare a motion which was tabled that evening at the forum.[10]

In my presentation to the forum of the South I referred to Karl Barth's 1925 address to the WARC in Cardiff on 'The desirability and possibility of a universal Reformed creed'. As in 1925, I argued that the churches of the South must now reluctantly accept that the World Alliance is, for the same three crucial reasons, not yet ready to declare a *status confessionis* on global economic injustice. The Alliance (a) does not have a shared theological category to judge the current global economic reality; (b) although it has so many member churches from the South in its consciousness the Alliance does not come from an illuminating contextual position to understand the *kairos*; and (c) I questioned whether it had the combined political will to act on this matter in the nature of a confessing community. From the perspective of the South, the question is no longer whether we are in a *status confessionis* of a global economic nature. However, based on the criteria required for the declaration of such a state of confession, we must conclude that it is not yet possible. The World Alliance would, therefore, do better if it declared a process of learning, education, confession and action. Ulrich Möller was appointed secretary for the Section II Report responsible for a final recommendation to the WARC's 23rd General Council, Debrecen, Hungary (1997). Based on the recommendation of the Section II Report, the WARC, at its meeting in Debrecen subsequently declared a *processus confessionis* with regard to economic injustice in the context of globalisation. In the past, we have called for *status confessionis* in cases of blatant racial and cultural discrimination and genocide: 'We now call for a committed process of progressive recognition, education and confession (*processus confessionis*) within all WARC member churches at all levels regarding economic injustice and ecological destruction' (Opocensky 1997:198).

The exclusionary nature and the principle of triage in the global context served as epicentre for this development. The decision took the issue of exclusion in the realm of economic globalisation beyond the boundaries of the ethical. Indeed, it took ethical challenges and translated them in terms of faith affirmation. The Alliance has invited member churches and Christians everywhere to embark on a journey in which we continued to study the global phenomenon, its impact on

---

10   This motion was adopted by delegates of churches from the South with only one person voting against it because of the absence of a reference to 'economic destruction' in the call for a *processus confessionis*. The motion, as prepared by me, was adopted by the forum and became part of the proceedings of the WARC 23rd General Council. See Appendix 22 of the report in Opocensky (1997:245).

people and nature to come to a better understanding of the theological centre of the global challenge which could lead to faithful action for global transformation.

The WARC 24th General Council took place in Accra, Ghana in 2004. In a presentation to the council, I focused on the notion of God's covenant as a theological construct in the discernment of human dignity and the integrity of creation. This construct is useful in the engagement of global economic realities in the context of globalisation (Botman 2005).

In a document entitled *Covenanting for Justice in the Economy and the Earth*, the WARC General Council (2004) agreed on a choice for confession in response to the call of Debrecen (1997) and to show the necessity and urgency of an active response to the current challenges of our time (WARC 2004a). The WARC 24th General Council (2004) Public Issues Committee Report reflected on economic and environmental justice with a call to action within churches, towards governments, the private sector, international organisations and other faith-based and secular organisations (WARC 2004c). The Policy Committee of the WARC 24th General Council (2004) is responsible for reviewing the work of the WARC since Debrecen (1997) and for proposing future priorities and directives. The Policy Committee Report recognised the work that was done on covenanting for justice in the economy and the earth (*processus confessionis*) and recommended work on this subject as a priority issue for the future (WARC 2004b).

Beyond the Declaration of Barmen, hovering in Barmen's own proud tradition stands the Confession of Belhar. This confession belongs to the ecumenical Christian community. The Uniting Reformed Church in Southern Africa is merely the present trustee of this great confessional treasure which is relevant to the neo-capitalist global economy. I think that Belhar has much more to say to the present situation in Germany and the context of economic globalisation than even, perhaps, the Barmen Declaration. Perhaps, beyond Barmen, the journey of the confessing community is leading to Belhar and thus back to the younger Karl Barth.

Bibliography

Primary sources

Dutch Reformed Church (DRC). 1990. *Minutes of Synod, October 1990, Appendix 1 to Moderator's report.*

Dutch Reformed Church (DRC). 1996. *Minutes, General Synodical Committee, 29-30 October 1996.*

Opocensky, M. (ed.). 1997. *Debrecen 1997: Proceedings of the 23rd General Council of the World Alliance of Reformed Churches, Presbyterian and Congregational, held in Debrecen, Hungary, 8–20 August 1997.* Geneva: World Council of Churches Publications.

Secondary sources

Arens, E. 1989. *Bezeugen und bekennen: Elementare handlungen des glaubens*. Dusseldorf: Patmos-Verl.

Barth, K. 2003/1940. *Church Dogmatics* (Vol. 2, Part 1). Translated by G. Bromily & T.F. Torrance. Edinburgh: Bloomsbury T&T Clark.

Barth, K. 2004/1958. *Church Dogmatics* (Vol. 4, Part 2). Translated by G. Bromily & T.F.Torrance. Edinburgh: Bloomsbury T&T Clark.

Boesak, W.A. and Fourie, P.J.A. (eds). 1998. *Vraagtekens oor gereformeerdheid?* Belhar: LUS Printers.

Botman, H.R. 1998. Gereformeerdheid en die Belydenis van Belhar? In W.A. Boesak & P.J.A. Fourie (eds.), *Vraagtekens oor gereformeerdheid?* Belhar: LUS Printers.

Botman, H.R. 2000a. Discipleship and practical theology: The case of South Africa. *International Journal of Practical Theology* 4:231-242. https://doi.org/10.1515/ijpt.2000.4.2.201

Botman, H.R. 2000b. Is blood thicker than justice? The legacy of Abraham Kuyper for southern Africa. In L.E. Lugo (ed.), *Religion, pluralism, and public life: Abraham Kuyper's legacy for the twenty-first century*. Grand Rapids, MI: William B. Eerdmans.

Botman, H.R. 2004. 'Globalisation's threat to human dignity and sustainability'. Paper presented at the World Alliance of Reformed Churches 24th General Council, Accra, Ghana (30 July–13 August).

Botman, H.R. 2006. Barmen to Belhar: A contemporary confessing journey. *Nederduitse Gereformeerde Teologiese Tydskrif* 47(1/2):240-249.

Cloete, G.D. & Smit, D.J. (eds). 1984. *A moment of truth: The confession of the Dutch Reformed Mission Church 1982*. Grand Rapids, MI: William B. Eerdmans.

de Gruchy, J.W. 1984a. Barmen: Symbol of contemporary liberation? *Journal of Theology for Southern Africa* 47:59-71.

de Gruchy, J.W. 1984b. *Bonhoeffer and South Africa: Theology in dialogue*. Grand Rapids, MI: William B. Eerdmans.

de Gruchy, J.W 1990. From Cottesloe to the 'Road to Damascus'. Confessing landmarks in the struggle against apartheid. In G. Loots (ed.), *Listening to South African voices: Critical reflection on contemporary theological documents*. Pretoria: Woordkeur.

de Gruchy, J.W. 1991. *Liberating Reformed theology: A South African contribution to an ecumenical debate*. Grand Rapids, MI: William B. Eerdmans.

de Gruchy, J.W. & Villa-Vicencio, C. (eds). 1983. *Apartheid is a heresy*. Claremont: David Philip Publishers.

Durand, J. 1988. Church and state in South Africa: Karl Barth vs Abraham Kuyper. In C. Villa-Vicencio, *On reading Karl Barth in South Africa*. Grand Rapids, MI: William B. Eerdmans.

Dutch Reformed Church (DRC). 1976. *Human relations and the South African scene in the light of Scripture*. Official translation of the report 'Ras, volk en nasie en volkeverhoudinge in die lig van die Skrif'. Approved and accepted by the General Synod of the Dutch Reformed Church, October 1974. Cape Town: Dutch Reformed Church Publishers.

Goudzwaard, B. 1998. *Globalisation, regionalisation and sphere sovereignty*. Unpublished conference paper.

Horn, N. 1984. Die Barmen Verklaring – 'n Belydenisskrif? In D.J. Smit (ed.), *Teologie-belydenis-politiek: Die referate, response en besprekings van die dogmatologiese werksgemeenskap van Suid-Afrika*. Bellville: University of the Western Cape.

Horn, N. 1988. From Barmen to Belhar and kairos. In C. Villa-Vicencio, *On reading Karl Barth in South Africa*. Grand Rapids, MI: William B. Eerdmans.

Huber, W. 1991. The Barmen Declaration and the Kairos Document: On the relationship between confession and politics. *Journal of Theology for Southern Africa* 75:48-60.

Möller, U. 2005. The Accra Confession and its ecclesiological implications, in *Reformed World* 55(3):202-212.

Nederduits Gereformeerde Sendingkerk in Suid-Afrika. 1986. *Die Belydenis van Belhar, 1986: Bybelse versoening en 'n statutêr geskeide gemeenskap*. Belhar: Nederduits Gereformeerde Sendingkerk.

Smit, D.J. 1984. What does *status confessionis* mean? In G.D. Cloete & D.J. Smit (eds), *A moment of truth: The confession of the Dutch Reformed Mission Church 1982*. Grand Rapids, MI: William B. Eerdmans.

Smit, D.J. 1992. Reformed theology in South Africa: A story of many stories. *Acta Theologia* 12(1):88-110.

Strauss, P.J. 1995. Abraham Kuyper, apartheid and Reformed churches in South Africa in their support of apartheid. *Theological Forum* 23(1):4-27.

THE RELEVANCE OF PEDAGOGICAL NARRATIVE MAPS

The Confession of Belhar as a practical theological narrative searching for a pedagogic-therapeutic methodology

Gordon Dames[1]

Introduction

This chapter presents a new narrative pedagogy methodology to offer a therapeutic praxis and social consciousness. The aim is to introduce us to new liberating spaces, perspectives and people. Narratives are instrumental in the formation of personal and communal identity and character. The Confession of Belhar, as an embodied narrative, is offered as pedagogy of formation and transformation. Especially, in terms of post-1994 communities confronted with the psychosocial and socio-economic scars of apartheid.

One of the mental and systemic obstacles in South Africa today is the inability of leaders to address deep questions and to search for deep answers. In the search for transformation, my resolve is not to opt for easy answers or results, but rather to face head on difficult or deep issues and challenges. This chapter offers such a perspective for this book and leaves it up to the reader to make an informed decision on how to apply practical theology in South Africa today.

The chapter views the relevance of pedagogical narrative maps: The Confession of Belhar as a practical theological narrative searching for a pedagogic-therapeutic.

This chapter explores the pedagogic value of the Confession of Belhar within a practical theology narrative framework as a potential therapeutic practice for (pre- and post-1994) traumatic racial experiences (Dames 2012). Recurring and hidden

---

[1] Gordon Dames is a professor of practical theology in the Department of Philosophy, Practical and Systematic Theology, School of Humanities, Social Sciences and Theology, at the College of Human Sciences, University of South Africa. As a research leader, he is actively engaged in a research project in practical theology and research in the Department of Theology Philosophy, Practical and Systematic Theology in collaboration with Prof. Chris Hermans of the Department of Empirical Science of Religion, Radboud University, Nijmegen, in the Netherlands.

occurrences of oppression, injustice, inferiority and disunity engender psychosocial dysfunctionality in church and society (De Beer & Van Niekerk 2009:50-52) and the chapter endeavours to deconstruct structuralist hegemonic paradigms. A contextual analysis of liberating poststructuralist paradigm/s serves as foundation for the chapter and the chapter explores the appropriation of narrative pedagogical maps. Different narrative maps within a pedagogical framework are applied to illuminate two (Koopman 2008; Strauss 2005) opposing narratives. Finally, the chapter suggests the ways that narrative pedagogy could be applied to address pre- and post-1994 conditions of oppression, injustice and disunity. The confession is proposed as a narrative pedagogical model for addressing ecclesial and psychosocial dysfunctionalities. The aim is to explore how racial trauma can be addressed and hegemonic conditions transformed into alternative possibilities for living.

Recurring oppressive challenges

The living conditions of many South Africans, it can be agreed, are still the result of the hegemonic practices, trauma or stress caused by apartheid and need transformation and healing (Koopman 2008:164-165; Landman 2009a; 2009b; Van Rooi 2010:176-180). Racism feeds on hegemonic power and fosters cultural and knowledge inferiority (Koopman 2008:160). Koopman (2008:159) concurs that his identity and humanity were deformed during the apartheid era through the direct and indirect violence of racism. The Confession of Belhar, with its formative and transformative nature, embodies both the historical and the contemporary suffering of marginalised communities (Dames 2009a:125-127; De Beer & Van Niekerk 2009:56-57; Koopman 2008:162-164). The current racial depiction (on the internet – 'The Facebook Racist') and generational conflict in society highlights the dangers of racial fundamentalism and growing leadership intolerance (Nair 2011; Malema-Luthuli-hearing 2011). Young leaders in South Africa need a proper historical framework and members of society require conversations of remembrance and re-authoring if we are to treasure the 1994 democratic achievements of a new South Africa. It is sufficient to argue here that these conditions are fostered by the failure to address the pre- and post-1994 hegemonic practices of apartheid using pedagogic and therapeutic interventions. The hidden powers or unintentional rationalisation of racism among black, 'coloured' and white communities complicates and even duplicates historical apartheid-like oppression, injustice and inferiority (Koopman 2008:159-162; Strauss 2005:563). A recent inappropriate argument about the confession illuminates the potential re/production of pre-1994 hegemonic and inferiority notions: Therefore, a confession must correlate with the core issues of 'God's revelation in Jesus Christ' without entertaining '*beuselagtighede*' [nonsense] (Strauss 2005:563).

Strauss's (2005:563) reference to '*beuselagtighede*' or nonsense could be regarded as a paternalistic attempt to disregard the audience's authentic faith expression and values embodied in the confession. It characterises 'white' supremacy enacted in the re/production of oppression, injustice and inferiority through hegemonic discourse (Van Dijk 1993). What or who defines the abovementioned 'core issues of God's revelation in Jesus Christ'? Strauss's (2005:563) notion of 'core issues' reminds one of the historic paternalistic discourses within Dutch Reformed Church (DRC) circles (Botha & Naudé 1998:77-89). Koopman's (2008:162) depiction of decades of unbearable suffering and the emergence of a new transforming story constitutes 'the core issues of God's revelation in Jesus Christ' for millions of black, 'coloured' Indian and white South Africans during and after apartheid. Bam declares a *status confessionis* on the basis of apartheid and apartheid theology's threat to the Gospel of Jesus Christ (cited in Botha & Naudé 1998:34-37). Apartheid and apartheid theology engineered collective and structural contexts of violence through racial prejudice, separation, discrimination, exclusion, alienation, enmity, injustice, humiliation and dehumanisation. It culminated in the DRC's racially based missionary policy and nationalist ('*volksgesentreerde*') ecclesiology (De Beer & Van Niekerk 2009:56-57).

Status confessionis as a pedagogical transformation narrative

A transformed narrative, however, dawned with the declaration of a *status confessionis* in 1982 and the adoption of the confession in 1986 (Botha & Naudé 1998:27-37). It was this very same faith response of the confession that sought consolation, comfort, redemption, liberation, hope and healing for all South Africans (Koopman 2008:162). Koopman's notion of the confession as the God-given event of consolation, liberation, hope, and so forth, illuminates the confession's formative, transformative nature and therapeutic function. We concur that the confession embodies both a therapeutic and pedagogical function in fostering unity, reconciliation and justice. The pre-1994 apartheid context was renowned for separation, discrimination, alienation, enmity, racism, injustice and oppression. The confession redressed these ideological and structural hegemonies with liberational intent (Botha & Naudé 1998:24-37). A new narrative or discourse on 'solidarity and cohesion, embracing and participation, compassion and human rights' was later introduced (Koopman 2008:162-164). This therapeutic narrative transformed structural injustice, separation and racism and engendered the formation of a new kind of citizenship and/or Christianity (McLaren 2001:40, 138), particularly in the light of Polany's notion of meaning formation for everything in life within its location/context in society (cited in McLaren 2001:151).

The hypothesis of this chapter holds that hidden pre-1994 hegemonic practices continue to threaten the moral and spiritual fibre of churches and society; that this requires a narrative pedagogical methodology in reaffirming our Christian and democratic ideals and values, and in fostering healing for psychosocial dysfunctionality in church and society.

Narrative pedagogical methodology

Goodson, Biesta, Tedder and Adair (2010:133) refer to unexplored and underdeveloped methodologies in engendering narrative learning, and call for the exploration of new learning resources and new learning environments. This chapter seeks to address familiar and critical issues within a new methodological framework. Narrative pedagogy reveals deeper perspectives of life and interprets and analyses data from reality in engendering social consciousness (Clough 2002:8). Postmodern conditions require methodological accountability for complex moral issues. According to Richardson, 'Self-reflexivity [within the written story] unmasks complex political/ideological agendas' (cited in Clough 2002:9).

Narrative pedagogy from faith traditions constitutes an important method for redressing old and informing new worldviews (Ploeger 1995:275). In his book *Shaped by the Story: Helping Students Encounter God in a New Way*, Novelli offers a new pedagogical framework based on a narrative methodology. Narratives are powerful in incorporating people into new spaces – they open up new perspectives and places and introduce us to new people. Narratives illuminate and form a personal and communal identity and character. Narratives are a dialogue-centred approach to forming new knowledge, values and praxis Novelli (2008:6-8). Novelli argues that narratives are 'guided by imaginative listening, creative retellings, and interactive discussions' (Novelli 2008:7). This is an inspirational method by which learners can discover themselves in sequences of events that include characters, dialogue, context and plot. Narrative pedagogy engenders a revised perspective; a new reorganised and prioritised style and mode of living. Nevertheless, this is not intended to disregard the conceptual, theoretical principles of the Confession of Belhar in favour of a mere imaginative methodological project (Murphy 2007:1). We contend, with Novelli, that the confession, as an embodied narrative, is pedagogy of formation and transformation – especially considering post-1994 communities confronted with the psychosocial and socio-economic scars of apartheid. Narrative therapy is ideal for redressing tangible, hidden and silent re/occurrences of oppression, injustice, discrimination and isolation (Freedman & Combs 1996:5-18; Landman 2009b; Morgan 2000:1, 8-9, 13-15; White 2007:24-27).

Life stories are linked through certain events and are in sequence over time: 'The key distinction that emerges is that between the use of life narratives as tools for learning, agency and identity construction and the ongoing process of narration itself as a site for learning' (Goodson et al. 2010:131). Plots are formed for dominant or alternative stories to inculcate and engender new meaning. 'A narrative is like a thread that weaves[2] the events together, forming a story' (Morgan 2000:5). Narrative therapy attends to the self and the other regarding personal and communal life stories. We tell stories to make sense of ourselves and our circumstances (Winslade & Monk 1998:1). Narrative pedagogy is a respectful, non-blaming approach that centres people as the experts on their own lives. People have various skills, competences, beliefs, values, commitments and abilities. These traits could help them to change their relationship towards injustice, inequality and hegemony. Narrative pedagogy is determined by people or communities in terms of their own outcomes (Morgan 2000:4).

Narrative pedagogical therapy and social construction

The narrative metaphor represents a discontinuous paradigm within hegemonic structuralist social and institutional contexts. This paradigm shift is also referred to as 'post-structuralism, deconstructionism, the interpretive turn, new hermeneutics, and postmodernism' (Freedman & Combs 1996:14).

Structuralism and/or objective study methods were developed to analyse the laws/ structures in life and physical phenomena to provide supposedly reliable, valid and universally applicable knowledge of the physical world (Thomas 2002:85). This objective worldview emphasises facts, replicable procedures, and rules. It, however 'ignores the specific, localized meanings of individual people' (Freedman & Combs 1996:9; Thomas 2002:85). We contend that the uniqueness of the former Dutch Reformed Mission Church (DRMC) and the Uniting Reformed Church in South Africa's (URCSA)[3] members were and are still being disregarded by some white supremacy practices (Strauss 2005:563, 572-575). Structuralism implies that people are studied, perceived and treated objectively through paternalistic pedagogical guidance and therapy (Koopman 2008:161; Strauss 2005:563-564; Thomas 2002:86).

---

2   See also Kotze (2000).
3   References to both the former Dutch Reformed Mission Church and the new Uniting Reformed Church in South Africa are used to describe its rich historical and contemporary narratives. The DRMC was founded on racially segregated grounds – the URCSA was formed as a decentralised ecclesial denomination between the Dutch Reformed Church in Africa and the DRMC (reserved for black and 'coloured' people, respectively). The Dutch Reformed Church (DRC – for white people) previously referred to itself as the 'Mother' of the aforementioned 'daughter' churches. The DRC was the brain child of the apartheid ideology/narrative.

Today, poststructuralism or postmodernity challenges the abovementioned assumptions of structuralism. The French philosophers, Michel Foucault[4] and Jacques Derrida,[5] are the founding fathers of poststructuralism. They influenced disciplines in which hegemonic objective/structural methodologies are applied (Thomas 2002:86).

Social realities, the taken-for-granted, conditions in life (injustice, etc.), are constructed by the members of a particular culture through reciprocal relationships. Social construction provides individuals and communities with hegemonic or liberating frameworks through which they interpret their world.

We contend that the confession, as theological and social construction, functioned as a liberating and a pedagogical therapeutic framework during the pre-1994 period – it reconfigured the lives and world views of DRMC/URCSA members (De Beer & Van Niekerk 2009:50-53; Freedman & Combs 1996:12; Hartney 2011:103; Koopman 2008:162). Narrative pedagogy, within a postmodern and social constructionist worldview deconstructs power, knowledge and truth and informs how it works in diverse communities and cultures (Freedman & Combs 1996:22). The confession, for instance, as a deconstruction of hegemonic structuralist and objective worldviews, reframed the realities into poststructuralist, intersubjective, postmodern life-giving worldviews (Koopman 2008:162; Hartney 2011:97, 99, 103; Ploeger 1995:302-303, 316-317).

The transformation of structuralist practices

The Belhar Confession transformed the structuralist philosophy, identity and culture of apartheid ideology and its theological justification. The confession embodies Christ's creativity, transformation, social cohesion, compassion, reconciliation, love, hope and peace (Koopman 2008:166; Louw 2008:74-76, 270,553). The confession assisted the former structuralist DRMC to decentre itself and to embrace a new identity with an alternative narrative (Koopman 2008:162-166). The following perspectives of Thomas (2002:88) underline the pedagogical contribution of the confession in terms of alternative possibilities (De Beer & Van Niekerk 2009:54-58),

---

4   Foucalt's (in Morkel 2008) contribution should be noted. He focuses on language as an instrument of power; distinguishes between the tension of normal/abnormal, power/resistance, life-giving/life-taking; dominant narratives as units of power and meaning; truth claims which constitute discourses that dehumanise and objectify people.

5   Derrida (in Morkel 2008) is also essential in this regard. He argues for the following: the meaning of any symbol, word or text is inextricably bound up in its context; deconstruction of structuralist's meaning systems; the absent but implicit in meaning; taking a term under erasure, to undo not to destroy; and the binary opposition of not either/or but both/and possibilities in meaning.

namely: (1) identities are not fixed, but in a constant process of being created; (2) identity is being created in relation to changes to which others are reacting and witnessing; (3) identities are socially (by history, culture, gender, sexuality, class and power relations) created; (4) people's identities cannot be known by the truths of scientific methods; (5) therapists do not possess objective, neutral or value-free understandings, and should not impose their perspectives on others; and (6) the (un-harmful) quirks of people's lives (times, places, events, ways of being that do not fit the normal) and their formative meaning in people's lives. To concur with Thomas, the Belhar Confession therefore shaped the lives and conditions of the marginalised majorities in our country through existential, social and communal identity formation and transformation. The confession remains appropriate in the reconfiguration of dysfunctional identities (xenophobia, homosexuality, HIV and Aids) and hegemonic discourses (Dames 2014:1-8, 2010:1-7; De Beer & Van Niekerk 2009:63; Koopman 2008:164-166).

New possibilities for coexistence and co-operation

Poststructuralism can open up new possibilities for creative forms of listening to and working with [URCSA and DRC] people (De Beer & Van Niekerk 2009:58; Thomas 2002:88). Theological deconstruction through the confession demonstrates the value of a poststructuralist pedagogical methodology (Koopman 2008:162-164). It illustrates how theological transformation as well as deformation could exist between two identical, but different confessional narrative versions (Koopman 2008:159-164; Strauss 2005:569-575), albeit, from the same confessional tradition, the traditional confessions (Strauss 2005:560) and the new status of *confessionis* (Koopman 2008:162). The essence of the comparison between the two narratives is that the confessions' traditional confessional text did not change. The way the traditional and new *confessionis* narratives were read reflects the way in which the DRC audience have objectified the confession as a political discourse or just as another 'document' ('*stuk*') (De Beer & Van Niekerk 2009:63; Strauss 2005:569). Members of the DRMC, however, embraced it as an intersubjective (liberation, communal) life-giving praxis (Hartney 2011; Koopman 2008). The setting in which the Belhar Confession and the traditional *confessionis* narrative functioned changed, but not the traditional confessional textual intent. The new status of *confessionis* demonstrated that a poststructuralist culture is essential for a transformed worldview. Traditional confessions were projected by the DRC as a preferred culture of structuralism, certainty and normativity – it was claimed as the product of a preferred paternalistic institutionalised community (Strauss 2005:560-572; Taylor 2005:19-29). The confession represents a changed worldview, a postmodern culture in which narrative pedagogical therapy has a distinctive function. It gives a new vision and therapy for audiences within their local and particular social and cultural poststructuralist contexts (De Beer & Van Niekerk 2009:58, 63). A break between the way things used to be and the way they are today, has been realised. De Beer and Van Niekerk (2009) presume to capture the confession for the DRC's ecclesiological and missionary legitimacy; instead of embracing it as a liberating witness in confessing the atrocities of apartheid and the theological justification of apartheid. The pre-1994 context of the confession provides us with a good example of how a therapeutic pedagogical community (DRMC/URCSA) engaged in and through mutual formative and transformative opportunities with its fellow members and the public.

We will consequently apply the confession as a therapeutic narrative pedagogical methodology within a growing poststructuralist context.

Defining narrative maps

White (2007:5-6) believes that maps for therapeutic practice should serve as a critical reflective guide in the development of therapeutic conversations. Maps as a metaphor could inform narrative pedagogy in addressing existential the psychosocial concerns, dilemmas and problems of communities. Narrative therapy within a pedagogical perspective could empower communities to reconfigure their goals or to embrace new objectives to transform their lives (White 2007:4). Partnerships for transformation result in the acknowledgement and embracing of diverse cultural relationships (White 2007:5; Ploeger 1995:97ff, 183). Maps engender opportunities for people to explore neglected life events and existential psychosocial problems. They foster constructive and creative engagement with oppressive, unjust and existential problems (White 2007:5). Narrative pedagogical therapy maps can be constructed in terms of White's narrative frameworks, namely, by externalising, re-authoring, re-membering, unique outcomes, and scaffolding conversations (White's (2007:5, 9ff). White's framework is ideal for addressing pre- and post-1994 hegemonic conditions by helping suffering communities to externalise, re-author and re-member the past in recreating a new hopeful future by scaffolding conversations of unity, reconciliation and justice as unique outcomes.

Externalising conversations identifying the thin descriptions in narrative pedagogy

White (2007:9) proposes the externalising conversations map as an antidote (not as a skill/technique) to psychological self-understandings. Externalising conversations detach the person/community from their problem or suffering (injustice, separation and inferiority). They deconstruct practices of injustice, discrimination and the objectification of people or organisations as inferior. The collective existential experience of the DRMC during the 1980s characterised such practices and perceptions (Freedman & Combs 1996:47; Koopman 2008:159-162; White 2007:9). Narrative pedagogy should help oppressed people or communities to separate their personalities, identities and culture from hegemonic conditions (Morgan 2000:17; White 2007:9). In the context of externalising conversations, inferiority ceases to represent the truth about people's identities (White 2007:9). Narrative pedagogy helps people to name their problems (plots of suffering, inferiority, injustice and separation) in search of tangible problem resolution (Koopman 2008:159-162; Morgan 2000:17; White 2007:9).[6] This is realised through the confession as an example of creative and authentic linguistics with a therapeutic narrative and pedagogical intent and orientation. The confession, however, was initially and may still be perceived as a 'mistaken problem-identity' of the former DRMC and the contemporary URCSA (Strauss 2005:572). Bam (cited in Botha & Naudé 1998:34-37) concurs, however, that it is a confession on the same level as the other confessions of the church. The Belhar Confession is ultimately the personification of liberation from injustice, separation and inferiority and the embodiment of its rich ecclesial and confessional identity. The shift in the confession's narrative plot during 1982/1986 constituted it as a pedagogical therapeutic and transformative agent.[7]

The development of externalising conversations

Externalising conversations focus on different aspects such as psychosocial, cultural, economic-political and theological challenges between people, diverse cultures and social practices, as well as complex ideological, philosophical and metaphorical problems (Morgan 2000:20-21). The internalisation of communities' problems (apartheid and their theological justification) impact negatively on their philosophical disposition (their attitudes, values, character and beliefs) (De Beer & Van Niekerk 2009:50-52). An untransformable DRC has become a stuck and maintenance institution with a silo mentality and culture (De Beer & Van Niekerk 2009:57; Strauss 2005:560,574-575). These dynamics could lead to a cycle of pathological problems without alternative outcomes (White 2007:9, 24-25). However, the confession's poststructuralist theological context and inclusive denominational culture (shared by the SACC, the US Presbyterian Church, Germany, the Netherlands, broader society, etc.) have proved to shape its newfound theological conviction (Koopman 2008:162). This socially and culturally influenced church developed its own self-understanding, habits of thought and faith, and moral practices. The URCSA has a natural tendency to instruct its self-understanding due to the mere thought habits

---

6   People should name their own problems, and not the therapist (Morgan 2000:20).
7   The use of historical and contemporary symbols and art like films could be applied to address 'unpleasant, serious, chronic and intractable problems in their social consequences' (White 2007:23-24).

of her moral, cultural and theological heritage (Hartney 2011; Koopman 2008:162; Morgan 2000:9; White 2007:25). The confession was and remains a hermeneutical practice embodying core truths of Scripture (Hartney 2011:103). McLaren (2001:151) refers elsewhere to 'the story of God's work in the human community'.

Externalising conversations are counter-practices to the objectification of people's/communities' identities (Koopman 2008). The notions of inferiority, disorder, dysfunctionality, incompetency or inadequacy are challenged (White 2007:26). The confession as an externalising conversation acted as a counter-practice in distinguishing the DRMC/URCSA from the DRC and the former oppressive National Party regime. De Beer and Van Niekerk (2009:56) hold that it exposed the DRC's integrity crisis and its crisis of missionary relevance. It decentred the DRMC/URCSA from pathologically inferior philosophies and opened up new possibilities for redressing the theological justification of apartheid and its psychosocial effects (De Beer & Van Niekerk 2009:56-57; Freedman & Combs 1996:56; Koopman 2008:162; White 2007:26).

This language partnership provided the Confession of Belhar with the necessary scaffolding to cross pathological (political and theological) zones to new life possibilities (White 2007:263) and created a new reality of meaning (Freedman & Combs 1996:29). The deconstruction of oppressive and inferior philosophies is the ultimate objective of externalising conversations (Morgan 2000:24; White 2007:27). Koopman avers that 'our deepest convictions in the words of the Belhar Confession ... helped us to resist apartheid with resilience and hope, and that eventually helped us to overcome this evil system' (Koopman 2008:162).

The intention is 'not so much problem-solving or direct power struggles, but rather actions of 'cool engagement' in expressing anonymous (oppressive) previous life (pre- and post-1994) experiences (White 2007:27-29). Communities' sense of vulnerability in existential life problems and stressful circumstances decrease as a result (White 2007:29). The DRMC has been empowered/liberated through the confession and has accepted responsibility for being socio-politically conscious in deconstructing the DRC's discriminatory theology, antisocial ideas, beliefs and actions (Koopman 2008:160-164; Morgan 2000:45).

The Belhar Confession re-authored the DRMC's sense of being part of a preferred democratic community and multiracial church. The notion of the confession that God is in a special way on the side of the sufferer, poor and oppressed (Botha & Naudé 1998:4-5) opened public space for a concrete understanding (a catharsis moment) of her life and identity in constructing new stories (Freedman & Combs 1996:56ff; White 2007:31). Metaphors are basically not intended as battle and contest metaphors to defeat or vanquish injustice, separation and inferiority (White

2007:30-31). The DRC's constant tendency to totalise problems (negative perception) of the confession should be challenged (De Beer & Van Niekerk 2009:50-53; Strauss 2005:569ff). Relentless theological discourse by the DRC obscured the context of apartheid, injustice and its effect during the 1980s until today (De Beer & Van Niekerk 2009:61). It attempts to invalidate the DRMC's/URCSA's identity, humanity and culture (Koopman 2008:161; White 2007:35).[8] Strauss's (2005:572-573) remark that the confession occupies itself with peripheral issues and not with central faith issues totalised the DRMC/URCSA's pre- and post-1994 authentic experience into moral and peripheral issues (Hartney 2011:94). Metaphors of battle and contest and a totalisation of the confession as a problem are only appropriate for some people in the DRC – those who are fighting for the survival of white supremacy since 1982 and beyond (De Beer & Van Niekerk 2009:60-63; Strauss 2005:571-575; White 2007:35).

Externalising conversations were used in the revising and redeveloping of the DRMC's strengths and resources (Koopman 2008:159-162; Van Rooi 2010:176-178; White 2007:38). Koopman's post-1994 observation embodies an externalising conversation in the DRMC and URCSA: 'In the quest for the restoration of human dignity, i.e. in the quest to build an ethos of social solidarity and social cohesion, embrace and participation, compassion and justice we drink from the wells of the Christian tradition' (Koopman 2008:166). Koopman goes on to say that the threefold office of Christ might enrich our theological contents.

It might help the DRC to begin revisioning her life and to gain renewed strength in herself – to 'tap' into her traditional neighbourhood and friends as a therapeutic and narrative pedagogical resource (De Beer & Van Niekerk 2009:58, 61). The different, absent but implicit metaphors used by both Koopman (2008:166): restoration of human dignity; and Strauss (2005:574-575): the confession's *'afgeleide gesag'* (assumed authority), illustrate the therapeutic and hegemonic power of externalisation conversations. Strauss's (2005:575) notion of the assumed authority of the Belhar Confession resonates with hegemonic dominance and power that led numerous times to power in the form of harassment (De Beer & Van Niekerk 2009:53; Van Dijk 1993:255). Bam redressed white hegemony and spearheaded the DRMC's 1982 status confessionis in witnessing:

> I came to a place where I understand apartheid regulations as a contradiction to the Gospel of Jesus Christ. I experience this faith clash so sharply that it forces me to witness and reject the false doctrine that threatens me. I find myself in a situation where I either witness confrontationally against the powers which threaten to neutralise and disempower my faith confession,

---

[8] 'This totalising of the problem is founded upon the dualistic, either/or habits of thought that have been quite pervasive in Western culture' (White 2007:35).

or am silenced and crumble to nothingness. When I find myself in a *status confessionis* then the word which speaks in this situation should have the status and character of a confession. (cited in Botha & Naudé 1998:34-37)

The appropriation of Bam's external conversation for the URCSA in the previously mentioned and in the following paragraphs is crucial for inculcating the values of the confession and in redressing complex contemporary issues.

Position map: Four categories of inquiry

The 'statement of position' map applied to a narrative pedagogy context facilitates externalising conversations distinguished by four principal categories of inquiry (White 2007:38-39). The 'statement of position' map functions as a narrative pedagogical therapeutic inquiry guide; where people present problem-dominated life issues and or individual/relational pathological identities. Narrative pedagogy takes on a decentred position in helping people to name their own problems and to voice their concerns in their positioning to their problems (White 2007:39).

Naming the problem

The first task of narrative pedagogical therapy is to assist both the URCSA and DRC members in the naming of their current existential problems. Their existential and psychosocial problems are richly characterised through their problems experienced at a distance (global) by rendering them problems experienced nearby (particular) (White 2007:40). The URCSA's unique knowledges, capabilities and skills are central in readdressing existential problems (De Beer & Van Niekerk 2009:62-63; White 2007:43). Pedagogical therapy, in this instance, could use language in a particular way to foster decentred specific conversations about problem identity (Morgan 2000:18). The confession as a missional witness (De Beer & Van Niekerk 2009:63) is not *'n liriese ontboeseming of emosionele ontlading nie'* – it is a daring act of conflict (Bam cited in Botha & Naudé 1998:37). The confession became the DRMC's/URCSA's liberating moment and renamed and transformed its own pathological position into one of unintentional care, compassion and healing for the DRC and broader public (De Beer & Van Niekerk 2009:62-63; Koopman 2008:163-164).

Mapping the effects of the problem

It was and is still important to address the effects or influence that apartheid had and continues to have on people's lives (De Beer & Van Niekerk 2009:52-53; Koopman 2008:164; Van Rooi 2010:176-177). Narrative pedagogy should appropriate the impact of the dominant (apartheid) story in people's lives (Morgan 2000:39-40; White 2007:43). The tactics/methods and consequences of apartheid, discrimination and unjust conditions should be addressed. For example, how has the confession affected the way in which the DRMC functioned during the 1980s and thereafter? (Botha & Naudé 1998; Koopman 2008:159-162; Morgan 2000:40). The DRMC/URCSA critiqued the DRC's hegemonic tactics of influencing discourse and meaning regarding the confession (Hartney 2011:94,103; Koopman 2008; Morgan 2000:33-38, 40). The confession constituted an alternative story. The way that the DRMC/URCSA coped in the face of injustice and oppression was due to her psychosocial and spiritual competence (Koopman 2008:159-162; Morgan 2000:41). The transition from internalising conversations in the DRMC/URCSA became clear in its public missional witness (Botha & Naudé 1998:34-37; de Beer & Van Niekerk 2009:56-57; White 2007:43). Externalising conversations shift pathological philosophies to enable decentred identity formation and transformation (White 2007:44).

The effects of oppressive/unjust practices

Apartheid and its effects on contemporary people's lives should be redressed (Koopman 2008:166). Appreciative enquiry should be applied in guiding people to consider and articulate their opinions in this regard (Morgan 2000:42; White 2007:44). Therapeutic narrative pedagogy should articulate the complexities of peoples' positions on the effects of apartheid (Morgan 2000:42; White 2007:46). The Truth and Reconciliation Commission (TRC) started this process, but left a narrative therapeutic vacuum after it was dissolved.[9] The DRC's prophetic and pastoral voice in terms of the 'what, why and how' questions of apartheidwould have helped to transform its identity (Koopman 2008:166; Morgan 2000:42). However, the DRC's attitude (Strauss 2005:569ff) towards the Belhar Confession inspired the URCSA's missional witness, informed and emphasised its meaning in life (De Beer & Van Niekerk 2009:58).

Evaluating the effects of apartheid

The 'why' question motivated or justified how people evaluate the effects of apartheid in their lives (Morgan 2000:43; White 2007:48). It is not associated with moral judgement and values (Hartney 2011:103), but gives people a voice and develops their framework (intentions, values, skills, competences, preferences and praxes) for living (Koopman 2008:165; Morgan 2000:43; White 2007:49). It also helps to develop positive identity and preferences for living. People can decentre themselves from (apartheid-) saturated stories to aspire for rich story development and alternative stories (Morgan 2000:43; White 2007:49, 51). The Belhar Confession succeeded in decentring itself from the DRC's justification of apartheid (De Beer & Van Niekerk 2009:51-52).

---

9   See the Truth and Reconciliation Commission website at http://www.justice.gov.za/trc/

Thickening the alternative stories

Towards a renewed role of the confession in the URCSA – the introduction of narrative pedagogy in churches, schools and communities could support communities to stay connected to their new and preferred stories (Van Rooi 2010:179-183). Thickening and enriching the alternative stories of unity, reconciliation and justice may involve witnessing the articulation of new stories (De Beer & Van Niekerk 2009:51, 56-58; Koopman 2008:164ff; Morgan 2000:74-75). De Beer and Van Niekerk (2009:56ff) interpret the confession in terms of its missional value/witness and emphasise its value as an alternative narrative. The confession cannot, however, be reconfigured through creative linguistics to argue for an alternative confessional identity in advancing church unity, especially for those DRC members who continue to resist the confession's original intention and full implications. According to Bam, the confession is by nature subversive and prophetic (cited in Botha & Naudé 1998:35). Re-authoring conversations, re-membering conversations and the unique outcomes methodology will henceforth be applied in order to thicken the pedagogical therapeutic value of the confession as the URCSA's alternative narrative (Koopman 2008:159-162). These narrative frameworks are crucial in fostering authentic historical memory and pedagogical therapeutic space for the leaders of the younger generation and for generations to come.

Re-authoring conversations

Narrative pedagogy should explore unique outcomes for pathological socio-economic, political and theological conditions through historical analysis and hermeneutics (Hartney 2011:95-103). New plots and alternative stories could emerge – described with new meaning and linked to past events (De Beer & Van Niekerk 2009:52, 62-63). In the retelling and reliving of stories lies the rediscovery of a story which relates to a new situation (Freedman & Combs 1996:33). People can shift from oppressive-saturated living to a reconnection with communal preferences, hopes, dreams and ideas (Morgan 2000:59). According to White:

> These themes often reflect loss, failure, incompetence, hopelessness, or futility. Along with this, people routinely refer to the figures or protagonists that feature in the story, and they share with therapists their conclusions both about the identity of these figures or protagonists and about their motives, intentions and personal characteristics. (White 2007:61)

The embodiment of White's (2007:61) notion of communal praxis was demonstrated in the TRC process. The TRC initiated an unprecedented project of reconciliation and social justice, but failed to sustain its work. Current socio-political and moral conditions in the country require similar projects to facilitate reconciliation and social justice (Dames 2009a:121ff). The URCSA should renew its own confessional vocation to redress contemporary challenges. This re-authored DRMC/URCSA situation (1982/1986) was a defining moment in search of reconciliation, restitution and justice from both the DRC and the apartheid government. Such re-authoring conversations are crucial for traumatised and fragmented societies as a result of ongoing violence, corruption, poverty, xenophobia and renewed instances of discrimination and prejudice.

Re-authoring conversations is defined by landscape of action and landscape of identity questions (White 2007:78, 81-82). Events, actions and beliefs which do not fit with the URCSA's dominant story are explored (Morgan 2000:60; Strauss 2005:569-575). Landscape of action and landscape of identity create a context or open space in which South Africans can give meaning to and assimilate overlooked, but significant, events in their lives into a coherent storyline (White 2007:83). The landscape of action develops over time through a sequence of experiences, events and contexts by creating a specific plot. The landscape of identity seeks to understand the knowledges, thoughts, or feelings, or absent knowledges, thoughts or feelings in people's actions (White 2007:78). De Beer and Van Niekerk's (2009:63) notion of the missionary value of the confession, if authentically appropriated, is an example of its pedagogical and therapeutic potential. The potential outcome is God's preferred future – people become engaged with many of the lost experiences and events in their own living contexts (Keifert 2006; White 2007:81). The refinement and development of future conversations become critical (White 2007:81). People's lives become multi-storied as their landscape of identity is identified and thickened (White 2007:81). We can distinguish between interactive plots in the narratives of Koopman (2008) and Strauss (2005). The most significant landscape of action and of identity played itself out in Koopman's (2008:159-166) narrative; after decades of suffering, injustice and oppression he posed an open externalised question to his fellow theologian colleague, Strauss (2005:569-575). His question signalled a catharsis moment in the whole story, but in the views of his colleague, one could sense the perplexity of being confronted with reality and personal agency and responsible action. (White 2007:266)

Koopman's narrative is the catalyst for pedagogic-therapeutic healing and reconciliation between the URCSA and DRC.

Re-membering conversations

Re-membering conversations anchor on an understanding that identity is grounded in communities (Morgan 2000:77; White 2007:129). Isolation and disconnection from meaningful relationships are generally experienced by postmodern people faced with problems. Dominant apartheid stories minimised the collective histories of black and 'coloured' communities. Re-membering conversations deconstruct these dominant apartheid stories. It 'powerfully incorporates and elevates significant people's contribution in the lives of those consulting the [narrative pedagogy] therapist' (Morgan 2000:77). The confession's voice was formative with regard to the construction of DRMC/URCSA's own new identity (De Beer & Van Niekerk 2009:57-58; Koopman 2008:162ff; Morgan 2000:83ff; White 2007:129).

Re-membering conversations give the URCSA and the DRC an opportunity to critique the authentic membership of the church. Suffice it to say that silent voices gain authority in claiming their community identity and in challenging other hegemonic [unjust and oppressive DRC] voices (White 2007:129). Historical events, experiences and contexts that stand outside the influence of apartheid are sought through the landscape of action and the landscape of identity (Morgan 2000:78). In so doing, communities can re-engage with their history or revise their relationships with significant others. New contemporary identities and projected futures are constructed (De Beer & Van Niekerk 2009:57-58; White 2007:136). The Belhar Confession became a therapeutic narrative pedagogical agent and an outside audience for the others' [DRC, society] stories (De Beer & Van Niekerk 2009:58; White 2007:208ff).

Conversations that highlight unique outcomes

It could be contended that many DRMC/URCSA members still live consciously/ unconsciously with the scars of unconscious hegemonic stories of suffering (Koopman 2008:159-162; Van Rooi 2010:176-178). Hidden or unconscious stories could be significant and are defined as unique outcomes or exceptions in favourable circumstances. Unique outcomes do not necessarily fit with the dominant story; but may be an action, statement, thought, belief, ability and commitment (Morgan 2000:52). Their identification engenders alternative storylines. Many neglected unconscious, lived experiences of the URCSA became public through the Belhar Confession (Koopman 2008:159-162; White 2007:219). Unique outcomes functioned in the past, present and future – free from dominated apartheid-saturated stories (Botha & Naudé 1998:90-100; De Beer & Van Niekerk 2009:52; Morgan 2000:54). People are liberated or healed to voice their own intentions, values (White 2007:220), alternative stories and rich descriptions of their lives and social relationships (Morgan 2000:55). These facets become motivators for transformative action in the DRMC/URCSA (De Beer & Van Niekerk 2009:51; White 2007:220). Unique outcomes are related to events that are linked to both people's dominant and invisible storylines – towards collective and preferred values (De Beer & Van Niekerk 2009:52-53; Morgan 2000:55; White 2007:232-233). Alternative storylines are generated and transcend the dominant and oppressive-saturated storylines (White 2007:233-243). A new DRMC/ URCSA community identity resulted with reconstructed social meaning (De Beer & Van Niekerk 2009:51).

Drinking from our own wells

The shift from structuralism to poststructuralism has a direct theological implication. Theology itself has made paradigm shifts, which have influenced society on many levels. Liberation theology, black theology and feminist theology have changed the way people, society and institutions should be perceived, approached and valued (Beyers Naudé in Berkhof et al. 1985; Boesak 1975, 1977; Cone 1975; Wimberley 1979). This shift represents a departure from traditionally held assumptions and philosophies about life, people, the church, and so forth. Key to such a paradigm shift is the fact that the church or theology does not hold all the truth and authority in people's lives. In therapeutic narrative pedagogy, the existential context of any society and its people should duly be recognised and respected (Bonino in Berkhof et al. 1985:139-155; Cone 1975:39-80; De Beer & Van Niekerk 2009:52-53; Wimberley 1979:20).

Conclusion

The missional nature of church unity should not substitute the authentic witness of the Belhar Confession and its subversive enactment against hidden apartheid and paternalistic theological ideologies and practices. Such is the potential for narrative therapy; that it unlocks the hidden treasures that lie dormant in the rich lives of people who are blindfolded by both modern and postmodern hegemonic, structuralist religious beliefs. The confession of Belhar holds and exposes such hidden, albeit publicly practical, theology treasures to engender pedagogic narrative therapy for divided, broken and traumatised communities.

We are yet again called to be prophetic in our time and space:
> [P]rophetic religion is a fugitive affair – an empathetic and imaginative power that confronts hegemonic powers always operating. Prophetic religion is a profoundly tragicomic affair ... For prophetic religion the condition of truth is to allow suffering to speak ... It does not last too long, because the powers-that-be are not just mighty, but they're very clever and they dilute and incorporate in very seductive ways – or sometimes they just kill you! (West 2011:97-99)

A contextual transformative practical theology within a liberational post-foundational praxis in South Africa could play a critical role in answering the complex questions raised in this book by offering deep answers. The next practical theology quest should be about a practical theology of spiritual and moral transformational leadership in southern Africa. We are our practices, complex and socially extended. This leads to the formation of a way of life, the following of Christ in concrete contexts of cultural and socio-economic dimensions. The communicative community is formed through its participation in these 'co-operatively formed' and 'socially extended' practices. The way of overcoming the chasm between content and intent of the confession (*status confessionis*) and theology of the 'Black Church' in South Africa is through a Christo praxis defined as a 'coherent and complex form of socially established co-operative human activity' which involves every believer of the communicative community. In this way, the dream of a people's church may be realised. As such, the poor of the townships will be empowered to go into the future as part of the crew of the ship, rather than as slaves in the galleys of religious traditions. They will participate in practices that have inherent to them the 'goods' of a theological struggle for liberation and the redemption of humanity. In this way, South Africa will feel the public effect of the practices of church unity, reconciliation, social justice and a critical-loyalty to the state. These are the practices of the Confession of Belhar (Botman 2000:212).

Bibliography

Belhar Confession. 1986. The official English translation of the Belhar Confession 1986 approved by the General Synod of 2008. Belhar: LUS Printers.

Berkhof, H. et al. 1985. *Met de moed der hoop: Opstellen aangeboden aan Dr C.F. Beyers Naudé* (With courage for hope: Essays contributed to Dr C.F. Beyers Naudé). Baarn, Netherlands: Ten Have.

Boesak, A.A. 1977. *Afskeid van de onschuld. Een sociaal-ethische studie over zwarte theologie en zwarte macht.* Kampen, Netherlands: J.H. Kok.

Boesak, A.A. 1975. *Om het zwart te zeggen. Een bundel opstellen over centrale thema's in de zwarte theologie* (To be black: A compilation of essays on central themes in black theology). Kampen, Netherlands: J.H. Kok.

Boff, L. 1986. *Ecclesiogenesis: The base communities reinvent the church.* Glasgow: Collins.

Botha, J. & Naudé, P. 1998. *Op pad met Belhar: Goeie nuus vir gister, vandag en môre* (On route with Belhar: Good news for yesterday, today and tomorrow). Pretoria: Van Schaik Publishers.

Botman, H.R. 2000. Discipleship and practical theology: The case study of South Africa, *International Journal of Practical Theology* 4:201-212. https://doi.org/10.1515/ijpt.2000.4.2.201

Clough, P. 2002. *Narratives and fictions in educational research: doing qualitative research in educational settings.* Philadelphia, PA: Open University Press.

Cone, J.H. 1975. *God of the oppressed.* New York: The Seabury Press.

Dames, G.E. (ed.). 2009. *Ethical leadership and the challenges of moral transformation.* Stellenbosch, SUN PReSS. https://doi.org/10.18820/9781920338350

Dames, G.E. 2010. The dilemma of traditional and 21st-century pastoral ministry: Ministering to families and communities faced with socio-economic pathologies. *HTS Teologiese Studies/Theological Studies* 66(2), Art. #817, 7 pages. [Online] Available at http://www.hts.org.za (Accessed 11 October 2015). https://doi.org/10.4102/hts.v66i2.817

Dames, G.E. 2012. The relevance of pedagogical narrative maps: The Confession of Belhar as a practical theological narrative searching for a pedagogic-therapeutic methodology. *Dutch Reformed Theological Journal* 53(1):25-38. [Online] Availablle at http://ngtt.journals.ac.za (Accessed 11 October 2015).

Dames, G.E. 2014. Spiritual and ethical transformational leadership: Critical discourse analysis within a practical theology praxis. *Koers Bulletin for Christian Scholarship* 79(2), Art. #2116, 8 pages. http://dx.doi.org/10.4102/koers.v79i2.2116

de Beer, J.M. & van Niekerk, A.S. 2009. Die missionêre waarde van Belhar en die NG Kerk-familie se herenigingsgesprek: The missional value of Belhar and the DRC family's reunification talks. *Dutch Reformed Theological Journal* 50(1/2):50-65.

Freedman, J. & Combs, G. 1996. *Narrative therapy: The social construction of preferred realities*. New York: Norton.

Hartney, J.N.M. 2011. Eksegeties-teologiese ondersteuning van die Belydenis van Belhar (Exegetic-theological analysis of some biblical concepts in the Confession of Belhar). *Dutch Reformed Theological Journal* 52(1/2), 94-104.

Institute for Justice and Reconciliation. 2004. *Interfaith solidarity: A guide for religious communities*. Cape Town: Amazon Media.

Keifert, P. 2006. *We are here now: A new missional era, a missional journey of spiritual discovery*. Eagle, ID: Allelon Publishing.

Koopman, N. 2008. On violence, the Belhar Confession and human dignity, *Dutch Reformed Theological Journal* 49(3/4):159-166.

Kotzé, E. (ed.). 2000. *A chorus of voices: Weaving life's narratives in therapy and training*. Pretoria: Ethics Alive.

Landman, C. 2009a. 'Gender-based violence and God-talk'. Paper presented at the Joint Conference of Academic Societies in the Fields of Religion and Theology, Faculty of Theology, Stellenbosch University, Stellenbosch (22–26 June).

Landman, C. 2009b. *Doing narrative counselling in the context of township spiritualities*. [Online] Available at http://www.unisa.ac.za/library (Accessed 11 October 2015).

Louw, D.J. 2008. *Cura vitae: Illness and the healing of life*. Wellington: Lux Verb.

Malema-Luthuli-hearing, 2011. [Online] Available at http://www.news24.com/Multimedia/MyNews24/Malema-Luthuli-hearing-20110916 (Accessed 11 October 2015).

McLaren, B.D. 2001. *A new kind of Christian: A tale of two friends on a spiritual journey*. San Francisco CA: Jossey-Bass.

Morgan, A. 2000. *What is narrative therapy? An easy-to-read Introduction*. Adelaide: Dulwich Centre Publications.

Morkel, E. 2008. Post-modern epistemology: MTh pastoral care and counselling workshop notes.

Murphy, F.A. 2007. *God is not a story*. Aberdeen: University of Aberdeen. [Online] Available at www.oxfordscholarship.com (Accessed 30 August 2011). https://doi.org/10.1093/acprof:oso/9780199219285.001.0001

Nair, N. 2011. Facebook-racist-lashed. [Online] available at http://www.timeslive.co.za/politics/2011/08/29/facebook-racist-lashed (Accessed 11 October 2015).

Novelli, M. 2008. *Shaped by the story: Helping students encounter God in a new way*. Grand Rapids, MI: Zondervan.

Ploeger, AK. 1995, *Inleiding in de godsdienstpedagogiek* (Introduction to religious pedagogy). Kampen, Netherlands: J.H. Kok.

Strauss, P.J. 2005, *Belydenis, kerkverband en Belhar* (Confession, denomination and Belhar). *Dutch Reformed Theological Journal* 46(3/4):560-575.

Taylor, S. 2005. *The out of bounds church? Learning to create a community of faith in a culture of change.* Grand Rapids, MI: Zondervan.

Thomas, L. 2002. Poststructuralism and therapy – what's it all about? *The International Journal of Narrative Therapy and Community Work* 2:, 85-89.

van Dijk, T.A. 1993. Principles of critical discourse analysis. *Discourse & Society* 4(2):249-283. https://doi.org/10.1177/0957926593004002006

van Rooi, L. 2010. Identity, boundaries and the eucharist: In search of the unity, catholicity and apostolicity of the church from the fringes of the Kalahari Desert. *Dutch Reformed Theological Journal* 51(1/2):176-185.

West, C. 2011. Prophetic religion and the future of Capitalist civilisation. In J. Butler, J. Habermas, C. Taylor & C. Wes (eds), *The power of religion in the public sphere* (Kindle edition). New York: Columbia University Press.

White, M. 2007. *Maps of narrative practice.* New York: Norton.

Wimberley, E.P. 1979. *Pastoral care in the black church*, Nashville, KY: Abingdon.

Winslade, J. & Monk, G. 1998. *Narrative counselling in schools: Powerful and brief.* Thousand Oaks, CA: Corwin Press. 'Narrative therapy in a nutshell' – notes taken from the book.

BARMEN AND BELHAR IN CONVERSATION
A South African perspective

Dirkie Smit

Abstract

This chapter is taken from a paper read at the Barmen/Belhar Consultation, 18 October 2004 and the article, 'Reformed Churches in South Africa and the Struggle for Justice – Remembering 1960-1990' published in the *Nederduitse Gereformeerde Teologiese Tydskrif* (Smit 2006)

Claiming that the South African Confession of Belhar should be understood in the tradition of the Barmen Theological Declaration, this chapter points to historical continuities, formal similarities and shared theological viewpoints.

A central section focuses on the theses of Barmen, to reflect on the question why Barmen influenced and inspired so many South African Christians in the struggle against apartheid. The chapter concludes buy considering the possible contemporary relevance of Barmen and Belhar by asking three questions concerning their potential impact and influence today, namely if their claims are still regarded as true, how they could be embodied, and whether they could contribute to a new language.

A long and ongoing conversation

The Belhar Confession is the product of a conversation with the Barmen Declaration. Without Barmen, there would have been no Belhar in its present form. Belhar was born in a long, intense struggle with Barmen – with its own historical context, its insights and contributions, the theologies, theologians and church movements informing and inspiring it, the evangelical claims expressed in it, and its own ambiguous history of reception during the decades to follow, in Germany and far outside its birthplace. Since its inception, Belhar was both a product of this long conversation with Barmen and a further historical moment in this conversation itself.

This history has often been told. It therefore suffices to remember that Belhar would not have been born without the role of, among many others, Beyers Naudé, the Christian Institute and its many supporters, from church leaders to many believers, and church members who increasingly understood the struggle against apartheid in continuity with the church struggle in Germany. Also, Belhar would not have come about without the South African Council of Churches (SACC) with several of its member churches, church leaders and theologians, like Desmond Tutu, Wolfram Kistner, John de Gruchy, Douglas Bax, and many others, its *Message to the People of South Africa*, and the role of the broader ecumenical movement; without South African Reformed theologians like Jaap Durand, Willie Jonker, David Bosch and many others, who worked, thought and witnessed in the theological tradition of Karl Barth; without especially Allan Boesak, who played a major role as church leader, theologian, ecumenical figure and activist, also in the tradition of Calvin, Barth, Bonhoeffer and Barmen, and without whom the struggle against apartheid certainly would not have developed the way it did; without movements like the '*Broederkring*', later the '*Belydende Kring*', and the Alliance of Black Reformed Christians in Southern Africa (ABRECSA), all consisting of sisters and brothers who again thought and acted very consciously in this theological and ecclesial tradition; without a whole generation of other theologians and church leaders, like Daan Cloete, Chris Loff, Shun Govender, Hannes Adonis, Johan Botha, Welile Mazamisa, Takatso Mofokeng and many of their contemporaries (to mention only a few from my own small world of personal experience, although there are many others who deserve to be mentioned whenever the full story is told); without a still younger generation of then students and younger ministers, like Russel Botman, James Buys, Leonardo Appies, and again many more, most of them not celebrated and publicly well-known, who through their insights and convictions, commitment and witness, even suffering and fate, stood in the tradition of Barmen. Everyone who knows this history will be able to add many other names of people who deserve to be mentioned, but the point here is very simple. It is a reminder that Belhar itself is the product of a long and intense conversation with Barmen, with Barth, Bonhoeffer, the German Confessing Church, and the history of its reception and interpretation.

It is therefore understandable that there are indeed many formal similarities between Barmen and Belhar – structural elements, positive claims and negative rejections, appeals to Scripture, direct allusions (especially in the preface and conclusion of Belhar), the shared dependence on the Heidelberg Catechism, and many more. Both were documents of the church, not of individuals; both targeted false doctrine, not specific people; both were binding and authoritative and not optional, not mere theological opinions and contributions to a discussion, born in a *status confessionis*, a moment of truth, when the gospel itself was at stake, according to those who confessed. Both therefore did not cause the crisis but were responses to an already existing crisis.

There are even deeper commonalities, such as the deliberate absence of any reference to these historical contexts or crises that gave rise to the respective confessions, except for being implied in the rejections. The latter characteristic was based on the same understanding of what a confession is – not a political statement, but a positive expression of the truth of the gospel, applicable elsewhere and afterwards. The accompanying letter to Belhar, according to the original decision of the Confessing Synod an integral part of the confession and always to be read together with it, even shows direct influence from the Barmen history. Scholars could therefore easily develop a conversation between the two documents by looking for similarities and possible differences.

However, much more important is that the two documents share a common theological tradition, a common faith position, a common confessional viewpoint and claim. Although there were similarities even between the historical struggles in which they were born, in the challenges they addressed and the false convictions they sought to unmask and rejected, the much more important agreement is given in the fact that they do that from the same theological and confessional position. Both Barmen and Belhar responded to specific, and in some ways similar, historical challenges, but both regarded these as symptoms of deeper, more fundamental theological and ecclesiological problems and temptations that had been growing over a long period, and that could again manifest itself in history in perhaps different symptoms – and both wanted to affirm positively, against this fundamental but hidden false understanding of gospel and church, the wonderful news of the living, Triune God.

The most interesting conversation could, therefore, be one that seeks to understand this common confessional and theological ground between Barmen and Belhar, and then continues to ask about the continuing challenges embedded in that confessional viewpoint, if any. To understand this theological and confessional tradition, it may be helpful to start the conversation by listening anew – from a South African perspective – to the central theological claims of Barmen. Why did the Barmen Theological Declaration so powerfully inspire and inform so many South African Christians during the struggle against apartheid?

Listening to Barmen

Like every confession, Barmen must be heard as a single, albeit complex claim. It is important to read Barmen not as six separate and distinct theses – precisely as it is true of Belhar – of which we can adhere to some while ignoring and neglecting others. Only in their joint claim do they confess what is truly at stake. Therefore, the internal structure, the overall thrust of Barmen is of extreme importance. However, to understand that thrust it is indeed necessary first to listen carefully to the way it seemingly fans out into six different directions. The central claim of Barmen concerns the church. It is found in theses III and IV. The message of the church, the faith of the church, has to be reflected in the order of the church, in the form of the church – this is the point. The church, belonging to Jesus Christ, may not proclaim one message but practice another one. This central ecclesiological claim is given a Christological foundation in the form of a preface in theses I and II. Jesus Christ is the one Word of God, he is the content of the message and faith of the church, and he frees us and claims us. He should therefore determine the form and order of this church that belongs to him (III and IV). The final two theses draw practical implications from this central Christological and ecclesiological conviction, namely for the public and political role of the church (V) and for the mission and proclamation of the church to the whole world (VI). This structure is seemingly so simple, but the implications are powerful and dramatic – for then and there, and for today.

The first thesis claims that 'Jesus Christ, as he is attested for us in Holy Scripture, is the one Word of God which we have to hear and which we have to trust and obey in life and in death.'[1] Jesus Christ is the one Word of God – there is no other. Which Jesus? The Jesus as is attested for us in Holy Scripture, which includes both the Old and New Testaments. In this Jesus Christ we know God, and in him alone. The three verbs – we have to 'hear', 'trust' and 'obey' him, and in that order – are of crucial importance. We have to do this 'in life and death,' which is a clear allusion to the Heidelberg Catechism, and which in fact plays a major role in the overall argument and theology of Barmen (and Belhar). The verbs even suggest allusions to the threefold ministry of Jesus Christ, as prophet, priest and king. What is rejected by this foundational Christological claim? The answer is clear, namely any form of natural theology, claiming that there are also other ways of knowing other gods, other words, that we have to hear, trust and obey. When the implications are drawn for the form and nature of the church (III and IV), and also for the public role and the mission of the church (V and VI), the radical implications of this rejection will be clear, and at stake. Or put differently, behind the seemingly practical – even innocent, debatable, and theologically contestable? – arguments of that time concerning Christian ethics (II), the church order (III), the ministries of the church (IV), the public role of the church (V) and the missionary task of the church (VI), lies hidden a fundamental conflict; between natural theology on the one hand and hearing, trusting and obeying Jesus Christ as the one Word of God, in life and death, on the other hand. To whom is this thesis addressed? Clearly not to outsiders, but to the church itself, internally, self-critically. What is at stake is the

---

1 All quotations from the English translation of the Declaration of Barmen are taken from *The Church's Confession Under Hitler* (Cochrane 1962:237-242).

theological basis of the church itself, the very ground on which it exists, the very gospel which it believes and confesses. In characteristic confessional style, Barmen (like Belhar) speaks in the first place to the speakers themselves, to the church who utters these words. Anyone who knows the history of the 'church struggle' in South Africa knows that this fundamental theological conflict, between forms of natural theology and pleas for a Christological theology based on the Word alone, was at the heart of our struggle. There is no other way to understand the theological contributions of people like Jonker, Durand, Boesak, and many others. I remember a visit at the Jonker home with Allan Boesak and an ecumenical visitor, during which Jonker explained how he saw his own calling as teaching this Christological theology to a new generation of students, in the hope that the prevailing natural theology undergirding apartheid will, in the long run, not be able to withstand this truth revealed to us in Jesus Christ.

The second thesis claims that 'As Jesus Christ is God's assurance of the forgiveness of all our sins, so in the same way and with the same seriousness is he also God's mighty claim upon our whole life.' It adds, in a second clause, 'Through him befalls us a joyful deliverance from the godless fetters of this world for a free, grateful service to his creatures.' The rejection is very important: 'We reject the false doctrine, as though there were other areas of our life in which we would not belong to Jesus Christ, but to other lords – areas in which we would not need justification and sanctification through him.' Barmen II is nothing less than 'a foundation for Christian ethics' (Busch 2004:38) – and Christian ethics is 'an ethics of freedom' (Huber 1991:48-60). It is at the same time a theological protest against doctrine (I) without ethics (II), and against ethics separated from doctrine and theology (Huber). It is again a summary of the overall structure of the Heidelberg Catechism, where salvation and liberation flow over in lives of obedience and gratitude. It describes the nature of discipleship (Busch 2004:39). Since the church belongs to Jesus Christ, we should live like people who belong to him. He is at the same time God's assurance of forgiveness of all our sins and God's mighty claim upon our whole life. The addition 'our whole life' is of particular importance, as the explicit conclusions of the rejection show, calling it false doctrine if anyone should claim that there are 'other areas of our life in which we do not belong to Jesus Christ, but to other lords.' This is a rejection of all versions of the so-called autonomy ('*Eigengesetzlichkeit*') of different spheres of (modern) life, understood in such a way that the gospel of Jesus Christ has no implications for those spheres of reality. Again, these were precisely the theological and ethical claims at work in the theology and sermons of, for example, Allan Boesak, often with appeals to other traditions as well, particularly Reformed ones, including Kuyper, but mostly with explicit reference to Barth and Bonhoeffer.

The third thesis comes to the heart of Barmen. It claims that 'the church has to testify with its faith as with its obedience, with its message as with its order, that it is solely the property of Jesus Christ,' and rejects 'the false doctrine, as though the church were permitted to abandon the form of its message and order to its own pleasure or to changes in prevailing ideological and political convictions.'

Here one hears the voices of Barth and Bonhoeffer very clearly. According to some, this thesis offers what Protestantism had been lacking since the Reformation, namely 'an evangelical definition of the church' – the church belongs to Jesus Christ, and this should be reflected in its order, in its visible form and structure as well. The living Christ is working as Lord in word and sacrament through the Holy Spirit, and this should become visible and practical in the so-called 'real church.' The truth and the form, the message and the social structure of the church belong inextricably together. The latter should not contradict and deny the former, because of the influence and impact of whatever prevailing ideological, social, cultural, political and economic convictions, practices and policies. The church is therefore a congregation of brothers and sisters, belonging to Jesus Christ and therefore to one another, given to one another by Jesus Christ himself, and not chosen on the basis of their race, ethnicity, skin colour, sex, class or whatever cultural and social characteristic. The extraordinary relevance of this theological position for South Africa is for everyone to see, then and now. It is also confessed at the heart of Belhar's claims about the unity of the church. In fact, these convictions have a long tradition in Reformed thought and practice. Since the earliest days of the Calvinist Reformation and ever since, Reformed confessions were always intended to be embodied, also in the form of church orders and practical arrangements. In South Africa, these arguments were, for example, powerfully made by Willie Jonker, in several of his small but extremely influential, although deeply controversial, publications during the apartheid years, and they were again developed in great detail by people like Hannes Adonis in his work on the wall of separation rebuilt.

The fourth thesis is closely related to the third, still deals with the church, and describes the nature of ministry in this church belonging to Jesus Christ, claiming that 'the various offices do not establish a dominion of some over others, but on the contrary, are for the exercise of the ministry entrusted to and enjoyed upon the whole congregation'. There are no special rulers in or over this church and none with vested ruling powers. The brothers and sisters are all and jointly called to mutual service, to one another and the world. The 'various offices' do not lead to personal authority, but only to functional authority, and this function is one of service. In Belhar's description, with a whole series of biblical allusions, of the way in which the wonderfully rich diversity of gifts, backgrounds, opportunities and abilities present in the members work together in the one – *not* uniform – church to enrich and strengthen its life and witness, one hears the same theological convictions at work. In the new Church Order of the Uniting Reformed Church in Southern Africa, precisely these confessional convictions and their practical implications have been employed to open up possibilities for a church to order and organise itself practically on the basis of this Protestant ecclesiology of Barmen and Belhar.

The fifth thesis considers theologically the public role of this church, its political responsibility and its relationship with the state, and claims that 'Scripture tells us that' in the 'as yet unredeemed world' in which both church and state exist, the state has 'by divine appointment' the task of providing for 'justice and peace,' and should do this 'according to the measure of human judgement and human ability.' The church 'acknowledges the benefit of this divine appointment in gratitude and reverence before God,' and calls to mind the kingdom of God, God's commandment and righteousness,' and thereby the responsibility of both rulers and ruled – trusting in and obeying 'the power of the Word by which God upholds all things.' It therefore rejects both the false doctrine of the totalitarian and usurping state and the false doctrine of the church itself becoming state-like and an organ of the state. Again, the historical context is clearly implied and present, but even more fundamental for Barmen are the theological convictions at stake and the false doctrines that had become powerful and pervasive, even in the church itself. Thesis five should be heard against the backdrop of theses one and two, about Jesus Christ as the one Word and both God's assurances and mighty claim upon our whole life. A Christ-like church may not become a state-like church, employing state-like methods and demonstrating state-like characteristics. In its political ethics, describing both the task and the boundaries of the state theologically, Barmen affirms the strengths of both the two-kingdoms and the lordship-of-Christ understandings. The oft-construed tension between these two rests, mistakenly, on only a seeming contradiction, since both represent elements of truth. Church and state should be distinguished, but not totally separated. The arrogant hubris of both state and church should be resisted in the name of the kingdom. The state is not the kingdom and the church is not the state. The state is not the kingdom, but exists in the unredeemed world by God's appointment – in German, '*Anordnung*', a clear allusion to and rejection of the totalitarian '*Ordnung*', the total order usurped by the totalitarian state, exceeding its divine appointment, as the rejection says. Appointed by God, the state has a task, namely to serve justice and peace. The state should do this humanly and humanely, and the church should thank God for this. The church is not the state, but also exists in and as part of the as yet unredeemed world – reminding both rulers and ruled of their respective responsibilities. Many commentators, including already Barth himself, and later Wolfgang Huber, have argued convincingly that political ethics today should go beyond the insights and claims of this thesis, although in the same theological direction. In a very definite way, Belhar and again the Uniting

Reformed Church in Southern Africa (URCSA) church order have already done this to some extent, for example by not concentrating on church and state relations, but rather situating the church in more complex spheres of public life, civil society, the formation of public opinion and economic life, but specifically by focusing explicitly on real reconciliation and compassionate, caring justice.

The sixth thesis addresses the missionary task of the church, claiming that 'the church's freedom' is founded upon its commission to deliver 'the free grace of God to all people in Christ's stead,' which leads to a rejection of the false doctrine 'as though the church could place the Word and work of the Lord in the service of any arbitrarily chosen desires, purposes, and plans.' Again, this is clearly a further implication of the Christological claims that the church belongs to Jesus Christ (I and II) and should therefore visibly demonstrate this belonging to him in its own order, life and ministry (III and IV) – which also involves its public witness (V) and its mission and proclamation (VI). The mission of the church may also, like the church order, never be instrumentalised to serve other desires, purposes and plans, whether political, cultural, social or economic. The expression 'to all people' ('*an alles Volk*') was extremely controversial at the time, and has remarkably remained so in the history of Barmen's reception, until today. Particularly important is the way in which the freedom of the church – a central theme right through Barmen – is understood in relation to the mission of the church. The church's deepest freedom is given in its calling to proclaim the message of the free grace of God – 'to all people'! Any other message, however religious and pious, moral and serious, despite any restriction of the addressees to only some, to a specific '*volk*' or to only some in the '*volk*', or any refusal or reluctance to proclaim this good news of God's free grace, or any denial of this wonderful missionary task of the church, is nothing less than a loss of freedom. Again, it is abundantly clear how this confessional stance was at stake in the theological and ecclesial developments legitimating apartheid and therefore in the theological opposition against this alien influence and power in the church and its proclamation, and the resultant loss of the freedom of the church. It was precisely the ministry of Christ's Word and work through sermon and sacrament 'to all people' that was compromised – so that this wonderful freedom was lost.

Even through this superficial reminder of the content of Barmen, its central and powerful claim becomes obvious. The church belongs to Jesus Christ, who assures the church of joyful deliverance and claims the church with a mighty claim. The church is not simply a religious organisation of like-minded people who can decide for themselves how to organise themselves, what to do and whom to serve. The order, the structure, the ministries, the offices of the church should all visibly serve the truth of his message, the content of his good news. The church should hear, trust and obey Jesus Christ in every aspect of its whole life, and should therefore freely proclaim this wonderful truth of God's free grace in the public spheres and to all people. In almost every respect, this central claim was being denied by the thought, practices and structures of the official church and its leaders at the time – a denial in which the confessing believers recognised false doctrine and false theological convictions that had grown among them over many decades until their moment of decision. It is also obvious why so many South African Christians would recognise similar thought patterns, practices and structures in the church during the days of apartheid, and why the theological stance and tradition of Barmen would help them to discern similar fundamental theological and confessional choices present here, in our moment of decision. Perhaps the more intriguing question is whether this longstanding conversation between Barmen and Belhar still presents us with challenges today?

Listening to Barmen and Belhar, today?

It is possible to list a whole range of crucial themes and issues for us today in the light of this conversation. I would like to invite such reflections by pointing to three possible clusters of themes and issues. Recently, as part of the 70-year anniversary of Barmen, Eberhard Busch wrote:

> Confession does not mean clinging to a confessional text that has once been called forth from the church. Confession rather means new witness to the gospel of Jesus Christ in the light of present challenges. A church that does not faithfully practise its own confession, does not thereby make this confession invalid, but is instead called to repentance by its own confession. The worst that could happen, would then be that such a church, instead of such repentance, with unrepenting hearts, proudly exhibits their confession as a golden memory in a glass display cabinet. It has happened often enough that the church has not understood that the confession does not belong at home in a museum, but that it must be carried in front of them and that they must follow their confession whenever facing new challenges and struggles. It is not enough for the church to *have* a confession. The church should *live* from and with its confession. (Busch 2004:9-10, italics added)

The first question one could ask is whether we still hear and trust these claims, today; whether we still hear this one Word of God, Jesus Christ, in our churches and in our lives; and whether this is indeed still the good news, the gospel, that we trust, in life and death? The symptoms of the temptation, the visible manifestations of the false doctrine and the deviant theology differ through the years – they do not appear in the same form again – but do we have the spiritual discernment, the theological skill and gospel sense to read the signs of the times and to recognise the new temptations and false teachings, which we may be facing today in our contemporary societies and world? Or are we still caught in the struggles that lie behind us, unable to discern the present ones? Are we able to recognise the possibly new forms of natural theology, of natural religiosity, of idolatry, of cultural usurpation of gospel and church, of the church becoming state-like? Do we really trust and worship the one Word of God, according to the Scriptures, or do we celebrate and worship, trust and follow other promises, other claims of self-fulfilment, happiness, and success? Do we see the (possibly) new ways in which the church is tempted today to take on cultural form, rather than the form of Christ? Which kind of freedom do we truly celebrate and trust – the joyful deliverance from the godless fetters of this world for a free and grateful service to his creatures (Barmen II), the freedom based on the church's commission to proclaim the message of the free grace of God to all people (VI), or a different kind of freedom, offered to us by other events and powers, figures and truths (I)?

These are self-critical questions, addressed to the church itself, in particular, churches who stand – sometimes seemingly proudly and smugly, even self-righteously – in the tradition of Barmen and Belhar. Therefore, many commentators like Busch have repeatedly stressed that having a confession is not the point, but confessing it, and ever anew. A true confession of this nature becomes a self-critical voice, also addressed to those who think they have and possess this confession. A church with a confession is not necessarily a confessing church. From the beginning the Dutch Reformed Mission Church (DRMC) knew this very well. That is why it, from the very beginning, officially and publicly distinguished between the fact of Belhar and the content of Belhar. The DRMC did not expect any other church, including the members of the DRC family, but also more widely in the ecumenical church, to accept Belhar as their own confessional document. That would have been contrary to the century-old Reformed practice and custom concerning confessional documents. It would have been contrary to the fact that it was precisely the confession born in the heart of the DRCM itself, expressing its own identity, understanding of the gospel, and commitment. It also would have been contrary to what we learned from the reception of Barmen over decades, in many churches all over the world, where the exact status of the text and the diverse ways in which churches affirmed, appropriated and adopted Barmen correctly never became the major issue, not even in the different evangelical churches in Germany itself. This would also be contrary to the firm conviction – expressed again and again in discussions with other churches by the so-called '*Gesprekskommissie*' – that the 'fact' of Belhar should not be a hindrance in the way to achieve what Belhar is about. Having a confession and formally accept a confession was not the point. What the DRMC did take very seriously, however, was the content of Belhar. We wanted to hear what other churches said about the content, and in the official conversations that was what we asked from other churches in the DRC family and in ecumenical circles. We wanted our ecumenical brothers and sisters to advise us and to help us to hear the one Word of God, and we wanted to know where we stood with the other member churches of the family. We explained officially that, as far as we were concerned, the unity we longed for so much was only to be found on the basis of this content. Therefore, we needed to know whether our brothers and sisters also heard the same gospel, trusted the same promises, and wanted to obey the same claim on our lives– and only on that basis could we reunite, we said. Merely clinging to a document as document, to a text as text, and expecting others to accept that text formally as their text as well, has never been what Reformed confessions, what Barmen and what Belhar was about. In fact, doing that could ironically and sadly even become a form of the church becoming state-like, attempting to deal with others primarily by legal and judicial means, by dominion rather than service, which Barmen so clearly rejects (V and VI). It has therefore indeed been an encouraging and often wonderful experience over the last decades to hear from so many churches, ecumenical bodies, and groups of Christians, in South and southern Africa, in larger regions, in other countries and continents, that they indeed hear in Belhar the one Word of God, his liberating assurances and his mighty claim, and that this helps them in their own contexts, with their present challenges and struggles, and our joint struggles in the world today – this is indeed the first and important question.

The second question is whether we truly obey these claims, today? The ongoing conversation has made it abundantly clear that Protestant – very definitely Reformed – confessions call for embodiment. The one Word we hear and trust must be practised in all areas of our life (Barmen II), in our church structures and order, including our material and financial structures, as Huber rightly underlines (III), in our ministries and services (IV), in our public witness through word and deed (V), and in our mission and proclamation (VI). Regarding Barmen, Huber developed 'an ethics and ecclesiology of freedom,' asking how Christian freedom can achieve concrete form and body in such ways that it is really experienced. Answering this question, he develops a practical vision of the church *'als Raum und als Anwalt der Freiheit,'* as both the space where freedom is practised and experienced as well as the advocate who publicly speaks for freedom whenever and wherever necessary. Regarding Belhar, it similarly should be possible to develop an ethics and ecclesiology of living unity, real reconciliation and compassionate justice, according to which the church becomes both the place where unity, reconciliation and justice are really practised and experienced in the church itself, as well as the voice that actively and publicly speaks and pleads for these forms of unity, reconciliation and justice, whenever and wherever necessary. What would this truly mean in our world, our societies, today – to be a church like this, to embody the claims and convictions of our own confession? The question is how we – together, jointly – live these convictions today, in our church order and structures (Barmen III), but also in our ethics (II), in our mutual acceptance and service (IV), in our public witness, presence, actions and style (V), in our mission and our proclamation, through sermon and sacrament, through word and deed, in many and rich ways at our disposal in the contemporary world (VI). This is our acid test, also for a new, reunited church in our family – not whether we find the best formulations for including Belhar in the confessional basis, since that will be easy, and certainly not whether we use a confessional document in un-Reformed, inquisitional ways to test the personal faith of individual members, but whether this new church hears, trusts and obeys this faith, today. For a reunited church, this faith could never be optional, to choose or to ignore, to live and embody, or not.

This leads to a final question. Following Ernst Lange's famous description of the church as 'Sprachschule für die Freiheit', as the school where we learn to speak the language of freedom, Huber expresses the hope that Barmen could maybe provide us with a new common language, with a new and more adequate way to talk about our world and our shared responsibilities. Regarding Belhar, that could perhaps also be a realistic hope. The ongoing ecumenical conversation in the tradition of Barmen and Belhar will certainly not provide us with the answers to our present challenges, but perhaps it can indeed help us to find a common language, a language of freedom, unity, reconciliation, justice and responsibility, a language of discipleship and hope that could help us better to see and recognise, better to understand and describe, and better to respond together to the new challenges of our common and radically changing world, today.

Bibliography

Adonis, J.C. 1982. *Die afgebreekte skeidsmuur weer opgebou*. Amsterdam: Rodopi.
Adonis, J.C. 1988. 'n Gereformeerde kerkorde? Opmerkings oor die kerkorde van die Verenigende Gereformeerde Kerk in Suider-Afrika In W.A. Boesak & P.J.A. Fourie (eds.), *Vraagtekens oor gereformeerdheid?* Belhar: LUS Printers.
Barth, K. 1935. *Das Bekenntnis der Reformation und unser Bekennen*. München: Chr. Kaiser Verlag.
Barth, K. 1960. *The humanity of God*, Richmond, VA: John Knox.
Barth, K. 1990. Wünschbarkeit und Möglichkeit eines allgemeinen reformierten Glaubensbekenntnisses. In K. Barth, *Vorträge und kleinere arbeiten 1922-1925. Gesamtausgabe III*. Zürich: Theologischer Verlag.
Barth, K. 1998. *Die Theologie der reformierten Bekenntnisschriften 1923. Gesamtausgabe II*. Zürich: Theologischer Verlag.
Barth, K. 2004. *Texte zur Barmer Theologischen Erklärung*. Zürich: TVZ Theologischer Verlag.
Berkhof, H. 1964. Die toekoms van die Gereformeerde konfessie. *Pro Veritate* III/6:1-2.
Berkouwer, G.C. 1963. Vragen rondom de belijdenis. *Gereformeerd Theologisch Tijdschrift* 63:1-41.

Boesak, A.A. 1984. *Black and reformed*, Maryknoll, NY: Orbis.
Botha, J.G. & Naudé, P.J. 1998. *Op pad met Belhar. Goeie nuus vir gister, vandag en môre!* Pretoria: Van Schaik Publishers.
Büning, M.B. 2002. *Bekenntnis und Kirchenverfassung*. Frankfurt: Peter Lang.
Burgsmüller, A. & Weth, R. 1998. *Die Burmer Theologische Erklärung*. Neukirchen-Vluyn: Neukirchener Verlag.
Busch, E. 2004. *Die Barmer Thesen 1934-2004*. Göttingen: Vandenhoeck & Ruprecht.
Cloete, G.D. & Smit, D.J. 1984. *'n Oomblik van waarheid*. Cape Town: Tafelberg.
Cochrane, A.C. 1962. *The church's confession under Hitler*. Philadelphia, PA: Westminster Press.
EKU. 1975. *Zum politischen Auftrag der christlichen Gemeinde – Barmen II*. Gütersloh: Gütersloher Verlag.
EKU.1980. *Kirche als 'Gemeinde von Brüdern'. Barmen III, Bd. I und II*. Gütersloh: Gütersloher Verlag.
EKU. 1986. *Für Recht und Frieden sorgen: Auftrag der Kirche und Aufgabe des Staates nach Barmen V* (1986). Gütersloh: Gütersloher Verlag.
EKU. 1993. *Das eine Wort Gottes – Botschaft für alle. Barmen I und VI. Bd. I und II*. Gütersloh: Gütersloher Verlag.
EKU. 1999. *Der Dienst der ganzen Gemeinde Jesu Christi und das Problem der Herrschaft. Barmen IV. Bd. I und II*. Gütersloh: Gütersloher Verlag.
Freudenberg, M. 1997. *Karl Barth und die reformierte Theologie*. Neukirchen-Vluyn: Neukirchener Verlag.
Huber, W 1985. *Folgen christlicher Freiheit. Ethik und Theorie der Kirche im Horizont der Barmer Theologischen Erklärung*. Neukirchen-Vluyn: Neukirchener Verlag.
Jonker, W.D. 1962. *Die sendingbepalinge van die NG Kerk van Transvaal*. Bloemfontein: Sendingboekhandel.
Jonker, W.D. 1965a. *Aandag vir die kerk*. Potchefstroom: Die Evangelis
Jonker, W.D. 1965b. *Om die regering van Christus in sy kerk*. Pretoria: University of South Africa Press.
Jonker, W.D. 1993. Die moderne belydenisbeweging in Suid-Afrika – en Calvyn. *In Die Skriflig* 27(4):443- 461. https://doi.org/10.4102/ids.v27i4.1472
Jonker, W.D. 1994. *Bevrydende waarheid*. Wellington: Hugenote-Uitgewers.
Lange, E. 1980. *Sprachschule für die Freiheit*. München: Kaiser Verlag.
Link, H.G. 1998. *Bekennen und Bekenntnis*. Göttingen: Vandenhoeck & Ruprecht.
Möller, U. 1999. *Im Prozeß des Bekennens*. Neukirchen-Vluyn: Neukirchener Verlag.
Plasger, G. 2000. *Die relative Autorität des Bekenntnisses bei Karl Barth*. Neukirchen-Vluyn: Verlag.
Plasger, G. & Freudenberg, M. 2005. *Reformierte Bekenntnisschriften*. Göttingen: Vandenhoeck & Ruprecht.
Rohls, J. 1987. *Theologie reformierter Bekenntnisschriften*. Göttingen: Vandenhoeck & Ruprecht.
Smit, D.J. 1984. Wat beteken *status confessionis*? In G. Cloete & D. Smit(eds), *'n Oomblik van waarheid: Opstelle rondom die NG Sendingkerk se afkondiging van 'n status confessionis en die opstel van 'n konsepbelydenis*. Cape Town. Tafelberg.
Smit, D.J. 2000. Social transformation and confessing the faith? *Scriptura* 72(1), 76-86.

Smit, D.J. 2002. Bely en beliggaam (Confess and embody). In P. Coertzen (ed.), *350 jaar Gereformeerd/350 years Reformed*. Bloemfontein: CLF.

Smit, D.J. 2003 No other motives would give us the right – Reflections on contextuality from a Reformed perspective. In M.E. Brinkman & D. Van Keulen (eds), *Studies in Reformed theology*. Zoetermeer, Netherlands: Meinema.

Smit, D.J. 2006. Barmen and Belhar in conversation – a South African perspective. *Nederduitse Gereformeerde Teologiese Tydskrif* 47(1/2):291-301.

Weth, R. 1984. *'Barmen' als Herausforderung der Kirche. Beiträge zum Kirchenverständnis im Licht der Barmer Theologischen Erklärung*. München: Chr. Kaiser Verlag.

TO STAND WHERE GOD STANDS

Reflections on the Confession of Belhar after 25 years

Allan Boesak

Introduction

The Confession of Belhar was first adopted by the Dutch Reformed Mission Church (DRMC) Synod in 1982, and then formally accepted as a fourth confession in 1986. Since then, it has become the bedrock of theological reference and reflection as well as a salient point of theological identity within the Uniting Reformed Church in Southern Africa (URCSA). However, it has not escaped controversy, and today has become quite the most visible point of conflagration in the tortuous process of reunification of the Dutch Reformed Church (DRC) family. Over the past twenty-five years, the Confession of Belhar has been accepted as the formal confession of a number of churches within the Reformed family worldwide. The confession is studied seriously as an important theological contribution to the thinking of the ecumenical church and significantly informs documents such as the Accra Confession, adopted by the World Alliance of Reformed Churches (WARC) General Council in Accra, Ghana, 2004. This chapter, offers historical and theological reflections on the Confession (Boesak 2008:1-29). It endeavours to show the relevance of the Confession in the different contexts into which it came into being and how the confession challenges those contexts. It considers the theological understanding upon which the Confession rests, and argues that it remains of great relevance to and theological importance for the churches in South Africa and worldwide, and is an absolute necessity for the theological integrity of the church unification process (Boesak 2008).[1]

A rare and precious occurrence

Twenty-five years ago, the church in which I serve, the then DRMC (now the URCSA), adopted a new confession known as the Confession of Belhar, named after the 'coloured' township where the synod was held. It was the first confession of faith to be formulated in almost 300 years within the Reformed family of churches and the

---

1 This chapter was first presented in a lecture series and published in article by Alan Boesak in *Studia Historiae Eccelsiasticae* (Boeasak 2008). Also available at http://uir.unisa.ac.za/handle/10500/4539

first to come from a church in Africa in modern times.[2] It was a rare and precious occurrence, and one that has impacted significantly on the theological landscape in South Africa and elsewhere. It changed the life of especially the churches in the Reformed family, and increasingly, it emerges now, represents a parting of the ways. What follows is narrative analysis and theological reflection on the meaning of this document for the life of the church in South Africa and beyond. Like all true confessions, Belhar was born out of the hearts of the faithful, and into a situation of deep despair and uncertainty, of trial and tribulation, of crisis and testing, a time in which the fundamental tenets of the gospel and the heart of our faith were under so severe a threat that no mere religious statement or even a theological declaration, no anxious repetition of doctrinal certitudes would suffice: the church could only turn to the rare and radical act of confession to proclaim the gospel anew. It was a moment of truth and of *kairos*, of being overpowered by the Word of God and being empowered by the Spirit of God. It arose in a specific situation, but like all true confessions, because of its rootedness in the Scriptures, it spoke of a universal reality. Its necessity was parochial, its application was ecumenical. The gospel was at stake, our very lives were at risk and the testimony of the church was in jeopardy. We could only call upon the One who is the source of it all. Hence the confession spoke and still speaks to the human situation everywhere.

Like all true confessions, the Confession of Belhar seeks neither to attack nor to defend, but to uphold and affirm. It does not condemn or rationalise, but testifies and proclaims. Like all true confessions, it responds to heresy, that wilful and deliberate turning of the truth away from the light of the gospel into the shadow of human distortion and satisfaction. The rediscovery and recognition of that truth is not a moment of triumphalist gloating, but rather of profound and humble joy: the truth has found, recovered, and reclaimed us. We are not the light; the light illumines and leads us. We do not announce, we proclaim; we do not pontificate, we confess. For that reason, joy is the most visible, sustained and enduring trait of the confession.

---

2   The last official confessions from within the churches of the Reformation are the Westminster Confession of the Church of Scotland (1647), and the *Formulae Concordiae* (1657). The Barmen Declaration of the Confessing Church in Germany followed in 1934, but the church itself saw this as a theological 'declaration' and not a 'confession' as traditionally understood. The Barmen Declaration was, however, in the decades following, accepted by many churches as a confession of faith, since in their particular situations it spoke so much to the heart of their faith. The Confession of Belhar was the conclusion of a process of *status confessionis* announced by the Dutch Reformed Mission Church and adopted by the synod as an official fourth confession on a par with the traditional confessions from the churches of the Dutch Reformed tradition, viz the *Confessio Belgica*, The Heidelberg Catechism and the Canons of Dordt. See Botha and Naudé (1998).

That joy reverberates vibrantly throughout the Confession of Belhar. From the first sentence, 'We believe in the triune God, Father, Son and Holy Spirit, who through the Word and Spirit gathers, protects and cares for the church from the beginning of the world and will do to the end' to the last, 'To the one and only God, Father, Son and Holy Spirit, be the honour and the glory for ever and ever!'[3] Joyfully it claims with all the saints the affirmation of the unity of God's people as gift and obligation, the message of reconciliation God has entrusted to the church and the truth that through Jesus Christ we are the light of the world and the salt of the earth, called to be peacemakers. It celebrates the good news that God is a God who brings true justice among humankind and that the church as the possession of God must stand where God stands, against all injustice and with the wronged and the powerless against the powerful. It sings joyfully that we are called to confess all these things, not through earthly power, arrogance or recklessness, but in obedience to Jesus Christ, even though doing so may provoke the wrath of earthly authorities and human laws, because above all we know that Jesus is Lord.

Belhar, then as now, proclaims the victory of Christ and through him ours, over the power of sin and death, fear and powerlessness. We shall no longer be afraid.

From among the poor and the downtrodden

To understand the power of this confession and the reason for our joy, one must understand something of the situation into which the Confession of Belhar was born. Not unlike the crises that gave birth to some of the ancient Reformed confessions, the *Confessio Scotica* for instance, or the *Confessio Belgica*, the crisis that moved us to the moment of confession was both political and spiritual.

South Africa was then in the grip of the apartheid system, a system of racial oppression, domination and economic exploitation that held sway over every area of our lives. It dehumanised black people while according an idolatrous status to whites. Skin colour determined everything: from education to employment, from the courts of law to the definition of human dignity. It caused immense suffering among millions. It was a system inherently violent and indescribably destructive, and needed ever more draconian laws and growing physical violence to keep it in place. The impact of these laws, the wide range of powers given to the police, security apparatus and the military, and sequential states of emergency proclaimed by the government arguably made the 1980s the darkest period of the apartheid

---

3   All quotations from the Confession of Belhar in this chapter are taken from the English translation at Addendum 15, The Confession of Belhar. Also available at http://urcsa.net/wp-content/uploads/2016/02/Belhar-Confession.pdf

era. However, at the same time it called forth the strongest and most persistent resistance to the system.

But South Africa was not the only place in the world where racist oppression, social discrimination and economic exploitation were the daily bread of the poor and defenceless. What made our situation unique was the role of the Christian Church, not just in creating openness to racial prejudice, or in justifying racial prejudice after the fact, but in the actual shaping of policy based on racial prejudice and oppression. The policy of apartheid was in its essence the legacy of English colonial rule, and although it gives none of us any comfort, it is only fair always to remind ourselves that the ideology and practises of racial superiority were not Afrikaner inventions. It was, however, also the logical political outcome of the so-called 'mission policy' of the DRC (see Botha 1982:264).[4] But it was more than that. It was presented to both white and black people as an all-embracing, soteriological-loaded, God-given solution to what was seen as 'the race problem'. It was not just willy-nilly presented as God's will; there was a complete theological rationale, a comprehensive 'apartheid theology' for its biblical, moral and theological justification. As such it became more than just a political ideology and system or a socio-economic construct. It became in fact a pseudo-gospel, challenging and replacing the truth and the authority of the true gospel in our personal lives, in the life of the church as well as in the corporate life of the nation.

The church of which I am now specifically speaking is the DRC of South Africa. That church was (and to a large extent still is) divided on the basis of race and skin colour. This is not to say that other churches did not, overtly or covertly, support apartheid (see, for example, Villa-Vicencio 1994).[5] That fact is hardly contested. But this is the church that came with the colonisation of South Africa, into which the first natives and the slaves who became Christians were baptised and became members. In time, this church increasingly became the church of the colonist and slave owner, the church of the white, 'European' (as distinct from the 'heathen Christian') whose superior position in the political and socio-economic hierarchy of colonial society had to be reflected in the church. As society became more and more conscious of race, skin colour and social status, there was less and less room for those who were not white, and who were considered 'heathen' even though they confessed Jesus Christ as their Lord and Saviour. As political and economic tensions

---

4   Botha makes the point that the ideology of apartheid represents a 'revolution' in the thinking and life of Afrikaner nationalism and argues strongly that no other institution in the Afrikaner community, including the Afrikaner Broederbond, did as much as the Dutch Reformed Church to prepare the Afrikaner for the acceptance of apartheid and its radical consequences for politics, society as well as the church.

5   Villa-Vicencio explores the dilemmas of English-speaking churches in South Africa during apartheid.

arose, Christian fellowship withered. The strains of power and powerlessness, of enforced superiority and inferiority, of ownership and being owned, could no longer be hidden. As white Christians laid more and more claim to land, destroyed whole communities and people, slaves and native people reacted contradictorily, as can be expected under such circumstances. Some began to reassert ownership of their land and to demand recognition of their human dignity, other communities and individuals simply began to fall apart.

In the end, for those in the community of the church, the contradictions proved too much. The same Bible that proclaimed the childhood of God justified the subjugation and ownership of human souls. The bondage of slavery and the bonds of Christian love could not live side by side. The 'slave-holding, the woman-whipping, the mind-darkening, the soul-destroying religion' in the words of Frederick Douglass (cited in Boesak 1984:38), could not share the same baptism, break the same bread and drink of the same cup at the Lord's table, nor make the same confession that Jesus Christ is Lord, with those who sought a religion which is 'first pure, then peaceable, then gentle, without partiality and without hypocrisy Could one rape a woman on Friday, whip a man to death or lynch him on Saturday because he sought his freedom, and on Sunday be witness to the baptism of his child and celebrate a oneness in Christ?' Could the oppressor listen to the psalms that sang of the God who will 'protect the stranger and support the downtrodden, crush the oppressor' while standing next to the oppressed who are promised freedom, who lifted their heads high because they would be 'lifted up from the dust of the earth'? Could the message of Jesus be heard while the cries from the slave lodge across the street could not be drowned out?

By the middle of the 19th century, these contradictions, embodied as they were in the very bodies and voices of the slaves and former slaves, simply became unbearable. And since the church could not ignore them nor deny their existence, it sought to remove their presence. The church found it easier, even though it knew and acknowledged that what the gospel demanded was different, first to opt for separate baptisms and a separated communion, then for separate worship services altogether, then finally for separate, race-based church formations. Now the justification for slavery or slave-like conditions could be preached without the accusing presence of those whose woundedness constituted society's wealth. Now Communion could be served without the broken body of Christ reminding congregants of the broken bodies of 'chastised' slaves. Now Baptism would no longer be a reminder that all were, in equal measure, sinners before God, and that, through the redeeming grace of God, all belong to Christ. Now the 'slave catechism' would be less embarrassing, slaves could be taught that even though their lot was unjust, dismal and undeserved, the things that seemed unbearable to them were the will of God for their own good. And that indeed, if they had remained in their home countries they would never have heard of the saving grace of their Lord and on dying would have been lost forever (cited in Boesak 1984:104-105).[6]

The rationalisations abound: racial separation was 'preferred' by the 'heathen Christians'; it would be better for the 'mission' of the church, it was 'the more practical way', and as formulated in an official decision of 1857, the church did it to accommodate 'the weakness of some' (white members). This decision stands as the crucial moment in the history of the church in South Africa. Henceforth, not faith in Jesus Christ alone, but race, culture and pigmentation would begin to define membership of the church. This moment is, in the words of church historian Chris Loff, 'the birth of a heresy' (Loff 1983:17-20).[7] The painful consequences of that decision have been with us for 150 years now. But stripped of all pretence, this fateful decision essentially provided a haven for a conscience that would not bend to the will of Christ. I have dwelt somewhat longer on this particular historical context, for it is my belief that this history is indeed the birth of the heresy against which the Dutch Reformed Mission Church proclaimed its *status confessionis* more than a century later. But history is more than the record of events and facts. History is also about the living memory and the continuing story of the people. The people of whom British scientist Robert Knox asks the following:

> What signify these races to us? Who cares particularly for the Negro, or the Hottentot, or the Kaffir?... Destined by the nature of their race to run, like animals, a certain limited course of existence, it matters little how their extinction is brought about. (cited in Magubane 1999:26)

These people Knox talks about were our ancestors. Bereft of land, dignity and everything they held dear, they sought and found comfort and strength in the gospel even if, as the blind African poet and catechist John Ntsikana confessed in 1884, that gospel was a 'fabulous ghost' they sought to embrace in vain (see Boesak 2005:136-137).[8] Their struggles with the presence of evil and the absence of God are largely unknown. Neither have we, in contrast to African-Americans, much of a record of how they felt when they heard those slave-holding preachers tell them about the God of Jesus Christ or when they were told that they were no longer welcome in the church where they had learned to know their Lord.

But the gospel always asserts itself. It might be manipulated and distorted, but its truth cannot be denied. It might be perverted, but it cannot be buried. Crushed to earth, that truth shall rise again. Here and there, almost as lost echoes down

---

6   The views of Rev. M.C. Vos, 19th century Dutch Reformed minister and missionary.
7   Loff calls this a 'sinful disposition' nurtured by a 'deluded theology'.
8   See Boesak (2005) for for Ntsikana's poem and the relevant discussion.

the dongas and valleys of our history and in the stories handed down through the generations, there is witness of those who found in the words of the prophets and the message of Jesus the power of the gospel, that Word of life that cannot be bound, that empowers and provides for justice and freedom, for dignity and peace. They spoke, and in their words, we, their children and their children's children, discovered the continuity with the prophets and Jesus of Nazareth. Carried and sustained by their faith, we walked the wilderness and drank the water from the angel's hand with Hagar; we climbed to the mountain top with Moses and slept under the broom tree with Elijah. We cried in the Temple with Hannah and wept with Elisha for the coming destruction. Our voices rose with that of the psalmist, 'How long Lord?' and with Isaiah and Jeremiah we heard, and believed, the promise of salvation and restoration. With Mary we sang the 'Magnificat' and with Jesus we suffered on a cross made by human hands. In prison, we learned to sing with Paul and Silas, and with the ancient church we discovered that there is no power in heaven or on earth, not even death, that can separate us from the love of God which is in Jesus Christ: Jesus is Lord.

But we must consider further that the historical contexts of slavery and apartheid are not the only contexts within which the Confession of Belhar speaks powerfully. The Confession lives by the affirmation that concludes Article 2, which deals with the unity of the church, namely that 'true faith in Jesus Christ is the only condition for membership of this church'. This affirmation, I believe, has much more radical consequences than might hitherto have been admitted to, perhaps because the confession is too readily read as a document responding to a 'racial' situation. Notice that the 'forced separation of people on the grounds of race or colour' is mentioned for the first time and only in Article Three which speaks to the 'enforced separation of people on a racial basis' and in the 'rejection' which follows. The 'true faith in Jesus Christ' affirmation is related first to the rejection of any absolutisation of 'either natural diversity or the sinful separation of people' that 'hinders or breaks the visible and active unity of the church', and next to the kind of belief that professes that genuine spiritual unity is truly being maintained 'in the bond of peace while believers of the same confession are in effect alienated from one another for the sake of diversity and in despair of reconciliation'.

This goes far beyond the issue of race. In my view, this addresses quite profoundly the historical and actual contexts of oppression, rejection and exploitation of both gay persons and women. This begins with the recognition that Belhar's understanding of the diversity mentioned above is a holistic, positive, enriching one, as opposed to an understanding of 'diversity' that is negative and therefore leads to 'natural' separation that should be enforced by law and then sacralised by the church. Belhar rejects the sinful absolutisation, which aims to separate, oppress and render some inferior, but expressly celebrates the diversity that affirms humanity and welcomes it as a gift from God for the life of the church. Belhar embraces that enriching diversity that unites and builds the church. In this regard, the rejection of gay persons or the degradation of women as if their 'true faith in Jesus Christ' is not enough but is in reality subjected to some form of human approval and something 'extra', is part of the sinful 'doctrine' Belhar rejects. Not only is their rejection a sin, but, according to the Confession it is also a sin to refuse 'earnestly to pursue this visible unity as a priceless gift'. This strong language is inclusive. All manifestations of the sinfulness that 'breaks the visible unity', 'despairs of reconciliation', causes 'alienation from one another', and blesses the 'enforced separation of people' on whatever grounds are as applicable to gay persons and women as they are to the realities of racial oppression.

Moreover, the whole of Article 4, which deals with God as the 'One who wishes to bring about justice and true peace on earth', speaks to the situation of gay persons and women. In their woundedness, their vulnerability, the enmity of many in society and the rejection of their true and full humanity, women and gay persons have an unalienable right to call upon the God 'who in a special way [is] the God of the destitute, the poor and the wronged.' Their suffering is no less than the suffering of widows and the orphans and it is in regard to their right to justice that God wishes to teach the people of God to do what is good and to seek the right. 'Therefore, in the struggle for the recognition of the right of gay persons and women to full humanity, the church too must learn 'to stand where God stands', and to witness and strive against 'any form of injustice' perpetrated against these members of the body of Christ so that 'justice may roll down like waters, and righteousness like an ever-flowing stream'.

As the church seeks to follow Christ in the struggle for justice for the poor and those who are discriminated against, so the church must follow Christ in this matter. This not only means that the church ought to support, uphold and implement those rights afforded women and gay persons in the Constitution of South Africa in the public square, but it ought to seek actively to safeguard and promote those rights within its own structures, its preaching and living, its worship and witness. Rejecting, as Belhar enjoins us, 'any ideology which would legitimate forms of injustice and any doctrine which is unwilling to resist such an ideology in the name of the gospel', means by the same token, or better still, by the same conviction, rejection of any form of oppression of women, or any form of homophobia, blatant or subtle.

This is the way in which the inclusiveness of the Confession of Belhar reflects the inclusiveness of the embrace of God. Article 5 declares:

> We believe that, in obedience to Jesus Christ, its only Head, the church is called to confess and do all these things, even though the authorities and human laws might forbid them and punishment and suffering be the consequence. Jesus is Lord.[9]

And so, from among the poor and oppressed, the despised and the voiceless, the dejected and downtrodden, came the Confession of Belhar, and this is, perhaps, it is most eminent, and to some, it is most offensive characteristic. In other words, and in the unguarded, heated moments of debate we see this emerging more and more, the real reason for the rejection of Belhar is that it is the voice of those who had no voice, who, in fact, had no right to speak; the least of those whom God should have chosen to speak prophetically to the powerful. That those with no name in the streets could dare to name the Name of God in the sanctuary as well as in the public square, not just to their 'own people' in their ordained separated spaces, but to the world church – that seems to be too much. Its birthplace was not the palaces of the privileged or the high-steepled stain glass-windowed sanctuaries of white power. It gave voice to the voiceless and power to the powerless. Nor was it the child of esoteric academic debate; it emerged from the struggles of ordinary people living in the presence of evil and with the promises of God and it spoke with the eloquence of faith. It was not commissioned by the powerful to legitimise earthly power. It places earthly power under the critique of heaven and earth: of the outraged God and the suffering people. In its words pulsates a life, lived not under the protection of the throne but in the shadow of the cross. In it one will not find the arrogance of certitude; it is the trembling steadfastness of those who walk by faith, not by sight. In essence, this is what those who embrace the Confession of Belhar embrace, and this is what they share with those who accept the Confession as their own. The point I am making is not so much socio-economical or political – it is profoundly theological. In this sense, Belhar is a unique representation of God's identification with the poor, the voiceless and the dispossessed. Embracing it both reveals and preserves the integrity of the process of reunification with which the DRC family is now engaged. In this embrace lies not so much correction as redemption.

Bending our will to the mind of Christ

Belhar does not see the need to repeat the deep doctrinal truths inherited from the ancient church, and some use that to argue that Belhar is therefore not 'a true

---

9   Extracts from the Confession of Belhar in this chapter are taken from the English translation at Addendum 15, The Confession of Belhar. Also available at http://urcsa.net/wp-content/uploads/2016/02/Belhar-Confession.pdf

confession'. That, however, is a false argument. There are some revered confessions in the Christian tradition that are not at all solely concerned with doctrinal matters. Besides, the first known confession of the Christian Church, 'Jesus is Lord', was made not as a doctrinal statement, but as living testimony against an idolatrous state and the claims of divinity of the Roman Caesars. The commitment of those at Belhar to these truths has never wavered. That Jesus of Nazareth was the Son of God was not the issue; rather the question was: how seriously do we take God's incarnate presence in Jesus Christ? We were called to revisit, for ourtime again and anew, the question Jesus had asked his disciples, 'Who do you say I am?' (Mark 8:29), so well understood and asked again by Dietrich Bonhoeffer in a time likewise filled with pain, suffering and vexing contradictions: 'Who is Jesus Christ for us today?' (Bethge et al. 1986-1998:8, 42). That is the question with which we grappled. For what value does it have formally to confess Jesus as the Christ when the church loses its way on the moral, socio-economic and political consequences of the gospel, and even while confessing Christ, the church makes common cause with the destructive powers of the world? So, too, what does it mean when the doctrine is piously repeated, but the life of the church, even as it affirms the doctrine, denies the message and the very life of Jesus?

We struggled with our Christian identity: what did it mean to be Christian when one of the most systematically exploitative and oppressive systems of the twentieth century, was being proudly claimed by the Christian Church as its own?[10] What did it mean when, in blind and sinful submission to a race-obsessed society, race and skin colour, rather than faith in Jesus Christ alone, was made the criterion of membership of the church? The response was a confession that 'true faith in Jesus Christ is the only condition for membership of this church'. This was a time when the divinity of Jesus was not denied, but the humanity of the poor was, and hence the good news for the poor that Jesus brought. The continued impoverishment of the poor was the result of deliberate policy and the church, rather than seeking the justice that rolls down like waters, and the righteousness that flows like a mighty stream, chose to benefit from the exploitation of the poor and justified their plight as God's will. In such a situation, we are called to confess, boldly and publicly,

> that God has revealed Godself as the One who wishes to bring justice and true peace on earth; that in a word full of injustice and enmity God is in a special way the God of the destitute, the poor and the wronged ... that the church belonging to God, should stand, namely against injustice and with the wronged.

---

10 See as just one example among many over many years, *Die Kerkbode*, official organ of the Dutch Reformed Church, 22 September 1948.

The church affirmed Christ as mediator, but preached the irreconcilability of people based on race, culture and skin colour. The church administered the sacraments, but allowed racist prejudices to disempower the efficacy of the sacraments. The church affirmed the unity of the church, but insisted on its division on the basis of race. The church supported missions, but rejected the reciprocity of all-transcending love that should characterise the life of the followers of Jesus. So, we are called to confess that we 'share one faith, have one calling, are of one soul and mind; have one God and Father, are filled with one Spirit, are baptised with one baptism, eat of one bread and drink of one cup, confess one Name.'

The church confessed the sinfulness of all humankind, but in effect made an idolatry of racial identity and denied the equality of all before God that that same confession expressed. It rebuilt the walls of enmity that Christ has broken down with a deliberate political and theological purposefulness that belied the affirmation of that central biblical truth. When this happened, we were called to confess that

> Christ's work of reconciliation is made manifest in the community of believers who have been reconciled with God and with one another; that that unity is, therefore, both gift and obligation for the church of Jesus Christ … that this unity must become visible so that the world may believe that separation, enmity and hatred between people and groups is sin which Christ has already conquered.

The church professed its dependence upon the triune God, but in reality, relied on and made common cause with worldly power, political privileges, economic exploitation and military might so that the church itself became a powerful force in the justification and safeguarding of the system and of its own power, privilege and survival. Hence, we could not but confess that in standing where God stands, 'the church must witness against all the powerful and privileged who selfishly seek their own interests and thus control and harm others'.

Should some seek to hide behind the sinfulness of humankind and the brokenness of the world, Belhar in turn reminds them that 'God's life-giving Word and Spirit have conquered the powers of sin and death' and so made us all conquerors through Jesus Christ, and that God's life-giving Word and Spirit 'enable the church to live in a new obedience which can open new possibilities of life for society and the world'. And should we be reminded of the wrath of the state, the relentlessness of its violence, the wide range of its powers and the reach of its security apparatus, we in turn remind ourselves that 'we believe that, in obedience to Jesus Christ, its only Head, the church is called to confess and to do all these things, even though the authorities and human laws might forbid them and punishment and suffering be the consequence.' In this Belhar does no more, but no less than echo the *Confessio*

Scotica, which calls upon Reformed Christians to 'save the lives of the innocent, to repress tyranny, to defend the oppressed'. And then we said: 'Jesus is Lord.'

I should make one or two more important remarks in this regard. As we made this confession, even as we spoke, many of us had been imprisoned without charge; many under false charges. Lives had been threatened, lost and otherwise destroyed. Many had disappeared. Our youth were on the streets of the nation in flaming protest, risking their lives every day in clashes with police and the army. The casualties numbered in the thousands. Under the most draconian of laws security police had free reign to harass and torture hundreds of those who resisted. Parents saw their children flee without hope of ever seeing them again. Years later the Truth and Reconciliation Commission would uncover small parts of the realities we lived with then. We lived in daily fear of our lives. Trust in each other was destroyed; many were bought, or coerced into becoming spies for the police. Enmity, hatred, distrust and fear were the most natural of responses. Our country was becoming less and less our mother and more and more our grave.

Yet in the midst of all this, the Confession of Belhar, constantly giving account of the hope that is within us, and having grounded itself in the Word, the tradition and faith of the ancient church, calls first and foremost upon Christ's work of reconciliation, proclaiming to those who suffer oppression not to be tempted by hatred, enmity and self-justifying revenge but to remember 'that we are obligated to give ourselves willingly and joyfully to be of benefit and blessing to one another, [since] we share the one faith'. In South Africa at the time, whites and blacks were fearsome and fearful enemies. In politics, talk of reconciliation was considered premature, if not traitorous. Hatred was natural, enmity was a virtue. And even though most of our members were crucially engaged in the struggle for liberation, it was not the call of politics that dictated our conduct, but the call of the gospel. The reality of our oneness in Christ overrode the political necessity to see the other as an enemy, even if there was blood on the streets. Here popularity with our struggling masses was not the issue, our obligation to Christ was.

Despite all this, the confession never once mentions the word 'apartheid', for the issue never was apartheid, but justice, unity, reconciliation, the integrity of the gospel, the faith of the church and the Lordship of Jesus Christ. Focusing on apartheid would have fatally moved the focus from Christ and would, both spatially and historically, have parochialised the confession beyond redemption. It is important to remember that those who stood up that day in solemn acceptance of the confession included whites as well as blacks, and conversely, those who did not also included both white and black. Those whites who stood up that day did not just come from nowhere. They stood there because that is where they had been standing all along, namely, where God stands. It never really was about race and pigmentation; it was always about faith and commitment and conviction. In the cauldron of white/black polarisation this was and still is an amazing testimony to true non-racialism, but it was more: it was a testimony to reconciliation and the oneness of the church so central to Belhar. Then, as now, those who were there were not driven by political correctness. They were, as they still are, driven by the love of Christ and their passion for unity, reconciliation and justice. That is why it is utterly facetious, if not disingenuous in the extreme to argue that the rejection of Belhar by some black people is an invalidation of the confession.

But note something else: the obligation of worship, reconciliation, unity and standing with the poor is firstly directed at those who confess, and only in second instance at those who might listen. The faith Belhar espouses is not a self-justifying faith; it is a self-critical faith. Furthermore, those who are called to confess are also called to obedience. The act of confession is an act of commitment – it allows for no arrogance, disengagement or sense of spiritual superiority. And it is this humble submission to the Word of God, this bending of our mind and will to the obedience of Christ that strengthens and emboldens us to say 'Therefore, we reject'. That act of rejection does not mean the spiritual elimination of a person or group; far from it. The rejection does not stand on its own; it is embedded in the obligation to love, forgive and reconcile. Without this obligation, it is invalidated. We must have, said John Calvin in his *Institutes*, the humility to realise that we stand and are upheld by God alone, that 'naked and empty-handed we flee to his mercy, repose entirely in it, hide deep within it, and seize upon it alone for righteousness and merit' (Calvin 1975/1536, Book 2, Ch. 7.8). Calvin continues that in Jesus Christ, God's face shines in perfect grace and gentleness, even upon those who profane God's name, betray God's trust, and dishonour our baptism. It is in that spirit that Belhar was written, discussed, and finally adopted as a fourth confession in our church. For that reason, we have asked that the accompanying letter should be read before one reads the confession. And it is in that spirit that we have offered it to the ecumenical church. And once offered thus, the Uniting Reformed Church no longer owns it. It cannot be used to judge, humiliate or annihilate the other. It cannot ever be the measure of our spiritual superiority, neither can it be cross upon which the other is nailed, and kept hanging. In doing that we would crucify Christ all over again. It is not a weapon to brandish; it is a staff on which to lean. Belhar symbolises, indisputably and sublimely, the inclusive, merciful and loving embrace of Jesus the Messiah. All notions of exclusivity, in whatever shape or form, are alien to it.

There are encouraging signs that a significant number from within the DRC are ready to fully embrace the Confession of Belhar, and that they are even ready to move beyond the decision made by the 2004 General Synod that Belhar should be part of the confessional basis of a reunited church. They intend not to be accidental, but purposeful inheritors of the confession. The impact on the unification process within the DRC family could be profound. Even more profound would be if that meant the emergence of a new community of faith, based upon renewed theological convictions and convergence of understanding, a different understanding and interpretation of Scripture and the Reformed tradition. This would be a community beyond the boundaries of race and culture, beyond the resurgent but fatally flawed 'identity politics', which threaten to drag South Africans back to the vagaries of ethnic mobilisation, and the dangerous undercurrents of racial stagnation. It does not matter if the whole of the church throughout South Africa does not immediately follow this course of action. The church shall be known, and judged, not by the reticence of the many but by the faithfulness of the few, not by the hesitations of its legions, but by the courage of its prophets.

Standing where God stands

The Confession of Belhar helped us then, and it helps us now, as we face the new challenges of the 21st century.

First, Belhar helps us to see the value of the tradition within which we stand. In an age of amazing arrogance, when a new Christian fundamentalism disengages itself completely from the heritage of the early church, finds refuge and legitimacy in alliances with worldly powers and measures itself and its success by its acceptance by those powers, Belhar reminds us of the true meaning of the confession that Jesus, and Jesus alone, is Lord. This does not mean Jesus and our struggle, nor Jesus and our national pride, nor Jesus and our economic prosperity, nor Jesus and our patriotic fervour. That is the very first confession of the Christian Church and it stood against the imperial claims of absolute power, against the claims of divinity by the Caesar, and against the belief that true power lies in military might and that military might may be a handmaiden of the cross exercised in the name of Jesus. It binds us to the early church which understood that true power lies in the powerlessness of the cross, in the willingness to give one's life for the sake of others, and in the love that overcomes evil.

Second, Belhar refocuses us on our inescapable bond of and call to unity – its source is the triune God; its reality the one, visible body of Christ; its life: sharing and receiving the gifts of the Spirit; its driving force the love of Christ; its goal: 'so that the world may believe'. It destroys our sense of self-sufficient, opinionated, self-deluding isolation. It seeks to engrave upon the faces of the brothers and sisters the face of Christ, so that, to speak again with John Calvin,

> [None of them] can be injured, despised, rejected, abused or in any way be offended by us, without at the same time inuring, despising, and abusing Christ by the wrongs we do ... that we cannot love Christ without loving him

in the brothers (and sisters) ... for they are members of our (own) body. (Calvin 1975/1536, Book 4, Ch. 17.38)

Third, Belhar helps us to understand that in standing where God stands, the church in a particular situation, however pressed or isolated, never stands alone. We are ensconced in the womb of the church universal, bound together by the Spirit of the Lord in a solidarity and love that knows no borders – cultural, political, socio-economic or physical. In rediscovering the heart of the gospel, we discovered the communion of the saints and found ourselves opened to their correction, support and love. There were few things in those dark and dismal days that strengthened us more than the knowledge of ecumenical solidarity. And there were few things more humbling than the realisation that our words, spoken in our suffering, pain, hope and faith, were words spoken into the heart of the universal church. In our powerlessness, we empowered the church to respond and do bold things in the name of the Lord.

Fourth, Belhar helps us to find our voice and place globally, as we face the momentous changes and challenges globalisation is forcing upon countries and peoples, as we struggle with new idolatries and with the immense temptations of imperial alliances confronting us today. In our globalising world with its powers and myths of power, its distortions of reality and neglect of truth, Belhar helps us to discern the difference between gospel and ideology, between genuine good news and propaganda, between truth-telling and myth-making, between the dictates of so-called 'political realism' and the reality of the kingdom of God. It helps us to distinguish between half-hearted vacillation and commitment, between obedience and Christian solidarity. In the Bible, 'standing where God stands' was the guarantee for the prophets to distinguish between the myths of the idols, the demands of the palace, and the 'whispers' of the Lord. And as we ourselves have discovered, while it is by no means the safest place to stand, it is without doubt the right place to stand. It is the only place from where we can make the affirmation to which the Confession of Belhar clings: 'Jesus is Lord'.

Fifth, Belhar helps us because it affirms that unalterable biblical truth that the God of Jesus Christ is in a special way the God of the poor, the weak, the destitute and the wronged. This is the claim of the exodus, of the Commandments, of the prophets and the song writers of the Hebrew Bible; and this is the song of Hannah, of Mary in the 'Magnificat', and the message and life of Jesus of Nazareth. Next, it helps us to understand that the poor are not poor because of some historical accident, genetic traits or because it is the will of God. The poor are poor because they are wronged. They are poor because of injustice. They are victims, not of an act of God, but of deliberate historical, political and economic decisions through which injustice was done to them, in a systematised and systemic fashion. These decisions were and are still made by human beings in positions of power who fully understand the consequences of their actions. In recognising that the poor are 'the wronged', Belhar also recognises that the struggle for the poor is the struggle for the rights of the poor. The poor are not just deprived of livelihood and dignity; they are deprived of rights.[11]

In the first place, to stand with the poor means to stand up and be counted. To stand not just where, but as God stands: not just in front of the poor in protection of them; but alongside in solidarity with their struggle. Not just in sympathy with, but in empathetic identification with them. In Matthew 25, Jesus becomes the poor, the prisoner, the naked and the hungry. What we have done to them, is done to him. In not doing what is right we wrong God. What we do for and with the poor is done for and with him. With the cry 'how long, Lord', John Calvin again reminds us, as it emanates from among the poor and the downtrodden, that it actually comes from the heart of God. 'It is', Calvin asserts, 'the same as though God heard Himself when he hears the cries and groaning of those who cannot bear injustice' (Calvin 1847, On Habbakuk 2:5).

Dietrich Bonhoeffer has taught us yet another truth which illustrates how intimately Belhar reflects our understanding of John Calvin on this point. To 'stand where God stands' does not only mean to stand with the poor and the destitute. It means, Bonhoeffer says, to 'stand with God in the hour of God's grieving' (Bethge et al. 1986–1999:8, 515-516). We must be 'caught up in the way of Christ'. It is not our religion that makes of us believers and followers of Christ, but our participation in the sufferings of God. We are called to share the sufferings of God at the hands of a hostile world. That, Bonhoeffer maintains, is what distinguishes not from people of other faiths but from pagans. But here Bonhoeffer does not criticise pagans, but Christians whose religiosity, symbols and rituals have become the hallmark of their life. They are those who think that it is more important to be religious than to be followers of Christ.

We are disciples of Christ when we stand by God in the hour of God's grieving. God's grieving is not in the pain of God for God, but in the pain of God at the suffering of humanity. That pain inflicted by people on people, is inflicted upon God. When Bonhoeffer speaks of the pain of God, he does not look towards heaven, but around him, at the pain of people created in God's image. When we fail to stand with them, we fail to stand with God. We do not ask whether their pain is the pain of heathen or pagans or enemies. It is the pagan within us who asks that. We stand by them

---

11 I owe this insight to Nicholas Wolterstorff, whose continued developments of these thoughts I find entirely convincing. See Wolterstorff (1999:107-130); also Boesak (2005:204-205).

because their pain is the pain of a grieving God. That is discipleship, because it is being caught up in the way of Jesus Christ. It is for that reason that the Confession of Belhar is embraced by Palestinian Christians as well as North American Christians who are marginalised, poor and voiceless, and by those who hear their voice. It will give comfort to the suffering people of Iraq as it will to those brave fighters for democracy in Burma, as to us still. It empowers women, gay and lesbian persons and all those who are relegated to the sidelines of society. And in their struggles we stand with them, because we are disciples of Christ, caught up into the way of Christ.

We are the possession of God, says Belhar, and therefore, driven by God's love and compassionate justice. Belhar helps us to continue to remember this, to continue to remember who we are and what we are called for; to reclaim in our life and work that spirituality without which we cannot face the challenges before us, to bring about the transformation that reaches out for justice, human dignity and freedom; for the responsibility for the earth, for the very things most necessary in our global reality. It is a spirituality that is not captive to triumphalism, not dependent upon earthly powers to gain acceptance in the world. It is not locked up in a desire to escape the realities of this world, a privatised, inner experience of God while shutting out the voices of pain.[12] It is the trembling of the soul before God, so that we are sent out to seek the glory of God and the Lordship of Jesus Christ in all areas of life. It leaves us open to the woundedness of others and makes us take the risk of vulnerability ourselves. It is sharing the pain of God in the pain of humanity, but it is also sharing the rage of God against injustice and all forms of inhumanity.

Two years before the Confession of Belhar was written, at an intensely personal level, I realised something that is truer today than even then. It was a dismal and difficult time – our struggle seemed in vain – death and terror was all around. It was as if all humanity had fled. I discovered then in the ancient Reformed confessions something that provided me with prophetic faith and pastoral comfort.

It came from the Heidelberg Catechism, Lord's Day One, in answer to that most crucial question, 'What is your only comfort in life and death? The Catechism answers:

> That I, with body and soul, both in life and death, am not my own, but belong to my faithful Saviour Jesus Christ; who with his precious blood has fully satisfied for my sins and delivered me from all the power of the devil, and so preserves me that without the will of my heavenly Father not

---

12 I have worked out my understanding of spirituality in Chapter 7 of my book, *The Tenderness of Conscience: African Renaissance and the Spirituality of Politics* (Boesak 2005).

a hair can fall from my head; yea, that all things must be subservient to my salvation, wherefore by his Holy Spirit he also assures me of eternal life, and makes me heartily willing and ready henceforth, to live unto him. (Heidelberg Catechism)

I said then that this is a revolutionary spirituality without which our being Christian in the world is not complete, and without which the temptations that are part and parcel of the liberation struggle will prove too much for us. I believe this is how Belhar blesses us at this time. The 'authoritarian audacity' I ascribed then to the powers in South Africa is once again seen in the destructive powers that are rampant today. 'The market' is spoken of as if it were a god – human life seems to be easily expendable. People do not matter but profits do. These destructive powers claim with totalitarian arrogance a place in our lives that only God can. Then, as now, it is of vital importance that we never forget to whom our ultimate allegiance and obedience are due. I said then and I believe it now, that our lives have meaning only when they are in the hands of the One who has given his life for the sake of others. And although he is the Lamb who is slaughtered, for those who call him Lord, he is also 'Jesus Christ, the faithful witness, the firstborn from the dead, the ruler of the kings of the earth'. It is to this Jesus that Belhar testifies. It is this Spirit who empowers us. It is this God whom it calls us to worship. As the confession ends, 'To this God be glory and honour and praise for ever and ever'.

Bibliography

Anthony, W. 1992. *Lessons of struggle: South African internal opposition, 1960–1990.* Cape Town: Oxford University Press.

Barth, K. 1938. *The knowledge of God and the service of God according to the teaching of the Reformation.* London: Hodder & Stoughton.

Bethge. E. et al. (eds). 1986–1999. *Dietrich Bonhoeffer werke.* 17 volumes. Munich and Gütersloh: Kaiser-Gütersloher Verlagshaus.

Boesak, A.A. 1984. *Farewell to innocence: A socio-ethical study on Black Theology and Black Power.* New York: Orbis.

Boesak, A.A. 2005. *The tenderness of conscience: African Renaissance and the spirituality of politics.* Stellenbosch: SUN PReSS.

Boesak, A.A. 2008. To stand where God stands: Reflections on the Confession of Belhar after 25 years. *Studia Historiae Ecclesiasticae* 34(1):143-172.

Botha, D.P. 1982. Church and kingdom in South Africa. In J.H.P. Serfontein (ed.), *Apartheid, change and the NG Kerk.* Extracts, Annexure M. Emmerentia, South Arica: Taurus.

Botha, J. & Naude, P. 1999. *Op pad met Belhar: Goeie nuus vir gister, vandag en more,* Pretoria: Van Schaik Publishers.

Calvin, J. 1847. *Commentaries on the Twelve Minor Prophets* (Vol. 4). Edinburgh: Calvin Translation Society.

Calvin, J. 1975/1536. *Institutes of the Christian religion*. Translated and annotated by Ford Lewis Battles. London: Collins.
Christian Classics Ethereal Library (n.d). Heidelberg Catechism (extended). [Online] Available at https://www.ccel.org/ccel/anonymous/heidelberg.ii.html (Accessed 4 April 2016).
Loff, C. 1983.The history of a heresy. In C. Villa-Vicencio & J.W. de Gruchy (eds), *Apartheid is a heresy*. Claremont: David Philip Publishers.
Magubane, B. 1999. African Renaissance in historical perspective. InW.M. Malegapuru (ed.), *African Renaissance: The new struggle*. Cape Town: Tafelberg and Mafube.
Wolterstorff, N. 1999. The contours of justice: An ancient call for Shalom. In L. Barnes Lampman (ed.), *God and the victim: Theological reflections on evil, victimisation, justice and forgiveness*. Grand Rapids, MI: William B. Eerdmans.

ADDENDA

ADDENDUM 1

WARC Resolution on racism and South Africa[1]

God in Jesus Christ has affirmed human dignity. Through his life, death and resurrection he has reconciled people to God and to themselves. He has broken down the wall of partition and enmity and has become our peace. He is the Lord of his church who has brought us together in the one Lord, one faith, one baptism, one God who is the father of us all (Eph. 4:5, 6).

The gospel of Jesus Christ demands, therefore, a community of believers which transcends all barriers of race – a community in which the love for Christ and for one another has overcome the divisions of race and colour. The gospel confronts racism, which is in its very essence a form of idolatry. Racism fosters a false sense of supremacy, it denies the common humanity of believers, and it denies Christ's reconciling, humanizing work. It systematizes oppression, domination and injustice. As such the struggle against racism, wherever it is found, in overt and covert forms, is a responsibility laid upon the church by the gospel of Jesus Christ in every country and society.

At the present time, without denying the universality of racist sin, we must call special attention to South Africa. Apartheid (or 'separate development') in South Africa today poses a unique challenge to the church, especially the churches in the Reformed tradition. The white Afrikaans Reformed churches of South Africa through the years have worked out in considerable detail both the policy itself and the theological and moral justification for the system. Apartheid ('separate development') is therefore a pseudo-religious ideology as well as a political policy. It depends to a large extent on this moral and theological justification. The division of Reformed churches in South Africa on the basis of race and colour is being defended as a faithful interpretation of the will of God and of the Reformed understanding of the church in the world. This leads to the division of Christians at the table of the Lord as a matter of practice and policy, which has been continually affirmed save for exceptional circumstances under special permission by the white Afrikaans Reformed churches. This situation brings a particular challenge to WARC.

---

1   WARC General Council *Ottawa Proceedings of the 21st General Council, Geneva: WARC*, 1983, pp. 176-180; *Called to Witness to the Gospel Today, Studies from the World Alliance of Reformed Churches* 1, Geneva: WARC, 1983:26-30.

This is not the first time that the Alliance has dealt with this issue. In 1964 the general council, meeting in Frankfurt, declared that racism is nothing less than a betrayal of the gospel: 'The unity in Christ of members, not only of different confessions and denominations, but of different nations and races, points to the fullness of the unity of all in God's coming kingdom. Therefore, the exclusion of any person on grounds of race, colour or nationality, from any congregation and part of the life of the church contradicts the very nature of the church. In such a case, the gospel is actually obscured from the world and the witness of the churches made ineffective.' In 1970, the general council held in Nairobi confirmed this stance: 'The church must recognise racism for the idolatry it is ... The church that by doctrine and/or practice affirms segregation of peoples (e.g. racial segregation) as a law for its life cannot be regarded as an authentic member of the body of Christ.' This strong language by WARC was not heeded by the Nederduitse Gereformeerde Kerk and the Nederduitse Hervormde Kerk who were mentioned by name, and it was not given any follow-up by WARC itself.

The WARC General Council meeting in Ottawa 1982 declares:
> The promises of God for his world and for his church are in direct contradiction to apartheid ideals and practices. These promises, clearly proclaimed by the prophets and fulfilled in Christ, are peace, justice and liberation. They contain good news for the poor and deliverance for the oppressed, but also God's judgement on the denial of rights and the destruction of humanity and community. We feel duty bound by the gospel to raise our voice and stand by the oppressed. 'None of the brethren can be injured, despised, rejected, abused, or in any way offended by us, without at the same time injuring, despising and abusing Christ by the wrongs we do ... We cannot love Christ without loving Him in the brethren' (Calvin). In certain situations, the confession of a church needs to draw a clear line between truth and error. In faithful allegiance to Jesus Christ it may have to reject the claims of an unjust or oppressive government and denounce Christians who aid and abet the oppressor. We believe that this is the situation in South Africa today. The churches which have accepted Reformed confessions of faith have therefore committed themselves to live as the people of God and to show in their daily life and service what this means. This commitment requires concrete manifestation of community among races, of common witness to injustice and equality in society, and of unity at the table of the Lord. The Nederduitse Gereformeerde Kerk and the Nederduitse Hervormde Kerk, in not only accepting, but actively justifying the apartheid system by misusing the gospel and the Reformed confession, contradict in doctrine and in action the promise which they profess to believe.

Therefore, the general council declares that this situation constitutes a *status confessionis* for our churches, which means that we regard this as an issue on which it is not possible to differ without seriously jeopardising the integrity of our common confession as Reformed churches. We declare, with black Reformed Christians of South Africa that apartheid ('separate development') is a sin, and that the moral and theological justification of it is a travesty of the gospel, and in its persistent disobedience to the word of God, a theological heresy.

The WARC General Council affirms earlier statements on the issue of racism and apartheid ('separate development') in 1964 and 1970, and reiterates its firm conviction that apartheid ('separate development') is sinful and incompatible with the gospel on the grounds that:
- it is based on a fundamental irreconcilability of human beings, thus rendering ineffective the reconciling and uniting power of our Lord Jesus Christ;
- in its application through racist structures it has led to exclusive privileges for the white section of the population at the expense of the blacks; and
- it has created a situation of injustice and oppression, large-scale deportation causing havoc to family life, and suffering to millions.

Apartheid ('separate development') ought thus to be recognised as incurring the anger and sorrow of the God in whose image all human beings are created.
- The general council expresses its profound disappointment that despite earlier appeals by WARC general councils, and despite continued dialogue between several Reformed churches and the white Dutch Reformed churches over twenty years, the Nederduitse Gereformeerde Kerk (in the Republic of South Africa) and the Nederduitse Hervormde Kerk Van Afrika have still not found the courage to realise that apartheid ('separate development') contradicts the very nature of the church and obscures the gospel from before the world; the council therefore pleads afresh with these churches to respond to the promises and demands of the gospel.
- The general council has a special responsibility to continue to denounce the sin of racism in South Africa as expressed in apartheid ('separate development'). It is institutionalized in the laws, policies and structures of the nation; it has resulted in horrendous injustice, suffering, exploitation and degradation of millions of black Africans for whom Christ died; and it has been given moral and theological justification by the white Dutch Reformed churches in South Africa who are members of WARC and with whom we share a common theological heritage in the Reformed tradition.
- Therefore, the general council, reluctantly and painfully, is compelled to suspend the Nederduitse Gereformeerde Kerk (in the Republic of South Africa) and the Nederduitse Hervormde Kerk Van Afrika from the privileges of membership

in WARC (i.e. sending delegates to general council and holding membership in departmental committees and commissions), until such time as the WARC executive committee has determined that these two churches in their utterances and practice have given evidence of a change of heart. They will be warmly restored to the full privileges of membership when the following changes have taken place:

- Black Christians are no longer excluded from church services, especially from Holy Communion;
- Concrete support in word and deed is given to those who suffer under the system of apartheid ('separate development');
- Unequivocal Synod resolutions are made which reject apartheid and commit the church to dismantling this system in both church and politics.

The general council pays respect to those within the Nederduitse Gereformeerde Kerk (in the Republic of South Africa) and the Nederduitse Hervormde Kerk Van Afrika who have raised their voices and are fighting against apartheid; the general council further urges member churches to pray that these efforts bearing witness to Christ, who frees and unites, may prevail within their churches. The general council asks the WARC executive committee to keep this whole issue regularly under review. Even as we say these things, we, delegates at the general council, confess that we are not without guilt in regard to racism. Racism is a reality everywhere and its existence calls for repentance and concerted action. And so, certain questions emerge for our churches:

- How do we combat racism in our own societies and our own churches?
- How do we come to understand our complicity in the racist structures of South Africa through the economic involvement of especially Western European and North American countries and churches?
- How do we remain sensitive to the insidious way in which racism and social injustice are so often excused in the name of economic interest and national security?
- How can we give concrete manifestation to our concern for and solidarity with the victims of racism in South Africa and elsewhere in their struggle for justice, peace, reconciliation and human liberation?
- Churches should endeavour to develop relationship with black Reformed churches in South Africa and with churches and Christians (black and white) who are engaged in this struggle.
- In expressing solidarity with those who struggle for justice in this situation, we also ask the churches to struggle with the painful and difficult questions of how to witness to the reconciling grace of God for those whom we see as oppressive and in error.

ADDENDUM 2

WARC Seoul statement on the DRC and the status confessionis[1]

WARC noted the following:

The conditions set by the Ottawa General Council for the re-admission of the DRC to full membership were that:

1. Black Christians are no longer excluded from church services, especially from Holy Communion.
2. Concrete support in word and deed is given to those who suffer under the system of apartheid (or separate development).
3. Unequivocal Synod resolutions are made which reject apartheid and commit the church to dismantling this system in both church and politics.
4. The Synodical decisions of the DRC in 1986, relating to the above conditions for re-admission, which endorsed the document *Church and Society*.
5. The minutes of the WARC executive committee held in Belfast, in October 1988 which, *inter alia*, state: 'Recently, the DRC published a Church and Society document which, on the surface might reveal a significant repentance from and revision of its earlier position. That document at its best, may indicate that the church is ready to consider so-called reforms of the apartheid system, which, however, do not alter the present situation. The church refused recently to declare apartheid a sin and its theological justification a heresy. The latest startling revelation is that the church is now suggesting that those calling for a dismantling of apartheid do not belong to the church.'
6. The official statement, known as the Vereeniging Declaration, issued by the representatives of the various member churches of the DRC family after a consultation held in Vereeniging, in March 1989, under the auspices of Reformed Ecumenical Council (REC). This declaration unequivocally rejects apartheid in all its forms as sin and commits the DRC family of churches to dismantle apartheid in both church and state by accepting unification of the various churches into one non-racial Reformed church in southern and central Africa, and by calling on the state to repeal all racist laws and repressive security legislation. All the

---

1 Text from WARC General Council in *Seoul Proceedings of the 22nd General Council*, ed. Edmond Perret, Geneva: WARC, 1990:279-281.

representatives present, with the notable exception of the white DRC, adopted this declaration.

7. The decisions of the General Synodical Commission of the DRC on the Vereeniging consultation and declaration which clearly indicate that the DRC position at Vereeniging had not moved beyond the official position expressed in *Church and Society* as well as in the 1986 Synodical decisions.

Having noted the above, WARC concludes that

1. by its own admission the white DRC has not moved further forward than the position adopted at its Synod on the basis of its *Church and Society* document. Furthermore, the WARC executive committee meeting in Belfast from 19 to 26 October 1988 clearly stated that this position failed to meet the conditions laid down at Ottawa, particularly those in clause (b) and (c), and recommended that suspension be maintained.

2. the other churches in the DRC family have strengthened their witness and have succeeded, despite all the pressures to the contrary, to make a unanimous and unequivocal stand on the rejection and dismantling of apartheid as well as a commitment to the unification of the church into one non-racial church.

Recommendations

Therefore, the WARC General Council meeting in Seoul in August 1989 resolves

1. The statement on racism adopted by the Ottawa General Council (From Ottawa to Seoul, pp. 34-39) was shared with all member churches with the request for an official response. The replies received (ibid., p. 44) show that the statement reflects the conviction of the large majority of the member churches. In the light of these replies the general council feels entitled to reaffirm the statement as being representative of the position of member churches of the Alliance.

2. Having considered that the DRC was silent on too many crucial issues relating to the dismantling of the system of apartheid and that it failed to call and work for the abolition of discriminatory and unjust laws, especially the Land Act, Group Areas Act, Separate Amenities Act and the Population Registration Act; an end to the practice of detention without trial; the lifting of the state of emergency, the unconditional release of all political prisoners and detainees; the unbanning of all organisations opposing apartheid; genuine negotiations with authentic leaders which will lead to a transfer of power to the majority by free and fair election; one, united, non-racial Reformed Church in southern and central Africa. WARC consequently maintains the suspension of the DRC pending its response at its Synod in 1990 and mandates the executive committee to act accordingly.

3. Cognizant of the very difficult circumstances of many churches, to urge churches with direct links with the DRC to review their relationship with the DRC in view of the declaration of the *status confessionis* and report back to the WARC executive committee. Furthermore, to request all the WARC member churches to support the efforts of the younger DRC churches in SA towards independence from the DRC.

4. To pledge support to individuals, congregations and churches, that experience intimidation and pressure from the white DRC; individuals within the DRC who have adopted the *status confessionis* declaration and are being victimized because of this conviction.

5. To urge the DRC to stop its practice of intimidation and adopt a proper ecclesiastical attitude.

6. To commend the 'younger churches' of the Dutch Reformed family of churches for taking the unanimous stand on resistance to apartheid and towards unification of the Reformed churches in southern and central Africa as expressed in the Vereeniging declaration, March 1989.

7. To encourage all the churches that participated in Vereeniging to pursue the pledges in the Vereeniging declaration, March 1989.

8. To facilitate a consultation on church unification of the Dutch Reformed churches in one, non-racial Reformed church during 1990 or early 1991, as well as to prepare the way towards the greater unity of all the Reformed churches in southern and central Africa.

9. To appeal to the DRC to join the church unification process started at Vereeniging and to return to the fellowship of the Reformed churches in southern and central Africa and thus also into community with the common confession of the global Reformed community.

10. To commend those many members of the DRC who individually and jointly adopted the status confessionis position and the official declaration of Vereeniging and call on other members and congregations of this church to take this courageous step.

Status confessionis

The term *status confessionis* came into the vocabulary of the Alliance at the Ottawa meeting of the general council in 1982. The specific occasion (*casus confessionis*) was the issue of apartheid. The general council issued a carefully-worded statement reflecting its conviction that a matter can be declared as having *status confessionis* within the Reformed tradition, but only when the integrity of the proclamation of the gospel is at stake. To declare a *status confessionis* is to affirm that the issue in question bears so directly on the centre of Christian faith that the decision taken on it is one for or against the gospel of Jesus Christ.

The general council meeting in Seoul recalls that the Ottawa General Council, after setting out with care the theological grounds for its concern, declared:

> The churches which have accepted Reformed confessions of faith have therefore committed themselves to live as the people of God and to show in their daily life and service what this means. This commitment requires concrete manifestation of community among races, of common witness to justice and equality in society and of unity at the table of the Lord. The Nederduitse Gereformeerde Kerk and the Nederduitse Hervormde Kerk in not only accepting, but actively justifying the apartheid system by misusing the gospel and the Reformed confession, contradict in doctrine and in action the promise which they profess to believe.
>
> Therefore the general council declares that this situation constitutes a status confessionis for our churches, which means that we regard this as an issue on which it is not possible to differ without seriously jeopardising the integrity of our common confession as Reformed churches. We declare with black Reformed Christians of South Africa that apartheid (separate development) is a sin, and that the moral and theological justification of it is a travesty of the gospel and, in its persistent disobedience to the word of God, a theological heresy. [1]

Decisions approved and actions taken by member churches since the Ottawa statement have supported this decision of the Ottawa council. The general council meeting in Seoul has reviewed the situation and affirms that the decision on *status confessionis* taken in 1982 was and still is appropriate.

The question has been raised about the role of the general council of the Alliance in making a declaration of *status confessionis*. While the council has no authority over its member churches, it is able to act in a representative way on behalf of the churches and bring to their attention for decision matters which they may not have been able to focus clearly for themselves. In this particular case the Alliance has played a crucial role. *Status confessionis* when declared by the council is effective to the degree it is appropriated by the churches with their assent or consent. The declaration may act in a prophetic way, challenging member churches to become more faithful to the gospel by recognising and acting on matters that are decisive for life in faith.

---

1   See *Ottawa 1982, Proceedings of the 21st General Council*, pp. 177.

There are many concerns in today's world which call for loyalty and obedience to the gospel. The church responds to these challenges by witnessing to and confessing Jesus Christ. The church calls its members to bring the gospel of Jesus Christ, which transcends the horizons of human thought, to bear upon these challenges. The church has to testify unambiguously to Jesus Christ in every human context. The question has been raised since Ottawa whether some of the other crucial issues facing humankind might also force the church to declare itself to be in status confessionis. However, the church can do this only in situations that impinge on the heart of the Christian gospel, where confusion is present in the church and where a clear and unambiguous affirmation of the gospel is forced upon it.

The events prior to the 1982 declaration by the Alliance illustrate the process that can lead to a declaration of *status confessionis*. The Alliance has been a major forum for churches of the Reformed family to share their concerns about apartheid over an extended period. After many years of dialogue with the churches in South Africa, there was a broad conviction that the council, acting in the name of the Reformed community, needed to act decisively. This it did by declaring apartheid to be a sin and its theological justification a heresy. It was only at the end of a long process of reflection, dialogue, debate and negotiation within the Alliance that its general council made this declaration. It was forced on the church at the point where it needed to stand for the integrity of the gospel against a declared position which was hostile to and distorted the gospel. The general council is therefore advised to treat all further proposals for the declaration of a *status confessionis* with considerable caution, and to weigh carefully the implications of such a declaration.

The following guidelines are suggested for future reference

Jesus Christ sets us free to confess our faith, to confess our sins and hear God's word of forgiveness, to witness to him and to live in love towards God and our neighbour. This is the primary meaning of Christian confession. Any declaration of a *status confessionis* stems from the conviction that the integrity of the gospel is in danger. It is a call from error into truth. It demands of the church a clear, unequivocal decision for the truth of the gospel, and identifies the opposed opinion, teaching or practice as heretical. The declaration of a *status confessionis* refers to the practice of the church as well as to its teaching. The church's practice in the relevant case must conform to the confession of the gospel demanded by the declaration of *status confessionis*. The declaration of a *status confessionis* addresses a particular situation. It brings to light an error which threatens a specific church. Nevertheless the danger inherent in that error also calls in question the integrity of proclamation of all churches. The declaration of a *status confessionis* within one particular situation is, at the same time, addressed to all churches, calling them to concur in the act of confessing.

When church bodies declare a *status confessionis*, they declare first of all that they themselves are in a situation in which a clear decision for the truth of the gospel must be made. The declaration of *status confessionis* therefore has the character of self-obligation. A declaration of a *status confessionis* must therefore be treated as a matter of high seriousness. The fragmented history of Reformed churches is a sober warning against declaring a *status confessionis* on issues that are less than central to the gospel.

It is not appropriate to declare a *status confessionis* in order to emphasise commitments which are primarily based on current ethical, social or political concerns. Such concerns do regularly call for Christian witness and challenge the church to consider what is the proper response to them in the light of the gospel. But that alone does not constitute a *status confessionis* in the sense outlined above. It is quite unjustifiable to declare a *status confessionis* in order to exert moral pressure upon Christian sisters and brothers who take the call to Christian discipleship as seriously as we do, but give different answers to such ethical, social or political challenges.

Christian confession is always and inevitably particular and historical. It reverberates beyond the particular historical context when it authentically echoes the claim and promises of God, our Creator, redeemer and sanctifier. In this sense, every act of punctual confession and witness has universal import and contributes to the life of the church as a community of witnesses.

ADDENDUM 3

The Declaration of faith of the Presbyterian Church of Southern Africa[1]

The Presbyterian Church of Southern Africa approved the Declaration of Faith for use in 1973. It adopted an amended version as a subordinate standard in 1986 (and amended it again in 1993 and 1994). The Declaration was not meant to replace the traditional ecumenical creeds or to be a summary of the whole Christian faith, but to express the Christian response to two contemporary problems in the Church and society. The first problem was racial discrimination and segregation and the ideology that underpinned this. The second was the way of thinking that excluded political issues from the concern of the gospel and the Church and from Christ's sovereignty. In that the privatization of the gospel and racial prejudice still disfigure Church and Society, this historic declaration remains pertinent.

The declaration is cast in the Trinitarian form of a brief creed, longer than the Apostles' Creed but shorter than the Nicene. This is so that congregations can use it as a common statement of faith in response to the Word of God, read and proclaimed, in services of worship, as an alternative to the traditional ecumenical creeds.

We believe in the one true God, Father, Son and Holy Spirit.

We believe in the Father, who created and rules all the world, who will unite all things in Christ and who wants all his people to live together as brothers and sisters in one family.

We believe in Jesus Christ, the Son, who became human and lived and died and rose in triumph to reconcile both the individual and the world to God, to break down every separating barrier of race, culture or class, and to unite all God's people into one body.

He is exalted as Lord over all, the only Lord over every area of life.

He summons both the individual and society, both the Church and the State, to seek justice and freedom for all and reconciliation and unity between all. We believe in

---

1   *Manual of Faith and Order of the United Presbyterian Church of Southern Africa* (2007:2.5).

the Holy Spirit, the foretaste of God's coming reign, who gives the Church power to proclaim the good news to all the world, to love and serve all people, to strive for justice and peace, to warn the individual and the nation God's judgement and to summon them both to repent and trust and obey Jesus Christ as the King who will come in glory.

ADDENDUM 4

Covenanting for the reunification of the DRC family – Esselenpark Declaration[1]

The General Synodical Commission of the URCSA and the Moderamen of the General Synod of the DRC (extended Executive Committees) met the past three days to discuss the reunification process of the family of Dutch Reformed Churches. It was an historical gathering – the first time that such a representative group of the leadership of the two churches met together. In the meeting we soon became aware of a new spirit of reconciliation and togetherness and a willingness to reach out to one another. We have experienced that all of us are humbler, more willing to listen to one another and to assist one another on the road to reunification. We also sensed a new urgency that we could no longer delay reunification.

In the opening session the DRC leadership apologised once more for the pain and hurt that they had caused the URCSA and its members in the past. This confession was movingly accepted by the URCSA leadership, an act that set the tone for the whole meeting. On the final day the URCSA leadership apologised in turn for the pain that the URCSA had caused the DRC. This experience of humility and heartfelt reconciliation was sealed in a celebration of the Lord's Supper at the end of the meeting. We are deeply grateful to the Lord for this new spirit among us. We know that this comes from God. At the end of the meeting we as leadership group unanimously committed ourselves to guide our churches resolutely in the process of reunification – in agreement with the wish expressed by our churches on numerous occasions. It is our intention that this process will be completed within three years.

We use the term 'covenanting' with hesitance – in the knowledge that 'covenant' in Scripture is a key and loaded word. We use this term because we want to bring ourselves and the reunification process under the authority of the word of God and the will of Christ. We covenant together, not from our own will or under pressure from social and political processes, but because we believe that the Lord, who graciously committed himself to us, requires this of us. We envisage a new organically united reformed church, organized according to Synodical-Presbyterian principles, which lives mission ally and is committed to the biblical demands of love, reconciliation, justice and peace. At the same time we are committed to non-

---

[1] Adopted 22 June 2006 at Esselenpark (*Acts General Synod URCSA 2008*).

racialism, inclusiveness and the acceptance and celebration of our multicultural composition. The different languages in our churches will be treasured.

From within our common faith in the triune God we commit ourselves anew to Africa, the continent where the Lord has placed us, and particularly to Southern Africa. We wish to take up this calling together to make a difference to the life-threatening problems facing our countries. In the process of spreading the gospel, we covenant to work together in concrete ways to:
- combat poverty
- give assistance and support to the vulnerable and the sick (e.g. HIV and Aids sufferers)
- follow and promote the moral values of Scripture
- promote justice for all
- achieve reconciliation, which is more than mere tolerance of one another
- oppose violence of all kinds in our society.

In the spirit of reconciliation and helping another on the way the GSC of URCSA declared that the Belhar Confession should not be a stumbling block in the process of reunification. Their full decision reads:

> We accept the challenge to become one united church in three years time. In this regard the Confession of Belhar shall not function as a precondition for unity. Instead the message of Belhar shall continue to be the inspiration and guide of both the process towards and the formation of the new church. In accordance with the decisions of both churches the Confession of Belhar shall function as a confession in the new church and we shall work together to help the church as a whole grow towards its complete acceptance. We shall take this decision for full ratification to our next Synod.

In their response to this initiative of the GSC of the URCSA the DRC leadership expressed their deep appreciation and gratitude for this bold move and assured the URCSA of their deep and firm commitment to the biblical imperatives of unity, justice and reconciliation, the three main themes of the Belhar Confession. The leadership expressed the opinion that this statement brings the positions of the two churches on Belhar virtually in line with one another. In the process of reunification our churches covenant together to actively engage in:
- establishing combined/uniting ministries at the local level, where congregations are willing and ready for this;
- creating provisional structures of unity between congregations, presbyteries and Synods that are ready for this;

- launching joint projects through which we express our common calling, as set out above;
- creating opportunities for our members to get to know each other better, to listen to each other's fears and dreams, to discuss our differences, and to overcome prejudice;
- give urgent attention to the court cases in the Free State, Phororo and elsewhere and to do our utmost to reconcile the groups outside of court by way of a structured reconciliation process;
- to develop acceptable ways of dealing with issues related to the confessional basis, Church Order and administration of the new church; and
- to work out a proper process that will inform congregations and members on the unity process and all its implications, and give them opportunities to respond to it.

The leadership commit themselves to meet regularly, to make joint decisions as far as possible, and to act together – as a concrete expression and symbol of our commitment to one another and to the reunification process. This covenanting has grown out of bilateral meetings between the URCSA and DRC leadership. We wish and pray that the other two churches of the DRC family will become part of the reunification process as soon as possible. The family will not be complete without their presence. They will be contacted as soon as possible. We also express the hope that our reunification will be a step towards the formation of an inclusive and united Reformed Presbyterian Church in Southern Africa.

ADDENDUM 5

Declaration of Laudium[1]

Biblical gospel

We affirm that the biblical Gospel is God's enduring message to our world and we determine to defend, proclaim, and embody it. We affirm our commitment to the primacy of evangelism, of the preaching of the Gospel to every creature. We affirm that evangelism is not an option but an imperative. We affirm that men are born in sin and guilty and lost without Christ and totally depraved. We affirm that other religions and ideologies are not alternative paths to God, and that there is no other name given among men whereby we can be saved but the name Jesus. We reject as derogatory to Christ and the Gospel every kind of Syncretism and dialogue that implies that Christ speaks equally through other religions and ideologies. To proclaim Jesus as the Saviour of the world is not to affirm that all men are either automatically or ultimately saved.

Holy Spirit's witness

We affirm that the Holy Spirit's witness to Christ is indispensable to evangelism and that without his supernatural work the new birth and the new life, evangelism is not possible and all our endeavours fruitless. We affirm that we who proclaim the Gospel must exemplify it in a life of holiness and love, otherwise out testimony loses its credibility. We affirm the constant need for revival and determine to seek God's face for revival in our lives, in the life of the RCA and in the church of South Africa at large. We affirm that nothing commends the Gospel more eloquently than a transformed life and that nothing brings it into more disrepute than personal inconsistency. We determine to live worthy the gospel of Christ.

Evangelistic witness and compassionate service

We affirm that the congregation of believers should turn itself outwards to its local community in evangelistic witness and compassionate service. We affirm that God has committed the whole Gospel to the whole church and to every member the task of making Christ known throughout the world. We long to see all lay and ordained persons mobilised and trained for the task. We determine to proclaim the Gospel

---

1 Available at http://www.rcacharisma.org/laudium-declaration (Accessed 11 April 2015).

faithfully, urgently, passionately, and sacrificially until He comes. We affirm that we must demonstrate God's love visibly by caring for those who are deprived of justice, dignity, food, and shelter. We affirm that governments, religious bodies, and nations will continue to be involved with social responsibilities, but should the church fall in her mandate to preach the Gospel, no other body will do so.

Unity

We affirm our God-given unity at the deepest level with all born again blood washed believers. We determine to foster such unity across all denominational boundaries. In the immediate circle of our church we will foster structural unity with those who share the same confession, provided that such structural unity will not stifle the evangelical witness of the Reformed Church in Africa. We affirm that we who proclaim that we are members of the body of Christ must transcend within the church the barriers of race, gender, and class. We affirm that racism within the church constitutes a denial of the Gospel and a deterrent to evangelistic witness.

Prophetic witness

We affirm that the proclamation of God's kingdom of justice, peace and holiness demands the denunciation of all injustice, oppression, and immorality. We will not shrink from this prophetic witness. We affirm the freedom in Christ of the Church of Jesus Christ and refuse the alignment of the church to any ideology or current political trend, power, or movement. We affirm our solidarity with those who suffer for the Gospel and will seek to prepare ourselves for the same possibility. We affirm the right of the believer to conscientious objection. In our demonstration and witness against evil we determine not to use carnal weapons but to act in the Spirit of Christ and through spiritual warfare and constant prayer enter into Christ's victory over the principalities and powers of evil.

ADDENDUM 6

The testimony of Vereeniging March 1989[1]

Preamble

It is with gratitude to God that we churches of the Dutch Reformed family, under the leadership of the Interim Committee of the Reformed Ecumenical Council, could meet in a brotherly discussion on social and ecclesiastical issues which trouble our churches. We were reminded at the opening of the consultation of our need for full reliance on God in whose image we are made and whose representatives we are. We met in the awareness that He has given us a ministry of reconciliation in our troubled society as agents of justice and love. The spirit of love prevailed, even when there was a clear difference of opinion expressed on issues such as apartheid and the unity of the church. It was in the confrontation on the issues that the demands of social justice emerged most clearly.

In the discussions, it soon became apparent that, in spite of the different positions between the Dutch Reformed Church and the other churches in the same family, there was a solid basis on which we all could accept one another as fellow servants of God, as we seek for the coming of His kingdom and its righteousness in this area of the world. This mutual acceptance prevailed, even though delegates were all aware of the different perceptions of the political situation in South Africa and of the different responses to it. A key feature of this mutual acceptance was the expression of guilt by delegates of the Dutch Reformed Church for its complicity in the system of apartheid.

It appeared at first that there was a far-reaching and unprecedented unity. But this perception was soon placed in doubt as the discussion progressed. For it soon became apparent that in spite of the basic oneness, the differences in perception and response could not easily be brought into a consensus statement that reflected a common mind. Rather, at the end of the second day the diverging perceptions assumed such a high profile that many were constrained to speak not only of different perceptions and different responses, but of two worlds in the one family of churches. Reference was made to the possibility that the black churches might

---

[1] This is the text of the testimony adopted by the consultation on race relations among Dutch Reformed churches organised by the Reformed Ecumenical Council in Vereeniging, South Africa, from 6–10 March 1989.

have to go their own way without the company of the Dutch Reformed Church. The euphoria of the first days gave way to a feeling of near despair one day later. But just when a break threatened, a consensus emerged, not one that reflected a common mind on all issues, but one that was deeper and better founded than the one earlier. For now the conviction prevailed that whatever the differences, and they should not be minimised, the churches needed to consult together and wanted to remain together. The areas of agreement and those where more discussion is needed and the way ahead for the Dutch Reformed family of churches are explained in the pages that follow.

The testimony

The consultation adopted the following motion in which it expressed its view of apartheid and the unity of the church:

On apartheid

We have heard from the representatives of the DRC repeated confessions to guilt with regard to the establishment, maintenance and justification of apartheid. We have heard their plea for forgiveness. We too confess that we have not always been willing to speak out clearly enough against apartheid through fear. We now respond by reaching out in forgiveness and brotherhood and assure our brothers from the white DRC that, well aware of our own weakness and sin, we 0do not intend to hold the past against them, but together seek a way forward to find God's will for all of us. We say clearly and unequivocally that we regard apartheid in all its forms as a sin, as contrary to and irreconcilable with the gospel of Jesus Christ. We agree that apartheid in all its forms cannot be reformed, but must be totally eradicated from the life of the South African nation and church.

In the light of this, we commit ourselves to work together towards the dismantling of apartheid. Therefore we believe that all discriminatory and unjust laws should be abolished, especially the Land Act, Group Areas Act, Separate Amenities Act and the Population Registration Act. We call upon the Government to cease immediately the practice of detention without trial; lift the state of emergency; release all political prisoners and detainees; unban all organisations opposing apartheid; as a matter of urgency start negotiations with the authentic leaders of the majority in our country. Here we are not speaking of co-optation and consultation, but of genuine negotiations which will lead to a transfer of power to the majority by free and fair elections. We believe that 'sharing of power' means full and meaningful participation of all the people at all levels of government. We pledge continued support for non-racial, non-violent opposition to apartheid.

On church unity

We confess that, even though we should be one in Christ, in fact we are divided on the basis of race, ethnicity and colour. We pledge ourselves to become one, united, non-racial Reformed Church in southern and central Africa.

On the future

We recognise that the people of South Africa are one nation. Political change is necessary, but we recognise that political change alone is not enough. We therefore commit ourselves to work towards genuine reconciliation based upon the demands of the gospel for justice for all. We will work towards an open, non-racial democratic society. We realise that this is not an easy task, indeed for some it may be more difficult that for others. But we pledge solidarity to each other and obedience to God. We do this, not in our own strength, but in faith in Jesus Christ our Lord and depending upon the guidance of his Holy Spirit.

The content of this motion represents the official standpoint of the consultation. It became evident that the representatives of the DRC could not identify with the motion as it was adopted. They felt that this motion went beyond what was agreed upon by the DRC in Church and Society and that this document determines their present mandate. At our request, however, they were prepared to make some statements in which they expressed their own view of the burning issues at hand. They too realise that there are laws, such as the Land Act, Group Areas Act, Separate Amenities Act and the Population Registration Act, which are the four pillars of apartheid and are experienced by millions as degrading and as violating the human dignity, and they are willing, in co-operation with the other churches, to bring these matters to the attention of the present Government.

In a statement presented to the consultation by the DRC delegation we found several biblical principles that are accepted by all of us. The consultation, however, is of the opinion that this statement, just as Church and Society, stops short at the principles and fails to implement them in a practical and concrete way, by clearly indicating what is to be done. As long as this has not been done the credibility of the DRC remains at stake. As members of this consultation we urge the DRC to go beyond the position of Church and Society and spell out clearly and concretely what is the task of Christians in this day and in this land. In the meantime we expect from the DRC delegates that they will present the motion adopted by the consultation to all the official church meetings for discussion and we also expect that the DRC, when and where possible, will act upon it. On the unity of the church the motion states unambiguously: 'We pledge ourselves to become one, united, non-racial Reformed church in Southern and Central Africa'. The delegates of the

DRC, however, stated that they could not identify with this pledge, because their church, while recognising the need for spiritual and visible unity, is not yet ready to say what the structural model of the one-church-to-be will be. The consultation was deeply disappointed by this and therefore urges the DRC delegation to bring our pledge to their church as a matter of the greatest urgency.

The future

As agreed at the beginning of the consultation we all commit ourselves to bring all the matter decided upon to our churches and seek from them the approval of these decisions. Unless disagreements have been indicated to the consultation, we will defend the resolutions of the consultation.

We also plead with all the member churches, as a matter of priority, to bring the outcome of the consultation, with all the relevant documents (The Statement of the DRC, The Statement of the NGKA, 'The Struggle for Liberation between the Two Worlds in South Africa'), before their respective congregations and church bodies in order to involve in these discussions people belonging to the various churches.

Once again we say with the motion: 'We realize that this is not an easy task, indeed for some it may be more difficult than for others. But we pledge solidarity to each other and obedience to God. We do this, not in our own strength, but in faith in Jesus Christ our Lord and depending upon the guidance of his Holy Spirit'.

ADDENDUM 7

A pastoral letter to the moderamen and our brothers and sisters of the Dutch Reformed Church (NGK) from the 23rd WARC General Council, meeting in Debrecen, Hungary, August 1997[1]

We greet you in the name of Jesus Christ, giving thanks that the Holy Spirit has created new opportunities for restoring fellowship. Through our visits with you and through other contacts with you over recent years, we have rejoiced to see significant changes in the life of your church which place you well on the way to restoration of full fellowship with the churches of WARC. Of the three requirements laid down by the 21st general council at Ottawa in 1982 for lifting of your membership suspension, we can recognise your compliance with the first two: you have opened your worship to Christians of all races and given aid to victims of apartheid. It has been more difficult to find 'unequivocal Synod and moderamen resolutions' rejecting apartheid and committing the church to dismantling this system in both church and state. Even recent statements, including Journey with Apartheid of May 1997, suggest that the errors and sinful actions of apartheid reside more in the implementation of apartheid than in its fundamental nature. Because the very nature of forced separation of people of differing races denies fundamental biblical teaching that all humanity is equally created in the image of God, teaching so central to the Christian faith that it cannot be denied by Christians without denying their Christian commitment, we still seek an official resolution from the NGK stating unequivocal rejection of apartheid. The proposed joint resolution, if approved by the NGK, would meet that last requirement.

As the officers of the Alliance indicated during the 1993 visit to South Africa, we believe that your engagement in the unification process with the Uniting Reformed Church in Southern Africa is itself a significant mark of your turning away from apartheid. Through that engagement and particularly your church's study of the Belhar Confession, we believe that you will continue to grow in your understanding of the reasons why the churches of the world felt it necessary to declare *status confessionis* against the theological justification of apartheid. We eagerly await the day when you will be able to confess the Belhar Confession with conviction as

---

1 Available at http://www.ngkerk.org.za/documents/answerurcsaletter (Accessed 11 April 2015).

your confession as a united church. We urge your energetic engagement in the unification process so that that day of confession will come soon.

There has been some confusion over what the Ottawa General Council meant when it called the theological justification of apartheid 'heresy'. This term should not be understood to imply 'excommunication'. WARC is not a church but a fellowship of churches; therefore, it possesses no authority to excommunicate. WARC does not presume to judge whether those who in the past taught the rightness of apartheid will be damned or saved. Reformed people leave the dead to the merciful judgement of God. WARC intended to convey its profound concern for the responsibility of the living church to teach faithfully the gospel of Jesus Christ, for the teachers of the church stand under God's judgement, accountable for their stewardship of the mysteries of God. 'Heresy' is persistent and deliberate teaching of false doctrine after the error has been pointed out by the wider church. This term conveys WARC's conviction that the theological justification of apartheid was not simply an 'error' in stating doctrine or a disagreement in matters where there is freedom to disagree but rather a fundamental perversion and deformation of the heart of the gospel. We pledge to continue to accompany you and the other churches of southern Africa as you continue your journey towards fuller unity. May God give you wisdom, strength, and courage.

ADDENDUM 8

Joint Resolution of the World Alliance of Reformed Churches and the Dutch Reformed Church[1]

Both the World Alliance of Reformed Churches and the Dutch Reformed Church express their desire to lift the suspension imposed by the 21st general council in Ottawa, and to see the Dutch Reformed Church welcomed back into active membership with full privileges in the family of the World Alliance. As part of this action, the Alliance, meeting in Debrecen in 1997, reaffirms its repudiation of any theological justification of apartheid as a matter of status confessionis for the churches inasmuch as such a theological justification is a travesty of the gospel and in its persistent disobedience to the word of God, a theological heresy.

As part of this action, the Dutch Reformed Church through its General Synod in 1998, within the framework of the decision of WARC (para 1 above), assures the churches of the Alliance that it rejects apartheid as wrong and sinful not simply in its effects and operations but also in its fundamental nature. WARC pledges to continue to work pastorally with the Dutch Reformed Church and other churches in southern Africa in the process of unity and reconciliation. Upon approval of this joint resolution by both the General Council of the World Alliance of Reformed Churches in 1997 and the general Synod of the Dutch Reformed Church in 1998, the suspension of the Dutch Reformed Church in the Alliance will be lifted.

Both the World Alliance of Reformed Churches and the Dutch Reformed Church give thanks to God for this act of reconciliation and pray that it will strengthen the joint witness of all Reformed churches both in southern Africa and throughout the world.

---

1   *Agenda Algemene Sinode van die Nederduitse Gereformeerde Kerk* 1998:413/414. Available at http://www.ngkerk.org.za/documents/answerurcsaletter (Accessed 11 April 2015).

ADDENDUM 9

Resolutions of the moderamen (expanded) of the DRC on church reunification 11–12 June 2008 Carmelite Retreat Centre

These resolutions were approved by an expanded meeting of the Moderamen of the General Synod. The moderatures of Synods were invited to this meeting. The agenda of this meeting was the reports of the Task Team for Church Reunification on the Consultation Process 2007 as well as the Moderamen's actions on it. This meeting was held in accordance with a resolution of the General Synod. The Moderamen (Expanded) decided that these resolutions of the Dutch Reformed Church, as proposals for further negotiations, must first be communicated to the family of DR Churches before it is dealt with further (the exception is the section on The Church we want to be... – it was also sent to the Synods of the DR Church to communicate to congregations for further discussion). The last section contains suggestions with regard to communication within the DR Church on the matter of church reunification. It is included for notification and comments by the family of Churches.

The church we want to be...

Calling

In our commitment to the Triune God we, the Dutch Reformed Church in Southern Africa, reaffirm our clear calling in Africa.

Sent to the World (Missiology)

We are convinced that the church in the first instance does not exist for her own sake or for the sake of her members, but to the glory of God and the sake of all people. We understand that it is our calling to make a difference here and now. We want to exercise it by sharing the hope and reconciliation alive in us with everyone around us.

An inclusive church (Ecclesiology)

God chose us as believers, corporately and individually, out of the entire human race to be His Church. Through His Spirit and Word He brought us together, from the beginning of the world to its end, united in true faith. Each member, therefore, should consider it his or her duty to use his or her gifts readily and cheerfully for the service and enrichment of the other members of the church (as well as those outside the church). (Heidelberg Catechism Sunday 21 Q & A 54 and 55.)

Context

The context in which we are called reflects the tragic testimonies of violence, the devastating extent of poverty, famine, crime, the Aids pandemic and the lack of respect for God, humans, animals and the environment. Added to this is the fact that many people live and die without Christ and without hope every day.

Reconciliation

We cannot understand the reason for the church's existence differently than that it is to be the carrier of God's reconciliation with Himself, with one another and with the world. We cannot and will not accept this big challenge alone, because this ministry of reconciliation (2 Cor 5:19-20 NIV) is bigger than the Dutch Reformed Church. The extent of this issue is so large that the assistance and co-operation of all co-believers are necessary. As church we commit ourselves to greater visible unity with other churches, but especially with the members of our own family of Churches. We find our unity in our calling, and we are convinced by the Bible/Gospel that it is God's will.

Diversity

We celebrate our diversity, as God's gift to us, within this unity because our differences help us to better understand and appreciate the full extent of God's grace and love. If one member suffers, all the members suffer; if one member is honoured, all the members rejoice together (1 Corinthians 12:26).

Relationships

We want to travel along this exciting road with honesty, transparency, integrity and in obedience. On this journey of faith mutual relationships in our own circle as well as with members of the family of Dutch Reformed Churches will be of crucial importance.

Challenges

We are aware of the fact that this journey may well hold uncertainty, hurt and self-renunciation. Our comfort is that this new unity is a celebration of our connectedness to the Triune God, Himself being our example of true unity (Mark 12:29-30).

Joint projects and unity structures on congregational, presbytery and Synodical levels, and other fields of the ministry of the church

Introduction

The following proposals are additional to the resolutions about joint projects which were already taken by Achterbergh 1 and 2, as well as by the General Synod of the Dutch Reformed Church (2007) and the Moderamen of the General Synod; are suggested in the light of the very positive reaction received from congregations on joint projects in their feedback on the unity process (Nov 2007); are in obedience to Scripture, in which it is clear to us that the unity of the church is not only in formal ecclesiastical structures or denominations, but also in the exercising of our joint calling, our joint witness, true koinonia, joint worship and the celebration of our unity in Christ. With great gratitude we took cognisance of a multitude of examples of joint projects and unity structures – spontaneous and organised, on a variety of levels – that already exist between the churches in the DR Church family. We want to encourage members and congregations to participate enthusiastically in these joint projects, and to further it.

Some guidelines:

- Joint projects are not viewed as an alternative to the reunification process but actually express the unity even further. It reflects a shared calling and joint ministries leading towards unity structures on a variety of levels.

- The way in which we work together is determined by each specific context and the nature of the projects. It can be only networks, ad hoc projects or spontaneous collaboration, but it can also lead to permanent agreements between two or more partners. It can also include partnerships with other churches than the churches of the DR Church and non-church organisations.

- Members and congregations are encouraged, for the sake of the joint calling, to establish all kinds of permanent partnership agreements in which the following values will be adhered to: It is all about mutual support in the exercising of a joint calling. Partners acknowledge one another's independence and respect each other's differences. Any prescriptiveness and dependence must be avoided. Transparency, honesty and mutual trust are important cornerstones for this relationship. The partners have a say in decisions: it will be taken on the basis of consensus between the partners. Take time to 'listen' to one another and together to Scripture and the context (see *Season of Listening*). The concrete results of the planned project are not only what the partnership relationship is all about. The relationship itself also needs to be enhanced and sustained. Agreements must preferably be in writing and partners must keep to what was agreed upon (the writing an agreement together already embodies the first steps in the building of relationships).

- Congregations, presbyteries and Synods are encouraged to execute existing resolutions about open membership, open structures on the level of the congregation, presbytery and Synod, the calling of pastors between the churches, etc.
- Joint meetings of church councils, presbyteries and Synods, joint events, pastors invited to preach in one another's churches, etc. are encouraged.
- The discussion on a growing number of members, pastors, wards, groups and even congregations of the sister churches of the family 'moving' to the Dutch Reformed Church must be conducted honestly with our sister churches. This process can also be one of 'moving' from the Dutch Reformed Church to our sister churches. This is accepted as a spontaneous and positive process, and is encouraged, but then in consultation with the relevant parties.
- Processes where congregations, presbyteries and other ecclesiastical structures form unity structures in an orderly way are encouraged.
- Due to the growing number of vacancies in congregations and the growing inability to afford pastors, in-depth discussions must be held on various levels with regard to effective and sustainable ministry structures, empowerment of members, theological training and the sharing of pastors.

Confessional basis

- The Three Forms of Unity is without question the confessional basis of reformed churches.
- The Moderamen understands that the Confession of Belhar has significant theological value and sentiment for URCSA and some members of the Dutch Reformed Church. At the same time we know, especially after the consultation with the congregations, that for the majority members and congregations of the Dutch Reformed Church the Confession of Belhar is not acceptable as fourth confession.
- The Moderamen resolves that both these viewpoints must continue to be respected in any future handling of this matter.

New denomination (kerkverband) – (model)

- Two alternative models (i.e. an additional Synod and a replacing Synod) are taken to an Achterbergh 3 for further negotiations with the family of Dutch Reformed Churches.
- As an unalienable part of both models congregations, presbyteries and Synods are encouraged to strive in the meantime for meaningful forms of unity on every level.
- Achterbergh 3 deliberates about the possibility to consider, as an interim measure, a Joint Synod of the four member churches. The mandate of this Joint Synod would be to deal with the further process of church reunification. We suggest that all (regional) Synods of the four member churches send representatives to this Joint Synod.
- The momentum of the other reformed churches in Southern Africa are sought to help us out of our impasse by calling a Southern African Synod of Reformed Churches.

ADDENDUM 10

A Statement by the Delegation from the World Alliance of Reformed Churches 2009[1]

We, the delegation from the World Alliance of Reformed Churches (WARC), have come to South Africa as a consequence of invitations from both the Uniting Reformed Church in Southern Africa (URCSA) and the Dutch Reformed Church (DRC). We pray that all we say may clearly spring from a love for God and for God's people in this place, particularly in the DRC and URCSA. We have learned that this is a painful time in the life of those churches and that the process of unification between them has not proceeded satisfactorily. With the leadership of both churches, who have spoken to us with great candour, we lament the apparent breaking of once shining hopes. Nevertheless, we do not lose heart. For the Lord Jesus Christ, whose prayer is that all who know him may be one, is with us and he, in the end, will overcome all that hurts and divides us.

WARC has long sought to foster unity among Reformed churches in all countries so that their witness to the Gospel may be strong and their call to justice effective. In particular, WARC has been closely involved in the affairs of the Reformed churches of South Africa for more than a century and, with respect to apartheid, since 1964. Five key principles have emerged, particularly following the declaration in 1982 that apartheid is a sin and its theological justification a heresy:

I. Churches must openly invite all people, regardless of race or class, into full participation in the life of the church. Further, they must welcome all believers to the Lord's Table.

II. We reject apartheid in church or society as contrary to the will of God.

III. We call on all churches to reach out with justice and compassion to the victims of apartheid.

IV. We are committed to pastorally accompanying the churches of the Dutch Reformed family of churches through the reunification process.

V. We support the Belhar Confession as a common confession of the reunited church.

---

1 Drafted on March 6, 2009 by Clifton Kirkpatrick, President of WARC, Setri Nyomi, General Secretary of WARC, Jerry Pillay, General Secretary of the Uniting Presbyterian Church in Southern Africa, Stephen Farris, Alexander Horsburgh, Peggy Kabonde, Rommie Nauta and Egbert Rooze.

All we say here is consistent with those long held principles.

- We lament the pain caused in both churches by the dashing of the hopes for a quick reunion raised by the Esselenpark and Achterbergh conferences. Nevertheless, we give thanks that this pain has not been hidden nor has responsibility for present troubles been evaded. In particular, we have heard and acknowledge with gratitude the confession by DRC leadership of their part in the failure of those hopes.

- The Belhar Confession has emerged repeatedly as a central issue in the present difficulties. We wish to state first that the Belhar Confession is not a problem; it is a gift. It is not an obstacle to be surmounted but a blessing to be enjoyed. As a way forward, we urge URCSA and the DRC to engage in a serious study of the Belhar Confession, which should be accompanied by a study guide. The study should clearly be supported by the leadership of both churches and designed jointly by leaders and adult education experts of both churches. We have been told that the content of the Belhar Confession has been recognised by both churches as Biblical and that the problems with receiving it have to do with history. We suggest that the study guide address questions of historical context directly. We offer the services of WARC to convene the meeting that initiates this process and can provide resources on the Belhar Confession from other churches.

- We applaud a common interest by both churches in a truth and reconciliation process and a commitment to restorative justice. We are thankful that, despite the moratorium on unity talks, the leaders of URCSA have expressed willingness to help the DRC understand these deep matters. We trust that the DRC family of churches will take the necessary steps to set up this process promptly, since hope delayed can too easily turn into cynicism and mistrust.

- We believe that change can and must happen at both the leadership and grassroots level and would support efforts to affect that change at all levels.

- We applaud what appears to be increasingly temperate and reflective language as the process of consultation has progressed in our time together. We urge all to continue, whether in person or through the media, to use language appropriate to those who will one day minister together in one church under the Lordship of Jesus Christ.

- We respect and understand the decision of URCSA to initiate a moratorium on unity talks. We hope, however, that this moratorium will be short in duration.

- We look forward with hope to the unity of all four churches of this Reformed family in South Africa, the Uniting Reformed Church in Southern Africa, the Dutch

Reformed Church, the Reformed Church in Africa, the Dutch Reformed Church in Africa, and affirm the value of unity discussions among them.

- We wish to renew our commitment to the process of pastoral accompaniment of these four churches. We therefore commit ourselves to a process of monitoring, facilitated by Dr. Jerry Pillay, here in South Africa, but also involving, from a distance, the other members of the team. With the permission of the executive Committee of WARC, team members may be able to visit from time to time to encourage the process of unification. We will remain available, as the Lord permits, for further consultation.

We sense through all this a clear commitment to unity in the Dutch Reformed family of churches and share that deep yearning for the day when all will be one. In particular we celebrate and affirm five commitments made by both churches at the conclusion of our meeting:

1. Respect for the moratorium called by URCSA
2. A shared commitment to reunification
3. Assistance to one another in a serious and positive study of the value and importance of the Belhar Confession for the reunified church
4. A common effort for restorative justice and reconciliation
5. Intentional efforts to build relationship between the members of the churches
6. We acknowledge that this is a difficult time in the lives of the churches and for church leaders who have invested their time, energy and, indeed, their very selves in the process of unification. We will remember you our prayers. Do not give up hope, we urge you. Remember your only comfort in life and in death and know that, with God, all things are possible.

ADDENDUM 11

Memorandum of Agreement between the DRC and URCSA[1]

Introduction

The Executives of URCSA and DRC has met in November 2011, February and July 2012 to discuss the way forward after the DRC General Synod accepted the Belhar Confession and started a process to get the Belhar Confession to be included as a confession in a church orderly way. From these meetings and a mutual discernment of God's will, the Executives has agreed to draw up a Memorandum of Agreement, sign it and present it to our various church structures for acceptance.

Preamble

We as churches have decided to covenant together, because we believe that the Lord, who graciously committed himself to us, requires this of us. We use the term covenanting because we want to bring ourselves and the reunification process under the authority of the word of God and the will of Christ. As the family of churches we already decided together at Achterberg to journey together.

We envisage a new organically united reformed church, organized according to Synodical-Presbyterial structures, which lives missionally and is committed to the biblical demands of love, reconciliation, justice and peace. At the same time we are committed to non-racialism, inclusiveness and the acceptance and celebration of our multicultural composition. The different languages in our churches will be treasured.

From within our common faith in the triune God we commit ourselves anew to Africa, the continent where the Lord has placed us, and particularly to Southern Africa. We wish to take up this calling together to make a difference to the life-threatening problems facing our countries. In the process of spreading the gospel, we covenant to work together in concrete ways such as:
- inviting people to life in fullness in Christ
- promoting of healing and wholeness for all of life
- engaging in prophetic dialogue with others on societal matters

---

1 Report on Ecumenical affairs in the *Agenda of the General Synod of URCSA*, October 2012.

- embodying, modelling and promoting moral values of Scripture
- seeking and advocating justice for all
- achieving reconciliation, which is more than mere tolerance of one another
- opposing violence and abuse of power of all kinds in our society
- promoting and embracing human dignity and gender equity.

On church unity

We commit ourselves to the following model of unity:

From the different models for church unity in different churches, we intentionally choose a Presbyterial-Synodical church body (i.e. organic) that supports the Gospel of Jesus Christ who broke down the wall of separation between people (Ephesians 2:14-16).

> *Ephesians 2*
>
> *14 For he himself is our peace, who has made the two groups one and has destroyed the barrier, the dividing wall of hostility,*
>
> *15 by setting aside in his flesh the law with its commands and regulations. His purpose was to create in himself one new humanity out of the two, thus making peace,*
>
> *16 and in one body to reconcile both of them to God through the cross, by which he put to death their hostility.*

We believe that this proposed model is a Scriptural embodiment of unity in the Southern African context. This model we believe can help the church on different levels to be the living body of Christ in the world.

As reformed churches we believe that the local congregation is the expression of the church of Christ in a local community, but we also believe that local congregations live in communion with one another and this communion is expressed in various manners e.g. presbyteries, Synods.

We agree that getting the church to be fully one will be a process and that it will ask of us to commit ourselves to journey and grow together.

We propose that the churches start a process to obtain the permission of all the congregations of the churches (in the exact way currently prescribed in the church order of the particular church) for the following:
- the forming of a new General Synod as expression of new denominational ties (kerkverband)
- the formulating of the confessional basis for the reunited church
- to approve amendments to existing Church Orders needed for the formation and restructuring of a reunited church
- to approve that, after the forming of a new General Synod, a process will follow by which the regional Synods and presbyteries engage in processes of expressing the reunited church at their respective levels
- the name of the reunited church
- the church orderly position of congregations with regard to ministry, property, etc.

The actuarii of the General Synods form a task team to evaluate the existing church orders and to start a process to amend them in the correct way in order to make such a process possible.

On the Confession of Belhar

- We agree that the Confession of Belhar will be taken up in the confessional basis of the reunited church.
- We understand that the Dutch Reformed Church decided to make the Confession of Belhar part of the confessional basis of the Dutch Reformed Church in a church orderly way and we also understand that it proposed to do it in the following way:
  - The doctrine which the Church confesses in accordance with the Word of God, takes place in communion with the confession of our tradition as it is expressed in
  - the Apostles Creed, the Nicene Creed and the Athanasian Creed through which the Church expresses her connectedness with the catholic Christian Church, and
  - the Heidelberg Catechism, Confession and Canons of Dordt through which the church expresses her connectedness with the reformed tradition.

In connectedness with our own context we acknowledge the Confession of Belhar.
- We understand that the Dutch Reformed Church will have to follow the Dutch Reformed Church's Church Order to make the Confession of Belhar part of the confessional basis of the Dutch Reformed Church.
- We agree that the churches will journey together in this process of acceptance and renewed engagement of the Confession of Belhar.
- We understand that the decision of the 2011 General Synod of the Dutch Reformed Church is a journey towards full acceptance of the Confession of Belhar as part of the confessional basis of the Dutch Reformed Church.
- Where congregations, ministers, and members of the Dutch Reformed Church do not underwrite the Confession of Belhar as an article of faith, we are committed to journey with them.

On restorative justice and reconciliation

We acknowledge that church unity and the Belhar Confession urges us to also speak about restorative justice and reconciliation. As churches we have therefore decided to embrace the following:
- Restorative justice should not be an end in itself but always lead to reconciliation. Reconciliation should be the restoration of communities at different levels of society: personal, social, political, denominational, economical, emotional and spiritual reconciliation between God and us.
- We believe that restorative justice is a Biblical imperative that restores life in its fullness. It restores imbalances of the past and imbalances in God's creation and glorifies God through our restored unity and reconciliation.
- We accept that restorative justice is a complex process which will ask some sacrifices. We will therefore need good stewardship but also a clear vision on the possible outcomes of such a process.

Regarding reconciliation we agreed on the following statements:

- We believe that true reconciliation is a deeply spiritual process. Christian principles like sacrifice and forgiveness should not be neglected. Without the necessary spiritual maturity, it could fail dismally.
- We accept the reality that conflict, bitterness, hatred, racism, ethnicism, classism, sexism and a lot of emotional pain is still very much part of society. We must address some of the core reasons for conflict like: misunderstandings and poor communication, bad and corrupt leadership, language, culture and religion,

ideologies and the greed for political power, injustices, personalities, scarce resources and imbalances in society.

In order to effect reconciliation we believe that:

- We need to take the emotions of our people very seriously.
- We will have to develop greater passion and willpower to really make a difference. We will have to name the areas of conflict, face it and engage in the situation.
- At the heart of reconciliation is the matter of spirituality and the reconciliation that has already taken place in Jesus Christ.
- We will have to grow in integrity.
- We will have to define a common cause for all our people and enhance the principle of interpathy.

On restorative justice we want to propose the following practical measures:

- Some initial successful examples which could be a model for future actions.
- Co-operate with URCSA in the important 5 year strategic plan of URCSA. We believe that this plan could give us entry points into the restorative justice process.
- To conduct a property audit.
- To propose and undertake some concrete actions.

We firmly believe that any process of restorative justice and reconciliation must be guarded and guided by good stewardship, discipline, work ethic and healthy moral values.

We believe that essential to restorative justice and reconciliation is a need for a change of heart and attitude. This will only be possible if we engage with one another and are guided by the overwhelming power of the Holy Spirit.

Conclusion

We believe that this process should be accompanied by a specific and focused process that creates safe spaces for listening to God and one another and spiritual discernment on how we need to address all the challenges facing us on this journey and acknowledging our different experiences and stories.

In the spirit of this covenant, we agree to encourage agreements on different levels of the church that will embody this new unity.

We do this in obedience and dependence in Jesus Christ who is the Lord of the church.

ADDENDUM 12

The roadmap to church reunification: DRC and URCSA[1]

Stage 1
Point of departure. Signing of *Memorandum of Agreement* by Executives and ratification by General Synods.

Stage 2
Formal decision taken by General Synods or General Synodical Commission mandated by General Synod to start the church orderly process to church reunification. An urgent effort to be made to get the two other churches in the DRC family on board before proceeding to stage 3.

Stage 3
Convene joint meetings of the churches' Executives, Moderatures and/or Synodical Commissions and continue to do so.

Stage 4
General Synods of the churches mandate the following commissions to act on their behalf ad interim: (a) The Leadership of die Churches (Executive, Moderamen and/or General Synodical Commission) to take preliminary or in principle decisions on behalf of the Church and report back to General Synod; (b) The Steering Committee for Church Reunification constituted by a majority of members not acting in the Leadership. The Steering Committee must be composed to ensure continuity and credibility, to maintain objectivity and to dispose of persuasiveness; (c) The Task Teams, among a Church Order Commission responsible for the drafting of an Common Set of Rules (Tussenorde) for the Churches see foot note, the Concept Church Order for a Reunited Church and the obtaining of legal advice from a Panel of Legal Advisors. The principles already agreed on in the *Memorandum of Agreement* must be contained in the Concept Church Order (organic Synodical-Presbyterian structure, missional structure, diversity of language and culture, unification of congregations, presbyteries and Synods, the autonomy of the local congregation

---

1 *Minutes General Synodical Commission URCSA*. November 2013:1-2.

combined with the authority of the presbytery, Synod and General Synod and the confessional basis with the inclusion of the Belhar Confession).

Stage 5
Convene a joint General Synod, take joint decisions regarding church reunification and related issues, and ratify decisions by own General Synod. First joint General Synod may coincide with a General Ministers Conference. First General Synod shall be a celebration and festive occasion. In future general Synodical meetings will take place on the same date and at the same venue. Joint decisions will be taken and be ratified as soon as possible afterwards in own meeting.

Stage 6
Report back to the General Synods (joint and singly) on the Common Set of Rules, on proposed amendments to the existing Church Orders to make church reunification church orderly and legally possible, and on the Concept Church Order. General Synods take the decision to approve, apply and later to amend the Common Set of Rules. The Common Set of Rules has authority over the Churches' own Church Order on a spelled out issue.

Stage 7
All Synods and Congregations enjoy the opportunity to respond to the content of the Concept (Draft) Church Order by making their proposal and/or accepting it in principle. A time is set therefore. The final draft for the Concept Church Order is approved by the Churches' Synods and Church Councils/Consistories, with the approbation/consent of the members of the Congregation. A time is set therefore. The decision of each Church Council and Synod, taken in terms of the applicable Church Order, is conveyed to existing General Synod of the Church.

Stage 8
The General Synod of the Church takes a final decision to reunite and approve the Concept Church Order with a two-thirds majority. The General Synod of the Church takes the necessary transitional decisions regarding the transfer of activity, property, funds, etc. The General Synod of the Church takes a decision to dissolve the General Synod as meeting (not as juristic person, that may continue to exist) and appoints delegates to a Conventus and the General Synod of the Reunited Church.

Stage 9
The Conventus convenes on the date and time set forth by Steering Commission. Report back from the General Synods of the Churches is given and the Church Order of the proposed Reunited Church is approved.

Stage 10
The General Synod of the Reunited Church is constituted.

Common Set of Rules

- The Common Set of Rules is provided to serve the process of reunification and represents an important phase in the process of the churches to know each other, while experiencing and growing together in unity, reconciliation and justice.
- The Common Set of Rules is a set of church orderly provisions which give a legal base to co-operation between the churches on the road to reunification.
- The Common Set of Rules does not remove/abrogate the articles, regulations or rules of the churches. The articles, regulations or rules stated in the Church Order are applicable as they stand, except in case where the Common Set of Rules specifically arranges exceptions.

ADDENDUM 13

Response of the URCSA with regard to the acceptance/ (non) acceptance of the Belhar Confession in the DRC 2015[1]

Dear all, we have just learned that the proposal to add the Belhar Confession to the PCUSA Book of Confessions has just cleared a crucial hurdle with 75% of their presbyteries voting to approve the addition. As you know the URCSA presented the Belhar Confession as a gift for the church worldwide. The decision of the PCUSA will still need to be ratified by the 222nd General Assembly next June, but that seems likely to be just a formality at this stage. We know they also paid a huge price to come thus far. We as the moderamen of URCSA are grateful that one of the largest denominations in the USA accepted the gift of the Belhar Confession. Praise is to God from whom all blessings flow. This wonderful news ironically serves to emphasise the tragedy of what is unfolding in South Africa. History will judge the DRC harshly with regard to the reasons tabled during the course of time at the DRC Synods for not accepting the Belhar Confession.

The URCSA however want to emphasise that we applaud the efforts by the DRC on General Synod level, Regional Synod level as well as congregational level to take up the Belhar Confession in your confessional basis. We cherish your efforts. We affirm that we will still avail ourselves to accompany the DRC in this regard. We know that it could not been an easy task to embark on this very difficult process to change the confessional basis of the DRC. We took cognisance that the current wording of the DRC's Church Order makes the change of the confessional basis of the DRC almost impossible (see Article 44.1 and 44.2). According to Article 44.1 The amendment of the Confession is only possible only after each regional Synod of the DRC approved with a two-thirds majority and two-thirds of all church councils, each with a two-thirds majority in favour of the resolution. 44.2 states that Article 44.1 and 44.2 of the church Order of the DRC is amended after each Synod with a two-thirds majority voted in favour of the resolution, the General Synod then afterwards by a two-thirds majority vote in favour of it. The DRC gone on this extremely difficult church judicial process to change their confessional basis, knowing the limitation in their

---

1   Official response to the DRC drafted and presented on behalf of the URCSA by the moderator of the URCSA, Prof. Rev Dr Mary-Anne Plaatjies-Van Huffel at the church reunification talk between the DRC and the URCSA under the facilitation of Jerry Pillay 23-24 April 2015 in Kempton Park at Kempton Park (*Agenda General Synodical Commission* 2015).

own Church Order, which allows that if only one Synod would agree dismissively, that would mean that the amendment of Article 1 will not be possible in the coming General Synod. The amendment of Article 1 of the Church Order of the DRC is, after all, limited by Article 44.1 and Article 44.2. It seems to us that the DRC is again facing a critical time in its history, that you are rent apart by two streams in your church, that you are being confronted with forces in your church, that you need to make a courageous stand for justice, reconciliation and unity, meaning the biblical principles even if you would not being able to accept the Belhar Confession, that the DRC has not been able to fully confront their past. Maybe we are wrong in our interpretation of what is unfolding in the DRC. With much anticipation we had been watching you embarking on the church judicial process to amend your confessional basis. We must admit that we are hugely disappointed at the results of the voting. We as the URCSA believe that the Confession of Belhar is a profound statement on unity, reconciliation, and justice for church and society and we again are offering it to you. We want to say categorically: In not accepting the Belhar Confession the DRC are rejecting the URCSA.

The URCSA want to rectify understanding in die DRC and some of their ministers that the Belhar Confession is a gun which the URCSA is holding against their head. It is not a gun forcing you. We are not forcing it down your throat. The leaders/ministers of the DRC should be careful not to affirm the grand narrative in South Africa that we as the URCSA are forcing you to accept the Belhar Confession. It is a historical fact: The Confession of Belhar was born in the struggle against apartheid. The URCSA still sees the Belhar Confession as the acid test for the DRC to show that she has broken with integrity with her past. The biblical affirmation that all human beings are created in the image of God is being articulated in the Confession of Belhar. This should be conveyed tirelessly to the members of the DRC. It is not the URCSA forcing you to accept the Belhar Confession. It is God himself who are forcing/challenging you to confront the elephant in the house. We repeatedly said in the past that the Belhar Confession is a staff to lean on in our joint journey to church reunification. We say tirelessly that it should be part as a fully-fledged confession in the envisioned unified church. We understand confession as both the church's response to human sin and as witness to our faith. This is what the DRC has to face. We admit, the church at large, are called to confess that the sin of racism is still like Durand once said is lurking in our hearts. We as moderamen see this as a time of Kairos for the DRC. You are dared in a time like this to speak with unusual clarity. We, however, cannot force or coerced anyone to confess. Rather, the compulsion to confess is imposed by God himself.

We as the URCSA do not want to be paternalistic therefore we do not want to give guidance to the DRC how to attend to this issue. Twenty years after the dismantling of apartheid the Dutch Reformed family of churches is still being dived along racial, cultural, and class divisions. (Rev Godfrey Betha shared with us numerous stories conveyed to him by ministers of the Word in the Northern Synod inter alia that it not possible for them to tell for example the farmers to accept the Belhar Confession, because they assume that after church reunification the URCSA would take hold of their land as well as the resources of the DRC). The Belhar Confession is currently challenging the DRC regarding the theological presuppositions in the DRC with respect to unity, justice and reconciliation, ecclesiology as well as their understanding of the status of confessions in a Reformed church (*quia or quatenus*). We, both the DRC and the URCSA, should admit that we are still being divided into separate spheres. We, both as us, should not sanction the rationales for this division. We as moderamen believe that Belhar directs us, the DRC and us, to look at what has led to where we are now. The question is: What is the deep divides that still haunt us all? We believe it is only the gospel of God, who alone can bring us together as one family of Christ. Therefore we reaffirm that we will still prayerfully embrace each other and will pastoral accompany you.

We are committed to church reunification. We are members of the one family of God. We are brothers and sisters in Christ. We believe all of us should embody God's ministry of reconciliation. We however want to say load and clear that Jesus Christ calls us to a costly discipleship of dying to ourselves. '*When Christ calls a man, he bids him come and die.*' (Dietrich Bonhoeffer). We heard numerous stories during yesterday of the DRC moderamen and individual members of the DRC's pain. This however is part of the uneasiness to confess. We cannot as the URCSA ease this pain. It is part of your own journey. Bonhoeffer once said: 'The messengers of Jesus will be hated to the end of time. They will be blamed for all the division which rend cities and homes. But the end is also near, and they must hold on and persevere until it comes.' We can only say as the ambassadors of Christ's reconciling love the apostles often met resistance and persecution. This we believe is where the DRC is now. This, however, is a journey you should embark on alone. It is your process to confession (*process confessionus*). The overall process currently in the DRC with regard to the amendment of their confessional basis *inter alia* the numerous Bible studies, sermons, articles, hymns, debates, voting is actually nothing else a process to confess. Whatever choice the of the DRC, (affirmative or dismissive) we are sure that ultimately the DRC will never be the same after the conclusion of the process. Even if the DRC dismissively finally decided on the Confession of Belhar, the DRC's future as a church will be determined what she during the process of confession (processus confessionus) accepted, endorsed, tacitly sanctioned or rejected. That is how the history will judge the position choice of the DRC with regard to the Belhar Confession. We can only pray for the DRC.

With regard to the joint ventures nothing changed because there are legal agreements between the legal entities in the DRC and the URCSA. With regard to the Memorandum of Agreement, nothing changed. With regard to the Common Set of Rules we want to convey to the DRC that the URCSA already approved the principles of such a Common Set of Rules at their last Synod. We can only urge the DRC to on their own account approve principles of such a Common Set of Rules at their upcoming Synod. We are at a crossroad. What we are going to in the meanwhile? We will only wait and keep you in our prayers at the crossroad until the upcoming General Synod of the DRC October 2015. We are waiting with anticipating for your decisions on the way ahead. We are only pausing at the crossroad. We do not want to be misinterpreting on the issue. We are not abandoning the process. We are still committed to the process of church reunification. We as the URCSA do not want to be seen paternalistic in our joint journey towards church reunification. Therefore we do not want to give church judicial advice to the DRC at this point of time on the way ahead. We will be waiting for the DRC at the crossroad. It is your task to overcome the hurdles in the DRC. This is the plea from the side of the URCSA. We, therefore, want to close with the ringing affirmation found in the final words from the Confession Jesus is Lord. He is the one whom will ultimately unify us.

ADDENDUM 14

Press statement of the URCSA on xenophobia[1]

Introduction

The URCSA takes cognisance of the emergence of Xenophobia and Afrophobia in South Africa since 2008 as well as the recent Xenophobia and Afrophobia onslaught which is tarnishing our newly founded democracy. Research undertaken by the Forced Migration Programme shows that sections of the South African population are highly xenophobic. The URCSA calls upon government to confront the rising tide of racism, ethnocentrism and xenophobia in South Africa. The wider issues at stake are how to handle difference, respond to the 'other', and negotiate plurality. Firm action from the government is necessary. The URCSA urges all fellow South Africans to acknowledge 'others' in their difference, to welcome strangers even if their 'strangeness' sometimes threatens us, and to seek reconciliation even with those who have declared themselves our enemies.

Call to the church

We believe in the words of the Belhar Confession (Article 3) *that God has entrusted to his Church the message of reconciliation.* Therefore we believe that how we react to stranger in our midst is not an optional, supplementary issue. It touches the heart of the church's teaching about who God is, who we are and who the earth and the land belong to. In the Old Testament hospitality towards the strangers whom they encountered is emphasised.

The Bible is full of accounts of people who are on the move, who are strangers, immigrants or refugees, and who have nowhere they can call home (Philippines 4, 5 NRSV). Jesus was also a stranger, without a home, with nowhere to lay his head (Matthew 8:18-20, John 1:11, Luke 2:7, Matthew 2:13ff, Matthew 25:31ff NRSV). Jesus expects and demands that his disciples will care for strangers. The Bible emphasises that strangers or refugees should be met with friendliness and caring (Leviticus 19:9-10, Deuteronomy 6:20f, Exodus 20:10, Exodus 23:10-12, Ruth 2:2-3 NRSV). In a time like this when foreigners are treated unjustly we believe that the Confession of

---

[1] The statement was drafted by moderator of the General Synod of the URCSA, Prof Mary-Anne Plaatjies-Van Huffel, and was issued on 16 April 2015. The statement is published in German as Wie wir auf Fremde in unserer Mitte reagieren, das berührt das Herz der kirchlichen Lehre In *Für das Recht streiten. 30 Jahre Bekenntnis von Belhar.* http://www.reformiert-info.de/15410-0-0-1.html (2016)

Belhar Article 4 urges us to *affirm that God is in a special way the God of the destitute, the poor and the wronged and that He calls his Church to follow Him in this...;* We believe that the triune God called us together on earth to share our common humanity. God called us to embody Christ's work of reconciliation towards fellow human beings not withstanding race, culture of creed. The church believes in one God who created everything and gives life. The earth, nature and the land that provides the necessities of life are all God's gifts. Christian hospitality involves seeing the 'other' not as a threat but as a 'gift'. When the 'other' comes to our country, we are challenged to share these gifts with them, in thankfulness to God. Those who come as aliens are to be received kindly and treated as one of our own people (Deuteronomy 26, 5-8, Exodus 22, 21-7, Leviticus 19:33-34 NRSV).

We urge all to pursue community with one another; to fight against all which may threaten or hinder this common humanity. We should earnestly pursue and sought a common citizenry. To give shelter to the stranger in our midst is ultimately a question of preserving our own human dignity. The dignity of human beings is thus not bound to ethnic, cultural, religious or national identity (Leviticus 23, 22, Deuteronomy 24, 19; 14, 28f; 26, 12; 24, 17f; 10, 18; 24, 14f; Exodus 12, 49 NRSV). God cares for everyone and regards each individual human being as infinitely valuable.

All human beings are created in the image of a righteous and loving God. We therefore reject xenophobia and afrophobia. We believe that God is in a special way the God of the stranger in our midst and that He calls his Church to follow Him in this; that He protects the stranger and that the church must therefore stand by the stranger in our midst in any form of suffering (Colossians 3, 11; Ephesians 2, 14; Romans 15, 7; 12, 13 NRSV). God's love and compassion includes all humankind. Christ has already conquered separation, enmity and hatred between people and groups (Galatians 3, 27-29 NRSV). Without embracing the 'other' there can be no dignity of all.

Therefore the Church must witness against all those who selfishly seek their own interests and harm others on ground of their nationality. We have an imperative to serve as the voice of the voiceless. We should speak out, judge righteously, and defend the rights of those whose rights are being inflicted upon (Proverbs 31:8-9 NRSV). We believe that, in obedience to Jesus Christ, its only Head, the Church is called to love the stranger, for we all had been strangers in the land (Deuteronomy 10:18-19 NRSV). Jesus is Lord!

ADDENDUM 15

Confession of Belhar

The Accompanying Letter

1. We are deeply conscious that moments of such seriousness can arise in the life of the Church that it may feel the need to confess its faith anew in the light of a specific situation. We are aware that such an act of confession is not lightly undertaken, but only if it is considered that the heart of the gospel is so threatened as to be at stake. In our judgement, the present church and political situation in our country and particularly within the Dutch Reformed Church family calls for such a decision. Accordingly, we make this confession not as a contribution to a theological debate nor as a new summary of our beliefs, but as a cry from the heart, as something we are obliged to do for the sake of the gospel in view of the times in which we stand. Along with many, we confess our guilt, in that we have not always witnessed clearly enough in our situation and so are jointly responsible for the way in which those things which were experienced as sin and confessed to be so or should have been experienced as and confessed to be sin have grown in time to seem self-evidently right and to be ideologies foreign to the scriptures. As a result many have been given the impression that the gospel was not really at stake. We make this confession because we are convinced that all sorts of theological arguments have contributed to so disproportionate an emphasis on some aspects of the truth that it has in effect become a lie.

2. We are aware that the only authority for such a confession and the only grounds on which it may be made are the Holy Scriptures as the Word of God. Being fully aware of the risks involved in taking this step, we are nevertheless convinced that we have no alternative. Furthermore, we are aware that no other motives or convictions, however valid they may be, would give us the right to confess in this way. An act of confession may only be made by the Church for the sake of its purity and credibility and that of its message. As solemnly as we are able, we hereby declare before everyone that our only motive lies in our fear that the truth and power of the gospel itself is threatened in this situation. We do not wish to serve any group interests, advance the cause of any factions, promote any theologies or achieve any ulterior purposes. Yet, having said this, we know that our deepest intentions may only be judged at their true value by God before whom all is revealed. We do not make this confession from God's throne and from on high, but before God's throne and before other human beings. We plead therefore, that this Confession should not be misused by anyone with ulterior

motives and also that it should not be resisted to serve such motives. Our earnest desire is to lay no false stumbling blocks in the way, but to point to the true stumbling block Jesus Christ the rock.

3. This confession is not aimed at specific people or groups of people or a church or churches. We proclaim it against a false doctrine, against an ideological distortion that threatens the gospel itself in our church and our country. Our heartfelt longing is that no one will identify themselves with this objectionable doctrine and that all who have been wholly or partially blinded by it will turn themselves away from it. We are deeply aware of the deceiving nature of such a false doctrine and know that many who have been conditioned by it have to a greater or lesser extent learnt to take a half-truth for the whole. For this reason we do not doubt the Christian faith of many such people, their sincerity, honour, integrity and good intentions, and theirs in many ways estimable practice and conduct. However, it is precisely because we know the power of deception that we know we are not liberated by the seriousness, sincerity or intensity of our certainties, but only by the truth in the Son. Our church and our land have an intense need of such liberation. Therefore it is that we speak pleadingly rather than accusingly. We plead for reconciliation, that true reconciliation which follows on conversion and change of attitudes and structures. And while we do so we are aware that an act of confession is a two-edged sword, that none of us can throw the first stone and none is without a beam in their own eye. We know that the attitudes and conduct that work against the gospel are present in all of us and will continue to be so. Therefore this Confession must be seen as a call to a continuous process of soul-searching together, a joint wrestling with the issues, and a readiness to repent in the name of our Lord Jesus Christ in a broken world. It is certainly not intended as an act of self-justification and intolerance, for that would disqualify us in the very act of preaching to others.

4. Our prayer is that this act of confession will not place false stumbling blocks in the way and thereby cause and foster false divisions, but rather that it will be reconciling and uniting. We know that such an act of confession and process of reconciliation will necessarily involve much pain and sadness. It demands the pain of repentance, remorse and confession; the pain of individual and collective renewal and a changed way of life. It places us on a road whose end we can neither foresee nor manipulate to our own desire. On this road we shall unavoidably suffer intense growing pains while we struggle to conquer alienation, bitterness, irreconciliation and fear. We shall have to come to know and encounter both ourselves and others in new ways. We are only too well aware that this confession calls for the dismantling of structures of thought, of church, and of society that have developed over many years. However, we confess that for the sake of the gospel, we have no other choice. We pray that our brothers

and sisters throughout the Dutch Reformed Church family, but also outside it, will want to make this new beginning with us, so that we can be free together, and together may walk the road of reconciliation and justice. Accordingly, our prayer is that the pain and sadness we speak of will be pain and sadness that lead to salvation. We believe that this is possible in the power of our Lord and by God's Spirit. We believe that the gospel of Jesus Christ offers hope, liberation, salvation and true peace to our country.

The Belhar Confession

www.vgksa.org.za/documents/The%20Belhar%20Confession.pdf

[Note: The Synod of the former Dutch Reformed Mission Church (DRMC) adopted the draft Confession of Belhar in 1982 with an accompanying letter. These two documents should always be read together. In 1986 the DRMC adopted the Confession of Belhar in its final version in Afrikaans. The 2008 General Synod of the Uniting Reformed Church in Southern Africa (URCSA), which resulted from the reunification between the former Dutch Reformed Church in Africa (DRCA) and the DRMC, declared the 1986 Afrikaans version to be the original source document. The 2008 URCSA General Synod in addition adopted the English translation that follows here as the official English version.]

1. **We believe** in the triune God, Father, Son and Holy Spirit, who through Word and Spirit gathers, protects and cares for the church from the beginning of the world and will do to the end.

2. **We believe** in one holy, universal Christian Church, the communion of saints called from the entire human family.

    We believe that Christ's work of reconciliation is made manifest in the church as the community of believers who have been reconciled with God and with one another (Eph. 2:11-22);

    that unity is, therefore, both a gift and an obligation for the church of Jesus Christ; that through the working of God's Spirit it is a binding force, yet simultaneously a reality which must be earnestly pursued and sought: one which the people of God must continually be built up to attain (Eph. 4:1-16);

    that this unity must become visible so that the world may believe that separation, enmity and hatred between people and groups is sin which Christ has already conquered, and accordingly that anything which threatens this unity may have no place in the church and must be resisted (John 17:20-23);

that this unity of the people of God must be manifested and be active in a variety of ways: in that we love one another; that we experience, practice and pursue community with one another; that we are obligated to give ourselves willingly and joyfully to be of benefit and blessing to one another (Philem. 2:1-5;1 Cor. 12:4-31);

that we share one faith, have one calling, are of one soul and one mind; have one God and Father, are filled with one Spirit, are baptised with one baptism, eat of one bread and drink of one cup, confess one Name, are obedient to one Lord, work for one cause, and share one hope; together come to know the height and the breadth and the depth of the love of Christ; together are built up to the stature of Christ, to the new humanity; together know and bear one another's burdens, thereby fulfilling the law of Christ that we need one another and up build one another, admonishing and comforting one another; that we suffer with one another for the sake of righteousness; pray together; together serve God in this world; and together fight against everything that may threaten or hinder this unity (John 13:1-17;1 Cor. 1:10-13; Eph. 4:1-6; Eph. 3:14-20;1; Cor. 10:16-17; 1 Cor. 11:17-34; Gal. 6:2; 2 Cor. 1:3-4);

that this unity can be established only in freedom and not under constraint; that the variety of spiritual gifts, opportunities, backgrounds, convictions, as well as the diversity of languages and cultures, are by virtue of the reconciliation in Christ, opportunities for mutual service and enrichment within the one visible people of God (Romans 12:3-8; 1 Cor. 12:1-11; Eph. 4:7-13; Gal. 3:27-28; James 2:1-13);

that true faith in Jesus Christ is the only condition for membership of this church.

Therefore, we reject any doctrine

which absolutises either natural diversity or the sinful separation of people in such a way that this absolutisation hinders or breaks the visible and active unity of the church, or even leads to the establishment of a separate church formation;

which professes that this spiritual unity is truly being maintained in the bond of peace whilst believers of the same confession are in effect alienated from one another for the sake of diversity and in despair of reconciliation;

which denies that a refusal earnestly to pursue this visible unity as a priceless gift is sin;

which explicitly or implicitly maintains that descent or any other human or social factor should be a consideration in determining membership of the church.

3. **We believe** that God has entrusted the church with the message of reconciliation in and through Jesus Christ; that the church is called to be the salt of the earth and the light of the world that the church is called blessed because it is a peacemaker, that the church is witness both by word and by deed to the new heaven and the new earth in which righteousness dwells (2 Cor. 5:17-21; Matt. 5:13-16; Matt. 5:9; 2 Peter 3:13; Rev. 21-22);

   that God's life-giving Word and Spirit has conquered the powers of sin and death, and therefore also of irreconciliation and hatred, bitterness and enmity;

   that God's life-giving Word and Spirit will enable the church to live in a new obedience which can open new possibilities of life for society and the world (Eph. 4:17 – 6:23; Romans 6; Col. 1:9-14; Col. 2:13-19; Col 3:1 – 4:61:9-14);

   that the credibility of this message is seriously affected and its beneficial work obstructed when it is proclaimed in a land which professes to be Christian, but in which the enforced separation of people on a racial basis promotes and perpetuates alienation, hatred and enmity; that any teaching which attempts to legitimate such forced separation by appeal to the gospel, and is not prepared to venture on the road of obedience and reconciliation, but rather, out of prejudice, fear, selfishness and unbelief, denies in advance the reconciling power of the gospel, must be considered ideology and false doctrine.

   Therefore, we reject any doctrine which, in such a situation sanctions in the name of the gospel or of the will of God the forced separation of people on the grounds of race and colour and thereby in advance obstructs and weakens the ministry and experience of reconciliation in Christ.

4. **We believe** that God has revealed Godself as the One who wishes to bring about justice and true peace on earth; that in a world full of injustice and enmity God is in a special way the God of the destitute, the poor and the wronged and that God calls the church to follow in this; that God brings justice to the oppressed and gives bread to the hungry; that God frees the prisoner and restores sight to the blind; that God supports the downtrodden, protects the strangers, helps orphans and widows and blocks the path of the ungodly; that for God pure and undefiled religion is to visit the orphans and the widows in their suffering; that God wishes to teach the people of God to do what is good and to seek the right (Deut. 32:4; Luke 2:14; John 14:27; Eph. 2:14; Isaiah 1:16-17; James 1:27; James 5:1-6; Luke 1:46-55; Luke 6:20-26; Luke 7:22; Luke 16:19-31);

   that the church must therefore stand by people in any form of suffering and need, which implies, among other things, that the church must witness against and strive against any form of injustice, so that justice may roll down like waters, and righteousness like an ever-flowing stream (Psalm 146; Luke 4:16-19; Romans 6:13-18; Amos 5);

that the church belonging to God, should stand where God stands, namely against injustice and with the wronged; that in following Christ the church must witness against all the powerful and privileged who selfishly seek their own interests and thus control and harm others.

Therefore, we reject any ideology which would legitimate forms of injustice and any doctrine which is unwilling to resist such an ideology in the name of the gospel.

5. **We believe that**, in obedience to Jesus Christ, its only Head, the church is called to confess and to do all these things, even though the authorities and human laws might forbid them and punishment and suffering be the consequence (Eph. 4:15-16; Acts 5:29-33; 1 Peter 2:18-25; 1 Peter 3:15-18).

Jesus is Lord.

To the one and only God, Father, Son and Holy Spirit, be the honour and the glory for ever and ever.

ADDENDUM 16

Responsive Litany of the Belhar Confession[1]

L: We believe in one God, Father, Son and Holy Spirit, Who gathers, protects and nourishes the church from the beginning of the world to the end

C: *The church is one; The church is holy; The church is universal; It is the community of God's children, called together from the whole of humanity to proclaim God's wonderful deeds*

L: We believe that the reconciling work of Christ gives birth to a uniting church, because church unity is a gift from God and a goal we need to strive for

C: *The unity of the church must become visible so that the people around us can see how separation and hatred are overcome in Christ*

L: We believe that genuine faith in Jesus Christ is the only condition for membership in this Christian church

C: *We praise God that race, class, gender, or culture does not determine who belongs to this church*

L: We believe that God has entrusted to the church the message of reconciliation; and that the church is called to proclaim and embody this reconciliation; to be peacemakers; and to believe and to witness that God conquers all powers of sin and death, of hate, bitterness and enmity, through his life-giving Word and Spirit

C: *We praise God that the gospel does not separate people on the basis of race, gender, class, or culture, but is the power of reconciliation in Christ*

L: We believe that God wants to bring about true justice and lasting peace on earth; We believe that God is, in a special sense, The God of the suffering, the poor and the downtrodden

C: *We praise God who gives justice to the oppressed and bread to the hungry; Who sets captives free and makes the blind to see; Who protects strangers, orphans and widows and obstructs the plans of the wicked*

L: We believe that the church belongs to God and that it should stand where God stands: against injustice and with those who are wronged

---

1 *URCSA Worship Book 2016.*

C: *We commit ourselves to reject all forms of injustice in ourselves and amongst us; and to struggle against all forms of injustice and every teaching that allows injustices to flourish*

L: We are called to confess and to do all this in obedience to Jesus Christ, our only Lord; even if authorities or laws oppose this; even if punishment and suffering may be the consequence.

C: *Jesus is Lord! We will follow Him! To the one God, Father, Son and Holy Spirit, be honour and glory for ever and ever!*

Amen

WEBSITES WITH MATERIAL ON THE BELHAR CONFESSION

The URCSA is in debt to the churches, theologians, individuals who painstakingly developed material regarding the Belhar Confession which are available for public assumption on various search engines. The Internet has become an invaluable tool for learning and researching on the Belhar Confession and related issues. Voices from both sides of the spectrum can be found on various websites regarding the Belhar Confession. These websites are great sources for information on the historical events timelines, background material, presentation, archival material of Synods presentations, statements, newspaper articles and letters, study material, sermons, books, videos, songs, litanies, scholarly articles, blogs, speech archives, discussions and links to relevant sites regarding the confession. Knowing that not all information on the research engines is reliable, the URCSA has to admit that the benefits outweigh the challenges. The Internet has contributed significantly to the dissemination of information regarding the Confession. The downloadable resources material assists easy access to information on the Belhar Confession and contributions to a better understanding of the Confession. Furthermore, the Internet helps in having access to information on the Belhar Confession not feasible in the URCSA's own archives; lastly it helps in having up-to-date information about the Confession.

In future visiting search engines might become one of the principal ways to engage in an informative manner in the discourse regarding confessions in general and the Belhar Confession specifically. Below you will find a list of websites which are not exhausted at all.

Websites with downloadable material on the Belhar Confession

Http://www.belydenisvanbelhar.co.za
http://www.calvin.edu/library/database/crcpi/fulltext/banner/2011-0600-0037.pdf
http://www.crcna.org/
http://www.crcna.org/pages/belhar.cfm
http://www.googlescholar
http://www.hierstaanek.com/.../teologiese-kritiek-op-belhar/
https://internal.calvinseminary.edu/pubs/forum/10fall.pdf#page=10
http://www.ngkerkas.co.za
http://www.kerkargicf.co.za
http://www.ngkerk.org.za
http://www.ngkok.org.za

http://www.kerkargief.co.za
http://www.ngkerk.org.za
http://www.ngkerkvrystaat.co.za
http://www.ngkerkas.co.za/.../besluite-en-studiestukke-Van-die-algemene-sinode/
http://oga.pcusa.org/section/ga/ga221/ga221-belhar/
http://oga.pcusa.org/section/ga/ga221/ga221-belhar/
https://www.pcusa.org/.../belhar-confession/
http://www.pcusa.org/belhar
http://www.oikoumene.org/en/resources/documents/wcc-programmes/unity-mission-evangelism-and-spirituality/just-and-inclusive-communities/racism/statement-from-the-wcc-conference-on-racism-today
http://pres-outlook.org/2015/04/confession-of-belhar-approved-by-presbyteries
https://www.rca.org/resources/belhar-confession-study-center
https://www.rca.org/resources/confession-belhar
http://www.steedshervormers.co.za
http://www.upcsa.org.za/upcsa-home-docs-archived.html
http://www.urcsa.org.za
https://www.wat-is-die-belhar-belyapk.co.za/index.php/laaikas/die-ng-kerk-en-belhar
http://www.maroelamedia.co.za/.../die-belhar-debat-die-bely%

INDEX

A

Accra Confession 29, 176, 421
Achterbergh Declaration 52, 73-75, 468, 470
Allan Aubrey Boesak vii, xii-xiii, 13, 17, 19, 21, 23, 29, 111, 113, 185, 189, 200, 238-241, 243, 258, 268, 279, 283-284, 287, 291, 349, 356, 358, 377, 408, 411, 421, 425-426
Alliance of Black Reformed Christians in Southern Africa (ABRECSA) 20, 348, 408

B

Barmen Theological Declaration 29, 193, 349, 350, 355, 371, 375-378, 384, 407-409, 411, 414, 418
Belgic Confession xi, 38, 55, 61, 66, 73, 259, 351, 376, 380
black theology 17, 113, 201, 377, 403

C

Calvin Protestant Church 10-11, 25-26
Christian Reformed Church in North America 25, 32
church unity 8, 17, 46, 50-52, 59, 65, 67-70, 74, 79-80, 98, 101, 109, 115, 128-129, 135-137, 139-140, 145, 148, 150, 159, 199-200, 212, 275, 313-314, 332, 334, 355, 358, 361, 376, 377, 400, 403-404, 461, 475, 477, 495
compassion 65, 85, 87, 155, 175, 178, 204, 210-211, 224, 232, 238, 288, 296, 297, 300-302, 347, 366, 369, 381, 389, 392, 397-398, 471, 488
compassionate justice xiii, 68, 239, 241, 296-297, 301-302, 417, 437
Confessing Circle 17, 20-21, 348

Cottesloe Declaration 7, 190, 217-218
covenant 24, 29, 36, 49, 70, 79, 126, 192, 241, 251-252, 254, 260, 270, 274, 384, 454-455, 474, 479
Covenanting for the Reunification of the Family of DRC - Esselenpark Declaration 49, 66, 71-72, 454

D

Declaration of faith of the Presbyterian Church of Southern Africa 39, 452
Declaration of Laudium 51, 64, 457
Dirkie Smit xiii, 19-20, 161, 200, 366, 407
Dutch Reformed Church (DRC) xi, 1, 44, 51, 97, 119, 141, 146-147, 163, 189, 199, 222, 256, 275, 347, 352, 356, 358, 360, 364, 375, 389, 421, 459-460, 465-469, 471-472, 476-477, 489, 491
Dutch Reformed Church in Africa (DRCA) ix, xi, 4, 25, 44-45, 47, 111, 120, 124, 142, 200, 207, 222, 305, 315, 321, 348, 357, 360, 364, 473, 491
Dutch Reformed Mission Church (DRMC) ix, 4-6, 8-14, 16-24, 26, 32, 44-45, 47, 50-53, 55-56, 66, 82, 111, 114, 119-120, 125-127, 142, 149, 161, 189, 191, 193, 195, 200, 206-207, 215, 224, 238, 241, 258-259, 277-278, 284, 307, 315, 321, 348-350, 356-364, 368, 376, 391-399, 401-402, 416, 421, 426, 491

E

Ecumenical Faith Declaration 25, 34-35
embodiment 186, 243, 305, 365-366, 371, 395, 400, 417, 475
Esselenpark Declaration
    See Covenanting for the Reunification of the Family of DRC - Esselenpark Declaration
Eucharist xii, 1-2, 143, 251-255, 257, 259, 260-261, 263, 265-268, 321
Evangelical Reformed Church in Africa (ERCA) 25-28, 360, 362

G

Gustav Bam xiii, 19, 23, 357

H

hate speech 44, 87, 163, 170-175, 177
Heidelberg Catechism xi, 38, 47, 55, 61, 66, 73, 259, 376, 380, 408, 410-411, 422, 437-438, 467, 476
heresy 12-14, 16-19, 22, 32, 50, 53, 56, 114, 189, 200, 218, 256, 258, 350-351, 357-358, 375-376, 378, 422, 426, 444, 446, 449-450, 464-465, 471
Holy Communion 1, 2, 12, 14, 54, 97-98, 103, 105-110, 115, 136, 189, 194, 445-446

I

Iglesia Rerformada Dominicana 25, 37
inclusivity xii, 84, 87, 97, 153-154, 156-159, 254, 365, 368-369
internal unity 115, 220, 305, 307-316, 319
Isaac David Morkel 8-11
Isak Mentor xiii, 19, 23

J

Jaap Durand xiii, 12, 19, 55, 81, 276, 375, 379, 408
joint ventures 26, 59, 69-70, 73, 300, 486

K

Kairos Document 102, 255, 257
Kerk en Samelewing 53, 146

L

Lesotho Evangelical Church 25

M

Memorandum of Agreement 50, 64-65, 79-80, 149, 168, 300, 352, 474, 480, 486
multiculturalism xiii, 225-226, 314, 319, 324
multi-ethnic ix, 320, 322-325, 327

N

narrative pedagogical 388, 390, 393-394, 397-398, 402

P

pastoral care xii, 73, 273, 277-278, 281-282, 284-286, 289-291, 301
Presbyterian Church in the USA 25, 38, 42, 175, 395, 452, 456
Programme to Combat Racism 12, 165, 218
provisional order 63-65

R

Ras Volk en Nasie en Volkereverhoudinge in die Lig van die Skrif (RVN) 6-8, 17
Reformed Church in Africa xi, 4, 25, 44, 49-51, 64, 111, 142, 162, 186, 222, 305, 337, 344, 360-361, 457-458, 473
Reformed Church in America (RCA) xi, xiii, 11, 25, 30-32, 35, 37-38, 45, 49-52, 55, 61, 64, 72-74, 78, 82, 111, 125-129, 186, 212, 300, 305, 337, 344, 360-361, 457
Reformed Ecumenical Council (REC) 11-12, 14, 24, 32, 53-54, 66, 446, 459

Reformed Nederduitsche Zendingkerk of South Africa 4, 13, 47, 53
Resolution on Racism and South Africa 13-14, 199-200, 215-216
restorative justice 44, 66, 79, 87-88, 148, 150, 168, 472-473, 477-478
Roadmap to Church Reunification 64-65, 79, 352, 480

S

Seattle First Christian Reformed Church 25
separate development 6-8, 13-14, 111, 193-194, 200, 215, 218, 357, 442, 444-446, 449
sexist language xiii, 353, 363-364, 367-369
South African Council of Churches (SACC) 12, 114, 142, 189, 258, 348, 395, 408
status confessionis 13-16, 18-19, 45, 53-56, 114, 146, 159, 193, 200, 218, 224, 229, 258-259, 355-358, 360, 376-377, 382-383, 389, 397-398, 404, 408, 422, 426, 444, 448-451, 463, 465
Submission of the URCSA to the Truth and Reconciliation Commission 9, 17, 21

T

theological justification of apartheid xii, 4, 8-10, 16, 21 22, 50, 56, 111, 123, 191, 199, 207, 215-218, 256-257, 350-351, 357, 362, 376, 378-379, 392, 394-396, 424, 442, 444, 463-464, 465
theological training 25, 27, 50, 308, 310-311, 469
theology of development xii, 231-232, 236-239, 243-246
Tomlinson Report 121, 122, 124

U

United Protestant Church in Belgium (UPCB) 25, 28
Uniting Presbyterian Church in Southern Africa (UPCSA) 25, 38-42, 64, 77, 300
Uniting Reformed Church of Southern Africa (URCSA) 35, 125

W

World Alliance of Reformed Churches (WARC) xii-xiii, 12-16, 18-19, 29, 50, 52-58, 66, 77-78, 114, 189, 199, 200, 215-219, 228-229, 258, 351, 356-357, 376-377, 382-384, 421, 442-448, 463-465, 471,-473
World Council of Churches xii, 7, 165, 190, 217, 228-229, 258

www.ingramcontent.com/pod-product-compliance
Lightning Source LLC
Chambersburg PA
CBHW080611230426
43664CB00019B/2857